Lecture Notes in Computer Science

Commenced Publication in 1973
Founding and Former Series Editors:
Gerhard Goos, Juris Hartmanis, and Jan van Leeuwen

Editorial Board

David Hutchison
   Lancaster University, UK
Takeo Kanade
   Carnegie Mellon University, Pittsburgh, PA, USA
Josef Kittler
   University of Surrey, Guildford, UK
Jon M. Kleinberg
   Cornell University, Ithaca, NY, USA
Alfred Kobsa
   University of California, Irvine, CA, USA
Friedemann Mattern
   ETH Zurich, Switzerland
John C. Mitchell
   Stanford University, CA, USA
Moni Naor
   Weizmann Institute of Science, Rehovot, Israel
Oscar Nierstrasz
   University of Bern, Switzerland
C. Pandu Rangan
   Indian Institute of Technology, Madras, India
Bernhard Steffen
   TU Dortmund University, Germany
Madhu Sudan
   Microsoft Research, Cambridge, MA, USA
Demetri Terzopoulos
   University of California, Los Angeles, CA, USA
Doug Tygar
   University of California, Berkeley, CA, USA
Gerhard Weikum
   Max Planck Institute for Informatics, Saarbruecken, Germany

Martin Wolpers   Paul A. Kirschner
Maren Scheffel   Stefanie Lindstaedt
Vania Dimitrova (Eds.)

Sustaining TEL: From Innovation to Learning and Practice

5th European Conference
on Technology Enhanced Learning, EC-TEL 2010
Barcelona, Spain, September 28 - October 1, 2010
Proceedings

Volume Editors

Martin Wolpers
Fraunhofer Institute for Applied Information Technology FIT
53754 Sankt Augustin, Germany
E-mail: martin.wolpers@fit.fraunhofer.de

Paul A. Kirschner
Open Universiteit Nederland
6419 AT Heerlen, The Netherlands
E-mail: Paul.Kirschner@ou.nl

Maren Scheffel
Fraunhofer Institute for Applied Information Technology FIT
53754 Sankt Augustin, Germany
E-mail: maren.scheffel@fit.fraunhofer.de

Stefanie Lindstaedt
Know-Center Graz
8010 Graz, Austria
E-mail: slind@know-center.at

Vania Dimitrova
University of Leeds
Leeds LS2 9JT, UK
E-mail: V.G.Dimitrova@leeds.ac.uk

Library of Congress Control Number: 2010934728

CR Subject Classification (1998): H.4, H.3, I.2, C.2, H.5, J.1

LNCS Sublibrary: SL 2 – Programming and Software Engineering

ISSN	0302-9743
ISBN-10	3-642-16019-0 Springer Berlin Heidelberg New York
ISBN-13	978-3-642-16019-6 Springer Berlin Heidelberg New York

This work is subject to copyright. All rights are reserved, whether the whole or part of the material is concerned, specifically the rights of translation, reprinting, re-use of illustrations, recitation, broadcasting, reproduction on microfilms or in any other way, and storage in data banks. Duplication of this publication or parts thereof is permitted only under the provisions of the German Copyright Law of September 9, 1965, in its current version, and permission for use must always be obtained from Springer. Violations are liable to prosecution under the German Copyright Law.

springer.com

© Springer-Verlag Berlin Heidelberg 2010
Printed in Germany

Typesetting: Camera-ready by author, data conversion by Scientific Publishing Services, Chennai, India
Printed on acid-free paper   06/3180

Preface

These proceedings of the fifth European Conference on Technology Enhanced Learning (EC-TEL 2010) exemplify the highly relevant and successful research being done in TEL. Because of this great work, this year's conference focused on "Sustaining TEL: From Innovation to Learning and Practice." The last decade has seen significant investment in terms of effort and resources (i.e., time, people, and money) in innovating education and training. The time has come to make the bold step from small-scale innovation research and development to larger-scale and sustainable implementation and evaluation. It is time to show the world (i.e., government, industry, and the general population) that our field has matured to the stage that sustainable learning and learning practices – both in schools and in industry – can be achieved based upon our work.

The present day TEL community now faces new research questions related to large-scale deployment of technology enhanced learning, supporting individual learning environments through mashups and social software, new approaches in TEL certification, and so forth. Furthermore, new approaches are required for the design, implementation, and use of TEL to improve the understanding and communication of educational desires and the needs of all stakeholders, ranging from researchers, to learners, tutors, educational organizations, companies, the TEL industry, and policy makers.

And the TEL community has taken up this challenge. As one can see in this volume, in its fifth year the conference was once more able to assemble the most prominent and relevant research results in the TEL area. The conference generated more than 150 submissions which demonstrates a very lively interest in the conference theme, thus significantly contributing to the conference's success. After detailed deliberations, 24 submissions were selected as full papers; in other words EC-TEL 2010 has an acceptance rate of less than 24%! That is just one indicator of how quickly this conference has established itself as one of the main research dissemination venues in the field.

Apart from this highly competitive scientific program, the conference also solicited keynote presentations from

- Judy Kay, Director of CHAI – Computer Human Adapted Interaction Research Group, University of Sydney, who presented a visionary talk on personalization, HCI, and learning. Her vision is to support a highly personalized way for people to interact with the computers that they carry, those embedded within the environment as well as desktop computers.
- José Ángel Martínez Usero, Director of International Projects, Technosite-Fundación ONCE, who presented state-of-the-art research trends in accessible elearning: interoperability of solutions, ubiquity of resources, and personalization of services.

- Pat Manson and Marco Marsella, from the European Commission, Unit 'Cultural Heritage and Technology Enhanced Learning', who presented the future funding of TEL from an EC point of view, focusing on the updated Framework 7 work program, relating to new calls for proposals and other funding instruments.

Other highlights of the conference were:

- TEL in Spain: A track on TEL driven by researchers from Spain and their projects.
- Industry: In this track, industry took up the opportunity to discuss urgent needs, recent developments, and new findings with research regardless of their origin and market interests.
- STELLAR round table: A discussion of the STELLAR network of excellence on new and emerging topics in TEL, including a lively discussion of the grand challenges of TEL.
- DATATEL lounge: Discussion on how to strengthen TEL research by exchanging data sets of research findings in the lovely atmosphere of the Barcelona yacht harbour and beach.
- Hotel Garden Poster Reception: EC TEL again opened with a poster exhibition (in the marvellous hotel garden). Participants had the opportunity to enjoy high profile posters with often very provocative topics while having a lovely sip of Cava.
- Demo Session: For the first time, EC-TEL allowed selected researchers to demonstrate their achievements live. Participants were able to walk up and actually try out new developments, findings, and algorithms.
- ICT 2010 cooperation: Using the latest video conferencing technology, participants of the simultaneous ICT 2010 event in Brussels, Belgium, were able to participate in EC-TEL 2010 in Barcelona, Spain. Thus, EC-TEL was present at the biggest general European research event.

Preceding the program, a number of high-profile workshops and a doctoral consortium took place. The workshops focused on specific topics in a more interactive fashion, thus deepening and developing topics. The doctoral consortium provided a unique opportunity for advanced PhD students to present their work in progress in front of experienced and reputable researchers in the field of technology enhanced learning.

In conclusion, we need to remind ourselves that technology enhanced learning is there to be actively used in the real world. While sustainability is often seen or experienced as an unwanted "have to do" for many researchers, it is clear that the real-world application of TEL will significantly contribute to helping overcome many current societal problems. It is, therefore, the responsibility of researchers to ensure the uptake of their TEL-related findings in real life. This conference has shown that research has taken up this challenge and that the first efforts show good results.

September 2010

Paul A. Kirschner
Martin Wolpers

Organization

Executive Committee

General Chair	Vania Dimitrova, University of Leeds, UK
Program Chairs	Paul A. Kirschner, Open Universiteit Nederland, The Netherlands
	Martin Wolpers, Fraunhofer FIT, Germany
Organizing Chair	Martin Wolpers, Fraunhofer FIT, Germany
Local Chair	Marta Enrech, Open University of Catalonia, Spain
Dissemination Chair	Carlos Delgado Kloos, Carlos III University of Madrid, Spain
Workshop Chair	Daniel Burgos, ATOS Origin, Spain
Demo Chair	Stefanie Lindstaedt, Know-Center Graz, Austria
Industry Chair	Gabriel García-Prieto, International University of La Rioja, Spain

Program Committee

Vincent Aleven
Heidrun Allert
Julio Alonso
Charoula Angeli
Sylvester Arnab
Roger Azevedo
Nicolas Balacheff
Noaa Barak
Katrin Borcea-Pfitzmann
Bert Bredeweg
Francis Brouns
Peter Brusilovsky
Lorenzo Cantoni
Mohamed Amine Chatti
Ulrike Cress
Alexandra Cristea
Paul De Bra
Christian Depover
Darina Dicheva
Pierre Dillenbourg
Yannis Dimitriadis
Peter Dolog
Hendrik Drachsler

Benedict du Boulay
Erik Duval
Markus Eisenhauer
Dieter Euler
Christine Ferraris
Dragan Gasevic
Denis Gillet
Fabrizio Giorgini
Christian Glahn
Monique Grandbastien
Begona Gros
Christian Gütl
Jörg Haake
Anne Helsdingen
Knut Hinkelmann
Ulrich Hoppe
Emmanuel Jamin
Patrick Jermann
Sanna Järvelä
Marco Kalz
Nikos Karacapilidis
Liesbeth Kester
Michael Kickmeier-Rust

Barbara Kieslinger
Joris Klerkx
Tomaž Klobučar
Rob Koper
Nicole Krämer
Milos Kravcik
Karel Kreijns
Barbara Kump
Susanne Lajoie
Lydia Lau
Effie Lai-Chong Law
Ard Lazonder
Teemu Leinonen
Andreas Lingnau
Rose Luckin
George Magoulas
Maggie McPherson
Riichiro Mizoguchi
Paola Monachesi
Pablo Moreno-Ger
Pedro Muñoz-Merino
Mario Muñoz-Organero
Wolfgang Nejdl

Roumen Nikolov
Roger Nkambou
Reinhard Oppermann
Viktoria Pammer
Abelardo Pardo
Jan Pawlowski
Roy Pea
Eric Ras
Peter Reimann
Uwe Riss
Vicente Romero
Maren Scheffel

Tammy Schellens
Hans-Christian Schmitz
Judith Schoonenboom
Peter Scott
Mike Sharples
Peter Sloep
Marcus Specht
Slavi Stoyanov
Pierre Tchounikine
Stefaan Ternier
Martin Valcke
Jan Van Bruggen

Christine Vanoirbeek
Katrien Verbert
Aisha Walker
Gerhard Weber
Armin Weinberger
Wim Westera
Fridolin Wild
Katrin Wodzicki
Andreas Zimmermann
Volker Zimmermann

Additional Reviewers

Johanna Bertram
Maria Blanca Ibanez
Emmanuel G. Blanchard
Luca Botturi
Ilknur Celik
Luis de la Fuente Valentín
Norberto Fernandez Garcia
Jonathan Foss
Martin Friedrich
Adam Giemza
Iassen Halatchliyski
Yusuke Hayashi
Christoph Held

Sonia Hetzner
I-Han Hsiao
Sebastian Kelle
Uwe Kirschenmann
Barbara Kump
Derick Leony
Anja Lorenz
Moffat Mathews
Manolis Mavrikis
Johannes Moskaliuk
Danish Nadeem
Katja Niemann
Ferry Pramudianto

Kamakshi Rajagopal
Isabella Rega
René Reiners
Christoph Richter
Sandrine Sarre
Eva Schwämmlein
Craig Stewart
Stefano Tardini
Jozef Tvarozek
Nicolas Weber
Michael Yudelson
Sabrina Ziebarth

Supporting Partners

imc AG, Germany
Universidad Internacional de la Rioja, Spain
Fraunhofer Institute for Applied Information Technology FIT, Germany
European Association for Technology Enhanced Learning (EA-TEL), Germany
Springer-Verlag, Germany
University of Leeds, UK
Center for Learning Sciences and Technologies, The Netherlands
Atos Origin, Spain
Spanish Network of Technology Enhanced Learning Initiatives (Telspain), Spain
eMadrid, Spain
Universidad Carlos III de Madrid, Spain
elearningeuropa.info, UK
European Network of Excellence STELLAR, EU
Integrated Project ROLE, EU

Table of Contents

Section 1. Invited Papers

Tackling HCI Challenges of Creating Personalised, Pervasive Learning Ecosystems 1
    Judy Kay and Bob Kummerfeld

Section 2. Full Papers

Maintaining Continuity of Inquiry Learning Experiences across Contexts: Teacher's Management Strategies and the Role of Technology 17
    Stamatina Anastopoulou, Yang Yang, Mark Paxton, Mike Sharples, Charles Crook, Shaaron Ainsworth, and Claire O'Malley

Ultra-Personalization and Decentralization: The Potential of Multi-Agent Systems in Personal and Informal Learning 30
    Ali M. Aseere, David E. Millard, and Enrico H. Gerding

Learning Spaces as Representational Scaffolds for Learning Conceptual Knowledge of System Behaviour 46
    Bert Bredeweg, Jochem Liem, Wouter Beek, Paulo Salles, and Floris Linnebank

Investigating Teachers' Understanding of IMS Learning Design: Yes They Can! 62
    Michael Derntl, Susanne Neumann, Dai Griffiths, and Petra Oberhuemer

Task Performance vs. Learning Outcomes: A Study of a Tangible User Interface in the Classroom 78
    Son Do-Lenh, Patrick Jermann, Sébastien Cuendet, Guillaume Zufferey, and Pierre Dillenbourg

Content, Social, and Metacognitive Statements: An Empirical Study Comparing Human-Human and Human-Computer Tutorial Dialogue ... 93
    Myroslava O. Dzikovska, Natalie B. Steinhauser, Johanna D. Moore, Gwendolyn E. Campbell, Katherine M. Harrison, and Leanne S. Taylor

Authenticity in Learning Game: How It Is Designed and Perceived 109
    Celso Gonçalves, Marie-Caroline Croset, Muriel Ney, Nicolas Balacheff, and Jean-Luc Bosson

Orchestrating Learning Using Adaptive Educational Designs in IMS
Learning Design 123
  Marion R. Gruber, Christian Glahn, Marcus Specht, and Rob Koper

Management of Assessment Resources in a Federated Repository of
Educational Resources.. 139
  Israel Gutiérrez Rojas, Derick Leony, Andrés Franco,
  Raquel M. Crespo, Abelardo Pardo, and Carlos Delgado Kloos

Knowledge Maturing Activities and Practices Fostering Organisational
Learning: Results of an Empirical Study 151
  Andreas Kaschig, Ronald Maier, Alexander Sandow,
  Mariangela Lazoi, Sally-Anne Barnes, Jenny Bimrose,
  Claire Bradley, Alan Brown, Christine Kunzmann,
  Athanasios Mazarakis, and Andreas Schmidt

Demands of Modern PLEs and the ROLE Approach.................... 167
  Uwe Kirschenmann, Maren Scheffel, Martin Friedrich,
  Katja Niemann, and Martin Wolpers

How to Share and Reuse Learning Resources: The ARIADNE
Experience 183
  Joris Klerkx, Bram Vandeputte, Gonzalo Parra, José Luis Santos,
  Frans Van Assche, and Erik Duval

Towards Improved Support for Adaptive Collaboration Scripting in
IMS LD 197
  Florian König and Alexandros Paramythis

Providing Varying Degrees of Guidance for Work-Integrated
Learning... 213
  Stefanie Lindstaedt, Barbara Kump, Günter Beham,
  Viktoria Pammer, Tobias Ley, Amir Dotan, and
  Robert de Hoog

Automatic Detection of Local Reuse................................. 229
  Arno Mittelbach, Lasse Lehmann, Christoph Rensing, and
  Ralf Steinmetz

Developing and Validating a Rigorous and Relevant Model of VLE
Success: A Learner Perspective 245
  Daniel Müller and Stefan Strohmeier

The Design of Teacher Assistance Tools in an Exploratory Learning
Environment for Mathematics Generalisation 260
  Darren Pearce-Lazard, Alexandra Poulovassilis, and Eirini Geraniou

Representing the Spaces When Planning Learning Flows 276
  Mar Pérez-Sanagustín, Davinia Hernández-Leo, Raúl Nieves, and
  Josep Blat

Studying the Factors Influencing Automatic User Task Detection on
the Computer Desktop 292
    Andreas S. Rath, Didier Devaurs, and Stefanie N. Lindstaedt

Learning 2.0 Promoting Innovation in Formal Education and Training
in Europe 308
    Christine Redecker and Yves Punie

Extended Explicit Semantic Analysis for Calculating Semantic
Relatedness of Web Resources 324
    *Philipp Scholl, Doreen Böhnstedt, Renato Domínguez García,
    Christoph Rensing, and Ralf Steinmetz*

Leveraging Semantic Technologies for Harmonization of Individual and
Organizational Learning 340
    *Melody Siadaty, Jelena Jovanović, Dragan Gašević,
    Zoran Jeremić, and Teresa Holocher-Ertl*

Learning from Erroneous Examples: When and How Do Students
Benefit from Them? 357
    *Dimitra Tsovaltzi, Erica Melis, Bruce M. McLaren,
    Ann-Kristin Meyer, Michael Dietrich, and George Goguadze*

Enhancing the Learning Process: Qualitative Validation of an Informal
Learning Support System Consisting of a Knowledge Discovery and a
Social Learning Component 374
    *Eline Westerhout, Paola Monachesi, Thomas Markus, and
    Vlad Posea*

Section 3. Short Papers

Pattern-Mediated Knowledge Exchange in Non-Governmental
Organizations 390
    *Franziska Arnold, Johannes Moskaliuk, Till Schümmer, and
    Ulrike Cress*

Modelling a Stakeholder Community via a Social Platform: The Case
of TELeurope.eu 396
    *Noaa Barak, Daniel Burgos, Anthony Fisher Camilleri,
    Fred de Vries, Marcus Specht, and Caroline Windrum*

Scenario-Based Multi-User Virtual Environments: Productive Failure
and the Impact of Structure on Learning 402
    Shannon Kennedy-Clark, Michael J. Jacobson, and Peter Reimann

Experimentation and Results for Calibrating Automatic Diagnosis Belief Linked to Problem Solving Modalities: A Case Study in Electricity. 408
  Sandra Michelet, Vanda Luengo, Jean-Michel Adam, and Nadine Mandran

Exploring Mediums of Pedagogical Support in an across Contexts Mobile Learning Activity 414
  Jalal Nouri, Johan Eliasson, Fredrik Rutz, and Robert Ramberg

Overview and Preliminary Results of Using PolyCAFe for Collaboration Analysis and Feedback Generation 420
  Traian Rebedea, Mihai Dascalu, Stefan Trausan-Matu, Dan Banica, Alexandru Gartner, Costin Chiru, and Dan Mihaila

A Framework for the Domain-Independent Collection of Attention Metadata 426
  Maren Scheffel, Martin Friedrich, Katja Niemann, Uwe Kirschenmann, and Martin Wolpers

Who Students Interact with? A Social Network Analysis Perspective on the Use of Twitter in Language Learning 432
  Carsten Ullrich, Kerstin Borau, and Karen Stepanyan

Conditions and Effects of Teacher Collaboration within a Blended Professional Development Program for Technology Integration 438
  Albena Todorova and Thomas Osburg

Enhancing Learning with Off-Task Social Dialogues 445
  Jozef Tvarožek and Mária Bieliková

Section 4. Poster Papers

Audience Interactivity as Leverage for Effective Learning in Gaming Environments for Dome Theaters 451
  Panagiotis Apostolellis and Thanasis Daradoumis

Free-Riding in Collaborative Diagrams Drawing 457
  Furio Belgiorno, Ilaria Manno, Giuseppina Palmieri, and Vittorio Scarano

Affordances of Presentations in Multi-Display Learning Spaces for Supporting Small Group Discussion 464
  Brett Bligh and Mike Sharples

Recommending Learning Objects According to a Teachers' Contex Model 470
  Jorge Bozo, Rosa Alarcón, and Sebastian Iribarra

Preferences in Multiple-View Open Learner Models	476
Susan Bull, Inderdip Gakhal, Daniel Grundy, Matthew Johnson, Andrew Mabbott, and Jing Xu	
Supporting Free Collaboration and Process-Based Scripts in PoEML ...	482
Manuel Caeiro-Rodríguez, Luis Anido-Rifón, and Roberto Perez-Rodriguez	
A Simple E-learning System Based on Classroom Competition	488
Iván Cantador and José M. Conde	
Computerized Evaluation and Diagnosis of Student's Knowledge Based on Bayesian Networks	494
Gladys Castillo, Luís Descalço, Sandra Diogo, Eva Millán, Paula Oliveira, and Batel Anjo	
An Interoperable ePortfolio Tool for All	500
Fabrizio Giorgini	
Disaster Readiness through Education – Training Soft Skills to Crisis Units by Means of Serious Games in Virtual Environments	506
Nina Haferkamp and Nicole C. Krämer	
Ambient Displays and Game Design Patterns	512
Sebastian Kelle, Dirk Börner, Marco Kalz, and Marcus Specht	
PWGL, Towards an Open and Intelligent Learning Environment for Higher Music Education	518
Mika Kuuskankare and Mikael Laurson	
Vicarious Learning from Tutorial Dialogue	524
John Lee	
Computer-Supported Argumentation Learning: A Survey of Teachers, Researchers, and System Developers	530
Frank Loll, Oliver Scheuer, Bruce M. McLaren, and Niels Pinkwart	
End-User Visual Design of Web-Based Interactive Applications Making Use of Geographical Information: the WINDMash Approach	536
The Nhan Luong, Patrick Etcheverry, Thierry Nodenot, Christophe Marquesuzaà, and Philippe Lopistéguy	
Supporting Reflection in an Immersive 3D Learning Environment Based on Role-Play	542
Nils Malzahn, Hanno Buhmes, Sabrina Ziebarth, and H. Ulrich Hoppe	
Facilitating Effective Exploratory Interaction: Design and Evaluation of Intelligent Support in MiGen	548
Manolis Mavrikis, Sergio Gutierrez-Santos, and Eirini Geraniou	

GVIS: A Facility for Adaptively Mashing Up and Representing Open
Learner Models 554
    Luca Mazzola and Riccardo Mazza

Introducing a Social Backbone to Support Access to Digital
Resources 560
    Martin Memmel, Martin Wolpers, Massimiliano Condotta,
    Katja Niemann, and Rafael Schirru

Towards an Ergonomics of Knowledge Systems: Improving the Design
of Technology Enhanced Learning 566
    David E. Millard and Yvonne Howard

Using Personal Professional Networks for Learning in Social Work:
Need for Insight into the Real-World Context 572
    Kamakshi Rajagopal, Desirée Joosten-ten Brinke, and Peter B. Sloep

Deep Learning Design for Sustainable Innovation within Shifting
Learning Landscapes 578
    Andrew Ravenscroft, Tom Boyle, John Cook, and Andreas Schmidt

Evaluation of the Software "e^3-Portfolio" in the Context of the Study
Program "Problem-Solving Competencies" 584
    Thomas Sporer, Magdalena Steinle, and Johannes Metscher

Components of a Research 2.0 Infrastructure 590
    Thomas Daniel Ullmann, Fridolin Wild, Peter Scott,
    Erik Duval, Bram Vandeputte, Gonzalo Parra, Wolfgang Reinhardt,
    Nina Heinze, Peter Kraker, Angela Fessl, Stefanie Lindstaedt,
    Till Nagel, and Denis Gillet

Exploring the Benefits of Open Standard Initiatives for Supporting
Inquiry-Based Science Learning 596
    Bahtijar Vogel, Arianit Kurti, Daniel Spikol, and Marcelo Milrad

Monitoring and Analysing Students' Systematic Behaviour – The SCY
Pedagogical Agent Framework 602
    Stefan Weinbrenner, Jan Engler, Astrid Wichmann, and
    Ulrich Hoppe

Section 5. Demonstration Papers

iAPOSDLE – An Approach to Mobile Work-Integrated Learning 608
    Guenter Beham, Fleur Jeanquartier, and Stefanie Lindstaedt

A Haptic-Based Framework for Chemistry Education 614
    Sara Comai, Davide Mazza, and Lorenzo Mureddu

Intelligent Tutoring with Natural Language Support in the BEETLE II
System 620
   Myroslava O. Dzikovska, Diana Bental, Johanna D. Moore,
   Natalie B. Steinhauser, Gwendolyn E. Campbell,
   Elaine Farrow, and Charles B. Callaway

ScenEdit: An Intention-Oriented Authoring Environnment to Design
Larning Scenarios 626
   Valérie Emin, Jean-Philippe Pernin, and José Luis Aguirre

Skill-Based Scouting of Open Management Content 632
   Katja Niemann, Uta Schwertel, Marco Kalz,
   Alexander Mikroyannidis, Marco Fisichella, Martin Friedrich,
   Michele Dicerto, Kyung-Hun Ha, Philipp Holtkamp, Ricardo Kawase,
   Elisabetta Parodi, Jan Pawlowski, Henri Pirkkalainen,
   Vassilis Pitsilis, Aristides Vidalis, Martin Wolpers, and
   Volker Zimmermann

The Complexity of Integrating Technology Enhanced Learning in
Special Math Education – A Case Study 638
   Ann Nilsson and Lena Pareto

TAO – A Versatile and Open Platform for Technology-Based
Assessment 644
   Eric Ras, Judith Swietlik, Patrick Plichart, and Thibaud Latour

Author Index 651

Tackling HCI Challenges of Creating Personalised, Pervasive Learning Ecosystems

Judy Kay and Bob Kummerfeld

School of Information Technologies, University of Sydney, Sydney, NSW 2006, Australia
{Judy.Kay,Bob.Kummerfeld}@sydney.edu.au

Abstract. This paper explores two classes of emerging technology that offer the promise to provide radically improved ways to support lifelong learning. We particularly focus on the human computer interaction (HCI) challenges that must be addressed if that promise is to be realised. One technology is *personalisation*, based on a *long term learner model* which captures the learner's knowledge, preferences and other attributes. We discuss the roles of an *explicit learner model* that is a first class software entity, with APIs for programmers as well as effective user interfaces that can give users control over their model and its use. We present the PLUS framework that provides the infrastructure for personalised learning, and how its Accretion-Resolution representation supports both flexible reasoning for personalisation by programs and provides the foundation for users to control the whole personalisation process. We link the PLUS framework to a second class of technology, the fast-changing and increasingly ubiquitous *personal mobile devices* and the emerging *embedded surface computing devices*, such as tabletop and shared wall displays. We show how we have tackled several of the HCI challenges that are key to both these technologies.

Keywords: personalisation, lifelong learning, human-computer interaction, mobile, surface computing, tabletops.

1 Introduction

Recent and emerging progress in hardware technologies is creating important new possibilities for learning, be it in formal settings or as part of broader lifelong learning [46]. The key is the increasing number of *personal* devices owned by individuals. One important class of these is the mobile phone, which has become truly ubiquitous in the developed and, increasingly, in the developing world. We can confidently predict that these will have an increasing potential role for personalised learning, especially with the fast growing proportion of *smart* phones. In 2009, 172 million smart phones were sold, 24% more than the previous year, representing 14% of the 1.2 billion phones bought that year[1].

---
[1] http://techcrunch.com/2010/02/23/smartphone-iphone-sales-2009-gartner/

Other emerging classes of *personal* mobile internet devices are tablet computers and ebook readers, providing screens large enough for many learning tasks. Yet another important class of *personal* technology is the range of inexpensive sensors that can readily capture digital information about a person's activities. Some of these may be integrated into phones, as in the case of accelerometers, while others are inexpensive devices that can easily be worn, for example in a shoe or like a watch. At a very different level, there is a move toward powerful *personal* laptops. Together, such collections of personal devices can hold large archives of digital artifacts. They also track the individual's digital footprints, a potentially valuable, currently under-exploited resource. These personal devices mean a learner can, at all times and many places, access large repositories of information, both from their own devices and the internet.

At the same time, a quite different form of emergent technology is the *embedded* devices such as interactive whiteboards that are becoming increasingly common in classrooms and informal learning spaces, such as museums. Similar technology can be used for tabletop interaction, so that a small group of people can work collaboratively around a table with their digital artifacts. For example, at the left of Figure 1, we show three users collaborating, by sharing and discussing information at a touch-based tabletop, with a linked wall display; they can *throw* objects from the table to the wall. At the right of the figure, we show learners using pen-based whiteboard technology. This time they are working with their personal information. This figure illustrates the nexus between the personal device and the embedded tabletop. They use their mobile phones as a private workspace, in contrast to the shared workspace of the tabletop. So they can check out things privately if they wish. The phone also enables them to determine which of their personal information appears at the tabletop [19].

There are many other ways that we can bring personal and embedded technologies together to support learning. For example, suppose that Alice and Bob are students doing a group project, where Alice's role involves doing research on spiders. Her mobile phone holds a model of her current interests, including a *persona* that holds just those interests associated with the project. The phone also

Fig. 1. (Left) Three learners using a touch-based tabletop and linked wall display. (Right) Two users work at a pen-based tabletop, using their mobile phones to control what personal information they release to the table.

can access information she has collected for the project. She visits the museum to learn more. When she stops at the their tabletop, she releases her *persona*, to the tabletop. It is represented by the image shown at the left of Figure 2 and this appears on the tabletop. When she dwells on it, the tabletop searches all the devices currently connected to it, including her phone and the museum's repository. This provides the results shown at the right of Figure 2. If her friend, Bob, has his phone also connected to the tabletop, the search operates across the files that he makes searchable to the table. This could be the information he collected for the project, including some he came across on spiders, since he thought Alice might find that useful.

Fig. 2. (Left) Alice's persona, as displayed on the tabletop. (Right) The information displayed after Alice dwells on her persona; a search is conducted to find all available information of interest to Alice.

These examples illustrate some of the possibilities for combining recent and emerging technologies for new ways to learn. One particularly promising possibility is to personalise teaching and learning, with the goal of moving towards the benefits of individualised expert teaching [9]. The new technologies make personalisation feasible in ways that have not existed in the past. An important reason for this relates to relative ease of storing large amounts of information about a learner and having it readily available when and where the learner might need it. Then the new technologies can keep this in a form that can be useful for the learner, their human peer or teacher, and for the emerging personalised teaching systems. This creates the need to create an explicit *learner model*, a collection of the information about a person that can be useful for personalising their learning. It should be a *first class citizen* in the sense that it is independent of any particular application. To support learning of skills that take years to acquire, a *lifelong learner model* could facilitate personalisation for many different learning tools. Such models can drive personalisation within educational tools that can take account the learner's existing knowledge, learning goals and preferences [42]. In the next section, we show how we have designed the PLUS framework to do this. We then discuss some of the associated interface challenges and opportunities of these two technologies.

2 *PLUS* Framework

The *PLUS* framework describes the elements in this vision for personalised learning that is available on a range of devices. The elements of *PLUS* are Personalisation, Pervasive computing, Lifelong Learning, Learner model, Ubiquitous computing, User model and Scrutability. The *PLUS* framework is a foundation for creating the set of tools and the infrastructure needed to support powerful and flexible personalisation broadly, but particularly for learning. The notions of *pervasive* and *ubiquitous* computing reflect the goal that the learning can occur when and where the learner wishes or needs to learn, making effective use of a range of devices, be they carried, embedded or conventional. *Lifelong learning*, with support for personalisation, means that there needs to be a long term *learner model* or, more broadly, *user model*, that holds the information used to drive the personalisation to match the learner's long term knowledge, beliefs, goals, preferences and other attributes as well as their short term context and current needs. Finally, the personal nature of the learner model means that *PLUS* must aim for *scrutability* as the basis for the user maintaining control over their own personal information in the learner model. This means that the personalisation, in terms of the learner model, the mechanisms that inform it and the ways that it is used should be scrutable, that is *capable of being understood through study and observation; comprehensible*[2] or *understandable upon close examination*[3]. The goal to support scrutability drove the design of *PLUS* and creates the need for effective user interfaces for scrutability. We introduce a scenario, to illustrate the key ideas in PLUS.

Alice has long wanted to be a software engineer. She studied computing at high school and is now nearing completion of a degree in Software Engineering. In her school, university and private studies she used many forms of learning technology such as learner management systems (LMSs) and personalised learning tools. She mainly used these on desktop computers, at home and on campus. She also used some on her phone. This was particularly useful for her long commutes. She will continue lifelong learning about software engineering throughout her career.

Alice is also keen to be healthy and fit. This means learning and tracking her long term progress towards her goals. She has wireless scales and a pedometer. Each uses wireless communication to send information to her user model. She has a display of her activity as a background on her phone, so she can easily see

---

[2] http://www.thefreedictionary.com/scrutable
[3] http://www.tiscali.co.uk/reference/dictionaries/difficultwords/data/d0011288.html

how she is doing on that. She uses a *personalised coaching system* which helps her learn more and improve her fitness.

We have been working towards creating a framework based on an Accretion-Resolution representation, that can support the reasoning needed for such scenarios. The earliest implementation [29] provided a toolkit library for use within a single application, with the user model residing in the user's own filespace. The demonstrator application supported concept mapping [38] as a means to modelling a learner's conceptual knowledge. Each mapping activity could contribute to a growing learner model that could be used by other applications that the user ran. We extended this to various applications, such as a movie recommender and for long term modelling of a learner's knowledge of a text editor, based on their use of it [30] as well as an Open Learner Model [20]. We refined its mechanisms for reasoning and for compacting or deleting parts of the model [31]. We then took AR to a server architecture [32], making it accessible from any machine. A major shift was to generalise the use of AR to give a consistent approach to modelling users, devices and places in pervasive computing [31,15]. In the most recent major work [7], we made it truly distributed and added new reasoning mechanisms that can also drive external devices, making it able to drive pervasive applications. We have created a version for a mobile phone [25], as the basis for client-side personalisation. We now describe the core ideas, with a particular focus on the user perspective and the HCI issues.

2.1 Evidence Sources

This scenario illustrates a long term user model that is derived from many sources. This is the type of user modelling that will characterise lifelong user modelling. Figure 3 provides a high level overview of the *PLUS* framework designed to support the personalisation in the scenario. Every learning tool that Alice used is a potential source of evidence about her knowledge and other relevant information. For example, the wireless scales and pedometer are examples of *sensors* shown at the upper left of the figure. The next box, showing arbitrary *applications that add information* to the model may include learning technology such as an LMS or a system that automatically graded her programming assignments. Note that both of these have lines only *into* the model since they can only provide evidence about her learning.

The next box shows *personalised applications*. These, too, can provide evidence to her learner model. In addition, they need to access some part of her model to drive their personalisation. Note that this operates only through the box labelled, *filters, resolvers*. Before we explain this, we note that OLMs, *Open Learner Models* are another important class of application: these are interfaces that enable Alice to see relevant parts of her learner model. An example from the scenario is the phone background showing her activity model. These may operate as a source of evidence, based on the learner interacting with them. Importantly, like the personalised applications, they need to make use of the model.

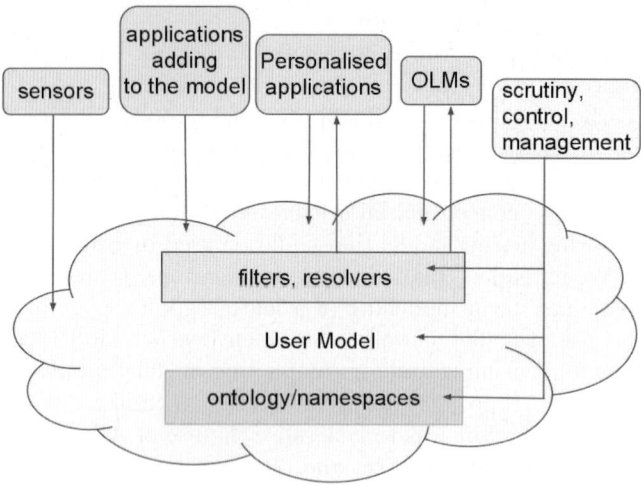

Fig. 3. *PLUS* overview. The cloud is the user model, with its underlying ontology. Some classes of applications only contribute evidence to the user model. Others do this but also make use of it, via a resolver. at the right is the subsystem for controlling the model.

2.2 Evidence as the Atomic Elements of Reasoning

Figure 3 illustrates some aspects of the way that *evidence* is the atomic reasoning element within the PLUS approach. This is in line with many approaches to reasoning under uncertainty and for user modelling (for example, [14]). We take a somewhat different approach to that work because the design of our representation was driven by a focus on the user's perspective and the goal of supporting scrutability of the reasoning processes, at the same time as powerful and flexible reasoning. The PLUS design aimed to support explanations and user control over personalisation, both in terms of the evidence used and the reasoning about it. In the figure, we illustrate one important difference between different classes of evidence, relating to *user-awareness.* In the diagram, the four blue round-edged sources of evidence about the user are ordered, with the left-most being lowest in user-awareness and those further right being higher. So, for example, the whole goal of emerging sensor technology is that it captures evidence that is useful for reasoning about the user, without bothering the user, meaning that the user becomes unaware of it. At the other extreme, OLMs involve direct interaction between the learner and part of their model, so that evidence from this mechanism was given directly by the user, meaning that at that time, they were aware of providing it. The PLUS framework implementations distinguish each source of evidence. This is particularly important for privacy management. Notably, we have found that users tend to be far more cautious about allowing applications acccess to the evidence from low-awareness sources.

2.3 Ontology, Namespace

We now discuss the cloud shaped user model. The bottom part shows the *ontology, namespace*. This defines the *components* of Alice's model. In a programming course, these includes key learning elements such as *iteration* and the learner model collects *evidence* that can be used to reason about whether she knows about iteration to the required standard for a particular context or situation. The user model may be able to structure such concepts to represent the relationships between them. In this case, it may model *iteration* as a specialisation of *control structures*. The notion of *namespace* simply means that the concepts can be grouped into different namespaces. This makes it feasible for some personalised systems to operate with their own part of the user model and to use a concept differently from the way another application uses it.

2.4 AR: Accretion-Resolution Representation

Our core representation aims to be as simple as possible, so that we will be able to explain the personalisation to a user. The PLUS framework has two central actions. The first is *accretion*, meaning the addition of evidence to a named *component* in the model. So, for example, if Alice correctly solved a test task about loops within an LMS, that evidence could be added to the *iteration* component of the model (with the details of the evidence source and a timestamp). Applications that are allowed to contribute to the user model do so with a *tell* operation. One of the distinctive aspects of AR is that, by default, evidence is kept "forever". AR's design makes use of the low cost of storage. Importantly, this approach supports historic queries, so the user can determine how a personalised system would have responded in the past. This distinguishes it from most approaches to reasoning under uncertainty.

When an application needs to query the model, it performs an *ask* operation. This causes the second action, *resolution*, which is the interpretation of evidence based on a *resolver*. In Figure 3, we see that all such operations that take information out of the model do so via a *resolver*. For example, one resolver might conclude that Alice knows about *iteration* based on her success at the test task above. Another resolver may conclude that it does not have enough evidence because it does not consider that evidence sufficient.

The figure also shows a *filter*. This is a mechanism that determines which sources of evidence are allowed for a particular application. For example, Alice may want her OLM to make use of all the evidence about her. By contrast, she may not want information from a personal practice activity to be available to her teacher. In that case, applications associated with her teacher could make use of various resolvers but these would operate only with the evidence allowed to them. The filtering should be thought of as part of the resolution process. We implemented them separately because this gives the user two simple tasks. They can think about each in isolation, to control the use of their model. Each filter and resolver is one small piece of code. We have created systems where the user can decide which resolver to use, to best match their current preferences and needs [28].

In essence, our approach is to accrete evidence into the model as it becomes available, *without interpreting it*. Only when it is needed is the resolution process applied. At that time, the application can make use of a resolver that applies its preferred assessment of the reliability, or credibility of different evidence sources. Some resolvers are very simple. For example, a Point Query algorithm takes just the last piece of filtered evidence [37]. Others can be quite sophisticated, for example incorporating ontological reasoning [37] to deal with noisy and conflicting evidence. For the case of learner models, the A/R approach means that different applications can easily apply different standards, as one would expect as a learner develops maturity and has more robust knowledge of the fundamentals, but more fragile levels of knowledge of recently learnt more advanced topics.

2.5 Where Does the User Model Reside?

The user model in Figure 3 is shown as a cloud-like shape to emphasise that it might be spread across different machines. Alice's full user model might be held on her nominated machine, perhaps at her home. A partial model is held on her phone [25], so supporting client-side personalisation on the phone, a goal that is being recognised for the always connected user [2]. Other parts of her user model for a particular context might be accessed via her phone, which connects back to her home machine [24].

2.6 The Need to Unify an Individual's Learner Model

There is growing recognition of the problems of fragmentation of information about a learner [46]. One aspect of this relates to the semantic, ontological issues [14]. Another key issue relates to user control. We have explored an approach which places the user in control of their own user model [33], and they determine which applications may contribute to it or access it, as well as where each part of it is stored. This means that the learner should be able to aggregate the relevant information about their learning in one place, their lifelong learner model.

2.7 Scrutiny, Control and Management

This is the last element we need to describe in Figure 3. It is shown as a box at the upper right in the same colour as the user model itself. This is the user interface for managing the model. We have explored several ways to provide effective interfaces that enable the user to navigate around their own model, for example [33]. Unlike OLMs, which also present part of the model and should be designed to support learning, this interface enables the user to define new parts of the model, define the applications that may use it, the filters and the set of available resolvers for each application that the learner allows to access their model.

Of course, this risks the learner creating false models. We have explored ways to avoid this. We provided mechanisms for authorities to define signed, authenticated models [27]. The learner can decide whether they will allow these into their model. They could also alter them, but if an altered model were exported, that would not be authenticated. So the application receiving it may choose not to trust it.

Importantly, Alice should be able to define *personas* [32] which define a subset of her model for a purpose, such as in the case of tabletop personalisation example in the Introduction. A persona defines a subset of components within her model. The filters and resolvers allowed for a particular application are then used with the persona to control release of the user model.

3 Human Computer Interface Challenges

Although the discussion to this point has been primarily technical, the fundamental drivers for the design of the PLUS framework were driven by HCI concerns. Key among these was the goal of supporting scrutability as a foundation for user control over their personal information in their user model and the ways that it is used. In addition to the actual framework, we have been exploring some of the HCI challenges associated with deploying it for personalised lifelong learning.

3.1 OLMs - Open Learner Models - Making Models Meaningful

The SMILI framework [12] has defined and analysed key roles for OLMs: improving accuracy by enabling learners to contribute to the model; supporting learner reflection; helping learners to plan and monitor their learning; facilitating collaboration or competition between learners; supporting navigation of the learning system; addressing the learner's right of access to their personal data, supporting learner control and increasing trust in a system; for assessment. The success of these depends upon the availability of suitable interfaces. Bull has conducted extensive evaluations of several such interfaces, for example exploring ways to support parents and their children, each with different interfaces [13] and mobile access to OLMs for private study and revision [11].

Bull also explored ways to use an OLM to improve the accuracy of the learner model [10], allowing the learner to challenge the system and negotiate with it. If the learner considers they know an aspect that the system models them as not knowing, the learner can simply opt to do an assessment task to convince the system its model should be changed. The PLUS framework takes a different approach. We simply accrete the evidence from the learner about their perception of their knowledge and let the application resolver interpret this. In the case of modelling long term learning of a text editor [20] some learners did use the OLM to add such evidence.

Concept mapping offers a promising way to build a learner model based on the learner's own externalisation of their knowledge [29]. We have explored a way to do this that maintains our goal of scrutability, based on verified concept maps [16], where the learner is informed of the ways that their concept map has been used to build the learner model. The same concept map interface could operate as a form of OLM for that part of the model. In that case the learner model should maintain the detailed layout of the concept map.

We have explored interfaces for OLMs to large user or learner models [5]. Users could navigate the models with high accuracy and satisfaction where models had up to 700 concepts. This means that we could provide an overview model for all the learning topics in a four-year graduate medical programme. It supported reflection for a semester long HCI course with over 100 concepts [35].

One of the challenges that deserves more exploration for OLMs concerns effective ways to help a learner make sense of their own learner model. One widely used approach to present results, for example in LMSs, shows the individual's data in comparison with the whole class, as we did in our HCI course [35]. This poses two key problems. First, it means that the individual's data is, effectively shared with the whole class. While this is accepted practice, and commonly done in LMS reports of student results, it can be a problem for small classes and it does not map well to informal and lifelong learning where the learner must agree to release their own data. Another problem is how to tackle the Boomerang Effect [41] which might have the undesirable effect of making a student complacent when they see their relative performance in the class.

We note that the AR representation creates a challenge for design of OLM interfaces. This is because there are potentially many interpretations of the evidence about the learner. As different applications may make use of the model, via different filters and resolvers, it makes sense to link the OLM to those applications or enable the learner to explore it with different interpretations. Our work with large user models [5] did this in terms of the judgement of the level of knowledge, allowing the user to determine how strict the requirements are to assess a concept as known.

We have seen rather limited use of the OLM to support navigation of information spaces. Notably, ELM-ART [47] provided a contents page that used a traffic light metaphor to indicate which material the learner was ready to learn (green) and which they should not tackle (red) as they lacked required knowledge. This is a simple and useful form of overview OLM. At the same time, it serves as a way for the learner to navigate the information space. We realised this navigation role applied in our Narcissus OLM [45] which was designed to show relative contributions in small groups. Although our primary goal had been to create a model that could be used in group planning meetings, particularly those with the group facilitator, we found that it was often a very useful way to navigate to information. This seems to be a promising role for OLMs and could make them very broadly applicable, particularly for lifelong independent learning.

3.2 Scrutiny of Personalisation Processes

While there has been considerable work on OLMs, there has been little work on supporting scrutiny of personalisation processes. After a series of formative prototypes [22], we demonstrated that users could determine how personalisation operated in a scrutable hypertext that had been built using the SASY framework. This supports authoring of adaptive hypertext so that the user can then scrutinise and control their learner model and its use [21]. In a quite different personalisation framework, users of a just-in-time training system [28] were able to use its scrutiny interface to control the personalisation processes. In both cases, our evidence-based reasoning, with accretion and resolution enabled people to work through the elements of their user model, its interpretation and its use [23].

3.3 Sharing Models for the Community Good

We have already noted the importance of individuals sharing their learner models to help define norms, that support the learner in making sense of their own model. There are also potential benefits if we can mine large collections of learner's data, performing educational data mining [8]. For example, taking this approach to analysing activity by members of teams in a software engineering project course, we identified useful patterns of activity which can predict potential problems [40]. Based on this analysis of larger numbers of users, we can provide valuable information to teachers, mentors, as well as the learners themselves. There is also the potential to make contributions to understanding of learning. All this relies on the learner making their their data available and this poses HCI challenges. This is exacerbated because it is often difficult to achieve effective anonymisation and to foresee all the potential uses of even carefully limited sets of one's information.

3.4 Pragmatic Ontologies, Vocabularies and Granularity of Evidence

There are several important roles for ontologies in the PLUS framework. Figure 3 shows these as the basis for the learner model, defining the aspects to be modelled about the learner. The first challenge associated with this is the need to define the ontology for the learner model for a particular context. In keeping with our goal of scrutability, we wanted do this in a way that could support explanations of ontological reasoning. So we mine existing resources such as dictionaries to build the ontology [3]. Interestingly, this means that we can create personalised ontologies [37] based on mining just the resources relevant to the particular user. Even more importantly, this enables a teacher to add local concepts to the ontology. For example, we added the concepts *basics* and *advanced* [34]. We simply created dictionary definitions for these, linking them to the relevant learning objectives. These were useful as a part of the class glossary as well as the learner modelling.

Another critical ontological challenge is to model *competencies*, including the generic skills that are critical goals of a broad education but which have had little attention in personalised learning research. We have taken a pragmatic, lightweight approach to this task, based on the actual natural language texts the institutions and accreditation bodies use to describe these [26]. We have used a lightweight approach to mapping the competency descriptions, in terms of the actual concept and the descriptions of different levels of competence. We have deployed it at the University of Sydney, for diverse discipline areas which include Engineering, Architecture and Health Science. It enabled the academics responsible for more than 1000 subjects to map their learning outcomes to the institutional competency models, with details of the assessments and learning activities associated with these learning outcomes. This framework will provide the basis for modelling the individual learner's progression over the three to five years of their degree.

Ontologies can play many important roles for personalisation. One of these is to reason across granularity levels [35]. For example, even if evidence is only available for fine grained concepts (such as *iteration*), we can make some inferences about coarser grained concepts (such as *control structures*). Similarly, we can make somewhat riskier inferences in the opposite direction if that is needed. Scrutability of the ontological reasoning should enable the learner to understand such processes.

A very similar role for ontological reasoning can aggregate evidence that comes from different sources, especially where those sources use different vocabularies. Ontological reasoning can support reasoning across different learner models [14].

Another important role for ontologies is in support of tagging Learning Objects (LOs) such as a test item or other learning resource. This is critical for learner modelling since a learner's successful interaction with each LO contributes evidence about learning progress. We found that an interface to the ontology for the subject made it faster and easier to tag learning objects reliably [4].

A key role for ontologies is in conjunction with OLMs for domains with large numbers of concepts. If we want to provide effective interfaces for scrutinising such models, we need to structure the model so that the interface can present closely related concepts so the learner can focus on these. We used our lightweight, scrutable ontologies as the structuring mechanism for this purpose [5].

3.5 Rethinking Interaction with New Personal and Embedded Devices

We now turn to the second technology, the emerging personal and embedded devices and their associated interfaces. Each class of these devices has distinct characteristics, limitations and affordances. This calls for rethinking the user interface that these provide for the most basic of interactions that an operating system normally provides at desktops. Notably, all theses devices need to provide interfaces to the filesystem and the relevant operating systems actions, such as changing applications, changing the dataset used by the current application and altering settings for the application. Existing desktop interfaces for these interactions have been stable with increasingly standardised WIMP interfaces. There is no reason to suppose that these are the best way for the user to work with devices such as mobile phones or embedded tabletops.

We have been exploring ways to support tabletop interaction that makes it easy for a small group of people to work together at the table [6]. One of the challenges of this work is the fast changing nature of the hardware, with some based on touch interaction, some using special pens and some being able to distinguish which of the users has performed each action. We need to build a greater understanding of the nature of interaction that works well with the range of current hardware, as well as that likely to be created.

Taking these issues into account, we have explored ways to support the most fundamental actions at a tabletop [6]. We have also explored a new *associative* file access mechanism that enables a user to dwell on one file at the tabletop to retrieve all related files on all the systems connected to the tabletop [17]. We have explored ways that mobile phones can provide a private space for controlling this process [19]. As indicated in the tableshots in Figure 2, we used this process to drive personalisation [18]. At a quite different level, we have explored the nature of the core operating system functions that are relevant for tabletop interaction and the interfaces that can support them effectively [1].

To make such technology effective for education is still a very new area of research [44]. We have begun to explore ways to enable a non-programmer to create a rich collection of linked learning resources [43], curating a collection of learning resources, easily adding hot-spots to any of them, so that tapping that spot retrieves the linked materials. A similar approach has been used for the informal learning context of museums where experts can create content by defining links between physical *things* and digital resources [36].

4 Conclusions

The recent and emerging advances in personal and embedded devices create new possibilities for personalised learning and new ways to interact. We have outlined the key ideas in our PLUS framework, its foundation in the AR representation and the many HCI concerns that have informed its design and driven research into pragmatic interface solutions. The very nature of the learner model means that it contains personal information about the learner and this is subject to legal requirements [39]. This means the learner must be able to manage their own long term learner model: what evidence is allowed to go into it and what information about them is available to which applications. In brief, this makes scrutability essential. It is also really useful for learning, especially if we can create the right interfaces to OLMs. We have touched on some of the uses of long term modelling. One key driver for our work comes from the potential value of personalised learning [9]. New drivers come from the possibilities offered by the emergence of widely available *personal* and *embedded* devices that enable a learner to always have ready access to their learner model and their personal collections of digital artifacts.

Acknowledgments. This research was supported by Australian Research Council Project DP0877665. It also describes work funded by the Smart Internet Technology and Smart Services Technology Co-operative Research Centres.

References

1. Ackad, C.J., Collins, A., Kay, J.: Moving beyond the tabletop as an appliance. In: Adjunct Proceedings of ITS 2009, the ACM International Conference on Interactive Tabletops and Surfaces (2009)

2. Ankolekar, A., Vrandecic, D.: Kalpana - enabling client-side web personalization. In: Proceedings of the nineteenth ACM conference on Hypertext and hypermedia, Pittsburgh, PA, USA, pp. 21–26. ACM, New York (2008)
3. Apted, T., Kay, J.: Mecureo ontology and modelling tools. International Journal of Continuing Engineering Education and Lifelong Learning (Special Issue on Concepts and Ontologies in WBES) 14(3), 191–211 (2004)
4. Apted, T., Kay, J., Lum, A.: Supporting metadata creation with an ontology built from an extensible dictionary. In: De Bra, P.M.E., Nejdl, W. (eds.) AH 2004. LNCS, vol. 3137, pp. 4–13. Springer, Heidelberg (2004)
5. Apted, T., Kay, J., Lum, A., Uther, J.: Visualisation of ontological inferences for user control of personal web agents. In: Banissi, E., Borner, K., Chen, C., Clapworthy, G., Maple, C., Lobben, A., Moore, C., Roberts, J., Ursyn, A., Zhang, J. (eds.) Proceedings of IV 2003, 7th International Conference on Information Visualization, Washington, DC, USA, pp. 306–311. IEEE Computer Society, Los Alamitos (2003)
6. Apted, T., Kay, J., Quigley, A.: Tabletop sharing of digital photographs for the elderly. In: CHI 2006: Proceedings of the SIGCHI Conference on Human Factors in Computing Systems, pp. 781–790. ACM Press, New York (2006)
7. Assad, M., Carmichael, D., Kay, J., Kummerfeld, B.: PersonisAD: distributed, active, scrutable model framework for Context-Aware services. In: Pervasive Computing, pp. 55–72 (2007)
8. Baker, R.S.J.D., Yacef, K.: The state of educational data mining in 2009: A review and future visions. Journal of Educational Data Mining (JEDM) 1, 3–17 (2009)
9. Bloom, B.S.: The 2 sigma problem: The search for methods of group instruction as effective as one-to-one tutoring. Educational Researcher 13(6), 4–16 (1984) (1209 cites November 2009)
10. Bull, S., Brna, P., Pain, H.: Extending the scope of the student model. User Modeling and User-Adapted Interaction 5(1), 45–65 (1995)
11. Bull, S., Mabbott, A.: 20000 Inspections of a Domain-Independent Open Learner Model with Individual and Comparison Views. In: Ikeda, M., Ashley, K.D., Chan, T.-W. (eds.) ITS 2006. LNCS, vol. 4053, pp. 422–432. Springer, Heidelberg (2006)
12. Bull, S., Kay, J.: Student models that invite the learner in: The SMILI open learner modelling framework. IJAIED, International Journal of Artificial Intelligence 17(2), 89–120 (2007)
13. Bull, S., Kay, J.: Metacognition and open learner models. In: The 3rd Workshop on Meta-Cognition and Self-Regulated Learning in Educational Technologies, at ITS 2008 (2008)
14. Carmagnola, F., Dimitrova, V.: An Evidence-Based Approach to Handle Semantic Heterogeneity in Interoperable Distributed User Models. In: Nejdl, W., Kay, J., Pu, P., Herder, E. (eds.) AH 2008. LNCS, vol. 5149, pp. 73–82. Springer, Heidelberg (2008)
15. Carmichael, D.J., Kay, J., Kummerfeld, R.J.: Consistent modelling of users, devices and sensors in a ubiquitous computing environment. User Modeling and User-Adapted Interaction 15(3-4), 197–234 (2005)
16. Cimolino, L., Kay, J., Miller, A.: Concept mapping for eliciting verified personal ontologies. International Journal of Continuing Engineering Education and Life-Long Learning 14(3), 212–228 (2004)

17. Collins, A., Apted, T., Kay, J.: Tabletop file system access: Associative and hierarchical approaches. In: TABLETOP 2007: Proceedings of the Second Annual IEEE International Workshop on Horizontal Interactive Human-Computer Systems, Washington, DC, USA, pp. 113–120. IEEE Computer Society, Los Alamitos (2007)
18. Collins, A., Coche, H., Kuflik, T., Kay, J.: Making the tabletop personal: employing user models to aid information retrieval. Technical report, School of Information Technologies, University of Sydney (2010)
19. Collins, A., Kay, J.: Escaping hierarchies and desktops: Associative, pervasive file access with user control. Technical Report 649, School of Information Technologies, University of Sydney (2010)
20. Cook, R., Kay, J.: The justified user model: a viewable, explained user model. In: Kobsa, A., Litman, D. (eds.) Proceedings of Fourth International Conference on User Modeling UM 1994, pp. 145–150. MITRE, UM Inc. (1994)
21. Czarkowski, M., Kay, J.: Bringing scrutability to adaptive hypertext teaching. In: Gauthier, G., VanLehn, K., Frasson, C. (eds.) ITS 2000. LNCS, vol. 1839, pp. 423–432. Springer, Heidelberg (2000)
22. Czarkowski, M., Kay, J.: A scrutable adaptive hypertext. In: De Bra, P., Brusilovsky, P., Conejo, R. (eds.) AH 2002. LNCS, vol. 2347, pp. 384–387. Springer, Heidelberg (2002)
23. Czarkowski, M., Kay, J.: Giving learners a real sense of control over adaptivity, even if they are not quite ready for it yet, pp. 93–125. IDEA Information Science Publishing, Hershey (2006)
24. Dolog, P., Kay, J., Kummerfeld, B.: Personal lifelong user model clouds. In: Proceeding of the Lifelong User Modelling Workshop at UMAP 2009 User Modeling Adaptation, and Personalization, pp. 1–8 (2009)
25. Gerber, S., Fry, M., Kay, J., Kummerfeld, B., Pink, G., Wasinger, R.: PersonisJ: mobile, client-side user modelling. In: De Bra, P., Kobsa, A., Chin, D. (eds.) User Modeling, Adaptation, and Personalization. LNCS, vol. 6075, pp. 111–122. Springer, Heidelberg (2010)
26. Gluga, R., Kay, J., Lever, T.: Modeling long term learning of generic skills. In: Aleven, V., Kay, J., Mostow, J. (eds.) Intelligent Tutoring Systems. LNCS, vol. 6094, pp. 85–94. Springer, Heidelberg (2010)
27. Hitchens, M., Kay, J., Kummerfeld, R.J., Brar, A.: Secure identity management for pseudo-anonymous service access. In: Hutter, D., Ullmann, M. (eds.) SPC 2005. LNCS, vol. 3450, pp. 48–55. Springer, Heidelberg (2005)
28. Holden, S., Kay, J., Poon, J., Yacef, K.: Workflow-based personalised document delivery (just-in-time training system). Journal of Interactive Learning 4(1), 131–148 (2005)
29. Kay, J.: Um: a user modelling toolkit. In: Second International User Modelling Workshop, p. 11 (1990)
30. Kay, J.: The um toolkit for cooperative user modelling. User Modeling and User-Adapted Interaction 4, 149–196 (1995)
31. Kay, J.: Accretion representation for scrutable student modelling. In: Gauthier, G., VanLehn, K., Frasson, C. (eds.) ITS 2000. LNCS, vol. 1839, pp. 514–523. Springer, Heidelberg (2000)
32. Kay, J., Kummerfeld, B., Lauder, P.: Personis: a server for user models. In: De Bra, P., Brusilovsky, P., Conejo, R. (eds.) AH 2002. LNCS, vol. 2347, pp. 203–212. Springer, Heidelberg (2002)
33. Kay, J., Kummerfeld, B.: Portme: Personal lifelong user modelling portal. Technical Report 647, School of Information Technologies, University of Sydney (2010)

34. Kay, J., Li, L., Fekete, A.: Learner reflection in student self-assessment. In: Proceedings of ACE 2007, 9th Australasian Computing Education Conference, pp. 89–95. Australian Computer Society, Sydney (2007)
35. Kay, J., Lum, A.: Exploiting readily available web data for reflective student models. In: Proceedings of AIED 2005, Artificial Intelligence in Education, pp. 338–345. IOS Press, Amsterdam (2005)
36. Koleva, B., Egglestone, S.R., Schnadelbach, H., Glover, K., Greenhalgh, C., Rodden, T., Dade-Robertson, M.: Supporting the creation of hybrid museum experiences. In: Proceedings of the 27th international conference on Human factors in computing systems, Boston, MA, USA, pp. 1973–1982. ACM, New York (2009)
37. Niu, W.T., Kay, J.: PERSONAF: Framework for personalised ontological reasoning in pervasive computing. User modeling and User-Adapted Interaction: the Journal of Personalization Research 20(1), 1–40 (2010)
38. Novak, J.D.: Concept maps and Vee diagrams: Two metacognitive tools to facilitate meaningful learning. Instructional science 19(1), 29–52 (1990)
39. Palen, L., Dourish, P.: Unpacking" privacy" for a networked world. In: Proceedings of the conference on Human factors in computing systems, pp. 129–136 (2003) (331 cites November 2009)
40. Perera, D., Kay, J., Yacef, K., Koprinska, I., Zaiane, O.: Clustering and Sequential Pattern Mining of Online Collaborative Learning Data, vol. 21, pp. 759–772. IEEE Computer Society, Los Alamitos (2009)
41. Schultz, P., Nolan, J.M., Cialdini, R.B., Goldstein, N.J., Griskevicius, V.: The constructive, destructive, and reconstructive power of social norms. Psychological Science 18(5), 429 (2007)
42. Self, J.: The defining characteristics of intelligent tutoring systems research: ITSs care, precisely. International Journal of Artificial Intelligence in Education 10(3-4), 350–364 (1999)
43. Sprengart, B., Collins, A., Kay, J.: Curator: A design environment for curating tabletop museum experiences. In: ITS 2009 Demonstrations, the ACM Conference on Interactive Tabletops and Surfaces (2009)
44. Tse, E., Schöning, J., Rogers, Y., Shen, C., Morrison, G.: Next generation of hci and education: workshop on ui technologies and educational pedagogy. In: CHI EA 2010: Proceedings of the 28th of the international conference extended abstracts on Human factors in computing systems, pp. 4509–4512. ACM, New York (2010)
45. Upton, K., Kay, J.: Narcissus: interactive activity mirror for small groups. In: Houben, G.-J., McCalla, G., Pianesi, F., Zancanaro, M. (eds.) UMAP 2009. LNCS, vol. 5535, pp. 54–65. Springer, Heidelberg (2009)
46. Van Merrienboer, J., Kirschner, P., Paas, F., Sloep, P., Caniels, M.: Towards an Integrated Approach for Research on Lifelong Learning (2009)
47. Weber, G., Brusilovsky, P.: ELM-ART: An adaptive versatile system for Web-based instruction. International Journal of Artificial Intelligence in Education 12(4), 351–384 (2001)

Maintaining Continuity of Inquiry Learning Experiences across Contexts: Teacher's Management Strategies and the Role of Technology

Stamatina Anastopoulou, Yang Yang, Mark Paxton, Mike Sharples, Charles Crook, Shaaron Ainsworth, and Claire O'Malley

Learning Sciences Research Institute, Exchange Building, University of Nottingham, Jubilee Campus, Wollaton Road, Nottingham NG8 1BB, UK
{stamatina.anastopoulou,lpxyy,mark.paxton,mike.sharples, charles.crook,shaaron.ainsworth, claire.o'malley}@nottingham.ac.uk

Abstract. An inquiry-led investigation with technology was designed and implemented, aiming to enhance our understanding of how inquiry learning takes place within a personal, socio-cultural and institutional context. Children used personal technologies across contexts, to plan and collect evidence, analyse and share their work. These technologies are boundary objects, connecting students' experiences across the classroom, out-of-class activities, a fieldtrip and the home, and enabling students to carry out inquiry activities autonomously. The science teacher aimed to maintain a sense of continuity across contexts by utilising specific management strategies: interchanging between highlighting and constraining technology use, ensuring that all students know what they need to do in and out of class, communicating interdependencies among groups and by translating group data to an overview of the whole class data. These strategies are identified as prerequisites for any successful inquiry learning experience to take place.

Keywords: personal technologies, inquiry learning, science education.

1 Introduction

Inquiry learning has a long history (e.g. [1]), which focuses on exploring meaningful and productive approaches to the development of children's knowledge of the world. Inquiry learning calls upon the ability to plan, carry out and interpret investigations. Science educators note that inquiry represents a view of science education that carries with it an increased emphasis on process skills and presents a number of challenges for teachers and students.

Millar [2] argues that for teachers to communicate inquiry learning in their classrooms, they need to shift from perceiving their role as one of transmitting information to a role in which they are the facilitators of opportunities. Sandoval et al. [3] suggest that many teachers, as well as their students, currently see science as being the discovery and collection of facts about the world, rather than as being theories that have been created by people. Practical work in classrooms is often about communicating the known rather than exploring the unknown [4]. Experiments are seen to create answers rather than to test ideas, because often students are not aware of where the ideas come from. This suggests that the focus of practical work in science education should be on communicating ideas such as scientific models and methods, and to provide an opportunity for students to use scientific language and to learn how to see the world from a scientific perspective.

In the Personal Inquiry project, we explore ways to support scientific investigations through discussing scientific methods and inquiry questions in the light of data collected and analysed. Students are provided with software (the PI Toolkit) running on netbook computers to guide and structure science investigations related to curriculum topics, such as 'healthy eating' and 'microclimates'. The teacher needs to accommodate these technologies, adjusting her teaching to fit the new situation. Following an ecological approach, we anticipate that disruptions will arise, as with any school intervention with technologies, which tend to undermine existing practices and demand new ones. We aim to understand how technologies and their related activities influence the personal, socio-cultural and institutional context where learning takes place and how the immediate learner experience within these contexts blends with or confronts existing practices to lead to new practices [5]. By providing students with netbooks that they use in the science class, outdoors and at home, we focus on how class practices change. We regard these issues of outmost importance, to achieve the aim of developing innovative learning experiences into widespread learning and teaching practices.

In this paper we discuss the challenges faced by one teacher and her strategies to address them as a part of a research intervention with personal learning technologies. Based on an intervention with a science class, we examine the teacher's view of how the introduction of a new technology in the classroom shapes students' experiences across different contexts (i.e. the class and outside, during a fieldtrip) and how the teacher orchestrates these experiences. In particular, we discuss the teacher's management strategies to maintain the continuity of students' inquiry learning across contexts.

2 Relevant Research

Previous research on personal mobile devices has denoted personal learning technologies as a boundary objects [6]. A boundary object is an object or construct that is claimed by a group of actors who occupy divergent viewpoints. They are both plastic enough to adapt to local needs and the constraints of the several parties employing them, yet robust enough to maintain a common identity across sites [7]. For example, a personal technology can be utilised to support students' individual needs, e.g. to play games or access social networking sites, but also to carry out activities set out by school investigation. As a result, personal learning technologies may become a focus for conflict between children and teachers because they interpose between informal and formal contexts of learning [6].

Since it is designed to enhance both the autonomy and communication between worlds [7], we consider the PI toolkit as a boundary object. It was used to connect students' experiences across the classroom, out-of-class activities, a fieldtrip and the home, enabling students to carry out inquiry activities autonomously. However, disruptions may occur and it is the teacher's role to either anticipate or react to them.

Boundary objects mediate between different groups; they do not provide a common understanding, or consensus between participants. Instead, they serve a dual function, supplying common points of reference at the same time as serving to distinguish differences [8]. Therefore some students used the netbook to engage in the activities of the lessons while others also played games.

We designed and implemented an inquiry-led investigation with technology aiming to enhance our understanding of how learning takes place within a personal, sociocultural and institutional context. Children used their netbooks across contexts, at home for example to show to their parent what they did as well as access the software to review previous activities. These opportunities further supported the sense of continuity that the science teacher aimed for. However this boundary object brought disturbances in the classroom practices as well as enjoyment. For example, as with any classroom laptop activity, children could 'hide' behind the netbook screen and engage in irrelevant to the class activities but they could also visualise information in new informative ways. In this paper we address and study such disturbances from a teacher's perspective. We explore how she anticipated or reacted to them and how she utilised technology to facilitate the transition between different contexts, e.g. between the class and the fieldtrip or outdoors. The aim is to understand how existing learning and teaching practices are confronted and what new practices arise.

3 Method

We designed a study in an inner city secondary school to investigate how the PI toolkit supports students in learning in a science classroom, in a fieldtrip or other outdoors.

3.1 The Intervention

Over a period of 4 weeks, 10 science lessons and a day trip to a nature reserve took place. The educational aim was for the children to carry out investigations into the effect of noise pollution on the feeding habits of birds. The topic was devised through discussions amongst the researchers, teachers, students and wildlife experts, to be relevant to the UK national curriculum while also being of personal interest to the students. Participants were 28 students of 13 years of age (UK Year 8) and their science teacher. The Science teacher had taught the particular students for more than a year and she has been using desktop PCs as part of her science teaching regularly. She has been fully engaged with the project and contributed to lesson planning sessions and this is the second intervention with the PI Toolkit that she facilitated.

Table 1 describes the place and learning objectives of the lessons and the fieldtrip. An objective across the lessons was for the students to understand the inquiry process as a whole and how each lesson was connected to the previous and the next.

Fig. 1. Students using the PI toolkit in the science class

Students went through an inquiry process on the topic of pollution and wildlife, which is part of the UK Key Stage 3 curriculum. Their inquiries were structured in eight phases that enabled the students to:

- Gain a broad understanding of pollution and wildlife,
- Narrow down their focus to specific inquiry questions,
- Plan the methods and procedures they need to use in order to answer these questions,
- Collect evidence,
- Perform an analysis of the collected data,
- Draw inferences based on evidence,
- Prepare a leaflet,
- Evaluate their inquiries.

To avoid misunderstandings of these phases being in a sequence, inquiry phases were communicated as iterative and interconnected. Students experienced three different methods of data collection (observation, correlation and experiment) handling different sets of data each time. Therefore, they started with a generic inquiry question which was specified further in the course of the investigation, through iterations of the inquiry phases.

During the fieldtrip students carried out an observation of wildlife to make them think of a man-made habitat that was friendly to wildlife and they pursued a sound data mapping activity to explore how sound may or may not affect wildlife. In the afternoon, students discussed their activities and visualised their findings (Figure 2).

In the school yard, students collected data regarding their surroundings, weighed bird food and fill up bird feeders (Figure 3). They had also the opportunity to repeat their activities if they collected erroneous data.

Table 1. The outline of lessons, their objectives and where they took place

Time Period	Learning Objectives	Place
Lesson 1:	Specifying the topic of inquiry	Science classroom
Lesson 2:	Giving out and explore the technology. Finding out how it can support their investigation	Science classroom
Lesson 3:	Discuss about observations as a scientific method. Coming up with an inquiry question	Science classroom
Fieldtrip	Carry out observation method (describe the habitat and collect environmental data of the nature reserve), Analyse results	Nature reserve
Lesson 4	Describe school habitat. Reflect on observation as a method and introduce correlation as a method. Set up a more specific inquiry question. Hypothesis formation Make predictions of the school study	Visit school yards to consider them as habitats
Lesson 5	Data collection (phase 1) Reflection on data collection.	Visit School yards
Lesson6	Discuss interim findings, and reflect on correlation as a method. Introduce experiments as a method. Discuss independent and dependent variables.	Science classroom
Lesson7	Data collection. Data analysis of school study, Drawing conclusions from school study. Introducing garden experiment	Visit School yards
Lesson 8	Data analysis of experimental data Drawing conclusion from all studies Answering inquiry question	Science classroom
Lesson 9:	Making a leaflet communicating one of the methods	Science classroom
Lesson 10	Return equipment Questionnaires Give bird feeders to students to continue their investigations at home.	Science classroom

Fig. 2. Students collecting sound data and a screenshot of the GoogleEarth visualising all groups data

3.2 The Personal Inquiry (PI) Toolkit

To support children's personal inquiries across contexts, the PI 'toolkit' was designed and installed on Asus EEE netbooks. Implemented to work across different devices, from netbooks to shared classroom displays, the toolkit supports students through a sequence of activities including planning, collecting data, data analysis, conclusions and communication of results.

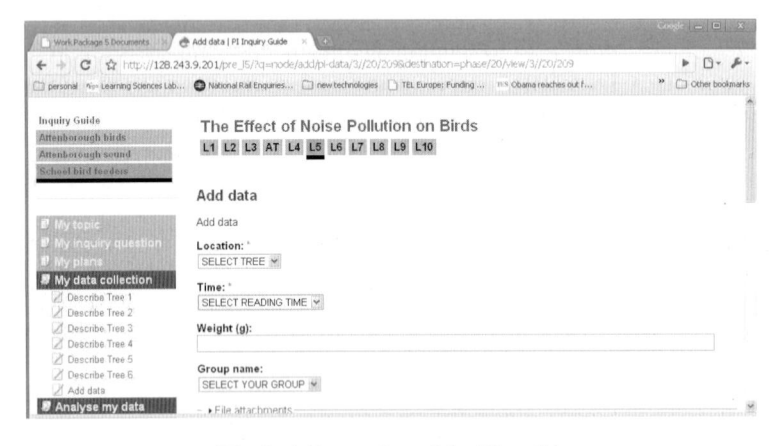

Fig. 3. A Screenshot of the PI toolkit

Activities may be created as individual tasks, or group and class tasks where the activity is completed as a group. In addition, outputs of an activity can be viewable only by the authors and the teacher, or made available for the whole class to see. The activities are assigned to inquiry phases, appearing in a navigation menu on the right hand side of the screen, the activities are further assigned to a number of stages, representing individual lessons [9]. As students pursued their inquiries, different activities, inquiry phases and stages were highlighted.

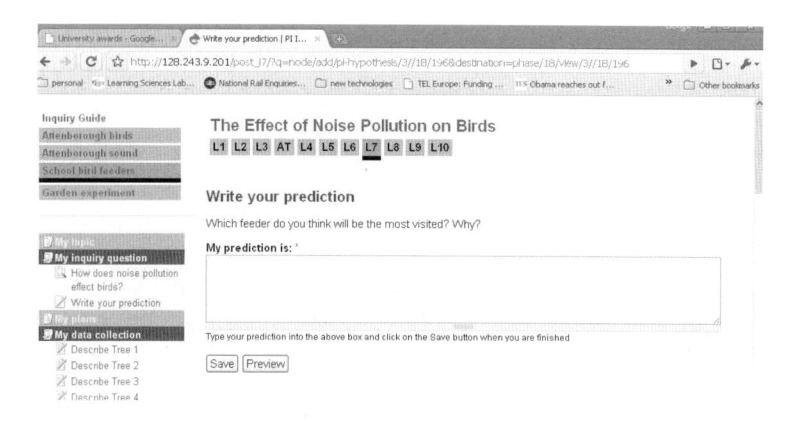

Fig. 4. The PI Toolkit showing a text entry page

The PI toolkit is a web based application, built upon Drupal, an open source content management platform. During the intervention, the toolkit was deployed in two configurations; during classroom activities participants used their netbooks to access a single installation. A web server and wireless network was deployed in the classroom to achieve this (and avoid the administrative overhead of accessing the schools wireless network and restricted internet connection). This configuration allowed all the class data to be stored in a single place so that participants could work collaboratively and changes to the toolkit could be rapidly deployed. Out of the classroom, when participants were engaged in data collection activities, the toolkit was installed directly on to a set of group work netbooks, one per group. This configuration allowed the participants to work in the field (where network access was not available), though the data then had to be transferred to the central installation post-hoc. The group work netbooks were separate from their individual devices, so this (and preparation of the machines) could be done in the background whilst the participants worked on their own computers.

To carry out the sound data mapping activity in the field trip, students used data loggers (ScienceScope Logbooks) with sound level sensors, a GPS receiver and a digital camera. The GPS unit recorded position information which were synchronised with photographs and the sound levels after the activity. At the same time, the netbooks were used to record observations during the data collection. In the second part of the field trip the data was projected onto the whiteboard and inspected by the class on a Google Earth 3D map (Figure 2). This map brought all the groups' data together into one view and each group's files was then available to download via the website to further viewing.

3.3 Procedures

Each student was given a netbook which was used in class and also taken home for the duration of the intervention. Students also used the netbooks when they were out of the class, in the school yard, the nature reserve and the home. Out of the classroom, the students engaged with netbook-supported inquiry activities, such as data collection and visualisation of data.

When in the class, the teacher used her laptop which also run the PI toolkit to facilitate the class activities. She guided students' access to the toolkit, as well as the sharing, analysis and presentation of findings.

From the pool of data collected during the intervention, this paper focuses on teacher interviews, commenced right after every lesson in her classroom. The interviews illustrate the teacher's perspective, her challenges and how she addressed them. The interviews were semi-structured and designed to be 20-30 minutes long. They aimed to elicit the teacher's reflection on the lesson, its successes and problems, the extent to which it had met her expectations and capture her future plans.

4 Results and Discussion

We followed inductive thematic analysis of the interviews [10] which consists of six phases: (1) Familiarisation with data; (2) Generating initial codes; (3) Searching for themes; (4) Reviewing the themes; (5) Defining and naming themes and (6) writing up. In this process, the following codes came up: Teacher's adoption and emotions towards technology, Teacher's highlight of successful moments, Teacher's concerns, Teacher's strategy towards technology management, Continuity of teaching, Teacher's general reflections on the technology intervention. Six themes emerged from these codes, which are discussed below and they are grouped in three clusters according to the situation they describe.

In particular, they describe classroom management issues arisen from the introduction of technology, management of activities across contexts, and management of students' data as they shift in different sized groups. These themes reflect the teacher's management strategies which are identified as a prerequisite for any successful inquiry learning experience to take place.

4.1 Situation 1: Tempering Technology Temptation

Every time the netbooks are brought in the classroom from home or outside, the teacher needs to accommodate the netbooks within her classroom. The 'temptation of the technology' is one of the concerns most frequently mentioned by the teacher, so she develops strategies to manage technology use. The teacher interchanges between two strategies to support and constrain technology use by a) harnessing the students' excitement and b) coordinating technology use class-wide.

Harnessing students' excitement. When the netbooks are first brought in the classroom, students' emotional responses to the netbooks are openly communicated between the teacher and students. In the teacher's point of view, these emotions needed to be acted upon strategically in her classroom, for the successful implementation of the lessons. So, she accommodated students' excitement, by giving students time to play with them and also by discussing openly technical problems, which they may have encountered out of class.

In particular, before the technologies were given out to the children, and while they were lying at one bench of the class, the teacher used the computers to attract students' attention.

> EX1: 'There was a lot of excitement before the class about the technology...... I thought maybe I will show them the computer, because I was thinking 'people are getting a bit rowdy now' and then I thought 'oh, maybe I can talk about the computer, it can get them listening and let them [engaged].'

She devoted lesson time to explore the technologies and viewed the activity as necessary and important: She characterise it as a 'slack lesson' but she considered it as an acceptable trade-off for the familiarisation of technology.

> EX2: 'Part of me feels like it a bit of a slack lesson or there was slack time but I think in some respects, that is quite important to allow them to have time to play on the computer and find out everything that is on there.'

During subsequent lessons, she recognised technology as boundary object and decided to spend time on the technical problems that the students encountered at home. Therefore, she accommodated the students' problems with the netbooks out of the classroom. She did not disconnect technology use in different contexts. She suggested that doing so would help her to start the lessons quicker and smoother, and she proved herself right.

> EX3: 'Maybe that's something with the computers [5-10 minutes helping students with their technical problems with netbooks at home] that needs to be built into each lesson in a way, because if you don't build something in and they've got problems, they'll shout out and try and get the answers and stop you from starting the lesson as quick as you can...'

Coordinating technology use and access class-wide. Although she appreciated the opportunities offered by the netbooks, she also indicated that students cannot self-regulate netbook use. To sustain the teaching flow and good classroom behaviour, the teacher decided to constrain netbooks use only when it is needed. But, having personal devices for each student undermined her efforts to achieve this across all students in the class. So she utilised peer pressure to coordinate the technology use and access.

In each lesson, students should log into the PI toolkit but this often took a few minutes because of high load on the network and the server. Therefore this necessary activity was disruptive and challenged classroom behaviour, e.g. students would play games while they waited for other students to log in. The teacher was aware of this disruption from lesson 2 onwards and started to develop and test her strategies to cope with this disruption:

> EX4: 'maybe we get them 'log on' as soon as they get in. So they'll be logging on at the same time but slightly different. But then to say 'right, once you've logged on,[...] you can shut your screen'. ...... Or I can tell them 'you don't get your computer out until we need it' and then at the point in the lesson, they can all get the computers out and use them but I just thought it might be less disruption'

She also puts effort into switching students' attention from game playing to using the learning toolkit.

> EX5: Maybe I have to highlight 'log onto the toolkit' instead of going on games first to make sure that everyone can get on.'

Moreover, when an activity without the netbooks needs to be carried out, she wants the students to close the netbooks lids at the same time. To succeed in that, she makes clear to the students that technology use is a class-wide activity. However, having personal devices brings extra challenges to the teacher. So, the teacher utilises peer pressure as a trigger to achieve more cooperative use of the netbooks.

> *EX6:* '*Apart from a few of them, they're getting better at closing the computers. They still don't do it instantaneously which we would like them to do, however unrealistic that may seem. They're getting better at doing that and I think they'll nag each other a bit. I think maybe they can start to see 'if I get on with this, then we do get to open them again and do another activity and we will do that quicker if we do all shut our computers faster'.*

To summarise, when personal technologies enter the classroom, the teacher sometimes accommodates and sometimes manages technology use and access. Therefore, students' reactions to technology are strategically highlighted by the teacher, but on some occasions technology use is constrained. As a result, the teacher subtly balances the usefulness of the technology in class and interchanges her strategies to achieve the lesson objectives.

4.2 Situation 2: Preparing Students for the Transition across Contexts

When students go out of the class (to the fieldtrip or to the school yard), they change roles. From being monitored by the teacher, they become more autonomous and they need to carry out activities responsibly. The toolkit as a boundary object is present at all times, but the way students need to interact with it changes: from text entry (Figure 4), they move to form-like interaction (Figure 3), e.g. they need to add their data. The teacher prepared the transition across contexts by 'making inroads' into other contexts. Before the student went to the fieldtrip, she navigated the students through their future activities in order to facilitate their use of netbooks outside the class. She revealed that preparing the students for their out-of-classroom activities was a major lesson objective by saying '*it was important that they saw all the things that they had to record onto and in for [the nature reserve]. That will make a bit of an inroad into [the nature reserve].*' This section, therefore, discusses how the teacher prepares the transition across contexts by encompassing all students and by supporting proper use of netbooks when out of the classroom. These two themes are associated and influenced by each other since she addresses both themes with one strategy.

Encompassing all when out of class. Including all students is the teacher's major concern, when the students go out of the classroom. During the interviews, 'incorporate everyone' and 'encompass all' are frequently mentioned by the teacher and she continuously assessed if she held the attention of all the students and maintained their involvement during her lessons. To make sure the students understood what they needed to do with the netbooks during the fieldtrip, she used the interactive whiteboard to demonstrate step by step how to navigate the system in order to carry out the inquiry activities. Although it may have been a laboured method, she reported that she valued the importance of showing all pages to everyone.

> *EX7:* '*The way we did it may have been a bit more laboured but I think everybody found the right things, they knew they'd found the right things,*

they got a chance to see it properly and I know that everyone's done all those steps. So even if they do struggle on Monday [during the fieldtrip], you know that they have done it.

She also explained why she chose to demonstrate the use of the netbook on classroom whiteboard over distributing written instructions to the students.

> EX8: 'I think the other method [giving written instructions to the students and asking them to read it and prepare individually]; it does allow some students to work quicker than others and the ones who worked at home maybe who are slightly more focused and work quicker. They could have gone at their own pace and then done something different but it might have been less easy to ensure that you knew that everyone had got to the right place.'

Proper use of netbooks when out of class. Using the netbooks out of class was a new challenge for the teacher and the students so she wanted to make sure that everyone knew what they need to do prior to being there. Prior to the fieldtrip and the outdoors activities, she focuses on the practical and functional aspects of the netbook use, instead of the conceptual understanding of the netbook use for inquiry activities, probably because she understood that unless they used it 'properly' they would not be able to have useful data to discuss. Therefore, she put substantial effort into the demonstration of the netbook use on the interactive whiteboard.

> EX9: 'it would have been too much, too overwhelming with logistics or whatever on Monday [during the fieldtrip]. The use of the computers would have been too much of a hassle, whereas we have taken some of that hassle away now. So it will be 'let's use them properly to make the recordings onto [the PI toolkit]. I think we had to do it but I don't know if there is a better way of going.'

To summarise, to support children's outdoors activities, the teacher prepared their transition by 'making inroads' between the activities in the class and outdoors. Two strategies that the teacher employed were 'encompassing all' and 'proper use of netbooks', by ensuring that all the students know what they need to do and how to navigate the toolkit.

4.3 Situation 3: Preparing Students for the Transition between Different Sized Groups

As students moved from out-of-class to class activities, they experienced transitions between individual, group and class activities. The teacher prepared students for the transition between different sized groups by taking advantage of technology's networking capabilities to bridge the out-of-class group work and the in-class class-wide work. The teacher perceived the networking capabilities of the PI toolkit as a means to strengthen cooperation among groups, and as tools to translate group data to an overview of the whole class data.

Interdependence among Groups. From the teacher's point of view, successful data collection depends on the students' proper use of technology. For students to enact their activities responsibly, the teacher connects the group contributions to a class level. They should, therefore, be dependent on each other, instead of competitive.

The students went out to collect data in groups and as a result, they needed to record the data in the netbooks. The teacher indicated that it was essential for students to use the technologies properly: when some groups did not collect data the consequences would affect the rest of the class.

> *EX10: I was thinking 'oh no, if they don't press those last two buttons at the end'. I thought some groups might not have managed to record anything or they'd gone wrong with the GPS thing, [...]. At least everyone did record data.*

Moreover, the teacher promoted interdependence among the different groups by introducing the group activities to the students in Lesson 5, as follows: 'the whole class relies on your data'. With the recognition of this need, she tried to externalise the interdependence among the groups and to communicate possible breakdowns.

A Variety of Group Contributions. The networking capabilities of the PI toolkit strengthen the interdependence among the groups by synthesising their contributions. The teacher highlighted a broad spectrum of contributions made by different groups, instead of identifying errors. Her major interest lay in synthesising the whole class' performance and acknowledging the wide spectrum of the data the students had collected.

After data collection out of the classroom, the teacher retrieved the data from the groups rapidly in the shared classroom display through a table which summarised the group data. Thus, the teacher could discuss with the class the meaning of their data. Revealed in the interview, the children enjoyed the moment as did the teacher:

> *EX11: I think they were quite wowed by that at the start, seeing exactly where you were on Google Earth and mapping that.*
> *EX12: It [The data table] worked pretty well on the board and was quite amazing that [a researcher] managed to get it there.*

In summary, as students moved from out-of-class to class activities, they not only changed location but also style of collaboration. The teacher orchestrated the class interactions at group and class level and prepared students for the transition between different sized groups by communicating the interdependencies among groups. She also took advantage of technology's connectivity to strengthen the cooperation among groups and to translate group data to an overview of the whole class data.

5 Conclusions

During a research intervention with personal learning technologies in a science class, a teacher developed management strategies and overcame challenges, in order to maintain continuity of student experiences across contexts. In this paper we studied these strategies, following an inductive thematic analysis of the teacher's interviews. We examined the teacher's view of how the introduction of a new technologies in the classroom shapes students' experiences across different contexts (i.e. the class and outside, during a fieldtrip) and what new practices she employed in her class. The PI toolkit, as a boundary object, supported but also disrupted classroom practices by visualising information in new informative ways but also allowing children to engage in irrelevant to the class activities.

When personal technologies enter the classroom, the teacher sometimes accommodates and sometimes constrains technology use and access. She subtly balances the usefulness of the technology in class and interchanges her strategies to achieve the lesson objectives. When students go out of the class, they become more autonomous and they are responsible to carry out inquiry activities. By ensuring that all the students know what they need to do and how to navigate the toolkit, the teacher made inroads into the fieldtrip while in the classroom so that students are prepared for the transition across contexts. The teacher also orchestrated individual, group and class-wide activities to support a sense of continuity of their experiences. As students move from out-of-class to class activities, they experienced changes in collaboration style and the teacher orchestrated these changes by communicating the interdependencies among groups and by translating the group contributions to an overview of the class.

Acknowledgements. We would like to thank the teacher and pupils of Hadden Park High School that participated in our study and our cooperate partner Sciencescope. This project is supported by an ESRC/EPSRC Technology Enhanced Learning Grant for Personal Inquiry (PI): Designing for Evidence-based Inquiry Learning across Formal and Informal Settings, reference: RES-139-25-0382.

References

1. Dewey, J.: How we think: a restatement of the relation of reflective thinking to the educative process, Boston, MA, Heath (1933)
2. Millar, R.: Towards Evidence-based Practice in Science Education 3: Teaching Pupils 'Ideas-about-science', June 2003. Teaching and Learning Research Briefing, vol. 3. Teaching and Learning Research Programme, London (2003)
3. Sandoval, W., Deneroff, V., Franke, M.: Teaching, as learning, as inquiry: moving beyond activity in the analysis of teaching practice. Presented at Annual Meeting of the American Educational Research Assn., New Orleans, LA, April 1-5 (2002)
4. Millar, R.: Thinking about practical work. In: Amos, S., Boohan, R. (eds.) Aspects of secondary science. Routledge/Falmer and the Open University, London and New York (2002)
5. Vavoula, G., Sharples, M.: Meeting the Challenges in Evaluating Mobile Learning: a 3-level Evaluation Framework. International Journal of Mobile and Blended Learning 1(2), 54–75 (2009)
6. Sharples, M., Corlett, D., Westmancott, O.: The Design and Implementation of a Mobile Learning Resource. Personal and Ubiquitous Computing 6, 220–234 (2002)
7. Star, S.L., Griesemer, J.R.: Institutional Ecology, 'Translations' and Boundary Objects: Amateurs and Professionals in Berkeley's Museum of Vertebrate Zoology, 1907-39. Social Studies of Science 19, 387–420 (1989)
8. Harvey, F., Chrisman, N.: Boundary objects and the social construction of GIS technology. Environment and Planning A 30(9), 1683–1694 (1998)
9. Scanlon, E., Anastopoulou, S., Kerawalla, L., Mulholland, P. (under review). Scripting personal inquiry: using technology to represent and support students' understanding of personal inquiry across contexts. Manuscript submitted to Journal of Computer Assisted Learning
10. Braun, V., Clarke, V.: Using thematic analysis in psychology. Qualitative Research in Psychology 3(2), 77–101 (2006)

Ultra-Personalization and Decentralization: The Potential of Multi-Agent Systems in Personal and Informal Learning

Ali M. Aseere, David E. Millard, and Enrico H. Gerding

School of Electronics and Computer Science,
University of Southampton, Southampton, UK
{ama07r,dem,eg}@ecs.soton.ac.uk

Abstract. Agents are autonomous software components that work with one another in a decentralized fashion to achieve some end. Agent systems have been used in Technology Enhanced Learning (TEL) before, but these applications seldom take advantage of the fact that each agent may have its own goals and strategies, which makes agent systems an attractive way of providing personalized learning. In particular, since agents can solve problems in a decentralized way, this makes them an attractive way of supporting informal learning. In this paper we use scenarios to examine how common problem solving techniques from the agents world (voting, coalition formation and auction systems) map to significant challenges for personalized and informal learning in the TEL world. Through an agent simulation we then show how an agent system might perform in one of those scenarios and explore how different agent strategies might influence the outcome. Based on this work we argue that agent systems provide a way of providing ultra-personalization of the learning process in a decentralized way and highlight equitability and scrutability as two key challenges for future investigation.

Keywords: Agent Systems, Personalized Learning, Informal Learning.

1 Introduction

Agents are special software components that work together in an agent framework to achieve some end. Their main features include autonomy, reactiveness, proactiveness and social ability [1]. Multi-agent systems, where several such agents interact, are being used in a wide variety of applications, ranging from comparatively small systems for personal assistance, to open, complex, systems for industrial applications [2]. In Technology Enhanced Learning (TEL) they can provide new models of learning and applications, such as personal assistants, user guides and alternative help systems, which are helpful for both students and teachers [3]. It has also been argued that using multi-agent systems to design educational systems lead to more versatile, faster and lower cost systems [4].

We believe that the major potential in multi-agent systems has yet to be fully explored, and that it relates to the ability of agent systems to support personalized and informal learning. In the e-learning domain we are increasingly seeing a move from a world of VLEs (Virtual Learning Environments) into a space where students are taking more control of their learning in the form of PLEs (Personal Learning Environments), either as monolithic applications to help students manage their resources and time, or as a collection of online tools (such as Google calendar to manage time, 43 Things to manage goals, etc). In this personalized learning context agent technology becomes even more appropriate because agents are good at representing the requirements of users, and negotiating a more personalized experience. There is also a lot of potential to support informal learning, because in a decentralized agent system there is no need for a central authority (such as a tutor or academic institution) to orchestrate collaborations and learning activities.

In this paper we explore the potential of multi-agent systems for personalized and informal learning. We first present a number of scenarios that show how common problem solving techniques in the agents world (voting systems, coalition formation and auction systems) could map to problems in TEL, and explore how agent technologies could lead to ultra-personalization and decentralization, enabling new scenarios that are not possible with today's technology.

We then present a multi-agent simulation of the first of these scenarios (students making module choices) in order to demonstrate how a multi-agent system can solve problems in a decentralized way where an autonomous software agent votes on a student's behalf according to the student's preferences. In so doing, we are the first to apply voting procedures in an e-learning scenario. In particular, we introduce a novel voting protocol, consisting of multiple rounds that allows the student agent to accurately represent the student's preferences, and that can learn from previous rounds. In a comparative experiment we also explore how different student strategies (the algorithms that individual agents use to negotiate with each other) affect the outcome.

Our research demonstrates how agent systems could be applied to TEL to support personalized and informal learning, but it also highlights a number of key issues that may be of concern to educators.

The rest of this paper is organized as follows. Section 2 describes related work focusing on personalized and informal learning and the existing use of agent technology in TEL. Section 3 presents three scenarios that show how solutions from the agent domain might be used to solve problems from the TEL domain in a novel way. Section 4 describes an agent simulation of the first of these scenarios, and an experiment to compare the performance of three different student strategies. Section 5 analyses our findings and argues that while agent systems enable ultra-personalization and decentralization they also present new problems of equitability and scrutability. Section 6 concludes the paper and discusses our future work plans.

2 Background

2.1 Personalized and Informal Learning

Personalization in an educational setting is about working in partnership with the learner to tailor their learning experience and pathways according to their needs and personal objectives. Personalization is perceived as the task of providing every learner with appropriate learning opportunities to meet individual learning needs supported by relevant resources that promote choice and advance learner autonomy [5]. The concept of personalized learning emerged as a result of several developments. Partly, it is a reflection of living and working in a modern society, the developments of new technologies, and in particular how they can enable learners to break down institutional barriers and become a part of a global society.

There is also a growing recognition that current educational provision may be to narrow and restrictive and is not meeting the individuals learners or society needs as a whole [6]. Current learners see technology as core to their learning environments in particular computer and mobile devices. They use the Internet usually to support their learning, to find information and to discuss work with other students and teachers. They are comfortable working with multiple representations, are digitally literate, and happy to turn to Internet-based tools to help achieve their learning [5].

Sampson [7] has suggested that e-learning benefits from the advanced information processing and the Internet technologies to provide the following features which could be considered as lineaments of personalized learning:

- *Personalization*, where learning material are customized to individual learners, based on an analysis of the learners objectives, status and learning preferences.
- *Interactivity*, where learners can experience active and situated learning through simulations of real-world events and on-line collaboration.
- *Media-rich content*, i.e. educational materials presented in different forms and styles.
- *Just-in-time delivery*, i.e. support systems that can facilitate training delivery at the exact time and place that it is needed to complete a certain task.
- *User-centric environments*, where learners take responsibility for their own learning.

Although personalized learning is increasingly recognized as important in formal settings, it is key for informal learning. There are many definitions of formal and informal learning, however the key distinction is that formal learning is typically described as learning that is managed in some manner by an authority (for example, a School or University), while informal learning is less managed, or may be managed by the learner themselves [8-9]. A survey by Cross showed that 70 percent of adult learning is self-directed learning [10] and informal learning is increasingly recognized as a key domain for TEL.

There have been a number of technologies and approaches to solving personalized learning such as intelligent tutoring systems (ITS) and adaptive hypermedia (AH). The goal of ITS is to interact with the student based on a deep understanding of the student's behavior. ITS systems assess each learner's actions in his learning environment and develops a model according to his or her knowledge, skills and expertise [11]. AH systems similarly personalize the learning experience by modifying content and links according to a user model. AH systems can be useful in e-learning areas where students have different goals [12]. However, these are typically centralized solutions and provide only limited autonomy to users.

Based on this work we believe that agent technology is a good approach to support personalized and informal learning. This is because of the characteristics of intelligent agents, which are autonomy, social ability, adaptability, and reaction. Because of these characteristics agents are a powerful way of representing learners in system, adapting content and acting autonomously on their behalf. In addition, they can interact with multiple students and agents at the same time in order to facilitate collaborative and team learning [1] without the need for a formal centralized authority.

2.2 Agent Technologies

The term agent has been in existence in a number of technologies and been widely used, for example, in artificial intelligence, databases, operating systems and the marketplace [2]. Researchers in the agent technology field have proposed a variety of definitions of what comprises an agent but all agree that a key feature is autonomy. One of the most common definitions is that proposed by Jennings and Wooldridge: "*An agent* is a computer system situated in some environment that is capable of autonomous action in this environment in order to meet its design objectives" [13]. *An intelligent agent* is a flexible agent that is pro-active, reactive, or social and able to learn to improve its own performance [14].

While agents work in the same *agent framework* (and often work together) they are inherently autonomous, and may have different and conflicting goals. This means that in their interactions they are trying to maximize their own benefit (this is more formally described as maximizing a utility function). There is therefore a need to establish the rules by which agents can converse and negotiate with one another; this is called the *agent protocol*. For example, in situations where a group of agents need to come to a common decision a voting protocol can enable them to reach agreement as a group while taking into account individual preferences [15].

Voting theory is an active area of research in multi-agent systems and one example of how agents can make decisions together in a decentralized way. It is part of the general area known as *social choice*, which is concerned with procedures for making collective decisions that maximize the *social welfare* (the sum of utility of individual agents), while at the same recognizing that agents are self-interested and act in a way that maximizes their own individual preferences [15]. In the agent experiment described in Section 4 we use a novel voting procedure that combines two approaches: the *single transferable vote* STV[1] and *cumulative voting*[2].

2.3 Agents in Technology Enhanced Learning

In TEL, multi-agent systems appear to be a promising approach to deal with the challenges of educational environments. A number of researchers have applied agent technology to e-learning, however they often use the agents as advanced components, focusing on the individual agent and/or its relationship with an individual student, rather than looking at a system of agents that works together to achieve some goal.

---

[1] This is a multi-agent voting procedure when the alternative that is ranked lowest is removed. Votes that had this alternative ranked first will now have another alternative ranked first. This is repeated until one alternative remains.

[2] Here, each voter receives a number of points (usually the number of points is equal to the number of candidates), and they are free to choose how many points to allocate to each candidate. The candidates with the highest cumulative points are selected as winners.

In this context, De Meo et al. [16] proposed the X-Learn system, an XML-based multi-agent system for adaptive e-learning based on user preferences and requirements. However, rather than the multi-agent aspect, they focus on the adaptation itself and how to exploit XML technology facilities for handling and exchanging information related to e-learning activities.

Shi et al. [17] designed an integrated multi-agent systems for computer science education that focuses on two introductory courses where the learning process is student-centered, self-paced and highly interactive. They use Java RMI, JavaSpace and JATLite to create a web-based system; in this case they use personal agents to manage student's data and their interactions with course material.

Furthermore, Yang et al. [18] proposed to apply an intelligent system to enhance navigation-training systems that consists of the client portion and server portion using JADE framework. Like most work in this area, this paper focuses on the intelligence of individual agents themselves, rather than communications between agents. One exception to these approaches is Soh et al. [19] who have shown a system called Intelligent Multi-agent infrastructure for Distributed Systems in Education to support students in real time classroom where a buddy group is formed dynamically to support the members to achieve common goals.

Although these papers apply agents to e-learning, only Soh et al. demonstrates any kind of self-organization, and none of them applies any fundamental agent theories, such as mechanism design or social choice theory, to guide their design choices. In contrast, our approach is to explore how agent systems can be used for decentralization as well as personalization. For example in our experiment we examine how voting mechanisms can be used in an e-learning scenario where a University agent represents all the modules available, and where student agents can vote in any way he or she prefers. Thus our work explores, for the first time, voting procedures in an e-learning setting, and the consequences of the resulting system behavior for learners in that scenario.

3 Motivational Scenarios

We believe that agents have the potential to transform Technology Enhanced Learning by enabling scenarios that are simply not feasible with today's technology. This is possible because of some of the key features of agent systems such as distributed control and agent autonomy. In this section we illustrate this potential through three different TEL scenarios that show how agent technologies could be used in e-learning to take full advantage of the agent's ability to communicate and negotiate. Each case is composed of a *description* of the scenario, an analysis of the *agent solutions* that make the scenarios possible, and more speculative *variations* of the scenario that would share the same features.

Through the scenarios we hope to show how certain types of problem in Technology Enhanced Learning fit with known agent solutions (Voting systems, Coalition Formation, and Auction systems). We also hope to show how agent systems enable a very high level of personalization, and to start a discussion about the implications for education in the future.

In Section 4 we will take the first of these scenarios and describe a prototype agent system that supports it, along with a suitable voting protocol, and analysis of how potential strategies perform. In Section 5 we reflect on the scenarios and experiment in order to identify key issues and challenges that will arise from the use of agent systems in education.

3.1 Scenario One: Module Selection

Description. This scenario concerns a University that wants to support students who are interested in a wider variety of modules than it is possible for the University to offer. The University must therefore somehow choose which subset of modules to run. This is a common scenario with Higher Education degree courses, where often students are offered a number of modules, and for economic reasons only the most popular modules are run. However, current solutions are centralized, requiring students to hand over their preferences to a central algorithm controlled by the University. In addition students are unable to respond to cancelled modules by changing their preferences. From a personalized learning point of view this is undesirable, as despite the tension between the goals of the institution and the students (the institution really wants to run as few modules as possible whereas each student wants to get the modules in which he or she has most interest) the student must hand over almost all control to an opaque process managed by the University.

Agent Solutions. In agent systems this scenario can be characterized as a **voting problem**. It occurs whenever agents are required to invest in or vote for a limited number of options within a greater number of more or less attractive possibilities. There are numerous potential solutions to voting problems where the outcome impacts all the agents (sometimes described as problems of **social choice**) but through transparent protocols they offer fairness, decentralization and independence (as they allow agents to choose their own voting strategies). This distribution of control fits well with personalized learning.

Variations. This scenario describes students making choices about modules within a single institution, however because agent solutions are decentralized an agent solution could also work in situations where students were choosing modules from multiple institutions (for example, as part of a personalized degree programme across Bologna compliant Universities). In this case, the factors taken into account in an individual agents voting strategy might also include issues such as institutional reputation, distance from home and student facilities.

3.2 Scenario Two: Group Formation

Description. In education it is often necessary for students to arrange themselves into groups for learning, for example to share equipment, to help with timetabling, or for pedagogical activities such as discussion. Students can group themselves, or be grouped by a teacher either randomly or based on some criteria. Group formation is important because although all students need to be allocated to a group, the mix of students might be important. For instance, it may be desirable to have a mix of abilities, so that no one group has an advantage over another in assessment.

Current solutions are normally centralized, meaning that students cannot have different criteria for group selection (for example, some students might wish to be in the most effective groups, while others would rather learn with existing friends) – similarly to Scenario One this one-size-fits-all approach is at odds with personalized learning and requirements to consider the learner experience.

An interesting aspect of this scenario is that sometimes the goals of the teachers are at odds with the goals of the students. The students may wish to be placed in groups with their friends or with students that will help them to achieve good marks, while the teacher may want to arrange students in groups that will help them to learn more material or to learn it more quickly. This means that even non-centralized solutions may need to be mediated by a central authority.

Agent Solutions. In agent systems an appropriate metaphor for this scenario is **coalition formation** - a process by which agents form, join and switch groups until a stable set of coalitions is made. There are numerous potential protocols for this, for example by having an initial allocation, perhaps based on criteria set by the teacher, and then for the students to negotiate exchanging their places with students in other groups. The agent framework provides the conversational mechanism for this negotiation, but the agents need some self-organization. For example, each coalition might produce a virtual leader agent to negotiate with the leaders of the other groups. At the same time, each leader agent has to negotiate with the teacher agent because any changes made in group membership still have to conform to the constraints set by the teacher agent.

Variations. This scenario envisages group formation occurring under the supervision of a teacher or lecturer, and therefore implies a more formal educational context. However, distributed group formation enabled by agents could enable informal learners to also benefit from group work, by helping them form coalition with other (potentially remote learners) who share similar pedagogical goals. Such distributed agent-based group formation systems could be of great help to life-long learners, and could form the basis of informal group work and peer assessment without the need for a mediating teacher or institution.

3.3 Scenario Three: Personalized Learning

Description. Different students may have different personal preferences about the way they want to learn or to be assessed. These preferences may be because of preferred learning styles, but could also be for other practical reasons (such as time commitments in their personal lives, or different project requirements). An institution has difficulty catering for these preferences, due to the mixed cost of providing different activities (for example, lectures are cheaper than tutorials), resource restrictions (such as time commitments of staff, or access to specialized equipment or information sources) and their own guidelines and regulations about having a mixed set of assessment styles (for example, many Universities are cautious about having modules assessed totally by course work).

It is therefore rare for an institution to allow much flexibility at an individual level, although there are limited solutions that allow a cohort to make choices about how they will be taught or assessed, but these tend to be managed directly by teachers and are therefore of limited complexity (for example, it might be possible for the students to negotiate with their teacher about the methods of learning or assessment that will be used).

Agent Solutions. In this kind of scenario there are a number of limited resources (tutorial slots, lab equipment, seminar places, etc.) and many individuals competing for them. In agent systems this situation is characterized as an **auction**. The institution associates a cost with each type of activity and wants to minimize the total cost, or at least prevent it from rising above an agreed level. This cost need not be only financial; it could include factors such as value to external assessors or complexity for staff to manage.

There are many different kinds of auction, and therefore different solutions to this problem. But as an example we can define a utility function for each agent that calculates their student's satisfaction with the activities that they have been allocated. Following an initial allocation, agents could then bargain (negotiate) with their institution, exchanging items according to their cost until their utility function is maximized within the constraints of the institution's cost level.

Variations. Using an economic model allows a University to adjust the wealth (and therefore purchasing power) of certain students according to circumstances. For example, students with learning differences, such as dyslexia, could be given more credit, allowing them to tailor their learning experience within the same economic framework as other students. More controversially students might actually be allowed to purchase additional credit, in effect buying themselves more expensive tuition through the University fees system.

4 Agent Simulation and Experiment

In Section 3 we described a number of TEL Scenarios and described how agent technologies could be used to solve them in a decentralized way. But what would be the performance of such a system, how would it behave and what would be the consequences for the learners and the institution? In this section we attempt to answer these questions by presenting an agent simulation of Scenario One (decentralized module selection using a voting protocol). To do this we must describe the context for our simulation (number of students, modules, etc.), the agent protocol (the rules under which the agents negotiate), and the strategies taken by individual agents. We can then use the system to demonstrate how a decentralized approach compares to an optimal centralized solution, and to compare the performance of different student strategies.

4.1 Context for the Simulation

In our experiment we considered three different cases. These differ in terms of the number of students, the number of total modules, and the number of running modules. Table 1 shows the settings for these cases. We choose these cases to reflect the kind of modules typical in UK computer science departments. The column *# modules (m)* shows how many modules there are for each case. We consider a large (undergraduate), medium (smaller undergraduate) and small (postgraduate) module. The column *#running modules (r)* shows the number of modules that will eventually run. The column *#students (n)* shows the number of students in the experiments.

Table 1. Different settings for each case

Case	# modules (m)	#running modules (r)				#students (n)
1	51 (undergraduate)	10	20	30	40	100
2	33 (smaller undergraduate)	9	18		27	60
3	15 (postgraduate)	4	8		12	20

In our system, each agent is autonomous, that is, it is in control of its own actions and responses. The system consists of two types of agents: student agents (SAs) and the university agent (UA). SAs and the UA use a voting procedure to interact with each other and to choose which modules to run. To this end, the UA manages the votes cast by the student agents and decides, based on the voting procedure and the votes received, which modules will be cancelled. Furthermore, after completing the entire process, it will provide the SAs with a final list of running modules.

4.2 Protocol

In general, a protocol is the set of rules that controls the interactions between agents and determines the beginning and end conditions of a given conversation [20]. The protocol we used in our system works in several stages. In each stage, the student agents cast their votes for the modules by allocating points to each module. The module that receives the lowest number of cumulative points is cancelled, and the points that were allocated to the cancelled module are refunded. In the next round, the students can use these points (and any points that they did not use in the previous rounds), to vote again. Furthermore, in each round, the students are informed about which module is cancelled and the total number of points that have been allocated to the remaining modules so far. Note that, once allocated, a student agent cannot retrieve its points, unless the module is cancelled. The advantage of this iterative approach is that votes are not wasted since points allocated to the cancelled module can be reused for the remaining modules. Furthermore, the student agent can use the information about the current "popularity" (i.e. the current cumulative points) of the modules to guide its voting behavior (we discuss the potential strategies of student agents in more detail in Section 4).

For example, if there are 40 modules available in total, but the university only has sufficient resources (e.g. staff and lecture rooms) to run 30 modules, then the voting will proceed for 10 iterations or rounds. At the end of each of these rounds, the module with the least number of cumulative points is cancelled.

4.3 Strategies

Abstractly, a strategy determines the agent's plan of action to achieve a particular goal. It specifies the way in which an agent behaves in a given environment [15] . In our scenario, the strategy determines the number of points to allocate to the modules in each voting round, given the preferences of the agent and the information received by the UA about the voting process. In this experiment we compared three different strategies for the SAs in order to explore what would happen to students that adopted different strategies. These strategies were: proportional, equal share and intelligent.

Proportional: The proportional strategy was included as an example of a simple but sensible strategy. Consequently, it provides a good benchmark that we can use to compare the performance of more sophisticated strategies. The main idea behind a proportional strategy is that, in each round of voting, the student agent distributes its points proportionally to the student's preferences for each module. This strategy is simple in that it does not consider the information received by the UA about the current number of points allocated to the modules.

In more detail, the number of points allocated to module j is calculated as follows. Let RP denote the total number of points remaining and IP denotes the number of initial points (in the first round $IP=RP$), m is the total number of available modules available, and the vector $\vec{v} = \{v_1, v_2, ..., v_m\}$ denotes the student preferences. Then, the total number of points to be allocated to module j, b_j is:

$$b_j = \frac{RP}{\sum_{i=1}^{m} v_i} \cdot v_j \tag{1}$$

Equal share: The equal share strategy is included as an example of a very simple and ineffective strategy, and provides a good lower bound on the performance of the system. An equal share strategy is based on the principle that the SA gives all modules an equal number of votes, regardless of the student's preference. The following formula was used to calculate voting points each module:

$$b_j = \frac{RP}{m} \tag{2}$$

Intelligent: The intelligent strategy is included as an example of what can be achieved with a more sophisticated strategy that learns as the voting procedure progresses from one round to the next. The main idea behind this strategy is that, in each round, the agent tries to predict the probability that a module will be cancelled based on the number of points currently awarded to each module from previous rounds. Then, based on this probability, it can calculate its *expected satisfaction* for a given allocation of points, and it will allocate the points such that the expected satisfaction is maximized.

In more detail, the probability of a module being cancelled is estimated using a *softmax* function, which is commonly used in discrete choice theory to make decisions in the case of incomplete information [21]. The probability that a module i is going to be cancelled in the future is given by:

$$ProbCancel_i(\vec{b}) = \frac{e^{\frac{-(cp_i+b_i)}{\sum_{j=1}^{m}(cp_j+b_j)} \cdot \beta}}{\sum_{k=1}^{m} e^{\frac{-(cp_k+b_k)}{\sum_{j=1}^{m}(cp_j+b_j)} \cdot \beta}} \tag{3}$$

Where cp_i is the *cumulative* number of points which have so far been allocated to module i, and b_i is the number of points that the student agent is planning to allocate to module i in the current voting round, and $\vec{b}$ is the vector of points to be allocated. Furthermore, β is constant which weights the importance of the current point allocation (for example, if $\beta = 0$, then each module is equally likely to be cancelled, but as $\beta \to \infty$, the module with the lowest total number of points will be cancelled with probability 1, and all other modules will be cancelled with probability 0).

We can use this probability to calculate the *expected satisfaction*, ES, of the student. The expected satisfaction is given by:

$$ES(\vec{b}) = \sum_{i=1}^{m}(1 - ProbCancel_i(\vec{b})) \cdot v_i \qquad (4)$$

The next step is then to find the allocation that maximises this expected utility. We estimate this using a search algorithm based on *random sampling*:

1. We randomly generate an allocation vector $\vec{b}$ subject to the constraint that the total number of points is equal to the maximum number of points that we would like to spend in the current round.
2. The student agent calculates the expected satisfaction.
3. If the current solution has a higher expected satisfaction than any previous solution, then keep the solution. Otherwise, discard it.
4. This process is repeated for 1000 times and the solution with the highest expected utility is kept.

In our experiments, the number of points allocated in any round was 50%, except in the last voting round where we allocate all remaining points. In the first round (where there is no existing allocation of points) we use the proportional strategy (but only use 50% of the available points).

4.4 Comparing Agent Strategies to the Optimal

In the first part of our experiment we compared the agent strategies explained above to the optimal case in which the University Agent has access to all of the preference information and makes the decisions centrally. Our objective is to discover if the decentralized agent solutions can match a centralized approach

In each of the experiments that follow, each scenario was run 30 times with different preferences. Thus, the results shown are the average results over these runs.

Figure 1 shows the results for cases 1, 2 and 3 respectively. Here, the y axis shows the *percentage of student satisfaction*. This is calculated by the total satisfaction of the running modules, as a percentage of the total satisfaction if all the modules would be running. Furthermore, on the x axis we vary the total number of running modules (while keeping the other parameters in the scenarios fixed). The graphs show the differences in the satisfaction of the agents using different strategies and also compares this with the satisfaction of the optimal solution.

These results show that the outcome of the proportional strategy is almost identical to the optimal strategy (although this is not visible in the figure, there is some difference but this is not statistically significant), and the intelligent strategy does slightly less well but is still very close to optimal. On the other hand, we see that the equal share strategy does significantly worse. This suggests that a decentralized solution using voting results in high quality solutions that are comparable to optimal.

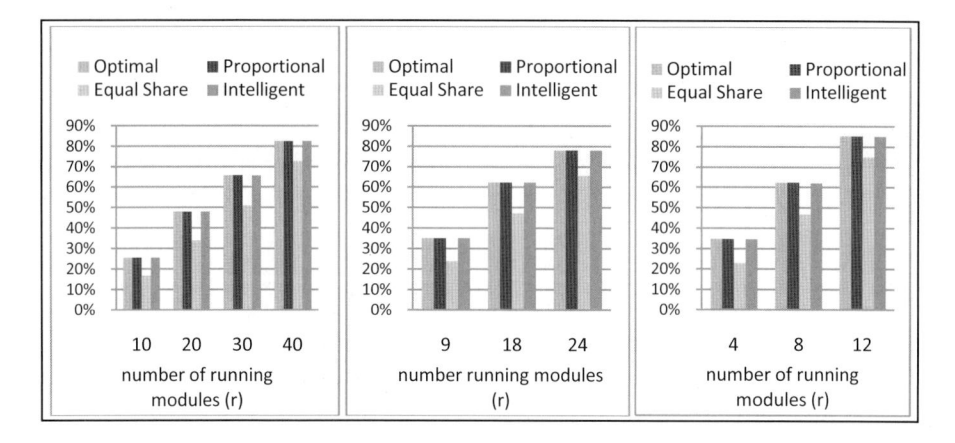

Fig. 1. Results for Case 1 (left), Case 2 (centre), Case 3 (right)

4.5 Comparing Agent Strategies to Each Other

In the next set of experiments we compare the case where a proportion of the students use one strategy, and the remainder of the students uses another strategy. This allows us to see what would happen if students used a mixture of strategies to choose their options. We might expect some strategies to work better than others.

If all the students had random preferences then the agents would cancel each other out regardless of their strategy choice, so in order to show the effect of strategy we biased the preferences in such a way that the students using the same strategy are also likely to have similar preferences. In this way each group of students with the same strategy is pulling in the same direction. We can then measure the comparative success of each strategy by looking at the satisfaction within each group. We can also compare the power of the strategies by varying the size of the group.

In the results that follow, the y axis shows the percentage of satisfaction for each group of agents using a particular strategy. The x axis shows the proportion of students using a particular strategy. For example, in Figure 2, 90-10 means that 90 students use the proportional strategy, and 10 students use the equal share strategy.

The results in Figures 2 show that the intelligent and proportional strategies are both significantly better than the equal share, irrespective of the proportion of students that use this strategy. On average, the improvement is around 8% compared to the equal share strategy. The results shown are for case 1 (see Table 1) with 40 students, but the results for other cases are very similar and not shown to avoid repetition.

Figures 3 show the results of comparing the intelligent strategy and the proportional strategy for the 3 different cases. The result show that, as the number of students allocated to a particular strategy increases, the student satisfaction for these students also increases. However, this is mainly because of the bias that has been introduced; since students with the same strategy have similar preferences, when more students have these preferences they have greater voting power since they act as a group. The difference in the effectiveness of the strategies can be seen by comparing the number of students needed in a group for it to become the most successful.

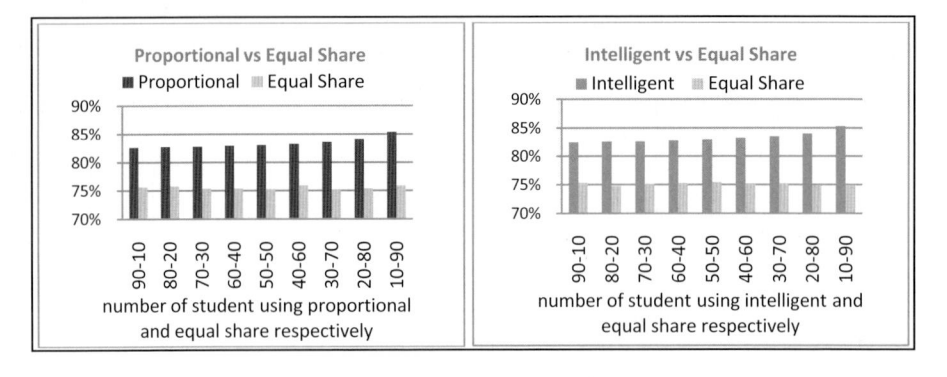

Fig. 2. Left: Proportional vs. Equal Share, Right: Intelligent vs. Equal Share

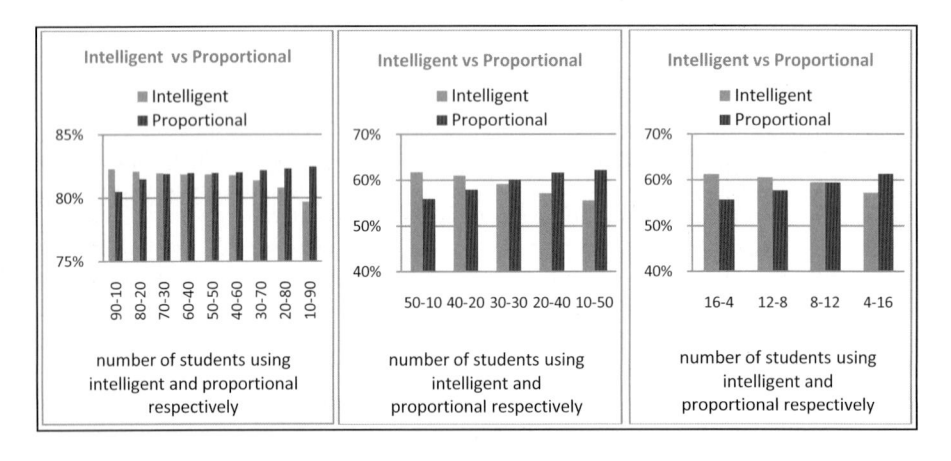

Fig. 3. Intelligent vs. Proportional. Case 1 (left), Case 2 (centre), Case 3 (right).

Comparing the intelligent and proportional strategies, it can be seen that there is not much difference between them. Although in Case 3 the intelligent strategy slightly outperforms the proportional strategy (given the same number of students are using that strategy), in the other two cases, the proportional strategy outperforms the intelligent strategy. We have also tried to vary the parameters of the intelligent strategy (such as the beta parameter), but the results do not change significantly. This suggests that a learner who takes a more advanced intelligent strategy cannot easily exploit the system.

5 Discussion

Through the Scenarios described in Section 3 and the experimental simulation in Section 4 we have explored how multi-agent systems could be used for TEL. While others have focused on agents as containers of student information and user interface adaptation, we have focused on their ability to act autonomously in a system and to negotiate with one another to reach an agreed outcome.

Our work shows that when used in this way agents provide two key advantages:

- **Ultra-personalization** – In a multi-agent system autonomous agents allow for unprecedented levels of personalization. Not only can students have preferences about any given learning scenario, but by selecting different strategies they can change the way in which their agents negotiate. For example, in the module selection scenario students have different preferences and in our experiment can choose different strategies for negotiating based on those preferences. But it would also be possible to introduce other student agents that had a completely different basis for choosing modules (for example, based on the choices of their friends, or on the requirements of some qualification framework). Multi-agent systems provide the necessary level of abstraction for the tailoring of every aspect of the negotiation, including the basis for making choices (e.g. preferences or some other criteria), the individual's personal data (e.g. the preferences themselves), and the algorithm that uses that data to negotiate (e.g. how to vote according to those preferences).
- **Decentralization** – In Section 3 we argued that agent systems could provide decentralized solutions to a number of key TEL problems. In Section 4 we have demonstrated that not only is this possible, but that if students choose sensible strategies the results tend towards an optimal solution (calculated as the result of a centralized approach).

However, we also believe that our work highlights potential concerns:

- **Equitability** – In situations of ultra-personalization it is very difficult to guarantee that all students will have the same potential for satisfaction. This is because, although the agents are handled equally, the system relies on the agents themselves making sensible choices and selections. Power and responsibility are both transferred from a central authority (the institution) to the individual agents (the students). If an agent makes irrational choices, or chooses a bad strategy, then their student will be disadvantaged when compared to others. In Section 4 we demonstrated this by showing how a foolish equal share strategy penalized students who acted in that way, however we also showed how a well-designed protocol had made it difficult for a more intelligent (or intentionally subversive strategy) to gain advantage over a sensible strategy.

- **Scrutability** – in decentralized systems it can be very difficult for any individual in the system to see and understand the big picture, making accountability and transparency difficult. Although in our experiment the University Agent was in a position to see the voting behavior of all the students, it is possible to imagine situations where no single agent understands the sequence of events that lead the system as a whole reaching a decision (for example, if multiple institutions had been involved in our scenario then no one of them would have seen all the voting behavior). Institutions in particular may find it difficult to engage in a system where they cannot fully account for the outcome.

6 Conclusions and Future Work

The main aim of this work was to investigate how the autonomy and negotiation aspects of multi-agent technology might impact on the domain of Technology Enhanced Learning. Using three scenarios we have shown how common multi-agent solutions (voting, coalition formation and auction systems) map to problems in TEL. We argue that multi-agent technologies could allow genuine *decentralization* and *ultra-personalization* allowing these scenarios to be extended to include types of personal and informal learning that are difficult to support with today's systems.

As an illustration we took the first of these scenarios (module selection) and presented a multi-agent simulation that uses a suitable voting protocol to support module selection. Using our simulation we have been able to show that a decentralized agent approach not only works, but that with reasonable agent strategies it approximates an optimal centralized solution. We have also been able to show how different agent strategies compare to one another, revealing that with this particular protocol simplistic strategies are penalized, but that it is difficult to use intelligent (subversive) strategies to significantly improve on a naïve sensible strategy.

Based on the scenarios and experiment we believe that agent systems have a great deal of potential for TEL, but that their use raises concerns about the *equitability* of results (as agents become responsible for their own performance) and the *scrutability* of the process (as no single agent understands the system as a whole). Depending on the context this may impact on the acceptability to stakeholders of using an agent-system in a given scenario.

In our future work we intend to explore more sophisticated versions of the module choice scenario, where agents use different selection criteria and where there are multiple institutions vying for student interests. Our aim is to help establish the characteristics of agent protocols that makes them either equitable or scrutable, and to investigate the feasibility of more ambitious scenarios.

References

1. Sampson, D., Karagiannidis, C., Kinshuk: Personalised Learning: Education, Technological and Standardisation Perspective. Interactive Education Multimedia 4, 24–39 (2002)
2. Bellifemine, F.L., Caire, G., Greenwood, D.: Developing multi-agent systems with JADE. Wiley series in agent technology, p. 286. John Wiley, Chichester (2007)

3. Kommers, P., Aroyo, L.: Special Issue Preface - Intelligent Agents for Educational Computer-Aided Systems. Journal of Interactive Learning Research 10(3), 235–242 (1999)
4. Silveira, R., Vicari, R.: Developing Distributed Intelligent Learning Environment with JADE — Java Agents for Distance Education Framework. In: Cerri, S.A., Gouardéres, G., Paraguaçu, F. (eds.) ITS 2002. LNCS, vol. 2363, pp. 105–118. Springer, Heidelberg (2002)
5. Bariso, E.U.: Personalised eLearning in Further Education, in Technology-Supported Environments for Personalized Learning: Methods and Case Studies. In: O'Donoghue, J. (ed.), pp. 138–156. Information science reference, London (2009)
6. Conole, G.: Personalisation through Technology-Enhanced Learning, in Technology-Supported Environments for Personalized Learning: Methods and Case Studies. In: O'Donoghue, J. (ed.), pp. 30–44. Information science reference, London (2009)
7. Sampson, D.: Current and Future Research and Technology Developments in e-Learning. In: The 2nd International Conference on New Horizons in Industry and Education. Technological Educational Institute of Crete, Milos Island (2001)
8. Coombs, P.H., Ahmed, M.: Attacking rural poverty: how nonformal education can help, p. 292. Johns Hopkins University Press, Baltimore (1974)
9. McGivney, V.: Informal learning in the community: a trigger for change and development. National Institute of Adult Continuing Education (1999)
10. Cross, K.P.: Adults as learners: increasing participation and facilitating learning, p. 300. Jossey-Bass Publishers, San Francisco (1981)
11. Corbett, A.T., Koedinger, K.R., Anderson, J.R.: Intelligent Tutoring Systems. In: Handbook of Human-Computer Interaction, Amsterdam, ch. 37 (1997)
12. Brusilovsky, P., Eklund, J., Schwarz, E.: Web-based education for all: A tool for developing adaptive courseware. In: Proceedings of Seventh International World Wide Web Conference, pp. 297–300 (1998)
13. Jennings, N.R., Wooldridge, M.: Applications of intelligent agents, in Agent technology: foundations, applications, and markets, pp. 3–28. Springer, New York (1998)
14. Soh, L.-K., Jiang, H., Ansorge, C.: Agent-based cooperative learning: a proof-of-concept experiment. In: Proceedings of the 35th SIGCSE technical symposium on Computer science education. ACM, Norfolk (2004)
15. Wooldridge, M.J.: An introduction to multiagent systems, 2nd edn., p. 461. Wiley, Chichester (2009)
16. Meo, P.D., et al.: Personalizing learning programs with X-Learn, an XML-based, user-device adaptive multi-agent system. Information Sciences: an International Journal 177(8), 1729–1770 (2007)
17. Shi, H., Shang, Y., Chen, S.-S.: A multi-agent system for computer science education. In: Proceedings of the 5th Annual Conference on Innovation and Technology in Computer Science Education (ITiCSE 2000), vol. 32(3), pp. 1–4 (2000)
18. Yang, C., Lin, H., Lin, F.O.: Designing Multiagent-Based Education Systems for Navigation Training. In: 5th IEEE Int. Conf. on Cognitive Informatics, ICCI 2006 (2006)
19. Soh, L.-K., Jiang, H., Ansorge, C.: Agent-based cooperative learning: a proof-of-concept experiment. SIGCSE Bull 36(1), 368–372 (2004)
20. Beer, M., et al.: Negotiation in Multi-Agent Systems. Knowledge Engineering Review 14(3), 285–289 (1998)
21. Hensher, D.A., Rose, J.M., Greene, W.H.: Applied choice analysis: a primer. Cambridge University Press, Cambridge (2005)

Learning Spaces as Representational Scaffolds for Learning Conceptual Knowledge of System Behaviour

Bert Bredeweg[1], Jochem Liem[1], Wouter Beek[1], Paulo Salles[2], and Floris Linnebank[1]

[1] University of Amsterdam, Informatics Institute, Amsterdam, Netherlands
{B.Bredeweg,J.Liem,W.G.J.Beek,F.E.Linnebank}@uva.nl
[2] University of Brasília, Institute of Biological Sciences, Brasília, Brazil
psalles@unb.br

Abstract. Scaffolding is a well-known approach to bridge the gap between novice and expert capabilities in a discovery-oriented learning environment. This paper discusses a set of knowledge representations referred to as Learning Spaces (LSs) that can be used to support learners in acquiring conceptual knowledge of system behaviour. The LSs are logically self-contained, meaning that models created at a specific LS can be simulated. Working with the LSs provides scaffolding for learners in two ways. First, each LS provides a restricted set of representational primitives to express knowledge, which focus the learner's knowledge construction process. Second, the logical consequences of an expression derived upon simulating, provide learners a reflective instrument for evaluating the status of their understanding, to which they can react accordingly.

The work presented here is part of the DynaLearn project, which builds an Interactive Learning Environment to study a constructive approach to having learners develop a qualitative understanding of how systems behave. The work presented here thus focuses on tools to support educational research. Consequently, user-oriented evaluation of these tools is not a part of this paper.

Keywords: Conceptual knowledge, Qualitative reasoning, Architecture, Scaffolding, Knowledge representation.

1 Introduction

One of the goals of the DynaLearn project (http://www.DynaLearn.eu) is to provide an instrument for studying the interactive characteristics under which learners develop conceptual knowledge. There is ample research that points out the importance of learners constructing conceptual interpretations of system's behaviour (e.g., [9,14,21,26,33]). There is a need for software that 'goes beyond data handling' and supports learners in actively dealing with the theoretical concepts involved. This can be done by having learners create models and perform concept prediction and explanation [16,22,26]. However, such techniques are only sparsely available or too complex to use, and therefore seldom part of prescribed learning activities [25].

This paper addresses issues concerning the knowledge representation for articulating conceptual knowledge. Particularly, it discusses the idea of a set of representations, which act as scaffolds to support learners in developing their conceptual knowledge. The representations are referred to as Learning Spaces (LSs) and based on Qualitative Reasoning (QR) technology (cf. [13]). A qualitative model provides formal means to externalize thought. It captures the explanation the creator of the models believes to be true of *how* and *why* a system behaves. The approach is domain independent.

In DynaLearn we utilize the full expressiveness and potential of the QR formalism. This allows us to divide the qualitative system dynamics phenomena over a range of LSs of increasing complexity, implementing a progression where at 'the next level' learners are confronted with additional and alternative expressive power for representing and reasoning about the behaviour of systems, and hence facilitating the construction of a better understanding of the phenomena involved.

The remainder of this paper is organised as follows. The subsections below position our work in the context of related research. Section 2 enumerates the knowledge representation and reasoning vocabulary that is typically used in QR software. Section 3 discussed the LSs as defined and implemented in DynaLearn's Interactive Learning Environment (ILE). Section 4 provides a wider scope of how the representational scaffolds can be used in educational settings, particularly addressing ongoing work in the DynaLearn project [5].

1.1 DynaLearn Project Context

The DynaLearn project is motivated by the need from the field of science education to have learners construct conceptual knowledge, particularly for secondary and higher education. The project seeks to address these needs by integrating well established, but currently independent technological developments, and utilize the added value that emerges from this integration. The main project objective is to develop an ILE that allows learners to construct their conceptual system knowledge. The workbench is based on three strategic characteristics: (a) accommodate the true nature of conceptual knowledge, (b) be engaging by using personified agent technology, and (c) react to the individual knowledge needs of learners [8].

In the DynaLearn ILE, learners construct knowledge by manipulating icons, and their inter-relationships, using a diagrammatic representation. The diagrams represent models that can be simulated confronting learners with the logical consequences of the knowledge they represented. Alongside this workspace embodied conversational agents are situated, available for learners to analyse and reflect on their expressions. This interaction is steered using knowledge technology that connects learners to diagrammatic representations created by peers, teachers and/or domain experts.

1.2 Learning by Building Qualitative Models

Modelling is regarded fundamental to human cognition and scientific inquiry [33]. It helps learners express and externalize their thinking; visualize and test components of their theories; and make materials more interesting. Modelling environments can thus make a significant contribution to the improvement of science education. In the past two decades, since Papert published *Mindstorms* [27], different kinds of modelling environments have been created. Environments such as StarLogo [30] (later NetLogo), Stella [31], and Model-It [17] are some examples that offer innovative environments in which students can construct their own simulations to solve problems that interest them. These environments allow learners to view the invisible and examine complexity in new ways (cf. [3]).

Despite its value for learning, the use of these technologies for handling conceptual knowledge is hampered by a number of issues. First, the underlying representation is quantitative, which means that in order to obtain simulation results, numerical details have to be provided (or to be assumed by the software). However, the required numerical details may not be available. Moreover, having to deal with numbers distracts learners from focusing on the real issue (which is developing their conceptual understanding of how systems work). Second, there is discrepancy between the key characteristics of conceptual knowledge and the vocabulary provided by modelling environments based on numerical simulations. Many crucial notions are not explicitly represented in such approaches [10,19], such as landmark values, causality, qualitatively distinct states of behaviour, processes, etc. This has two negative consequences. First, when learners cannot use the appropriate language to develop their knowledge, the learning is deemed to be suboptimal. It has been shown that learners develop a better understanding (which also improves transfer to new situations) when they are given the opportunity to use causal relationships to represent system behaviour [32]. Second, when the underlying representation does not capture certain crucial distinctions, it will be difficult to create interactive tools that teach learners the key conceptual insights that explain the behaviour of a system. Hence, the automated feedback that can be provided is suboptimal (see e.g. [34]).

Today there are techniques originating from Artificial Intelligence that overcome the above-mentioned problems. These techniques can be employed to provide learners with interactive tools for handling conceptual knowledge that actually fit the characteristics of this kind of knowledge. More specifically, the technology known as QR is well suited for this purpose (see [4,7] for overviews). The vocabulary used in QR not only suits the nature of conceptual knowledge, but due to the explicit representation of these notions in the software it also provides the necessary handles to support an automated communicative interaction that actually discusses and provides feedback at the conceptual level.

QR should thus not be seen as 'just another kind of simulation technology'. On the contrary, its objective and its implementation are fundamentally different. Simulation technology mimics the behaviour of a system such that the simulated variables have continuously changing values that closely match observable (measurable) variables. The goal of simulation is thus to obtain a close match between the model (in fact the underlying mathematical equations) and the real system in terms of matching variable values. **QR**, on the other hand, **captures human interpretation of reality**, and provides a **conceptual account** that **explains why** a system has certain behaviour. The goal of QR is thus to **map closely with human cognition**. The QR terms (in fact a symbolic logic-based vocabulary) used in the model **mimic the way humans understand and explain** the observable behaviour.

1.3 Interactive Qualitative Models

QR works without using any numerical information and excels in representing cause-effect knowledge and other conceptual notions crucial to systems thinking. Conceptual models based on QR can either function as standalone artefacts developed for understanding, predicting, and explaining system's behaviour, or as primordial frameworks in which quantitative knowledge can be interpreted. Such conceptual models are also 'animated', as they capture the dynamic aspects of a system by reasoning about quantities that change over time, using a well-defined set of modelling primitives grounded in a mathematical foundation.

Recent advancements have delivered diagrammatic representations to interact with QR software, e.g. Betty's Brain [1], Vmodel [12], and Garp3 [7]. Such external representations help reduce the working memory load (known as cognitive offloading [11,23], thereby enabling learners to address more complex problems than they would be able to handle otherwise. It also enables learners to more easily and accurately share their conceptual ideas with others for discussion and collaboration. However, to further enhance usability, approaches such as Betty's Brain and Vmodel reduce the amount of primitives available in the model-building software. Although this 'makes things simpler', it has the obvious drawback of not using the full potential of QR and the means it provides for representing conceptual knowledge.

In DynaLearn we use the Garp3 software (http://www.garp3.org) developed in the NaturNet-Redime project (EU, FP6), which does utilise the full expressiveness and potential of the QR formalism. Experts have used Garp3 intensively to create advanced conceptual models [6]. These results support the hypothesis that the software is able to capture advanced explanations of system's behaviour. The ambition of the DynaLearn project is therefore to cover the whole gamut of conceptual knowledge acquisition, from the simplest of conceptual structures to the most complex. The DynaLearn ILE is specifically targeted towards secondary and higher education.

2 Baseline Representation: Qualitative Reasoning Vocabulary

Garp3 is used as the basis for the design and implementation of the different LSs in the DynaLearn ILE. Table 1 enumerates the main ingredient categories that can be used to create models (see also Fig. 1). The means for users to inspect the simulation results of such models are enumerated in Table 2 (see also Fig. 2).

3 Learning Spaces – Knowledge Representation Scaffolds

The knowledge representation scaffolds developed in the DynaLearn project are organised as a set of LSs with increasing complexity in terms of the modelling ingredients a learner can use to construct knowledge. Six LSs have been designed and implemented (see Fig. 3 and Table 3):

- Concept map (LS1)
- Basic Causal Model (LS2)
- Basic Causal Model with State-graph (LS3)
- Causal Differentiation (LS4)
- Conditional Knowledge (LS5)
- Generic and Reusable Knowledge (LS6)

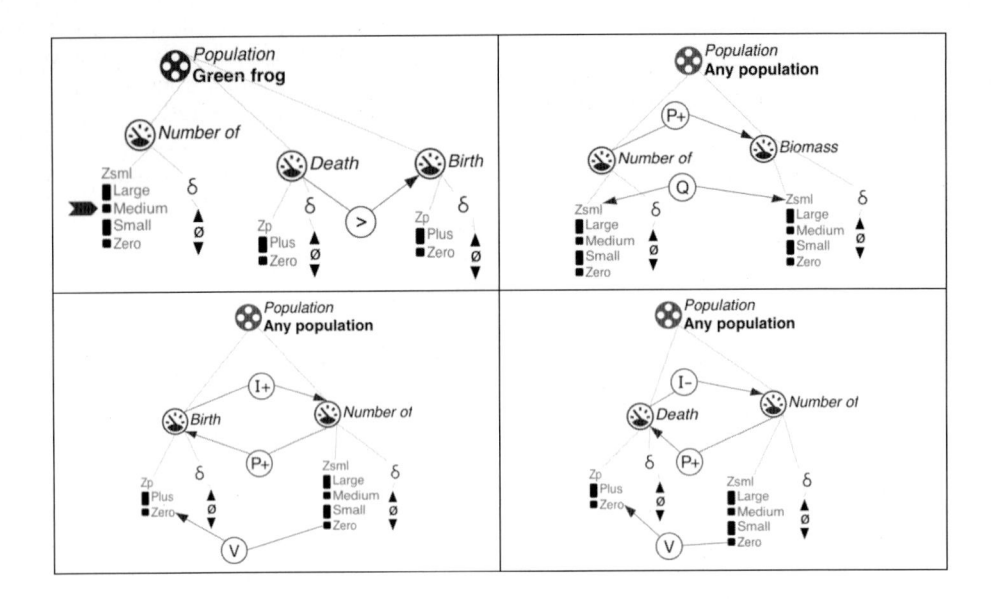

Fig. 1. The LHS top shows the scenario of a *Green frog Population* starting at value *Medium*, while *Death > Birth*. RHS top shows a model fragment detailing that *Number of* determines *Biomass* (proportionality, P+ and correspondence, Q). The LHS bottom shows a fragment capturing the idea that the *Birth* process positively influences (I+) the *Number of*, while changes in the latter cause changes in the former (P+, positive feedback). The RHS bottom shows mortality (*Death*), which is similar to birth, but it has a negative influence (I-). Both processes represent that they have no impact in the case of a non-existing population (value correspondence on *Zero*, V, saying that *Birth* is *Zero* whenever *Number of* is.).

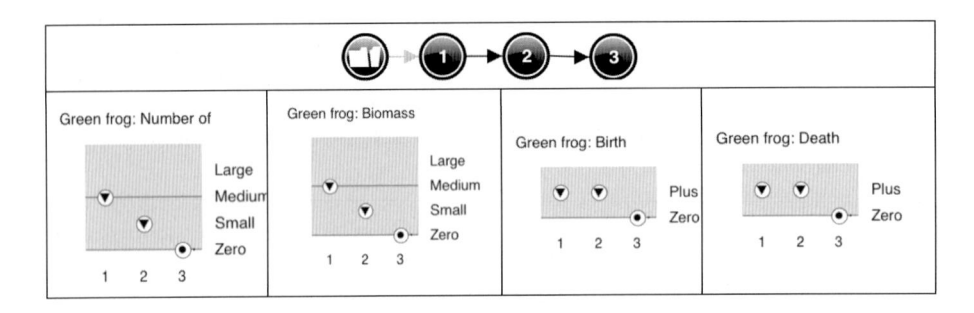

Fig. 2. The top box shows a state-graph (this simulation produced three states). The four boxes below the state-graph show the value history for *Number of*, *Biomass*, *Birth* and *Death*. E.g. *Number of* decreases ($\partial = -$, shown by the downward arrow) from *Medium* (in state 1), via *Small* (state 2) to *Zero* (in state 3); in which the value becomes steady ($\partial=0$).

Table 1. Model ingredients of a Qualitative Reasoning model in Garp3 (see also Fig. 1)

Ingredient	Description
Entity	Physical objects or abstract concepts that constitute the system.
Agent	Entities influencing the system (without being affected themselves).
Assumption	Labels indicating that certain conditions are presumed to be true.
Configuration	Structural relations between entities (including agents).
Quantity	Changeable features of entities represented as variables. Its qualitative value is represented as a pair of 'magnitude' (amount of stuff) and 'derivative' (direction of change).
Quantity space	Range of possible quantity values. Default derivative QS is {–, 0, +}, meaning decrease (inc), steady (std), and increase (inc), respectively.
Influence	Primary cause of change, due to a process being active (I+, I–).
Proportionality	Propagation of change, as cause by direct influences (P+, P–).
Correspondence	Relations specifying co-occurring qualitative values (Q, V).
Inequality	Ordinal relations (<, ≤, =, ≥, >), and subtraction & addition)
Scenario	Initial state of a system.
Model fragment	Reusable chunk of knowledge composed of multiple ingredients.

Table 2. Simulation results of a Qualitative Reasoning model in Garp3 (see also Fig. 2)

Ingredient	Description
State	Specific situation of a modelled system, reflecting qualitatively unique behaviour that holds during a certain period of time.
State-graph	Set of states and the possible transitions between them.
Behaviour path	A particular sequence of successive states within a state graph.
Value history	Diagram representing the quantity values for a sequence of states.
Equation history	Ordinal relations between variables for a sequence of states.
Causal model	Diagram representing the causal relations among quantities (notably, influences and proportionalities) active in specific state of behaviour.

Two aspects guided the design of the LSs: the logic of the representation and the ability for a representation to capture relevant system behaviour (for the latter, see the goals mentioned below in the sections describing each LS). Defining the LSs from a representational perspective was done as follows. The formal context and starting point for developing the LSs is the QR software Garp3. LS1 is the smallest subset of ingredients that constitute a meaningful subset from the representation used by this engine. Effectively this subset of modelling ingredients allows the construction of concept maps, consisting of nodes connected by arcs (referred to as entities and configurations in Garp3, respectively). Defining a higher LS is done by augmenting the current space with the smallest subset of possible modelling ingredients while ensuring that the next level is self-contained. Self-contained implies that the representational primitives available within a LS form a logical subset of all the primitives available. Hence, they allow for automated reasoning on behalf of the underlying software. It also implies that from a Qualitative System Dynamics perspective, learners are able to create meaningful representations of the phenomena they perceive when observing the behaviour of a real-world system. What learners express at a certain LS has consequences for what the software can infer. Hence, learners can be confronted with the logical consequences of their expressions, which either may or may not match the observed system behaviour or the learner's expectations thereof. Particularly in the case of a mismatch between logical consequences and expectations there is ample room for interactive learning.

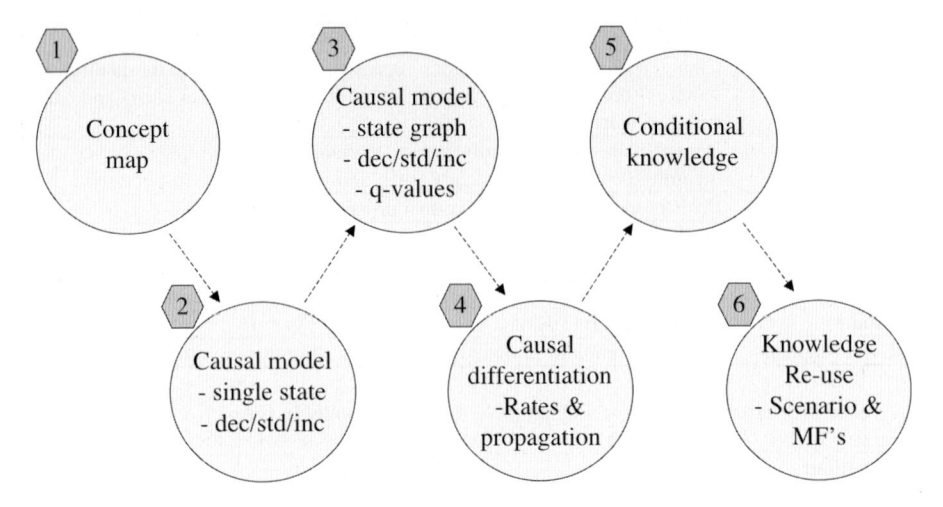

Fig. 3. Schematic representation of the six LSs. The LSs can be traversed in the indicated order. However, alternative routes are also possible. Moreover, each LS can be regarded as a scaffold by itself and can be used as a standalone instrument for acquiring a specific kind of knowledge. (Notice, dec = Decreasing, std = Steady, inc = Increasing, q-values = Qualitative values, MF = Model fragment.)

3.1 Concept Map (LS1)

A concept map (an entity-relation graph) is a graphical representation of ideas that a person believes to be true [24]. A concept map consists of two primitives: nodes and arcs. Nodes reflect important concepts, while arcs show the relationships between those concepts.

The relevance and use of concept maps in education is well understood. Once developed, concept maps can be used to discuss their contents with other model builders. During this process the map can be further adjusted to accommodate alternative ideas, and may ultimately reflect a shared understanding among model builders. By making concept maps learners not only externalise thought, but by doing so they also further specify and organise their own knowledge.

Although very useful for organizing the learners' ideas, concept maps do not capture system dynamics. Hence, concept maps cannot be simulated. However, LS1 provides the basis on top of which more complex knowledge representations can be built. Therefore, a simple version of such a workspace is available in the DynaLearn software (see Fig 4).

Table 3. Overview of ingredients available at each LS. The LS are cumulative; each LS includes the representational details from the preceding LS (but are not enumerated in the table for each LS). Learners create a single expression at LS 1 to 4. At LS5 one or more conditional expression can be added to that. At LS6 learners create multiple reusable expressions, including a scenario. Expressions at LS 2-6 can be simulated.

Nr	Learning Space (LS)	Model Ingredients
1	Concept map *Which concepts are involved and how are they related?*	• Entities • Configurations
2	Causal model *What constitutes the system (structure vs. behaviour)? How do changes propagate through the system?*	• Attributes • Quantities • Value assignments • Derivatives • Causal relationships (+ and –)
3	Causal model with state graph *Which quantities may reach which critical landmarks?*	• Quantity spaces • Correspondences

4	Causal differentiation
	What is the initial cause of change? What processes are involved? Are there external influences?
		• Causal relationships (+ and –) refined
		  o Influences
		  o Proportionalities
		• Inequalities
		• Operators (+ and –)
		• Agents
		• Assumptions

5	Conditional knowledge *Are there behaviours that only occur under specific conditions?*	• Conditional expressions

6	Generic and reusable
	System independent descriptions facilitating simulation of scenarios with an arbitrary set of system features.
		• Multiple expressions
		  o Model fragments
		  o Scenarios

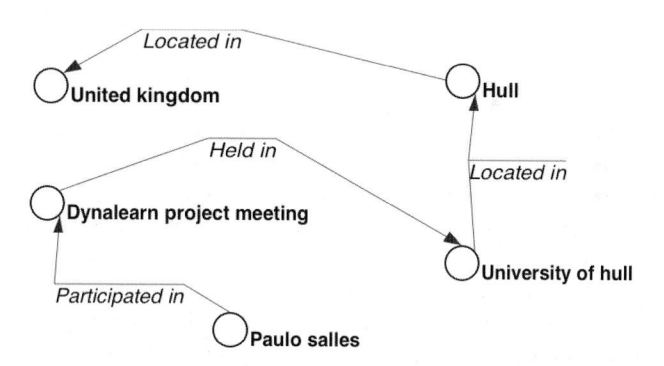

Fig. 4. A concept map representing the idea of a person participating in a meeting, held in the University of Hull, located in Hull, which is located in the UK

3.2 Basic Causal Model (LS2)

The goal of LS2 is that learners acquire an overall understanding of the cause-effect relationships governing the behaviour of a system. LS2 focuses on quantities, how they change, and how those changes cause other quantities to change. Quantities are associated to entities, the structural units in the model. The simulator calculates for each quantity the direction of change: decrease, steady, increase, ambiguous (because of opposing influences), or unknown (because of missing information). Augmented with a teachable agent LS2 closely relates to Betty's Brain [1].

When constructing knowledge at LS2 the learner works in a single workspace. Simulation results are shown in the same workspace, and have the form of derivative values generated by the software. Fig. 5 shows the workspace content after simulating an expression.

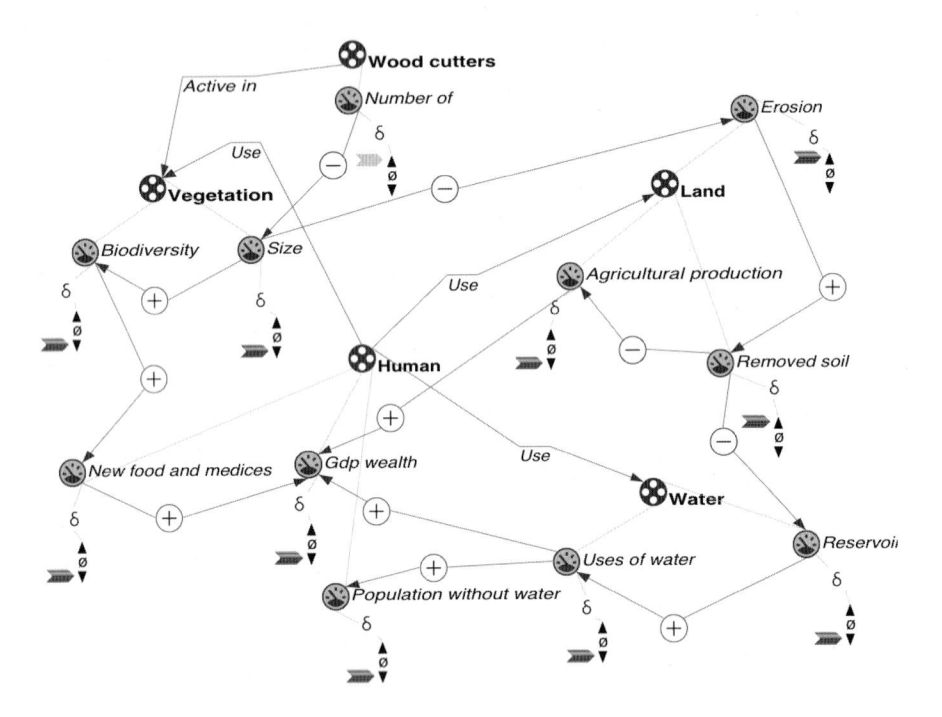

Fig. 5. A model of deforestation. The diagram captures a model and its simulation results, showing the effect of an increasing number of woodcutters on the wealth (GDP) of humans. In this representation each entity (e.g. *Vegetation*) has one or more quantities (e.g. *Size*). Each quantity has an indicator for its direction of change (stack of: arrow up, zero, arrow down). In simulation mode the values the learner assigned become grey (e.g. increase, for the quantity *Number of* belonging to *Wood cutters*). Directions of change that are generated during simulation are shown in blue (e.g. decrease, for quantity *GPD wealth* of the entity *Human*). There are two types of causal dependencies in this LS: + and −, that propagate changes between quantities.

3.3 Basic Causal Model with State-Graph (LS3)

The goal of LS3 is to have learners acquire the notion of state and state-change, and to discover that state-variables change values causing the system to move into different states, possibly undesired ones. Are there quantities that may reach critical landmarks? LS3 augments LS2 with the notion of *quantity space*, which can be assigned to one or more quantities. Adding this feature has an important impact on the simulation results, since quantities can now change values. This introduces other notions such as the *state* of the system, *transitions* from one state to another, and sequences of states along time and the history of values across states (*value history*). Notice that at LS2, only the direction of change can be simulated (the derivative of a quantity), and that this information is displayed in the same workspace as in which the model is created. At LS3 however, values (the magnitude of a quantity) are assigned to quantities and these may change, hence representations are required that shows the behaviour of a system changing over time. This is what the notions of a state-graph (consisting of states and transitions) and the value history do (see also Fig. 6).

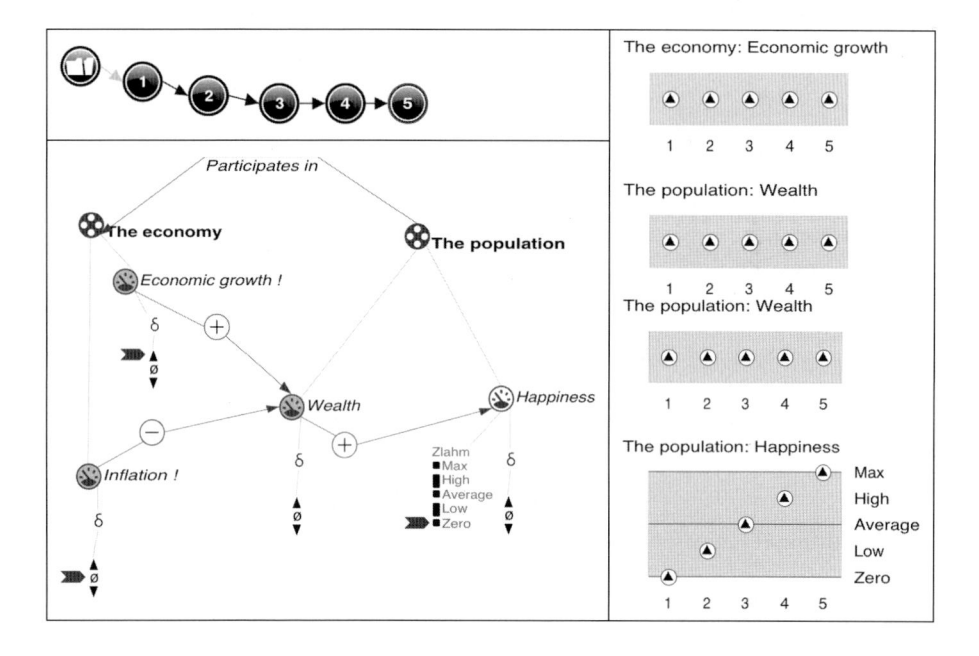

Fig. 6. The state-graph is shown at the top. It consists of 5 states, constituting a single behaviour path: [1 → 2 → 3 → 4 → 5]. The model that produced this state-graph is shown on the LHS. The representation is largely similar to that of LS2 (Fig. 5), except for the quantity space assigned to the quantity *Happiness*: {Zero, Low, Average, High, Max}. The value Zero has been assigned as initial value. During the simulation the value of *Happiness* increases from Zero to Max, as is shown on the RHS in the value history.

3.4 Causal Differentiation (LS4)

The goal of LS4 is to have learners acquire detailed understanding of processes. What is the initial cause of change? How is this triggered? How do changes propagate through the system? How do systems change due to the processes that are active? Causal differentiation refines the notions of causality. Processes are introduced, requiring a differentiation between influences (I) and proportionalities (P) (see table 1, Fig. 7 and 8). Also different from LS 2 and 3 is that the notion of exogenous quantity behaviour is introduced. This means that agents can be added to the model, allowing learners to include causal influences that enter the system from without, thereby differentiating between system and system environment.

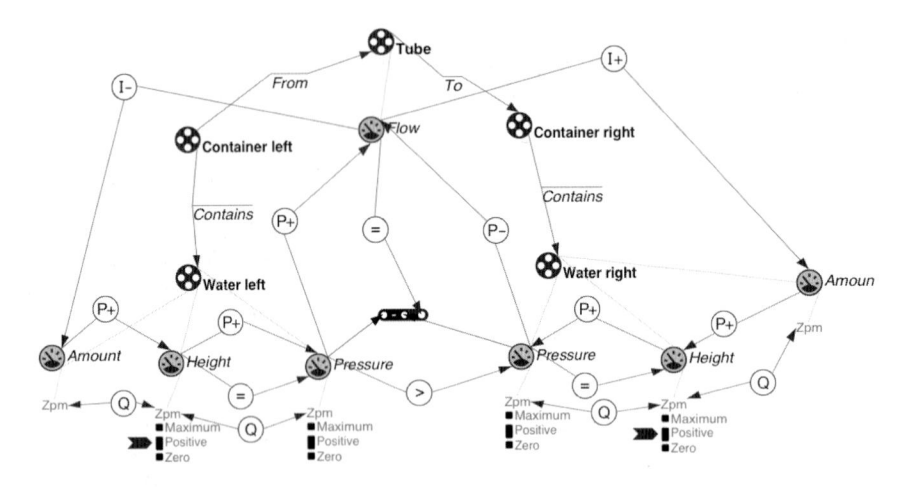

Fig. 7. A model of liquid flow (between two containers containing water). In this model Pressure difference determines Flow. Flow (initial cause of change) influences the amounts in the left (negative, I-) and right container (positive, I+). This influence is propagated via proportionalities to Height and Pressure (implementing a feedback loop). The pressures change causing the pressure difference to disappear and with that the flow. Notice that the flow can be towards the RHS (positive flow), but also towards the LHS (negative flow).

3.5 Conditional Knowledge (LS5)

The goal of LS5 is to have learners acquire a more refined understanding of the conditional aspects of processes. LS5 refines LS4 by making it possible to specify conditions under which specific subsets of the model are true, and are triggered by other subsets of the model being true. In the preceding LSs expressions created by learners were always assumed to be true. However, some facts (e.g. an evaporation process) only happen when certain conditions are satisfied. To represent conditional knowledge learners create one expression that is always true (as in LS4). But in addition to that they can add as many conditional expressions as needed. Colour coding is used to distinguish between the conditions and consequences of a model.

3.6 Generic and Reusable Knowledge (LS6)

LS6 provides the full range of representation and reasoning as is available in Garp3 (see Section 2). Learners create *scenarios* and *model fragments*. In contrast to expressions (containing both scenario and model fragment aspects), which always become active in a simulation, in LS6 a simulation is based on a scenario (describing the initial state of the system). The model fragments (which contain both conditions and consequences) can be seen as rules (IF [*conditions*], THEN [*consequences*]). If the scenario fulfils the conditions of a model fragment, the fragment becomes active, and the ingredients represented as consequences of the fragment are introduced to the description of the initial situation.

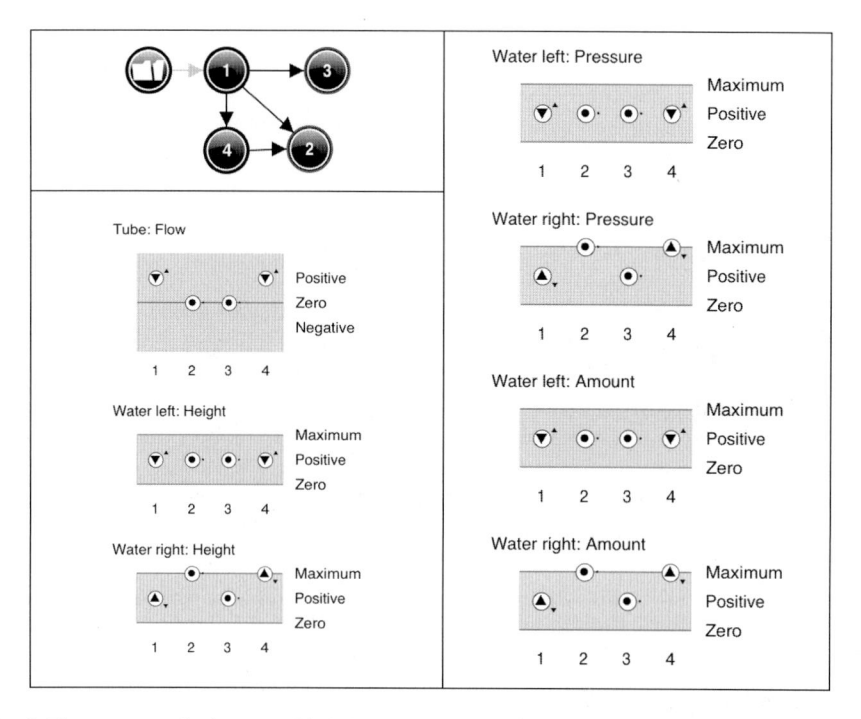

Fig. 8. The state-graph shows multiple behaviour paths [1 → 3], [1 → 4 → 2] and [1 → 2]. The path to state 3 is the one most learners expect: from unequal to equal columns. The path to state 2 is often forgotten by learners, but possible: equilibrium at the moment that the LHS container is completely filled. Finally, the path via state 4 shows the possibility of the LHS container overflowing before equilibrium is reached. Notice that additional information between the heights of the liquid columns would remove the ambiguity.

The goal of LS6 is to have learners acquire generic knowledge of processes and system behaviour, and how that generic knowledge instantiates to particular situations. Being able to handle the notion of inheritance is also essential at this space. LS6 models are rather advanced, reflecting expert level of understanding (see [6] for models expressed at this level by domain experts).

Finally notice that when used in educational practice, LSs can be used individually to focus on a particular phenomenon, or in a sequence to gradually refine someone's understanding of a phenomenon.

4 Reflective Interaction and Ongoing Development

This section briefly describes the wider view on how the software described above can be used in educational practice, as well as the additional functionality that is currently being developed in the project. The DynaLearn software consists of three main components. Firstly, the conceptual modelling environment, discussed in this paper. This is where learners construct conceptual knowledge and run simulations in order to predict the behaviour of systems based on the created model. Secondly, the semantic technology that allows the models that were created in the former component to be compared with one another. Thirdly, the virtual characters, a group of animated agents that interact with the learner.

In the DynaLearn software we bring together different interaction modes, aimed at inducing reflective thought in learners and thereby further supporting them in developing their conceptual knowledge. The interactions are implemented using virtual characters. The following modes are being developed[1]:

- *Basic help*. The user can ask the basic help character (a) how the DynaLearn software should be used and (b) what knowledge has been modelled so far.
- *Recommender*. This agent compares a learner's expression to models that were previously created by learners, teachers and/or experts. These models are stored in an online repository. Based on these models, recommendations are given for ways to improve the learner's model.
- *Critic*. This agent engages the learner in a critical analysis of the learner's conceptual model implementing a kind of Socratic dialogue.
- *Teachable agent*. After choosing a virtual student character, the learning creates a model representing that virtual character's knowledge state [2]. The learner can question the virtual student character in order to verify whether it has been taught the right knowledge, and the character can take a quiz[2]. This mode implements a *learning-by-teaching* paradigm (cf. [15,29]).
- *Quiz*. A quizmaster asks questions about a model and its simulation results that the learner must answer. The model created by the learner can be used for this (the learner must then be able to interpret the answer from the simulation results), or a model created by a teacher or an expert (learning by interacting with a predefined model). The quiz is also used in the Teachable agent model. The questions the quizmaster asks are then based on an available teacher model. Hence, the learner's ability to teach the teachable agent is evaluated. The results of the various teachable agents can be compared

---

[1] The interactions are implemented using the semantic technology and virtual characters components.
[2] Note that this is a special mode, which applies only to LS2.

with one another, based on the quizmaster's assessment. E.g. in a classroom setting the 'best model' can be identified.
- *Diagnosis*. In this mode the learner specifies simulation *expectations* with respect to the self-created model. The diagnostic virtual character addresses the discrepancies between the learner's expectation and the simulated behaviour. Based on the character's feedback, the learner is able to make adjustments to either the model or the expectations thereof (or both). In this way, learners can interactively refine their conceptual ideas.

The interaction modes can in principle be combined with one another, thus allowing the learner to interact with multiple virtual characters, receiving their feedback [28]. This way, learners can plan and control their own development [18]. Steering the communicative dialogue via the virtual characters is expected to increase the engagement of learners [20].

5 Conclusions and Discussion

To be effective, science education should focus on understanding scientific concepts and innovations; on the application of scientific knowledge to everyday life; on developing skills for problem solving, decision-making and argumentation building; and on strengthening the capacity for elaborating proposals. To engage learners in learning-by-doing activities, these aspects should be developed by adopting open curricula and participative educational methodologies. DynaLearn uses QR technology as the basis for creating such an engaging learning environment. Taking this approach unleashes valuable potential for learning. Learners can use diagrammatic representations to enhance their conceptual knowledge. Automated feedback can be provided that actually addresses the contents expressed by learners. The motivational factor is brought into play by 'routing' the interaction via virtual characters that engage the learner in various interaction modes.

The DynaLearn project is an ongoing activity. At this moment the following components have been realized: the conceptual modelling environment (including the LSs), the grounding of the created models, a simple version of the corrector interaction mode, as well as the teachable agent and quiz modes. Ongoing research addresses the remaining interaction modes, a more advanced grounding method, incorporating more information from external sources, and the development of an integrated and coherent multi-agent dialogue (currently each character has its own interaction schema with the learner). Considerable effort will be put into classroom evaluation of the different modes of interaction. The research will particularly focus on blending in with ongoing classroom learning activities so that undesired disturbances are minimized as much as possible, while the positive impact and learning enhancements caused by the DynaLearn innovation are maximized.

Acknowledgements. The work presented in this paper is co-funded by the EC within the 7th FP, Project no. 231526, and Website: http://www.DynaLearn.eu. We would like to thank Andreas Zitek for his stimulating comments.

References

1. Biswas, G., Schwartz, D., Leelawong, K., Vye, N., TAG, V.: Learning by Teaching: A New Agent Paradigm for Educational Software. Applied Artificial Intelligence, Special Issue on Educational Agents 19(3), 363–392 (2005)
2. Blair, K., Schwartz, D., Biswas, G., Leelawong, K.: Pedagogical Agents for Learning by Teaching: Teachable Agents. Technical report, School of Education, Stanford University (2006)
3. Blauvelt, R.G.: A design environment for automata: supporting children's construction of mechanical reasoning and spatial cognition. Doctoral dissertation, University of Colorado at Boulder, USA (2001)
4. Bredeweg, B., Forbus, K.: Qualitative Modeling in Education. AI Magazine 24(4), 35–46 (2003)
5. Bredeweg, B., Gómez-Pérez, A., André, E., Salles, P.: DynaLearn - Engaging and Informed Tools for Learning Conceptual System Knowledge. In: Pirone, R., Azevedo, R., Biswas, G. (eds.) Cognitive and Metacognitive Educational Systems (MCES 2009), AAAI Fall Symposium, Arlington, Virginia USA, November 5-7. Technical report FS-09-02, pp. 46–51. AAAI Press, Menlo Park (2009a)
6. Bredeweg, B., Salles, P.: Qualitative models of ecological systems — Editorial introduction. Ecological Informatics 4(5-6), 261–262 (2009b)
7. Bredeweg, B., Linnebank, F., Bouwer, A., Liem, J.: Garp3 — Workbench for Qualitative Modelling and Simulation. Ecological Informatics 4(5-6), 263–281 (2009c)
8. Bredeweg, B., André, E., Bee, N., Bühling, R., Gómez-Pérez, J.M., Häring, M., Liem, J., Linnebank, F., Thanh Tu Nguyen, B., Trna, M., Wißner, M.: Technical design and architecture. DynaLearn, EC FP7 STREP project 231526, Deliverable D2. (2009d)
9. Elio, R., Sharf, P.B.: Modeling novice-to-expert shifts in problem solving and knowledge organization. Cognitive Science 14, 579–639 (1990)
10. Forbus, K.D.: Qualitative process theory. Artificial Intelligence 24, 85–168 (1984)
11. Forbus, K.D., Feltovich, P.J.: Smart Machines in Education. AAAI Press / MIT Press, Cambridge (2001a)
12. Forbus, K.D., Carney, K., Harris, R., Sherin, B.L.: A qualitative modeling environment for middle-school students: A progress report. In: The 15th Int. Workshop on QR, San Antonio, Texas, May 17-18 (2001b)
13. Forbus, K.D.: Qualitative Modeling. In: Harmelen, F.v., Lifschitz, V., Porter, B. (eds.) Handbook of Knowledge Representation, vol. 3, pp. 361–393 (2008)
14. Frederiksen, J.R., White, B.Y.: Conceptualizing and constructing linked models: creating coherence in complex knowledge systems. In: Brna, P., Baker, M., Stenning, K., Tiberghien, A. (eds.) The Role of Communication in Learning to Model, pp. 69–96. Lawrence Erlbaum Associates, London (2002)
15. Gartner, A., Conway Kohler, M., Reissman, F.: Children Teach Children: Learning by Teaching. Harper&Row, New York (1971)
16. Hucke, L., Fischer, H.E.: The link of theory and practice in traditional and in computer-based university laboratory experiments. In: Psillos, D., Niedderer, H. (eds.) Teaching and learning in the science laboratory, pp. 205–218. Kluwer, Dordrecht (2002)
17. Jackson, S.L., Krajcik, J., Soloway, E.: The design of guided learner-adaptable scaffolding in interactive learning environments. In: Proceedings of ACM CHI 1998, pp. 187–194. ACM Press, New York (1998)
18. de Jong, T.: Technological Advances in Inquiry Learning. Science 312, 532–533 (2006)

19. de Kleer, J.H., Brown, J.S.: A qualitative physics based on confluences. Artificial Intelligence 24, 7–83 (1984)
20. Lester, J.C., Converse, S.A., Kahler, S.E., Barlow, S.T., Stone, B.A., Bhogal, R.S.: The Persona Effect: Affective Impact of Animated Pedagogical Agents. In: Proceedings of the SIGCHI Conference on Human Factors in Computing Systems, pp. 359–366. ACM Press, New York (1997)
21. Mettes, C.T.C.W., Roossink, H.J.: Linking factual and procedural knowledge in solving science problems: A case study in a thermodynamics course. Instructional Science 10, 333–361 (1981)
22. Niedderer, H., Aufschnaiter, S., Tiberghien, A., Buty, C., Haller, K., Hucke, L., Seter, F., Fischer, H.: Talking physics in labwork contexts - A category based analysis of videotapes. In: Psillos, D., Niedderer, H. (eds.) Teaching and learning in the science laboratory, pp. 31–40. Kluwer, Dordrecht (2002)
23. Norman, D.A.: Things that make us Smart. Perseus Books, Cambridge (1993)
24. Novak, J.D., Gowin, D.B.: Learning How to Learn. Cambridge University Press, New York (1984)
25. Osborne, J., Simon, S., Collins, S.: Attitudes towards science: a review of the literature and its implications. Int. Journal of Science Education 25(9), 1049–1079 (2003)
26. Otero, V., Johnson, A., Goldberg, F.: How Does the Computer Facilitate the Development of Physics Knowledge Among Prospective Elementary Teachers? Journal of Education 181(2), 57–89 (1999)
27. Papert, S.: Mindstorms: Children, Computers, and Powerful Ideas. Basic Books, NY (1980)
28. Picard, R.W., Papert, S., Bender, W., Blumberg, B., Breazeal, C., Cavallo, D., Machover, T., Resnick, M., Roy, D., Strohecker, C.: Affective Learning: A Manifesto. BT Technology Journal 22(4), 253–269 (2004)
29. Renkl, A.: Lernen durch Lehren. In: Rost, D. (ed.) Handwörterbuch Pädagogische Psychologie, vol. 3, pp. 416–420. Beltz Verlag, Auflage (2006)
30. Resnick, M.: Changing the centralized mind. MIT press, Cambridge (1994)
31. Richmond, G., Peterson, S.: STELLA II: An Introduction to Systems Thinking, High Performance Systems, Hanover, N.H (1992)
32. Schumacher, R.M., Gentner, D.: Transfer of training as analogical mapping. IEEE Transactions of Systems, Man, and Cybernetics 18, 592–600 (1988)
33. Schwarz, C.V., White, B.Y.: Metamodeling Knowledge: Developing Students' Understanding of Scientific Modeling. Cognition and Instruction 23(2), 165–205 (2005)
34. Winkels, R., Bredeweg, B. (eds.): Qualitative Models in Interactive Learning Environments. Interactive Learning Environment (special issue) 5(1-2), 1–134 (1998)

Investigating Teachers' Understanding of IMS Learning Design: Yes They Can!*

Michael Derntl[1], Susanne Neumann[2], Dai Griffiths[3], and Petra Oberhuemer[2]

[1] University of Vienna, Faculty of Computer Science, Austria
michael.derntl@univie.ac.at
[2] University of Vienna, Center for Teaching and Learning, Austria
{susanne.neumann-heyer,petra.oberhuemer}@univie.ac.at
[3] University of Bolton, Institute for Educational Cybernetics, UK
dai.griffiths.1@gmail.com

Abstract. In order to understand whether conceptual obscurity is truly the reason for the slow uptake of IMS Learning Design (LD), we have initiated an investigation into teachers' understanding of IMS LD outside of technological environments. Using paper representations ("snippets") of IMS LD component and method elements at levels A and B, 21 higher education teachers from nine countries recreated a prescribed textual learning design. Results showed that the teachers achieved an average conformity of 78% with a prototypical expert solution after watching a 45-minute IMS LD introduction. Despite successfully using IMS LD's elements, teachers reported having difficulties understanding the concepts environment, property, role-part, and condition. We conclude that the specification per se does not present an insuperable obstacle for teachers, and that from a usability perspective the calls for a new or modified LD specification might be premature, since most obstacles can be overcome with appropriate abstractions in LD tools.

1 Introduction

The ICOPER project [1] is tasked with making recommendations for interoperability specifications for e-learning in Europe. In the area of learning activities a key specification is IMS Learning Design (LD) [2], as it is the only interoperability specification which supports the definition and orchestration of complex learning flows. However the adoption of the specification has been poor, and largely restricted to research projects and pilot implementations. It is therefore necessary to consider if this is due to shortcomings in the specification, to implementation issues, institutional aspects, or to other factors. This is a complex question which is discussed in greater breadth in [3], who identify four aspects to adoption of the specification, considered as a modeling language, interoperability specification, infrastructure and methodology. In this paper we focus on the first of these, and seek to separate it from the influence of the other factors.

---

* This research was supported by the ICOPER Best Practice Network, which is co-funded by the EC under the eContent*plus* programme, ECP 2007 EDU 417007.

As a modeling language, IMS LD is intended to provide a means of defining a wide range of pedagogic strategies. Its performance in this regard has been evaluated by van Es and Koper [4], who conclude that it fulfills this requirement to a high degree. This is largely confirmed by practical experience, as few reports have been published of designs which it is not possible to represent in IMS LD. Some aspects which have been identified as being open to improvement include drawbacks in the definition of groups which are not specified in advance, and in the handling of document flows. However these are not impossible to achieve with IMS LD, but rather are tricky to implement, and it can also be argued that they are, in whole or in part, implementation issues. We therefore take as our point of departure the assumption that a lack of expressivity is not a significant barrier to the adoption of IMS LD.

However some critics—most notably [5]—have maintained that while the specification may be sufficiently expressive, it is too conceptually complex to be comprehensible and to be used in practice by authors who are not technical specialists. If true this critique would not of itself disqualify IMS LD as an effective specification, as it could still be a valuable means of transferring learning activities between systems. Nevertheless, the conceptual structure of the specification informs many of the authoring applications and runtime systems so far developed [6]. If the conceptual structure of the specification were indeed to be too complex for authors to understand then this would have implications for the way in which it can be used. Therefore we seek to answer the following questions:

1. Does the conceptual structure of IMS LD present a serious challenge for teachers to understand?
2. Which conceptual structures present the most significant challenges to teachers' understanding?

The challenge in answering these questions is to separate out the various potential causes of confusion and obscurity which could be experienced by authors. The specification is primarily intended for use by developers of authoring applications, rather than as a document which will be read and understood by authors. The *information model* [7], which contains the conceptual structure, is lengthy and formal, and this is still more true of the XML binding. Thus it is reasonable to investigate the way in which authors engage with the specification when mediated by an authoring application. However, the interfaces of authoring applications introduce usability issues which are hard to quantify. It is easy to compare two applications and conclude that one is more usable or effective than the other [8], but it is hard to assess the degree to which they transparently provide access to the conceptual structure of IMS LD. Moreover, the applications can take the modeling task out of the teachers hands, e.g. by providing templates [9] or by providing a new set of metaphors [10] and treating IMS LD simply as a file format. In this use authors may have little (or no) contact with the conceptual structure of IMS LD, and their effectiveness with the applications tells us little about the comprehensibility of IMS LD as a modeling language.

The original contribution of this paper is to directly evaluate the comprehensibility to teachers of IMS LD's conceptual structure through a evaluation activity which sidesteps the difficulties identified above. We are aware that the design of learning activities is often carried out by professional instructional designers or technical experts, but we choose to work with teachers as the most challenging case. Building on the information model of the specification we identified the key concepts which need to be assimilated in order to build a model, while missing out some of the associated detail (cf. Section 3.3). The elements of the conceptual structure of IMS LD were then represented in paper "snippets". These require the teacher to provide information which shows that they understand how the elements can be used in creating an IMS LD unit of learning.

The rest of this paper is structured as follows. In Section 2 the research design and methodology for collecting and analyzing data on teachers' use of IMS LD is set out. In Section 3, the results of quantitative and qualitative analyses are presented along with limitations and findings. Section 4 concludes the paper and discusses the findings in the light of current developments around IMS LD. Note that the core parts of this paper require solid knowledge of the IMS LD specification. IMS LD novices are kindly referred to an excellent general introduction openly available in [11], and to the full specification of the IMS LD information model in [7].

2 Research Design and Methodology

2.1 Data Collection and Participants

The data were collected in two workshops with an identical setup. One workshop was held in late 2009 in Kaunas, Lithuania ($N_K = 12$) and a second workshop was held in early 2010 in Vienna, Austria ($N_V = 9$), for a total of $N = 21$ participants. In Kaunas, all participants came from the Baltic States or Russia, while in Vienna the participants came from Austria, France, Sweden, Estonia, Germany, Slovakia, and the United Kingdom. Participants' background data were collected through a survey at the beginning of the workshops.

The average teaching experience is 9.9 years, so participants may generally be characterized as experienced teachers. The range of subject areas in which participants are teaching was quite diverse. However, most participants had a rather technical background: 16 of the 21 participants provided one or more subject areas with a technology focus, e.g. computer science, information (communication) technology, or engineering (see a word cloud of the provided teaching areas in Fig. 1). The vast majority (81%) of participants were teaching in the higher education sector, with a few occurrences of secondary, primary and other educational sectors (e.g. vocational training). Fig. 2 shows that only five of the 21 participants had previous experience with IMS LD authoring tools, with only two of them having seen an IMS LD unit of learning running in a player. That is, three out of four participants have never "done" anything with IMS LD.

2.2 Workshop Setup

Each workshop started with a demonstration of IMS LD. The objective of the demonstration was on the one hand to acquaint participants with IMS LD at

Fig. 1. Word cloud of participants' teaching backgrounds

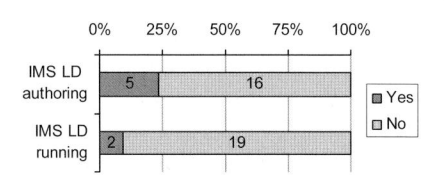

Fig. 2. Participants' previous experience with IMS LD

levels A and B, and on the other hand to provide guidance for the following hands-on design task. The demonstration took the form of a 45-minute presentation with PowerPoint slides including (1) a brief general introduction to IMS LD, (2) a demonstration of IMS LD components and method elements based on a simple, one-role example that required the use of all IMS LD level A and B elements, and (3) guidelines for using the paper snippets in the design task.

After the demonstration, every participant had the task of transferring the learning scenario shown below in italics into representations of IMS LD elements without any assistance. The scenario was more complex than the example shown during the demonstration, so that participants would have to perform more than a simple transfer of identical concepts from the example to the task.

> *The following scenario is an online learning scenario. The instructor gives a presentation to learners via a presentation conferencing service about coal-burning power plants as well as their positive and negative side effects. After the presentation, learners can choose to do one of the two following activities:*
> 1. *set up controversial questions regarding coal-burning power plants (to be used during a later discussion round), or*
> 2. *collect credible sources on the World Wide Web regarding new developments in coal-burning power plants (to be used during a later discussion round).*
>
> *The outputs learners created in the previous activities will be used during the subsequent discussion activity: The learners engage together with the instructor in the discussion using the questions and materials. After the discussion, learners rate their own agreement with the statement "Coal-burning power plants have a future in Europe's energy production" (scale of 5, where 5 is the highest agreement). Learners, who rated themselves with a level of at least 3, will next do an activity involving the creation of a (digital) poster on one positive aspect of coal-burning power plants. Learners, who rated themselves at a level of 2 or lower, will next create a (digital) poster on one negative aspect of coal-burning power plants.*

Every participant received an envelope with paper snippets, each representing one instance of an IMS LD level A or B element (see Fig. 3). Each paper snippet is divided into boxes which represent information about the element. Participants were told that those boxes with a bold, all-capitals label must be filled out, whereas those boxes labeled with a plain text format are optional. The snippets with their information boxes were designed as an immediate, slightly simplified representation of the IMS LD elements as specified in the IMS LD Information Model [7]. For instance, plays were not considered in the method, only one type of property was offered to be used as needed, and there were no self-contained items for activity descriptions, learning objects, and service instructions.

Each element had its own unique color. In order to guide participants in placing connections between elements (e.g. link an environment to an activity), the reference box of the snippet was colored with the color that represents the target element (e.g. the "environments to display" box on the activity snippet is colored with the signature color of the environment snippet, since it should reference an environment's ID). Each act was represented as a letter-size sheet of paper. The assignment of a role-part to a particular act was achieved by sticking a role-part snippet onto the sheet representing the act with provided paper glue or tape. Participants had to number the acts consecutively. Conditions were also to be glued onto the act sheets to simplify the workshop setup, although we are aware that in IMS LD conditions are captured as part of the IMS LD method.

During the task, participants had several "cheat sheets" available. One cheat sheet showed the conversion to IMS LD elements for the sample learning scenario used in the IMS LD demonstration. Another sheet offered a tabular overview of IMS LD elements (snippets) including a description and a use example for

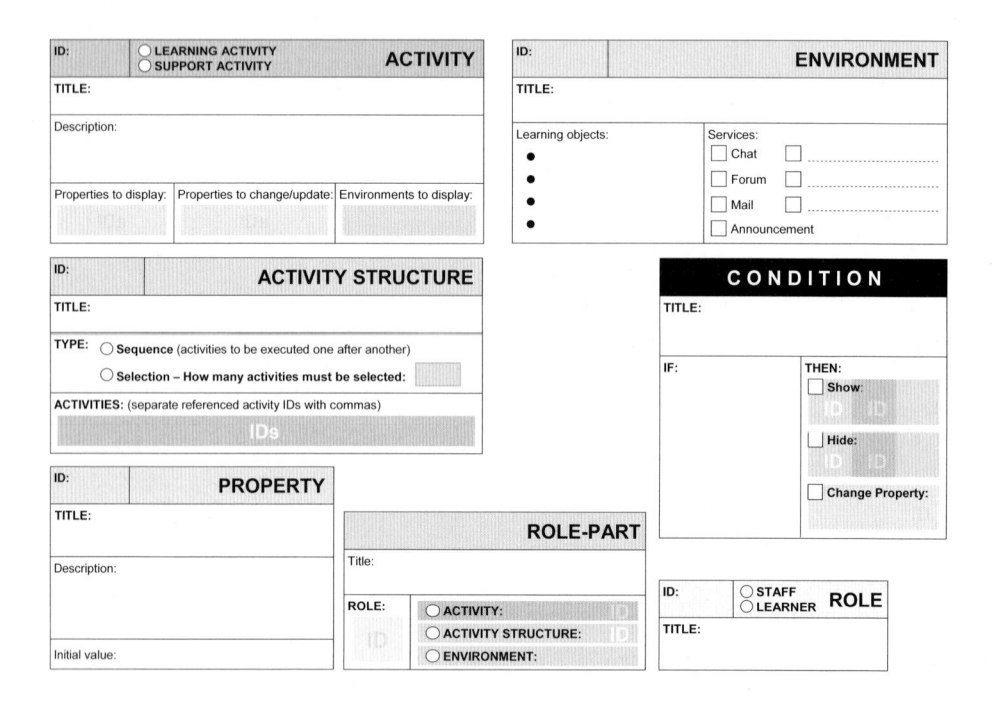

Fig. 3. Paper snippets representing the IMS LD components and method elements

each element. This information (snippet description and use example) was also printed on the back side of each snippet, e.g. the back side of the *role* snippet read, "A role expresses the function that a person carries out in a learning design. Example: Learners can take the roles of moderator, group member, or learner."

Participants were not offered any help or guidance during the task other than personal answers to questions for clarification. They were thus asked to keep a task protocol by writing down any issue, problem or question they encountered during the task on a protocol sheet. They were also asked to indicate for each identified issue whether or not they were able to solve this issue on their own.

After the design task was completed participants were asked to fill out a survey, which aimed to collect information about what gave participants the most trouble in completing the task. The purpose of the post-task survey was to complement the task solutions with additional qualitative information about participants' problems and perceptions of IMS LD.

2.3 Data Analysis

Two IMS LD experts created a prototype solution for the design task. This solution was decomposed into 81 solution parts by specifying a checklist of actions that needed to be performed to obtain the solution. For example, the checklist for the activity structure where material for the discussion is to be collected includes the action items: create activity structure, define type (selection of one activity), and link activities (two activities to choose from). The two experts independently analyzed all participants' solutions and matched them with the prototype solution by assigning a correct/incorrect flag for each item on the checklist. For 21 solutions with 81 checklist items each, the experts had to make a total of 1,701 judgments each. The two experts independently agreed on 1,617 (95%) of these judgments. The interrater reliability as calculated using Cohen's Kappa is very high ($\kappa = .87, p < .001$). The 84 judgments, on which the experts had disagreed, were reconciled and the decisions recorded in a protocol.

The resulting solution checklist data were analyzed using the layered model depicted in Fig. 4. The left-most layer comprises the IMS LD element instances required for completing the task solution. These element instances are connected with general actions to be performed with IMS LD elements at the IMS LD Action Layer. Essentially, each connection between these two layers refers to one item on the solution checklist. During the creation of this model, some actions that appeared on the original checklist were removed, added, or merged with the objectives of (1) improving focus on solution-relevant actions, and (2) simplifying the model. Of the 81 original checklist items, 60 "survived" this cleanup. Each action on the IMS LD Action Layer was assigned a level (A or B), and 18 of the 20 actions were connected with their corresponding IMS LD elements at the IMS LD Element Layer. While most of these connections are trivial, only the use of input to and output from activities were not linked to one specific element, since the linkage can—depending on the context of the action—relate to activities, environments and properties. The actions on the IMS LD Action Layer were also used to identify the performance of participants on IMS LD levels

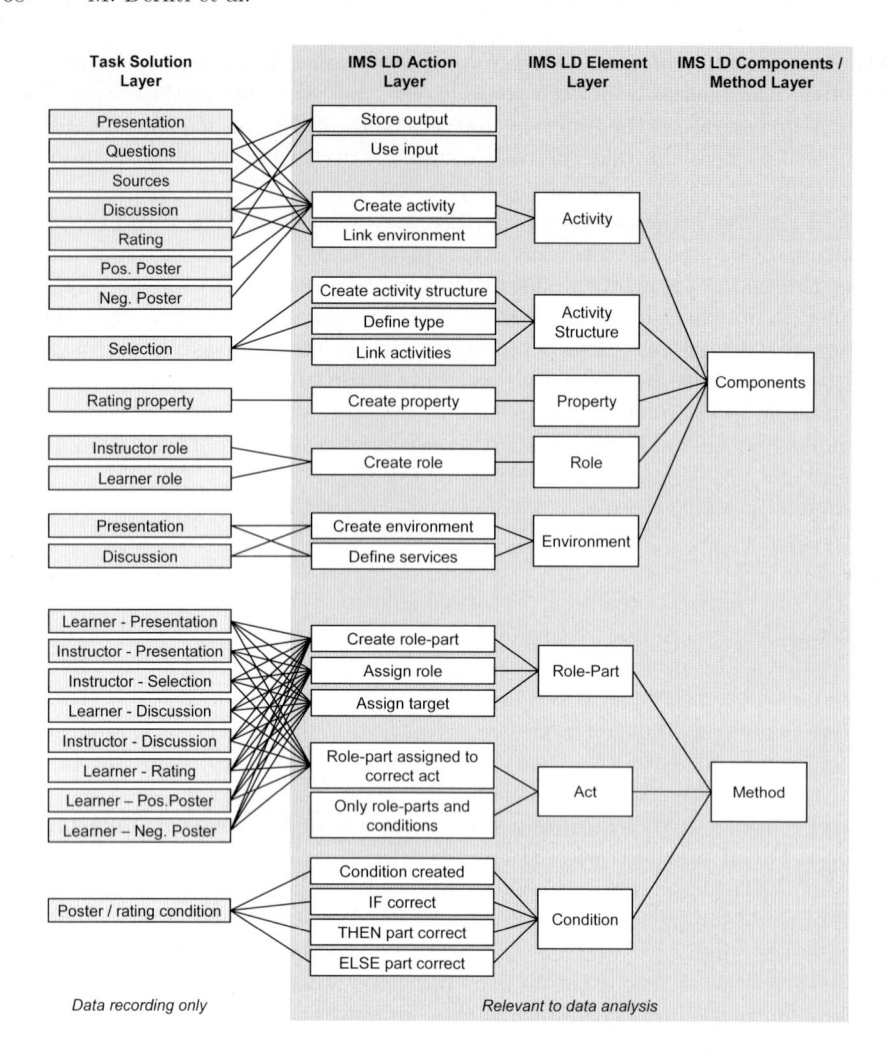

Fig. 4. Layers of data analysis and connections between the layers (solid lines)

A and B. The elements on the IMS LD Element Layer were used to analyze the performance of participants in regard to the different IMS LD elements. Based on these data, it is also possible to separately analyze the correct use of component elements and method elements. Finally, the actions at the IMS LD Action Layer were used to calculate the overall correctness of participants' solutions.

3 Results and Discussion

3.1 Quantitative Results

This section presents quantitative data analysis results and figures according to the layered data analysis structure presented in Fig. 4.

IMS LD Action Layer. The results of the IMS LD Action Layer (cp. Fig. 5) show that participants' solutions had a generally high conformity with the prototype solution created by IMS LD experts. Some actions in this layer depend on others. For instance, an environment can only be linked to an activity, if the activity was created first. These dependent actions (marked with an asterisk in Fig. 5) were only included in the analysis of a participant's solution if the participant had created the underlying element.

The percentage of conformity varies between 95% and 67%, whereby only 2 out of 20 actions realized less than 70% conformity. The actions "create [element]" rank on average among the highest actions that were successfully resolved. Participants were thus able to perform the most essential step of unit of learning authoring: They could recognize when an element needed to be created to represent a portion of the learning scenario, and for most of the elements they could adequately define this element with necessary parameters or descriptions. Role-parts were the element whose creation caused participants the most trouble. There may be several factors contributing to this. First, creating role-parts and gluing them onto the (correct) act sheets was presumably for most participants

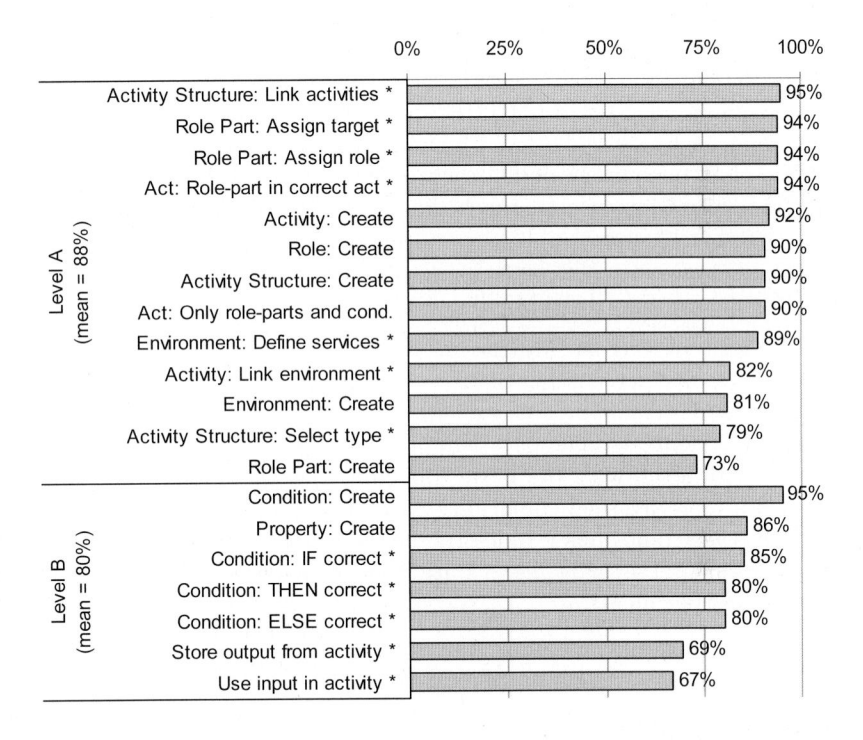

	Action	Conformity
Level A (mean = 88%)	Activity Structure: Link activities *	95%
	Role Part: Assign target *	94%
	Role Part: Assign role *	94%
	Act: Role-part in correct act *	94%
	Activity: Create	92%
	Role: Create	90%
	Activity Structure: Create	90%
	Act: Only role-parts and cond.	90%
	Environment: Define services *	89%
	Activity: Link environment *	82%
	Environment: Create	81%
	Activity Structure: Select type *	79%
	Role Part: Create	73%
Level B (mean = 80%)	Condition: Create	95%
	Property: Create	86%
	Condition: IF correct *	85%
	Condition: THEN correct *	80%
	Condition: ELSE correct *	80%
	Store output from activity *	69%
	Use input in activity *	67%

Fig. 5. Participants' solutions' conformity with the experts' prototype solution at the IMS LD Action Layer. Legend: The value 92% for "Activity: Create" means that on average each participant created 92% of the activities of the correct prototype solution. Dependent actions are marked with an asterisk (*); these actions could only be performed when the underlying element was created.

the final phase of authoring, and some of them may already have run into time constraints. Also, role-parts are complex elements since each role-part needs to be connected to one role and one target activity, activity structure, or environment. From a cognitive viewpoint, this is probably the most demanding element. However, once created, people were obviously easily able to assign a target and a role, and put the role-part into the correct act (94% average conformity each).

Fig. 5 shows that there are 8 percentage points difference between conformity scores of actions at level A (88% average conformity) and level B (80% average conformity). A significant share of this difference is accounted for by the level B actions related to activities, namely considering input to activities (67% average conformity) and output from activities (69% average conformity) using properties. In the task scenario this was the case, for instance, when students were to produce materials, and these materials were to be used during a subsequent discussion activity as demonstrated in the task description. Other than that, the use of level B elements added little to the task's complexity.

A separate view on the same data with focus just on IMS LD beginners (i.e. those 16 participants who have not had any previous experience with IMS LD authoring or playing) reveals little difference between beginners and the overall group. In fact, for most actions the results are almost identical (only $1-3$ percentage points difference). Actions where beginners perform worse by more than 5 percentage points are: selecting the correct type of activity structure (-8 percentage points), correct use of THEN and ELSE parts in conditions (-7 percentage points each), as well as creating environments and linking environments to activities (-6 percentage points each). The average difference of conformity between the overall group and the beginners is 3 percentage points. It seems safe to claim that beginners did not perform considerably worse on the IMS LD Action Layer, and, since this layer is the primary determinant of the scores on all subsequent layers, for IMS LD in general.

IMS LD Element Layer. Moving on to the IMS LD Element Layer, we averaged the conformity percentages of all actions at the IMS LD Action Layer that map to a particular element. This way, we obtained data on participants' success to use IMS LD elements. The data is represented in Fig. 6. All percentages are at a rather high level, with the most "difficult" elements being conditions and environments (85% average conformity each) and the "easiest" one being the act (92% average conformity). Since the difference between those two is only 7 percentage points, it seems valid to state that participants performed well with all level A and B elements.

IMS LD Components/Method Layer. IMS LD conceptually distinguishes elements belonging to the components part (i.e. activity, activity structure, environment, role, and property) or to the method part (i.e. role-part, condition, and act). While the component elements are frequently used concepts in several approaches to educational modeling and design, the method section is particular to IMS LD since it follows the metaphor of stage plays, where actors perform their role-parts in several consecutive acts. The average conformity scores for elements in the components and method sections are almost identical (87% and

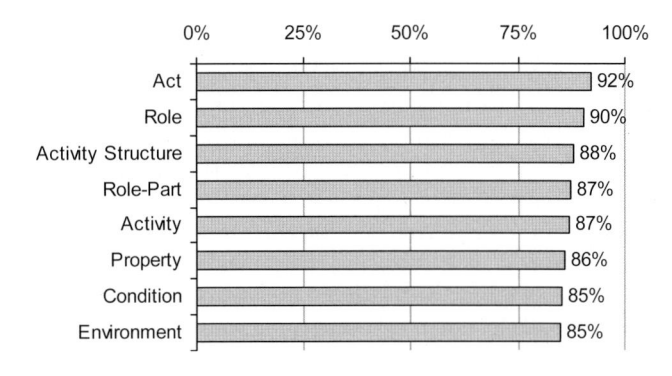

```
                    0%      25%      50%      75%     100%
             Act |████████████████████████████████████| 92%
            Role |███████████████████████████████████| 90%
Activity Structure|██████████████████████████████████| 88%
        Role-Part|█████████████████████████████████| 87%
         Activity|█████████████████████████████████| 87%
         Property|████████████████████████████████| 86%
        Condition|████████████████████████████████| 85%
      Environment|████████████████████████████████| 85%
```

Fig. 6. Participants' performance on the IMS LD element layer

88%, respectively), thus demonstrating that the stage-play metaphor of IMS LD does not pose any significant problems to its users.

Overall Quality of Solutions. The average overall conformity of participants' solutions with the IMS LD experts' prototype solution was computed using data from the IMS LD Action Layer for the following reasons: (1) The data on the IMS LD Element Layer was abstracted from the actions that had to be performed; and (2) using the checklist on the Task Solution Layer would assign more weight to those element types that occurred more frequently in the solution (e.g. since there were two environments and eight role-parts in the solution, the weight for creating role-parts would be four times as high as for creating environments). As an additional measure, all checklist data for dependent actions (i.e. actions that pre-require another action to be performed) were included in this calculation. This was considered necessary, since otherwise those participants who created an element but failed with the element's dependent actions could be "punished" more than participants who failed to create the element at all.

As a result, the average overall match of participants' solutions to the prototype solution based on correctly performed actions at the IMS LD Action Layer was 78.1% ($n = 21$; $s.d. = 20.2$ percentage points; $min. = 23.8\%, max. = 100\%$).

3.2 Qualitative Results

The IMS LD demonstration did not provide the entirety of information needed to perform the task. Some of the information was held back on purpose to see whether participants could figure out which IMS LD element should be used to perform specific actions. The two concepts that participants were not explicitly instructed about were (1) how to express that two roles perform a joint activity, and (2) how to reuse the output of an activity in a latter activity. Concerning this limitation, participants performed well in concluding which IMS LD elements it was correct to use to perform these actions. These two actions also represented the most difficult portion of the solution to complete successfully.

Role-Parts. As the quantitative results showed, participants were not as successful in creating role-parts correctly. This was especially true for activities, which were jointly performed by two roles. In the task, this was the case for the presentation activity (instructor presents while students listen during the presentation) and the discussion activity (the instructor and students discuss together). The anticipated way to express a scenario with two roles joining in an activity is to create two role-parts (one for each role) within the same act that both link to the same activity. Often, participants created just one of the role-parts. On average, participants were able to create 73% of the role-parts required for the task. Two role-parts which accounted for a large share of these difficulties were the instructor's role-part in the discussion activity (only 57% of the participants created this role-part) as well as the learners' role-part in the presentation activity (only 52% of the participants created this role-part). Obviously, participants were tempted to link only the "dominant" roles to these activities, i.e. the instructor with the presentation, and the learners with the discussion, respectively. Other role-parts that caused considerable trouble were the role-parts for the creation of a positive poster (57% created this role-part) and a negative poster (48% created this role-part). This was a complex part of the task, since participants had to use a condition to control the visibility of the poster-creation activities based on a property value set during a previous rating activity. While participants were highly successful in solving these challenges (86% created the property, 95% created the condition, and 85% referenced the property in the condition), they may have simply forgotten to create the needed role-parts for these activities. Another explanation could be that participants viewed the condition as being responsible for showing the activities, and therefore not deeming it necessary to create role-parts for the poster creation activities.

Activity Input and Output. One of the more difficult actions for participants was to store the product or output of an activity. In the task learning scenario, learners were supposed to collect credible sources on the web or set up controversial discussion questions. These items were then to be used during a later discussion activity. The difficulty for the participants was to decide how to store and reuse the learners' output. 16 of the 21 participants managed to create both output-generating activities. Of those, 12 participants stored the outputs of the pre-discussion activities. 67% of them used properties to store the output, while the rest used dedicated environments (e.g. for collecting the questions in a forum) to do so. 9 of them managed to link this property or environment as input to the discussion activity. Three additional participants linked an environment with outputs from preceding activities as input to the discussion activity; however, they did not link the environment to the output-generating activities. Either they forgot or failed to do this, or they considered it as redundant to link the environment to all involved activities. Although properties would be the correct way of expressing this solution in IMS LD, we regarded both ways as correct, since the technical constraints on properties and environments were not covered in detail in the introductory demonstration. In any case, the participants were obviously quite resourceful in finding a reasonable solution to this problem.

Conditional Activities. Participants further demonstrated problems when setting up the poster creation activities that were to be displayed or hidden automatically according to a condition. Most participants correctly set up the condition, which determines whether the learner will next see the activity for creating a pro-coal burning power plants poster or a con-coal burning power plants poster. Although the condition to control the display of one or the other activity was often set up correctly (80%), some participants additionally set up an activity structure of type selection referencing both poster activities. Seemingly, they did not trust that the condition will automatically arrange the display.

Referencing Elements. Uncertainty could also be recognized in regard to the link between activities and environments. Participants correctly linked environments to activities as the quantitative solution showed. However, the same environment was frequently linked twice: Participants referenced an environment in an activity on the activity snippet (correct action), but would then link the activity and again the environment to the role within the role-part (incorrect action). The same pattern, but not as frequent, appeared with activities and the activity structure: Participants would correctly set up the activity structure and reference the corresponding activities. However, when constructing the role-part, the participants would then link the activity structure, and link on the same role-part again the activities that were part of the activity structure. It appears that referenced elements caused uncertainty in their use and display.

Issues Protocol. In the protocol, participants recorded issues or problems they encountered while solving the workshop task. They were also to record whether they were able to solve the documented issue themselves. Fig. 7 shows the results of recorded issues, whereby issues were clustered in order to identify common themes in issue reporting. Clustering was performed whenever an item was mentioned more than once. Issue reports that only appeared once in all protocols, such as "not enough working space on the table" were omitted. Participants did not put down for every reported issue whether they were able to solve it or not. Therefore, for all non-marked issues we assume that these are unresolved issues.

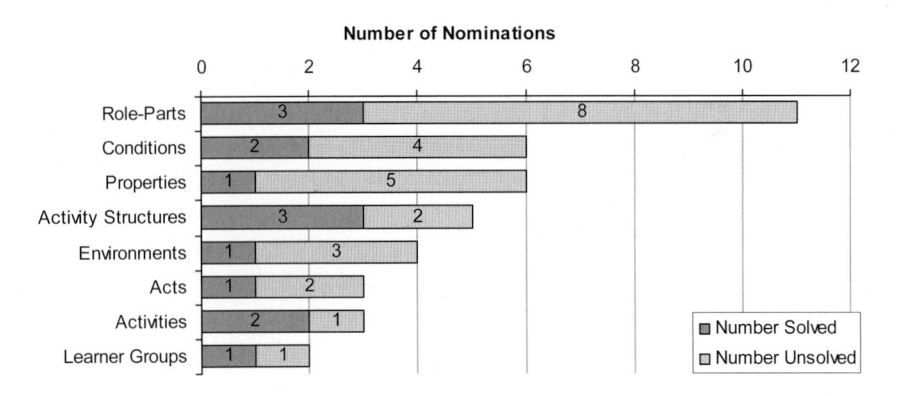

Fig. 7. Participants' reported issues and problems encountered while solving the task

Role-parts received the greatest number of nominations. Participants had most trouble with the 1:1 matching of a role and either an activity, environment, or activity structure. The protocol entries show uncertainty regarding this matching, and most often they reported that they were unsure whether to link the activity and the environment over again.

The second most reported problem related to conditions. Most often, the reported issue was whether conditions should be used to show and hide activities which could be represented in a sequence. This is in fact true, since conditions could be used instead of acts to structure a learning sequence. Participants understood that it is possible to use both elements to structure sequences. Properties were reported as the third concept that caused a significant number of unsolved problems. Participants reported that they were unsure whether they understood the concept of property. Specifically, some pondered whether the property is the appropriate element to use when storing the output of activities. One participant asked whether a property can be specific to a person (addressing the concept of personal properties, which was not explained in the IMS LD demonstration). This issue was reportedly unsolved to the participant.

Three Greatest Perceived Troubles. Test participants clearly had good understanding of using the IMS LD elements after only a brief introduction. When asked to name three things about the task that gave them the most trouble, they reported that the concepts environment (7 nominations), property (5 nominations), and condition (4 nominations) caused the most trouble. Another aspect that proved difficult for participants was the differentiation between some IMS LD components. The three confusions that were nominated most often were distinguishing between activity structure and act, between activity and activity structure, and between activity and environment. The question participants asked was, "when do I use which element?" They also had trouble understanding how to represent learner groups within IMS LD's role concept. This is a typical IMS LD problem, which has been reported elsewhere especially for building collaborative learning scenarios, e.g. in [12].

3.3 Limitations of the Study

Some comments on limitations inherent in this study are appropriate before arriving at general findings. The task carried out by participants required the use of virtually all level A and B elements. In order to manage the available workshop time, the task was kept moderate in terms of number and complexity of activities and was situated in a purely online context. Another reason for the positive results of this study could be that most study participants had a high technology affinity regarding their teaching backgrounds. Although the tasks carried out were not technological and most of the concepts used in IMS LD are also not technological (e.g. environment, activity structure, act ...), a technical background may have helped participants in understanding some details (for example in understanding the nature of properties). However, since IMS LD is meant for technology-enhanced learning and teaching, the workshop participants may in fact be representative of a typical audience that implements e-learning.

Compared to the IMS LD information model, the paper snippets representing the IMS LD elements were simplified in terms of structure (e.g. only one instead of five types of properties) and information content (e.g. textual instead of hierarchical IF-statements in conditions, or omitting to represent learning objects as paper snippets). We believe that this is appropriate in seeking to understand comprehension of the structure underlying the specification.

Last but not least, the demonstration of IMS LD at the beginning of the workshop was targeted at enabling participants to solve the given task using the paper snippets. Most of the actions required in the task were demonstrated. Actions not required in the task (e.g. employing several plays in a learning design, or employing a monitor service) were not demonstrated and were also not represented as paper snippets.

3.4 Answers to the Main Study Questions

The results indicate that teachers are able to handle level A and B elements presented in the IMS LD specification to an extent that enables them to solve a moderately complex learning design task. The problem is thus not to be seen in the specification itself, but in the tools and processes of using IMS LD.

In the introduction to this paper, two main research questions were stated: *"Does the conceptual structure of IMS LD present a serious challenge for teachers to understand?"* Based on the results in the empirical analyses this question can be answered with "no". Participants performed well on the components and the method sections of their solutions, and they performed equally well on level A and level B. They achieved at least 79% conformity with the correct prototype solution for 17 out of 20 distinct actions required to solve the design task.

The three actions with less than 79% conformity are used to answer the second research question, i.e. *"Which conceptual structures present the most significant challenges to teachers' understanding?"* The conceptual structures in the IMS LD specification that presented the most significant challenges to teachers' understanding were (1) the action related to using role-parts to link roles with activities, activity structures and environments; and (2) the handling of the "document flow" between activities, which is related to the actions of defining output of and input to activities.

4 Conclusions and Recommendations

In this paper we have presented an empirical study into the use of IMS LD by teachers to collect evidence for either maintaining or rejecting the common conception that IMS LD is too conceptually complex to be understood and used by teachers. To remove the bias introduced by IMS LD editors and tools, we adopted a paper-based approach: Elements of the conceptual structure of IMS LD were directly projected onto paper snippets. The qualitative and quantitative data analyses indicated that teachers were mostly able to create high quality solutions to a given design task which required the use of virtually all level A and B elements. Thus, our principal conclusion is that teachers were able to understand the elements, the structure, and the modeling metaphor of IMS LD after a brief introductory demonstration. Since the conceptual structure of IMS LD does not present a serious challenge for teachers to understand, the barriers to adoption may lie elsewhere. Suggested candidates for investigation are the length of time needed to develop mature tooling for a complex specification, and the social, professional and organizational changes required of an institution that is to adopt a learning design approach.

Secondly, we identified a number of conceptual structures which present the most significant challenges to teachers' understanding. We recommend that software developers be particularly aware of these when designing authoring applications. The first of these challenges, i.e. the management of role-parts, is largely resolved by existing authoring platforms. For example, the ReCourse LD Editor [6] and the Graphical Learning Modeller [9] hide the definition of role-parts from the learning designer with no loss of expressivity. The other principal aspects regarding the storage and reuse of user output should be investigated in greater detail: There is a need to identify the best way to show learning designers the consequences of conditions (what is being shown and what is hidden) and the most effective way of representing environments and their linkage to activities.

Additionally we note that obstacles to understanding such as the challenges presented above led some to conclude that radical changes to the specification are required or that a new and simpler specification should be developed. This is the position adopted by [5]: "it is complicated to create a learning design specification meeting both usability and technical needs. IMS LD tried to do that and it's maybe not the right way to proceed." In response they suggest that two new specifications should be developed. One of these, Simple Learning Design 2.0, would be a technical interoperability specification, while the other would be "a real UML for learning design."

Without entering here into a discussion of the perceived need for two specifications, we note that this is a path fraught with pitfalls. As Duval points out, "...the decision to develop a new standard is often taken without proper due diligence. The enthusiasm and will to create something useful is of course positive, but channeling that energy in the development of a new standard is often misdirected" [13, p. 229]. Developing a new standard and delivering the functionality to end users in a way that is useful and usable may take many years [13]. The study presented in this paper may be seen from the perspective of the due diligence. The appropriate response to a critique of a specification from the user's point of view is to thoroughly test if there is a problem with the existing specification itself, or if innovative and creative use and implementation can meet the requirements set out by the critique. For example, in our case we have identified that some teachers do not find the relationship between environment and activity in IMS LD to be intuitive. Due diligence requires us to consider if this can be resolved at the level of implementation metaphors, rather than at the level of the specification. In this case it seems clear that a graphical interface, which enables authors to place activities within an environment, could be mapped onto the specification. The tool would represent this as an association between an activity and an environment. In any event, it seems clear that this problem, one of the most challenging experienced by our participants in working with environments, does not necessarily require a change in the specification.

Extrapolating this example to the wider context the implication is that the development of usable authoring interfaces for simple learning designs is clearly welcome. However, it should be made clear that the evidence to date indicates that these conceptual mappings and simplifications can be achieved with only minor proposed modifications to the specification (e.g. as reported in [10]), and that our results provide direct evidence that the underlying elements, structure, and metaphors of the IMS LD specification are not an insuperable barrier to its effective use.

References

1. ICOPER: ICOPER Best Practice Network (2010), http://icoper.org
2. IMS Global: IMS Learning Design specification (2003), http://www.imsglobal.org/learningdesign
3. Griffiths, D., Liber, O.: Opportunities achievements and prospects for use of IMS LD. In: Lockyer, L., Bennett, S., Agostinho, S., Harper, B. (eds.) Handbook of Research on Learning Design and Learning Objects: Issues, Applications and Technologies, pp. 87–112. IGI Global, Hershey (2009)
4. van Es, R., Koper, R.: Testing the pedagogical expressiveness of IMS LD. Educational Technology & Society 9(1), 229–249 (2006)
5. Durand, G., Downes, S.: Toward Simple Learning Design 2.0. In: 4th Int. Conf. on Computer Science & Education 2009, Nanning, China, pp. 894–897 (2009)
6. Griffiths, D., Beauvoir, P., Liber, O., Barrett-Baxendale, M.: From reload to ReCourse: learning from IMS learning design implementations. Distance Education 30(2), 201–222 (2009)
7. IMS Global: IMS Learning Design information model (2003), http://www.imsglobal.org/learningdesign/ldv1p0/imsld_infov1p0.html
8. Griffiths, D., Beauvoir, P., Sharples, P.: Advances in editors for IMS LD in the TENCompetence project. In: 8th IEEE Int. Conf. on Advanced Learning Technologies, pp. 1045–1047 (2008)
9. Neumann, S., Oberhuemer, P.: User evaluation of a graphical modeling tool for IMS Learning Design. In: Spaniol, M., Li, Q., Klamma, R., Lau, R.W.H. (eds.) Advances in Web Based Learning – ICWL 2009. LNCS, vol. 5686, pp. 287–296. Springer, Heidelberg (2009)
10. Paquette, G., Leonard, M., Lundgren-Cayrol, K., Mihaila, S., Gareau, D.: Learning design based on graphical knowledge modelling. Educational Technology & Society 9(1), 97–112 (2006)
11. Koper, R., Olivier, B.: Representing the learning design of units of learning. Educational Technology & Society 7(3), 97–111 (2004)
12. Hernandez-Leo, D., Asensio-Perez, J., Dimitriadis, Y.: IMS Learning Design support for the formalization of collaborative learning patterns. In: 4th IEEE Int. Conf. on Advanced Learning Technologies, Juensuu, Finland, pp. 350–354 (2004)
13. Duval, E., Verbert, K.: On the role of technical standards for learning technologies. IEEE Transactions on Learning Technologies 1(4), 229–234 (2008)

Task Performance vs. Learning Outcomes: A Study of a Tangible User Interface in the Classroom

Son Do-Lenh, Patrick Jermann, Sébastien Cuendet,
Guillaume Zufferey, and Pierre Dillenbourg

CRAFT, Ecole Polytechnique Fédérale de Lausanne (EPFL)
1015 Lausanne, Switzerland
{son.dolenh,patrick.jermann,sebastien.cuendet,
guillaume.zufferey,pierre.dillenbourg}@epfl.ch

Abstract. Tangible User Interfaces (TUIs) offer the potential to facilitate collaborative learning in new ways. This paper presents an empirical study that investigated the effects of a TUI in a classroom setting on task performance and learning outcomes. In the tangible condition, apprentices worked together around an interactive tabletop warehouse simulation using tangible inputs. In the paper condition, they performed the same activity with only paper and pens. Results showed that the tangible condition resulted in better task performance (more alternative solutions explored and better final solution) but did not affect learning outcomes, i.e. understanding of important concepts and applying them to a problem-solving question. We discuss reasons for this in terms of task structure and type, nature of tangible user interfaces and effective interaction requirements.

Keywords: Tangible User Interface, Tabletop, Collaborative Learning, Augmented Reality, Technology-Enhanced Learning, Human Computer Interaction.

1 Introduction

With the fast development of technologies, educational scientists and practitioners have increased efforts to extend learning activities from traditional computers to other platforms, allowing richer experiences and more direct interactions. Among other paradigms, tangible user interfaces (TUI) have been actively researched recently. Very often, a TUI is augmented with visual information on a tabletop surface that works both as an input space and a display [28].

It is commonly believed that TUIs facilitate collaboration, especially collaborative learning scenarios, with learners not being constrained by obtrusive technologies and engaged in face-to-face, rather than mediated interactions. While it seems evident that TUIs provide new possibilities and enable many exciting activities [4,15,29], it remains unclear as to whether students really benefit from using them in learning settings.

Fig. 1. Two apprentices building a warehouse model with the TinkerLamp

In previous studies, we have observed qualitatively how apprentices at vocational schools collaborate around a TUI system called TinkerLamp (Figure 1) [13]. We also investigated the effects of this TUI when compared with a multi-touch interface on learning outcomes in a controlled experiment [24]. While feedbacks from teachers and apprentices are positive with regards to the learning activities that we developed, we do not have formal proof for its benefits in a real classroom setting. In this paper, we set out to answer this question and hope the findings will give more insights into the future designs and usages of TUIs in realistic environments.

To this end, we conducted a study with groups of logistics apprentices studying in a classroom setting, under two conditions: a tangible condition and a baseline condition with traditional paper and pens. The given task was to collaboratively design a warehouse layout to learn concepts of different types of surfaces used to describe a warehouse.

2 Related Work

Interactive tabletop computing (see e.g. [30,6]) is known for its support for fast and natural interactions. Among other things, people around a tabletop can interact with the system through various input styles, e.g. mouse or multi-mice [17], touch or hand gestures [6,23,10], or pens [18]. The horizontal nature of tabletop systems also affords users putting physical objects on the surface, and hence opens up the possibility for the intuitive manipulation of these tangibles (called Tangible User Interface) [28] which is the focus of our study.

The unique physical features of TUIs offer the potential to facilitate collaborative learning in new ways. They support building activities in which learners can interact directly with their hands by touching and manipulating objects. The benefits are manifold.

First, manipulation of physical objects is useful for students' understanding since they are real and can be manipulated. The added value of sensori-motor experience that TUIs offer has been described in the literature [22], relying on the idea that they support an enactive mode of reasoning [3] and enable empirical abstractions of sensori-motor schemes [19].

Second, TUIs can enable more participation. Learning outcomes are generally dependent on students' level of participation in the activity. Learning benefits can be impaired when some group members dominate the whole activity [25]. TUIs hence play an important role to bring about more equitable participation thanks to simultaneous inputs. In [27], Stanton et. al. concluded that simultaneous inputs can promote more equitable interactions between children. In [22], the authors also discussed how they were able to promote engaging, active and playful learning by developing digitally augmented physical spaces.

Third, TUIs with the integration of external concrete inputs and the abstract augmented information may be an excellent means to present Multiple External Representations (MERs)[1]. The arguments put forward by this learning approach is that presenting learners with several instances of the same information at different levels of abstraction will act as a scaffold allowing them to understand the more abstract representation by observing how it is related to the more concrete one.

Fourth, most TUIs are used around a tabletop which provides a larger display area and helps group members to be better aware of each other's actions. This has been confirmed by several studies [9,12]. For example, through a study comparing groups of three people using mice versus a multi-touch table [12], Hornecker et. al. suggested that the affordances of direct touch input and body movements in tabletop condition resulted in a better awareness of intention and action than mice.

Although previous research has reported on how tangible tabletop technologies are adopted by school communities [4,20,22,32,26], only a few applications are evaluated for learning outcomes [14,31,8]. Moreover, these studies have been mostly focused on young children, i.e. from primary-aged to about 14. Generally, the educational benefits of collaborative activities enabled by TUIs need further exploration and for different populations.

In this paper, we examine how effectively vocational apprentices, typically 17-20 years of age, study around a tabletop user interface using tangible objects as input. Before describing the study, we will first detail the educational context and our TUI system.

3 Context

3.1 Vocational Training

In countries like Germany, Austria and Switzerland, the prevailing organization of vocational training follows a dual approach: apprentices work three to four days per week in a company and spend one day per week in a vocational school. The dual model presents the advantage that apprentices gain experience by working in an authentic setting, and these experiences may be exploited in school courses. Likewise, the abstract concepts learned in school may also be referred to in their work environment.

The domain of interest was logistics, a profession that involves the storage and transportation of goods, the design of warehouses and transportation routes, as well as the management of inventories and information. Apprentices in logistics are students who usually have difficulties in reasoning skills. Consequently, it appears that many of them struggle to understand the logistics concepts presented at school.

Our field observations showed that the switching of context from the company (involving action) to the classroom (theory) potentially entails some difficulties for apprentices. Knowledge transfer from schools to the workplace is not automatic and would require specific training. Conversely, problems addressed in school appear as unspecific and inauthentic compared to the apprentices' daily practice. Bridging this abstraction gap is the focus of our research.

We developed a tangible tabletop environment, called the TinkerLamp. The main objective of this environment is to enable problem-solving activities which are as close as possible to the real context of a warehouse to help apprentices overcome the lack of abstraction skills.

3.2 TinkerLamp: A Tangible Tabletop Environment

The TinkerLamp system (Figure 2) is currently used in several vocational schools [33]. Apprentices and teachers interact with the TinkerLamp through a tangible user interface, consisting of two interaction modalities.

First, it involves using a small-scale model of a warehouse with miniature plastic shelves, loading docks, offices, etc. to build a physical warehouse layout (Figure 2b). Each element of the small-scale warehouse is tagged with a fiducial marker that enables automatic camera object recognition. This warehouse model is augmented with visual feedback and information through a projector above the table. The simplest augmentation is the drawing of navigation nodes around each shelf. When two shelves are placed too close, the navigation nodes turn red, showing that there is not enough space for a forklift to work in the alley between these shelves. It is therefore possible for apprentices to find the ideal alley width by trial and error.

Second, users use a paper-based interface (called TinkerSheet, Figure 2) to change parameters of the system or to run and control a simulation on top of the small-scale model. The simulation displays real-time information, e.g. various statistics about the warehouse inventory or storage management strategies. TinkerSheets are a set of paper pieces, used to set simulation parameters and visualize outputs on the same physical space which is used to build the warehouse model. Users can interact with a sheet in a couple of ways, using either physical tokens (e.g. magnets) or a pen by drawing a circle on an input area.

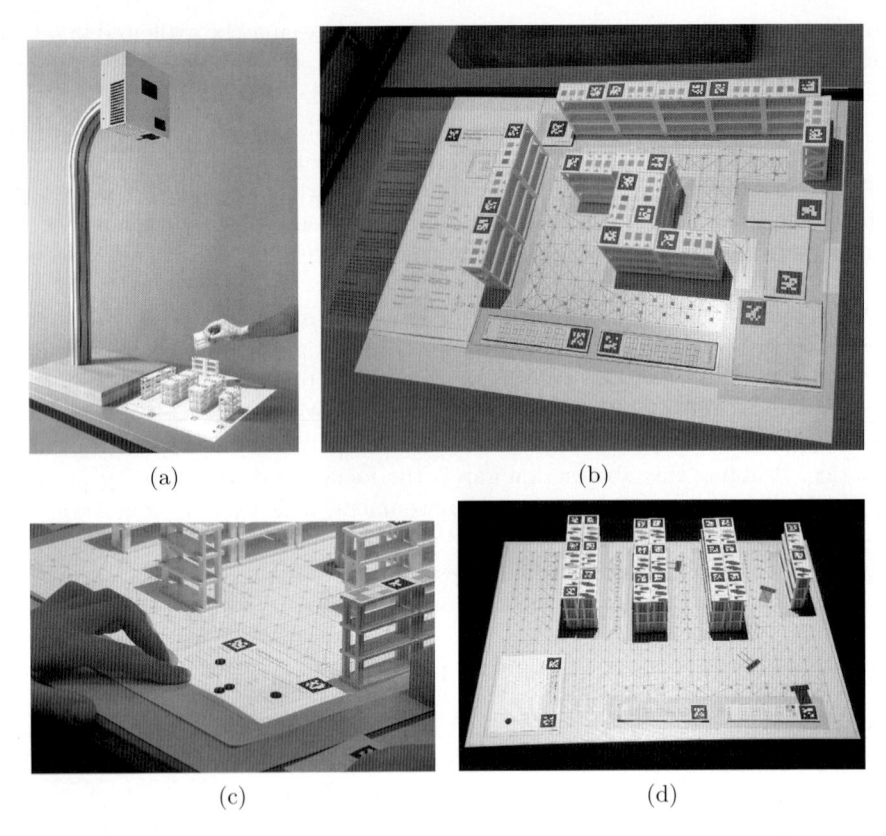

Fig. 2. Tinker systems: a) TinkerLamp. b)Small-scale model with a TinkerSheet to the left. c)Use TinkerSheet to change system's parameters. d) Simulation of the warehouse.

4 Research Hypotheses

We are interested in a problem-solving task, which is the design of a warehouse. This task is a common learning task in logistics classes. It requires the apprentices to explore the warehouse surfaces and problem-solve the placement of different warehouse elements (docks, storage shelves, administration offices, etc.) by taking into account various constraints. Drawing with paper and pens has been the traditional method to tackle this type of problems during the logistics apprenticeship. The aim of our contribution is to examine the impact of TUIs on learning outcomes compared to this method.

We conducted an experimental study in a classroom setting. Groups of apprentices in the experimental condition were provided with TinkerLamps and tangible inputs. The groups in the control condition were not provided with them, rather working together in a traditional way using paper and pens.

We expected that the physical and social natures of TUIs would result in both better task performance and better learning outcomes. More specifically, we tested the following hypotheses.

1. Tangible interface leads to better task performance (more alternative solutions, better final designs) than the traditional paper-and-pen approach.
2. Tangible interface leads to more positive learning outcomes (understanding and applying concepts in other situations better) than the traditional paper-and-pen approach.

Our aim with TinkerLamp is to develop a system that can be used in authentic settings without researcher's presence. Consequently, our study took place in a classroom and also involved teachers. We would like to explore how the TUI works in a setting as close to reality as possible.

5 Experiment Design

5.1 Participants

Four classes with a total of 61 apprentices participated in the study. Due to the logisctics domain characteristics, most of them are male (56 out of 61). The two experimental conditions were: (1) the tangible condition (hereafter called TAN condition, two classes of 15 students), in which the students collaborated around TinkerLamps; (2) the paper condition (PAP, a class of 15 students, a class of 16), in which the activity involved students drawing on paper with pens (Figure 3). There were two teachers, each managing a different class of 15 or 16 students in each of the conditions.

5.2 Learning Task

The objective of the learning task was to teach different types of surfaces that are used to design a warehouse: raw surface, raw storage surface and net storage surface. The *raw surface* is simply the surface of the whole warehouse. The *raw storage surface* is the raw surface minus annex rooms (offices, technical rooms, docks, etc.) The *net storage surface* is the raw storage surface minus the corridors where the forklifts travel on. The apprentices were required to understand what constitutes each type of surfaces and their impact on work effciency.

The task was to design a warehouse layout through several steps guided by an instruction paper, with the help from the teacher. At the beginning, groups of four apprentices, sitting around a table in the classroom, were instructed to design a warehouse with only ten shelves (which correspond to a very low usage of the warehouse surface), and compute the surfaces and the ratios. The next step required each group to try to augment the percentage of net storage surface by maximizing the number of shelves in the warehouse. Once they were done, they were asked to compute the surfaces and ratios again.

In the paper condition, they drew the warehouse on paper using pens, erasers and rulers. In the tangible condition, the group built the warehouse by placing tangible shelves under the TinkerLamp. The surface areas would also be automatically calculated and projected on the table by the system. The apprentices only needed to note down those statistics, instead of computing them. They also ran a simulation on the layouts they had built to see how the work efficiency are affected.

Fig. 3. Two experimental conditions: a,b) Paper condition. c,d) Tangible condition.

After completing the task, each group was asked to deduce some conclusions from their results. They would need to reflect on the layouts they had built, on the concepts of surfaces, e.g. see how different constraints affect surfaces areas and ratios, etc. At the end of the session, the teacher organized a debriefing session where the conclusions of each group were discussed.

The structure of the activity was a result of a participatory design process between researchers and the teachers participating in the study. While two conditions differ in a couple of ways due to the nature of the interfaces, the steps and contents to be transfered across two conditions are ensured to be very similar.

5.3 Procedure

Figure 4 shows an overview of the four phases of the study. First, apprentices did a brief individual pre-test in 10 minutes. It is a simple set of five math

| Pre-test (10 mins) | Introduction lecture (30 mins) | Group activity (60 mins) | Class debriefing (30 mins) | Post-test (20 mins) |

Fig. 4. Four phases in the study

questions, testing the apprentices of their basic knowledge of reasoning and math calculations.

After the pre-test, a typical session involved three steps: introduction lecture (30 mins), group activity (60 mins) and class debriefing (30 mins). During the lecture, the teacher gave the apprentices introduction about concepts that they were to learn.

The class was then divided into four groups to explore more about those concepts. There were paper instructions for apprentices as to how to proceed with the task. As presented in section 5.2, the groups had to collaborate to build warehouse models and discover how the concepts they had been introduced would be applied in these particular models.

The teacher toured around the room to respond to help requests. He used the last 30 minutes to recap the main points of the session. An individual post-test was administered at the end of the session to measure learning gains.

5.4 Usability Issues

Prior to this study, a series of usability tests had been conducted and major problems had been corrected. The system was also used during the last two years by the same teachers with other classes. Moreover, during the study, we noted that the apprentices encountered no problem understanding and using the system. Even though they were using it for the first time, they got quickly involved in the activity without much time asking interface-related questions.

5.5 Dependent Variables

Four dependent variables were used in this paper: (1) number of alternative solutions explored. (2) the quality of the final layout. (3) understanding score. (4) problem-solving score.

Task performance was determined by two variables (1) and (2). The number of alternative solutions is the number of warehouse layouts that the group tried out during the activity and was counted based on video and audio recordings. The quality of the final layout is computed based on the number of shelves that the apprentices succesfully placed in the warehouse. This variable implies that the warehouse will be able to store more goods with more shelves.

Learning performance was determined by two variables (3) and (4), both through the post-test. The post-test consisted of two parts, graded separately. The first part checks the understanding of the surface concepts, asking apprentices to compare different warehouses according to some aspect, e.g. to choose the one with the largest net storage surface. It consists of 12 multiple-choice questions, each of which included four possibilities with only one correct answer, and one to state "I don't know the answer". One correct answer corresponds to a point in the understanding score. There is no penalty for choosing a wrong answer.

In the second part, the apprentices had to answer an open-ended question with a realistic warehouse problem. They were told to consider a warehouse design and were asked to propose to the director how to maximize the efficiency of the warehouse. We consider it a problem-solving process since there are multiple possible solutions and the answer may be evaluated by multiple criteria. It involves, for example, taking into account the trade-off between two constraints: having as many shelves as possible and maintaining enough corridor space for forklifts to move around.

As the post-test is carried out with paper and pencil, it can be argued that there is a bias towards the paper condition. In fact, the first part of the post-test only involves multiple-choice questions and requires cognitive reasoning to solve, instead of performing a drawing activity. Paper and pencil are just a means to answer those questions, and hence will unlikely produce any effects on the results. The apprentices could have been asked to answer those same questions with a computer keyboard. The second part score was coded in a way to test only the understanding of the apprentices, and not the drawing skills. Moreover, testing on paper is also the traditional way of grading in these classes, and we were tempted to use the same measurement to judge the apprentices.

6 Results

6.1 Task Performance

Alternative Solutions. It is evident that in the course of collaboration, apprentices in the TAN condition explored more alternative layouts than those in the paper condition. Over the activity, groups who used the tangible interface completed 4.6 layouts on average (median = 4), which is higher than those who were in the paper condition (mean = 2.5, median = 2). This divergence in number of alternative layouts was significant, confirmed by a Wilcox-test, $W(14) = 8.0, p < .01$.

Quality of Final Solution. The apprentices in the TAN condition designed better final solutions compared to the PAP condition. A t-test revealed a significant higher number of shelves being placed in the final layout in the tangible condition ($t(14) = 2.36, p < .05$). They managed to use more space in the warehouse, succesfully placing 18.0 shelves on average in the final warehouse, compared to 15.1 shelves by those using paper and pens.

6.2 Learning Outcomes

Understanding Score. We found that the interface apprentices had used during the study had no signicant effect on the understanding score. A Wilcoxon test found no significant difference between individual scores in the two conditions, $W(59) = 506; p > .05$, though paper groups gained higher on average (M = 7.84 vs M = 7.43 for paper and tangible groups respectively).

We replicated the above test using another coding of the data, with which apprentices are penalized a point of -1 if they answer the question wrong and 0 if they mark "I don't know the answer". The results turned out to be no different. When using paper and tangible interface, the apprentices respectively scored on average 3.8 points and 3.1 points; not a significant difference: $W(59) = 504; p > .05$.

Problem-Solving Score. We graded the open-ended question in different aspects: whether the apprentices successfully augmented the net storage surface in the warehouse, how detailedly and correctly they justified their propositions, whether they remembered to put shelves in pair (an important concept when designing a warehouse), whether their propositions ensured enough alley space for forklifts' movements and manipulations, etc.

The final score is the average of all those partial scores. Apprentices in the PAP condition got an average score of 5.55, as opposed to 5.13 in the TAN condition, not a significant difference ($W(59) = 520, p > .05$).

7 Discussion

7.1 Task Performance

As expected, our findings showed that the task performance (number of alternative solutions explored and quality of the final solution) in the tangible condition is higher than that in the paper condition. This can be explained, first, by the direct interaction mechanism. Obviously, grasping a tangible shelf and placing it on the table to create the model is faster. Modifying the model is also facilitated by the fact that tangibles leave no traces behind. Apprentices could simply move shelves to another position, as opposed to erasing and re-drawing the layout with paper and pens. Simultanous actions also speed up the process. Design iterations were therefore done quickly which saved time for apprentices to try out other possible options.

Second, the task performance difference may concern the difference in information perception from the design space. The level of correspondence between a real warehouse and the design representation differs across the two conditions. The tangible small-scale model gives a concrete and 3D physical representation of a warehouse, in comparison with the more abstract representation offered by the 2D drawings in the paper condition. With difficulties in reasoning and abstraction skills, apprentices encountered problems in expressing their ideas into drawings [13]. Few of them were correct in terms of scaling. Hence, the tangible interface may have an advantage in this respect. An issue that can be further explored is the use of 2D PostIt-like paper pieces in the activity. It would be interesting to observe how the apprentices would exploit these objects instead of drawing as the 2D representation.

Third, we believe the different strategies adopted across the two condtions also play a role. Our observations revealed that those in paper condition tended to discuss about the solution first, then execute a perfect plan on paper. This differs with those in the tangible condition. They typically followed a bottom-up approach, incrementally added shelves on the table and tweaked their positions to choose the best layout. This strategy, made possible by the TUI, enables the apprentices to test small variations of the solution and come up with better ones.

7.2 Learning Outcomes

Contrary to our hypotheses, there is no evidence that the tangible condition had more effects than the paper condition on either the understanding or the problem-solving score. We discuss reasons for this in terms of task structure and type, physical properties of TUIs and effective interaction requirements.

The first dimension that we saw as important is how loosely or tightly structured the task was. In our study, it can be argued that the activity is not really a "group task" according to the definition of Cohen [5], in the sense that it could have been carried out by individuals separately (although roles did emerge). The type of the activity is another factor. The group activity is somewhat structured. That means that the apprentices did not need to exchange and discuss their own understanding to other group members and hence the collaboration that the tangible interface offers might not have been taken advantage. This finding is consistent with some of the literature in traditional collaborative learning [5]. Moreover, it is worth noting that the open-ended question was an ill-structured problem which takes time to be learned and the skills needed for it had not been trained during the activity.

The second dimension is the nature of TUIs. As much as it contributed to improve the task performance, this nature may have a detrimental effect on learning. First, the warehouse layouts were accomplished "too fast". It may have resulted in a less concentrated and intensive cognitive effort to make sense of the solutions and to understand deeper. Besides, previous studies have suggested that the physical properties of tangible tabletops and their support for parallel work can also lead to limited reciprocity and mutual understanding [16,7,11]. In [7], it has been found that students using a tangible interface gained fewer in test scores because group members tended to perform individual actions without discussing much with the others.

Another possible explanation for the lack of signicant effect is that students needed both social and cognitive skills for effective interaction [2]. While it is true that the tangible user interface encouraged the generation of more alternative options, the required skills (e.g. the social skills to modify and converge different viewpoints, or the cognitive skills to set up and test hypotheses when play around with various layouts, etc.) to use them are a real challenge for the logistics apprentices. Although we did not assess collaboration quality, we argue that their collaboration might not have been effective enough to bring about more understanding.

7.3 General Discussion

Our study is different from other related works in several aspects. First, we focus on a different student population, vocational apprentices to be specific, instead of younger children. Second, we wanted to look at the effects tangible interface have on learning outcomes, instead of only collaboration quality, strategy, conversations or task performance. Third, we ran our study in a classroom setting to ensure a realistic learning scenario. The study is also seen as complementary to our previous studies: qualitative analyses of how students collaborate around a tangible tabletop [13], and a controlled experiment comparing tangible and multi-touch interface in a lab setting [24]. We believe that by having a real scenario, the effects of artificial experiment factors on observed behaviours are reduced.

By focusing on these different variables and settings, we have found interesting results. Tangible tabletops, despite all of its potential, may require special designs when integrated in classrooms. While our findings about the better task performance measures in the tangible condition are in line with other studies [16,21,14], the results also suggested its learning outcomes are not necessarily better than the traditional paper-and-pens way of teaching and studying. In fact, a recent experiment also found a similar result[20].

We argue that the extent to which tangible user interfaces can improve learning is largely dependent on educational scenarios, involving different actors (the nature of the task, students's skills, teachers, group size, etc.), rather than an inherent characteristic of the technology. While TUI may have many benefits as stated at the beginning, when it becomes a part of classroom practice, many factors may well intefere in a complex way and contribute to the final effects.

8 Conclusion

We have presented our experiment in a classroom setting, comparing a tangible user interface against the traditional way of studying using paper and pens in terms of task performance and learning outcomes. As expected, apprentices who used the TUI scored better in task performance criteria. They explored more alternative solutions during the learning task and designed warehouse layouts with higher quality. However, we found no evidence of significant effects on learning outcomes. We discussed reasons for this in terms of the nature of the task, the physical properties of TUIs, and skills required for effective group learning.

It is arguable that more than a single factor affected the learning process in our study, and the inherent characteristics of tangible computing technology does not necessarily bring about more positive outcomes in classroom settings. Our findings have implications both for educational practitioners who are deploying similar technologies in classrooms and also for the designers of future tangible tabletops.

Acknowledgments. This research is part of "Dual-T: technologies for Vocational Training", a leading house funded by the Swiss Federal Office for Professional Education and Technology. We would like to thank the teachers and students from the vocational school for their enthusiasm to support our work, especially to Jacques Kurzo, Olivier Vonlanthen, André Ryser and the participants of our current study. We would like to thank Olivier Guedat for technical support during the study.

References

1. Ainsworth, S.: Deft: a conceptual framework for considering learning with multiple representations. Journal of Learning and Instruction (2006)
2. Barnes, D., Todd, F.: Communication and learning in small groups. Routledge & Kegan Paul, London (1977)
3. Bruner, J.S.: Toward a Theory of Instruction. Belknap Press, Cambridge (1966)
4. Cao, X., Lindley, S.E., Helmes, J., Sellen, A.: Telling the whole story: anticipation, inspiration and reputation in a field deployment of telltable. In: CSCW 2010: Proceedings of the 2010 ACM conference on Computer supported cooperative work, pp. 251–260. ACM, New York (2010)
5. Cohen, E.G.: Restructuring the classroom: Conditions for productive small groups. Review of Educational Research 64(1), 1–35 (1994)
6. Dietz, P., Leigh, D.: Diamondtouch: A multi-user touch technology. In: ACM Symposium on User Interface Software and Technology (UIST 2001), pp. 219–226 (2001)
7. Do-Lenh, S., Kaplan, F., Dillenbourg, P.: Paper-based concept map: the effects of tabletop on an expressive collaborative learning task. In: BCS HCI 2009: Proceedings of the 2009 British Computer Society Conference on Human-Computer Interaction, Swinton, UK, pp. 149–158. British Computer Society (2009)
8. Fernaeus, Y., Tholander, J.: Finding design qualities in a tangible programming space. In: CHI 2006: Proceedings of the SIGCHI conference on Human Factors in computing systems, pp. 447–456. ACM Press, New York (2006)
9. Ha, V., Inkpen, K.M., Mandryk, R.L., Whalen, T.: Direct intentions: the effects of input devices on collaboration around a tabletop display. In: First IEEE International Workshop on Horizontal Interactive Human-Computer Systems, TableTop 2006, p. 8 (2006)
10. Han, J.Y.: Low-cost multi-touch sensing through frustrated total internal reflection. In: Proceedings of the 18th annual ACM symposium on User interface software and technology, pp. 115–118 (2005) 1095054 115-118
11. Harris, A., Rick, J., Bonnett, V., Yuill, N., Fleck, R., Marshall, P., Rogers, Y.: Around the table: are multiple-touch surfaces better than single-touch for children's collaborative interactions? In: CSCL 2009: Proceedings of the 9th international conference on Computer supported collaborative learning, pp. 335–344. International Society of the Learning Sciences (2009)
12. Hornecker, E., Marshall, P., Dalton, N.S., Rogers, Y.: Collaboration and interference: awareness with mice or touch input. In: CSCW 2008: Proceedings of the ACM 2008 conference on Computer supported cooperative work, pp. 167–176 (2008)
13. Jermann, P., Zufferey, G., Dillenbourg, P.: Tinkering or sketching: Apprentices' use of tangibles and drawings to solve design problems. In: Dillenbourg, P., Specht, M. (eds.) EC-TEL 2008. LNCS, vol. 5192, pp. 167–178. Springer, Heidelberg (2008)
14. Khandelwal, M., Mazalek, A.: Teaching table: a tangible mentor for pre-k math education. In: TEI 2007: Proceedings of the 1st international conference on Tangible and embedded interaction, pp. 191–194. ACM, New York (2007)

15. Manches, A., O'Malley, C., Benford, S.: Physical manipulation: evaluating the potential for tangible designs. In: TEI 2009: Proceedings of the 3rd International Conference on Tangible and Embedded Interaction, pp. 77–84. ACM, New York (2009)
16. Marshall, P., Hornecker, E., Morris, R., Sheep Dalton, N., Rogers, Y.: When the fingers do the talking: A study of group participation with varying constraints to a tabletop interface. In: 3rd IEEE International Workshop on Horizontal Interactive Human Computer Systems, TABLETOP 2008, pp. 33–40 (2008)
17. Müller-Tomfelde, C., Schremmer, C.: Touchers and mousers: commonalities and differences in co-located collaboration with multiple input devices. In: CHI 2008: Proceeding of the twenty-sixth annual SIGCHI conference on Human factors in computing systems, pp. 1149–1152 (2008)
18. Nacenta, M.A., Pinelle, D., Stuckel, D., Gutwin, C.: The effects of interaction technique on coordination in tabletop groupware. In: GI 2007: Proceedings of Graphics Interface 2007, pp. 191–198 (2007)
19. Piaget, J.: The future of developmental child psychology. Journal of Youth and Adolescence 3, 87–93 (1974)
20. Piper, A.M., Hollan, J.D.: Tabletop displays for small group study: affordances of paper and digital materials. In: CHI 2009: Proceedings of the 27th international conference on Human factors in computing systems, pp. 1227–1236. ACM, New York (2009)
21. Piper, A.M., O'Brien, E., Morris, M.R., Winograd, T.: Sides: a cooperative tabletop computer game for social skills development. In: CSCW 2006: Proceedings of the 2006 20th anniversary conference on Computer supported cooperative work, pp. 1–10. ACM, New York (2006)
22. Price, S., Rogers, Y.: Let's get physical: the learning benefits of interacting in digitally augmented physical spaces. Comput. Educ. 43(1-2), 137–151 (2004)
23. Rekimoto, J.: Smartskin: an infrastructure for freehand manipulation on interactive surfaces. In: Proceedings of the SIGCHI Conference on Human Factors in Computing Systems (CHI 2002), pp. 113–120 (2002)
24. Schneider, B., Jermann, P., Zufferey, G., Dillenbourg, P.: Benefits of a tangible interface for collaborative learning and interaction. In: IEEE Transactions on Learning Technologies, under revision
25. Slavin.: Cooperative learning: theory, research and practice, 2nd edn. Allyn & Bacon (1995)
26. Stanton, D., Bayon, V., Neale, H., Ghali, A., Benford, S., Cobb, S., Ingram, R., O'Malley, C., Wilson, J., Pridmore, T.: Classroom collaboration in the design of tangible interfaces for storytelling. In: CHI 2001: Proceedings of the SIGCHI conference on Human factors in computing systems, pp. 482–489. ACM, New York (2001)
27. Stanton, D., Neale, H., Bayon, V.: Interfaces to support children's co-present collaboration: multiple mice and tangible technologies. In: CSCL 2002: Proceedings of the Conference on Computer Support for Collaborative Learning, pp. 342–351. International Society of the Learning Sciences (2002)
28. Ullmer, B., Ishii, H.: The metadesk: models and prototypes for tangible user interfaces. In: ACM Symposium on User interface Software and Technology (UIST 1997), pp. 223–232 (1997)
29. Underkoffler, J., Ishii, H.: Illuminating light: a casual optics workbench. In: CHI 1999: CHI 1999 extended abstracts on Human factors in computing systems, pp. 5–6. ACM, New York (1999)

30. Wellner, P.: Interacting with paper on the digital desk. Communications of the ACM 36(7), 87–96 (1993)
31. Zuckerman, O., Arida, S., Resnick, M.: Extending tangible interfaces for education: digital montessori-inspired manipulatives. In: CHI 2005: Proceedings of the SIGCHI conference on Human factors in computing systems, pp. 859–868. ACM Press, New York (2005)
32. Zuckerman, O., Resnick, M.: System blocks: A physical interface for system dynamics simulation. In: Proceedings of CHI 2003 (2003)
33. Zufferey, G., Jermann, P., Do-Lenh, S., Dillenbourg, P.: Using augmentations as bridges from concrete to abstract representations. In: BCS HCI 2009: Proceedings of the 2009 British Computer Society Conference on Human-Computer Interaction, Swinton, UK, pp. 130–139. British Computer Society (2009)

Content, Social, and Metacognitive Statements: An Empirical Study Comparing Human-Human and Human-Computer Tutorial Dialogue

Myroslava O. Dzikovska[1], Natalie B. Steinhauser[2], Johanna D. Moore[1],
Gwendolyn E. Campbell[2], Katherine M. Harrison[3], and Leanne S. Taylor[4,*]

[1] School of Informatics, University of Edinburgh, Edinburgh, United Kingdom
{m.dzikovska,j.moore}@ed.ac.uk
[2] Naval Air Warfare Center Training Systems Division, Orlando, FL, USA
{natalie.steinhauser,gwendolyn.campbell}@navy.mil
[3] Kaegan Corporation, 12000 Research Parkway, Orlando, FL 32826-2944
Katherine.M.Harrison.ctr@navy.mil
[4] University of Central Florida, 4000 Central Florida Blvd. Orlando, FL 32816
Leanne.Taylor.ctr@navy.mil

Abstract. We present a study which compares human-human computer-mediated tutoring with two computer tutoring systems based on the same materials but differing in the type of feedback they provide. Our results show that there are significant differences in interaction style between human-human and human-computer tutoring, as well as between the two computer tutors, and that different dialogue characteristics predict learning gain in different conditions. We show that there are significant differences in the non-content statements that students make to human and computer tutors, but also to different types of computer tutors. These differences also affect which factors are correlated with learning gain and user satisfaction. We argue that ITS designers should pay particular attention to strategies for dealing with negative social and metacognitive statements, and also conduct further research on how interaction style affects human-computer tutoring.

1 Introduction

Intelligent Tutoring Systems (ITS) are often used as part of technology-enhanced curricula, either on their own to help students practice skills [1] or in a wider context by providing support for exercises in an e-learning environment [2]. One approach to creating ITSs is to model them after a human tutor because human tutoring combined with classroom teaching has been said to be the most effective

---

* This work has been supported in part by US Office of Naval Research grants N000141010085 and N0001410WX20278. We would like to thank our sponsors from the Office of Naval Research, Dr. Susan Chipman and Dr. Ray Perez and five former Research Associates who worked on this project, Charles Callaway, Elaine Farrow, Leslie Butler, Lisa Durrance, and Cheryl Johnson.

form of instruction [3]. However, there remains a significant gap between the capabilities of a human tutor and the capabilities of even the best existing ITS, so the direct comparison between human-human and human-computer tutoring interactions may be difficult.

One of the key capabilities of human tutors is the ability to engage in natural language dialogue with students, providing scaffolding, explanations and motivational prompts. There are now a number of ITSs that engage in some form of natural language interaction with a student. These systems vary widely with respect to the type of natural language input they support and the kinds of feedback they provide. Student input may be restricted to short answers to questions (single words or phrases) [4,5][1], support a small set of longer sentences [6,7,8,9,10], or attempt to interpret extended answers to "Why" questions [8,11,12]. The feedback may be completely hand-authored [4,5,6,8], or generated automatically based on the system's internal representation [7,9,10,12].

This large space of possibilities can create very different interaction styles. For example, pre-authored feedback can provide the greatest flexibility in the form of the instructional strategies employed, but is mostly possible in systems that rely on short-answer questions or limited domain size. This greatly constrains the language that the system can understand, and means that interaction with such systems is not really similar to interaction with human tutors, even if the feedback is authored by humans. Pre-authored feedback is also difficult to adapt to the student model or past interaction history, sometimes leading to redundancy and student confusion [13]. In contrast, automatically generated feedback is more flexible and together with unrestricted language input, it may make the interaction more similar to human-human interaction. But such systems are currently more prone to errors, both in interpreting and in generating feedback, and may have to use a more constrained set of strategies due to limitations of existing reasoning and natural language generation techniques.

Given the large space of possibilities and tradeoffs between them, it is not clear which of the techniques used by human tutors will be effective in human-computer interaction. Moreover, implementing such techniques in computer systems relies on the assumption that students will react to the computer tutors in the same way they do to human tutors, and therefore that the same tutoring strategies will promote learning. To understand this problem better, we have performed a controlled experiment that compares three conditions: an ITS that asks students to explain their reasoning in their own words, and provides feedback targeted to the errors (if any), a version of the same system that gives away correct answers without specific feedback, and a human tutor using the same instructional materials in a computer-mediated learning environment.

We focus on two aspects of the interaction: the role of student-produced content, since it has been shown to predict learning gain with both human and computer tutors [14,15], and social and metacognitive utterances produced by students, since these are related to affective states, and have also been shown to

---

[1] The Why2-Atlas tutor is capable of interpreting long student essays, but restricts student input to short-answer questions in dialogue interactions.

predict learning gain [16]. Our results indicate that there are significant differences in human-human and human-computer interaction, and that in computer tutoring, different factors predict learning gain depending on the type of feedback given. This may have implications for devising appropriate feedback in computer-based learning environments.

This paper is organized as follows. In Section 2 we review the literature on differences between human-human and human-computer interaction, and factors which predict learning gain in tutorial dialogue. In Section 3 we discuss our human-human tutoring study, followed by the human-computer study in Section 4. The coding scheme used to analyze the data is described in Section 5. Section 6 discusses results and how the interaction and learning outcome differ in human-human and human-computer tutoring. We discuss the potential implications for technology-enhanced learning systems and future work in Section 7.

2 Background

Current research on how people respond to computers and computer entities, in comparison to humans, has produced mixed results. The work of Reeves & Nass [17] shows that people treat computers as social actors, i.e. they unconsciously follow rules of social relationships when interacting with media, and display emotions common in human-human relationships such as politeness or anger. Further studies demonstrated that people often respond to virtual humans similarly to how they respond to real people [18,19].

In contrast, more recent research using ITSs shows that students change the language they use in dialogue depending on whether they are interacting with humans or computers. When talking to a computer, students who were led to believe they were conversing with a human used more words and conversed longer than did students who knew they were talking to a machine [20]. Students also provided more explanations and longer turns when they thought they were conversing with a human versus a computer, even though they were conversing with a computer in both situations [21].

The use of natural language interaction has long been hypothesized as one of the factors that can contribute to improved learning outcomes with computer systems. There is a body of research suggesting that the kind of language the students are producing, both with human and with computer tutors, is important as well: a higher percentage of contentful talk is correlated with higher learning gain [14,15], and getting students to self-explain improves learning [22]. Yet studies comparing human tutors, computer tutors and carefully designed reading materials failed to demonstrate significant differences in learning gains [23], except when students were being taught by human tutors on content in their Zone of Proximal Development [24].

An open question when comparing human-human and human-computer tutoring results, however, is how much they are impacted by differences in human-human and human-computer interaction. For example, the systems in [23] all relied on short-answer questions, with rigidly defined dialogue structures, resulting in a very different interaction style than that observed in the human tutoring.

The goal of the experiment discussed in this paper is to provide a more controlled comparison between human-human and human-computer tutoring. For this purpose, we developed a computer-mediated learning environment where human tutors helped students work through a set of exercises. This framework fixed the choice of exercises, but let the tutors use their own strategies in providing feedback to students. Based on the data we collected from the human-human interaction, we developed a tutorial dialogue system that replaces the human tutor's feedback with automatically generated computer feedback, using natural language processing techniques to analyze student explanations. While the system does not achieve human competency in terms of interpreting natural language, the ability to accept less restricted input provides a closer comparison to the kinds of dialogue we have seen in human-human interaction, and therefore gives us a better opportunity to investigate whether the same factors are related to learning gain in the two situations.

Our initial studies comparing human-human and human-computer data demonstrated that two types of variables are important for learning. First, we found evidence that students who produce a higher percentage of content words learn more [15] (see also [14] for a similar result in another tutoring system). Second, we showed that different forms of non-content talk (social and metacognitive statements) are correlated with learning in human-human dialogue and in human-computer dialogue [16,25]. However, different factors are (positively or negatively) correlated with learning gain in human-computer versus human-human dialogue.

In this paper we extend our data analysis to explicitly compare three conditions: human-human tutoring, a computer tutor with adaptive feedback, and a computer tutor which gives away the answers without providing specific feedback. We examine the correlations between both content and non-content student statements and learning gain, and discuss implications for tutoring system design.

3 Human-Human Tutoring Study

3.1 Data Collection Environment

We constructed a curriculum incorporating lessons in basic electricity and electronics for use in computer-mediated instruction, including reading materials, interactive exercises with a circuit simulator, and general discussion questions. The curriculum covered topics including open and closed paths, voltage reading between components and positive and negative terminals, series and parallel configurations, and finding faults in a circuit with a multimeter. The students were asked to read slides, interact with a circuit simulator, and explain their answers, with questions like "explain why bulb A was on when switch C was open." The exercises also asked some high-level questions such as "What are the conditions for a bulb to light?".

Figure 1 shows a screenshot of the learning environment that the participants interacted with during the study. The screen is divided into three sections.

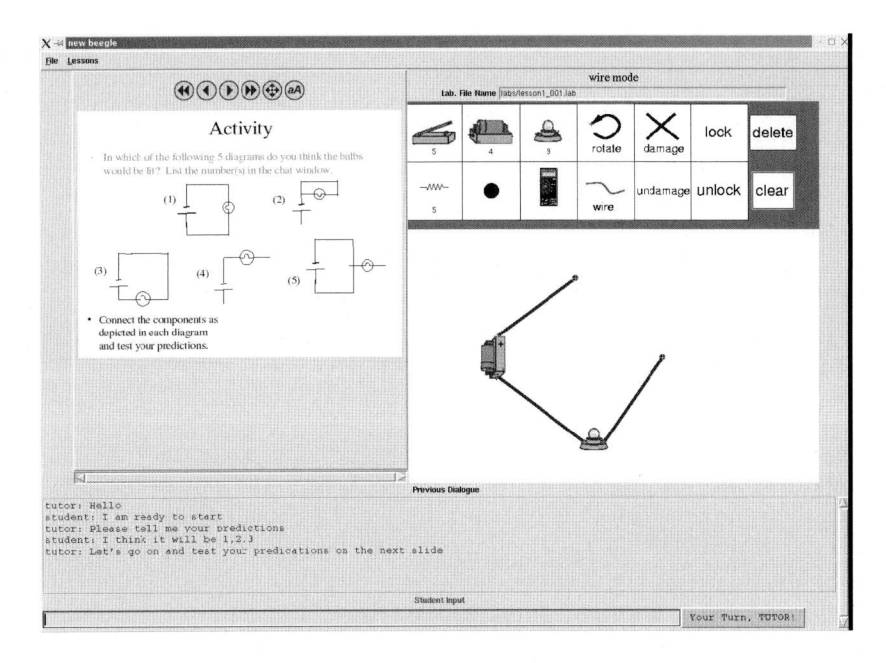

Fig. 1. Participant screen for human-human tutoring

The top left-hand section displays slides which deliver core lesson material including educational text, activities, and discussion questions. The participants were able to continue through the lesson slides at their own pace. The top right-hand section contains a circuit simulator which allows participants to construct and manipulate circuits as a supplement to the material in the slides. The bottom section is the chat window where the participants and tutor converse by typing.

The tutor and student were not co-located, however the tutor did have the ability to observe the student's learning environment and interact with the student through a chat window. The tutor gave feedback, technical assistance and encouragement as appropriate. Participants directed their answers, comments, and/or questions to the tutor throughout the curriculum. Each session with a system lasted approximately 4 hours.

3.2 Procedure

After completing informed consent paperwork, participants filled out a demographic questionnaire and took a pre-test consisting of 38 multiple choice questions. The participants were then introduced to their tutor and given a brief demonstration of how to operate the learning environment. The students spent the majority of the experimental session working through the lesson material and building circuits. At the conclusion of the experiment, participants completed a post-test which included 21 multiple choice questions and a satisfaction questionnaire. They were then debriefed and excused.

3.3 Corpus

Thirty undergraduate students from a large South-East US university participated in the study. The participants had little prior knowledge of the domain, and were paid for their time. They were randomly distributed across three experienced tutors. The average age of the participants was 22.4 years ($SD = 5.0$) and exactly half of them were female. The records of the sessions comprise the corpus for this study, which contains 8,100 dialogue turns taken by the student and tutor, and 56,000 words (including punctuation).

4 Human-Computer Tutoring Study

4.1 Data Collection Environment

To the extent possible, the same curriculum was used in the human-human study and in the computer tutoring system (BEETLE II). Small changes were made to the curriculum so that the computer would be able to understand student responses more easily. For example, multi-part questions were sometimes broken into series of single questions (e.g., the question "Explain your reasoning for those 5 diagrams" would be replaced with questions "Explain your reasoning for the circuit in diagram 1", "Explain your reasoning for the circuit in diagram 2" and so on). The user interface had the same functionality as the human-human tutoring environment.

Within the computer tutor, we implemented two different feedback policies corresponding to two different interaction styles. In the fully interactive condition (FULL), the computer tutor (ITS) used a subset of the most frequent strategies we observed in the human-human corpus. When the student answered a question correctly, the ITS confirmed the correct answer, occasionally restating it with improved terminology [12]. When the student was incorrect, the ITS provided hints at two levels of specificity, or suggested slides to re-read. The system responded to negative metacognitive statements by giving hints, or giving away the complete answer if the student appeared to be having significant difficulties. It ignored positive metacognitive and social statements. Finally, the system said "I am sorry, I didn't understand" in response to nonsense, and remediated by providing hints depending on the tutoring context [26].

An example of the interaction with the system in the FULL condition is shown in Figure 2(a). In their first turn, the student gives an answer which is partially correct, but incomplete: the student did not mention that a battery must be contained in the same closed path. The answer is analyzed with a natural language parser and semantic interpreter, and the diagnoser determines that the student correctly mentioned a bulb in a closed path, but is missing the relationship with the battery. The tutor then decides that, given that this is the first student error for this question, the appropriate tutoring strategy is to re-state the correct part of the answer, and give a content-less prompt for the missing information.[2]

---

[2] If a student was performing poorly, more specific hints would be used, for example "Here's a hint: your answer should mention a battery."

(a)
Tutor: What are the conditions for a bulb to light?
Student: It has to be in a closed path
Tutor: Right. The bulb must be in a closed path. Keep going.
Student: The battery must also be in a closed path.
Tutor: Right. A bulb must be contained in a closed path with the battery. When you are ready, go on to the next slide.

(b)
Tutor: What are the conditions for a bulb to light?
Student: It has to be in a closed path
Tutor: OK. One good way to phrase the answer is: A bulb must be contained in a closed path with the battery. When you are ready, go on to the next slide.

Fig. 2. Example interaction with the system a) in FULL condition; b) in BASE condition

The second student response completes the answer, but, since the answer was collected over multiple turns, the tutor restates it again as a complete sentence.

In contrast, in the baseline minimally-interactive condition (BASE), the ITS asks exactly the same questions, but does not provide specific feedback. Instead, it provides a neutral acknowledgment of the student's contribution, and gives away the correct answer. An example interaction is shown in Figure 2(b). As can be seen in this answer, the system provides the student with the correct answer, but makes no attempt to either acknowledge the correct part or point out specific problems. This condition is effectively equivalent to a non-interactive e-learning environment where students were asked to "write in" their answers and compare them with the system's answers. Students were not told that their answers weren't checked, in order to encourage them to provide meaningful answers.

Using the two conditions allows us to compare which factors correlated with learning gain and user satisfaction depending on the interaction style within a computer-based learning environment.[3]

4.2 Procedure

The procedure for the human-computer study was essentially the same as the human-human study with a few exceptions. The pre-test consisted of 22 multiple choice questions and the post-test consisted of 21 multiple choice questions. The same set of questions was used in the human-human and human-computer studies.[4] The participants were also given a usability and satisfaction questionnaire developed to measure their satisfaction with different aspects of the system.

---

[3] Our earlier study [25] examined data from FULL only, and served as a motivation for this extended analysis comparing all 3 conditions with additional variables of interest.

[4] The human-computer pre-test had fewer questions because in the human-human study, after taking the post-test the participants returned for a follow-up session with additional material. The pre-test covered the whole range of topics tutored by human tutors. In the human-computer study, only the first tutoring session was replicated by the ITS, and the pre-test questions were restricted to the material covered by the computer system and the first post-test.

4.3 Corpus

Seventy six undergraduate students without prior knowledge of the domain from the same university as the human-human study were paid for participating in the human-computer study. The average age of the participants was 21.05 years ($SD = 3.30$) and there were almost twice as many females as males. There were 37 participants in the FULL and 39 participants in the BASE condition. The interaction logs were converted into the same XML format as the human-human corpus. The corpus includes an estimated 57,600 total dialogue turns taken by the student and tutor, and an estimated 680,000 words.

5 Data Analysis

The human-human and human-computer tutoring studies were conducted at different times, however, as we discussed in Section 4, they were using comparable learning environments. Therefore, for purposes of this study we conducted a three-way comparison between three different conditions found in our data: human-human interaction, human-computer dialogue with detailed feedback in FULL, and minimally interactive human-computer dialogue in BASE. All data was annotated using the same coding scheme, to compare contentful and non-contentful student statements.

5.1 Coding

The coding scheme we used is presented in Table 1 (reproduced from [25]). All student utterances were classified as primarily content, metacognitive, social or nonsense. Note that nonsense is a special category for dialogue with computers, defined as statements that are made up of random letters or numbers that are not content related (e.g., "ufghp"). It never occurred in dialogue with humans. For purposes of data analysis, we treated nonsense as instance of negative social, because it often appeared to be an expression of student frustration with the system, similar in function to expletives. For the human-human data, two independent raters coded the student-tutor transcripts and were able to identify and distinguish between content, management, metacognitive, and social dialogue statements with a very high reliability (Cohen's kappa, $\kappa = 1.00$). In addition, raters were able to differentiate between positive and negative metacognitive statements made by the student with high inter-rater reliability ($\kappa = 0.99$).

For the human-computer data, four independent raters coded the student-tutor transcripts and were able to identify and distinguish between content, management, metacognitive, social dialogue, and nonsensical statements with high reliability ($\kappa = 0.88$), and to reliably differentiate between positive and negative metacognitive statements made by the student ($\kappa = 0.96$).

5.2 Variables of Interest

We analyzed and compared several properties of dialogue based on this coding. To investigate social and metacognitive aspects of the dialogue, we computed

Table 1. Coding Summary

Code	Definition	Example
Content	Statements including domain concepts that pertain to the lesson	"There is a battery and bulb in circuit 1." "1.5 volts."
Management	Dialogue that does not contain information relevant to the lesson material, but deals with the flow of the lesson	"I give up." "O.k." - Acknowledging the tutor's instructions to continue
Metacognition	Statements containing the student's feelings about his or her understanding, but does not include domain concepts	Metacognitive statements can be positive or negative.
Positive	Statements that express understanding	"I get it." "Oh, o.k."
Negative	Statements that express confusion	"I don't understand."
Social Dialogue	Dialogue that is not related to the content of the lessons or state of student's understanding, and expresses some form of social or emotional connection	Social statements can be positive or negative.
Positive	Statements that include humor, rapport, chit-chat, or saving face	"Ha-ha" "Hi, how are you doing?"
Negative	Statements that include frustration, refusal to cooperate with the system, or offending the system	"Because I said so." "No." "You're stupid." Expletives
Nonsense	Random sequences of letters or numbers	"oidhf" "dsfafadgdfh"

correlations between the learning gain and the number of metacognitive and social (including nonsense) statements submitted by the student during the course of each tutoring session. Management was left out of the analyses because it was not very prevalent in the computer tutoring data and in the few cases it did occur, it was ignored by the tutor. Also, it was not a relevant predictor of learning gain with the human tutor.

As mentioned in Section 2, we are also interested in the percentage of contentful talk, since it is known to be correlated with learning gain. There are multiple ways to define contentful talk [15]. For purposes of this study, we defined "content" as the number of student words present in a glossary compiled for the domain by instructional designers, normalized by the total number of words in the dialogue. We used the same glossary as [15].

6 Results

An initial study comparing 41 students in FULL to human tutors was presented in [25]. It demonstrated that there were significant differences in the distribution of metacognitive and social statements between FULL and human-human tutoring, as well as differences in which variables were correlated in learning gain. This study is extending results to compare different interaction styles, and the impact of contentful talk. However, in a small number of cases (4 participants) the data logs were incomplete due to technical failures, and did not contain the information necessary to compute measures of contentful talk. For consistency, we removed those participants from the set and replicated all our analyses, comparing measures of contentful talk, metacognitive, and social statements for the same set of participants.

6.1 Learning Gain

Pre and post-test scores were calculated in terms of percentage correct. A learning gain score normalized for pre-test performance was then calculated for each participant using the formula $gain = (posttest - pretest)/(1 - pretest)$.

6.2 Content-Learning Correlations

The summary of language statistics in the different conditions is shown in Table 2. As can be seen from the table, the numbers of words and turns in each session differed between conditions. This difference is due, in part, to splitting multi-part questions into individual questions (as discussed in Section 4). However, comparing average turn length and the percentage of contentful talk allows us to observe the differences in the student's dialogue behavior which are less affected by the differences in overall number of questions.

In human-human dialogue, students on average produced 5.68 words per turn ($SD = 2.22$). Overall, the percentage of content words produced by students (out of all words in the corpus) was significantly correlated with learning gain ($r = 0.40, p = 0.02$).

In human-computer dialogue, there were significant differences in terms of dialogue length and content between BASE and FULL (Student's t-test, $t(38) = 15.99, p < 0.0001$) However, students produced on average turns of similar length in the two conditions (Student's t-test, $t(71) = 1.61, p = 0.11$) and similar percentage of contentful words ($t(73) = 1.3, p = 0.20$). The proportion of contentful words out of all words in the dialogue was significantly higher than in human-human dialogue ($t(38) = 9.05, p < 0.0001$). This reflects a general difference

Table 2. Student language statistics for human-human and human-computer dialogue (Standard deviations in parentheses)

Condition	Turns per session	Words per session	Words per turn	Content words per session	% content
Human-Human	144(51.8)	816(357.3)	5.68(2.22)	381(173.8)	42.1(5.6)
BASE	156(6.3)	726(224.2)	6.13(0.68)	455 (108.3)	51.3 (1.2)
FULL	232(33.8)	1411(219.4)	5.66(0.57)	741 (102.5)	52.5 (1.1)

Table 3. Mean number of metacognitive and social statements per session in different conditions (standard deviation in parentheses)

Condition	Metacognitive		Social	
	Positive	Negative	Positive	Negative
Human	12.5 (8.16)	1.77 (1.94)	5.83 (6.99)	0
BASE	0	1.44 (2.93)	0.10 (0.68)	0.23 (0.84)
FULL	0.21 (0.48)	5.65 (4.24)	0.14 (0.54)	4.21 (8.03)

between the human-human and human-computer interaction styles. The interaction style of the computer tutor discouraged social comments by not reacting to them.

Even though students produced the same percentage of contentful talk in the two human-computer conditions, the proportion of contentful talk was only correlated with learning gain in FULL ($r = 0.42, p = 0.009$). In BASE, the proportion of contentful talk was not correlated with learning gain ($r = 0.19, p = 0.25$). We discuss possible reasons for this in Section 7.

6.3 Metacognitive Statements

The number of occurrences of metacognitive and social statements is summarized in Table 3. Students made metacognitive statements in all conditions, regardless of whether the tutor was a human or a computer; however the relative frequencies of positive and negative metacognitive statements depended on the type of tutor.

Students in FULL made significantly more metacognitive statements than students in BASE ($t(53) = 2.84, p < 0.01$). For either condition, this was significantly smaller than the number of metacognitive statements in human-human dialogue (FULL: $t(31) = -5.98, p < 0.001$; BASE: $t(29) = -6.58, p < 0.001$).

Students talking to a human tutor made significantly more positive metacognitive statements than negative metacognitive statements (paired t-test, $t(29) = 8.37, p < 0.001$). In contrast, students talking to both computer tutors, made significantly more negative metacognitive statements than positive metacognitive statements (FULL: $t(36) = -4.42, p < 0.001$; BASE: $t(38) = -3.05, p < 0.01$).

The condition also affected how the metacognitive statements were related to learning gain. For students interacting with a human tutor, the amount of positive metacognitive dialogue was significantly negatively correlated with learning gain ($r = -0.543, p = .002$), while the number of negative metacognitive statements was not correlated with learning gain ($r = -0.210, p = 0.266$). For students interacting with BASE, there were no positive metacognitive statements, and negative metacognitive statements were not correlated with learning gain ($r = -0.19, p = 0.25$). Finally, for students interacting with FULL, the number of both types of metacognitive statements were significantly negatively correlated with learning gain (positive statements: $r = -0.419, p = 0.006$; negative statements: $r = -0.537, p < .001$).

6.4 Social Statements and Nonsense

While students made social statements with both types of tutors, students interacting with a human tutor made exclusively positive social statements and students interacting with the computer tutor made exclusively negative social statements, either negative comments or submitting nonsense.

Again, students in FULL made significantly more social statements than students in BASE ($t(37) = 2.56$, $p = 0.01$). The overall number of social statements made with the computer tutor was significantly lower than in human-human dialogue (FULL: $t(30) = -2.80$, $p = 0.009$; BASE: $t(29) = -3.23$, $p = 0.003$).

In the human-human condition, the amount of social dialogue was not significantly correlated with learning gain. However, in FULL the average learning gain score of the students who generated any negative social dialogue, 52% ($SD = 26$), was statistically significantly lower than the average learning gain score, 67% ($SD = 12$), of students who did not ($t(38) = -2.43$, $p = 0.02$). Not surprisingly, the amount of negative social dialogue generated by the students in this condition was also significantly negatively correlated with the students' report of satisfaction with the computer tutor, $r = -0.55, p < 0.001$. There were too few instances of negative social in BASE to produce any meaningful statistical results.

6.5 The Impact of Interpretation Failures

While the FULL system attempts to model interaction with the human by accepting extended answers to "Why" questions and giving extended feedback, there are still significant differences in the system's capabilities compared to human-human interaction, due to the limitations of the natural language technology. Overall, the system failed to interpret 13.4% of student utterances ($SD = 5.00$). The frequency of interpretation problems was significantly negatively correlated with learning gain ($r = -0.47, p < 0.005$) and with user satisfaction ($r = -0.36$, $p < 0.05$). The interpretation problems encountered by students therefore present a major challenge for system implementation, and for comparison with human-human interaction. We discuss the implications in the next section.

7 Discussion and Future Work

As previously mentioned, it is common for ITSs to be modeled after human tutors, but it is uncertain if this is an effective technique because we are unsure if these interactions are similar and can be interpreted in the same way. The goal of developing the BEETLE II system was to provide a tutor that can accept a wider range of user language than existing tutors, and therefore deliver interaction style more similar to human tutoring.

While we have not completely achieved this goal (as evidenced by the impact of interpretation problems), the data we collected provide a new and significant comparison between human-human and human-computer interaction. Previously available studies compared human-human dialogue with a system that was only capable of asking short-answer questions during dialogue [27,23]. In these studies, the student's response when interacting with a human was on average 3 times longer than when interacting with a computer. Our system successfully interpreted a range of longer sentences, and the average turn length was more similar in human-human and human-computer tutoring.

Even as average turn length increased, factors correlated with learning gain also depended on the interaction style. In both human-human and FULL condition, the percentage of contentful talk was correlated with learning gain. This relationship did not hold for the BASE condition where students were not receiving targeted feedback. One possible explanation is that students often struggle with using appropriate terminology in this domain. At least one participant commented during the post-lesson interview that they found it difficult to figure out whether the difference between their answer and the answer given by the system was important or trivial. This indicates that it may not be enough to prompt students to explain their answers in an e-learning environment. The system actually needs to give them feedback that targets specific problems in their answer in order to "convert" the increases in contentful talk into learning gains.

The differences in interaction style had an impact on social and metacognitive dialogue as well. With a human tutor, the non-content statements were mostly positive acknowledgments and social statements used to build rapport; with computer tutors, students mostly used negative statements expressing confusion or showing frustration with the system's inability to interpret the user's input correctly or generate appropriate feedback.

We previously concluded that the differences in behavior between human-human and human-computer tutoring indicate that the negative social and metacognitive statements are more reliable indicators of student frustration in human-computer dialogue than in human-human dialogue, and therefore need to be addressed especially [25]. Adding BASE to this analysis introduces a new dimension, namely, interaction style. It is clear that students reacted with more social and metacognitive statements when the tutor (either human or computer) was listening and responding adaptively, while the neutral responses of BASE did not elicit either social or metacognitive statements.

An open question with respect to this analysis is to which extent the negative social and metacognitive statements are influenced by the limitations in the system's interpretation capabilities. Students used fewer negative social statements in BASE, where the system never indicated that they were not understood. To some extent frustration can be mitigated by improving language understanding components, thus reducing the number of misunderstandings. However, this may not be sufficient by itself. The negative correlation between learning gain and interpretation errors was observed in both BASE and FULL, despite students being more satisfied with BASE. These differences are further investigated in [28], where we conclude that special strategies are necessary for dealing with incorrect or vague use of student terminology.

Moreover, the role of motivational factors needs to be further examined. Previous research found that students' attitudes towards learning and expectations of computer systems affected their frustration and learning gain. Students who, before any interaction with the system, didn't believe that a computer system can help them learn were more frustrated with a computer tutor, even though they learned as much as the students who believed that a computer tutor would be helpful [29]. In a case-based learning environment, novice students didn't see the need to write down their explanations, therefore skipping this step when given an option. However, students who were forced to produce explanations learned more, even though they were less happy with the system [30]. Thus, reducing student frustration may not always have a positive effect on learning, and designers should focus on determining which negative metacognitive and social expressions indicate that learning is negatively affected and require action from the system. There is now some work in detecting and responding to student uncertainty in human-computer dialogue [31]. Future work should also investigate how students' prior attitudes to learning with computers affect their frustration with interpretation problems, and how to devise better error-recovery strategies to deal with the unavoidable limitations of natural language technology.

8 Conclusion

In this study we compared human-human tutorial dialogue with two different computer tutoring styles, focusing on features correlated with learning gain. We found significant differences between human-human and human-computer tutoring, but also in how students interact with different computer tutors teaching the same material. This could be partially explained by the limitations in computer system capabilities and frustration arising from problems in system interpretation. However, student attitudes to computers and learning may play an important role as well. Moreover, different factors are associated with learning gain depending on the system interaction style. Our results indicate that giving adaptive feedback changes which factors are correlated with learning gain compared to a system that simply gives away the answers. Further research should particularly focus on dealing with negative social and metacognitive statements, and address student beliefs which may be causing frustration, in addition to improving the system's ability to correctly interpret student's answers.

References

1. Aleven, V., Popescu, O., Koedinger, K.R.: Towards tutorial dialog to support self-explanation: Adding natural language understanding to a cognitive tutor. In: Proceedings of the 10th International Conference on Artificial Intelligence in Education, AIED 2001 (2001)
2. Goguadze, G., González Palomo, A., Melis, E.: Interactivity of exercises in activemath. Towards Sustainable and Scalable Educational Innovations Informed by the Learning Sciences Sharing. Good Practices of Research Experimentation and Innovation 133, 109–115 (2005)

3. Bloom, B.S.: The two sigma problem: The search for methods of group instruction as effective as one-to-one tutoring. Educational Researcher 13, 3–16 (1984)
4. Rosé, C., Jordan, P., Ringenberg, M., Siler, S., VanLehn, K., Weinstein, A.: Interactive conceptual tutoring in atlas-andes. In: Proceedings of AI in Education 2001 Conference (2001)
5. VanLehn, K., Jordan, P., Litman., D.: Developing pedagogically effective tutorial dialogue tactics: Experiments and a testbed. In: Proceedings of SLaTE Workshop on Speech and Language Technology in Education, Farmington, PA (October 2007)
6. Aleven, V., Popescu, O., Koedinger, K.: Pilot-testing a tutorial dialogue system that supports self-explanation. In: Cerri, S.A., Gouardéres, G., Paraguaçu, F. (eds.) ITS 2002. LNCS, vol. 2363, pp. 344–354. Springer, Heidelberg (2002)
7. Pon-Barry, H., Clark, B., Schultz, K., Bratt, E.O., Peters, S.: Advantages of spoken language interaction in dialogue-based intelligent tutoring systems. In: Lester, J.C., Vicari, R.M., Paraguaçu, F. (eds.) ITS 2004. LNCS, vol. 3220, pp. 390–400. Springer, Heidelberg (2004)
8. Graesser, A.C., Wiemer-Hastings, P., Wiemer-Hastings, P., Kreuz, R.: Autotutor: A simulation of a human tutor. Cognitive Systems Research 1, 35–51 (1999)
9. Callaway, C., Dzikovska, M., Matheson, C., Moore, J., Zinn, C.: Using dialogue to learn math in the LeActiveMath project. In: Proceedings of the ECAI Workshop on Language-Enhanced Educational Technology, pp. 1–8 (August 2006)
10. Khuwaja, R.A., Evens, M.W., Michael, J.A., Rovick, A.A.: Architecture of CIRCSIM-tutor (v.3): A smart cardiovascular physiology tutor. In: Proceedings of the 7th Annual IEEE Computer-Based Medical Systems Symposium (1994)
11. Nielsen, R.D., Ward, W., Martin, J.H.: Learning to assess low-level conceptual understanding. In: Proceedings 21st International FLAIRS Conference, Coconut Grove, Florida (May 2008)
12. Dzikovska, M.O., Campbell, G.E., Callaway, C.B., Steinhauser, N.B., Farrow, E., Moore, J.D., Butler, L.A., Matheson, C.: Diagnosing natural language answers to support adaptive tutoring. In: Proceedings 21st International FLAIRS Conference, Coconut Grove, Florida (May 2008)
13. Jordan, P.W.: Using student explanations as models for adapting tutorial dialogue. In: Barr, V., Markov, Z. (eds.) FLAIRS Conference. AAAI Press, Menlo Park (2004)
14. Purandare, A., Litman, D.: Content-learning correlations in spoken tutoring dialogs at word, turn and discourse levels. In: Proceedings 21st International FLAIRS Conference, Coconut Grove, Florida (May 2008)
15. Litman, D., Moore, J., Dzikovska, M., Farrow, E.: Using natural language processing to analyze tutorial dialogue corpora across domains and modalities. In: Proceedings of 14th International Conference on Artificial Intelligence in Education (AIED), Brighton, UK (July 2009)
16. Campbell, G.C., Steinhauser, N.B., Dzikovska, M.O., Moore, J.D., Callaway, C.B., Farrow, E.: Metacognitive awareness versus linguistic politeness: Expressions of confusions in tutorial dialogues. Poster presented at the 31st Annual Conference of the Cognitive Science Society, Amsterdam, Netherlands (July 2009)
17. Reeves, B., Nass, C.: The media equation: how people treat computers, television, and new media like real people and places. Cambridge University Press, New York (1996)
18. Zanbaka, C., Ulinski, A., Goolkasian, P., Hodges, L.F.: Effects of virtual human presence on task performance. In: Proceedings of International Conference on Artificial Reality and Telexistence (ICAT), pp. 174–181 (2004)

19. Pertaub, D.P., Slater, M., Barker, C.: An experiment on public speaking anxiety in response to three different types of virtual audience. Presence: Teleoper. Virtual Environ. 11(1), 68–78 (2002)
20. Shechtman, N., Horowitz, L.M.: Media inequality in conversation: how people behave differently when interacting with computers and people. In: CHI 2003: Proceedings of the SIGCHI conference on Human factors in computing systems, pp. 281–288. ACM, New York (2003)
21. Rosé, C., Torrey, C.: Interactivity versus expectation: Eliciting learning oriented behavior with tutorial dialogue systems. In: Proceedings of Interact 2005 (2005)
22. Chi, M.T.H., de Leeuw, N., Chiu, M.H., LaVancher, C.: Eliciting self-explanations improves understanding. Cognitive Science 18(3), 439–477 (1994)
23. VanLehn, K., Graesser, A.C., Jackson, G.T., Jordan, P., Olney, A., Rosé, C.P.: When are tutorial dialogues more effective than reading? Cognitive Science 31(1), 3–62 (2007)
24. Bransford, J.D., Brown, A.L., Cocking, R.R. (eds.): How People Learn: Brain, Mind, Experience, and School Committee on Developments in the Science of Learning. Commission on Behavioral and Social Sciences and Education of the National Research Council. National Academy Press, Washington (2000)
25. Steinhauser, N.B., Campbell, G.E., Harrison, K.M., Taylor, L.S., Dzikovska, M.O., Moore, J.D.: Comparing human-human and human-computer tutorial dialogue. In: Proceedings of the 32nd Annual Conference of the Cognitive Science Society poster session (2010)
26. Dzikovska, M.O., Callaway, C.B., Farrow, E., Moore, J.D., Steinhauser, N.B., Campbell, G.C.: Dealing with interpretation errors in tutorial dialogue. In: Proceedings of SIGDIAL 2009, London, UK (September 2009)
27. Litman, D., Rosé, C.P., Forbes-Riley, K., VanLehn, K., Bhembe, D., Silliman, S.: Spoken versus typed human and computer dialogue tutoring. International Journal of Artificial Intelligence in Education 16, 145–170 (2006)
28. Dzikovska, M.O., Moore, J.D., Steinhauser, N., Campbell, G.: The impact of interpretation problems on tutorial dialogue. In: Proceedings of the 48th Annual Meeting of the Association for Computational Linguistics (ACL 2010) (2010)
29. Jackson, G.T., Graesser, A.C., McNamara, D.S.: What students expect have more impact than what they know or feel. In: Proceedings 14th International Conference on Artificial Intelligence in Education (AIED), Brighton, UK (2009)
30. Papadopoulos, P.M., Demetriadis, S.N., Stamelos, I.: The impact of prompting in technology-enhanced learning as moderated by students' motivation and metacognitive skills. In: Cress, U., Dimitrova, V., Specht, M. (eds.) EC-TEL 2009. LNCS, vol. 5794, pp. 535–548. Springer, Heidelberg (2009)
31. Forbes-Riley, K., Litman, D.: Adapting to student uncertainty improves tutoring dialogues. In: Proceedings 14th International Conference on Artificial Intelligence in Education (AIED), Brighton, UK (2009)

Authenticity in Learning Game: How It Is Designed and Perceived

Celso Gonçalves[1], Marie-Caroline Croset[2], Muriel Ney[1], Nicolas Balacheff[1], and Jean-Luc Bosson[2]

[1] Laboratory of Informatics of Grenoble (LIG), CNRS and University Joseph Fourier
961 rue de la Houille Blanche, 38402 Grenoble Cedex, France
[2] Techniques for biomedical engineering and complexity management (TIMC),
University Joseph Fourier, Domaine de la Merci, 38710 La Tronche, France
{Celso.Goncalves,Marie-Caroline.Croset,Muriel.Ney,
Nicolas.balacheff,Jean-Luc.Bosson}@imag.fr

Abstract. A key concern in game-based learning is the level of authenticity games require in order to match what learners can expect in the real world, what keeps them engaged in the game, and what they need to learn. We examined authenticity or credibility in a game from the learner's perspective. There are very few studies on this aspect. We propose that authenticity is the result of a compromise between external authenticity (perceived likeness with real life reference), internal authenticity (perceived internal coherence of proposed situations) and didactical authenticity (perceived relevance about learning goals). Our empirical exploratory study investigated undergraduate students' perceptions of authenticity in healthcare game LoE. First, we suggest some attributes for learning games expected to favour game authenticity. We present the choices made for LoE as result of the compromise between the three aspects of authenticity. Second, we analyze students' behaviour and judgments on authenticity.

Keywords: authenticity, credibility, immersion, simulation, role-play, higher education, communication.

1 Introduction

Learning games are playing an important role for training people in real world situations. However, an entirely realistic simulation is neither practical nor desirable. On the one hand, game designers introduce realism in a situation by adding more and more elements, and thus bringing complexity to it. On the other hand, when students spend too much time to get familiar with too many details they can skip the main learning goals. In a learning context, a key concern is thus the level of authenticity the game requires in order to have an accurate match of what learners can expect in the real world with what they need to learn. Therefore, authenticity does not mean a perfect reproduction of reality. What need to be authentic are the main characteristics of the type of situations at stake, that is, those characteristics that require learners to mobilize the knowledge targeted in order to be successful in the game. High-fidelity simulators do not always lead to better performance in learning therefore when designing a learning situation one must consider an analysis on human perception and information process (e.g. [1]). Authenticity is both a function of the game and the perceiver, and we shall define them in the following, starting from a brief overview of related concepts.

Research in education started problematizing authenticity about a century ago, including the work of John Dewey who studied the relationship between learning and experience. To define authenticity in the context of learning games, we consider recent research on new technologies (see also [2]): video game research on immersion and engagement of players, human-computer interaction research on credibility of various computer environments, and communication research on perception of television content.

First, in video game research, many terms have been developed to try to account for these experiences, such as perceived realism [3], and immersion ([4], [5]). One mean to create authenticity in learning games is immersion, making learners feel a certain situation to be real although they know it is not. According to Brown [4] the main indicator of immersion by the user's perspective is the player degree of involvement. Game designers know players may engage in different ways in a game, mobilizing themselves differently, whether they are challenged on their ability to act rapidity, to find the best strategy, to communicate with different people, etc. To immerse in a game is to get involved in the context, not only physically but also mentally and emotionally. There have been numerous definitions of immersion in games based on different aspects of involvement (e.g. tactical, strategy or sensory immersion [5]). In this paper, we focus on immersion in a simulation of an authentic situation, and more specifically, a situation that involves many moments of interactions with people. We call "interactional immersion" such an immersion that relies mostly on interactions with other players or characters of the game [6]. We use engagement as one of many indicators of perceived authenticity, i.e. whether students play the game or not.

Secondly, authenticity can be linked to the concept of trust as developed in Human Computer Interaction studies, the second field of research from which we attempt to define authenticity. The use of the word trust refers to credibility as in "trust the information" or "believe the output", a meaning that is relevant to authenticity [2]. Tseng and Fogg [7] suggest various terms to assess trust or credibility in computer environments: believable, truthful, unbiased, reputable, well-intentioned. According to these authors there is a direct connection between "perceived lack of veridicality" (which we relate to authenticity) and lack of credibility. In the present paper, we shall treat perceived authenticity and credibility similarly. Indeed, users do not always have a personal experience of the simulated reality. The question of authenticity is thus: do they believe it or not. We will discuss in particular the credibility of the feedback from the environment to the learners.

Thirdly, in communication and media studies, several researchers have examined the perceived reality, or modality judgments, of television content ([8], [9]). These researchers identified various criteria involved in viewer judgments regarding the reality (or the realism) of media content. Chandler [8] proposes four criteria: possibility (possible to do in reality), plausibility (possible to do but highly unlikely that you would do it in real life), actual existence (could be done but nothing like this actually exists in reality), and constructedness (this is just a virtual situation and not a real one, it is pre-constructed). Interestingly, the judgments are measured on a likelyhood scale, which relates to the concept of credibility cited above. Furthermore, Brusselles and Bilandzic [10] offer a theoretical framework to explain circumstances under which perceptions of "unrealness" affect engagement in narratives and subsequent perceived realism judgments. They discuss three types of unrealness: fictionality, external realism (match with external reality), and narrative realism (coherence within a story). They show evidences that fictionality does not affect narrative processing unlike the two others.

We now come to a definition of authenticity that will be used both to design game authenticity and to analyze learners' perceived authenticity. We keep the notions of external and internal authenticity [10] and add a new one specific to our context of learning game, that is, didactical authenticity [6]. As summarized in figure 1, a learning game may be designed, and later perceived, as authentic from three points of view: it can be more or less realistic (perceived likeness with a real life reference), coherent (perceived internal coherence of the proposed situations) and relevant (perceived relevance with respect to learning goals).

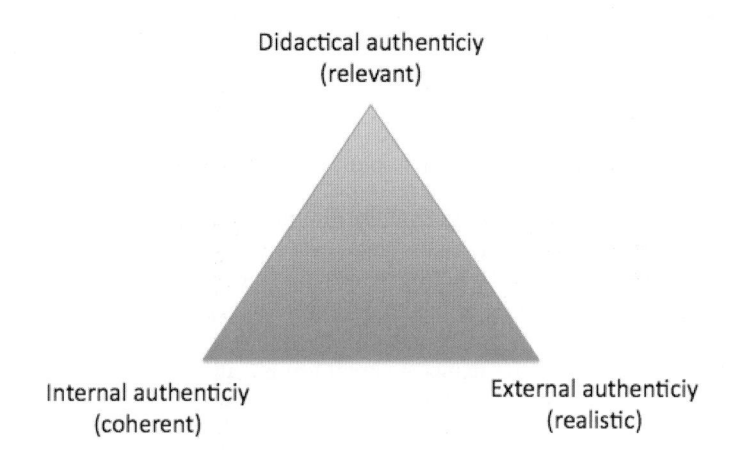

Fig. 1. Model of authenticity

Why should a learning game be authentic? Some fields are difficult to teach because students do not immediately see the purpose; they are not motivated because they do not relate the learning goals to their personal training project. This is often the case with mathematical teaching contents (e.g. statistics for medical students like in the game described in this paper, calculus for experimental sciences, etc). Like other approaches do (e.g. inquiry learning, problem-based learning), game-based learning gives an authentic context to the learning at stake. In our case, namely learning statistics, students will face a public health issue rather than directly a statistical issue. We shall now justify each of the three dimensions of the model (figure 1) one by one.

First, the context above mentioned should be authentic in the sense of external authenticity at least for professional training. Otherwise, students would not have the feeling of being prepared to react adequately in real professional situations. Second, the game must remain consistent with a logical sequence of events and feedback. This refers to the internal authenticity. Inconsistencies in the game may cause disengagement. Moreover, communication and media research suggest that one is more susceptible to persuasion or abstract lessons, when engage into a narrative. Third, didactical authenticity is related to appropriation, the fact that learners make the problem proposed their own, looking for their own solutions rather than finding strategies to do only what the teacher expects [11]. This will allow the learner to appropriate the meaning of the situation, i.e. what is the point in learning terms. Otherwise, the learner is just focusing on a particular solution of a particular problem with little ability to transfer to other similar problems.

After this definition of the nature and scope of authenticity, we introduce below the case study on the game LOE exploring various judgments expressed by learners after the game as well as their behaviour during the game. The following research questions guided our investigation:

(1) Do students perceive the game as authentic? How do students behave in (authentic) moments of interaction with characters of the game?
(2) What cues (within the game environment) enable students to make judgments of authenticity? What roles do these cues play in students' judgments?

2 Method

2.1 Description of the Game Environment Used in the Study

The Laboratorium of Epidemiology© (LOE) immerses learners into a full-scale, persistent and distributed simulation combined with a game scenario [6], [12]. It was collaboratively designed and used by researchers, teaching staff (hereafter called tutors), and students as both an educational project and a research project. The educational project forms part of a medical school course in biostatistics. The research project, to which we gave the name "Laboratorium", allows repeated data collection campaigns that are not unique events in students' or tutors' lives and is an attempt to reduce data collection biases and produce well-documented databases.

The game is based on a computerized simulation of various institutions (including hospitals) and role-play. Students play the role of public health physicians and are placed in an otherwise inaccessible professional situation involving the occurrence of a disease in several hospitals. Students have to design and carry out an epidemiological study, and write a scientific article to be presented at a congress. The main learning goal concerns the statistical analysis of a medical database. However, students are given a mission that contextualizes the problems of doing statistics. The mission is to design a diagnosis tool for VTED (Venous Thrombo-Embolic Disease) for hospital use. While working on this problem, students will learn statistics, understand the role they play, and more generally the function of statistics in public health.

The game is fully integrated into the standard medical school curriculum. It lasts four months including eight four-hour sessions in class. The main tasks for students, the learning goals and the main part of the computer environment connected to these tasks, are indicated in the following table. It is structured by the eight in-class sessions (left-side column). These tasks are performed in teams of three to four students.

Table 1. Analysis of the main tasks and learning goals of the game

	Main tasks	Goals	Computer environment
1	Bibliographical research, choose the main objective and make a plan	To gain knowledge about a specific disease as well as the methodologies used in epidemiological surveys	Virtual websites of various organization
2	Design an epidemiological survey and sent the protocol for validation	To construct and structure a survey (sample quality, indicator quality, ethical considerations, etc.)	E-mail application, Ethical Research committee web-site
3	Carry out the survey at one or several hospitals	To implement a survey (translate patient saying into data, control and organize data)	Virtual hospitals (online), Mobile phone
4 5	Analyze data	To analyze data with statistical tools and thus understand them	Statistical software, Spreadsheet application
5 6	Write an article and submit it to a congress	To understand how a scientific article is structured, and how to select and present evidences (statistics may come in different forms)	Text editor, Congress website
7	Prepare an oral presentation	To synthesize results taking into account a reviewer's comments	Slide editor, Congress website
8	Attend a (simulated) medical congress	To defend orally their decision tools based on statistical arguments	

One important challenge in this project was to design interactions with characters of the game that help students to appropriate different problems, acquire skills and engage in the game [6]. The system of interactions of Loe was inspired by recent work on embedded phenomena [12] and participatory simulations [13]. It is a persistent and distributed simulations, sharing several characteristics of pervasive games [14].

Between sessions 2 and 3 (table 1), students have to ask for authorization from the Head of each medical department of the hospital they wish to visit, in order to be able to interview patients. For this purpose, they have to make a phone call and, having listened to a brief message, they have to formulate their request in the way they think most appropriate. Later, a tutor listens to their message and replies by SMS giving them either permission or a documented refusal. A team of students can make several calls, either to have access to several departments, or to repeat their request after a refusal.

Students use their personal e-mail application on various occasions. For example, between session 2 and 3 (table 1) they send their protocol for validation by the Research Ethics Committee. They have access to the (virtual) website of this committee that gives an email address. This is compulsory since only approved protocols can be implemented at the hospital. The tutors behind these characters (experts of the Committee) use dedicated e-mail addresses and Webmail applications to answer to students.

During session 3, students interview patients in simulated hospitals each containing three wards and five patients per ward. The system allows the students to interact with the simulated patient by selecting one of five preformed questions: present illness, present lifestyle, past history, family/social history, and medications. For each question, an appropriate video clip provides the interviewer with the patient's reply. These clips are based on scripts made from real patient files: National Survey in Hospitals in France managed by J-L. Bosson.

In order to be able to participate to the simulated medical congress (session 8 in table 1), students have to upload their article on the virtual congress web site (between sessions 6 and 7). This is the least represented character of the game since not even a name is given to him/her. Later they will get a report on their article, visible on the web site. In many cases, they will be asked to revise their article and send it again. Articles are divided into two groups by the organizers of the congress and best articles are given a longer time of presentation.

The challenge was to make these interactions authentic according to the three dimensions of figure 1. Interactions should evokes the ones one would meet in a real hospital including feelings and constraints (realistic), they should also be useful and timely within the mission proposed (coherent), and finally they should help students acquire the knowledge and skills at stake (relevant).

2.2 Game Attributes with Regards to the Authenticity Model

We now give a list of attributes of the environment that were used to make the students' experience more authentic [6]. The game environment components were designed with different compromise within the triangle; part being predominantly on the realism dimension, other part being more oriented towards either the coherence or the relevance dimensions.

Table 2 summarizes nine attributes of authentic learning games based on a mission that implies interacting with characters. Below we give an example in LOE and an analysis using our model (figure 1).

Table 2. Environment attributes of authenticity

Themes	Attributes
Mission	Mission content and resources Original data
Mise en scene	Graphical representation Structure of the environment
User freedom	Constraints Level of control of the users
Interactions	Characters' personification Behaviour and feedback from characters Mode and media of communication

A mission. When starting the game, students are given a mission that gives context to the problems designed for learning. This mission has been designed to mimic a real situation with the help of an epidemiologist who conducted this mission in the past. It is presented to students in the form of text and video (of a meeting between professionals) on the commission's web site. This commission is the institution that gives the mission. We used real data (patients files) as stated above. Therefore, the external authenticity was the most important to design these attributes related to the mission.

Mise en scene. The environment that provides a mise en scene is for most parts online. Students find the websites of the different organizations they have ot interact with. This is designed following mainly the internal coherence principle. Indeed not all the organization one could encounter in real life are represented but the interactions are designed to flow logically within the game. Furthermore, the graphical representation, especially of the hospital, follows the didactical authenticity dimension. Instead of an avatar moving within a represented hospital with corridors and wards, we kept only those parts that are relevant for learning, in particular the patients talks (scripted).

User freedom. First, the constraints of the interaction may be considered. For instance, in the interaction with patients, it is important that a patient does not repeat at will his/her answers, which is a constraint that was reproduced in our system. This particular constraint is designed for didactical authenticity. Indeed, when a patient does not repeat oneself, students learn that they need to prepare their interview and also to look for ways to control their data, two learning goals of the course. Second, the level of control of the students on environment and tasks had to be defined. In LOE, the tutor is accompanying the students who discover by themselves what they have to do and how they can navigate into the environment. Students are physicians who can ask for help but who are relatively free otherwise (external authenticity).

Interactions with characters. Considering the authenticity of our system of interaction, we identified three attributes (see table 2). First, the characters students are interacting with may be more or less authentic. This is decomposed into two issues. First, the authenticity of the character refers to its personification: what information is available and in what form (text, photos etc). This is limited in LOE to satisfy mostly internal authenticity. Second, the content of the feedback the character gives to students may be more or less authentic, depending on how adapted to student's actions this feedback is. For didactical authenticity, this feedback is communicated verbally or otherwise (e.g. a patient with heavy breathing can be an important sign) and relevant or not (students need to sort information). Finally, another issue is the channel of communication (by email, phone, etc) and the mode (textual, verbal, visual). The latter was designed for external authenticity.

2.3 Data Collection and Data Analysis Methods

Our sample is composed by 170 second-year students of the medical school of Grenoble, France, in a compulsory biostatistics course they followed in 2009/2010. They are distributed over 45 teams of 3 or 4 students. Our first data set consisted of messages left on the answering machine of the hospitals by the 45 teams. There were

167 voice messages in total. Our second data sets consisted of transcripts of phone interviews with volunteer students. There were between 19 and 23 students from as many teams (one student per team) interviewed after each session.

We shall now explain our method with regards to the research questions asked. This is mostly an exploratory empirical study with two goals, one is to get a large variety of students' feedback, the other is to collect both what they do and what they say. For these reasons, we got data both during the game (students interact with characters of the game without explicit presence of researchers) and after (students talk to researchers and reflect on what they did). To answer question (1) on student perceived authenticity, we first analyzed student' behaviour as they interact with characters of the game. The goal was to look for signs of engagement into their role, in other words, see whether students behave as if the situation was real and/or useful for their training. Secondly, to answer question (2) on cues that enable students to make judgments of authenticity, we analyzed the phone interviews. We asked three questions during a phone interview that occurred about an hour after the end of each session: (i) what did you produce today, (ii) do you perceive what happened today as intuitively credible with regards to a professional reference or strange, and (iii) do you think what you did today useful for your professional training. Very little was said by the researcher-interviewer in order to let students spontaneously put issues on the table. In particular, participants were not notified about the realism of the environment (e.g. that data were real) or about how it would be for a professional.

Method of analysis of the voice messages. In a real life situation, the voice message would be formally addressed to the head of the department, indicating a relation of hierarchy which in turn fits the context proposed in this part of the game. Therefore, we could expect students to introduce themselves under the role of a medical doctor since this is the way they are assigned in the game by the public health commission "you are a doctor...". Here are the criteria used:

Attitude: their attitude towards the head of the hospital department (Formal or Informal).

Identity: the name and the role under which students introduce themselves (Medical Doctor, Medical Student or Themselves).

Context information: students give contextual information on the mission (e.g. the various organisations) or, conversely, on the course. Specify the objective of their survey to justify the request.

We also collected time and date of the phone call.

In order to analyse the nature of these messages we classified them into four groups: Successful, Unsuccessful or Partial, Mislead and Tryout massages.

Successful messages qualify the ones able to request an authorisation as well as to report students' main objective of their survey or at a pinch to mention it concerns a survey about the thromboembolic disease.

Unsuccessful or Partial messages: *Unsuccessful messages* were unfinished messages, incomplete messages (when students failed to identify themselves or their group), and ineffective messages (when students, despite requesting authorisation, failed to report a survey main objective). *Partial messages* were rectification partial messages or new authorisation request partial messages (when in a subsequent message students required an authorisation to access another hospital department without giving details of their survey oftentimes refereeing to a previous message).

Mislead messages were messages that presented only an authorization request following the instruction on the answering machine.

Tryout messages when students hung up the phone immediately after hearing the answering machine message.

A first grid of analysis emerged from previous pilot study. For this year, messages were coded by a PhD candidate in Cognitive Sciences and a PhD in Applied mathematics. This collaboration resulted in an adjustment of the criteria to the present sample through trials using 15 messages. Further on, we compared the results of 43 messages in order to check if there were any incongruities. Finally we double checked 167 messages and discussed a few incongruities especially concerning the classifications nature of some messages.

Method of analysis of the phone interviews. The phone interviews were transcribed. Then each unit of sense was associated to one of the nine game attributes (table 2), if any. There were approximately 8 hours of telephone interviews (representing all four first sessions of Table 1). Each unit of meaning (a topic addressed by a student after question) was then allocated to one of the nine attributes, when one of them was mentioned by the student. The analysis goal was to identify cues mentioned by students to explain a perception of authenticity (i.e. if a task seemed credible or not and why). We can also identify the positions taken by a majority of students, as well as individual variability.

3 Results

3.1 Analysis of the Voice Messages

The majority of the students (115 out of 136 messages that were not simple tests) have a formal attitude. This could be a sign of perceived authenticity by the students, whether it is because the task is realistic, coherent or relevant is another issue. However, there were 21 calls showing an informal register (mainly laughter), which would not have been allowed in reality (if calling a real hospital). Also, no team has assume the identity of a doctor, and only 40 of 136 callers introduced themselves as students. The 96 (71%) remaining, did not play their role as a doctor and did not even give sufficient status to justify their request. However, they all gave their name. Finally, 20 of 136 messages from 13 different teams told about the bio-statistics. None of the messages mentioned the organization they are working for in the game.

We looked for expected messages to assess students' perception of the relevance of the teaching situation, that is, those able to meet the educational goals. These messages should at least include information on the identity of the caller, the name of the department where the student wants to interview patients and the presentation of the main objective set by the team, all in a relatively formal language. If any of these criteria is not validated (e.g. informal attitude or lack of main objective), the message is rejected. The remaining messages indicate that the student perceived the issues underlying teaching (didactical authenticity). Among the 167 messages, 62 (37%) are coded as expected messages.

Each team has recorded several messages: 3 messages on average up to 17 messages for the same team. This shows their need to better understand the situation and the expectations of the game before reaching the goal. The evolution over time of the overall content of the messages, however, is positive: the five weeks the students have filed messages (see Figure 4), the proportion of messages considered expected grows from 15% to 50%. The messages of the first week were mostly incomplete (60%). However, eleven teams (of 45) leave no message corresponding to our expectation, during the five weeks.

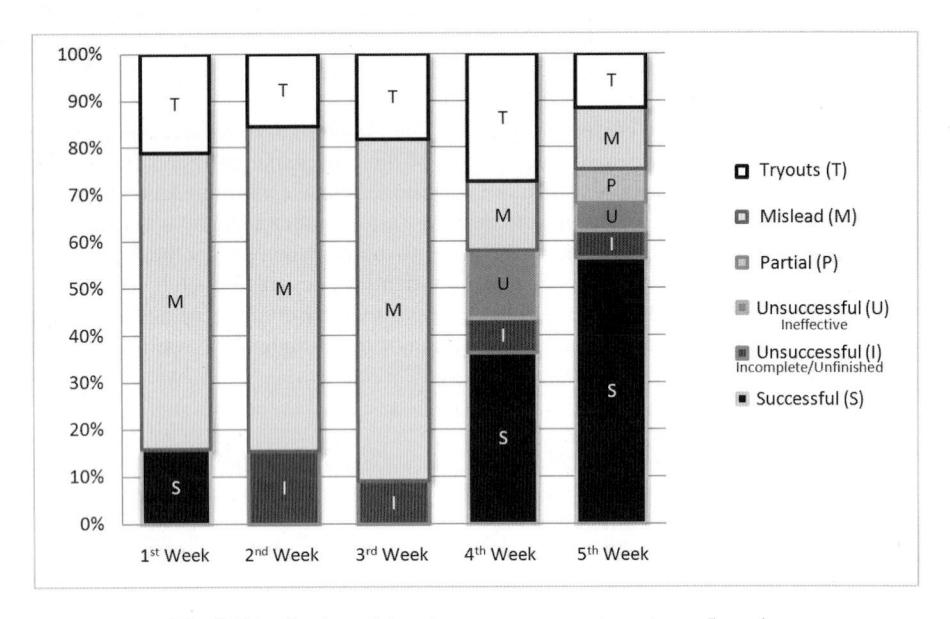

Fig. 2. Distribution of the phone messages nature across 5 weeks

To conclude, our combinations of indicators showed that most students did not perceived the situation as realistic nor relevant. These results will be confirmed by the comments made by students during phone interviews.

3.2 Analysis of the Phone Interviews

The following presentation and discussion of results is organized around the four groups of attributes of table 2. In keeping with the study's exploratory aim, we believe that the worth of our findings rests on the diversity of issues tackled and on a detailed exposition of differences among individual cases. Therefore, qualitative assessment of the relative importance of various issues for different individuals was a prevalent underlying process in our analysis.

A mission: given resources and original data. Students made judgments concerning the game mission mostly during the very first phone interview, at the end of the first session (table 1). Different cues were important to different participants and assessments of the game's authenticity diverged depending on what cues were perceived or taken into account by different individuals. On one hand, some students were ready to engage in the mission and believe in its authenticity. A realism comment from one of the student is "it looks like it was not made just for us". Some students said that the documents themselves look "serious". Students mentioned most often two cues: the figures in these documents, or the model of protocol, both look real. The video showing a meeting between physicians and introducing the issues of the mission was also taken as a cue by several students. One students added that it shows "… the importance of teamwork; it is not just a person who is going to change the world".

On the other hand, some students realize that they are going to make their own study but they know the results in advance (from a literature search in the virtual library). They think that they will "not be able to prove anything new" or that they have to "pretend that the patients are going to be interviewed but know that data have been collected already". The latter points out an internal incoherence perceived by some students: they have to write a protocol as if they were going to collect data, but at the same time they believe (at least for this session) that data will be given to them.

The data that are sent to student in the form of a table with patient in lines are real but students do not know it and most of them think that they are not but "look very real". Different cues are used to suggest the authenticity of the data: "the data are variable, with few repetitions", "there are many information", "it looks like a physician did the survey because all the different forms of the disease are distinguished", "there are a lot of details on each patient", " we did not get exactly what we wanted, it is not ideal, it is annoying", "the statistical test shows what we expected", " we got unexpected result". The latter shows that whatever the result, students do not question the authenticity of the data. This and the impact of the figures included in the document show the importance of figures as a crucial cues for student of the authenticity of their mission. One student even said that if the result is not what is expected from the literature review they will have to look for an error in their methodology.

Mise en scene (visual and graphical attributes). No comment is made about the site structure and graphical design. It may be that these aspects are not a source of evidence of authenticity for students. They appreciated the quality of the environment, but this raised not judgement on its authenticity (external, internal or didactical).

User freedom (constraints and level of control). One of our findings in this area is that a number of participants mentioned the constraints spontaneously and could even discern the value of the constraints with regards to one of the authenticity dimensions. For one student, two cues for what we called external authenticity were the fact they do not "have access to patients without asking for an authorization" and that " the more in advance they ask for data, the larger the number of patient files they get". By contrasts, for those students who got data too quickly, the interaction was not realistic. One important constraint with a didactical authenticity was the fact that students could not listen twice to the same patient answer. None of the students understand the value of this constraint (see previous section) and several of them even thought that it was not realistic since in real life it is possible to ask a patient to repeat an answer.

About the level of control, students mentioned that they got more help than in real life (a protocol model to start with, many resources in the virtual library, feedback on many aspects of their protocol in the e-mail, etc), which make the experience slightly less realistic. In other words, they see the didactical intention behind the feedback they get, event when they come from characters of the game. However, this is not seen as an internal incoherence or a factor of disengagement. A compromise between realism and relevance worked out in this case.

Interactions with characters. We present how students perceived the various interactions on a scale of personification, staring from the most personified character, namely the patients that appear to students in the form of actors on videos.

Patients look real to students "although we know they are actors" or that "they read a text, for some of them". The cues used by student to talk about the authenticity of the patient interactions are numerous: "patients do not say what we ask them to say", "it is not perfect", "not very clear", patients "use their own words", "there are old people telling their life story". According to a student, the "different types of patient are represented (cooperative or not, talkative or not, cranky or not...)". Comparing to real patient interview, one says that "it is the same; we have to sort what they say, and to translate it into medical terms".

As for the e-mail interaction with the experts of the Ethical Committee, some students thinks that "it looks like we talk to our teacher" because it asks for modifications like teachers do, "it looks like they say almost the same thing to everybody in part of the message". It is important to note that students try to compare with a real world reference they do not have. Therefore, realism is judge by what they think is realistic not by their prior experience. Most students say that they cannot judge the credibility of the situation because of that reason. One student thinks that "maybe one gets no explanation when the protocol is rejected, in real life". On the other hand, this interaction appears as authentic to most students, for reasons like "it looks real because the mail looks official", "the content is serious".

Considering the interaction with the Hospital, we get a different picture. Most students do not find it authentic, neither realistic nor relevant. From their point of view, "it does not look too serious when all of a sudden everybody gets an answer" (by SMS), " it is not credible to talk to an answering machine", "very bizarre", and it is the "same number for all hospitals". However, one student think that it looks realistic because it is like that when you want to get an appointment with a physician, you often get to talk to an answering machine. Several students think that it would be easier to know what to say with a real person, although more complicated to answer to his/her questions. It seems that it was hard for most students to play the game of this interaction, using an answering machine. On the other hand, only one student mentioned the SMS answer to say that 'to get an answer by SMS is not realistic'.

Finally, we examined how is perceived the interaction with the department of Information of the hospital. Student post a data request on the virtual hospital and get a short e-mail answer with a data file. Some students found it realistic, one because the e-mail is signed. However, most students did not remember to whom they had request their data from, although they were asked about it only one or two hours after they had done it. Only one student reflected about how the system of interaction works.

For this student, it was magic when "we got data right away, the file, the patients on videos, and just what we wanted".

4 Conclusion

In this work, we probed students' perceptions relative to the authenticity of a learning game environment (see also [2]). The qualitative method used has proven quite successful, as it allowed for the gathering and in-depth analysis of a wide variety of judgments concerning these matters. Overall, our results indicate that students authenticity judgments pertaining to the game LOE can be very complex and specific. In particular, we observed that given cues in the environment could play different, even contradictory, roles in the formation of these judgments. Students could use the same cue to make opposite judgment. This shows that it would be interesting to look for individual traits that could explain some of the authenticity judgments. We also found that, in some instances, unfavourable assessments could be promoted by cues designers had hoped would instead favour authenticity.

We performed a behavioural analysis as follows. The authenticity external (realism) is deduced from the fact that students behave in line with what they would do in "real" life. The internal authenticity was not measured through students actions, but it is analyzed in students' interviews or in discussions between students (not shown here). The didactical authenticity is finally linked to the recognition of the problem or not (wanted by teachers), and the deployment of a strategy to solve it.

We showed how our model (figure 1) can be used to study perceived authenticity. For instance, one may find students who perceive a learning game as externally and internally authentic but not relevant (e.g. students who rely strongly on the teachers and do not see the point of what they do in terms of learning). This model can also be used for the design of authentic games. Finally, the model can be used when the authenticity of the game has to be judged by different experts. For instance, external authenticity of the game (sometimes called fidelity) can be assessed by domain experts using more or less well established criteria. Didactical authenticity of the game can be assessed by teachers.

Our proposal is that the design of a game must result in a genuine compromise between the three dimensions of authenticity, namely, realism, coherence and relevance. This authenticity is particularly welcome in a biostatistics course for medical students. Indeed, a mismatch between students' perceptions of their future profession and the content of this type of course justifies an effort to contextualize the learning, i.e. to provide an authentic environment.

Regarding the example of the phone interaction with the hospital, interviews with students confirmed the findings of the analysis of their behaviour: two studies showed a lack of perceived authenticity. Several improvements are planned. To promote the didactical authenticity, we will make the problem more explicit (in particular, require a description of the main objective in the instruction provided by the answering machine). For internal authenticity, we will ask students to give a single call (to avoid repeated calls and responses received by SMS). Finally, for the sake of external authenticity, we will put a professional on the phone from time to time (instead of the answering machine). We hypothesize that these changes will lead to an indication of authenticity observable in student behaviour.

References

1. Scerbo, M.W., Dawson, S.: High Fidelity, High Performance? Simulation In Healthcare 2(4), 224–230 (2007)
2. Francis, A., Couture, M.: Credibility of a simulation-based virtual laboratory: An exploratory study of learner judgments of verisimilitude. Journal of Interactive Learning Research 14(4), 439–464 (2003)
3. Shapiro, M.A., Pena-Herborn, J., Hancock, J.T.: Realism, imagination and narrative video games. In: Vorderer, P., Bryant, J. (eds.) Playing Video Games: Motives, Responses, and Consequences. Lawrence Erlbaum Associates, Mahwah (2006)
4. Brown, E., Cairns, P.: A grounded investigation of game immersion. Paper Presented at the SIGCHI Conference on Human Factors in Computing Systems (CHI 2004), pp. 1297–1300. ACM Press, New York (2004)
5. Björk, S., Holopaine, J.: Patterns In Game Design, p. 423. Charles River Media, Hingham (2004)
6. Ney, M., Gonçalves, C., Balacheff, N., Schwartz, C., Bosson, J.-L.: Phone, Email and Video Interactions with Characters in an Epidemiology Game: towards Authenticity. In: Transactions on Edutainment, special issue on Simulation and Gaming in Healthcare. LNCS (in press)
7. Tseng, S., Fogg, B.J.: The Elements of computer credibility. In: Ehrlich, K., Newman, W. (eds.) Proceedings of CHI 1999, Pittsburgh, May 15-20, pp. 80–87. ACM Press, New-York (1999)
8. Chandler, D.: Children's understanding of what is 'real' on television: A review of the literature. [WWW document] (1997),
   http://www.aber.ac.uk/media/Documents/short/realrev.html
   (retrieved on April 10, 2010)
9. Busselle, R.W., Greenberg, B.S.: The nature of television realism judgments: a reevaluation of their conceptualization and measurement. Mass Communication and Society 3, 249–258 (2000)
10. Busselle, R., Bilandzic, H.: Fictionality and Perceived Realism in Experiencing Stories: A Model of Narrative Comprehension and Engagement. Communication Theory 18, 255–280 (2008)
11. Gonçalves, C., Ney, M., Balacheff, N., Bosson, J.-L.: Student's Problem Appropriation in an Epidemiology Game. Paper Presented at ECGBL 2009, European Conference on Game-Based Learning, Graz, Austria (2009)
12. Moher, T.: Embedded phenomena: supporting science learning with classroom-sized distributed simulations. Paper Presented at ACM CHI 2006 Conference on Human Factors in Computing Systems 2006, pp. 691–700 (April 2006)
13. Colella, V.: Participatory simulations: building collaborative understanding through impressive dynamic modeling. Journal of the Learning Sciences 9, 471–500 (2000)
14. Thomas, S.: Pervasive learning games: Explorations of hybrid educational gamescapes Simulation & Gaming. An Interdisciplinary Journal 37, 41–55 (2006)

Orchestrating Learning Using Adaptive Educational Designs in IMS Learning Design

Marion R. Gruber, Christian Glahn, Marcus Specht, and Rob Koper

CELSTEC, Open University in The Netherlands,
Valkenburgerweg 177, 6419AT Heerlen, The Netherlands
{marion.gruber,christian.glahn,marcus.specht,rob.koper}@ou.nl

Abstract. IMS Learning Design (IMS LD) is an open specification to support interoperability of advanced educational designs for a wide range of technology-enhanced learning solutions and other units of learning. This paper analyses approaches to model personalised learning experiences with and without explicit adaptive features in IMS LD. The paper has two main parts. The first part analyses the relation between orchestrating learning and IMS LD's semantic features. The second part compares modelling strategies for educational designs for personalised learning in non-collaborative learning units using IMS LD Level A and IMS LD Level B features. The analysis is based on two worked-out IMS LD units. The paper concludes with a comparison of the two modelling approaches and addresses gaps when integrating adaptation concepts at the levels of the specification.

Keywords: adaptation, IMS Learning Design, educational design, personalization, orchestrating learning.

1 Introduction

IMS Learning Design (IMS LD) is an open specification to support interoperability of advanced educational designs for a wide range of technology-enhanced learning solutions and other *units of learning* (UoL). The specification has been released in 2003 [1] and has been subject to a broad scientific discussion [2, 3]. Recent developments in the context of the TENCompetence project [4] have led to an improved set of tools and services for modelling and deploying educational designs in IMS LD [5] These developments extend the perspective on the capabilities of IMS LD and allow a better analysis of related educational design approaches.

IMS LD provides a semantic framework to formally express educational designs and to model learning processes with innovative technologies. Through scaffolding key parameters of learning IMS LD provides a framework for orchestrating learning processes and personalising competence development. The emphasis on modelling learning processes makes IMS LD a potentially useful framework for tackling the research challenges related to orchestrating learning that have been identified by the STELLAR project [6]. However, only a few research publications have addressed personalisation and adaptation with IMS LD in the past years [7, 8, 9]. Related research focused entirely on semantic structures of IMS LD for conditional modelling.

This focus is to narrow for reflecting the full potential of IMS LD's semantic framework for orchestrating learning.

This paper analyses the application of the conceptual structure of IMS LD for modelling personalised learning experiences. This analysis is based on the recent discussion on personalisation and adaptation in technology-enhanced learning using IMS LD, which is reflected in the background section. It is followed by a section that identifies the research question for this paper and identifies two underlying analytical problems: the relation of IMS LD to orchestrating learning and practical approaches and limitations of IMS LD for modelling orchestration scripts. The section orchestrating learning analyses the dimensions of orchestrating learning based on selected literature. It is followed by the analysis of what semantic features IMS LD refer to the different dimensions. Based on these insights two variations of a UoL analyse the modelling strategies at the different complexity levels of IMS LD. Finally, this paper compares the different approaches and discusses gaps that were identified with respect to the orchestration dimensions.

2 Background

Personalisation is increasingly important in technology-enhanced learning. However, personalised learning is not unambiguous. Two general viewpoints on personalisation can be identified. The first viewpoint defines personalised learning as individualised and tailored educational experiences [10]. The personal dimension in this viewpoint is directed towards facilitated educational processes that are unique to a learner. The second viewpoint emphasises the personal relevancy and involvement of individuals in learning processes [11]. From this perspective, personalised learning refers to those processes that support learners to take responsibility and control over their learning and enable them to reflect on the learning on a meta-cognitive level.

The two perspectives on personalisation are not mutually exclusive: learner-controlled learning processes may lead to unique learning experiences and automatically adapted educational environments may support deeper learning experiences that allow learners to feel more responsible for their learning. However, learner control can be provided in mass education and fully tailored educational processes can be provided without leaving any control to the learner.

Dron [12] argues that personalised learning does not require that learners have full control over their learning, but it requires that some control is left to the learners. Based on this premise, educational designs for personalised learning refer to those educational designs that enable learners to control and regulate their learning based on predefined tasks [13]. Educational designs are adaptive if their task arrangements can reflect the learners' control decisions. Such designs are orchestration scripts for the educational practice. Orchestrating refers to educational practices that organise and arrange learning activities and learning environments to guide learners through learning processes. In this sense the orchestration refers to control and regulation mechanisms for framing parameters of learning processes [14].

From an adaptive educational hypermedia perspective Brusilovsky [15] distinguishes between *adaptive presentation* and *adaptive navigation support* to categorise the different approaches for personalising and adapting information. Additionally, a third category has to be included: *adaptive sequencing*. Although adaptive sequencing is sometimes categorised under adaptive navigation support, adaptive sequencing focuses on the arrangement of processes whereas Brusilovsky's definitions of adaptive navigation support focuses on navigational features at information level. At this level orchestration scripts define the rules for using and combining the different approaches.

IMS LD provides a generic and flexible language to model educational designs in a machine-readable format. As an open specification it allows to prepare orchestration scripts for technology-enhanced learning. One of the requirements for IMS LD was that the language can describe personalization aspects within an educational design, "so that the content and activities within a unit of learning can be adapted based on the preferences, portfolio, pre-knowledge, educational needs and situational circumstances of the participants in educational processes. In addition, it must allow the designer, when desired, to pass control over the adaptation process to the learner, a staff member and/or the computer." [16, p. 14]

IMS LD has three complexity levels [17].

1. IMS LD Level A provides the core elements for creating educational designs. Conditional rules for controlling the learning process are limited to basic aspects of sequencing educational processes.
2. IMS LD Level B adds complex conditional elements that allow learner modelling, fine grained process control, and offers personalisation and adaptation features.
3. IMS LD Level C extends the process model by a notification feature that allows to model event-based processes.

Previous research on modelling adaptive educational designs with IMS LD has analysed approaches for modelling units of learning with basic adaptive and personalisation features. These approaches have been primarily guided by user-modelling and adaptation concepts from an adaptive hypermedia research perspective that is discussed by Aroyo et al. [10].

Paramythis and Loidl-Reisinger [18] reflect personalisation at the level of properties and conditions. The authors analyse these features for authoring fully dynamic adaptive processes. The authors conclude that IMS LD is most appropriate to transfer snapshots of adaptation logic between systems. Berlanga and Garcia [7] focus on content adaptation using meta-data fragments to define templates for learning resources. The arrangement of the resources is entirely based on the sequencing features of IMS LD. Instead of utilizing higher order control features of IMS LD for adaptation, the authors propose to store rules for adaptation separated from the educational design. Specht and Burgos [9] analyse what types of adaptation can be modelled using the language features of IMS LD. Their analysis includes partial user-modelling using properties and calculations as well as the application of conditions for adapting aspects of the educational design to the needs of the learner. The authors identify that IMS LD provides strong support for modelling adaptive sequencing, adaptive content presentation, and adaptive navigation support.

Van Rosmalen et al. [19] analyse the role of IMS LD in the lifecycle of adaptive e-learning courses. The authors propose that the educational design carries only general guidelines for personalising the learning experience. External modules of a runtime environment handle all other types of adaptation, such as recommendations or link adaptation. The authors describe the interrelation between the different system components for adaptive e-learning and discuss briefly the role of properties and conditions as connectors for personalisation and adaptation.

The semantic of IMS LD is based on an orchestration metaphor [16]. This metaphor means an abstraction from specific technologies, resources, tools, and services. This implies the emphasis of arranging and managing the communication between learners among each other and with their environment. Therefore, IMS LD supports designers to create orchestration scripts using a machine-readable notation for supporting learning processes under different technical conditions. Besides the commonly promoted property-condition-based approach of adaptation for personalisation that uses IMS LD Level B concepts, IMS LD offers alternatives for integrating personalisation facets into educational designs.

IMS LD is a modelling language for educational designs. Although its semantic structures share some characteristics with programming languages, several aspects that would be required for providing a full programming language were intentionally excluded from the specification. Consequently, it is not possible to model low level adaptation algorithms entirely in IMS LD. This restriction implies that some aspects of adaptive systems lie outside the scope of IMS LD. This is particularly the case for user-modelling concepts that reflect learner history at great detail. Low-level computational aspects are part of associated services. This approach is now researched in the GRAPPLE project in which external user-modelling services work together with authoring and run-time components to implement educational designs [20, 21]. With IMS LD Level B it is possible to integrate such services through so called global properties through which a service can expose certain information to the educational design [22].

3 Research Question

One aspect of orchestration scripts is to describe personalisation options. In this context, personalisation means dynamic adaptation of the learning support based on the learners' needs or previous learning experiences. Motivated by the related research objective of the GRAPPLE project to identify approaches and possible gaps related to modelling units of learning with adaptive features in IMS LD [23], this paper analyses personalisation concepts that are inherent in the IMS LD semantics. Consequently, the following research question provides the underpinning for this analysis.

How to use IMS LD to model concepts for modelling personalisation in the orchestration of educational designs for technology-enhanced learning?

This research question implies two aspects for the analysis.

1. It is required to understand how the semantics of IMS LD represent the different aspects of orchestrating learning and personalisation. The analysis of this aspect addresses the formal representation of orchestration scripts with the semantic concepts of IMS LD.
2. It is necessary to analyse how IMS LD concepts reflect personalisation in educational designs. This aspect addresses modelling concepts for representing variations of a generic educational approach.

By understanding the relation between the different concepts of modelling orchestrating scripts with their practical implications, it is possible to identify the gaps in the modelling concepts as well as concepts that fall outside the scope of the specification.

4 Orchestrating Learning

Dillenbourg [14] identifies three dimensions that are involved in orchestration. Firstly, *the interplay* of learning activities at different social planes. The planes are bound to the social connectedness of learners on the activity level and can include the individual, collaborative, collective (class wide) activities. Secondly, *the timing* of an educational script. Timing refers to the interrelation of the learning activities and the transitions from one activity to another. Finally, *the focus* on the learning process. Focus refers to emphasizing or hiding aspects of the learning objective in order to guide the students' attention. Integrating these dimensions allows teachers to manage the available environment for learning.

Orchestrating learning is closely related to educational design. According to Goodyear and Yang [13] educational design "is largely a matter of thinking about good learning tasks (good things for learners to do) and about the physical and human resources that can help learners to succeed with such tasks." [13: p169] When analyzing educational designs it is required to distinguish between *learning outcomes, learning activities, and learning tasks*. "Learning outcomes are the durable, intended, and unintended cognitive, affective, and psychomotor consequences of the learner's activity (mental or physical)." [13: p169] These outcomes are the result of what the learner does. In other words, learning outcomes are the direct consequence of the activity of a learner. According to Goodyear and Yang, learning activities are based on the learner's interpretation of the requirements of learning tasks. Teachers or instructional designers typically define learning tasks.

Van Merriënboer, Clark, and de Croock [24] structure the educational design process into four interrelated components: *learning tasks, supportive information, just-in-time information, and part-task practice*. Learning tasks are provided to learners in order to stimulate whole-task experiences for constructing knowledge (schema and rules). Supportive information is supportive with respect to the learning tasks. It bridges between learners' prior knowledge and the learning task. Just-in-time information refers to procedural rules of the educational design and the related information for communicating these rules to learners. Part-task practice items "are provided to learners in order to promote rule automation for selected recurrent aspects of the whole complex skill" [24: p43]. Educational design processes rely on aligning these components for generating coherent learning experiences that lead to higher transfer performance then designs that do not take all components into account.

While educational design is indirect to the learning situation, orchestrating learning implies also the direct management of performing learning tasks during runtime. From this viewpoint orchestrating learning includes the personalisation and the adaptation of learning tasks, because personalisation and adaptation refer to management decisions related to dynamic task arrangements in a learning environment. However, educational design and orchestrating learning go beyond defining rules for learning. Both concepts build on three pillars: learning tasks (and sub-tasks), learning environments, and procedural rules. Orchestrating learning crucially depends on the coordination of the relations between these pillars.

Koper and Specht [4] argue that related coordination problems can be identified at different levels of complexity of the learning environment. New tools and services can enrich the learning environment in ways that meet the learning needs of lifelong learners. Furthermore, the authors emphasize the relation between services and roles in learner communities at the different levels.

Based on the research on educational design, orchestrating learning refers to the coordination and the alignment of four dimensions.

– The *roles* that are involved in the educational activities and the interplay of the different social planes [14].
– The *learning tasks* include the main learning tasks [13], supportive tasks, and part tasks [24].
– The *learning environment* includes all kinds of services, knowledge resources [4], just-in-time and supportive information [24].
– The *rules and directives* for the educational process include the timing and the educational focus [14].

5 Modelling Concepts of IMS LD

The four dimensions of orchestrating learning are directly supported by the semantic structure of IMS LD across all complexity levels of the specification (see Table 1).

IMS LD provides two basic role types that are involved in a UoL: the learner role and the teacher role. The learner role refers to those participants of a UoL that follow the educational design in order to meet the learning objectives. The teacher role refers to those participants in a UoL that facilitate and moderate the educational process and support the learners. Based on these basic types a designer can model sub-roles for specific aspects of an educational design. One important feature of IMS LD's sub-roles is that they can be used for grouping.

Learning tasks are called "learning activities" in the IMS LD terminology. Based on the separation of learning and supporting roles, IMS LD provides the concept of "support activities". Each learning activity has a description and a completion rule. Additionally, learning activities may have prerequisites and learning objectives defined. The activity descriptions, prerequisites, and objectives provide information that helps the participants to interpret the activity and act according to the set expectations. The completion rule defines when a learning activity has to be considered as completed. A learning activity can either be infinite or completed by user choice, based on a time limit, or (for IMS LD Level B and C) if a predefined condition is met. For IMS LD Level B and C it is important to understand that the completion state of an activity is terminal. In other words, "completing" an activity is like a school degree: once it has been achieved, it cannot be repeated. At IMS LD Level A this constraint is not relevant because at this level it is only possible to define linear, loop free educational designs.

The concept of the learning environment is directly reflected in IMS LD. The learning environment is a concept for bundling resources, tools, and services in the terminology of IMS LD. Through this concept it is possible to model arrangements of resources and tools that can be used across learning activities. For example, if an environment contains a discussion forum that is linked to different learning activities, the learners will find the same postings that were posted in an earlier activity, in a later learning activity. If the discussion forum service is used in different environments, it means that different discussions are planned.

IMS LD provides several structures and semantic concepts for defining rules and directives for structuring the educational process itself. IMS LD Level A allows orchestration of learning activities, roles, and environments at the level of the educational design's method and at the level of *activity-structures*.

Activity-structures are constructs to arrange learning activities into more complex structures. From the design perspective, activity-structures are handled the same way as learning activities. IMS LD offers two types of structures: activity sequences and selections. Activity sequences define that the learning activities have to be followed in the order given in the activity-structure. Selections allow educational designers to model in a way that learners can choose one or more activities. For selections a designer can specify how many learning activities have to be selected from the structure before the structure is considered as completed. Through nesting of learning activities and activity-structures, designers can model basic processes.

Modelling personalization features using activity-structures is independent from the role that will perform the activity. Thus, this approach emphasizes the relation between learning activities. Modelling directives with activity structures commonly starts with conceptualising the process from the macro processes down to the individual learning activities. The initial step of modelling activity-structures is based on the decision of the initial step of processing the activity-structure.

In IMS LD the method may include more than one approach to reach the learning goal of a UoL. In the IMS LD terminology these approaches are called 'plays'. Each play connects the learning activities with a role that is expected to perform this activity in the current play. Different plays can refer to the same learning activities but assign them to different roles. By choosing alternative roles at the beginning of a UoL, learners can choose between different approaches. The actual association of learning activities to roles is done in *acts*. All plays in IMS LD have at least one act. Acts serve as synchronisation points for all participants in a play. This means that if an act is completed, it is completed for all participants in the same play.

The modelling strategy for role-play-based personalization requires for each play of the UoL a primary learner role. All learning activities within the play will be assigned to this role. In more complex scenarios in which learners are assigned to new roles in the process of the play at least the initial learning activities in this play have to be assigned to the primary role. Furthermore, it is necessary that also the subsequentially assigned roles are not connected to activities in multiple plays, otherwise the activities of the different play may appear out of the context to the learner. During the modelling of such a UoL, learners can either choose a role for their preferred approach or they are assigned to different roles. For example, the default of the CopperCore runtime engine is that learners can choose for themselves.

IMS LD Level B adds properties and conditions through which designers can include information models and logical constraints into their educational designs. The approach is related to generic user modelling [25]. Properties provide an abstraction for recording, representing, provisioning, and evaluating characteristics of learners and groups and their behaviour. Conditions allow expressing assumptions and generalising one or more types of learner characteristics in relation to the UoL. Three types of information models can be distinguished in IMS LD: the course information model, the group information model, and the user information model.

The *course information model* is based on generic properties. Within one instance of a UoL the value of these properties is shared with all participants. These properties can be used to model course wide contexts. The *group information model* is based on role-properties. The information of these properties is shared with all members of the same role – or if a role can have multiple instances within a UoL the information is shared with all members of the same instance of the role. This restriction allows to model group activity within a UoL. The *user information model* is based on personal-properties. Personal-properties refer to information that is different for every participant. These information models can be used to define rules for the orchestration. In IMS LD these rules are expressed through if-then statements. The conditional part of these statements refers to the property models or to a small number of process states for the UoL. Each condition has a consequence that is defined in the "then"-clause. An instructional designer can hide and show different parts of the educational design or set the value of properties. Hiding and showing includes learning activities, learning environments, plays, and HTML content fragments. Furthermore, authors can trigger notifications based on conditions on IMS LD Level C.

Table 1. Relation between orchestration dimensions and IMS LD concepts

Dimensions of Orchestrating Learning	IMS LD Semantic Concepts
Learning tasks	Learning activity
	Support activity
Learning environment	Environment
Orchestration rules	Activity-structure
	Play
	Act
	Role-part
	Personal-property[a]
	Role-property[a]
	Property[a]
	Condition[a]
	Notification[b]
Roles involved in the educational process	Learner role
	Teacher role
	(inherited roles)

[a]: only IMS LD Level B and Level C; [b]: only IMS LD Level C

6 Practical Aspects of Modelling Personalised Learning with IMS LD

The previous section analysed the relation between the dimensions of orchestrating learning and the semantic concepts of IMS LD. This section analyses how IMS LD concepts reflect personalisation in educational designs and orchestration scripts. This analysis is based on two variations of the UoL "Modern Architecture: Skyscrapers and Residential Homes" [26, 27]. This UoL has been developed on top of MACE Metadata Services [28]. The UoL provides a self-study course and does not include collaboration features.

The first variation of the UoL is entirely modelled on IMS LD Level A and illustrates personalisation concepts and service integration. This UoL is based on the MACE IMS LD Template [29]. The second variation of the UoL is modelled on IMS LD Level B and models an adaptive and personalised approach to the learning objectives of the UoL. Both variations are based on almost the same learning activities. This allows comparing differences in the modelling approaches for modelling personalised learning using the available concepts of IMS LD. Both UoLs were modelled with the ReCourse Editor [30] and tested with the SLED/CopperCore 3.4 runtime [31].

6.1 Common Outline of the Unit "Modern Architecture: Skyscrapers and Residential Homes"

The UoL "Modern Architecture: Skyscrapers and Residential Homes" focuses on modern architecture based on two construction styles – skyscrapers and residential homes. The selected buildings for representing the construction styles are from three architects: Frank L. Wright, Frank O. Gehry, and Ludwig Mies van der Rohe. For each architect one building of each construction style is discussed in the UoL. This leads to three tracks for the educational design. Every track brings different objects from one architect together.

The core design is based on a general introduction, followed by introductions into the main areas (skyscrapers and residential homes), a user selectable sequence of the architect tracks, and a final reflection activity.

Furthermore, the educational design is based on five learning activities that describe and define what the learner should do. The activities also require the learning process and help the learner to organise learning individually. The following learning activities are in both educational designs integrated: *search, explore, study, summarise,* and *reflect*.

Every learning activity has a provided learning environment in which all objects and tools for learning are available. MACE offers a set of various possibilities to utilise the MACE portal with its tools and services in education. MACE stands for 'Metadata for Architectural Contents in Europe'. In this project an Internet-based information system was developed that links up major international architectural archives with data records about completed and presently planned construction projects.

The MACE portal offers several possibilities to search and browse content: 'Filtered Search', 'Browse by Classification', 'Browse by Competence', 'Browse by Location', and 'Social Search'. But it also allocates various contents and real world objects from all over the world. Through these functions learners can search architectural content from different repositories, using metadata for filtering, visualizing results, or defining search parameters. MACE allows to navigate metadata in order to access content repositories through a toolset for a critical mass of digital content for learning with semantically well-defined metadata and associated formal descriptions that give meaning to metadata. Metadata enables new forms of explorative learning, integration of rich content in formal educational processes, or self-directed learning for ongoing professional development. These tools enable the application of quality-content-based services and are integrated in the learning environment of the UoL "Modern Architecture: Skyscrapers and Residential Homes" as well as related contents from MACE additionally to other online resources like documents, books or websites.

The learning objectives in this UoL are based on the standardised definition of architecture competences [32, 33]. The core targets for "Modern Architecture: Skyscrapers and Residential Homes" are

1. - Obtain adequate knowledge of the history and theories of architecture and the related arts, technologies and human sciences;
2. - Understand the relationship between people and buildings, and between buildings and their environment, and the need to relate buildings and the spaces between them to human needs and scale;
3. - Understand the profession of architecture and the role of the architect in society, in particular in preparing briefs that take account of social factors;
4. - Understand the structural design, constructional and engineering problems associated with building design.

These learning objectives define the learning outcomes that a learner should achieve through the UoL.

6.2 Orchestrating Learning on IMS LD Level A

IMS LD Level A structures are commonly not considered for personalization and adaptation. This does not mean that it is completely impossible to consider personalisation for an educational design. However, the available semantic structures at this level restrict the possible personalization to adaptive sequencing.

Three semantic features of IMS LD can be used at this level to define orchestration rules. These features are roles, plays, and activity-structures. In the terminology of IMS LD roles group participants that do different things or similar things differently than participants of other roles. Therefore, a separate learner role is required for each approach to reach a learning goal. Plays define the educational approach of a UoL. IMS LD does not limit the number of plays in a UoL. Each play refers to a distinct approach to meet the learning objectives. This means that typically learners will not change the play they have chosen or were assigned to. While plays are rather fundamental differences in the educational approach, activity-structures offer small-scale variations within one approach. This allows to model different pathways through a framing play. In real world scenarios, the two modelling approaches will be used in combination, as it is discussed below.

For the UoL "Modern Architecture: Skyscrapers and Residential Homes" all plays have a single act. This means that synchronization of the participants of an instance of this UoL is neither required nor possible.

The UoL consists of two plays that offer different pathways through the learning activities, while these plays are based on the same learning activities. The only difference between the approaches is the arrangement of the learning activities in activity-structures of the two plays.

The first play provides an architect-centred approach, in which the learners are guided through the curriculum based on the works of a single architect at the time once they have passed the introduction phase. Once all learning activities have been completed, the learner enters a reflection and assessment phase. Because of the sequential structure of this approach it is primarily based on a sequence structure. For the different sub-topics a learner can choose the learning activity or track to start with. In order to complete the activity-structures the learner has to perform all activities and follow all tracks within the structure.

The second play offers a building-type-centred approach that focuses on comparing similar buildings before learning more about the architects who designed the buildings. The reflection activities are aligned with the related topics. At the beginning of this approach, learners can choose the focus to start with. Therefore, the primary activity-structure is based on a selection of one out of two possible tracks.

The sequences of introducing, intensifying, and reflecting on a type of building can be found in both tracks in different arrangements within the two tracks of the second play. Therefore, these sequences were modelled as individual activity structures that can be reused in different arrangements. Typically, instructional designers define these structures in the interface of an IMS LD editor and do not bother about the underlying XML data format.

Because sequence and selection activity-structures depend on learning activities that are completed, the completion condition of all learning activities has been set to "user-choice". This allows the learners to indicate if they have finished a given activity and wish to proceed on their learning path.

6.3 Orchestrating Learning on IMS LD Level B

The options for modelling variations and personalisation of learning paths are limited in IMS LD Level A. IMS LD Level B introduces basic user-, group-, and concept-modelling features through properties and conditions. While these concepts provide more flexibility for including personalization and adaptive behaviour, it is also necessary to follow a different approach to model the adaptive behaviour.

The semantic features that are used at this level are plays, roles, properties, conditions, show, and hide. The modelling approach using plays and roles is the same as in IMS LD Level A. Instead of using different roles to define different learning approaches, personal properties are used to identify the learner's state within the process of the UoL. This allows the modelling of fine-grained personalized variations inside a play. The personalization is achieved through conditions. Conditions provide the underpinning for orchestrating a UoL and allow the modelling of more complex educational approaches. This includes didactical loops, content adaptation, conditional availability of learning activities, and interactive process control. The "show" and "hide" elements indicate if a learning activity should be made available or hidden for the learner.

For maximizing the flexibility for personalization and adaptation, properties and conditions replace activity-structures. Avoiding activity-structures for Level B UoLs allows easier integration of new adaptation and personalization rules. Furthermore, it is useful to mark all learning activities as "infinite" because of the terminal definition of the completion state in IMS LD. This step is required if learners are expected to repeat certain learning activities. Furthermore, only the initial learning activity is initially available, the visibility of all other activities is set as hidden.

The IMS LD Level B variation of the "Modern Architecture: Skyscrapers and Residential Homes" integrates the architect-track, the skyscraper-track, and the residential-home-track into a single play. The learners are allowed to freely work through the different tracks depending on their interests. After the general introduction of the UoL, the learner can set a preference of a topic to begin with. This preference can be either "skyscrapers" or "residential homes". This choice activates the introduction to the topic and as soon as the learner feels comfortable, the three related learning activities for this topic are activated as well. Each learning activity has a dedicated learning environment that includes a note-taking tool assigned. This allows the learner to take notes while performing a learning activity. When the learner has taken notes related to the active building, the biography of its architect and a related residential house from the same architect are activated. As soon as a learner has completed one of the three tracks a reflection activity for this track becomes available. This reflection activity is an assignment and includes all notes that have been taken in relation to the track. As soon as the learner is satisfied with the results of the reflection assignment the learner can submit the results. If all reflection assignments are submitted, the UoL is completed.

This educational design can be based entirely on personal-properties. Besides personal-properties for storing notes and choices, the UoL has some properties that are required for sequencing. These properties are used to compensate the "completed" flag: instead of completing a learning activity only a property 'task-complete-ID' is set, where ID is replaced by the mnemonic name of the related activity. For the learning activities with a note-taking environment, this flag is modelled through a condition that checks if the learner has taken a note. The task-complete-property is also used for the reflection activities to identify if the reflection assignment of this activity has been submitted. The properties are set and notes are stored by embedding global-elements in activity descriptions and in the note-taking tool. The difference is transparent to the learners, because in both variations the learners mark that they have finished an activity.

A set of 20 conditions handles the sequencing within the UoL. Most of the conditions are simple tests, on the task-complete-properties or if a note has taken. The more complex conditions are used to test if one of the main three tracks or the entire UoL has been finished. All conditions are required for making the next learning activities available to the learner by showing them.

7 Comparison and Gap Analysis

The previous section outlined the concepts for adaptive educational designs using IMS LD Level A and Level B. The first variation of the UoL was modelled using entirely Level A concepts. The example shows that it is possible to include elements of personalization into educational designs and to provide learners with (limited) control based on basic orchestration rules. The second variation of the educational design utilizes primarily IMS LD Level B concepts for defining the orchestration script. As reported by previous research the available semantic structure provides a powerful instrument for outlining the information of user models that are relevant for orchestration process and to model learning activities with great freedom for the learners.

The main difference between the two variants is that activity-structures are not used in the second UoL. The main problem with activity-structures within IMS LD

Level B designs is that selection and sequencing conditions of the structure rely on the completion state of the activities. This hinders learners to retry a learning activity, because once a learning activity has completed it cannot be uncompleted and thus not repeated. The second variation of the UoL discussed in this paper, allows learners to move back to previous learning activities if they realize that their notes are insufficient for mastering the reflection activity. In order to achieve this it is required that a learning activity cannot be completed in the sense of the IMS LD specification. Consequently, it is not possible to combine the two variants into a single UoL if both approaches use the same learning activities. In order to work around this problem, it would be necessary to "clone" the original learning activity so the cloned learning activity uses the same data items and environments as the original activity. However, this way of duplicating learning activities is not supported by the ReCourse editor. Moreover, this technique is prone to errors: e.g. if the instructional designer decides to replace items or environments of one of the learning activity, the other learning activity would not be aware of these changes.

From an orchestration perspective IMS LD includes all aspects for *prearranging* a learning scenario. For defining orchestration rules, IMS LD offers features for enabling instructional designers to define how a UoL can be personalized. The perspective of these rules is mainly task-centred with presentation related aspects. This has consequences for the orchestration related to roles and learning environment.

Roles in IMS LD are only defined as grouping mechanisms for the participants in a UoL. Many aspects related to the orchestration of roles are explicitly considered as external to the specification. Therefore, the specification is lacking of semantics for modelling role assignment and role structures. Consequently, it is not possible to model explicit rules for assigning learners to different roles based on the results of an assessment, so they can follow tailored learning paths. In IMS LD this can be achieved only implicitly by setting up a support activity.

Environments are used to connect learning activities with the learning tools that are required for an activity such as knowledge resources or educational services. IMS LD considers this relation as unidirectional, which means that the learning activity determines what environments are available. From an orchestration perspective the relation between activities and their environment appears bidirectional. This implies that being in an environment can also determine possible learning activities. Such behaviour can be partly modelled with special conditions and pseudo learning activities. Additionally, such a workaround would require interaction elements. Alternatively, external services might update "global" properties, which would trigger related conditions in a UoL. However, this second workaround is partly implicit for the orchestration process and it requires implementation of specific knowledge about the underlying property management system.

8 Conclusion and Future Work

This paper analysed the relation between the concepts of IMS LD and orchestrating learning in order to identify approaches and gaps for creating orchestration scripts. The research integrates perspectives from the research on adaptive systems and instructional design theory. Based on analyzing the previous research four fundamental aspects for orchestrating learning were identified. Based on this background a UoL for studying "Modern Architecture: Skyscrapers and Residential Homes" has been modelled in two variants with IMS LD Level A and Level B features for the integration of personalization aspects. It has been shown that even with IMS LD Level A it is possible to define UoLs with limited personalization features. For more flexible orchestration scripts IMS LD Level B offers richer semantics that allows the integration of basic user-modelling approaches. The variations of the UoL demonstrate possible personalization features. The gap analysis extended this view to those aspects of orchestrating learning that could not get modelled in IMS LD. The gap analysis indicates that IMS LD has a primarily task-centred approach to orchestration. Role- or environmental-centred orchestration can be only achieved with complex workarounds or have to be modelled implicitly.

The present research focuses on personalisation and adaptation aspects for orchestrating learning using the IMS LD specification. Future research will carry on these findings and analyses the identification of possible semantic extensions that allow simpler and more explicit orchestration scripts that can be based on IMS LD.

Acknowledgements. The research presented in this paper has been partly sponsored by the GRAPPLE project (www.grapple-project.org) funded by the European Commission's 7th Framework Programme and iCOPER best-practice network (www.icoper.org) within the European Commission's eContentPlus programme.

References

[1] IMS Global Learning Consortium: Learning Design Specification. Technical specification, IMS Global Learning Consortium (2003),
   http://www.imsglobal.org/learningdesign/
[2] Jeffery, A., Currier, S.: What Is ...IMS Learning Design? Cetis, Standards Briefings Series. JISC (2003),
   http://zope.cetis.ac.uk/lib/media/WhatIsLD_web.pdf
[3] Koper, R., Tattersall, C.: Learning Design: A Handbook on Modelling and Delivering Networked Education and Training. Springer, Heidelberg (2005)
[4] Koper, R., Specht, M.: TEN-Competence: Life-Long Competence Development and Learning. In: Cicilia, M.-A. (ed.) Competencies in Organizational e-learning: concepts and tools, pp. 234–252. IGI-Global, Hershey (2008)
[5] Sharples, P., Griffiths, D., Scott, W.: Using Widgets to Provide Portable Services for IMS Learning Design. In: Koper, R., Stefanov, K., Dicheva, D. (eds.) Stimulating Personal Development and Knowledge Sharing, Sofia, Bulgaria, October, 30-31, pp. 57–60 (2008)
[6] Sutherland, R., Joubert, M.: D1.1: The STELLAR Vision and Strategy Statement. Project Report. Stellar project. Unpublished Report, Stellar NoE (2010)
[7] Berlanga, A.J., Gracía, F.J.: IMS LD reusable elements for adaptive learning designs. Journal of Interactive Media in Education 2005(11), 1–16 (2005),
   http://jime.open.ac.ul/2005/11
[8] Burgos, D., Tattersall, C., Koper, R.: How to represent adaptation in eLearning with IMS Learning Design. Interactive Learning Environments 15(2), 161–170 (2007)

9. Specht, M., Burgos, D.: Implementing Adaptive Educational Methods with IMS Learning Design. In: Proceedings of the ADALE Workshop at the AH 2006 Conference (2006), http://hdl.handle.net/1820/718
10. Aroyo, L., Dolog, P., Houben, G., Kravcik, M., Naeve, A., Nilsson, M., et al.: Interoperability in Personalized Adaptive Learning. Educational Technology & Society 9(2), 4–18 (2006)
11. Verpoorten, D., Glahn, C., Kravcik, M., Ternier, S., Specht, M.: Personalisation of Learning in Virtual Learning Environments. In: Cress, U., Dimitrova, V., Specht, M. (eds.) EC-TEL 2009. LNCS, vol. 5794, pp. 52–66. Springer, Heidelberg (2009)
12. Dron, J.: Control and Constraint in E-Learning: Choosing When to Choose. IGI Publishing, Hershey (2007)
13. Goodyear, P., Yang, D.: Patterns and pattern languages in educational design. In: Lockyer, L., Bennett, S., Agostinho, S., Harper, B. (eds.) Handbook of Research on Learning Design and Learning Objects: Issues, Applications and Technologies, pp. 167–187. IGI Global, Hershey (2009)
14. Dillenbourg, P.: Integrating technologies into educational ecosystems. Distance Education 29(2), 127–140 (2008)
15. Brusilovsky, P.: Adaptive hypermedia. User Modeling and User-Adapted Interaction 11, 87–110 (2001)
16. Koper, R.: Current Research in Learning Design. Educational Technology & Society 9(1), 13–22 (2005)
17. IMS Global Learning Consortium: IMS Learning Design Information Model. Technical specification, IMS Global Learning Consortium (2003), http://www.imsglobal.org/learningdesign/ldv1p0/imsld_infov1p0.html
18. Paramythis, A., Loidl-Reisinger, S.: Adaptive learning environments and e-learning standards. Electronic Journal of eLearning, EJEL 2(1), 182–194 (2004), http://www.ejel.org/volume-2/vol2-issue1/issue1-art11-paramythis.pdf
19. Van Rosmalen, P., Vogten, H., van Es, R., Passier, H., Poelmans, P., Koper, R.: Authoring a full life cycle model in standards-based, adaptive e-learning. Educational Technology & Society 9(1), 72–83 (2006)
20. Harrigan, M., Wade, V.: Towards a conceptual and service-based adaptation model. In: Proceedings of the International Workshop on Dynamic and Adaptive Hypertext: Generic Frameworks, Approaches and Techniques (2009)
21. Van der Sluijs, K., Höver, K.M.: Integrating adaptive functionality in a LMS. International Journal of Emerging Technologies in Learning (iJET) 4(4), 46–50 (2009)
22. Vogten, H.: Design and implementation strategies for IMS Learning Design. Doctoral Thesis. CELSTEC, Open University in The Netherlands, Heerlen, The Netherlands (2008)
23. GRAPPLE project: Project summary (2009), http://www.grapple-project.org/summary
24. Van Merriënboer, J.J.G., Clark, R.E., de Croock, M.B.M.: Blueprints for Complex Learning: The 4C/ID-Model. Educational Technology. Research and Development 50(4), 39–64 (2002)
25. Kobsa, A.: Generic User Modeling Systems. User Modeling and User-Adapted Interaction 11(1-2), 49–63 (2001)
26. Gruber, M.R., Glahn, C.: IMS-LD Modern Architecture: Skyscrapers and Residential Homes Level A. IMS content package, Heerlen, The Netherlands (2010), http://hdl.handle.net/1820/2550

[27] Gruber, M.R., Glahn, C.: IMS-LD Modern Architecture: Skyscrapers and Residential Homes Level B. IMS content package, Heerlen, The Netherlands (2010), http://hdl.handle.net/1820/2551
[28] Stefaner, M., et al.: MACE. Joint Deliverable JD11: Evaluation of the MACE system. Project report (2009), http://dspace.ou.nl/handle/1820/2193
[29] Gruber, M.R., Börner, D., Ternier, S.: MACE for Educators (2009), http://www.mace-project.eu/index.php?-option=com_content&-task=blogsection&id=6&Itemid=87
[30] Beauvoir, P., Griffith, D., Sharples, P.: Learning Design Authoring tools in the TENCompetence Project. In: Koper, R. (ed.) Learning Network Services for Professional Development, pp. 379–387. Springer, Heidelberg (2009)
[31] TENCompetence Foundation: TENCompetence Learning Design Services for Coppercore Service Integration. TENCompetence Foundation (2009), http://tencompetence-project.bolton.ac.uk/-ldruntime/-index.html
[32] European Parliament & Council of the European Union: Directive 2005/36/EC on the recognition of professional qualifications. European Union, Brussels and Strasbourg (2005)
[33] Council of the European Union: Council Directive on the mutual recognition of diplomas, certificate and other evidence of formal qualifications in architecture, including measures to facilitate the effective exercise of the right of establishment and freedom to provide services (85/384/EEC). European Union, Strasbourg (1985)

Management of Assessment Resources in a Federated Repository of Educational Resources

Israel Gutiérrez Rojas, Derick Leony, Andrés Franco, Raquel M. Crespo,
Abelardo Pardo, and Carlos Delgado Kloos

Universidad Carlos III de Madrid, Telematic Engineering Department,
Av. de la Universidad 30, 28911 Leganés (Madrid) - Spain
{igutierrez,afranco}@inv.it.uc3m.es,
{dleony,rcrespo,abel,cdk}@it.uc3m.es

Abstract. This article tries to shed some light over the management of assessment resources in a repository of educational resources from an outcome-based perspective. The approximation to this problem is based on the ICOPER Reference Model, as a model to capture e-learning data, services and processes, addressing an interoperability approach. To demonstrate this proposal, a prototype has been implemented. This article also describes the design and development of this prototype that accesses a repository of educational resources (the Open ICOPER Content Space - OICS), the main features of the prototype, the development environment and the evaluation that is being performed.

Keywords: assessment resources, .LRN, federated repository, IMS QTI, OICS.

1 Introduction

Sharing assessment resources among teachers and course developers is a feature that has a great potential. The exposition in this article tries to shed some light over this feature and provides a solution by means of an application prototype. The learning management systems (LMSs) are the entry point for the mentioned stakeholders to the educational resources used by an institution. A possible solution for sharing assessment resources among learning management systems (LMSs) would be to use an information repository, such as the Open ICOPER [1] Content Space (henceforth referred to as OICS). By doing so, assessment content and information could be centralized and the material would be accessible from any other platform. All contents could be downloaded from a single centralized site, thus simplifying the integration of different LMS and interoperability.

There have been some initiatives for creating Open Educational Resources (OER) repositories, like the JISC OER program [2], which purpose is "make a significant amount of existing learning resources freely available online, licensed in such away to enable them to be used and repurposed worldwide." Some of these repositories contain assessment resources in several formats (e.g., IMS QTI [3]), like Fetlar [4] that collect maths assessment using IMS QTI and Bioscience UKOER project, whose resources can be accessed through JorumOpen [5].

In order to realize the exchange of assessment resources, a common assessment specification must be used. Although IMS QTI 1.2.1 presents deficiencies and limitations, as discussed in [6], it is nevertheless considered a de facto standard by the industry. It is also the most popular version nowadays and the one currently endorsed by the IMS Global Learning Consortium. Thus, this is the specification selected in order to widen the scope of the repository, accomplish universal access and allow it to provide services for both authoring tools as well as LMSs.

One important ICOPER task is to corroborate that the assessment model proposed in [7] fits properly in the ICOPER Reference Model (IRM). It is also needed to validate that the proposed model can support any kind of assessment scenario that a higher education institution may present. The process to perform this validation consisted of the development of a prototype of an assessment application that connects to the OICS. This prototype would help to demonstrate that the proposed IEEE LOM [8] profile, presented in the third section, provides a proper set of metadata information to exchange and work with learner assessments.

The ICOPER Reference Model (IRM) is a model based on the state-of-the-art in standards and specifications in the field that support learning outcome-driven content management in Technology-Enhanced Learning (TEL). The main objectives of this conceptual model are [9]:

- To describe the domain of outcome-based, technology-enhanced learning.
- To illustrate the structure of the reference model to support stakeholders to develop, use and improve (information and communication) systems for outcome-based learning.
- To initiate a discourse process on the reference model.
- To incorporate best practices to a common body of knowledge around this model.

The model consists of the following levels:

- Processes: key processes for the development, use, and improvement of outcome-based learning.
- Services: a classification and a description format as well as a collection of (technical) services that can be incorporated when developing outcome-based learning systems.
- Data: data models for data and information exchange between teaching and learning systems to improve interoperability.

This article is structured as follows: after the introduction of the problem and the ICOPER reference model, in section 2 the learner assessment is presented in the context of the IRM; after that, section 3 provides a perspective of the learner assessment and related concepts from the point of view of interoperability and proposes a metadata model for complementing the assessment resources; section 4 deals with the design and implementation of a prototype that permits teachers and course developers to manage and share assessment resources; finally, section 5 presents the conclusions of this work and the future works.

2 Learner Assessment in the ICOPER Reference Model

According to the ICOPER reference model presented in the previous section, the role of the learner assessment in the different levels is the following.

Processes. Two key processes have been identified related to the assessment process. The first one is the "Assessment planning" carried out by the learning supporter, i.e., a teacher or instructor. It consists of searching assessment resources that cover the intended learning outcomes of the learner. If the learning supporter finds a suitable resource (i.e., that addresses intended outcomes) from existing repository, it will be reused; otherwise, the learning supporter will create a new assessment resource. After that, the resources could be annotated, e.g., with student performance, and published if the learning supporter decides to do it. This process is represented in Fig. 1.

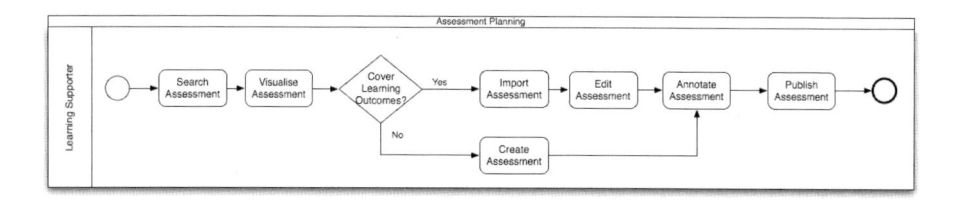

Fig. 1. Assessment planning process

The second process is the "Learner Assessment Activities" and describes the activities carried out by the learning supporter and the learner during the assessment process runtime. The delivery process is driven by the learning supporter, which allows the learner to visualize and answer the assessment, and then submit the response. Then is the turn of the learning supporter to appraise the learner response what generates some assessment results that could be visualized by the learner. This process is represented in Fig. 2.

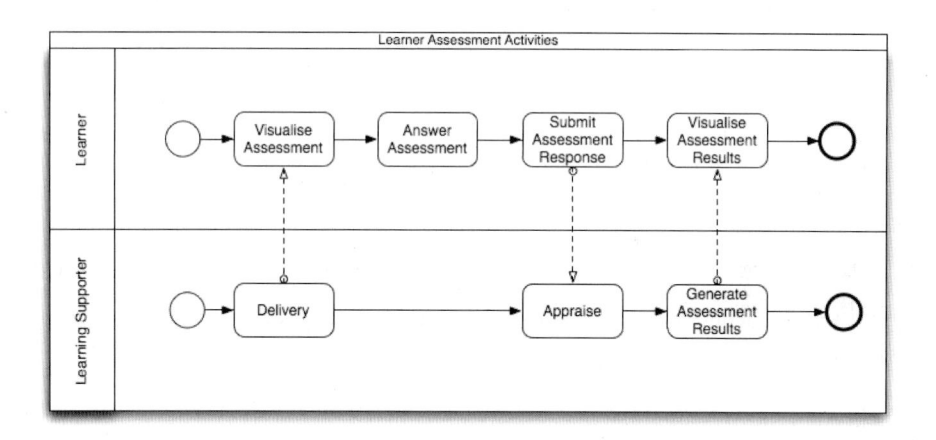

Fig. 2. Learner Assessment Activities process

Services. Three generic services have been identified for assessment purpose. These are a) the search and retrieval of resources, i.e., a service that allows search of assessment resources by some filter parameters; b) the publication of resources, i.e., a service that allows to publish resource information in a common shared virtual space; and c) a repository service, i.e., a service that allows storage of resources themselves. These generic services could be used as reference in concrete assessment use cases.

Data. At this level, there are two different parts to mention. The first one is an IMS QTI profile that is being developed in the ICOPER project as a best practice result. This profile is being developed taking into account the different implementations of the specification in European institutions. The second one is based on the relation of the assessment process to other e-learning aspects, like learning outcomes and units of learning. This result is presented in the next section as an IEEE LOM profile.

3 Learner Assessment Interoperability

The assessment interoperability proposal made in this section is twofold: on one hand, a connection to other e-learning concepts has to be achieved; on the other, a set of recommendations to simplify the IMS QTI usage has to be made due to the problems found in [6], like flexibility handicaps, version instability and incomplete support in assessment tools.

3.1 Learner Assessment Related Concepts

The IMS QTI data model does not include elements for representing or linking to concepts related to other learning aspects of the ICOPER Reference Model (IRM). For example, the unit of learning, the learning outcome or the assessment record are concepts that are related to assessment but not supported by IMS QTI data model. On the other hand, IMS QTI includes information about assessment resources (data level), but it does not provide information of learner assessment, like context (i.e., the set of educational elements that is external to and adds meaning to an achieved learning outcome or Learning Opportunity [9]). Learner Assessment was defined as the process of testing the learning outcomes (knowledge, skills and/or competences) attained by an individual learner and providing the corresponding information reporting about the student achievements and/or potential indications for improving them. As explained in [10], in Higher Education contexts it comprises identifying, collecting and preparing data to evaluate the achievement of program outcomes and program educational objectives.

The integration of assessment concepts and other e-learning process building blocks translates into a series of benefits. For example, the relation of learner assessment to learning outcomes results in the possibility of searching learner assessments in a repository based on the intended learning outcomes. On the other hand, the relation to units of learning stored in a repository results in getting assessment material attached to a specific unit of learning. Finally, the relation to assessment records (through assessment results) is necessary to access grades and feedback achieved by a learner attached to a particular assessment record, e.g., a certificate, and to update the learner profile or PALO (Personal Achieved Learning Outcomes) [11].

In Fig. 3, the Learner Assessment (LA) concept has been defined as an entity that contains all the data related to the assessment process. It includes the assessment resources and implements one or more assessment methods. Besides, the Unit of Learning

(UoL) is related to the Learner Assessment used in the UoL. Finally, the assessment results (using IMS QTI format) will be normalized into assessment records; this part is still work in progress in the context of ICOPER. The relation between learning methods (that include Teaching Methods and Assessment Methods, that are a special type of them) and the intended learning outcome definitions (LOD) is not going to be developed in the OICS prototype. The main reason is that the real linkage to the learning outcomes is already done from the unit of learning/learner assessment (contextualized versions of the learning methods). The only types of learning outcomes missing are the generic skills (e.g. presentation skills), which are acquired in several UoL/LA, but they are not the main objective of the UoL. An in depth research will be performed to determinate how to deal with this type of learning outcomes.

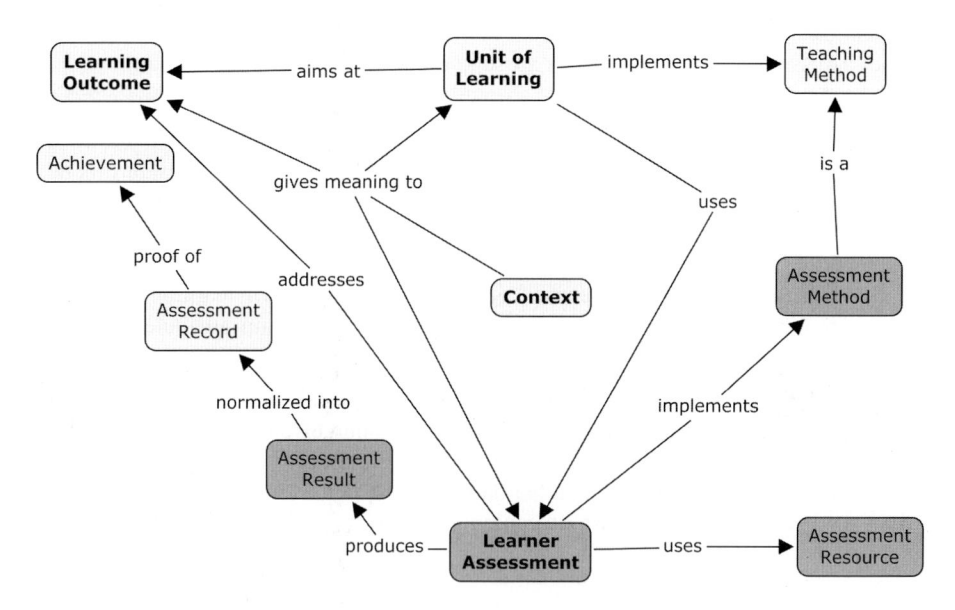

Fig. 3. Learner assessment and related concepts

Another concept not covered by the previous analysis is the assessment method. The assessment method describes the assessment methodology applied, completely specifying all the features that characterize the different dimensions of the assessment process. As explained in [12], there are several dimensions to define assessment methods like:

- Objective: summative or formative assessment.
- Collaboration: individual or collaborative assessment.
- Assessor: instructor-based, computer-based, peer or self-assessment.
- Channel: writing, oral, online, simulation assessment.
- Activity type: collaboration, questions and answers (MCQ, FIB, short answer), etc.

These list of assessment method dimensions is not complete, that is, there could be some other dimensions that make sense in a concrete assessment scenario. But the dimensions concept helps to define new assessment methods.

3.2 Interoperable Assessment Resources

In this subsection a LOM profile is presented that allows the connection of the assessment resources (e.g., using IMS QTI) to other e-learning aspects, like learning outcomes and learning designs. Implementing this profile guarantees high-level assessment interoperability, i.e., interoperable assessment services and processes.

Given these ideas, the IMS QTI data model should be extended in order to provide it with these connections, as explained in [6]. The new data model should include information of assessment resources, but also define the context and the process of the learner assessment. Two possibilities arose in order to perform this extension:

- Extending IMS QTI (what would be called x-QTI) to include new metadata using IMS QTI current concepts, e.g., the new data will be included in the same QTI file. Besides, a QTI schema should be defined to present this new utilization of elements.
- Using a complementary standard for metadata representation, such as IEEE LOM or Dublin Core, that covers the concepts that IMS QTI does not cover, e.g., relation between learner assessment and a unit of learning. The main problem of choosing this option is that some metadata attributes could be duplicated in the selected standard and IMS QTI.

The second option has been chosen because the extension of IMS QTI should be transparent for the system, i.e., current IMS QTI resources could be reused. For example, a system importing assessment data formatted in x-QTI and not supporting the defined schema should ignore extended data and will import just the assessment content in a proper way. But the current implementations in LMSs could not perform this behavior.

Due to that, it was decided to define the additional metadata using a metadata schema, in concrete, an IEEE LOM profile. The selection of IEEE LOM to represent assessment metadata was based on these reasons:

- It is a mature and widely adopted standard for learning objects metadata and allows connection to other e-learning domain concepts using the Relation attributes (for existing learning objects such as UoLs) and extensions (for non-LOM ones, like LODs).
- IEEE LOM relation to IMS QTI: there is a LOM profile defined in IMS QTI 2.X which the learner assessment profile could be based on.
- Homogeneity with other learning object metadata definitions, i.e., UoLs and TM in D3.1 [13]. In this document, the advantages of using IEEE LOM instead of Dublin Core (DC) or Dublin Core Educational for describing UoL and TM are exposed. Following the same reasoning, Dublin Core proposes a too general set of metadata elements; besides, Dublin Core Educational (a DC application profile for education) requires also some extensions to represent the assessment concepts.

- The IEEE LOM profile is already implemented in the OICS thus facilitating compliance and interoperability with other learning aspects.

The LOM profile proposed for ICOPER learner assessment metadata is defined in [13]. The main concepts of learner assessment are mapped into IEEE LOM profile as follows:

- Learner Assessment is defined by all LOM attributes and categories, including annotations (LOM Learning Resource Type: "Learner Assessment"). The learning resource type "Learner Assessment" is identified as the "Assessment Item" of Resource Discovery Network/Learning and Teaching Support Network (RDN/LTSN) resource type vocabulary [14]. This vocabulary is recommended in the IMS QTI profile.
- Learning resources are presented as IMS QTI files.
- Assessment Methods are related to Learner Assessment using IEEE LOM Relation.
- Units of Learning are related to Learner Assessment through IEEE LOM Relation.

Annotations could be done using the annotation part of LOM. In IMS QTI 2.X there are also mechanisms to define statistics of usage, but they will not be used to make it simpler.

Related to assessment methods, the implementations in the defined LOM profile are as follows:

- An instance of learner assessment can use one or more assessment methods. For this reason, the LOM Relation element will be used to link both concepts.
- An assessment method (AM) is a specialization of a teaching method (TM). Thus, an AM can be described using the same metadata. Besides, the IEEE LOM Educational Learning Resource Type (LRType) for a method instances could be AM, TM or both. Given a learning method, e.g., peer review, it could be considered as a TM and as an AM at the same time. That is the reason to allow multiple learning resource types.

In order to model this concept, IEEE LOM standard was used to describe its metadata elements in the OICS. As the assessment method concept inherits from the teaching method concept, the LOM profile used is the same for TM defined in [13].

4 Prototype Design and Implementation

The design phase of the .LRN prototype is based in a set of use cases. The use cases cover the services of the ICOPER Reference Model and the assessment planning process.

As the developed prototype is intended for assessment resources management, a set of assessment use cases have been implemented in the .LRN module.

4.1 Scenarios to Be Supported by Prototype Application

The design of the prototype for the assessment application was based on a set of assessment scenarios. This set contains three scenarios that involve the use of learner assessments during the design and enactment phases of a course. The scenarios taken into account for this set are the following:

1. Reuse of assessment resources available in the OICS.
2. Annotation of assessment resources by a learning supporter from a LMS.
3. Publication of assessment resources to the OICS from a LMS or authoring tool.

In order to provide a broader view of the process to validate the application prototype, an explanation of each one of these scenarios and their implications is presented as follows.

Scenario: Reuse of assessment resources during design phase. The first scenario is the reuse of an assessment resource during the Unit of Learning (UoL) design. This scenario describes a learning supporter that is planning the learner assessment that takes part of a UoL. He/she will search for assessment resources in the OICS according to a series of parameters like:

- The intended learning outcomes (knowledge, skill, competence) of the assessment
- The assessment method (e.g., type - summative, formative, diagnostic; or by assessor: instructor, peer, self or automatic).

The learning supporter could also search resources by language, author/contributor, date, name, description, format (e.g. PDF, MS Word Document), and rights (e.g.. Creative Commons – Share Alike).

The workflow of this scenario is described as follows:

1. Search assessment resources. This search can be based on keywords, learning outcomes or assessment methods.
2. Retrieval and review of results. The result view includes this information about the learner assessment: title, language, date, description, format and rights.
3. Selection of assessment resource.
4. Import of assessment resource into a course of the LMS.

Scenario: Annotation of assessment resources. The second scenario is the annotation of assessment resources by any teacher that has used the assessment resource in a real context. This scenario describes a learning supporter that wants to annotate assessment resources with information of students' average performance on the assessment. For example, the learner supporter wants to annotate a multiple choice question (MCQ) with the percentage of students who had selected each of the options. This information can help to detect ambiguous questions and also concepts particularly difficult for the students. Thus, this information can be applied by the learning supporter him/herself or other colleagues during the planning and design phase of the next course. These annotations contain date and time information (generated automatically), and possibly some data about the course in which the information was gathered. Annotation could be used also for peer reviewing of assessment resources.

Scenario: Publication of learner assessments to the OICS. The last scenario is the publication of assessment resources to the OICS. In this case, a learning supporter wants to publish assessment resources to the OICS. To do so, the required metadata should be aggregated to the assessment resource. Therefore, the only needed step in the workflow of this scenario consists of describing assessment resources with the corresponding metadata. For example, including information about intended learning outcomes, assessment method (e.g., type - summative, formative, diagnostic; the assessor: instructor, peer, self or automatic), language, author/contributor, date, name, description, format (e.g. PDF, MS Word document), and rights (e.g. Creative Commons – Share Alike).

One example of this scenario is the following: the assessment author has already created some assessment resources in the LMS (e.g. .LRN). This LMS supports the IMS QTI assessment specification to create and store the resources. When the author decides to share resources he has to annotate them with metadata, e.g., defining intended learning outcomes, defining who the author of the resource is and indicating that the assessor for this assessment should be an instructor, because this cannot be done automatically.

4.2 Use Cases Abstracted from Scenarios

The scenarios presented in the previous sub-section allow the abstraction of a set of use cases that can be aggregated into two:

- Search of learner assessments
- Publication of learner assessments

Use case: Search of learner assessments. The application prototype, which has been developed as a module of the .LRN LMS, supports the first use case: search of learner assessments. It also completely fulfils the first scenario described in this section, thus validating the general conceptual model for the exchange of learner assessments in a real scenario.

The implementation of this use case has been possible with a high level of simplicity due to the provision of an intermediate layer between the systems and the OICS. This intermediate layer has been defined as the Middle Layer API and is being documented in the deliverable D1.2 [15]. Basically, it provides a series of services needed for learning object management: search, publication, storage, etc.

Use case: Publication of learner assessments. Regarding the publication of learner assessments, the architecture and functionality of the OICS permits the publication of assessment resources enriched with IEEE LOM metadata. The mentioned metadata fields allow users to include information that is not present in the IMS QTI resources, like intended learning outcomes, teaching methods used and annotations. The union of assessment resources and metadata is called learner assessment (LA).

Regarding to the publication possibilities that the OICS permits, the institutions could share their own repositories by means of the OAI-PMH protocol [16]. But the option chosen for this development is to upload the assessment resources directly to the OICS by means of some middle layer API methods created for this purpose, because the University Carlos III of Madrid does not have already a repository of assessment resources.

4.3 Creation of Mockups

In order to define the concrete functionalities that the prototype was going to implement, a set of mockups was created before the actual implementation. These mockups are screenshots of the main important pages of the application and show the main functionalities and the user interface. An example of a mockup for this prototype is shown in Fig. 4. These application mock-ups were not evaluated just after their production, but when the functional prototype was evaluated.

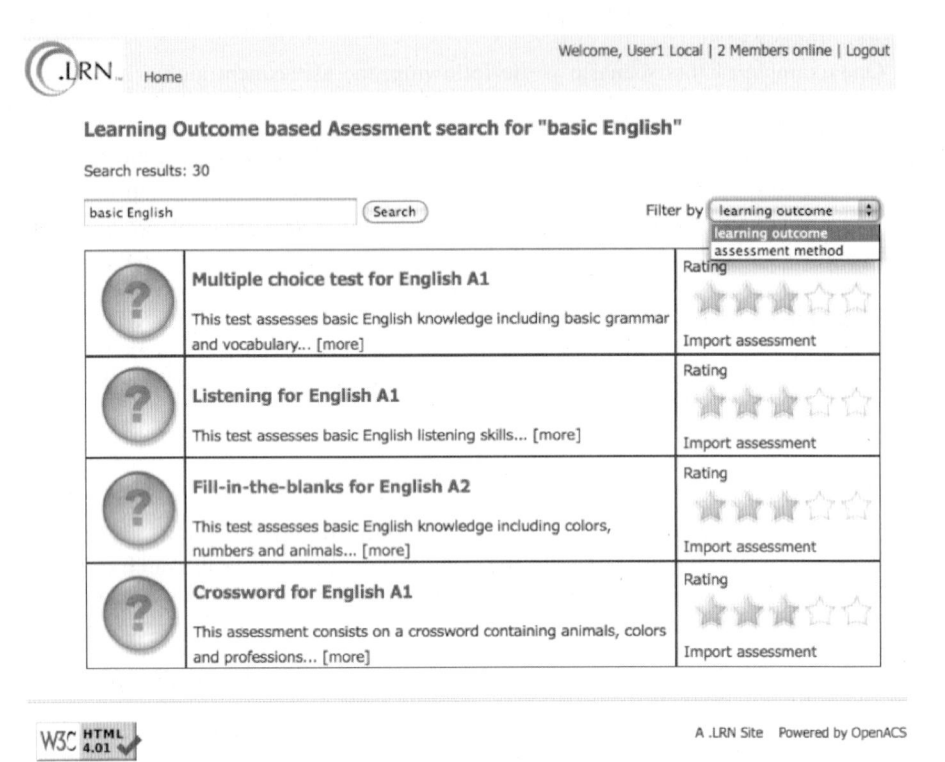

Fig. 4. Mockup of the search page of the .LRN prototype

4.4 Prototype Environment

The prototype has been implemented as a .LRN package. As stated in the .LRN website [17], .LRN is the world's most widely adopted enterprise-class open source software for supporting e-learning and digital communities. Originally developed at MIT, .LRN is used worldwide by over half a million users in higher education, government, non-profit, and K-12.

The selection of .LRN as the learning management system for the OICS prototype development has been quite clear, because this platform provides us with the required features for this development. For instance, it already has a package for authoring and managing assessment resources using IMS QTI 1.2.1, so the implemented prototype could make use of these capabilities. Another reason to choose this framework was the expertise and satisfactory results obtained from previous experiences with the platform in other research projects.

4.5 Prototype Evaluation

The prototype evaluation, according to the methodology defined in the ICOPER project, targets three types of audience (stakeholders):

- Engineering evaluation targeted to implementers, tool developers and technology providers.
- End-user evaluation targeted to instructors, learners, curriculum developers, administration or management.
- Epistemological evaluation targeted to researchers and standardization bodies.

The first one consists of a survey about the prototype implementation and the middle layer API. It will provide the perspective of these stakeholders from a technical point of view.

In the presented prototype, the end-user evaluation targets instructors and curriculum developers. It also consists of a survey that provides us the opinion about usability and utility of this targeted audience. This evaluation will be carried out in several training events, like ECTEL 2010.

5 Conclusions and Future Work

This article has presented the design and implementation of an application prototype that permits teachers and course developers manage and share assessment resources in an easy way. The development of the prototype also helped to prove that an application could connect and interact easily with a federated repository of educational resources, the Open ICOPER Content Space, through the use of the Middle Layer API.

The implemented prototype also satisfies the requirements established by the presented scenarios and use cases, so it is supposed to fulfill stakeholders' requirements in the assessment process.

On the basis of the experience gained from the development of this prototype, a series of recommendations for assessment interoperability have been proposed. These recommendations are related to the idea of extending the IMS QTI specification in order to link it to other e-learning fields. This integration brings some benefits, which emerge in the context of e-learning material repositories with several types of content, i.e., learner assessments, units of learning, learning outcomes, etc.

As future work, this prototype will be evaluated by relevant stakeholders like assessment authors (en users, like teachers and course developers) and implementers of learning tools, in order to obtain feedback about the proposed design and workflow.

A proposal of an IMS QTI profile will be done that will contain just a minimum set of elements that guarantee interoperability, based on the study of usage of the specification and stakeholders' needs in [12]. For example, features such as adaptive questions and templates are not implemented in the studied LMSs (Moodle and .LRN) [7], so the recommendation will be not to use them.

Acknowledgments. This work was partially funded by the Best Practice Network ICOPER (Grant No. ECP-2007-EDU-417007), the Learn3 project, "Plan Nacional de I+D+I" TIN2008-05163/TSI, and the eMadrid network, S2009/TIC-1650, "Investigación y Desarrollo de tecnologías para el e-learning en la Comunidad de Madrid".

References

1. ICOPER project, http://www.icoper.org
2. JISC UK OER program, http://www.jisc.ac.uk/oer
3. IMS Global Consortium: IMS Question & Test Interoperability Specification, http://www.ims.org/question/
4. Fetlar project, http://www.fetlar.bham.ac.uk/
5. JorumOpen, http://open.jorum.ac.uk/xmlui
6. Gutiérrez Rojas, I., Agea, A., Crespo, R.M., Pardo, A., Leony, D., Delgado Kloos, C.: Assessment interoperability using QTI. In: ICL 2009 Conference, Villach, Austria, September 23-25 (2009)
7. Agea, A., Crespo, R.M., Delgado Kloos, C., Gutiérrez Rojas, I., Leony, D., Pardo, A.: Production flow description and prototype for the two platforms under study (Moodle and.LRN) including the required steps to exchange the material in both platforms. ICOPER deliverable D6.2 (February 2010), http://icoper.org/results/deliverables
8. IEEE LOM, http://ltsc.ieee.org/wg12/
9. Kozlov, D., Pulkkinen, M., Pawlowski, J.: ICOPER Reference Model IRM. Conceptual Model. ICOPER deliverable D7.1 (October 2009)
10. ABET: Accreditation Policy and Procedure Manual (2008-2009)
11. Najjar, J., et al.: ISURE: Model for describing learning needs and learning opportunities taking context ontology modelling into account. ICOPER deliverable D2.1 (January 2010) http://icoper.org/results/deliverables
12. Agea, A., Crespo, R.M., Delgado Kloos, C., Gutiérrez Rojas, I., Leony, D., Pardo, A.: Analysis of existing specifications and standards for assessment and evaluation and their usage in Europe. ICOPER deliverable D6.1 (October 2009), http://icoper.org/results/deliverables
13. Derntl, M., Neumann, S., Oberhuemer, P.: Report on the Standardized Description of Instructional Models. ICOPER deliverable D3.1 (September 2009), http://icoper.org/results/deliverables
14. RDN/LTSN resource type vocabulary, http://www.intute.ac.uk/publications/rdn-ltsn/types/
15. Totschnig, M., et al.: Open ICOPER Content Space Implementations of 2nd Generation of Open ICOPER Content Space including Integration Mini Case Studies. ICOPER deliverable D1.2 (Work in progress, September 2010)
16. The Open Archives Initiative Protocol for Metadata Harvesting, http://www.openarchives.org/OAI/openarchivesprotocol.html
17. LRN, http://dotlrn.org

Knowledge Maturing Activities and Practices Fostering Organisational Learning: Results of an Empirical Study

Andreas Kaschig[1], Ronald Maier[1], Alexander Sandow[1], Mariangela Lazoi[2],
Sally-Anne Barnes[3], Jenny Bimrose[3], Claire Bradley[4], Alan Brown[3],
Christine Kunzmann[5], Athanasios Mazarakis[5], and Andreas Schmidt[5]

[1] University of Innsbruck, Universitätsstrasse 15, 6020 Innsbruck, Austria
{firstname.lastname}@uibk.ac.at
[2] University of Salento, Piazza Tancredi, N.7, 73100 Lecce, Italy
mariangela.lazoi@ebms.unile.it
[3] University of Warwick, Coventry CV4 7AL, UK
{firstname.lastname}@warwick.ac.uk
[4] London Metropolitan University, 35 Kingsland Road, London E2 8AA, UK
c.bradley@londonmet.ac.uk
[5] Research Center for Information Technology Karlsruhe (FZI), Haid-und-Neu-Straße 10-14, 76131 Karlsruhe, Germany
{lastname}@fzi.de

Abstract. Knowledge work is performed in all occupations and across all industries. The level of similarity of knowledge work allows for designing supporting tools that can be widely used. In this paper an activity-based perspective towards knowledge work is taken. Based on findings from a previous ethnographically-informed study, we identified valuable activities to be supported in order to increase knowledge maturing inside companies. The goal of this paper is to contribute to which knowledge maturing activities are deemed important, so that they can be supported by IT services. Quantitative and qualitative data have been collected in 126 organisations of different size, sector and knowledge intensity. Important feedback and issues emerged and need to be managed in order to support success in the knowledge maturing activities that allow improvement of organisational learning through the dissemination and application of the most appropriate knowledge.

Keywords: empirical study, knowledge maturing activities, knowledge work.

1 Introduction

The share of knowledge work [1] has risen continuously during recent decades [2] and knowledge work can be found in all occupations and industries with a level of similarity that is sufficient to allow the design of instruments to foster knowledge work independent of occupations or industries.

The systematic design of interventions aiming at increasing productivity of knowledge work [3] needs more information about how knowledge work is actually performed in real-world organisations. In clear opposition to the abundance of concepts, models, methods, tools and systems suggested for such interventions [4], many of which have failed to achieve their goals [5], information on how knowledge work is actually performed is scarce. Blackler et al. [6] recommend to study knowledge work by focusing on work practices or activities focusing on interactions between humans and computers, frequently referred to in the context of knowledge and learning management [7, 8].

This paper takes on a practice perspective towards knowledge work. Additionally, instead of integrated systems for workplace learning or knowledge management that support a prescribed, comprehensive process of handling knowledge and learning in organisations in their entirety, we focus on loosely coupled arrangements of services[1] supporting selected activities which are well aligned with the context of the work environment, i.e. the "spirit" [10], of the digital artefacts and tools available in the work environment and adopted by a community of knowledge workers that are jointly engaged in knowledge handling activities in an organisation. In this paper, so-called knowledge maturing activities (KM activities) are defined. Furthermore, we aim to contribute to the knowledge in the field about which KM activities are deemed important so that they can be supported by IT services. We employ a broad empirical study involving 126 European organisations. Collected data is analysed with a mixed-method approach using quantitative and qualitative methods. Section 2 of the paper introduces the context in which the study was conducted and details the study design which was employed. Section 3 elaborates on the results, utilizing a portfolio approach on the one hand and evaluating contextual data on the other. Section 4 discusses limitations, before a summary on the paper is given in section 5.

2 Background to the Study

2.1 The Context: The MATURE Project

The study has been conducted within the context of the MATURE Integrating Project (http://mature-ip.eu), which is based on the concept of knowledge maturing [11], i.e., goal-oriented learning on a collective level. The project investigates how knowledge maturing takes place in companies, which barriers are encountered, and how socio-technical solutions overcome those barriers with a particular focus on bottom-up processes. The project is characterised by four strands: the empirical strand conducting different forms of studies, the conceptual-technical strand conceptualising knowledge maturing support and implementing tools, the integration strand developing a flexible infrastructure and enabling loosely coupled solutions, and the evaluation strand which consists of participatory design activities, formative and summative evaluation.

Knowledge maturing has been analysed in terms of identifying the different phases of knowledge development, specifically 'expressing ideas', 'appropriating ideas', '

---

[1] A service is a building block of software systems that consists of contract, interface and implementation. It has a distinctive functional meaning, typically reflecting a high-level business concept covering data and business logic [9]. A service is an abstract resource that represents a capability of performing tasks that form a coherent functionality from the point of view of the provider's entities and requester's entities (www.w3.org/TR/ws-gloss/).

distributing in communities', 'formalising', 'ad-hoc training' and 'standardising', which are described in the knowledge maturing (phase) model [12, 13]. Within the first year of the project, an ethnographically-informed study [14] was conducted to understand real-world maturing practices and activities as well as design studies that explored different approaches to support KM activities. Based on these findings, the project has collaboratively defined use cases that correspond to important KM activities.

2.2 Study Design

In contrary to the ethnographically-informed study which researched a small number of organisations, the aim was to broaden the scope of organisations that were investigated in order to get a varied picture of perceptions held in companies of different size, sector and knowledge intensity about the results of the former study.

Therefore, we decided to conduct telephone interviews throughout Europe. Contacts were gained using a mixed approach of purposeful sampling and cold-calling. We asked for interviewees who have had work experience of at least three years, have been employed in the organisation for at least one year and have had responsibility for, e.g., knowledge management, innovation management or personnel development. The interview guideline was partly structured and partly semi-structured and was designed to focus on three subject areas: the phases of the knowledge maturing model [12], KM activities and knowledge maturing indicators. With respect to the knowledge maturing model, information was sought on the perception of importance, support from organisational and ICT measures, tools and infrastructures, barriers and motivational factors involved as well as perception of success.

The knowledge maturing model provides a new[2] and distinct lens for studying phenomena of knowledge conversion. Consequently, the empirical studies conducted in MATURE are exploratory in nature. This means that the study aimed at hypotheses generation rather than testing, and combines quantitative with qualitative elements in a mixed-method approach, so that phenomena of knowledge maturing, specifically about phases, KM activities and indicators, are investigated in more detail. However, some initial assumptions about relationships between concepts were also studied.

Within our project, we define KM activities as individual or group activities that contribute to the goal-oriented development of knowledge within an organisation. Knowledge activities in general have their roots in the perspective of practice of knowledge work as described above. Practice is the source of coherence of a community due to mutual engagement, joint enterprise and shared repertoire [18]. Practices formed by individuals that are part of semi-permanent work groups are examples of how knowledge work can be framed as a social process [19]. Knowledge work is characterised by practices such as acquiring, creating, gathering, organising, packaging, maintaining, systemising, communicating and applying knowledge [20-22], and by roles such as data gatherer, knowledge user and knowledge builder [23]. However, the practices proposed so far need to be detailed in order to offer starting points for information systems design. Schultze identifies informing practices in an ethnographic study of knowledge work in a

---

[2] There have been a number of models and theories for describing, analysing and studying knowledge handling in organisations, e.g., Nonaka's [15] SECI model, Wiig's [16] model for situation handling from a knowledge perspective or Sveiby's [17] knowledge conversions to create business value. However, none has an explicit focus on knowledge maturing.

large Fortune 500 manufacturing firm [24]: (1) ex-pressing, i.e. self-reflexive converting of individual knowledge and subjective insights into informational objects that are independent of knowledge workers, (2) monitoring, i.e. continuous non-focused scanning of the environment and the gathering of useful "just in case"-information, and (3) translating, i.e. creation of information by ferrying it across multiple realms and different contexts until a coherent meaning emerges, and later adds (4) networking, i.e. building relationships with people inside and outside the company that knowledge workers rely on [25]. In particular the work performed by [26], i.e. a series of 31 interviews with knowledge workers building on Schultze's practices, was considered useful to inform our approach to design a list of KM activities that are deemed important to be supported by MATURE software and services.

These knowledge activities, gained from a review of literature, were merged with results from the previous ethnographically-informed study (i.e. codes) and use cases created for the project, and then were further refined [27]. This resulted in a list of twelve KM activities, which can occur in each phase of the knowledge maturing model.

The concepts 'perceived importance', 'perceived support' and 'perceived success' are investigated with respect to each KM activity. KM activities have been explained to interviewees as activities of individuals or groups of individuals that contribute to the development of knowledge, which can occur within one knowledge maturing phase, e.g., 'distributing in communities', or between two knowledge maturing phases, e.g., from 'distributing in communities' to 'formalising'. Importance asks to what extent interviewees think that a KM activity is important for increasing knowledge maturity in the organisations they represent (question 12 of the interview guideline). Support refers to organisational or information and communication technological instruments that help individuals or groups of individuals perform an activity so that it contributes to the development of knowledge (question 13). Finally, success captures to what extent interviewees believe that a KM activity has been performed successfully in the organisations they represent (question 14). Each concept has been operationalised with the help of one statement per activity for which interviewees could mark to what extent they would agree to this statement on a 7-point Likert scale. We are well aware that the concepts of importance and, especially support and success would deserve a much more thorough investigation with the help of a number of variables that should be questioned for each of them, see e.g., [28, 29]. However, we are confident that the depth of these concepts has been explored in the course of the interviews by interviewer-interviewee dialogues that appropriated the concepts to the context of the organisations that the interviewees represent and that were documented on a per activity basis. Besides reflecting on each of the twelve proposed KM activities with respect to the three concepts, interviewees were also asked for additional ones. Moreover, comments of interviewees regarding the KM activities were collected.

3 Results

This paper focuses on evaluating data collected with respect to the three concepts described in the previous section. The following section 3.1 provides a quantitative analysis of the results. Additionally provided KM activities and comments from interviewees regarding existing KM activities are the basis for a qualitative analysis presented in section 3.2.

3.1 Knowledge Maturing Activities – Descriptives and Portfolios

In this section, the perceptions of interviewees are descriptively analysed and interesting facets of individual activities are highlighted. This detailed information is then further investigated with the help of portfolios opposing importance and support as well as importance and success of performance.

Importance, Support and Success of KM Activities. With respect to all three questions, a relatively high mean value of agreement can be observed. Looking at each question separately, the following aspects can be highlighted:

Perceived importance (question 12): According to the medians, at least 50% of respondents agreed or fully agreed that all of the twelve KM activities are important for increasing maturity of knowledge in their organisation (see table 1). The agreement to the importance of KM activities *'find relevant digital resources'*, *'reflect on and refine work practices or processes'*, *'find people with particular knowledge or expertise'* and *'communicate with people'* was even higher, as at least 50% of the respondents fully agreed. The KM activity with the highest standard deviation (2.15) is *'restrict access and protect digital resources'*. One reason for that is that 26.0% of respondents fully disagreed or disagreed with the statement that this activity is important for knowledge maturing in their organisation. The frequencies (see table 1) indicate that two different interpretations of this KM activity might exist which is analysed in more detail in section 3.2.

Perceived support (question 13): The agreement to the statement that the respective KM activity is supported in the respondents' organisations (see table 2) is not as high as the agreement to the importance of the respective KM activity (question 12). However, for ten out of twelve KM activities, according to the median at least 50% of interviewees agreed or fully agreed. With respect to the KM activity *'reorganise information at individual or organisational level'* 66.4% and with respect to *'assess, verify and rate information'* 69.9% of interviewees slightly agreed, agreed or fully agreed. Again, the most heterogeneous answers were given to the KM activity *'restrict access and protect digital resources'* (standard deviation is 1.81).

Perceived success of performance (question 14): Compared to the agreement to question 13 about support of KM activities, the level of agreement to the statement that the respective KM activity is performed successfully is lower (see table 3). However, more than 50% of interviewees (exact values after each activity) agreed or fully agreed that the KM activities *'familiarise oneself with new information'* (54.4%), *'share and release digital resources'* (51.2%), *'restrict access and protect digital resources'* (61.0%), *'find people with particular knowledge or expertise'* (52.4%) and *'communicate with people'* (58.7%), are performed successfully in their organisation. With respect to the remaining seven out of twelve KM activities, a median of five indicates that at least 50% of respondents slightly agreed, agreed or fully agreed. It is worth mentioning that the KM activity *'share and release digital resources'* has the highest standard deviation (1.67) closely followed by *'restrict access and protect digital resources'* (1.63).

The descriptions above are also mirrored in figure 1 where the mean values of the level of agreement to the three questions for each KM activity are shown.

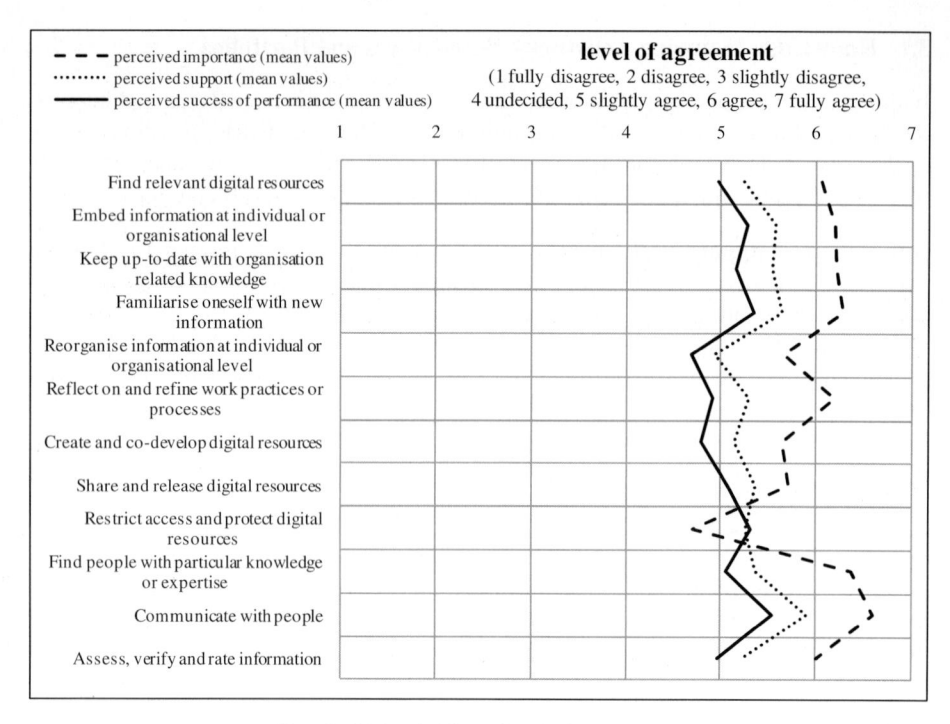

Fig. 1. KM activities – level of agreement

For eleven KM activities, the mean values of given answers decrease from question 12 over 13 to 14. Hence, though these KM activities are perceived to be important, they are actually less well supported. This might result in a less successful performance. In case of the remaining KM activity *'restrict access and protect digital resources'* the opposite is true: mean values increase from questions 12 over 13 to 14. For this KM activity, the perceived success of performance seems to be slightly higher than the perceived support and the perceived support seems to be higher than the perceived importance. We will investigate this further in section 3.2.

Portfolios. In order to support decisions in our project, it is of interest to identify KM activities that are, firstly, deemed important for increasing knowledge maturity, but perceived less supported and, secondly, deemed important, but perceived less successfully performed. In such cases, software or services could be (further) developed to enhance the support of such activities aiming at a more successful performance in organisations. To perform this analysis, we employed the mean levels of agreement. In order to avoid influences of the absolute height of mean values, we decided to concentrate on the relative values (i.e. mean level of agreement to one KM activity relative to the mean levels of agreement to other KM activities). This has also the advantage of retaining information about the relative mean height of agreement to each concept with respect to a specific KM activity, instead of reducing it to one single difference score. Therefore, mean values for each of the questions 12, 13 and 14, are divided into quartiles, comprising three KM activities each. These are then contrasted. Applying this approach makes explicit which KM activities are deemed to be more important, and at the same time, less supported or successfully performed than others. For investigating and for presenting results of this area of interest, we decided to create and evaluate portfolios.

Each of the portfolios described in the following opposes two dimensions. According to the number of possible pair-wise combinations of perceived importance, support and success of performance, three portfolios could be created. Based on the assumption that software or services can support KM activities and hence might have a positive influence on the success of performance, we concentrate on the deemed importance of KM activities and relate it to the perceived support and success of performance.

Knowledge maturing activities:
1. Find relevant digital resources
2. Embed information at individual or organisational level
3. Keep up-to-date with organisation-related knowledge
4. Familiarise oneself with new information
5. Reorganise information at individual or organisational level
6. Reflect on and refine work practices or processes
7. Create and co-develop digital resources
8. Share and release digital resources
9. Restrict access and protect digital resources
10. Find people with particular knowledge or expertise
11. Communicate with people
12. Assess, verify and rate information

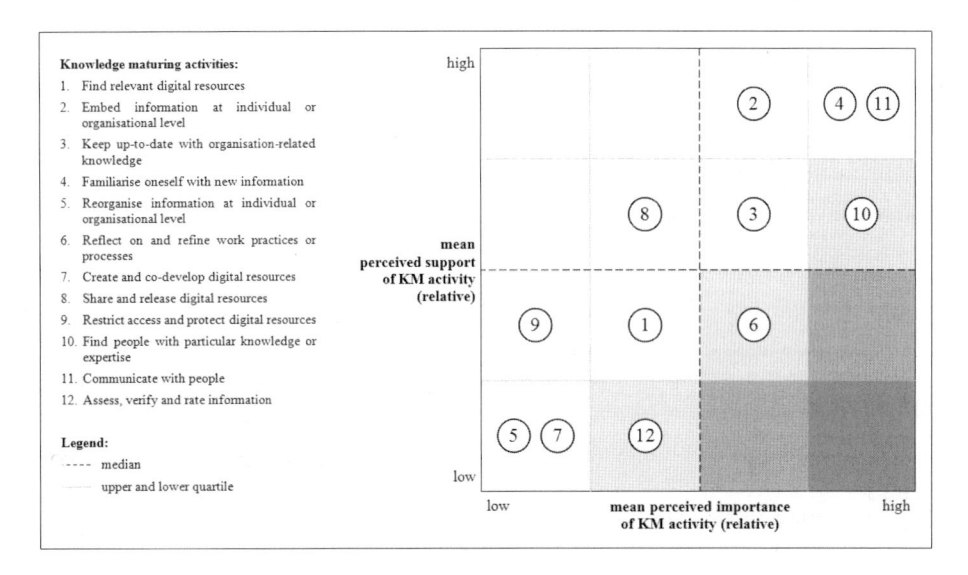

Legend:
---- median
—— upper and lower quartile

Fig. 2. KM activities portfolio importance – support

The portfolio displayed in figure 2 depicts on its x-axis the mean values of perceived importance and on its y-axis the mean values of perceived support. As quartiles were used for placing KM activities within the portfolio, the mean values of both, perceived support and importance are arranged relatively to each other.

The higher the perceived importance and the lower the perceived support, the worthier it is to focus on this KM activity. Following this, the background of the portfolio shown in figure 2 is coloured in different shades to show the strategy of investing into those activities that are in the lower right corner of the portfolio. The darker the background colour, the higher the importance and the higher the assumed lack of software or services that provide functionalities to support the KM activity.

Relatively to others, the KM activities '*4-familiarise oneself with new information*', '*11-communicate with people*' and '*10-find people with particular knowledge or expertise*' are deemed most important for increasing knowledge maturity in respondent's organisations. The latter is less supported and hence, would be most interesting for the MATURE project. The KM activities '*2-embed information at individual or organisational level*', '*3-keep up-to-date with organisation-related*

158   A. Kaschig et al.

knowledge' and *'6-reflect on and refine work practices or processes'* are deemed of secondary importance. The latter KM activity is deemed less supported, and additionally is the only one in this portfolio which belongs to both, the 50% of KM activities that are deemed more important and the 50% of KM activities that are deemed less supported than others. Hence, this KM activity would be of high interest for further consideration. With respect to perceived importance, the KM activities *'1-find relevant digital resources'*, *'8-share and release digital resources'* and *'12-assess, verify and rate information'* would fall into the third group. The latter of this group is less supported and would be a candidate to be facilitated with the help of software or services. The KM activities *'5-reorganise information at individual or organisational level'*, *'7-create and co-develop digital resources'* and *'9-restrict access and protect digital resources'* are part of the group that is deemed least important.

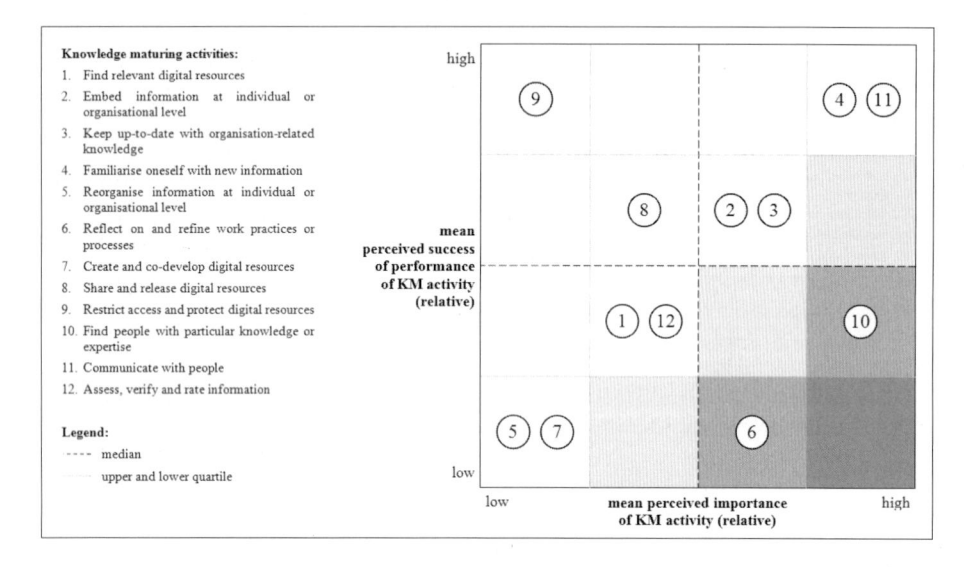

Fig. 3. KM activities portfolio importance – success of performance

The portfolio depicted in figure 3 displays the mean values of perceived importance on its x-axis and the mean values of perceived success of performance on its y-axis. Those activities deemed important and at the same time perceived to be performed less successfully would be most interesting for further consideration. Again, this area of interest is coloured in different shades to show the norm strategy of investing into those activities that are in the lower right corner of the portfolio.

According to this portfolio *'10-find people with particular knowledge or expertise'* and *'6-reflect on and refine work practices or processes'* would be most interesting for the MATURE project. The former falls into the group of most important KM activities and, at the same time, is part of the 50% of KM activities that are less successfully performed. The latter is deemed to be one of the 50% of more important and, at the same time, is perceived to be one of the three less successfully performed KM activities.

In summary, a comparison of both portfolios (depicted in figure 2 and figure 3) shows that *'6-reflect on and refine work practices or processes'* and *'10-find people with particular knowledge or expertise'* would be most interesting to be supported by software or services. *'12-Assess, verify and rate information'* could be considered as a third interesting KM activity, because it is one of the least supported and less successfully performed activities. Also *'1-find relevant digital resources'*, *'5-reorganise information at individual or organisational level'* and *'7-create and co-develop digital resources'* might be of interest. Although, in relation to others, these activities are deemed to be less important, their mean values calculated based on the Likert scale (6.06, 5.66 and 5.65) still indicate an agreement. Furthermore, compared to others, they fall into the group of less supported and less successfully performed KM activities.

3.2 Collected Evidences on Knowledge Maturing Activities

The KM activity *'restrict access and protect digital resources'* – a double perspective: The most controversial KM activity is *'restrict access and protect digital resources'*, as shown in the previous section. An analysis of a total of 42 comments related to this activity has revealed that two types of answers can be distinguished: (a) statements whether and why the organisation restricts access and (b) statements about personal opinion whether restricting access is beneficial to knowledge maturing.

From an organisational perspective, a mixed picture emerged. Some organisations have very few restrictions (related to an open organisational culture), whilst others are giving high priority to restricting access. In some cases, this is due to the fact that organisations are required to protect the information (e.g., data related to their customers), for others this is part of protecting their own competitive advantage.

In fact, several organisations in high technological sectors have recognized the importance of the KM activity *'restrict access and protect digital resources'*. In those organisations, this activity is perceived as a normal practice to channel the knowledge through the correct users and to avoid dissipating it. It seems a common practice to improve the structured knowledge and to support the diffusion among the employees correctly. This activity guarantees the right classification of knowledge and secures the diffusion with the most appropriate policy. On the personal side three reasons why individuals considered restricting access as important emerged from the data:

- **Trust as a prerequisite for knowledge sharing and collaboration.** Two interviewees mentioned that they consider restricting access as a measure to create a protected space in which you can more freely exchange knowledge because they trust each other. *"There are people who will share only in a limited way if they can trust that not everyone can see it."* The alternative they basically see is that knowledge is kept personally: *"But you have to restrict access, I think that restricting access as a functionality of a tool is an important prerequisite for exchanging knowledge. So if you restrict access, it is also good for knowledge exchange, not with those who don't have access, but for those who have access. Otherwise you wouldn't share anything if you couldn't restrict it to certain persons"*. This is in line with the general comment that *"human nature of the individual is very important and needs to be taken into account"*.
- **Information channelling and avoidance of information overload.** The underlying assumption of this line of argumentation is that shared knowledge and information

leads to a counterproductive overload situation: *"Knowledge is not something that has to be always distributed. With this activity the knowledge is channelled to the right users."*
- **Data security and fear of competition.** While in many cases, data security and fear of losing competitive advantage was seen as a given necessity, in some cases the interviewees also shared the company's position that this is essential. In other cases, there were more critical statements that this obstructs knowledge maturing: *"It does not help knowledge maturing, I would clearly say. Has also reasons of data protection that not everyone has access to everything. Having to restrict it: would rather disagree".*

Furthermore, interviewees also gave reasons against restricted access to resources (from the perspective of knowledge maturing). Overall, 14 comments suggest that restriction means obstructing people's access to knowledge which they view as a prerequisite for knowledge maturing to happen. Answers range from *"nonsense"* to critical reflection on their organisation's practice: *"The access rights are pretty strict, as extreme as personnel office not being able to see my drive, my drive cannot be seen by my colleagues, I find that unbelievable."* Or: *"We are destroying knowledge in this area".*

The KM activities *'familiarise one-self with new information'* and *'find relevant digital resources'*: *'Familiarise one-self with new information'* is a very important KM activity, and is also supported and realized with success (see section 3.1). When performing this activity the employees use internal knowledge and also external sources (e.g., participating webinar, searching information on internet or attending training course). However, internal initiatives to support the exchange of knowledge among employees also exist and allow familiarising with the organisation's knowledge. For example, an Italian ICT company has introduced a corporate training school in which employees are taught by colleagues. The aims are to share experiences about projects, to stimulate discussions and to exchange ideas. Thereby, knowledge and lessons learnt diffuse from a single team to a broad set of employees.

The lower support and success of the activity *'find relevant digital resources'* is often related to a lack of a common access point to organisational knowledge which, instead, could be easily supported by introducing specific ICT systems. The problem is, perhaps, in the high amount of knowledge that has to be structured and inserted into a unique platform or in different (for scope) platforms linked together. However, some organisations have introduced ad-hoc systems to classify organisational knowledge. Proprietary platforms manage that knowledge and the search and access to the most relevant and needed resources.

Description of critical KM activities: *'Find people with particular knowledge or expertise'* is one of the activities carried out with less support and less success, but it is deemed to be of high importance. The interviewees perceive that it is important to find the most useful people for giving help for certain issues and also for special needs faced during their daily tasks. The ability to find the most adequate people, e.g., to assign activities to, becomes also increasingly important. Some initiatives are undertaken by the organisations, but they are not a widely diffused practice, and better results have to be achieved. Another example is reported by an aerospace company which has introduced a Competence Management Roadmap. It has developed a methodology and software to trace the employees' competences, to elaborate the state of each activity in order to highlight gaps in the needed competences, and to simulate and forecast the situation of the organisational activities when changes in the team are hypothesized.

The activity *'reflect on and refine work practices or processes'* comprises thinking about tasks and processes within the organisation, and aims at their improvement. The most adequate knowledge can be highlighted and be "stored" in the company processes to be widely distributed and used daily. This activity allows for effective knowledge distribution amongst employees and to mature the organisational knowledge, learning how to apply it in work practices and processes. To better support this activity, initiatives oriented to the business process management can be useful. An example is a company which has applied business process management to reflect on the existing processes, analysing and mapping them, and to refine those processes through the mitigation of gaps and low performance. This allows them to have accurate processes that incorporate the learnt organisational knowledge and to improve the organisational performance. Furthermore, in that company, to support the application of the refined processes, a system has been developed automating the new processes. All the actions are traced and the employees are led in the execution, always being informed about the process task being performed and being up-dated about errors and performance. Therefore, the right application of the refined processes with the business process management is assured, using the ICT system in which each task can be digitally executed and traced.

The KM activity *'assess verify and rate information'* allows the organisation to make available the right and correct information for the organisational activities. A mechanism to verify and validate the information can be very useful in order to improve the quality of diffused information and to allow only the right knowledge to mature. In some companies, digital workflows are available to share, verify and approve documents. An Italian company, for example, invented a digital workflow for product design information. The files are verified and shared with other employees after approval. This digital workflow supports the *'assess verify and rate information'* activity and allows employees to learn from and apply the most adequate knowledge, reducing time due to wrong information and related errors. Therefore, this activity provides a clear view about what information is correct to learn from, and allows the most valid knowledge to mature.

General considerations: If organisations had top management support for explicit policies and practices for, e.g., innovation management, performance improvement or knowledge management, conditions for supporting collaborative KM activities were favourable. On the other hand, where innovation and improvement practices either did not have full top management support or were treated as (a series of) one-off events, then collaborative KM activities were also likely to be viewed in a similar fashion. The issue of how to cope with cases where expertise is distributed across organisations is an interesting challenge, as treating knowledge as something to be matured separately in single organisations could itself be problematic. Many organisations also saw movement towards more collaborative knowledge maturing processes as part of a 'bundle' of practices, inevitably bound up with the 'management of change' and significant shifts in the organisational culture.

Overall, it is clear that the stories told to us from a wide variety of organisations align with the view that the knowledge maturing model is one of a number of possible perspectives for engaging people in discussions about organisational change, learning and development. Further, some participants could see how collaborative knowledge maturing processes could be a key part of achieving a more fundamental transformation, where the quality of choice, information and commitment are improved in a move towards double-loop learning where broader questions about organisational goals are also addressed. Inter-organisational learning and knowledge development can be a particular challenge in this respect.

It is clear that innovation, learning and KM activities within and across organisations are essentially social processes and that both personal networks and cross-company networks need to pay attention to building relationships to support development, as well as focusing upon substantive issues. There is also a need to consider the interaction between formal and informal approaches to learning, skill development and knowledge creation as a particularly effective way forward, not only for enhancing personal professional development, but also as a means to improve organisational effectiveness.

Finally, there were some clearly differentiated answers related to the tension around external collaboration. Already identified as part of the ethnographically-informed study, knowledge and information exchange with external contacts in an individual's social network was a very essential part of everyday work (even to an unanticipated degree). Also, external sources have been seen by interviewees as essential for triggering change in an organisation. Organisations tend to be very cautious towards external collaboration, as they see the risk of losing competitive advantage, or need to ensure compliance to externally induced regulations for data protection. One balanced answer also indicated that you have to differentiate between different types of knowledge: *"Not all digital resources - I would here (and above) say all resources that influence the work process, the product, the organisational goals, here I would always say yes. If it is not influencing the work process, then it is stupid."*

4 Limitations

The topic of knowledge maturing is quite complex in general. This was known in advance as it is a distinct and new lens to look at the phenomena surrounding knowledge handling in organisations, and thus the concept certainly was new to all interviewees. This was also a primary reason why we decided to do interviews in the first place. Thus the interviewer-interviewee relationship and the interviewers' competence in appropriating an understanding of knowledge maturing in the context of the organisation represented by the interviewee were crucial. We spent substantial effort in preparing precisely and clearly defined concepts, with further explanations and examples to ease the task for the interviewer. Moreover, the study coordinators offered intensive interviewer training and kept in close contact with interviewers in order to transfer lessons learned and help overcome barriers of understanding. When interviews are conducted by different interviewers, there may be differences in answers. However, we found no significant differences between cases with respect to the interviewer that had performed them.

Although the interview aimed at (parts of) organisations, the personal scope (responsibility, interests) of the interviewee may have had an influence on the interviewees' perceptions. We performed statistical tests and could exclude the personal background (e.g., technical background versus business or HR background) as a factor influencing answers.

As we conducted one interview per organisation, different interviewees within the same organisation might have given different answers. However, as we carefully selected interviewees who had a good command of the knowledge and learning management in their organisation, this problem could at least be alleviated.

Another impression which arose as the interviews were carried out was that interviewees in leadership positions (i.e. CEOs) tended to provide an optimistic vision of the company, rather than pointing out shortcomings. Nevertheless, this factor could also be excluded by statistical tests we conducted.

5 Discussion and Conclusion

On average, all KM activities were deemed important for increasing knowledge maturity in interviewees' organisations. For eleven out of twelve KM activities, perceived importance is significantly higher than perceived support and perceived support is significantly higher than perceived success of performance. Based on these results, portfolios contrasting importance/support and importance/success were created. It seems, that the KM activities *'reflect on and refine work practices or processes'* and *'find people with particular knowledge or expertise'* are most interesting. Both are deemed to be important, but were less supported and less successfully performed.

The interviewees attribute high importance to the KM activities, and in general, to the knowledge which is perceived as a strategic resource to improve the actual practices and obtain competitive advantages. If the importance of a KM activity is shown to be very high from the study results, it may emerge that more support can be attributed to that activity in order to reach better results. Several initiatives have to be undertaken, in particular to improve the most critical KM activities (*'reflect on and refine work practices or processes'*, *'find people with particular knowledge or expertise'* and *'assess verify and rate information'*). For those activities, the importance is highly perceived but low support and lack of success are shown. When adequate support is given to a KM activity, performance is improved. Hence, organisations could support those KM activities through actions based, especially for the most critical ones, on the level of perceived importance and on the level of the existing initiatives. Therefore, in MATURE, it is planned to further investigate and take up these results to provide services embedded in the MATURE system for improving support of KM activities. Hence, support and success of KM activities allow organisational learning to improve because the right knowledge is disseminated and employees are able to acquire content and information and to apply them in their work.

However, not in all organisations, knowledge management initiatives were widely available and thus, effective and broader support is needed. Several interviewees have affirmed that their organisations are starting to think of knowledge as a strategic resource. They are actually working to improve knowledge management and to diffuse a culture based on sharing of appropriate knowledge, in order to capture what exists in the organisation and to learn how to apply it within daily work practices, thus capitalizing on their own intangible assets and getting higher profits. Today many organisations work in value networks and share knowledge, risks, costs and tangible assets with external actors who require a better and broader focus on the KM activities involving these external actors. In fact, the establishment of consortiums or project collaborations permit the development of a network with other actors, thus increasing the maturing of the knowledge of a single company. Working together, the knowledge is mutually influenced, and thus the potential to mature knowledge could increase. The exchange of best practices and initiatives with other actors can allow individual organisations to learn from others and to improve their application of organisational knowledge, creating new linkages between internal and external knowledge.

References

1. Blackler, F.: Knowledge, Knowledge Work and Organizations: An Overview and Interpretation. Organization Studies 16(6), 1021–1046 (1995)
2. Wolff, E.: The Growth of Information Workers. Communications of the ACM 48(10), 37–42 (2005)
3. Drucker, P.F.: The Age of Social Transformation. The Atlantic Monthly 274(5), 53–80 (1994)
4. Alavi, M., Leidner, D.E.: Knowledge Management and Knowledge Management Systems: Conceptual Foundations and Research Issues. MIS Quarterly 25(1), 101–136 (2001)
5. Bishop, J., et al.: Ensuring the effectiveness of a knowledge management initiative. Journal of Knowledge Management 12(4), 16–29 (2008)
6. Blackler, F., Reed, M., Whitaker, A.: Epilogue - An Agenda for Research. Journal of Management Studies 30(6), 1017–1020 (1993)
7. Boer, N.-I., Baalen, P.J., Kumar, K.: An Activity Theory Approach for Studying the Situatedness of Knowledge Sharing. In: 35th Annual Hawaii International Conference on System Sciences (HICS). Hilton Waikoloa Village, USA (2002)
8. Clases, C., Wehner, T.: Steps Across the Border – Cooperation, Knowledge Production and Systems Design. In: Computer Supported Cooperative Work, vol. 11, pp. 39–54 (2002)
9. Krafzig, D., Banke, K., Slama, D.: Enterprise SOA: Service-Oriented Architecture Best Practices. Prentice Hall, Englewood Cliffs (2005)
10. DeSanctis, G., Poole, M.S.: Capturing the Complexity in Advanced Technology Use: Adaptive Structuration Theory. Organization Science 5(2), 121–147 (1994)
11. Schmidt, A.: Knowledge Maturing and the Continuity of Context as a Unifying Concept for Knowledge Management and E-Learning. In: 5th International Conference on Knowledge Management (I-KNOW 2005), Graz, Austria (2005)
12. Maier, R., Schmidt, A.: Characterizing Knowledge Maturing: A Conceptional Model Integrating E-Learning and Knowledge Management. In: 4th Conference of Professional Knowledge Management (WM 2007), Potsdam (2007)
13. Kaschig, A., et al.: D1.1 - Results of the Ethnographic Study and Conceptual Knowledge Maturing Model, Innsbruck (2009)
14. Barnes, S.-A., et al.: Knowledge Maturing at Workplaces of Knowledge Workers: Results of an Ethnographically Informed Study. In: 9th International Conference on Knowledge Management (I-KNOW 2009), Graz, Austria (2009)

15. Nonaka, I.: A Dynamic Theory of Organizational Knowledge Creation. Organization Science 5(1), 14–37 (1994)
16. Wiig, K.M.: A Knowledge Model for Situation-Handling. Journal of Knowledge Management 7(5), 6–24 (2003)
17. Sveiby, K.-E.: A Knowledge-Based Theory of the Firm to Guide in Strategy Formulation. Journal of Intellectual Capital 2(4), 344–358 (2001)
18. Wenger, E.: Communities of Practice. Learning, Meaning, and Identity. Cambridge University Press, Cambridge (1998)
19. Daskalaki, M., Blair, H.: Knowing as an Activity: Implications for the Film Industry and Semi-Permanent Work Groups. In: Proceedings of the 3rd Conference on Organizational Knowledge, Learning and Capabilities, Athens (2002)
20. Davenport, T.H., Jarvenpaa, S.L., Beers, M.C.: Improving Knowledge Work Processes. Sloan Management Review 37(4), 53–65 (1996)
21. Kelloway, E.K., Barling, J.: Knowledge Work as organizational behavior. International Journal of Management Reviews 2(3), 287–304 (2000)
22. Holsapple, C.W., Whinston, A.B.: Knowledge-based Organizations. The Information Society 5(2), 77–90 (1987)
23. Snyder-Halpern, R., Corcoran-Perry, S., Narayan, S.: Developing Critical Practice Environments Supporting Knowledge Work of Nurses. Computers in Nursing 19(1), 17–23 (2001)
24. Schultze, U.: A confessional account of an ethnography about knowledge work. MIS Quarterly 24(1), 3–41 (2000)
25. Schultze, U.: On Knowledge Work. In: Holsapple, C.W. (ed.) Handbook on Knowledge Management 1 - Knowledge Matters, pp. 43–58. Springer, Berlin (2003)
26. Hädrich, T.: Situation-oriented Provision of Knowledge Services. In: Information Systems 2007. University of Halle-Wittenberg, Halle(Saale) (2007)
27. Kaschig, A., et al.: D1.2 - Results of the Representative Study and Refined Conceptual Knowledge Maturing Model (2010)
28. DeLone, W.H., McLean, E.R.: Information Systems Success: The Quest for the Dependent Variable. Information Systems Research 3(1), 60–95 (1992)
29. DeLone, W.H., McLean, E.R.: The DeLone and McLean Model of Information Systems Success: A Ten-Year Update. Journal of Management Information Systems 19(4), 9–30 (2003)

Statistical Data

Table 1. Measures and frequencies for perceived importance

	KM activity (perceived importance)	n	mean	median	std dev.	value on likert scale						
						1	2	3	4	5	6	7
1	Find relevant digital resources	125	6,06	7,0	1,40	3	3	4	2	14	35	64
2	Embed information at individual or organisational level	126	6,20	6,0	0,96	1		3	1	11	58	52
3	Keep up-to-date with organisation related knowledge	126	6,22	6,0	0,96			5	1	14	47	59
4	Familiarise oneself with new information	125	6,28	6,0	0,81			3		10	58	54
5	Reorganise information at individual or organisational level	125	5,66	6,0	1,33	1	3	7	11	19	48	36
6	Reflect on and refine work practices or processes	125	6,19	7,0	1,13	1	1	3	6	9	42	63
7	Create and co-develop digital resources	124	5,65	6,0	1,43	1	5	8	7	22	40	41
8	Share and release digital resources	124	5,72	6,0	1,61	6	4	4	4	15	45	46
9	Restrict access and protect digital resources	123	4,70	6,0	2,15	12	20	10	4	14	31	32
10	Find people with particular knowledge or expertise	126	6,37	7,0	0,92		2	1	1	9	45	68
11	Communicate with people	126	6,60	7,0	0,82	1		1	1	3	31	89
12	Assess, verify and rate information	125	6,00	6,0	1,01	1		1	9	15	58	41

Table 2. Measures and frequencies for perceived support

	KM activity (perceived support)	n	mean	median	std dev.	value on likert scale						
						1	2	3	4	5	6	7
1	Find relevant digital resources	125	5,25	6,0	1,55	3	7	11	8	27	44	25
2	Embed information at individual or organisational level	126	5,57	6,0	1,16	1	2	6	6	33	56	22
3	Keep up-to-date with organisation related knowledge	126	5,54	6,0	1,27	1	4	8	4	28	58	23
4	Familiarise oneself with new information	125	5,65	6,0	1,13		3	5	5	34	51	27
5	Reorganise information at individual or organisational level	125	4,93	5,0	1,50	1	9	15	17	33	31	19
6	Reflect on and refine work practices or processes	125	5,30	6,0	1,50	3	6	11	4	32	45	24
7	Create and co-develop digital resources	124	5,14	6,0	1,57	2	9	13	9	27	41	23
8	Share and release digital resources	123	5,36	6,0	1,62	4	7	10	5	20	48	29
9	Restrict access and protect digital resources	123	5,25	6,0	1,81	5	13	5	11	12	43	34
10	Find people with particular knowledge or expertise	126	5,36	6,0	1,55	2	8	11	6	22	49	28
11	Communicate with people	126	5,90	6,0	1,33	2	3	4	6	16	46	49
12	Assess, verify and rate information	123	5,23	5,0	1,53	4	3	7	23	26	30	30

Table 3. Measures and frequencies for perceived success of performance

	KM activity (perceived success of performance)	n	mean	median	std dev.	value on likert scale						
						1	2	3	4	5	6	7
1	Find relevant digital resources	125	4,96	5,0	1,59	2	9	18	11	28	37	20
2	Embed information at individual or organisational level	126	5,28	5,0	1,24	2	2	7	12	46	39	18
3	Keep up-to-date with organisation related knowledge	126	5,15	5,0	1,44	4	3	13	7	39	43	17
4	Familiarise oneself with new information	125	5,35	6,0	1,24	1	3	8	12	33	51	17
5	Reorganise information at individual or organisational level	125	4,70	5,0	1,51	1	11	17	22	36	21	17
6	Reflect on and refine work practices or processes	125	4,92	5,0	1,47	2	6	19	12	35	36	15
7	Create and co-develop digital resources	123	4,79	5,0	1,60	3	10	19	11	28	39	13
8	Share and release digital resources	123	5,07	6,0	1,67	2	9	19	9	21	36	27
9	Restrict access and protect digital resources	123	5,31	6,0	1,63	3	11	3	15	16	46	29
10	Find people with particular knowledge or expertise	126	5,06	6,0	1,58	1	8	22	8	21	45	21
11	Communicate with people	126	5,54	6,0	1,45	2	4	9	6	31	36	38
12	Assess, verify and rate information	123	4,97	5,0	1,44	5	2	8	26	35	30	17

Note: Missing data has been excluded pair-wise.

Demands of Modern PLEs and the ROLE Approach

Uwe Kirschenmann, Maren Scheffel, Martin Friedrich,
Katja Niemann, and Martin Wolpers

Fraunhofer Institute for Applied Information Technology,
Schloss Birlinghoven, 53754 Sankt Augustin, Germany
{uwe.kirschenmann,maren.scheffel,martin.friedrich,
katja.niemann,martin.wolpers}@fit.fraunhofer.de
http://www.fit.fraunhofer.de

Abstract. We present basic concepts and an outlook on current approaches and techniques of personal learning environments to point out their demands, focussing on recommendations in self-regulated learning scenarios as a major basic functionality of PLEs. In the context of the ROLE project, we explain how we plan to meet these demands by using user observations stored in the format of the contextualized attention metadata schema.

Keywords: personal learning environments, recommendations, attention metadata.

1 Introduction

Personal learning environments (PLEs) become more and more popular in the field of technology enhanced learning (TEL). In this paper, we refer to a PLE as a mix of applications (possibly widgets) that are arranged according to the learner's demands. A short example will illustrate this simple definition. Sara, a learner, wants to deepen her knowledge in calculus. As she does have some experience handling/constructing her PLE, she populates it with a widget that facilitates the use of a mathematics search engine. The widget displays important information about the characteristics of mathematical functions in which Sara is interested. The widget does not satisfy Sara's needs; she therefore also incorporates a specialized graphical widget that allows her to display the functions and to understand them more easily, e.g by manipulating the function graph manually. She also wants to know how to implement mathmatical functions in a programming language in order to calculate a range of values as well as some derivations; she includes a special programming course and a chat widget allowing her to discuss ideas with people whom she might not even know yet. The output of her calculations shall then be displayed by the graphical tool.

This example can easily be extended. It is apparent that the learner in our scenario already knows what she wants but that she has no clue where to find a widget that links a programming language (for example Java) with her special interest in mathematics. In this case she needs help on where to find the right tools and resources. The example also postulates that Sara has a running system at her hands letting her deal with different widgets on the same platform. Even more, the system takes care of Sara operating on a level that does not exceed her competencies at the time and that fits into her overall educational plan.

The above example about Sara illustrates the basic concepts of a PLE, that is the flexible compilation and reconfiguration according to the learners needs with suitable applications that are deemed useful by the learner, the teacher or the organization. In our theoretical work, we give an outlook on the current approaches and techniques in the development of PLEs in section 2. We explain the scenario in more detail in order to show the complex requirements that are imposed on such systems. We then focus on a basic functionality of PLEs, namley recommendations in section 3. As was shown in the example with Sara, it might be that a learner is totally at loss about where to find suitable learning content or services. Furthermore, a learner might not be aware of the knowledge she already has. In this situation, she needs help. Recommendations are a crucial component to convey that help. We therefore give a short introduction about recommendation techniques followed by an overview of present implementations of recommender systems in the field of TEL. Finally, we give an outlook on how we will meet some of the explained demands within the European project ROLE[1] in section 4.

2 Personal Learning Environments

A personal learning environment (PLE) is made up of technological, organizational as well as pedagogical concepts. We will focus on technologcial and pedagogical aspects while leaving organizational aspects for future work. From the pedagogical point of view a PLE should enable the learner to set her own learning goals.

In this sense the learner builds her own learning environment (therefore also called personalized learning environment) which includes choosing relevant contents, processes and services and being in control of them. This approach is opposed to the older paradigm of learning management systems (LMS) which have been introduced to institutions to address the needs of organizations, lecturers and of students [1]. This centralization also entails a predefinition of the learning processes and the used learning resources. Learners are restrained in their freedom to experiment and include new ways to achieve their individual goals or materials to learn from. The restrictions would not be too hard to accept in formal learning scenarios where learners simply want to pass the prescribed tests. If the interests of a learner change, however, such restrictions hamper learning success. The paradigm of lifelong learning (LLL) forces a shift in focus towards the individual interests of the learner [2]. This motivates further demands [3]:

---

[1] http://www.role-project.eu/

- a system with a standard interface to e-learning systems of different institutions
- maintenance of portfolio information
- transition and adoption of the learning environments across different systems – as for example mobile phones – and the possibility to have the environment available offline

In this line of thought we also find the need that a learning environment should support transitions not only of the technological kind but also of the learner's interests or changes in her social situations or educational paths. Obviously, the idea of PLEs has technological demands such as the integration of different e-learning platforms, the support of information exchange between and the adaptibility of systems, interoperability on different levels, privacy and security of data and user profiles, etc. In addition, direct communication between participants for the purpose of learning supports the constitutional part according to Web 2.0 ideology [4] while, at the same time, being a relevant item for the success of learning. Thus, communication is not restricted to certain topics or courses implemented within a LMS. From a social constructivist's point of view [3] learners create their subjects "bottom up" and in this way benefit from informal learning [5].

Schaffert and Hilzenshauer [6] formulate the demands and changes of PLEs. According to them, learning with a PLE leads to changes concerning: (a) the role of the learner as active, self-directed creators of content; (b) personalization with the support and data of community members; (c) learning content as an infinite 'bazaar'; (d) the role of social involvement; (e) the ownership of a learner's data; (f) the meaning of self-organized learning for the culture of educational institutions and organizations, and (g) technological aspects of using social software tools and aggregation of multiple sources.

We will briefly discuss these aspects by first looking at the pedagogical concept that comes with the PLE and second on how this concept is supported. Then we will shortly discuss the possibilities, requirements and problems of a technological solution.

2.1 The Pedagogical Point of View

The pedagogical point of view became recently popular among researchers of the social sciences as PLEs support the idea of the user centric learning approach that fits well with psychological and pedagogical concepts emphasizing, among other things, the importance of personal adaptation and individually adapted conveyance of learning contents [7].

Here, we focus on the self-regulated learning (SRL) paradigm. According to Zimmerman [8] "students can be described as self-regulated to the degree that they are metacognitively, motivationally, and behaviourally active participants in their own learning process". According to Aviram et al. [9] and Nussbaumer and Fruhmann [10], there are five common fundamentals in self-regulated learning models, namely (a) the learner is active, (b) the learner is able to control, monitor and regulate her cognition, motivational state and behaviour; (c) the learner can be hindered in her ability to monitor her motivation, behaviour, cognition or the context through constraints, like biological, developmental, contextual or individual constraints, (d) the learner sets goals, tries to achieve them through progress-monitoring and adaption of cognition, motivation, behaviour and context (learning process) and (e) "self-regulatory activities are mediators between personal characteristics and contextual features and actual performance, in the learning process" [9].

To put it shortly, the SRL approach can be understood as an umbrella term for various processes, such as goal setting, metacognition, etc. This approach assumes that learning will occur to a high degree in non-academic non-formal learning environments and that these less instructor- or teacher-oriented and primarily learner-oriented environments require a greater extent of self-regulated learning skills from learners [11]. To make it more concrete, we extract the following pedagogical demands for a PLE that is in line with Schaffert and Hilzenshauer [6]:

- goal setting must be supported
- activity of and control for learners must be enabled, giving the user the possibility to adapt her learning environment, learning contents and tools according to her needs
- progress monitoring and feedback of results: as the user is only on her way of becoming an expert and is – in the beginning – possibly not aware of her needs and goals yet, her actions are assumed to be faulty and she requires feedback about her actions in order to think of better ways to solve the problem at hand resp. learn.

2.2 The Technological Realization

Taraghi et al. [1] point out that LMSs as well as PLEs are technological concepts allowing for serveral pedagogical or personal learning strategies. Today, many Internet users set up their own environments to gain a personally relevant view on information in which they are interested. Examples of these personalized environments are iGoogle[2], Netvibes[3], Facebook[4] etc. Consequently, the underlying technologies have been transferred to the field of TEL and molded to the idea of the PLE. As they combine various Web 2.0 sources into one PLE, they are also called MUPPLEs, i.e Mash-Up Personal Learning Environments [5].

These MUPPLEs are put into effect using the technological bases of Rich Internet Application (RIA) technologies such as iGoogle and Facebook which implies strong allusions to the Rich Client Applications (RCA) [12]. In the case of RIAs the programming logic and presentation is done on the client-side whereas the server simply retrieves the raw data from the relevant servers and offers them to the client via an API [1]: "As it is not possible to integrate the entire set of services in the presentation layer, the PLE servers serve as a single entry point

---

[2] http://www.google.com/ig
[3] http://www.netvibes.com/
[4] http://www.facebook.com/

to provide the client programming logic with small applications or services", so called widgets. The user is then enabled to setup her own environment using the widgets that provide her with the needed resources and services.

Compared to standard RCAs, RIAs lack a standard solution for inter-component or inter-widget communication [13]. This is not surprising as they are intended as small self-contained applications. Contrary to the suggestions of the relatively new term, the idea behind RIAs dates back to the discussions about thin and rich clients as well as the 3-tier-architecture in the 1990s [14]. At the times there was a dispute about how to make Internet applications "rich". The first advance was done by Java and the strongly propagated applet technology [15]. Other client side technologies are Flash[5] and DHTML[6]. For Flash content, the user needs a separate runtime environment and DHTML is heavily dependent on the browser used. Both approaches intermingle the presentation logic with the business logic.

Three improvements to that general problem are Silverlight[7], JavaFX[8] and HTML5[9]. HTML5 and JavaFX seem to be good alternatives because of their wide or soon to be exptected wide distribution. With JavaFX, it is possible to drag widgets out of the browser window onto the desktop to make them available there. In addition it is possible to develop RIAs that can run across a wide variety of connected devices. The current release 1.2 enables building applications for desktop, browser and mobile phones. TV set-top boxes, gaming consoles, Blu-ray players and other platforms are planned. Widgets developed with the JavaFX scripting language can be integrated independent of the underlying PLE engine [1]. JavaFX also seems to hold the advantage of a more well-structured development process as the whole business logic that can be implemented in pure Java is separated from the presentation layer that later constitutes the user interface and is developed in the JavaFX scripting language. Java specific technologies can be used throughout the development cycle.

Putting this together there still exists a decisive disadvantage in standard RIAs: Although the W3C[10] is pushing the process of specifications so that widgets are supported in any environment that follows the W3C standards (see [16] and [17]), the widgets are per se not designed to enable communication from widget to widget as it is unclear which widgets a user will install. This is different from known RCAs [11] where "components must communicate with each other, for example to send user input to the business layer, and then to update the data store through the data layer".

The technologies are used to enable PLEs that are extendable, personalizable, integratable to enable smooth workflows in learning processes and easy to use. This last point is significant as there are no typical standards as of yet that

---

[5] http://www.adobe.com/products/flash/
[6] http://www.w3schools.com/Dhtml/dhtml_intro.asp
[7] http://www.silverlight.net/
[8] http://www.javafx.com/
[9] http://www.w3.org/TR/html5/
[10] http://www.w3.org/

guarantee a clearly arranged user interface. With too many widgets running at the same time, the danger of irritating rather than supporting the learner in her learning processes is high. The ROLE project aims at solving these problems.

2.3 Problems and Challenges

Within the European project ROLE (Responsive Open Learning Environments) the problems and challenges mentioned above are strategically addressed. This is mirrored in the configuration of the work packages that form the theoretical basis for integrating the technological and pedagogical demands [18].

ROLE aims at enabling the learner to compile her own learning environment and take this compilation with her across the various learning contexts, e.g. from university to workplace learning, or from employer to employer. Based on an organic requirements engineering process that incorporates learners, learning service suppliers, employers and political stakeholders, the necessary technologies, but also the required change processes in companies will be addressed. The developed solution is intended to be extendible by third party developers. During all these theoretical and practical ongoing processes, the goal is to integrate the pedagogical and technological demands of feeding the relevant information for her learning goals and activities back to the user.

The basic approach focuses on the intelligent mashup of learning services that are made available with current web-based technologies like widgets and inter-widget-communication-enabling frameworks like OpenSocial[11] or Graasp[12]. Furthermore, a widget store will enable learners to find, select and compile learning services into their learning environments. Learner communities will enable learners to exchange learning environment compilations, rating and commenting and also to identify best practices to ease the use of learning environment compilations.

Furthermore, ROLE aims at enabling personalization technologies, ranging from the recommendation of learning resources, learning paths and learning services to the support of learning paradigms like self-reflection and self-regulated learning. A major focus lies on SRL that gives the learner a greater responsibility and control over all aspects of TEL [19]. SRL is a prerequisite for the LLL paradigm [11].

In order to address the ROLE objectives, many technologies from different areas have to be combined, e.g. concerning the integration of services, data and tools. These issues are too complex and wide-ranged to be treated here. We therefore concentrate on the demands of recommendations. A common problem for PLEs is the danger of overwhelming learners with information in a short period of time [5]. Information here can mean the large amount of resources, tools or learning groups and goals to choose from for their individual competence development. This is counterproductive and opposite to the wanted effects of PLEs. In order to avoid this, especially new learners need guidance, e.g. in the form of recommendations.

---

[11] http://www.opensocial.org/
[12] http://graaasp.epfl.ch/

3 Recommendations

The quality of recommendations is integral for the success and acceptance of a PLE. "Good" recommendations ensure the user's trust in the system, "bad" recommendations lead to the opposite. In this chapter we give an overview of basic recommendation methods, followed by the implementation of recommender systems in the modern research field of TEL.

3.1 Recommendation Methods

Recommender systems are based on algorithms and used to suggest items to a user. An item can be anything of interest in the user's current situation, e.g. pictures, videos, documents, single files, sequences of files, websites, learning paths, specific tools and applications, people etc. Much effort has been put into the research, development and improvement of recommender systems in the last years. Most recommender systems used today are either based on content-based filtering or collaborative filtering or – so called hybrid approaches – on a combination of those two methods [20].

Users' preferences and items' attributes are the foundation for content-based recommender systems. There are several ways to create item profiles: it can either be done manually or automatically, e.g. by extracting keywords from text documents with extraction methods such as the very common TF-IDF measure [21]. To create user profiles there are also two different options as it can either be done explicitly by asking the users about their interests or implicitly by a user's given ratings. Once both profiles are built, they can be matched against each other and the most suitable items are recommended to the user. An example for a content-based filtering recommender system is PRES (Personalized REcommender System) [22]. To enable the user to more easily find relevant articles the system creates dynamic hyperlinks for web sites containing do-it-yourself home improvement advice. From each item sets of relevant terms are automatically extracted which are then used as item representations. A user model is created from the items she finds interesting and this model then enables the classification of unseen items as negative or positive. Another software agent that learns a user profile to rate pages on the World Wide Web based on explicit feedback is Syskill & Webert [23]. Based on the user profile the system suggests links to user and is also able to construct queries to help the user find other pages of interest to her. Two very common problems, however, that content-based filtering recommender systems suffer from are the new user problem, i.e. to suffice for recommendations user profiles first have to evolve, and overspecialization, that is a user hardly gets recommendations for classical music, eventhough listening to it from time to time, due to mainly listening to heavy metal music. Another problem with content-based filtering techniques is the time-consuming and expensive item profile maintenance.

The basis for recommendations of collaborative filtering techniques are items that have previously been rated by other users. Again, these ratings can either be implicit, e.g. visiting a site, listening to a song, or explicit, e.g. rating a book with three stars. One can differentiate between user-based and item-based collaborative filtering methods [24]. In user-based techniqes those items get recommended to a user that have been rated best by users most similar her, that is they try to find other users with interests most similar to those of the current user. The similarity of two users is calculated by comparing their previously rated items. MovieLens[13], a movie recommendation web site matching users with similar opinions about movies, is a prominent example for such a system. For each user of the system a set of like-minded users is created. The ratings of these neighbours are then used to create personalized recommendations for the user. While there is no need to create item profiles and while the identification of cross-genre niches is possible, the new user problem still exists and the new item problem, i.e. an item that is rated by a few users only will not be recommended, is introduced. Another problem of user-based collaborative filtering is scalability which cannot be compensated for by combining it with other approaches. Although reducing the data size might help with this problem and lead to better scaling, the recommendation quality usually worsens when doing so [25].

Item-based collaborative filtering approaches do not compare users, but calculate the similarity of items based on the users' implicit and explicit ratings as a basis for recommendations. These calculations can be done offline, making such algorithms quicker and scale more easily [26]. Amazon.com[14] uses this approach as it bases its calculations on an item-to-item similarity matrix. The more similar users the items share, the more similar they are. That is, items sharing the fact of often being bought by the same users (in general or during one session) are more similar than items not sharing so many users [25]. This, however, implies that items never being used or rated by the same users do not get a similarity value.

In order to obtain the advantages of several techniques, hybrid systems have been implemented. The drawbacks of single techniques can thereby be compensated for. It is mostly content-based and collaborative-based techniques that are combined in hybrid systems, knowledge-based or demographic-based methods, however, can be integrated as well [27]. Content-boosted collaborative filtering for example was introduced by Melville et al. [28]: for every member of a movie recommendation web site the system tries to predict a rating for every unrated film of the current user based on the ratings of similar users. Confidence values are assigned to each prediction. If this value is below a pre-defined threshold, e.g. due to only too few ratings for this movie, the textual description of the movie is compared to the descriptions of other movies rated by the user and the rating for the movie in question is then based on the rating of the movie with the most similar content. Combining the ratings using a weighting scheme as proposed in [29] or by showing the user the results from both techniques in a combined way as it is done in [30] are other approaches to integrate content-based and collaborative filtering.

---

[13] http://movielens.umn.edu/
[14] http://www.amazon.com/

3.2 Recommender Systems in TEL

Most of the existing recommender systems in technology-enhanced learning environments usually use collaborative filtering methods for recommending learning objects or sequences of them to recommend learning goals, people to collaborate with or even specific tools to use. The following paragraphs describe projects in the field of technology enhanced learning that deal with some form of recommendation.

The APOSDLE[15] project provides an environment to support individual learning to the user for work-integrated and life-long learning [31]. It supports three different types of recommendations: based on a user's task and prior knowledge artefacts such as texts and videos are recommended to the user. Other people within the network can be suggested to the user based on their skills (similar or more advanced). The third type of recommendations deals with learning paths: the system recommends activities and learning resources depending on a user's chosen learning path or prerequisites.

The iClass[16] project developed an open learning system and environment that is cognitive-based and adapts to an individual user's needs. According to a learner's predefined learning goals and her current knowledge, the system recommends activities or objects to the user [32].

Within the KALAIDOSCOPE Network of Excellence[17] the Trails project[18] aimed at investigating personalization and collaboration in an e-learning environment based on learning paths (trails). The Trails system accumulates usage statistics of individual learners or groups of learners for a set of learning objects (LOs) [33]. Already visited learning paths as well as recommended trails can be visualized. The visualizations can be based on individual or group usage and used for self-reflection or recommendation. The system not only recommends specific learning objects but also types of LOs a learner is interested in.

ActiveMath[19] is an adaptive learning system for mathematics that can be personalized corresponding to a user's preferences and her learning context. The system's course generator automatically proposes a sequence of learning materials according to the user's learning goals, skills and preferences [34]. Next to specific material exercises are recommended as well.

MUPPLE[20] comprises a personal learning environment within the iCamp[21] project. Its main focus is to support the learner by managing her learning tools and learning activities. The PLE is automatically harvested for typical action-outcome-tool triples which are then stored in a database [35]. When creating a new activity in the learning environment the system can suggest these triples

---

[15] http://www.aposdle.org/
[16] http://www.iclass.info/
[17] http://www.noe-kaleidoscope.org/
[18] http://www.dcs.bbk.ac.uk/trails
[19] http://www.activemath.org/
[20] http://mupple08.icamp.eu/
[21] http://www.icamp.eu/

to the user. Experienced users can get more detailed results than inexperienced ones.

The TENCompetence[22] project provides an open source, standards-based environment for life-long learning that can be personalized to individuals, groups or organizations. The system comprises the so called Hybrid Personalizer which recommends Units of Learning to the user based on her preferences, learning goals and current learning state [36].

QSIA[23] is a Questions Sharing, Information and Assessment system fostering learning and collaboration using recommendation. Items are recommended depending on a user's knowledge while people are recommended depending on the similarity of their disciplines [37].

The PALETTE[24] project supports three types of recommendations: collaborative filtering, user- as well as item-based, relying on explicit and implicit ratings, and also offers content-based and ontology-based filtering using domain-specific ontologies while the PROLIX[25] system, a framework to support organizations in improving the competencies of their employees, recommends content sequences based on the user's learning progress and skills.

4 Utilizing Usage Tracking

In this section we outline which benefits the analysis of usage metadata according to our approach provides and how this is done. We therefor outline CAM first before briefly describing three approaches to analyse CAM.

4.1 Contextualized Attention Metadata

In this context we use contextualized attention metadata (CAM) [38] for uniting the heterogenous approaches described in chapter 3. CAM provides the basic information about the activites of the user. In more detail: CAM is a schema that allows the usage tracking of learners while interacting with their computer-based applications. It describes the different actions a user is performing on digital objects within applications or widgets. Figure 1 shows the core elements of the CAM schema. The group element represents the user while applications are stored in the feed element. For all items additional information such as media type or title can be stored. The actions performed on the items and information about action type, session, context or content are stored in the event element and its sub-elements. By implementing listeners that observe the actions of users within a PLE, we are able to describe a holistic learning process that includes the sending and receiving of information. Using CAM in ROLE provides the means to represent the activities of learners within their learning environments on a well balanced level.

---

[22] http://www.tencompetence.org/
[23] http://qsia.haifa.ac.il/
[24] http://palette.ercim.org/
[25] http://www.prolixproject.org/

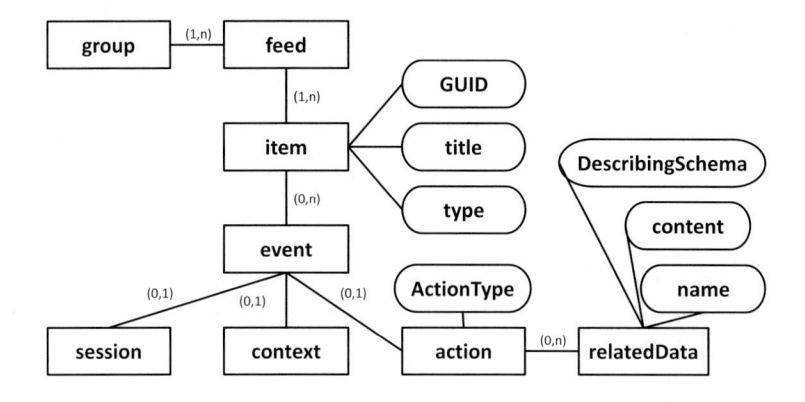

Fig. 1. Core elements of the contextualized attention metadata schema

The role of CAM in ROLE is two-fold: On the one hand, contextualized attention metadata will be combined with theories such as the Competence-based Knowledge Space Theory (CbSTK) [39] to enable self-regulated learning. While the CbSTK provides the means for adaptively assessing domain skills and devising personalized learning paths, CAM offers the means to identify the context of learners. The combination of both leads to a self-regulated learning approach that reflects on the learners' contexts and activities as a whole. Thus, it is not limited to a single learning system or environment. CAM provides the means to automatically assess the learner's behaviour, the learning success on the domain level, and to use self-estimation of the learner regarding learning tools.

On the other hand, CAM features the information necessary to detail or extend existing and to create new user profiles that base on today's user profiling standards like PAPI [40] and IMS LIP [41]. Often, such standardized profiles are created through existing LMSs and require learners to enter information about them by themselves. By mining the CAM information about users, their contexts and interests can be identified and included into the profiles. For example, CAM-based techniques allow the identification of the main interests of learners. A context might be formulated following the context definition of [42]. This means, by mining CAM, the context of a learner can be identified by her activities, her relations (and qualities thereof) with other learners and by describing her "individuality" in addition to time and location. Through clustering approaches, basic activities (represented in CAM) can lead to the identification of more complex activities. For example: when a user opens a document, copies some text and then pastes the text into another document, the more complex activity would be reading the copied text.

The learner's relations are directly deduced from her communication behaviour that is also captured in CAM. By monitoring and analysing emailing, chatting, teleconferencing and other means of communication behaviour, the communication patterns of the learner emerge. Relations to other learners are then easy to be identified. Even more, in specific cases, the quality of these relations can be estimated, e.g. through the use of emotional state recognition analysis. Consequently, the information forms the learner's relations context.

CAM also provides the information that is necessary to describe the human entity (individuality). By identifying the topics of the documents that a learner handles, creates and consumes, learner specific interests are identified. In combination with the relation analysis, the relations are then qualified according to the set of topics addressed in the respective communication. Furthermore, as CAM also provides information about the tools and services a learner uses, the individuality context also includes information about how a user handles which information with which tools.

Finally, by combining the contextual information about the learner with the respective learning domain, further information about the status of a learner in that respective domain is deducible. Using this information, we expect to be able to identify suitable learning paths, learning goals and recommend suitable tools.

4.2 Application Scenarios of CAM

CAM and assessment systems. We use CAM in order to provide help to students within an assessment system [43]. Assessment systems with the provision of hints have proven to be very useful in the teaching/learning process and many of such systems exist (e.g. [44] or [45]). While using assessment systems, students interact with exercises and hints. We use CAM to capture this information and use it for personalization, feedback or pattern detection. Using CAM we overcome the interoperability problem between various learning systems. Furthermore, we store more detailed information on the learner's activities in order to address the issue of varying measures across changing learning environments.

CAM and reflections of usage. Furthermore, as a first prototype, we developed and introduced a trend analysis of learner interactions [46] with the MACE learning environment [47] that we call Zeitgeist. The Zeitgeist application provides an overview on activities within the MACE system. In the context of the MACE system that sets up a federation of architectural learning repositories, large amounts of architectural contents from distributed sources are integrated and made accessible for architects, architecture students and lecturers. CAM is captured through the MACE portal and social community. Examples of the user actions that are captured within the system are search actions, downloads of metadata on learning resources and downloads of the learning resources themselves, modifications of metadata, etc. It gives users the possibility to reconstruct their learning paths by retracing which learning resources they accessed, how they found them and which topics have been of interest to them. This information can be used to make learning paths more explicit and to foster the learners' reflection on their activities.

CAM and usage pattern detection. Using a modification of the rough set theory – a mathematical framework for the analysis of data under uncertainty

– we identify patterns of usage [48] in CAM. The CAM is collected through the everyday learning and working environment of a number of users. By deducing a dependency between a user's frequent behaviour and her main interests while interacting with her computer, we make use of the rough set theory's indiscernibility relation to extract frequencies of a user's activities. Her actions can then be classified to be definitely in, possibly in and definitely out of her current interest. The thus discovered patterns can not only be used to find rough hypotheses of a single user but also to compare the activity patterns of several users. In both cases the results can be used to support self-regulated in reflective learning scenarios.

5 Conclusion

This paper discusses basic concepts of PLEs with a strong focus on recommendation in self-regulated learning scenarios. We identify an overlap between new technological developments and the educational demands of the self-regulation paradigm. SRL essentially determines the learning progress today.

There are many challenges that need to be addressed: On the technological side, applications used for learning have to be able to communicate with each other. They must be transferable to other environments and the selection or recommendation of various tools, documents and individuals must be adapted to the performance level and the interest areas of each learner. A basic requirement to satisfy this demand is extensive user monitoring. We suggest to use CAM as a standard as it serves as a basis for skill identification, user profiles and derivation of learning activities. The results of diverse CAM analyses then serve as a basis for an individualized recommendation as demonstrated in a number of example applications.

While theory indicates significant gains in learning effectiveness and efficiency, further research and evaluation is necessary to support this theoretical claim. First experiments already indicate that the chosen approach has the potential to significantly improve learning effectiveness and efficiency.

Acknowledgement

The research leading to these results has received funding from the European Community's Seventh Framework Programme (FP7/2007-2013) under grant agreement no 231396 (ROLE project).

References

1. Taraghi, B., Ebner, M., Till, G., Mühlburger, M.: Personal Learning Environment – a Conceptual Study. In: International Conference on Interactive Computer Aided Learning, pp. 25–30 (2009)
2. Field, J.: Lifelong Learning and the New Educational Order, 2nd edn. Trentham Books Ltd., Staffordshire (2006)

3. Harmelen, M.V.: Personal Learning Environments. In: ICALT 2006: Proceedings of the Sixth IEEE International Conference on Advanced Learning Technologies, pp. 815–816. IEEE Computer Society, Washington (2006)
4. O'Reilly, T.: What is Web 2.0: Design Patterns and Business Models for the next generation of software, http://www.oreillynet.com/pub/a/oreilly/
5. Drachsler, H., Pecceu, D., Arts, T., Hutten, E., Rutledge, L., Van Rosmalen, P., Hummel, H.G.K., Koper, R.: ReMashed - Recommendations for Mash-Up Personal Learning Environments. In: Cress, U., Dimitrova, V., Specht, M. (eds.) EC-TEL 2009. LNCS, vol. 5794, pp. 788–793. Springer, Heidelberg (2009)
6. Schaffert, S., Hilzensauer, W.: On the way towards Personal Learning Environments: Seven crucial aspects. Elearning papers 9, 1–10 (2008)
7. Sternberg, R.J., Williams, W.M.: Educational Psychology, 2nd edn. Ally& Bacon, Boston (2009)
8. Zimmerman, B.J.: A social cognitive view of self-regulated academic learning. Journal of Educational Psychology 81(3), 329–339 (1989)
9. Aviram, R., Ronen, Y., Sarid, A., Hagani, S., Winer, A.: iClass pedagogical model and guidelines (Final version). An FP6 K12 elearning integrated project, Deliverable Number: D3.1 (2008)
10. Nussbaumer, A., Fruhmann, K.: Common psycho-pedagogical framework. ROLE Deliverable 6.1 (15.02.2009)
11. Steffens, K.: Self-Regulated Learning in Technology-Enhanced Learning Environments: Lessons of a European Peer Review. European Journal of Education 41(3/4), 353–379 (2006)
12. Meier, J., Homer, A., Hill, D., Taylor, J., Bansode, P., Wall, L. (eds.): Rich Client Application Architecture Guide. Microsoft (2008)
13. Sire, S., Paquier, M., Vagner, A., Bogaerts, J.: A messaging API for inter-widgets communication. In: Proceedings of the 18th international conference on World Wide Web, pp. 1115–1116. ACM, New York (2009)
14. Allamaraju, S., Avedal, K., Browett, R., et al.: Professional Java Server Programming. Wrox Press, Birmingham (2001)
15. Krüger, G.: GoTo Java 2. Addison-Wesley, München (2000)
16. Widgets 1.0 Packaging and Configuration - W3C Working Draft, http://www.w3.org/TR/widgets/
17. Widgets 1.0 APIs and Events - W3C Working Draft, http://www.w3.org/TR/widgets-apis/
18. Ferdinand, P., Kiefel, A.: Survey on existing Models. ROLE Deliverable 2.1 (30.10.2009)
19. Kay, J.: Learner control. User Modeling and User-Adapted Interaction 11, 111–127 (2001)
20. Adomavicius, G., Tuzhilin, A.: Toward the next generation of recommender systems: a survey of the state-of-the-art and possible extensions. IEEE Transactions on Knowledge and Data Engineering 17(6), 734–749 (2005)
21. Salton, G.: Automatic Text Processing. Addison-Wesley, Reading (1989)
22. van Meteren, R., van Someren, M.: Using content-based filtering for recommendation. In: Proceedings of MLnet/ECML2000 Workshop, Barcelona, Spain (2000)
23. Pazzani, M., Muramatsu, J., Billsus, D.: Syskill & Webert: Identifying interesting Web sites. In: Proceedings of Thirteenth National Conference on Artificial Intelligence, AAAI 1996, Portland, OR, pp. 54–61 (1996)

24. Candillier, L., Jack, K., Fessant, F., Meyer, F.: State-of-the-Art Recommender Systems. In: Chevalier, M., Julien, C., Soule-Dupuy, C. (eds.) Collaborative and Social Information Retrieval and Access - Techniques for Improved User Modeling, 1st edn., ch. 1, pp. 1–22. Idea Group Publishing, USA (2008)
25. Linden, G., Smith, B., York, J.: Amazon.com Recommendations - Item-to-Item Collaborative Filtering. IEEE Internet Computing 7(1), 76–80 (2003)
26. Sarwar, B., Karypis, G., Konstan, J., Riedl, J.: Item-Based Collaborative Filtering Recommendation Algorithms. In: Proceedings of the 10th International World Wide Web Conference, pp. 285–295. ACM Press, New York (2001)
27. Burke, R.: Hybrid recommender systems: Survey and experiments. The Adaptive Web (2007)
28. Melville, P., Mooney, R.J., Nagarajan, R.: Content-Boosted Collaborative Filtering for Improved Recommendations. In: Proceedings of the 18th National Conference for Artificial Intelligence (2002)
29. Mobasher, B., Jin, X., Zhou, Y.: Semantically Enhanced Collaborative Filtering on the Web. In: Berendt, B., Hotho, A., Mladenič, D., van Someren, M., Spiliopoulou, M., Stumme, G. (eds.) EWMF 2003. LNCS (LNAI), vol. 3209, pp. 57–76. Springer, Heidelberg (2004)
30. Smyth, B., Cotter, P.: A Personalized TV Listings Service for the Digital TV Age. Journal of Knowledge-Based Systems 13(2-3), 53–59 (2000)
31. Lindstaedt, S., de Hoog, R., Aehnelt, M.: APOSDLE: Contextualized Collaborative Knowledge Work Support,
 http://www.ecscw09.org/proceedings/ecscw09_submission_116.pdf
32. Somech, S., Schellas, Y., Dotan, I., Ronen, Y.: iClass Methodologies, iClass Deliverable D3.3 (1.7.2007)
33. Schoonenboom, J.: Trails of Digital and Non-Digital LOs, Kaleidoscope Deliverable D22.2.2 (14.7.2004),
 http://www.dcs.bbk.ac.uk/trails/docs/D22-02-01-F.pdf
34. DFKI & Saarland University: ActiveMath - Tutorial Component (30.1.2008),
 http://www.activemath.org/Software/Tutorial-Component
35. Wild, F. (ed.): Mash-Up Personal Learning Environments, iCamp Deliverable D3.4 (January 2009),
 http://www.icamp.eu/wp-content/uploads/2009/01/d34_icamp_final.pdf
36. Drachsler, H., Herder, E., Kalz, M., Kärger, P.: The Hybrid Personalizer - Software Documentation (16.6.2008),
 http://dspace.ou.nl/bitstream/1820/1279/1/HybridPersonalizer.pdf
37. Rafaeli, S., Barak, M., Dan-Gur, Y., Toch, E.: QSIA - a Web-based environment for learning, assessing and knowledge sharing in communities. Computers & Education 43(3), 273–289 (2004)
38. Wolpers, M., Najjar, J., Verbert, K., Duval, E.: Tracking Actual Usage: the Attention Metadata Approach. Educational Technology and Society 10(3), 106–121 (2007)
39. Albert, D., Lukas, J. (eds.): Knowledge spaces: theories, empirical research, and applications. Lawrence Erlbaum Associates, Mahwah (1999)
40. Standard for Information Technology – Public and Private Information (PAPI) for Learners (PAPI Learner). IEEE Learning Technology Standardization Committee (LTSC) Version 8, draft (2001), CEN-WSLT,
 http://www.cen-ltso.net/main.aspx?put=230
41. IMS Learner Information Package Summary of Changes. Version 1.0.1, Final Specification. IMS Global Learning Consortium, Inc. (2005),
 http://www.imsglobal.org/profiles/lipv1p0p1/imslip_sumcv1p0p1.html

42. Zimmermann, A., Lorenz, A., Oppermann, R.: An operational definition of context. In: Kokinov, B., Richardson, D.C., Roth-Berghofer, T.R., Vieu, L. (eds.) CONTEXT 2007. LNCS (LNAI), vol. 4635, pp. 558–571. Springer, Heidelberg (2007)
43. Muñoz-Merino, P.J., Delgado Cloos, C., Muñoz-Organero, M., Wolpers, M., Friedrich, M.: An Approach for the Personalization of Exercises based on Contextualized Attention Metadata and Semantic Web technologies. In: Jemni, M., Kinshuk, Sampson, D., Spector, J.M. (eds.) ICALT 2010: Proceedings of the Tenth IEEE International Conference on Advanced Learning Technologies, pp. 89–91. IEEE Computer Society, Los Alamitos (2010)
44. Muñoz-Merino, P.J., Delgado Cloos, C.: A software player for providing hints in problem-based learning according to a new specification. Computer Applications in Engineering Education 17, 272–284 (2009)
45. Guzman, E., Conejo, R.: Self-assessment in a feasible, adaptive web-based testing system. IEEE Transactions on Education 48, 658–663 (2005)
46. Schmitz, H.-C., Scheffel, M., Friedrich, M., Jahn, M., Niemann, K., Wolpers, M.: CAMera for PLE. In: Cress, U., Dimitrova, V., Specht, M. (eds.) EC-TEL 2009. LNCS, vol. 5794, pp. 507–520. Springer, Heidelberg (2009)
47. Stefaner, M., Dalla Vecchia, E., Condotta, M., Wolpers, M., Specht, M., Apelt, S., Duval, E.: MACE - Enriching Architectural Learning Objects for Experience Multiplication. In: Duval, E., Klamma, R., Wolpers, M. (eds.) EC-TEL 2007. LNCS, vol. 4753, pp. 322–336. Springer, Heidelberg (2007)
48. Scheffel, M., Wolpers, M., Beer, F.: Analyzing Contextualized Attention Metadata with Rough Set Methodologies to Support Self-regulated Learning. In: Jemni, M., Kinshuk, Sampson, D., Spector, J.M. (eds.) ICALT 2010: Proceedings of the Tenth IEEE International Conference on Advanced Learning Technologies, pp. 125–129. IEEE Computer Society, Los Alamitos (2010)

How to Share and Reuse Learning Resources: The ARIADNE Experience

Joris Klerkx, Bram Vandeputte, Gonzalo Parra, José Luis Santos, Frans Van Assche, and Erik Duval

Katholieke Universiteit Leuven
Departement computerwetenschappen
Celestijnenlaan 200A, 3000 Leuven, Belgium
http://hmdb.cs.kuleuven.be

Abstract. ARIADNE is a European foundation that aims to foster "Share and Reuse" of learning resources. To support this goal, ARIADNE has created an infrastructure for managing learning objects in an open and scalable way. This paper describes the technical approach behind our open, standards based infrastructure, how content providers can connect to it, and the value they can derive from doing so. As such, the abundance that we help to unlock will act as a platform for innovation by tool developers, trainers and teachers and learners themselves.

Keywords: ariadne, learning objects, metadata, reuse, interoperability.

1 Introduction

ARIADNE is a European foundation that aims to foster "Share and Reuse" of learning resources. Reusing digital resources for learning has been a goal for several decades, driven by potential time savings and quality enhancements. To support this goal, ARIADNE has created a standards-based infrastructure for managing learning objects in an open and scalable way [33]. The overall goal of our infrastructure is to provide flexible, effective and efficient access to large-scale collections in a way that goes beyond what typical search engines provide[11]. Therefore, it provides

1. a set of services which allows the integration and management of learning objects, described in various metadata schemas in numerous repositories across the globe,
2. a toolset which allows end users to access the learning material in various ways through information visualization [16], mobile information devices [26], multi-touch displays and mash-up applications.

This paper explains how a content provider can unlock its learning objects through the ARIADNE services, thus ensuring that the material can be found in the "Global Learning Objects Brokered Exchange (GLOBE)" consortium; the largest federation worldwide which brings together content from over 70 learning object repositories provided by more than 50 organizations [13]. In this way, this paper describes the technical approach behind our open, standards based infrastructure, how content providers can connect to it, and the value they can derive from doing so.

This papers starts of in section 2 with an introduction of the key technologies used in ARIADNE. Secondly, section 3 provides an overview of the complete ARIADNE infrastructure with all the services and tools. Section 4 shows how a content provider can make his learning material available in GLOBE through ARIADNE. An evaluation of our infrastructure is presented in section 5. Related work is presented in section 6 and we conclude this paper in section 7.

2 Key Technologies

Over the last decade, ARIADNE has spent considerable effort on the development of standards and specifications for learning object repositories, with significant results. We consider the following standards and specifications as key technologies within the ARIADNE infrastructure.

2.1 Metadata

In order to enable flexible access to content, we need rich descriptions: these are typically called metadata. We focus on the automatic generation [21] and extraction of metadata as well as on so-called attention metadata [24] that describe interactions with content, rather than just the content itself [18]. For describing learning content, we mainly rely on IEEE LTSC LOM [14] but we support other standards like Dublin Core (DC) and ISO/IEC MLR as well, by automatically transforming metadata from one format into another (see section 3.1).

2.2 Harvesting

Frameworks for metadata harvesting (like OAI-PMH) enable harvesters to copy metadata from a repository and save this copy of the metadata locally [31]. On top of this local copy, search services can be added to enable search in the metadata of the contents of the content providers. We typically do not copy content itself. Therefore, we do not have to deal with intellectual property rights and digital access management for the content. We do make available metadata about the content by harvesting metadata with the OAI-PMH protocol. ARIADNE asks providers to release their metadata under a CC license (CC-BY-SA-NC) to improve discoverability of learning content because all harvested metadata is exposed again in an OAI-PMH target where it can be harvested by other federations and repositories.

2.3 Publishing

For publishing learning objects or their metadata into the ARIADNE infrastructure, we rely on the Simple Publishing Interface (SPI) specification. This model [36] has been designed such that it is interoperable with (i) the "Simple Web-service Offering Repository Deposit (SWORD)" profile [2], (ii) the "Package Exchange Notification Services (PENS)" [1] and (iii) the publishing specification that was developed in the ProLearn Network of Excellence [32]. With SPI, one can transfer digital educational resources from a variety of tools to the ARIADNE infrastructure.

2.4 Querying

The ARIADNE infrastructure provides a Simple Query Interface (SQI) [30] on top of the repository which can be used to issue queries in various query languages such as PLQL. SQI provides interoperability between search applications and various learning object repositories and is designed to support many types of search technologies. Other specifications such as SRU/SRW , O.K.I OSIDs, etc. do exist. SQI serves as a gateway to them.

3 The ARIADNE Infrastructure

Figure 1 shows a representation of the ARIADNE infrastructure which has three layers:

- The *Storage Layer* allows for storing both content and metadata in several databases.
- The *Middle Layer* offers persistent management of LOs and metadata through a set of services, such as an identifier service for providing unique identifiers for LOs.
- The *Toolset* layer hides protocols and standards for end users in a toolset that e.g. can be used for accessing LOs in the ARIADNE infrastructure.

The following sections focus on those services and tools that can be used by content providers to unlock their learning resources.

3.1 Middle Layer

From experience, we have learned that a set of services with specific goals are necessary for enabling share and reuse. ARIADNE has been improving these services constantly. However, with the inclusion of a number of new services such as the registry, the transformation and the identification service, ARIADNE has now reached a level of maturity leading to a much greater uptake.

The Repository services allow for the management of learning objects in an open and scalable architecture. To enable stable querying, publishing, and harvesting of digital learning material, all key technologies that have been discussed above are used in ARIADNEs repository services, which are described in detail in [33].

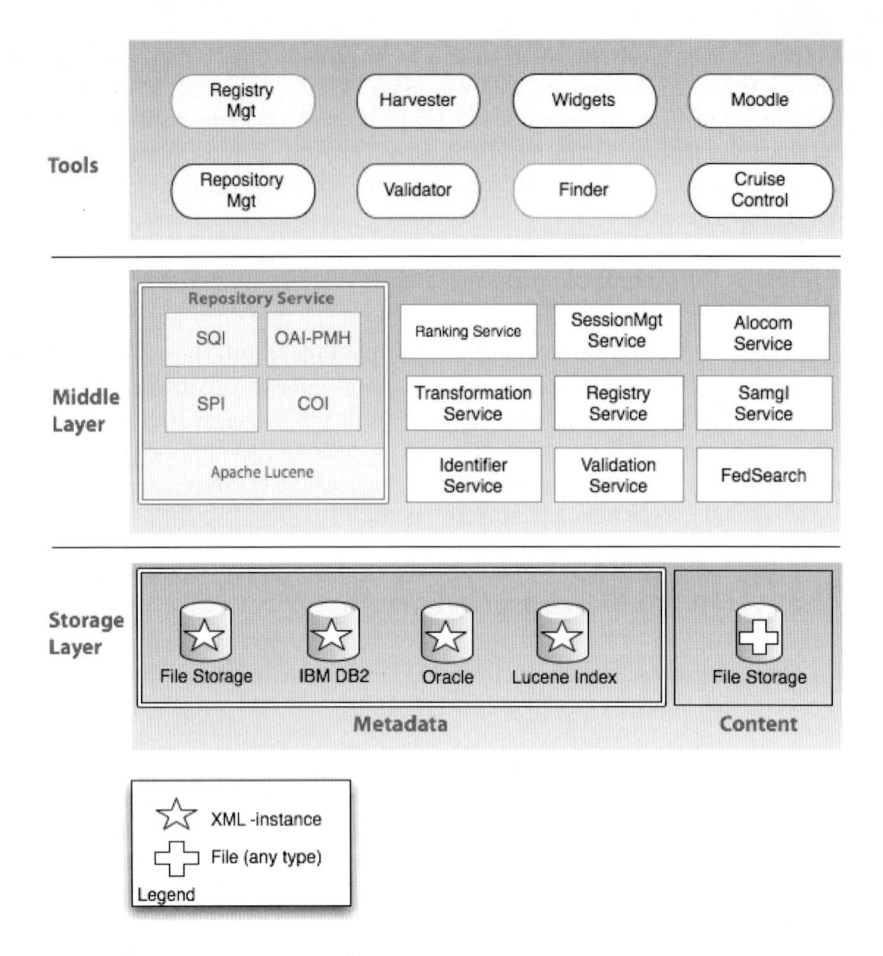

Fig. 1. The ARIADNE Infrastructure has three layers including a storage, middle and toolset layer

The Registry service is a catalog service that provides up-to-date information on learning object repositories (LORs). It provides the information necessary for systems to be able to select the appropriate protocols such as OAI-PMH, SQI, SPI, SRU/SRW [19] supported by a given learning object repository. The information is captured using the IMS LODE specification [12], that is based on the IMS Dublin Core Collections Application Profile, complemented with ISO 2146 and IEEE LOM.

The registry service facilitates interoperability between numerous learning object repositories. Besides that, creating a network of interoperable LOR registries, allows for the automatic discovery of new repositories with interesting material. Figure 2 illustrates the network of registries that has been set up in GLOBE. All information in the ARIADNE registry is exchanged with all registries in the network, with the consequence that if content provider X adds his target to the ARIADNE registry, client tools of the other registries like the

EUN [5] and LACLO [6] ones, can also discover the repository. The same goes for provider Y who adds his target to the LACLO registry. Therefore, it can be found by client tools of the ARIADNE and the EUN registries. Such client tools could for example be harvesters that would automatically harvest all targets from a registry.

The ARIADNE harvester uses the OAI-PMH framework [31] for harvesting metadata instances from an OAI-PMH target and publishes them with the Simple Publishing Interface (SPI) into (i) a specified component of the ARIADNE storage layer, (ii) any other repository that has an SPI target on top of its repository. As an illustration, in the ASPECT eContentPlus project, the ARIADNE harvester is used to harvest metadata from thirteen ASPECT content providers. The harvester then publishes their metadata in the Learning Resource Exchange (LRE) [10]. As a result, teachers can then discover these resources via the ASPECT portal. This is the client tool they are familiar with for searching learning material for their courses.

Once configured, the harvester can autonomously manage the addition, deletion and updates of metadata in a periodic and incremental way.

The validation service is available for providing validation of metadata instances against predefined application profiles, for example based on IEEE LOM. To ensure that only compliant metadata are stored in the ARIADNE repository, we use the validation service to check both the syntactic and semantic validity of the instances against the used profiles. The validation service has a modular approach, and combines different sorts of validation techniques including:

- XSD schema, mainly used for structural validation of xml metadata.
- Schematron rules [17], which are very flexible and are used for:
  - verifying the presence of mandatory elements.
  - checking the presence of empty attribute fields. For example, in the langstring datatype of LOM, the language of a string should be recorded in a non-empty attribute "language".
  - enforcing inter-field dependencies, like conditional fields.
  - checking for the correct use of the allowed terms in a vocabulary.
- validation of vcards present in the metadata with a separate vcard parser or validator.

The validation service is available as an online service where one single metadata record can be validated against the appropriate scheme. It is also integrated in the ARIADNE harvester for validating large sets of records. Reports are automatically generated which give an overview of all validation errors.

The transformation service converts metadata in one format, e.g Dublin Core (DC), into another format; e.g. the ARIADNE application profile in LOM. We need this transformation service due to the multiplicity of different metadata schemes that are used in various networks of learning object repositories [18].

For example if we want our end users to be able to discover content, described with DC metadata, in our IEEE LOM driven query tool, we need to transform the DC to IEEE LOM first and store this representation in the ARIADNE repository.

As there are a wide variety of standards and custom formats used, the transformation service works with a growing set of transformers. These transformers transform (i) metadata from one standard to another (like DC to LOM), (ii) from one AP to another within the same standard or (iii) they can combine both. Thus for every set of metadata the appropriate transformer needs to be selected, adapted or written if it does not exist yet.

The Identification service is used to provide persistent digital identifiers to resources in the ARIADNE infrastructure. The HANDLE system [27] is used as the backend service to create globally unique, persistent and independent identifiers. This system allows the assignment, management and resolution of persistent identifiers in a distributed environment. The lower level API provided by the HANDLE system is connected to an independent service interface that provides the basic functionality for persistent storage: Create, Resolve, Update and Delete (CRUD) identifiers. The identifiers created by the service are compliant with the Universally Unique Identifier standard [15]. For this purpose the Java Uuid Generator (JUG) [28] is used.

The SamgI service is able to semi-automatically generate metadata instances. Through automatic metadata generation, by extracting relevant information from contents and contexts, it is possible to significantly remove the need to fill in electronic forms when describing learning resources with metadata. This is essential if we want to make our approach scale up and become mainstream. The architecture of the SamgI service has been published in [21].

The Federated Search Service relies on SQI to offer transparent search to both ARIADNE and GLOBE. The architecture of the federated search service has been described in previous work such as [33], [34] and [30].

The Ranking service ranks search results according to Contextualized Attention Metadata (CAM)[25] which captures social data about the learning objects such as the number of times an object has been downloaded by an end user.

The ALOCOM service supports two processes: the disaggregation of learning objects into their components (text fragments, images, definitions, diagrams, tables, examples, audio and video sequences) as well as the automatic assembly of these components in real-world authoring tools [35].

3.2 Toolset

One of the main design principles in ARIADNE is to make everything disappear but the benefits. Within ARIADNE, we have therefore created a number of tools that are meant to make it easy to share and reuse learning resources.

The Moodle bridge is a module for the Moodle learning management system. If this module is deployed, users of the LMS can (i) issue a query to both ARIADNE and GLOBE, (ii) import a found resource directly from the GLOBE network into the LMS, and therefore (iii) make this resource available for other users.

The ARIADNE finder is a standalone search tool that lets users search learning material and browse the results. The finder hides protocols and standards that are used in the middle layer. Among its capabilities, it supports facetted searching in ARIADNE and GLOBE. The finder can be coupled on any repository that supports the SQI standard and describes its content with IEEE LOM.

The ALOCOM Powerpoint plugin can be used while creating a presentation from within powerpoint to find interesting material in ARIADNE and GLOBE, that can be included in the presentation. Besides that, it can be used to store a created presentation into the ARIADNE repository where it is available for users from GLOBE.

Both the Moodle bridge and the ALOCOM powerpoint plugin enable users to search for relevant content from within their usual environment, which

- offers opportunities to use their context for enriching their search criteria,
- enables us to integrate the services in their familiar workflow, so that they do not need to go to a web site to call the services.

4 From Content Provider to GLOBE

The different components in the ARIADNE infrastructure have been explained in the previous section. Figure 2 illustrates how those services and tools can be combined by content providers X and Y to interconnect their repository with GLOBE. Imagine that all contents from provider X have been described by Dublin Core (DC) - Educational metadata. The provider X has already implemented an OAI-PMH [31] target on top of the repository. To connect to GLOBE, the content provider registers his OAI-PMH target into the ARIADNE Registry (step 1a) where he adds information on his repository, such as title, description, contact person, the supported protocols used in his repository (OAI-PMH and DC metadata), etc. The registry uses an RSS feed to alert all (step 1.2) of its client tools about the new repository that has been added. In response to this alert, the ARIADNE harvester automatically issues a query (step 2) to the registry to get all relevant information about this repository. In step 3, the harvester performs the following steps:

- The DC metadata is harvested from provider X using the OAI-PMH protocol (step 3.1).
- From experience in different projects, we have learned that we cannot rely on the identifiers that are added by content providers because they are e.g. integers or descriptive titles. In a vast network of repositories, these are not

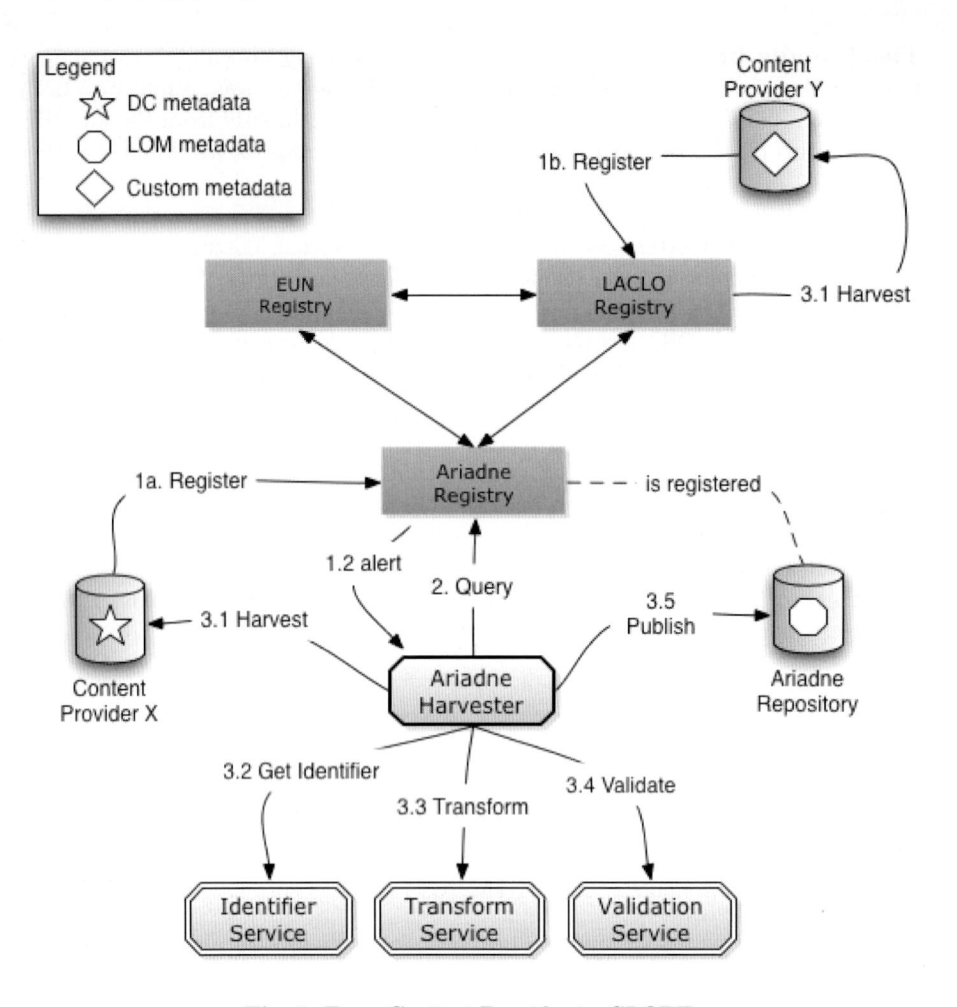

Fig. 2. From Content Provider to GLOBE

good identifiers because duplicates may arise. That's why the harvester calls the Identifier service (step 3.2) to generate a unique identifier and it adds those on-the-fly to the metadata instances of provider X.
– A call to the transform service takes care of the conversion from DC to IEEE LOM, the standard used in both the ARIADNE and the GLOBE network to describe learning resources. (step 3.3).
– At the moment, the GLOBE network brings together content from over 70 repositories. Mapping metadata from a local metadata scheme to a global one typically happens happens either by manually editing one record at the time, or in batch with a script written specifically for this mapping. Our experience has shown that both of these methods make this a very error-prone process. For example, in the eContent*plus* project MELT [22], there were originally over 90% validation errors in content providers' metadata. The reports of the

validation service helped the content providers to dramatically decrease this number to less than 5%. Faulty metadata instances often render errors or inconsistencies in tools and UIs when searching for resources. All metadata instances are therefore validated against the validation scheme in use (step 3.4), and invalid instances are discarded.
- The harvester uses the SPI specification to publish the harvested and validated metadata into the ARIADNE repository which is registered as well in the registry and therefore interconnected with GLOBE. All content from provider X can thus be found in GLOBE (step 3.5) after the harvester has completed the cycle from steps 3.1 to 3.5. The content is available through an SQI target that is connected with the federated search layer of GLOBE, as well as through an OAI-PMH target that exposes the metadata again.

5 Evaluation

Software Quality Attributes are benchmarks that describe the intended behavior of a system within the environment for which it was built [9]. The ARIADNE infrastructure has been evaluated by common quality attributes such as performance, reliability, interoperability, configurability and scalability. In the following paragraph, we describe which quality attributes are considered important for ARIADNE and which tactics we follow for optimising these attributes.

- *Interoperability* is defined as the ability of two or more systems to cooperate at runtime. ARIADNE is a modular service-oriented architecture built on the principle that interoperability and extensibility is best achieved by the integration of different interfaces as clearly defined modules. These interfaces interoperate by using open and interoperable standards and specifications such as IEEE LOM, SQI, SPI and OAI-PMH. For example, SQI serves as a gateway to existing search protocols such as SRU/SRW, O.K.I OSIDs, etc. Another interoperability example is the transformation service that allows mapping metadata instances from one standard into another. A third example is the ARIADNE registry that currently contains around 50 repositories with different access protocols and metadata schemas.
- *Scalability* refers to the ability to support large numbers of components, or interactions among components, within an active configuration. Scalability in ARIADNE is achieved by distributing services across many components with each of them their specific focus such as the identifier, transform or validation service. Besides that, the ARIADNE validator ensures that our approach is scalable by avoiding the publishing of erroneous metadata into the repository. At the moment, ARIADNE exposes 822.126 valid metadata instances from both ARIADNE and GLOBE.
- *Reliability* relates to the amount of time for the system being up and running correctly. To ensure the reliability of our infrastructure, we have integrated CruiseControl, an extensible framework for creating a custom continuous build process [4], to monitor the uptime and responsiveness of all services.

As a result, we are able to minimize the amount of time between failures. Furthermore, our tools and services are connected with a bug tracking system that allows users of e.g the ARIADNE finder to notify the technical support team when something is failing.

We have measured the degree to which the services are susceptible to failure by considering the presence of partial failures. The following calculations are based on the amount of time that the services were up and running correctly. By using the CruiseControl log data, we obtained the data required to analyze the reliability of ARIADNE services. This data has shown that all services have been up and running in 95% of the time during a period of 1 year, which is an acceptable outcome for service uptime. The log data also shows that most of the failures happened during the night which is due to the fact that during the day, technical partners are continuously aware of the system status.

- *Performance* measures the response time of the system to specific events. In the case of harvesting learning resources from content providers, the performance heavily depends on the performance of the OAI-PMH targets itself. For example, some providers might have been running the target on a slow machine which degrades the performance of a harvesting cycle. Besides that, performance is important for our tools on top of our repository such as the ARIADNE finder where we want to quickly find results in the repository if a users issues a query. To enable efficient, fast and facetted search, we make use of the combination of the open source Apache Lucene and SOLR frameworks. The authors from [23] show that Lucene performs well on keeping both the index size and the RAM usage small, and on providing powerful, accurate and efficient search algorithms.

   Apache JMeter, a load testing tool [3], has been used to collect quantitative data about the performance of ARIADNE services. We have measured the response time of our search services on top of the GLOBE repository. Our test simulated 15 parallel users doing 100 queries each. Figure 3 shows the results of our test: the average response time of the services is around 300 milliseconds, with some busy peaks of less than 2 seconds. Those results are acceptable for now but we know from Shneiderman [29], that systems should achieve a rapid 100ms interaction loop if we want the user perceived performance to be real good. Therefore, ARIADNE is currently investigating an in-memory search approach for further optimizing performance. First tests show us that this will allow ARIADNE to achieve a response time around 100ms in the near future.

- *Configurability* refers to post-deployment modification of components, or configurations of components, such that they are capable of using a new service. We have shown in section 4 that it is easy to configure the combination of ARIADNE services considering the scenario that is needed. For example, when the need arises to convert a custom metadata format from a content provider into e.g. the ASPECT Application Profile of IEEE LOM; a new module can easily be plugged into the transformation service. Another example is that the harvester can easily be configured to not use the

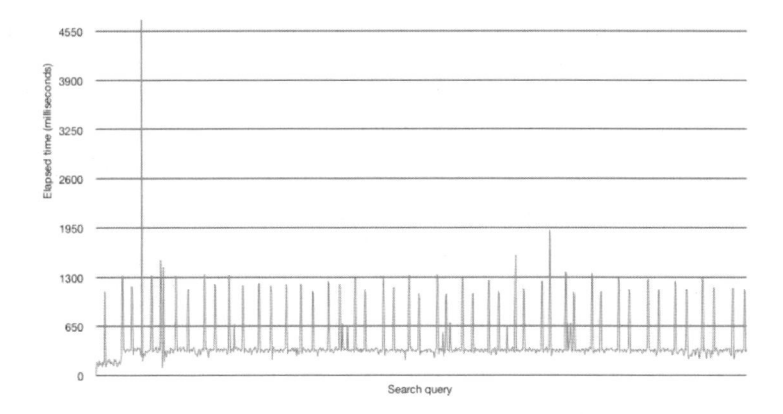

Fig. 3. Response time of ARIADNE Search service

transformation service if a content providers metadata is IEEE LOM. A third and last example is the storage layer; it is decoupled from the middle layer services which enables us to choose any database just by some small changes in a configuration file.

6 Related Work

As an open source, standards-based architecture for managing learning objects, ARIADNE has quite some technical commonalities with other architectures such as Fedora, LionShare, Edutella, and others. An extensive overview has been presented in [33]. Besides the technical aspects, ARIADNE shares quite some commonalities with numerous organizations all over the world like LORNET in Canada [7], the Learning Resource Exchange (LRE) of European Schoolnet [5], MERLOT in the USA [20], The Open University of Japan [8], KERIS in Korea, III in Taiwan, LACLO in Latin America [6], etc. This list is far from exhaustive.

All of those use various technologies and metadata schemes but they all strive to be interoperable with each other to make shared online learning resources available to educators and students around the world. ARIADNE is one of the founding members of GLOBE, a global alliance that has committed to work collaboratively on this shared vision of ubiquitous access to quality educational content.

7 Conclusion

ARIADNE has been improving its services constantly. However, with the inclusion of a number of new services such as the registry service and the identification service, ARIADNE has now reached a level of maturity leading to a much greater uptake.

The ARIADNE infrastructure has proven to be capable to provide flexible, effective and efficient access to large-scale collections. At the moment, ARIADNE exposes around a million learning resources through various repositories and networks of repositories that are registered in the ARIADNE registry. This number will undoubtedly increase in the coming months and years as more and more repositories are connecting to GLOBE.

This collection of learning resources allows for interesting research questions related to end users. Currently, we are focussing on accessing the learning material in various ways through information visualization [16], mobile information devices [26], multi-touch displays and mash-up applications.

In this paper, we have introduced a set of services which allows the integration and management of learning objects, described in various metadata schemas in numerous repositories across the globe. These services provide the backbone for an open learning infrastructure that provides access to impressive numbers of learning resources. As such, the abundance that we help to unlock will act as a platform for innovation by tool developers, trainers and teachers and learners themselves.

Acknowledgements

The work presented in this paper is partially supported by the European Commission eContentplus programme - projects ASPECT (ECP-2007-EDU-417008) and ICOPER (ECP-2007-EDU-417007).

References

1. Package exchange notification services (pens), http://www.aicc.org/docs/AGRs/agr011v1.pdf
2. Simple web-service offering repository deposit (sword), http://swordapp.org/
3. Apache jmeter (April 2010), http://jakarta.apache.org/jmeter
4. Cruisecontrol (April 2010), http://cruisecontrol.sourceforge.net/
5. European schoolnet, http://www.eun.org/ (last retrieved: April 2010)
6. The latin american community of learning objects (laclo), http://www.laclo.org/ (last retrieved: April 2010)
7. Lornet, www.lornet.ca (last retrieved: April 2010)
8. Open university of japan, http://www.u-air.ac.jp/eng/index.html (last retrieved: April 2010)
9. Bass, L., Clements, P., Kazman, R.: Software Architecture in Practice, 2nd edn. SEI Series in software engineering. Addison-Wesley Professional, Reading (June 2006) ISBN 0321154959
10. Baumgartner, P., Vuorikari, R., Van Assche, F., Duval, E., Zens, B., Massart, D., Vandeputte, B., Mesdom, F.: Experiences with the learning resource exchange for schools in europe. elearningeuropa.info (December 2009)
11. Duval, E., Hodgins, W.: Standardized uniqueness: Oxymoron or vision of the future? Computer 39(3), 96–98 (2006)

12. Massart, D., Smith, N., Tice, R.: D2.2 design of data model and architecture for a registry of learning object repositories and application profiles (2008), http://www.aspect-project.org/sites/default/files/docs/ASPECT_D2p2.pdf
13. Globe. The globe consortium (2008), http://globe-info.org/globe/go (last retrieved: April 2008)
14. IEEE. IEEE Standard for Learning Object Metadata. The Institute of Electrical and Electronics Engineers, Inc., 3 Park Avenue, New York, NY 10016-5997, USA (September 2002)
15. ISO/IEC. Iso/iec 11578:1996 information technology - open systems interconnection - remote procedure call (1996), http://www.iso.ch/cate/d2229.html
16. Klerkx, J., Verbert, K., Duval, E.: Visualizing reuse: more than meets the eye. In: Tochtermann, K., Maurer, H. (eds.) Proceedings of 7th International Conference on Knowledge Management, Graz, Austria, pp. 389–396 (2006)
17. Lee, D., Chu, W.W.: Comparative analysis of six xml schema languages. SIGMOD Rec. 29(3), 76–87 (2000)
18. Manouselis, N., Najjar, J., Kastrantas, K., Salokhe, G., Stracke, C., Duval, E.: Metadata interoperability in agricultural learning repositories: an analysis. Computers and Electronics in Agriculture 70(2), 302–320 (2010)
19. McCallum, S.: A look at new information retrieval protocols: Sru, opensearch/a9, cql, and xquery. Library of Congress, USA (2006)
20. McMartin, F.: Case study: MERLOT: A model of user involvement in digital library design and implementation. Journal of Digital Information 5(3) (September 2004)
21. Meire, M., Ochoa, X., Duval, E.: Samgi: Automatic metadata generation v2.0. In: AACE (ed.) Proceedings of World Conference on Educational Multimedia, Hypermedia and Telecommunications, pp. 1195–1204 (2007)
22. MELT. the melt project (2008), http://www.melt-project.eu
23. Middleton, C., Baeza-Yates, R.: Technical report: A comparison of open source search engines. Technical report, Universitat Pompeu Fabra, Barcelona, Spain (November 2008)
24. Najjar, J., Wolpers, M., Duval, E.: Contextualized attention metadata. D-Lib Magazine 13(9/10) (2007)
25. Ochoa, X., Duval, E.: Use of contextualized attention metadata for ranking and recommending learning objects. In: CAMA 2006: Proceedings of the 1st international workshop on Contextualized attention metadata: collecting, managing and exploiting of rich usage information, pp. 9–16. ACM, New York (2006)
26. Parra, G., Duval, E.: More! a social discovery tool for researchers. In: Proceedings of ED-MEDIA 2010-World Conference on Educational Multimedia, Hypermedia & Telecommunications (2010) (accepted)
27. PILIN Project. Pilin project: Project closure report (December 2007), https://www.pilin.net.au/Closure_Report.pdf
28. Safehaus. Java uuid generator(jug) (April 2010), http://jug.safehaus.org/Home
29. Shneiderman, B., Bederson, B.B.: The Craft of Information Visualization: Readings and Reflections. Morgan Kaufmann Publishers Inc., San Francisco (2003)
30. Simon, B., Massart, D., van Assche, F., Ternier, S., Duval, E., Brantner, S., Olmedilla, D., Miklos, Z.: A Simple Query Interface for Interoperable Learning Repositories. In: Proceedings of the 1st Workshop on Interoperability of Web-based Educational Systems, pp. 11–18 (2005)
31. Van De Sompel, H., Nelson, M.L., Lagoze, C., Warner, S.: Resource harvesting within the oai-pmh framework. D-Lib Magazine 10(nb. 12) (December 2004)

32. Demidova, E., Olmedilla, D., Memmel, M., Ternier, S., Massart, D., Duval, E.: D4.8 spi – the simple publishing interface. Technical report, Prolearn
33. Ternier, S., Verbert, K., Parra, G., Vandeputte, B., Klerkx, K., Duval, E., Ordonez, V., Ochoa, X.: The ariadne infrastructure for managing and storing metadata. IEEE Internet Computing 13(4), 18–25 (2009)
34. Ternier, S., Massart, D., Campi, A., Guinea, S., Ceri, S., Duval, E.: Interoperability for searching learning object repositories, the prolearn query language. D-Lib Magazine 14(1/2) (January/February 2008)
35. Verbert, K., Duval, E.: Alocom: a generic content model for learning objects. International Journal on Digital Libraries 9(1), 41–63 (2008)
36. CEN WS-LT. The simple publishing interface specification (cwa 16097), ftp://ftp.cen.eu/CEN/Sectors/TCandWorkshops/Workshops/CWA16097.pdf

Towards Improved Support for Adaptive Collaboration Scripting in IMS LD

Florian König and Alexandros Paramythis

Johannes Kepler University
Institute for Information Processing and Microprocessor Technology (FIM)
Altenbergerstraße 69, A-4040 Linz, Austria
{koenig,alpar}@fim.uni-linz.ac.at

Abstract. The IMS Learning Design specification is acknowledged as the most promising option available presently for the implementation of collaboration scripts in e-learning. Nevertheless, it has been criticized for a number of shortcomings, and, specifically for its lack of support for constructs that would enable comprehensive adaptive support to be effected over the collaborative learning process. In this paper we propose concrete extensions to the specification, which build upon prior work and address a wide range of problems and omissions. The most important modifications introduced include: explicit support for groups, and run-time member assignment; addition of a run-time model; introduction of concrete artefacts; introduction of an event-handling model; and, a modified sequencing and script organization model.

Keywords: collaborative learning, adaptive support, learning design, IMS LD, extension, sequencing, grouping, artifact.

1 Introduction

It is widely acknowledged that a large part of the success of the learning process lies with the opportunities of learners to interact with others: group work, exchanging ideas, and helping each other (thereby learning oneself) are standard "classroom" practices [1]. The establishment of online learning as a viable alternative to "traditional" approaches has resulted in the progressive lifting of geographical, temporal and other barriers to learning; but, at the same time, it has introduced obstacles in approaching learning as a social activity, due to the limited contact between learners that absence of physical collocation inevitably incurs [2].

The field of Computer-Supported Collaborative Learning (CSCL), which first appeared as a specialized direction in the area of Computer-Supported Collaborative Work (CSCW), is at the dichotomy between CSCW and e-learning, and seeks to support the various forms of collaborative learning in online settings [3]. A core focus of CSCL work is on ways in which collaborative learning supported by technology can enhance peer interaction and work in groups, and ways in which collaboration and technology facilitate sharing of knowledge and expertise among community members. A promising axis of work within CSCL is the scaffolding of productive interactions between learners by specifying in detail the 'collaboration' contract in a scenario

[1], in so-called CSCL scripts [4]. The later are external, computational representations of collaboration scripts, which are sets of instructions specifying how the members of a group should interact and collaborate to solve a particular problem [5].

The work reported in this paper falls within a line of research that seeks to further the principles underlying the use of CSCL scripts to guide the collaborative learning process, by introducing the dimension of adaptivity [6]. In this context, adaptivity concerns the provision of automated support within learning processes that involve communication between multiple learners (and, therefore, social interaction), and, potentially, collaboration towards common objectives. Furthermore, the support provided should be tailored to the specific requirements of both the participating individuals, and the social units in which they are involved (e.g., groups undertaking course projects). The goal of this line of work can then be stated as enabling the incorporation within CSCL scripts of constructs that would allow for expressing the types of adaptive support that a system can automatically offer to learners in the context of collaborative learning activities.

Unfortunately, the main starting point towards the above stated goal, namely a general modelling language for formalising collaboration scripts, is still missing [4]. At present, the most promising effort in that direction is the IMS Learning Design (IMS LD) specification [7], which evolved out of the Educational Modelling Language developed by the Open University of the Netherlands [8]. IMS LD is a learning process modelling language, fashioned on the theatrical play metaphor (e.g., with plays, actors, roles, etc.), and intended to formally describe any design of teaching-learning processes for a wide range of pedagogical approaches [8, 9].

IMS LD has been criticized both for its lack of support for sufficiently expressing aspects of the collaborative learning process [4], and for the absence of constructs that are vital in supporting adaptivity in scripts [10]. This paper builds upon that criticism, as well as on proposals for extensions of the specification that have appeared in the literature (discussed in the next section), to propose a comprehensive set of modifications and additions to IMS LD, aiming to address many of its general shortcomings and lay the foundations for improved support for adaptivity in CSCL scripts.

The rest of the paper is structured as follows. Section 2 presents an account of shortcomings of IMS LD and proposals for extensions that have appeared in the literature. Section 3 outlines the modifications and extensions proposed, relating them to two exemplary adaptive collaborative learning scenarios. Finally, section 4 summarizes the goals that can be achieved through the proposed amendments, and provides an outlook on issues that we want to address in future iterations.

2 Related Work

The IMS Learning Design modelling language has its strengths in specifying personalized and asynchronous cooperative learning. In the area of (adaptive) collaboration scripting, however, a number of shortcomings have been identified [4]: Modelling multiple groups independent from their role(s) is possible in IMS LD only with limitations, and manipulating groups at run-time is not supported. Miao and Hoppe [11] introduced an extension for modelling groups, which relies on newly defined operations for creating and deleting groups, member management and run-time state queries. However, they do not provide a high-level specification mechanism for run-time grouping, which would make it easy for both authors and adaptation engines to express and understand the semantics of group (membership) management.

In IMS LD there are also no means to specify how the members of a group interact within an activity, other than through a so-called "conference service" [12]. Hernández-Leo et al. [13] proposed the "groupservice" for specifying group collaboration spaces with communication facilities, floor control, support for different interaction paradigms and awareness functionality. This approach, however, suffers from the same limitations as the original IMS LD specification: the actual collaboration happens outside the script's specification and control. Miao et al. [4] proposed running multiple instances of activities, if required by the respective social plane (one per role/group/person) to allow, for example, groups to work in parallel on the same problem. Their approach, however, is still not geared towards maximum expressive flexibility. Even with these multiple instance activities, IMS LD provides insufficient support for (collective) artefacts [4] and no straightforward mechanism to model the flow of artefacts between activities [14]. Therefore, proposed already to some extent by Caeiro et al. [15], Miao et al. [4] also defined a possible model for artefacts, where the data flow is derived from the specification of creation-/consume- activities.

IMS LD's activity sequencing capabilities have been described as "quite simplistic" [16] and fine-grained splitting or synchronization of the control flow is not readily expressible [4]. Caeiro et al. [15] addressed some shortcomings by introducing a different model for the role-part in IMS LD. It would link elements according to the guiding question of who (roles) does what (act) in which way (operational role) where (environment) and towards which objective (outcome). The operational role would be independent from a person's roles in order to make varying responsibilities possible. They also proposed having conditional transitions between acts to allow more complex sequencing. Miao et al. [4] reiterated the need for advanced transition and routing constructs guided by approaches in the area of workflow management.

The features discussed until now form the basis for collaboration scripting. With respect to explicit support for adaptivity, IMS LD is missing a model of the run-time state of the script, and an event model, and has only a limited number of functions to modify aspects of the collaboration process while the script is running [10]. Paramythis and Christea [17] present some more requirements for adaptation languages in the area of collaboration support, none of which are supported by IMS LD: workflow- or process- based reasoning, temporal operators, policies for grouping and clustering, invoking system facilities / manipulating system state and support for "provisional" adaptation decisions. In our approach, we address a number of these requirements and lay the foundations for supporting more in the future. The following section describes our proposed extensions to IMS LD. We aimed to cover the aforementioned collaboration support requirements and the requirements with regard to adaptivity.

3 Proposed Extensions to IMS LD

Our approach combines ideas from many of the extensions proposed in related work, puts them into a coherent information model and introduces additional features that are intended to better support adaptivity. It encompasses the modelling of groups, run-time group and role membership assignment (section 3.1), group properties and property collections, a run-time model, an adapted and extended set of operators (section 3.2), an extensible modelling of services (section 3.3), artefacts, event handling, and new actions for effecting the scenario at run-time (section 3.4) as well as a flexible sequencing model (section 3.5). The relevant changes are depicted in diagrams of the information model, to be found in Fig. 1, 2 and 3, and resembling the diagrams in the original IMS LD specification [7]: child elements are either in a sequential (orthogonal connectors) or a choice (angular connectors) grouping; they are optional (question mark symbol) or required once (no symbol), zero or more times (star symbol), or one or more times (plus symbol). In the process of making the diagrams as space-efficient as possible, the order of the elements could not always be kept the same as in the textual description. Due to the complexity of both the original and the extended model, it is advisable to follow the diagrams in parallel to the explanations.

To explain our extensions in the context of real examples, we will use two well-known collaborative learning scenarios, JigSaw [18] and Thinking Aloud Pair Problem Solving (TAPPS) [19], that are often implemented as CSCL scripts. Both examples require features that cannot be modelled with the original IMS LD specification. Table 1 summarizes the unique requirements of each scenario, the limitations of IMS LD, and in which section the extension supporting the requirement is proposed.

Table 1. Limitations of IMS LD support for unique requirements of scenaria

Scenario	Requirement	IMS LD limitations	Extension
JigSaw	run-time grouping by characteristics	no concept of groups	section 3.1
	run-time casting of group leader	roles assigned before start	section 3.1
	(group) collaboration contexts	not in process model	section 3.1
		no group workspaces	and 3.5
	explicit artefacts, flow of artefacts	only properties	section 3.4
	flexible event handling (e.g., detecting when artefact delivered)	unstructured set of conditions with no semantics	section 3.4
TAPPS	service selection by criteria	only 3 types of "conference" service specified	section 3.3
	role rotation between participants	roles fixed during run	section 3.4
	multiple executions of activity (loop)	rigid sequencing model	section 3.5

In JigSaw, learners are grouped into mixed (ability, knowledge, …) groups of 5-6 members and a group leader is appointed. The material is split into 5-6 topics and each group member gets assigned to one. Students read their material individually and then come together in "expert groups" (one per topic), where they discuss their parts and how they are going to present them to their JigSaw groups. The students then reunite in the JigSaw groups, present their topic, and group peers can ask questions. In the end, each group collaboratively solves an assignment that involves all topics. The instructor collects the assignments and provides feedback. In TAPPS, students are paired and given a list of problems. One gets assigned the role of "problem solver", the other becomes the "listener". The problem solver tries to solve the problem while thinking aloud. The listener follows, identifies errors and asks questions. After solving a problem, they exchange roles and move on to the next problem.

3.1 Groups, Roles and Run-Time Member Assignment

In IMS LD, grouping participants can only be simulated by assigning them to predefined, static roles. Roles are expected to be populated before the unit of learning starts and role membership does not change thereafter. In our approach, groups can be directly modelled, and assignment of participants to both groups and roles is possible at run-time. There are statically defined groups and dynamic groups, which are created at run-time according to certain constraints (e.g., preferred size). Static groups are defined by *group* elements, which reside in *groups* in the *components* part of the script (see Fig. 1). Each group has a name (*title*) and can optionally have *information*, for example regarding its purpose. A *group-environment* (referencing *environment* elements) can be specified to give a group its own "group space", for example with communication facilities and shared material. In the JigSaw example, there would exist a group for each topic (the "expert group") with the material provided in the respective *group-environment*. Sub-groups can be defined via nested *group* elements.

The specification for creating dynamic groups and assigning participants to (static and dynamic) groups is located in *grouping* elements (see Fig. 1). A grouping consists of a set of groups and a mapping of participants to them. Groupings may be requested from an external provider (*provided-grouping*) or created at run-time (*runtime-grouping*). The first option allows re-using groupings, which exist for example in the LMS running the script. For a *runtime-grouping* the *partition* specifies, into which groups participants should be grouped. This can be a *static-group-set* containing references to existing *group* definitions or a *dynamic-group-set* with a set of constraints according to which groups are created automatically at run-time: The *number-of-groups* can be constrained to an *exact* number, a range (*from, to*) and/or to be *divisible-by* a specific value. The *group-size* element can be used to express equivalent constraints, so for the pairing in the TAPPS example an *exact* value of 2 can be set. In addition, one can specify a set of *proportions* to create, for example, groups with the size ratios of 1:2:4. Dynamic groups are automatically named and sequentially numbered (*group-names*) by specifying a *prefix* and/or *suffix* string around a *numbering* of *latin*, *roman* or *alphabetical* style (e.g., "Group III", "2. Gruppe", "Grupo k").

The *grouping-method* defines how the participants are assigned to groups. For a *manual* assignment, a *role* has to be referenced, which will be tasked to perform it manually. With *self-selected* assignment participants can themselves choose in which group they would like to be: a *direct* assignment is immediate; in a *prioritized* assignment participants can attach numeric priorities to each group to mark their (least) favoured choice and will then be assigned by balancing their preferences.

A totally *automatic* assignment can be *random*. Another possibility is *by-grouping-service* where a (possibly external) grouping service can be used to run a certain *grouping-strategy* with a set of *parameter* elements. This makes it possible to employ arbitrarily complex grouping algorithms and provide them with the required feature vector(s) of determinants. In the JigSaw example, where mixed groups are required, an algorithm could create them when provided with parameters detailing the relevant attributes (knowledge, interests, etc.) The *automatic* method *by-existing-grouping* can re-use the mapping of participants in *existing-groups* –represented by a *grouping* or a *static-group-set*– to create new groups. It is possible to *distribute* the members (approximately) equally over the new groups or *concentrate* them (i.e., keep them together). This is useful for example in JigSaw, where the JigSaw group members should be equally distributed across the groups representing the topics. With the method *role-selectable*, grouping methods can be specified, from which, at run-time, a member of the referenced *role* can choose one to perform the grouping.

For a *runtime-grouping* a *review* can be defined, which will present members of a referenced *role* with a certain *environment* to allow reviewing the result of the *grouping*. Like for single groups, a *group-environment* can be defined. Each group will be provided with its own group space according to this definition, which can also be set for a *provided-grouping*. Should a (static) group already have a group space, then the two will be merged with the one defined in *group* taking precedence.

The original definition of *roles* in IMS LD was kept, but a way has been added to specify how the assignment (i.e., "casting") of participants to them is to be performed at run-time. Similar to *grouping* there is a *casting* element, which also resides in the *method* part of the script (see Fig. 1). Under *roles-to-cast* multiple roles can be referenced, which will all get the same *role-environment*, if specified. The *casting-method* is similar to the *grouping-method*. With *by-vote* all eligible participants can vote (a) candidate(s) into a role either by a *direct* vote or *prioritized* by their preference to the candidates. The automatic *by-casting-service* method works like the *by-grouping-service* as described above, with one addition: for each role, multiple *role-requirement* elements can be used to specify criteria that prospective role members should fulfil. In JigSaw, this could contain information such as: the leader role should have an authority level above a certain threshold. Like for a grouping, a *review* can be defined for a casting as well. Depending on the scenario, not all roles can be cast at run-time, however. Any roles that need to be populated so that the learning-design can start must be referenced in the *initial-roles* element under *learning-design*.

3.2 Properties and Run-Time Model

Storing and accessing data inside a learning design using IMS LD is accomplished via properties. We have extended properties to account for groups and the need for collections (lists, sets). Additionally, we have defined a run-time model and means to use it in expressions, giving adaptation rules access to the run-time state of a scenario.

Groups can have a *locgroup-property*, which is local to the current run, as well as a *globgroup-property*, which is kept across runs. The owning group(s) need(s) to be specified in *owner* (see Fig. 1).

Static groups exist in every run and can have both local and global properties. Dynamically created groups can own only local properties, as the set of groups may change in every run. Groups of a *provided-grouping* may own global properties, which they keep as long as the external group exists.

Some extensions not related to collaboration have been added to the property model as well. They apply to every type of property, even though in Fig. 1 they are only shown in the context of the *locgroup-property*. Property and property group specifications now feature an optional *collection* element, where the type (ordered *list* or unordered *set*) can be specified. The *size* defines the maximum number of elements to be either *dynamic* or fixed to the result of an *expression*. The resulting property (group) is a collection of its defined data type. In order to constrain the content of a property of type *file*, the *restriction* now supports *mimeType* as a *restriction-type*. It takes a comma-separated list of MIME types (e.g. "text/html, text/xml, text/plain").

IMS LD allows only very limited access to run-time information via operators like *is-member-of-role*, *complete* or *time-unit-of-learning-started*. Most run-time modelling requires properties, but these custom-made models are not standardized or readily

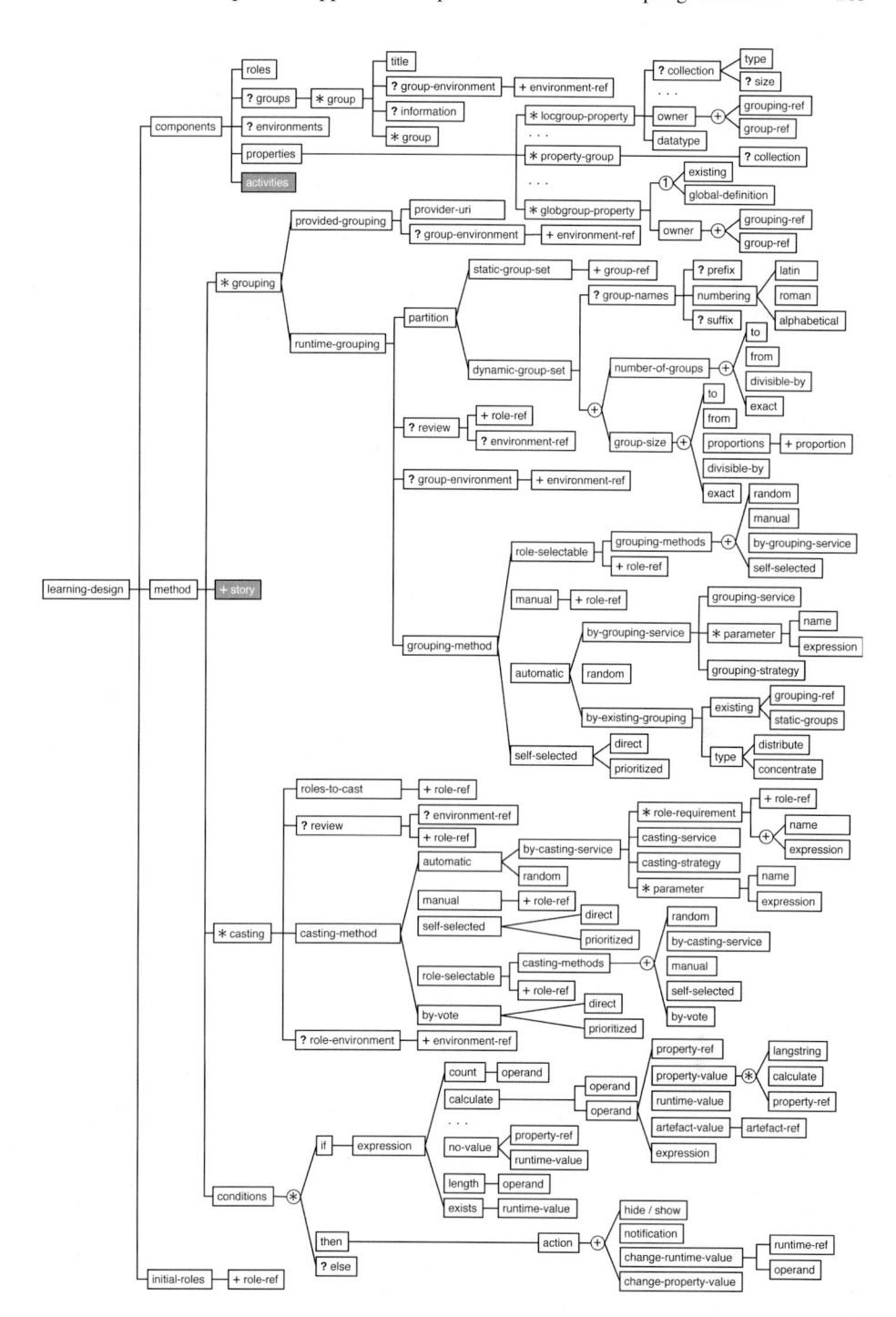

Fig. 1. Extensions to IMS LD (gray elements shown in following figures)

re-usable across scripts. The addition of a well-defined run-time model makes it possible to access a large part of the state information of a running script. The run-time model is structured like the static learning design and every statically defined element and attribute can be accessed. References are automatically resolved and the respective elements appear to contain the referenced ones. In addition, a range of run-time-only elements and attributes is added to the model (e.g., *members* in a *learner* role). One important (exclusively) run-time element, reachable for example via *members*, is *person*, which represents a participant. There is also a *system* element, which contains information about the run-time environment (e.g., *current-datetime*).

To access information inside the run-time model, the element *runtime-value* was added under *expression* in the *conditions* part as a new type of *operand* and in the *no-value* test operator. It expects a *run-time model access expression* following this syntax: *type[selector].property*. The *type* corresponds to the names of top-level-elements like *environment, learning-activity* or *group* and specifies which element(s) to access. In cases where there is no common type (e.g., *learner, staff*) the following "virtual" types can be used: *role, activity, property, condition*. If there exist more elements of the requested type in the run-time model, the *selector* can filter them with a logical or positional expression. Possible logical operators are =, !=, <, <=, >, >=, & (and), | (or) and ! (not). Parentheses can be used to group terms, and the precedence rules of the ANSI C programming language apply. Properties of elements to be filtered are accessed as *@property*. Literal values need to be enclosed in quotes (e.g., *role[@title = "leader"].members*). Positional expressions with integer results can be used as zero-based index in collections and do not need to be quoted (e.g., *group[@id = "grp1"].members[2]*). It is also possible to request collections, perform operations on them (see the end of this section), store them in collection properties (see above) or use them as parameters for adaptation actions (e.g., creating a group of participants which were retrieved from the run-time model). Selectors can contain nested run-time model access expressions. If the *property* in the expression is itself a structured element, it can be further filtered. Nested elements are accessed via the dot operator.

For writing to the run-time model, everywhere in the information model where *change-property-value* is permitted, the new element *change-runtime-value* can be used. It requires a *runtime-ref* containing a run-time model access expression pointing to the property that should be set. The value comes from an *operand* element.

Because the run-time model is dynamic, a new operator *exists* was introduced to check whether an object referenced by a run-time model access expression is present. When access to the run-time model is not guarded by an accompanying check with *exists*, accessing non-existing elements can result in exceptions. Therefore, script authors need mechanisms to detect exceptions and react accordingly. The specification of these exception handling mechanisms will be addressed in future work.

The following obsolete operators of the original IMS LD specification could be removed, because their results are now contained in the run-time model: *is-member-of-role, users-in-role, time-unit-of-learning-started, datetime-activity-started, current-datetime* and *complete*. The standard arithmetic *modulo* operator has been introduced, as well as a range of set (*contains, union, intersection, complement*) and temporal (*precedes, meets, overlaps, equals, includes*) operators, which have been omitted from the diagram for reasons of space efficiency. To support collections, a *count* operator for getting the number of elements has been added. The number of characters in a text string can be determined with the new *length* operator.

3.3 Services

The definition of services in the IMS LD specification has been criticized as being rather inflexible [15]. Our approach builds upon the *Generic Service Integration* approach of Valentin et al. [20] and provides three ways to specify a service: direct reference (URI), type selection (by a descriptor like *service:chat*) or constraint-based (requesting for example a direct, synchronous, speech-oriented communication service for the thinking aloud sessions in the TAPPS example). As the service specification is, very important in general, albeit not of direct relevance to the immediate support of collaboration in a learning design, we will not go deeper into this topic here.

3.4 Activities, Artefacts, Event-Handling and Actions

Grouping participants and casting them into roles conceptually fits neither in a *learning-activity* nor in a *support-activity*. Therefore, we have created two new activity types. A way to specify artefacts as one of the basic building blocks of collaborative work has been added as well. In order to support fine-grained means to react to runtime events, a mechanism to define event handling and perform actions is proposed.

Like for learning activities, there needs to be an element for describing acts of grouping participants or casting them into roles, that can be referenced when defining the sequencing of a learning design. We have extended the IMS LD specification by a *grouping-activity* and a *casting-activity* (see Fig. 2). Both reference a *grouping* or a *casting* respectively, can use a certain *environment* and have an *activity-description*. Their mode can be set to either "start from scratch" (*create-grouping* / *cast-roles*) or to *add-members* or *remove-members*, where existing groupings / castings need to be expanded or shrunk. These activities allow for creating groups and populating groups and roles. Disbanding groups and removing roles is part of the adaptation actions that will be defined in future iterations of this extension to IMS LD.

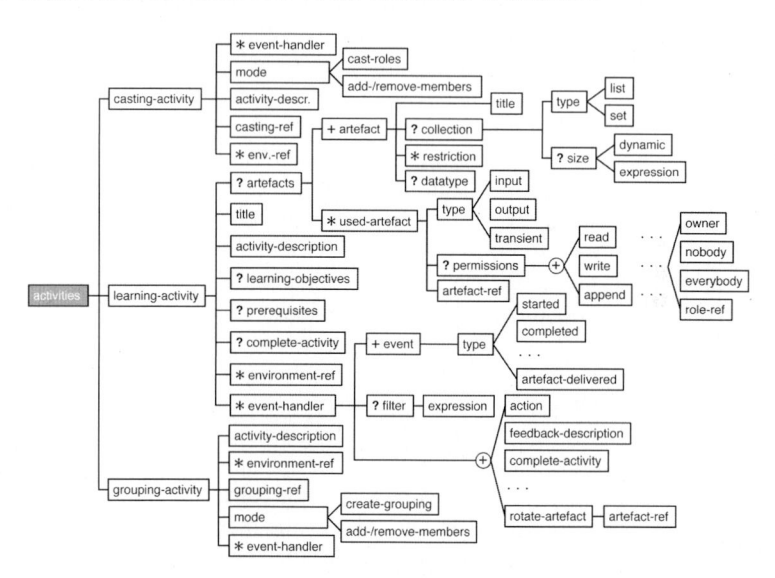

Fig. 2. Extensions to the *activities* element of IMS LD

In the original IMS LD specification, the results of work performed by participants are stored in and retrieved from properties. Access to them is possible via any referenced XHTML document through the use of special *global-elements* tags. The script itself, however, did not contain any explicit information about which result had to be created in which activity, and where else this result was used. In our approach, *artefacts* can be specifically defined in a *learning-activity*. An *artefact* has a *title* and the author can specify whether the artefact is a *collection*, or whether any other *restriction* applies (see definition of properties). If an artefact should be visible in a certain activity, it can be referenced as a *used-artefact*. An *output* artefact can be set during the activity, one of type *input* is only shown, and *input-output* artefacts can be both accessed and changed. Artefacts are owned by the entity that created them (participant or group). The default *permissions* (*read*, *write*, *append*) belong to the *owner*. However, it is also possible to give those permissions to either *nobody*, *everybody* in the current activity or members of a certain *role*. In the JigSaw example, students would create an output artefact as a solution to the assignment in one activity. In the next activity, this artefact could be used as an input artefact, and the instructor role could be given read access. The feedback artefact created by the instructor would be handled in a similar way. Finally, like properties, an artefact may be used in an *expression*. It can be either referenced directly as an *operand* via an *artefact-ref* or its value be read when referencing it inside the *artefact-value* element (see Fig. 2).

With the *on-completion* element in IMS LD one can specify that certain actions should be performed (e.g., *change-property-value*) when something (e.g., an activity) is completed. Two restrictions exist in this approach: it is not possible to perform an action when something starts (or some other event occurs); and, there are actions (e.g., *show* and *hide* for controlling the visibility of elements) that cannot be triggered. The first restriction was tackled by replacing *on-completion* with *event-handler* elements, each able to handle a certain event (e.g., *started*, *completed*, *artefact-delivered*, ...). The second restriction was resolved by collecting common actions in an *action* element in the *then* (and *else*) part of a *condition* (see Fig. 1). In an *event-handler*, any of those actions may be triggered. Depending on the element in which the handler is defined, additional actions (e.g., *complete-activity*) can be defined. The list of possible events is also specific to the surrounding element. Every *event-handler* can also have a *filter* with an *expression* to specify the exact conditions when it triggers actions. In the *expression*, the run-time event can be accessed via the special construct *$event*. Each event has a *timestamp* property and, depending on its type, it may have additional properties (e.g., *activity*: to access the activity that has completed). A complete list of events and their properties cannot be provided here due to lack of space.

Comprehensive support for adaptive interventions requires a large number of actions in order to change most parts of the run-time model and effect changes on the execution of the learning design. A number of actions has already been added to address shortcomings of IMS LD. Event handlers of a *learning-activity* can for example trigger a *rotate-artefact* action to effect a circular exchange of the referenced artefact among the entities (single participants or whole groups) currently performing the activity. The *rotate-roles* action rotates roles among participants of a certain *casting* (which must have assigned more than one role) or the members of a set of groups. In TAPPS, for each pair there would be a casting for the "problem solver" and "listener" roles. With the *rotate-roles* action, the roles can be switched between the members of each pair. In addition to these two examples, many other actions need to be defined, for example for creating and removing roles, groups, environments and activities, adding to and removing members from roles and groups, managing properties and altering the sequencing of activities, to name just a few.

3.5 Sequencing

For complex scenarios and even more so for adaptive collaboration scripts, which require flexible execution flows, the sequencing semantics of the original IMS LD specification have been found to be constraining [21] and difficult to understand [22]. Due to the lack of state-of-the art concurrency control features, one would often have to resort to custom-made mechanisms employing properties and conditions. In our approach, we have aimed at simplifying the constructs needed for sequencing, while at the same time supporting groups, allowing arbitrary transitions between activities and employing flexible concurrency controls from the area of workflow management.

The original metaphor of a theatrical play has been replaced by the following concept (see also Fig. 3): in a *story* there are *scene* elements, sequenced by directional transitions connecting them. Each scene has *actors* defined by their *role*, who perform a *task*: an *activity* or alternatively a nested *story*. In addition to the *environment* in the *activity*, one can be specified for each scene as well, possibly as an override.

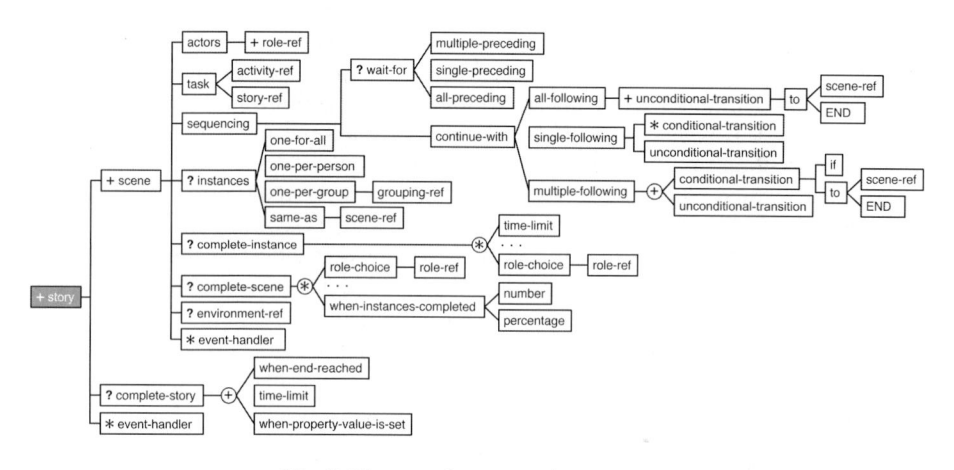

Fig. 3. Elements for sequencing activities

The multiplicity of a scene is a central concept of our approach. When a scene is run in a single instance (*one-for-all*), all actors share the same activity and, through it, environment and artefacts. Alternatively, a scene can be split into multiple instances: *one-per-person* or *one-per-group* with a respective reference to a *grouping*. For Jig-Saw, the reading and expert group scenes would be split by topic grouping, whereas the topic presentations and assignment solving scenes would be split to give each JigSaw group a separate instance. TAPPS pairs also act in individual instances. By specifying *same-as*, the multiplicity is inherited from the referenced *scene*. The multiplicity also defines how artefacts are aggregated or distributed: artefacts created in the activity of a multi-instance scene are collected and made available when they are used in the activity of a subsequent single-instance scene. Artefacts originating from a single-instance scene and used in a multi-instance scene, are copied to each instance. Other transfers are only possible when the multiplicity of both scenes matches.

Our model of sequencing has been influenced by common workflow control-flow patterns [23]. These represent generally acknowledged solutions to frequently encountered sequencing requirements in flow-oriented process models. Torres and Dodero [21] have found IMS LD to be lacking with regard to expressing certain workflow patterns. By modelling the patterns' basic building blocks as well as supporting some of them directly, improved support could be attained. Individual *scene* elements are connected by transitions to form a general graph. This provides maximum flexibility and makes it possible to model loops (required for example in the TAPPS scenario, see Fig. 4), which are not supported by IMS LD. As discussed by Gutierrez-Santos et al. [24], we also needed to amend the original semantics, so that activities can be completed multiple times when they are instantiated more than once in a loop.

Depending on the flow split mode, set via *continue-with* in *sequencing*, elements of *unconditional-transition* or *conditional-transition* are needed. The latter require an *if* element with a logical *expression* that evaluates to *true* to activate the transition. Both types can lead either to a referenced *scene* or (through the special value *END*) to the end of the current story. Using the flow split mode of *all-following* splits the flow to all outgoing transitions (AND-split). With *single-following*, the flow follows the first *conditional-transition* that has been set active by its condition, or alternatively the mandatory *unconditional-transition* (XOR-split). In *multiple-following* mode, the execution flow continues along all active transitions, resulting in multiple outgoing flows (OR-join). Conversely, with the element *wait-for* the mode of synchronizing incoming execution flows can be specified: It is optional by default and *all-preceding* is assumed, which synchronizes all incoming flows (AND-join). With *single-preceding*, the flow continues after arriving from a single incoming transition (XOR-join). The *multiple-preceding* mode has the following semantics: execution continues after one or more incoming flows have been received and there is no incoming transition left, over which another flow could arrive in the future (OR-join). This last mode, albeit useful and used for implementing a number of workflow patterns, is not straightforward to implement because it requires non-local semantics [23].

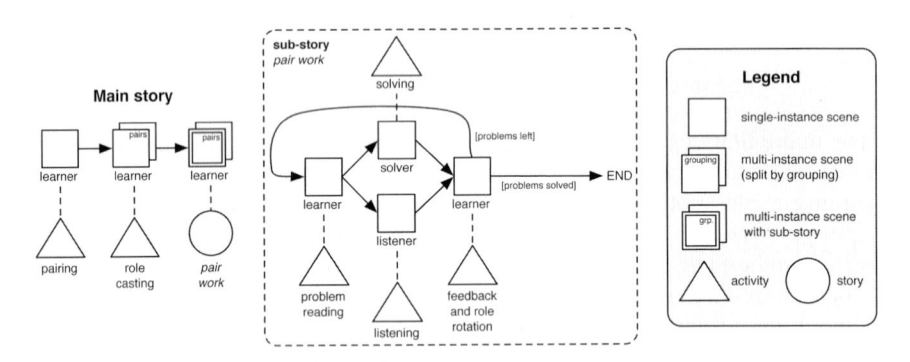

Fig. 4. Simple representation of TAPPS [19] with new sequencing semantics

By default, an instance of a scene (be it the only one or one of multiple) completes when its activity or nested sub-story completes. In the *complete-instance* element, however, multiple completion criteria can be defined. The options have been carried over from the IMS LD element *act*, and a new element has been added: *role-choice* gives members of the specified role a possibility for manual intervention. These options are also valid choices for the *complete-scene* predicate element. Additionally, with *when-instances-completed* one can specify how many or what percentage of instances are required for scene completion. This might be useful to express the following scenario: learners solve a problem and as soon as 80% have solved it, the whole class moves on to look at common solutions.

4 Summary and Outlook

In this paper, we have presented extensions to the IMS Learning Design specification that aim to better express collaboration scripts and allow for more comprehensive adaptation to individual learners and groups. The new elements of the information model support explicit modelling of (static) groups, their properties and group environments. Assignment of participants to static, as well as to dynamically created groups can be controlled via a number of policies; the same is true for the assignment to roles. Activity types for these grouping and role casting operations have been introduced. The extensions support a run-time model, giving access to all elements of the script and pure run-time data, such as information on participants, while it is running. Access to the run-time model is possible in expressions, making some operators obsolete. New set and temporal operators have been added. The service specification has been made more flexible to account for the plethora of possible services in today's learning management systems. Artefacts can be modelled explicitly, may be assigned a data type, and have restrictions associated with them, like properties. In the context of a learning activity, artefacts may be used as input, output or transient elements, optionally with access permissions (read, write, append) for different participants. An extensible event handling specification with event-condition-action (ECA) semantics has been introduced, and new actions (e.g., rotate artefacts, rotate roles) for adapting the scenario at run-time have been defined. Finally, the original sequencing model has been replaced with a more flexible one, which supports running multiple instances of activities according to the social plane (class, group, individual), offers (conditional) transitions for arbitrary sequencing of activities and uses workflow semantics for synchronizing and splitting the flow of action.

For future iterations of this information model, we plan to fine-tune its current features and provide new ones to enhance its expressiveness towards improved adaptivity. First, the run-time model needs to be fully and thoroughly specified, providing clear semantics for every element, its (data) type and multiplicity and introducing a temporal dimension to allow access to historic state information. Exception handling mechanisms need to be introduced to protect against script failure when non-existing elements of the run-time model are accessed. The run-time model needs to be made accessible from the client side (assuming the script is "executed" on the server side), in a way that conceptually extends (and ideally replaces) the *global-elements* of IMS LD. The main idea is to provide an implementation-independent interface specification similar to the SCORM run-time API [25], to allow for bi-directional data transfer between the learning design engine and the client (application). Another requirement is access from within the learning design script to external models like, for example, the personal learner models of participants in the learning management system. Making these models accessible via the respective element in the run-time model (e.g., person) would render them immediately usable by the mechanisms described so far.

For effecting adaptations, more actions are needed, especially for re-sequencing scenes, invoking system facilities (e.g., notifying participants) and manipulating the system state (e.g., controlling services). As suggested by Miao and Hoppe [11], a way to create expressions and action declarations needs to be modelled, in order to allow re-using sets of actions and complicated expressions. To support provisional adaptation decisions, a mechanism must exist to specify that certain participants (e.g., the instructor) should be consulted about whether to apply a specific adaptation or not. One of the benefits of such a model is that the instructor does not need to be present at all times, but can still monitor and control the scenario. Finally, the event model needs to be made more fine-grained to capture all possible events that occur during the run of a learning design and may be relevant for adaptation rules. This includes a basic event model for the different service types, so that participants' actions in them (e.g., chat entered, message posted, wiki page edited) can be reacted upon.

Once we have arrived at a mature specification that includes the additional elements described above, we intend to integrate a prototypical implementation of it into the Sakai e-learning platform [26]. This will then be employed in real-world student-based evaluations, where we will seek to establish the impact of the types of adaptive support that the new specification enables on the collaborative learning process.

Acknowledgements. The work reported in this paper has been supported by the "Adaptive Support for Collaborative E-Learning" (ASCOLLA) project, financed by the Austrian Science Fund (FWF; project number P20260-N15).

References

1. Dillenbourg, P.: What do you mean by collaborative learning? In: Dillenbourg, P. (ed.) Collaborative-learning: Cognitive and Computational Approaches, pp. 1–19. Elsevier, Oxford (1999)
2. Paramythis, A., Mühlbacher, J.R.: Towards New Approaches in Adaptive Support for Collaborative e-Learning. In: Proceedings of the 11th IASTED International Conference, Crete, Greece, pp. 95–100 (2008)
3. Lipponen, L.: Exploring foundations for computer-supported collaborative learning. In: Proceedings of the Conference on Computer Support for Collaborative Learning: Foundations for a CSCL Community, pp. 72–81. International Society of the Learning Sciences, Boulder (2002)
4. Miao, Y., Hoeksema, K., Hoppe, H.U., Harrer, A.: CSCL Scripts: Modelling Features and Potential Use. In: Proceedings of the 2005 Conference on Computer Support for Collaborative Learning – Learning 2005: The next 10 Years!, pp. 423–432. International Society of the Learning Sciences, Taipei (2005)

5. O'Donnell, A.M., Dansereau, D.F.: Scripted Cooperation in Student Dyada: A Method for Analyzing and Enhancing Academic Learning and Performance. In: Hertz-Lazarowitz, R., Miller, N. (eds.) Interaction in Cooperative Groups: The theoretical Anatomy of Group Learning, pp. 120–141. Cambridge University Press, London (1992)
6. Jameson, A.: Adaptive interfaces and agents. In: The human-computer interaction handbook: fundamentals, evolving technologies and emerging applications, pp. 305–330. L. Erlbaum Associates Inc., Mahwah (2003)
7. IMS Global Learning Consortium, Inc.: Learning Design Specification (Version 1.0 Final Specification) (2003), http://www.imsglobal.org/learningdesign/
8. Koper, R.: Modeling units of study from a pedagogical perspective: the pedagogical meta-model behind EML (2001), http://hdl.handle.net/1820/36
9. Koper, R., Olivier, B.: Representing the Learning Design of Units of Learning. Educational Technology & Society 7(3), 97–111 (2004)
10. Paramythis, A.: Adaptive Support for Collaborative Learning with IMS Learning Design: Are We There Yet? In: Proceedings of the Adaptive Collaboration Support Workshop, held in conjunction with the 5th International Conference on Adaptive Hypermedia and Adaptive Web-Based Systems (AH 2008), Hannover, Germany, pp. 17–29 (2008)
11. Miao, Y., Hoppe, U.: Adapting Process-Oriented Learning Design to Group Characteristics. In: Proceeding of the 2005 conference on Artificial Intelligence in Education: Supporting Learning through Intelligent and Socially Informed Technology, pp. 475–482. IOS Press, Amsterdam (2005)
12. Santos, O.C., Boticario, J.G., Barrera, C.: Authoring A Collaborative Task Extending the IMS-LD to be Performed in a Standard-Based Adaptive Learning Management System Called aLFanet. In: Proceedings of the Workshop on Adaptive Hypermedia and Collaborative Web-based Systems (AHCW 2004) held in conjunction with the International Conference on Web Engineering (ICWE 2004), Munich, Germany (2004)
13. Hernández-Leo, D., Perez, J., Dimitriadis, Y.: IMS Learning Design Support for the Formalization of Collaborative Learning Patterns. In: Proceedings of the IEEE International Conference on Advanced Learning Technologies (ICALT 2004), pp. 350–354 (2004)
14. Miao, Y., Burgos, D., Griffiths, D., Koper, R.: Representation of Coordination Mechanisms in IMS Learning Design to Support Group-based Learning. In: Handbook of Research on Learning Design and Learning Objects: Issues, Applications and Technologies, pp. 330–351. IDEA Group Publishing, Hershey (2009)
15. Caeiro, M., Anido, L., Llamas, M.: A Critical Analysis of IMS Learning Design. In: Proceedings of CSCL 2003, Bergen, Norway, pp. 363–367 (2003)
16. Dalziel, J.: From Re-usable E-learning Content to Re-usable Learning Designs: Lessons from LAMS (2005),
http://www.lamsinternational.com/CD/html/resources.html
17. Paramythis, A., Cristea, A.: Towards Adaptation Languages for Adaptive Collaborative Learning Support. In: Proceedings of the First International Workshop on Individual and Group Adaptation in Collaborative Learning Environments (WS12) held in conjunction with the 3rd European Conference on Technology Enhanced Learning (EC-TEL 2008), Maastricht, The Netherlands (2008). CEUR Workshop Proceedings, ISSN 1613-0073, online CEUR-WS.org/Vol-384/
18. Aronson, E., Blaney, N., Stephin, C., Sikes, J., Snapp, M.: The Jigsaw Classroom. Sage Publishing Company, Beverly Hills (1978)
19. Lochhead, J., Whimbey, A.: Teaching analytical reasoning through thinking aloud pair problem solving. New Directions for Teaching and Learning, 73–92 (1987)

20. de la Fuente Valentin, L., Miao, Y., Pardo, A., Delgado Kloos, C.: A Supporting Architecture for Generic Service Integration in IMS Learning Design. In: Dillenbourg, P., Specht, M. (eds.) EC-TEL 2008. LNCS, vol. 5192, pp. 467–473. Springer, Heidelberg (2008)
21. Torres, J., Dodero, J.M.: Analysis of Educational Metadata Supporting Complex Learning Processes. Metadata and Semantic Research, pp. 71–82 (2009)
22. Hagen, K., Hibbert, D., Kinshuk, P.: Developing a Learning Management System Based on the IMS Learning Design Specification. In: IEEE International Conference on Advanced Learning Technologies (ICALT 2006), pp. 420–424. IEEE Computer Society, Los Alamitos (2006)
23. Russell, N., Arthur, van der Aalst, W., Mulyar, N.: Workflow Control-Flow Patterns: A Revised View. BPM Center (2006)
24. Gutierrez-Santos, S., Pardo, A., Kloos, C.D.: Authoring Courses with Rich Adaptive Sequencing for IMS Learning Design. Journal of Universal Computer Science, 14, 2819–2839 (2008)
25. Advanced Distributed Learning Initiative: Sharable Content Object Reference Model (SCORM) 2004, 4th edn. Version 1.1 – Run-Time Environment (2009), http://www.adlnet.gov/Technologies/scorm/
26. Sakai Project. Sakai Foundation, http://www.sakaiproject.org

Providing Varying Degrees of Guidance for Work-Integrated Learning

Stefanie Lindstaedt[1,2], Barbara Kump[1], Günter Beham[1], Viktoria Pammer[1], Tobias Ley[1,3], Amir Dotan[4], and Robert de Hoog[5]

[1] Know-Center, Graz, Austria
{slind,bkump,gbeham,vpammer,tley}@know-center.at
[2] Knowledge Management Institute, Graz University of Technology, Austria
[3] Cognitive Science Section, University of Graz, Austria
[4] Centre for HCI Design, City University London, UK
amirdotan1@googlemail.com
[5] University of Twente, Nederlands
r.dehoog@gw.utwente.nl

Abstract. We present a work-integrated learning (WIL) concept which aims at empowering employees to learn while performing their work tasks. Within three usage scenarios we introduce the APOSDLE environment which embodies the WIL concept and helps knowledge workers move fluidly along the whole spectrum of WIL activities. By doing so, they are experiencing varying degrees of learning guidance: from building awareness, over exposing knowledge structures and contextualizing cooperation, to triggering reflection and systematic competence development. Four key APOSDLE components are responsible for providing this variety of learning guidance. The challenge in their design lies in offering learning guidance without being domain-specific and without relying on manually created learning content. Our three month summative workplace evaluation within three application organizations suggests that learners prefer awarenss building functionalities and descriptive learning guidance and reveals that they benefited from it.

Keywords: Work-integrated learning, learning guidance, informal learning, adaptive system, personalized retrieval, contextualized collaboration.

1 Introduction

In current business practice and eLearning research projects, most money is devoted to improving knowledge transfer of formal training interventions to the workplace. For instance, Haskell [1] informs us that in 1998, US$ 70 billion were spent on formal training. On the other hand, studies have shown that in today's economy only a small amount of knowledge that is actually applied to job activities comes from formal training. On average, people only transfer less than 30% of what is being learned in formal training to the professional workplace in a way that enhances performance. This is independent of the kind and quality of the courses taught, but is caused by not considering work environment needs during and after formal training efforts [2].

In the light of these findings, the CIPD – the professional body for both trainers and HR managers in the UK – has clearly articulated the need for a shift "from training to learning" (see [3] and [4]).

The question remains how this new type of workplace learning could look like and how it can be supported. Our approach builds upon the notion of Work-Integrated Learning (WIL, see Section 2) which has the potential to contribute to the above mentioned shift from training to learning by addressing continuous competency development during work. We engaged in a four year quest for building a computational environment which supports WIL. This quest was undertaken within the integrated EU-funded Project APOSDLE[1]. Applying a multitude of participatory design methods (shortly sketched in Section 3) we identified three key challenges: learning within real work situations, utilization of real work resources for learning, and learning support within real computational work environments.

This paper specifically addresses the first challenge (real time learning) and focuses on the open research question of "How much and what kind of learning guidance do people engaged in workplace learning desire, need, and actually use". Our participatory design studies indicated that learners require varying degrees of learning guidance in different situations. Section 4 introduces three different learning situations in the form of three WIL scenarios. These scenarios range from low to high learning guidance and introduce the different learning guidance functionalities provided within the APOSDLE environment.

Following this argumentation line a new research question on the more technical level arises: "How can we provide varying degrees of learning guidance without having to manually design all of them?" That is, we are looking for an environment which can provide varying degrees of learning guidance independently from the application domain and which utilizes knowledge resources from within an organization for learning – thus keeping costs and efforts for learning material generation low. Section 5 offers a conceptual view on the APOSDLE environment which represents our ontology-based approach to designing domain-independent learning support and offers varying degrees of learning guidance. In other words, we present a *design environment* [5] which enables the creation of environments for WIL support specifically tailored to the unique needs of a company and concrete learning domain. We see the "APOSDLE solution" as consisting of (a) modelling the learning domain and the work processes, (b) annotating documents and other sources of information available in the company repository, (c) training the prospective users of the APOSDLE environment, and (d) using the APOSDLE environment with its varying learning guidance functionalities at the workplace.

We have evaluated our approach to WIL by embedding the APOSDLE environment for three months into three application organizations – not only technically but also socially by building the relevant processes around it. Section 6 shortly summarizes the results of our summative workplace evaluation and discusses modelling efforts needed during APOSDLE instantiation in a specific application domain.

---

[1] Advanced Process-Oriented Self-Directed Learning, www.aposdle.org

2 Work-Integrated Learning

Building on theories of workplace learning (such as [6] and [7]) we conceptualize *learning as a dimension of knowledge work* which varies in focus (from focus on work performance to focus on learn performance), time available for learning, and the extension of learning guidance required. This learning dimension of knowledge work describes a continuum of learning practices which starts at one side with brief questions and task related informal learning (work processes with learning as a by-product), and extends at the other side to more formal learning processes (learning processes at or near the workplace). This continuum emphasizes that support for learning must enable a knowledge worker to seamlessly switch from one learning practice to another as time and other context factors permit or demand.

Research on supporting workplace learning and lifelong learning so far has focused predominantly on the formal side of this spectrum, specifically on course design applicable for the workplace and blended-learning. In contrast, the focus of our work is on the informal side of the spectrum, specifically covering work processes with learning as a by-product and learning activities located within work processes. In order to refer to this type of learning practices, we have coined the term work-integrated learning (WIL). By using this term we emphasize that we investigate *informal learning* at the workplace such that it is truly integrated in current work processes and practices. WIL is relatively brief and unstructured (in terms of learning objectives, learning time, or learning support). The main aim of WIL activities is to enhance task performance. From the learner's perspective WIL can be intentional or unintentional, and the learner can be aware of the learning experience or not [8].

WIL makes use of existing resources – knowledge artifacts (e.g., reports, project results) as well as humans (e.g., peers, communities). Learning in this case is a by-product of the time spent at the workplace. This conceptualization enables a shift from the training perspective of the organization to the learning perspective of the individual.

3 Distributed Participatory Design

This section gives an overview of the activities and their settings leading to the development of the APOSDLE environment. The development process involved three prototyping iterations lasting one year each and involving in-depth requirements elicitation, conceptual design, implementation, and evaluation phases.

3.1 Application Domains and Settings

The APOSDLE environment was designed in close cooperation and involvement of five different, knowledge intensive application domains of different enterprises. Three application domains were chosen in collaboration with enterprises participating in the project: simulation of effects of electromagnetism on aircraft (EADS - European Aeronautical Defence and Space Company, Paris), innovation management (ISN - Innovation Service Network, Graz), and intellectual property rights consulting (CCI Darmstadt - Chamber of Commerce and Industry, Darmstadt, Germany). Two additional domains refer to general methodologies that can be used in different settings and disciplines: the RESCUE process for the thorough elicitation and specification of consistent requirements for socio-technical systems, and the domain of Statistical Data Analysis (SDA).

3.2 Design and Development Process

The employed design process is an example of distributed participatory design, which has been carried out in the context of real-world project constraints on time and cost. The process consisted of instances of synchronous and asynchronous, distributed and non-distributed design activities, and also integrated activities designed to stimulate creative inputs to requirements. For example, the activities included workplace learning studies [9] and surveys [10], iterative use case writing and creativity workshops [11] resulting in 22 use cases and more than 1000 requirements, formative evaluations of the second prototype [12], a re-design of APOSDLE using the personas approach [13], extensive usability studies with students, application partners in real world settings and usability labs, and a variety of evaluations of individual components. A final summative evaluation spanning three months of real-world application concluded the process. The main findings of this summative evaluation are reported in Section 6 below.

3.3 Challenges for Supporting WIL

Based on the described participatory design and development activities, three major challenges for WIL support can be identified: real time learning, real knowledge resources, and real computational environment.

Real time learning: WIL support should make knowledge workers aware of and support them throughout learning opportunities relevant to her current work task. WIL support needs to be adapted to a user's work context and her experiences, and should be short, and easy to apply.

Real knowledge resources: WIL support should dynamically provide and make users aware of available knowledge resources (both human as well as material) within the organization. By providing 'real' resources the effort for learning transfer is reduced and the likelihood for offering opportunities to learn on different trajectories is increased.

Real computational environment: WIL support should be provided through a variety of tools and services which are integrated seamlessly within the user's desktop and allow one-point access to relevant back-end systems of her organization. These tools and services need to be inconspicuous, tightly integrated, and easy to use. They must support the knowledge worker in effortlessly switching between varieties of learning practices.

Concerning real time learning our participatory design activties and workplace learning studies suggest that learners need different support and guidance within different work situations. Specifically, it became apparent that learning guidance is needed on varying levels ranging from descriptive to prescriptive support. While *prescriptive* learning guidance has the objective of providing clear directions, laws, or rules of usage to be followed, *descriptive* learning guidance offers a map of the learning topic and its neighbouring topics, their relationships, and possible interactions to be explored. Specifically, prescriptive learning support is based on a clearly structured learning process which imposes an order on learning activities while descriptive support does not do so.

The learning guidance discussed here is applicable to WIL situations and covers the more informal side of the learning dimension of knowledge work. Clearly the spectrum of learning guidance could be extended to much more formal learning guidance approaches such as predefined learning modules and enforced learning processes. However, this is beyond the scope of our work and this paper. The learning guidance we consider and explore ranges from building awareness over descriptive learning support (exposing knowledge structures and contextualizing cooperation) to partially prescriptive (triggering reflection and systematically developing competences at work). The following section illustrates how these different degrees of learning guidance were realized within the APOSDLE environment.

4 Providing Varying Degrees of Learning Guidance

Within this section we present varying degrees of learning guidance functionalities in the form of three scenarios based on the ISN application case. These scenarios also provide an overview of the overall APOSDLE environment from the user's point of view.

ISN is a network of small consultancy firms in the area of innovation management. Consultants at ISN support customer cumpanies in the introduction of innovation management processes and the application of creativity techniques. Please meet Eva, a consultant for innovation management. Eva has been assigned to lead a new project with a client from the automotive industry. The objective is to come up with creative solutions for fastening rear-view mirrors to the windshield.

4.1 Building Awareness

Eva is in a hurry. She needs to plan the kick-off meeting for her new innovation project within the next hour. As Eva begins to create the agenda using her favorite word processor, APOSDLE automatically recognizes the topic of Eva's work activities, namely "moderation". A notification unobtrusively informs Eva that her work topic has been detected and that relevant information is available. Over the years the APOSDLE knowledge base has collected a large variety of resources (e.g. project documents, checklists, videos, pictures) about innovation management which Eva and her colleagues have produced or used. In the background, APOSDLE proactively searches the knowledge base utilizing the detected work topic together with information from Eva's User Profile (see User Profile and Experiences) to form a personalized query. Eva is interested in getting some help to speed up her work.

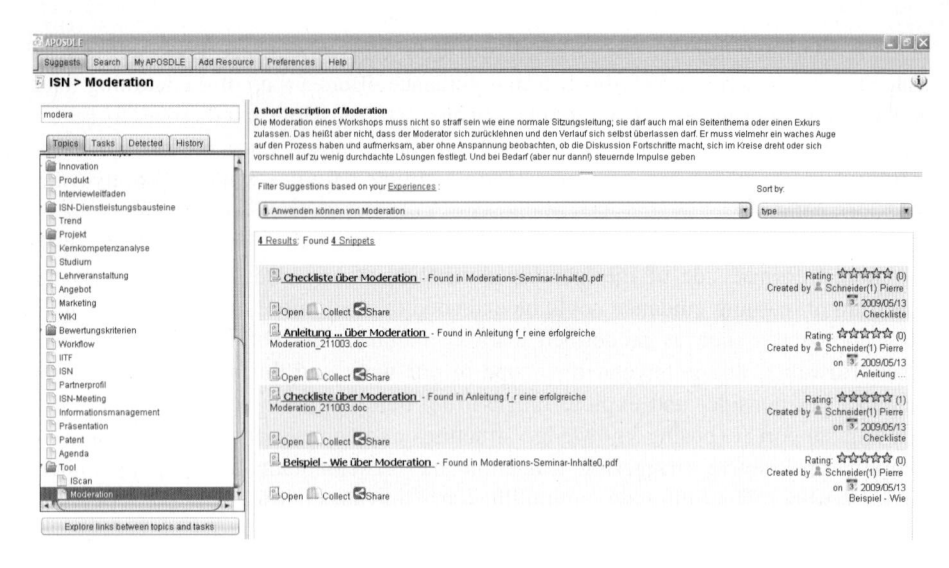

Fig. 1. "APOSDLE Suggests" recommends Knowledge Resources for Eva's current context (Topic "Moderation"). The tree view of Topics in the Browse Tab is shown on the left.

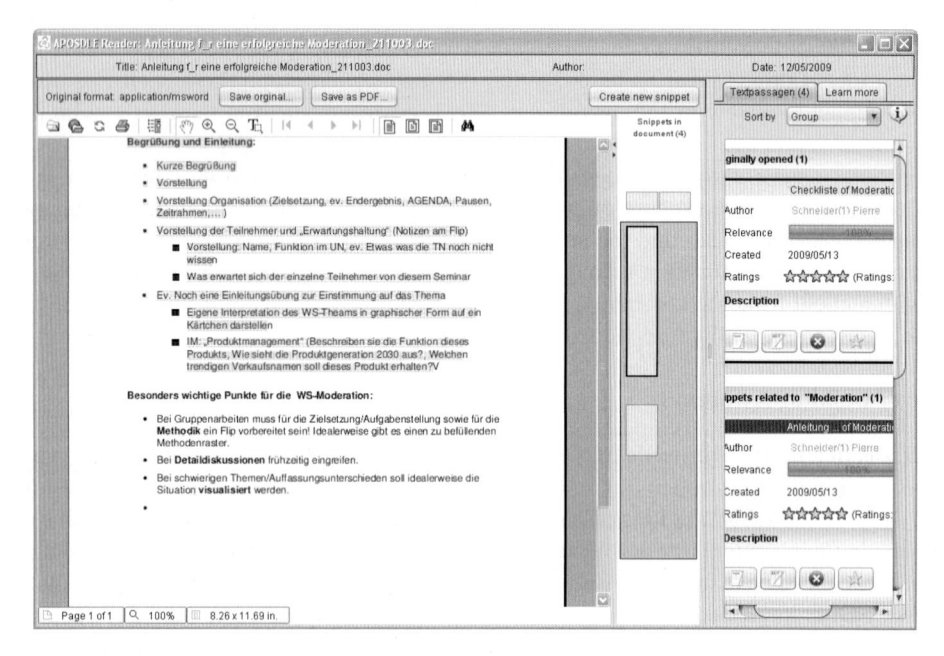

Fig. 2. APOSDLE Reader showing relevant information for Eva's context. It highlights the relevant part in a document (left), suggests other relevant parts (Snippets) throughout the document as a ThemeRiver (center), and offers a more detailed list view of Snippets (right) which can be sorted according to different criteria.

Therefore, she accesses APOSDLE Suggests by clicking on the notification or the APOSDLE tray icon. APOSDLE Suggests (Fig. 1) displays a list of resources related to the topic "moderation" (see Section 5.2). This list of resources is ranked based on her expertise in moderation techniques. Eva finds a checklist for moderating a meeting or a workshop which was put together by a colleague in the past. She opens the checklist in the APOSDLE Reader (Fig. 2) which highlights the most relevant parts (Snippets) for her. Eva finds some ideas suitable to her current project and integrates them into her own workshop preparation.

APOSDLE supports Eva in performing her work task without her even having to type a query. Moreover, her own expertise level is taken into account when making suggestions. This unobtrusive proactive information delivery raises awareness of knowledge resources (documents as well as people) which Eva would not have searched for otherwise. It provides learning guidance in that it highlights possible learning opportunities within the current work task without imposing constraints on the learner.

4.2 Descriptive Learning Guidance: Exposing Structures and Contextualizing Cooperation

After the kick-off meeting Eva prepares for the next step in the innovation project, namely a creativity workshop. Since she has never moderated such a workshop herself, she takes some more time to explore different possibilities and their implications. Eva opens APOSDLE Suggests and starts searching for the keywords "creativity techniques" and "creativity workshop". Eva selects the task "applying creativity techniques in a workshop". Eva refines the list of recommended resources by selecting a specific (predefined) Learning Goal (e.g. basic knowledge about creativity techniques in Fig. 3). She opens a video which contains an introduction about creativity techniques and creativity. The APOSDLE Reader again highlights relevant parts of the video and provides an overview of the video by displaying a theme river similar to the one shown in Fig. 2. The video helps Eva to get a better understanding of basic creativity theories and methods. But she still has some more concrete questions in particular in the context of the snippet she has found.

By simply clicking on the snippet, Eva contacts Pierre (another consultant in her company) to ask him about his experiences. APOSDLE supports Eva in selecting a cooperation tool by knowing Pierre's preferred means of cooperation (e.g. asynchronous vs. synchronous, tools he uses, etc.). APOSDLE also provides Pierre with the parts of Eva's work context which are relevant to her question. That is, Pierre can review which resources Eva has already accessed (assuming Eva's privacy settings allow this). Pierre accepts Eva's request and Pierre and Eva communicate via Skype (Pierre's preferred means of communication). Eva can take notes during the cooperation, and can reflect on the cooperation afterwards in a dedicated (wiki) template. If Eva and Pierre decide to share this cooperation results with other APOSDLE users, the request, resources, notes and reflections will be fed into the APOSDLE knowledge base. After talking to Pierre, Eva continues with preparations for the upcoming creativity workshop.

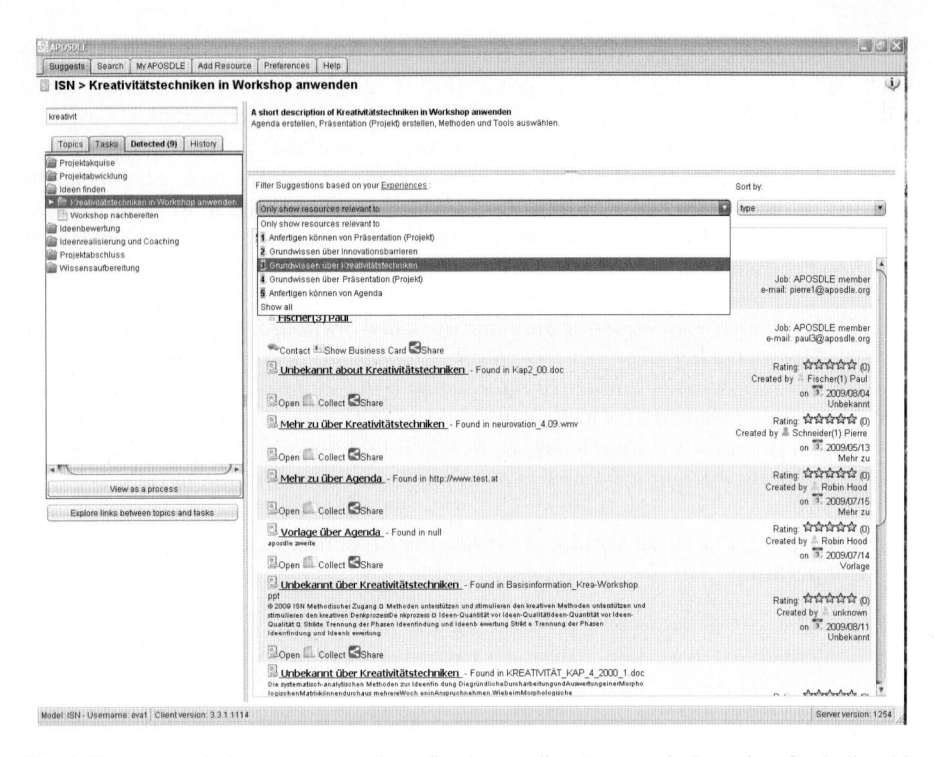

Fig. 3. Recommended resources can be refined according to a user's Learning Goals listed in the drop down box. Learning Goals allow narrowing down large lists of resources to specific needs of users.

By exposing the relationships between topics and tasks of the application domain the learner is enabled to informally explore the underlying formal knowledge structures and to learn from them. Specifically, users can be made aware of topics relevant to the current task. These might constitute relevant learning goals for the future. In addition, APOSDLE supports communication between peers by helping to identify the right person to contact, to select the preferred communication channel, to contextualize the cooperation, and to document it if desired. It is up to the user when, in which situations, and in which order to take advantage of this support.

4.3 Partially Prescriptive Learning Guidance: Triggering Reflection and Systematically Developing Competences at Work

Eva has some additional time which she wants to spend on acquiring in-depth knowledge about creativity techniques. She opens the Experiences Tab (find details in Section 5.5) of APOSDLE and reflects on her past activities. This tab (Fig. 4) visualizes her own User Profile indicating which topics she routinely works with (green, middle layer), which topics she needs to learn more about (orange, top layer), and in which topics she has expertise (blue, bottom layer).

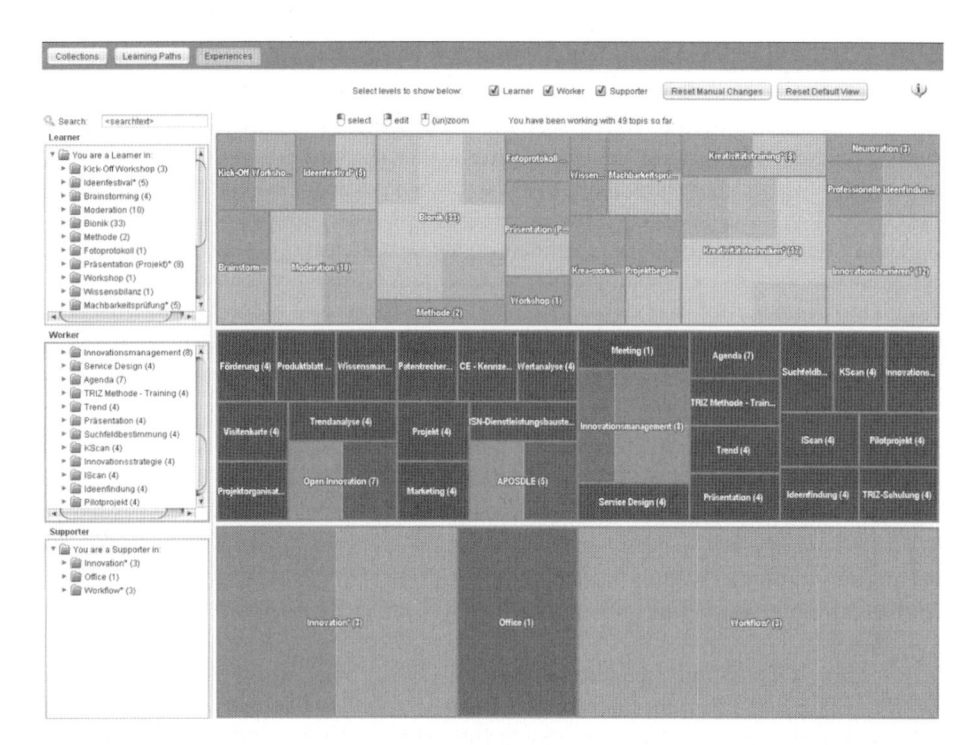

Fig. 4. The Experiences Tab provides users with an overview about their experiences with topics in the domain. APOSDLE uses three levels (Learner [orange, top layer], Worker [green, middle layer], Supporter [blue, bottom layer]) to indicate different levels of knowledge.

She realizes that she is learner in many of the common creativity techniques and therefore she decides to approach this topic systematically by creating a personalized Learning Path. Eva opens the Learning Path Wizard and browses through the task list. She selects the task "applying creativity techniques in a workshop". Based on this task, the Learning Path Wizard suggests a list of topics to include in her Learning Path (see Section 5.1.1), and Eva adds some more creativity techniques Pierre mentioned in their last conversation. Eva saves the Learning Path and also makes it public so that other colleagues can benefit from it. To execute the Learning Path Eva then activates it in APOSDLE Suggests. At this time APOSDLE Suggests recommends relevant knowledge resources for the topic she selected from her Learning Path. Eva now follows her Learning Path in dedicated times during her working hours. Whenever new relevant resources are added to the knowledge base Eva is made aware of them.

APOSDLE explicitly triggers reflective learning depending on learner activities (formal part) while the reflection process itself is not formally supported but left to the user's description. In addition, the creation of semi-formal Learning Paths for longer term and more systematic competency development is supported and partially automated. However, the time and method of Learning Path execution is not predetermined and can be performed flexibly.

5 A Conceptual View on the APOSDLE Environment

As was illustrated in the above scenarios the APOSDLE environment provides varying degrees of learning guidance. Within this section we present the four key components which implement them: APOSDLE Suggests, the APOSDLE Reader, the Cooperation Wizard, and the Experiences Tab. All four components have been designed and are implemented in a domain-independent fashion. That is, none of the components embody application domain knowledge and thus constitute a generic design environment for WIL environments. In order to create a domain-specific WIL environment for a specific company, all application-specific domain knowledge has to be added to APOSDLE in the form of three ontologies and the different knowledge resources within the knowledge base.

5.1 Knowledge Resources in APOSDLE

Different types of Knowledge Resources are presented to the user within APOSDLE: Topics, Tasks, Learning Paths, Documents, Snippets, Cooperation Transcripts, and Persons. All of these resources can be organized into Collections which can be shared with others and thus may serve as Knowledge Resources themselves.

5.1.1 Topics, Tasks and Learning Paths

Topics, Tasks and Learning Paths are structural elements which are presented to the users and which can be used for accessing further Knowledge Resources. All of them are encoded within an integrated OWL ontology within the Knowledge Base and provide the basis for intelligent suggestion of resources and for inferences on user's competencies [14].

Topics are core concepts which knowledge workers in a company need to know about in order to do their jobs. For instance, Topics in the ISN domain are creativity technique or workshop. Each Topic has a description. A Topic can be added to a Collection, its relations with other Topics and with Tasks can be browsed or it can trigger suggestions in APOSDLE Suggests.

Tasks are typical working tasks within a specific company. Examples for ISN Tasks include "applying creativity techniques in a workshop" or "identifying potential cooperation partners". Each Task has a description. In addition, to each Task a set of *Skills* is assigned which are required for performing the Task successfully. For instance, for the ISN task "applying creativity techniques in a workshop" one required Skill might be basic knowledge about creativity techniques. Each of these Skills is related to one Topic. That way, Tasks and Topics are inherently linked. Tasks in APOSDLE can be added to a Collection, its relations with other Tasks and with Topics can be browsed and it can trigger suggestions in APOSDLE Suggests.

In essence, a *Learning Paths* is a sequence of Topics for which suggestions can be obtained in APOSDLE Suggests. The sequence of Topics about which knowledge should be acquired shall maximize learning transfer and follows a prerequisite relation computed on the Task-Topic-Skills structure based on competency-based knowledge space theory [15]. Learning Paths are generated by APOSDLE users themselves with the help of a Learning Path Wizard (Section 4.3) starting from a Task, a Collection, or a Topic. Learning Paths can be shared with others or added to a Collection.

5.1.2 Documents, Snippets, and Cooperation Transcripts

Documents, Snippets and Cooperation Transcripts are the actual "learning content" within APOSDLE. They constitute previous work results of knowledge workers in the company which can be accessed by APOSDLE users. Such context-related knowledge artifacts improve the likelihood of offering highly relevant information which can be directly applied to the work situation with little or no learning transfer required. In addition, they have the advantage that no additional learning content has to be created.

By *Documents*, APOSDLE understands both textual and multimedia documents which can be accessed in the APOSDLE Reader. Documents can be opened and saved, shared with others, added to a Collection or rated.

Snippets are parts of (textual or multi-media) documents annotated with one Topic which can be viewed in the APOSDLE Reader. Users can share Snippets with their colleagues, add them to a Collection, or rate them. In addition, APOSDLE automatically generates Snippets fitting to the domain ontology provided.

Cooperation Transcripts are textual documentations of information exchanged during cooperations. Cooperation Transcripts can be fed back into APOSDLE and made available in APOSDLE Search.

5.1.3 Knowledgeable Persons

All APOSDLE users are potential sources of knowledge and hence constitute Knowledge Resources. Knowledgeable Persons are identified for each Topic. For instance, a person can be knowledgeable with respect to the Topic "workshop" might have little knowledge about the Topic "creativity technique". The information of who is a knowledgeable person at a certain point in time for a Topic at hand is obtained from the APOSDLE User Profile (see Section 5.4). Persons can be contacted directly or be added to Collections for future contact.

5.2 APOSDLE Suggests and Search: Access to Knowledge Resources

APOSDLE basically has two main entrance points from where Knowledge Resources can be accessed, namely APOSDLE Suggests and Search. While Search offers text-based search functionality within APOSDLE, the Suggests tab employs intelligent algorithms for delivering Knowledge Resources which are relevant to the user's work context and to his or her previous experiences.

5.2.1 Suggestions for Topics, Tasks, or Learning Paths

Suggestions can be obtained for single Topics, for Tasks, or for Learning Paths. If suggestions are requested for a Topic, APOSDLE presents all kinds of Knowledge Resources related to this Topic. Knowledge Resources can also be other Topics. The suggest algorithm is based on an associative network which combines a concept-similarity measures with text-based similarity measures [16].

For suggestions starting from a Task, Knowledge Resources of all different types are presented for all Skills (and hence all Topics) linked to the Task. Thereby, intelligent algorithms are applied for personalizing the ranking of Knowledge Resources: Information from the automatically maintained User Profile (see below) is used to compute a learning gap for the Task at hand. The learning gap expresses the difference between Skills needed for the Task and Skills the user possesses according to his or her User Profile. Based on this learning gap APOSDLE suggests relevant Skills as Learning Goals which the learner could pursue within her current work situations. These Learning Goals are offered ranked according to the inverse learning gap. That is, Learning Goals which are relevant to Topics with a high learning gap are displayed on top of the list while Learning Goals related to Topics for which the user already possesses some knowledge are displayed at the bottom of the list. If no Learning Goal is selected by the user, APOSDLE makes suggestions for all Learning Goals and ranks them according to their importance for the user. If the user selects a Learning Goal, only Knowledge Resources relevant for this Learning Goal are displayed.

Similarly, if suggestions are made starting from a Learning Path, the Topics in the Learning Path are interpreted as a sequence of Learning Goals. However, here, suggestions of Knowledge Resources are automatically presented for the first Learning Goal in the Learning Path; the user can change the Learning Goal.

5.2.2 Triggering Suggestions: Automated Context Detection or Manual Selection

As it becomes obvious from this description, suggestions in APOSDLE Suggests are always somehow related to one or several Topics. The Topics(s) can be identified by automatic context detection (Section 4.1), by means of manual selection of a Task or Topic (Section 4.2) or by activating a Learning Path (Section 4.3).

The APOSDLE context detection is able to detect Tasks and Topics which the user is currently working on [17]. In other words, the worker does its daily work with APOSDLE sitting silently in the background. Once APOSDLE has detected a Topic or Task, a small notification is displayed on the right bottom of the screen. Clicking on the notification, the users can access APOSDLE Suggests where they get Knowledge Resources directly related to what they are currently working on.

A Browse window in APOSDLE Suggests facilitates different views on the domain, a tree view of Topics, a tree view of Tasks, a process view of Tasks and an integrated view of Tasks, Topics and their interrelations. Descriptions of Tasks and Topics are also shown in all these views. From there, an element can be selected and sent to APOSDLE Suggests.

Eventually, clicking Topics and Tasks anywhere in the system can trigger suggestions in APOSDLE Suggests. A Learning Path is activated in APOSDLE Suggests via its context menu.

5.3 APOSDLE Reader: Central Access to Snippets and Documents

Snippets and Documents are viewed in the APOSDLE Reader (see Fig. 2). The APOSDLE Reader is based on the ADOBE PDF viewer and a video player for all standard audiovisual formats. In order to view documents, APOSDLE Converts them into *.pdf files. While the underlying document can only be viewed and not modified in the APOSDLE Reader, annotations with Topics can be viewed, created or edited.

For navigation, a ThemeRiver highlights the location of relevant Snippets (again based on the associative network [16]) within the opened document and a Snippet List gives an overview over all Snippets within the document. By clicking on bars in the ThemeRiver or Snippets in the Snippet list, the viewer or video player jumps to the corresponding position in the document. Snippet boundaries in text are defined by character positions. Snippet boundaries in videos are defined by temporal start and end positions. In the case of video lecture videos, additional metadata and PowerPoint slides, if available, can be displayed in additional Resource Viewer tabs. Additionally, the APOSDLE Reader provides means of access to learning guidance through a "Learn more" tab. Within the "Learn more" tab, a learning hints pane is shown which contains different types of Learning Hints which are automatically generated taking into account the Topic of the Snippet and the assigned Material Resource Types. These learning hints constitute more prescriptive types of learning guidance since they encourage the learner to explore certain aspects of a Topic or to relate its usage to other situations.

5.4 User Profile and Experiences Tab: Access to User-Related Data

The APOSDLE User Profile builds the basis for the system's adaptation, that is, for the ranking of Learning Goals and hence the recommendation of information within APOSDLE Suggests. In addition, the information in the User Profile is necessary for identifying Knowledgeable Persons for a Topic or Learning Goal at hand.

The APOSDLE User Profile is designed as an overlay of the Topics in APOSDLE. In other words, for each of the Topics, it is decided whether or not the user has knowledge or Skills related to it. The APOSDLE User Profile is automatically maintained applying the approach of knowledge indicating events (KIE). In a nutshell, different types of naturally occurring actions of users are observed and inferences are made on the user's underlying knowledge level in a certain Topic. For each Topic, three levels of expertise are distinguished in APOSDLE's third prototype: Learner, Worker and Supporter. For instance, "carrying out a task" is a KIE for the "Worker" level. Thus, whenever a user executes a task (e.g. prepares a creativity workshop) within the APOSDLE environment, the counter of all Topics related to that Task within his or her User Profile for the "Worker"-level is incremented. At any point in time, a weighted algorithm in the APOSDLE User Profile Service decides in which level of expertise a user is with respect to every Topic in the domain. A more detailed description of the APOSDLE User Profile and its User Profile Services has been given in [14].

Studies suggest that mirroring a learner's actions and their results can assist with the acquisition of meta-cognitive Skills which are important ingredients of self-directed learning. Therefore a visual component, the Experiences Tab (Fig. 4), was added where the users can reflect on their past actions and become aware of Topics which they might want to advance further in. This is in line with the idea of an open learner model as it has been suggested by a number of authors [18], [19]. Clearly, this overview also allows users to quickly check if the APOSDLE environment has inferred the right information from the observed activities and to provide feedback and corrections. Please note that the main goal of this functionality is not to "assess" the user in any formal or objective way, but to provide an overview of the past interactions with the systems in order to better make the user aware of and recommend activities in the future.

Figure 4 shows the Experience Tab for Eva, our consultant from above. The left hand pane of Experiences contains a tree view of the Topics with which Eva has been engaged in the past. The same Topics are also shown in the tree map visualization on the right where Eva's Topics are also grouped into three levels of expertise, Learner (brown), Worker (green) and Supporter (blue). The tree map view provides more details than the tree view: The size of a square related to a Topic summarizes the importance of the Topic for the user, frequency with which the user has been engaged with the Topic, the larger the square, the more frequent the engagement. The square of a Topic can be further subdivided into squares with different shades indicating different activities (KIE) the user has been engaged in.

6 Workplace Evaluation

As mentioned in the introduction, we see the "APOSDLE solution" as consisting of (a) modelling the learning domain and the work processes, (b) annotating documents and other sources of information available in the company repository, (c) training the prospective users of the APOSDLE environment, and (d) using the resulting domain-specific WIL environment with its varying learning guidance functionalities at the workplace. This means that a comprehensive summative evaluation of the APOSDLE solution requires a summative evaluation of each of these aspects. This is even more mandatory as the aspects depend on each other. If the domain modelling has not been done correctly, the annotation will fall short of what is needed; if the annotation is done badly retrieval of relevant information will be unsatisfactory; if the users are not well trained, their use of the APOSDLE system will be sub-optimal.

Within this contribution we shortly report on results of the workplace evaluation (step d) which were carried out at the sites of three application organizations and discuss the efforts required for model creation (step a). The modelling of the learning domain and the work processes were conducted over a period of two to three months. The workplace evaluation took about three months and involved nineteen persons. A multi-method data collection approach was followed using a questionnaire, interviews, log data, user diaries kept while working with APOSDLE, and site visits. This allowed for triangulation of results.

One conclusion of the workplace evaluation is that the APOSDLE solution has proven very useful for learners in highly-specialized domains such as EADS's Electromagnetism Simulation domain in which much of the knowledge to be learned is documented within work documents. In those circumstances, APOSDLE delivered an effective work-based learning solution that enabled relatively inexperienced knowledge workers to efficiently improve their knowledge by utilizing the whole spectrum of learning guidance provided. APOSDLE proved less effective for knowledge workers in broad customer-driven domains where knowledge was shared to a large extent in person and is typically not documented. One reason for this result probably was that in two domains the users worked in the same offices and thus there was no need for cooperation support.

Overall APOSDLE supported the acquisition of new knowledge by the users by making them aware of learning material, learning opportunities and by providing relevant material. In EADS especially, it was reported on numerous occasions in the user diary that explicit and implicit learning material enabled knowledge workers to gain useful insight, improve their knowledge and complete a task they were working on. In all application cases, users clearly favoured the awareness building and descriptive learning guidance (e.g. exposing knowledge structures) over the more prescriptive learning guidance (e.g. triggering reflection, learning paths). Learning Paths were only sporadically used and mainly to explore their functionalities; users did not use MyExperiences to reflect on their activities but rather to examine the environment's perception of their usage. On the other hand, learners extensively used the different functionalities to browse and search the knowledge structures (descriptive learning guidance), followed the provided content suggestions (awareness), and collected relevant learning content within Collections. Most other supporting facilities, like hints and notes, were rarely used. This suggests that prescriptive supportive measures derived from instructional theories which are focusing on formal learning contexts are not very relevant for learning at work.

Finally, we can conclude that the domain-independent WIL design environment approach was successful. Relying on existing material instead of tailor made learning material provided to be effective and cost efficient. Crucial for this is having good modelling tools, experienced modellers, and high quality annotations of snippets. EADS, CCI, and ISN reported modelling efforts between 59 and 304 person hours for domain, task, and learning goal models ranging from 94 to 145 Topics, 13 to 100 Tasks, and 59 to 291 Learning Goals. In a recent instantiation within a new application organization we were able to further reduce these efforts to 120 person hours for 51 Topics, 41 Tasks, and 124 Learning Goals. We believe that these efforts are quite competitive when comparing them to efforts needed to instantiate a traditional LMS at a site and to develop custom learning material.

Acknowledgements. The Know-Center is funded within the Austrian COMET Program - Competence Centers for Excellent Technologies - under the auspices of the Austrian Ministry of Transport, Innovation and Technology, the Austrian Ministry of Economics and Labor and by the State of Styria. COMET is managed by the Austrian Research Promotion Agency FFG. APOSDLE (www.aposdle.org) has been partially funded under grant 027023 in the IST work programme of the European Community.

References

1. Haskell, R.E.: Reengineering Corporate Training. In: Intellectual Capital and Transfer of Learning. Quorum Books, Westport (1998)
2. Robinson, D.: Skill and Performance: They are not equal. Apartment Professional Magazine (2003)
3. CIPD: Training and Development, Annual Survey Report 2005. CIPD, London (2005)
4. Reynolds, J.: Helping People Learn - Strategies for Moving from Training to Learning, Research Report. CIPD, London (2004)
5. Eisenberg, M., Fischer, G.: Programmable design environments: integrating end-user programming with domain-oriented assistance. In: Adelson, B., Dumais, S., Olson, J. (eds.) Conference Proceedings, Human Factors in Computing Systems, CHI 1994, pp. 431–437. ACM, New York (1994)
6. Lave, J., Wenger, E.: Situated Learning: Legitimate Peripheral Participation. Cambridge University Press, Cambridge (1991)
7. Eraut, M., Hirsh, W.: The Significance of Workplace Learning for Individuals, Groups and Organisations, SKOPE, Oxford & Cardiff Universities (2007)
8. Schugurensky, D.: The Forms of Informal Learning: Towards a Conceptualization of the Field, http://hdl.handle.net/1807/2733 (Retrieved July 10, 2010)

9. Kooken, J., Ley, T., de Hoog, R.: How Do People Learn at the Workplace. Investigating Four Workplace Learning Assumptions. In: Duval, E., Klamma, R., Wolpers, M. (eds.) EC-TEL 2007. LNCS, vol. 4753, pp. 158–171. Springer, Heidelberg (2007)
10. Kooken, J., de Hoog, R., Ley, T., Kump, B., Lindstaedt, S.N.: Workplace Learning Study 2. Deliverable D2.5, EU Project 027023 APOSDLE, Know-Center, Graz, Austria (2008)
11. Jones, S., Lindstaedt, S.: A Multi-Activity Distributed Participatory Design Process for Stimulating Creativity in the Specification of requirements for a Work-Integrated Learning System. In: Workshop at CHI 2008 (2008)
12. Lichtner, V., Kounkou, A., Dotan, A., Kooken, J., Maiden, N.: An online forum as a user diary for remote workplace evaluation of a work-integrated learning system. In: Proc. of CHI 2009 (2009)
13. Dotan, A., Maiden, N.A.M., Lichtner, V., Germanovich, L.: Designing with Only Four People in Mind? – A Case Study of Using Personas to Redesign a Work-Integrated Learning Support System. In: Gross, T., Gulliksen, J., Kotzé, P., Oestreicher, L., Palanque, P., Prates, R.O., Winckler, M. (eds.) INTERACT 2009. LNCS, vol. 5727, pp. 497–509. Springer, Heidelberg (2009)
14. Lindstaedt, S.N., Beham, G., Kump, B., Ley, T.: Getting to Know Your User – Unobtrusive User Model Maintenance within Work-Integrated Learning Environments. In: Cress, U., Dimitrova, V., Specht, M. (eds.) EC-TEL 2009. LNCS, vol. 5794, pp. 73–87. Springer, Heidelberg (2009)
15. Ley, T., Kump, B., Ulbrich, A., Scheir, P., Lindstaedt, S.: A Competence-based Approach for Formalizing Learning Goals in Work-integrated Learning. In: Proceedings of World Conference on Educational Multimedia, Hypermedia and Telecommunications 2008, pp. 2099–2108. AACE, Chesapeake (2008)
16. Scheir, P., Lindstaedt, S.N., Ghidini, C.: A network model approach to retrieval in the Semantic Web. International Journal on Semantic Web & Information Systems 4(4), 56–84 (2008)
17. Lokaiczyk, R., Goertz, M.: Extending Low Level Context Events by Data Aggregation. In: Proceedings of I-KNOW 2008 and I-MEDIA 2008, pp. 118–125 (2008)
18. Kay, J.: Learner Control. User Modeling and User-Adapted Interaction 11, 111–127 (2001)
19. Bull, S.: Supporting learning with open learner models (Keynote Speech). In: Proc. of 4th Hellenic Conference on Information and Communication Technologies in Education, Athens, Greece, September 29 - October 3, pp. 47–61 (2004)
20. Kelloway, E.K., Barling, J.: Knowledge work as organizational behavior. Int. J. of Management Reviews 2(3), 287–304 (2000)

Automatic Detection of Local Reuse

Arno Mittelbach, Lasse Lehmann, Christoph Rensing, and Ralf Steinmetz

KOM - Multimedia Communications Lab, Technische Universität Darmstadt,
Rundeturmstr. 10, 64283 Darmstadt
{firstname.lastname}@kom.tu-darmstadt.de

Abstract. Local reuse detection is a prerequisite for a multitude of tasks ranging from document management and information retrieval to web search or plagiarism detection. Its results can be used to support authors in creating new learning resources or learners in finding existing ones by providing accurate suggestions for related documents. While the detection of local text reuse, i.e. reuse of parts of documents, is covered by various approaches, reuse detection for object-based documents has been hardly considered yet. In this paper we propose a new fingerprinting technique for local reuse detection for both text-based and object-based documents which is based on the contiguity of documents. This additional information, which is generally disregarded by existing approaches, allows the creation of shorter and more flexible fingerprints. Evaluations performed on different corpora have shown that it performs better than existing approaches while maintaining a significantly lower storage consumption.

Keywords: Local Reuse Detection, Fingerprinting, Overlap Detection.

1 Introduction and Motivation

Detection of reuse is a prerequisite for a multitude of tasks. Duplicate or near duplicate detection plays an important role in web search and retrieval where it is, for example, used to filter result lists. However, there are several tasks that require not only the detection of near duplicate documents but the detection of local reuse, which we understand in the broad sense that *content is copied from one document to another* while possibly being adapted (see Section 2 for a more refined definition). Detection of plagiarism is an important use case [1] but also in the fields of web search or local desktop search several scenarios require techniques for detecting local reuse. Examples are retrieval of related documents or tracking of information flow for news stories [10,16], over different blogs [10,9] or in newsgroups or forums. Even in the field of Technology Enhanced Learning (TEL), the obtained information can be used to support authors as well as users of learning content (see Section 2). Generally, algorithms that efficiently handle the near-duplicate detection problem [7,4,5] do not work well for the detection of local reuse [19], while standard string matching approaches like Greedy String Tiling [22] or Local Alignment [6] usually suffer from bad runtime behavior or high storage consumption. There are so-called fingerprinting techniques that allow for the detection of local reuse while maintaining an acceptable runtime and storage behavior. However, most existing approaches concentrate on the detection of text reuse. Many documents contain not just text but also images, audio, video or other content types such as geometric forms or structures. Especially in the domain of Technology Enhanced Learning such object-based formats are commonly used. Presentation slides are a good example. They often contain many shapes and diagrams but comparably little text. Even documents generated by modern word processing tools usually contain objects like images or charts, which are completely neglected by text-based reuse detection methods.

In this paper we propose a flexible fingerprinting technique for the detection of local reuse based on the contiguity of a document's content (Section 4) that outperforms existing fingerprinting approaches (Section 3) in most aspects on the corpora used for evaluation (Section 5) including an annotated subset of the TREC newswire corpus and the LIS.KOM corpus created during the evaluation of the LIS.KOM framework [13]. In the following Section we define local reuse and show how local reuse detection can be applied to support different scenarios in the area of Technology Enhanced Learning.

2 Application of Local Reuse Detection to Support TEL

We define local reuse extending the definition for local text reuse by Seo and Croft [19] as follows: *Local reuse occurs when content is copied from one document to another.* In this definition, content can be anything from a part of a sentence to an image or an audio file. The reused content can be modified and may only make up a small fraction of the new document. It is apparent that local reuse relations are not transitive (a property often assumed for near-duplicate documents [7]), meaning that document A may reuse content from document B and B content from document C without A and C having anything in common.

The main use case for local reuse detection is to discover documents which overlap and thus are related to each other. This information can be used to support retrieval and generation of learning content. The resulting document relations can e.g. be used to generate recommendations, enrich given search results, or track the flow of information.

If one document is part of a search result or relevant for a user, e.g. because he is learning it, related documents might be potentially interesting too. Documents that are near-duplicates, are not useful for recommendation since the user already knows most of the content. They are thus usually filtered out by search engines like Google. However, this is not the case for documents that overlap in parts only. When a document A is relevant for a user and document B partially overlaps with document A, the content that document B contains in extent to the overlapping passages is probably relevant for a user or learner. Authors of learning content, like e.g. lecture slides or WBTs, can be provided with information about how a document is connected with other documents. This is especially helpful for authors who are not the creator of named document. If the document itself does not contain the content they need, one of the related documents might. Local reuse detection allows to find such relations and to give authors access to potentially relevant information.

Another way to support authors is to enable them to track their content. This applies mainly to commercial scenarios where an author has financial interest in his documents not being reused without permission. However even in open content scenarios authors might want to know where their content goes and who reuses it.

3 Fingerprinting Approaches for Local Reuse Detection

The given section covers the methodology for fingerprint generation and gives an overview on existing approaches for local reuse detection for text-based as well as for object-based documents.

3.1 Fingerprint Generation

While near-duplicate fingerprinting techniques generally produce one fingerprint per document, techniques for the detection of local reuse usually generate several fingerprints, i.e. hash values representing a document. How these fingerprints are put together depends on the approach used. Usually the following steps are performed during fingerprint creation: Initially a document is preprocessed. Common preprocessing steps for text include filtering of special characters, stopword filtering or stemming. Secondly chunks are extracted from the document. These chunks are then turned into numeric values using hash functions like MD5 [17]. In the final phase most approaches select a subset of the hashes resulting from the second step. This subset is then called fingerprint (or set of fingerprints) of the document. Most of the approaches described in this section use shingles as chunks. Shingles, as described by Broder [3], are sequences of k consecutive terms that are generated by extracting the contents of a sliding window with fixed size k running stepwise over the text.

3.2 Containment Calculation

To quantify the reuse between two documents, most approaches use an asymmetric measure as such a measure reflects differences in length of the documents. The containment of document A in document B is defined by Broder [3] as:

$$C(A,B) = \frac{|F_A \cap F_B|}{|F_A|} \qquad (1)$$

F_A and F_B are the sets of fingerprints of documents A and B respectively and are usually treated as sets in the mathematical sense (e.g. by [8], [18] and [19]) meaning that every fingerprint only occurs once in the selected set of fingerprints, even if it has multiple occurrences in the document. However, taking duplicate fingerprints into account and thus treating F_A and F_B as multisets [20] can be beneficial in some scenarios.

3.3 Approaches for Text-Based Documents

K-gram. K-gram is the first and simplest of several approaches that use shingles as chunks. It serves as the basis for most of the following fingerprint schemes. It is based on the n-gram overlap approach [14] and simply uses all shingles of a document generated by a sliding window with size k as fingerprints. Therefore the number of fingerprints generated by k-gram for a document with n tokens is calculated as $N_{k-gram} = n - k + 1$. This, however, only applies when a multiset approach is used. When using k-gram in a set-wise fashion, as it is usually done, the given formula represents an upper bound for the number of fingerprints. The following four approaches take the fingerprints generated by k-gram and reduce their number by selecting a representative subset. Since a subset of k-gram's fingerprints may never provide as accurate results as the whole set, k-gram is usually used as a benchmark to evaluate these approaches.

0 mod p. For a selection algorithm to work properly, it is required to select the identical subset of fingerprints for identical documents. A random selection algorithm would not fulfill this requirement. 0 mod p [15] selects every hash value that is dividable by p out of the hashes generated by k-gram. Thus the average number of fingerprints 0 mod p selects is $N_{0\ mod\ p} = N_{k-gram}/p$. One drawback of this approach is that if very common shingles are dividable by p the results can be effected negatively. Moreover it is not guaranteed that if two documents contain identical chunks that these chunks will be selected in both documents. Therefore, reuse may not be detected. The guarantee given by 0 mod p is that if a chunk is selected in one document it will be selected in every other document as well.

Winnowing. Winnowing [18] uses a second window with size w sliding over the shingles resulting from k-gram. In each winnowing window the lowest hash value is selected as fingerprint. If there is more than one lowest hash value, the rightmost one within the window is chosen. Schleimer et al. have shown that winnowing yields slightly better results than 0 mod p and give a lower bound for the number of fingerprints chosen as $N_{winnowing} \geq 2/(w+1) \cdot N_{k-gram}$. While the selection 0 mod p performs is global, winnowing's selection of fingerprints depends on the other hash values within the same winnowing window. This means that even if two documents share a common shingle, winnowing does not necessarily select that shingle's fingerprint in both documents. However, if two documents share a chunk that is at least as large as the winnowing window w, at least one common shingle out of that chunk is selected in both documents.

Other Approaches: Hailstorm [9] combines the results of winnowing with a better and more global coverage of the document. Each token (i.e. word) of a document is hashed separately before applying k-gram to the document. Each shingle is then examined whether the token with the lowest hash value is the leftmost or rightmost token within the shingle. If this is the case, the shingle is selected as fingerprint. It is necessary to use a large window size to reach high compression rates with Hailstorm. However, the quality of k-gram for detection of local reuse usually decreases for big window sizes (e.g. $k > 6$), since the sensitivity of k-gram for small changes increases with an increasing window size. Originally, Hailstorm has been developed for origin detection. In that use case content is often cited and fully copied from document to document, with relatively long parts of text remaining unchanged. In such a scenario larger values for k - like 8, as proposed in [9] - work well, which is not the case for detection of local reuse.

Hash-breaking [2] is not based on k-gram and thus does not use shingles. A document is divided into non-overlapping chunks. Every word of the document is hashed and if a resulting hash value is dividable by a given parameter p, the text is divided at this point. The resulting text chunks are then hashed and used as fingerprints of the document. While a chunk of text selected by hash-breaking is on average p tokens long, it might be very short or very long in practice, depending on the distribution of hash values. Specifically, when a sequence is very short and consists of very common words, the results Hash-breaking provides are influenced badly. Seo and Croft have modified hash-breaking such that it only selects chunks that are at least p tokens long (revised hash-breaking) [19].

Since the chunks hash-breaking selects can be very long, the approach is rather sensitive to changes. If only one character in a chunk is changed, the hash values and thus the outcome of the approach is completely different. Seo and Croft use **Discrete Cosine Transformation** (DCT) to make it more robust against small changes [19].

3.4 Approaches for Object-Based Documents

Object-based documents are documents whose main content is non-textual. Typical examples for object-based documents are presentations, web based trainings, documents from modeling tools (like e.g. Visio or ARIS), project charts or the output of various design tools (like Adobe InDesign or MS Publisher). While there are many existing approaches for the detection of reuse for text-based documents, very few approaches for detecting reuse between object-based documents exist or have been researched.

In [11] Klerkx et al. evaluate the reuse of PowerPoint presentations in the ALOCOM repository [21]. To detect reuse, Klerkx et al. utilize the cosine measure for textual content, hash functions for images and a mix of both for the content of slides. No specifics are given and, since different techniques are used for text and images, no common fingerprint can be generated.

Basic approaches like k-gram or the selection algorithms based on k-gram can be adapted for object-based documents. If it is possible to extract ordered features from a document it is possible to extract fingerprints from it. For instance, to generate k-gram fingerprints for a PowerPoint presentation, the objects need to be extracted in the order they occur in the document. To be able to process both objects and textual content at the same time it is necessary to generate individual hash values for each of them and then apply the k-gram window to the resulting bit string. Hence, the preprocessing used on an object-based document is different, but the principle mechanisms of the approach are the same as in the text-based case.

4 MiLe Approach

Documents possess an inherent order. In text documents, for example, the order in which words occur is (for most languages) an eminent aspect of the text's semantics. That is, if the word order is changed, either a nonsense sentence is created or semantics are changed: E.g. *Tom protects Lisa* has a different meaning than *Lisa protects Tom* or *protects Tom Lisa*.

Existing fingerprinting approaches do not consider documents as a contiguous entity but as a set of individual chunks (or features) which forms the basis for the fingerprint generation. While it is possible to store additional offset information for each shingle or chunk (see e.g. [9]), utilizing this information requires additional storage and computational effort, e.g. reconstructing the order of a document's k-gram fingerprints would approximately take $O(n \log n)$ steps, depending on the algorithm used.

We propose a new fingerprinting algorithm called MiLe that utilizes the contiguity of documents. The main idea behind MiLe is to not break up documents into chunks and select a subset to calculate a resemblance measure but to transform the resemblance estimation problem into a string-matching problem, thereby benefiting from the additional information taken from the contiguous nature of documents.

The comparison of documents using document fingerprints usually consists of two steps: First a fingerprint is generated for every document, which is then used to estimate the resemblance. This is also the case for MiLe. However, while all local reuse detection approaches described in Section 3.3 generate a set of fingerprints, MiLe creates only one fingerprint per document.

4.1 Fingerprint Generation

While the generation of fingerprints for text-based and object-based documents is different, the calculation of containment is not, i.e. once a MiLe fingerprint has been created it can theoretically be compared to any MiLe fingerprint regardless of the underlying document type. Therefore we first describe the two different methods of fingerprint generation before proceeding with the general calculation of containment measures.

Generating MiLe Fingerprints for Text-Based Documents. The resulting bit sequence of a MiLe fingerprint is created from a text-based input document by performing the following steps:

1. The document's text content is extracted and preprocessed. Preprocessing can, for example, involve case folding, stop-wording or stemming. For the evaluation (Section 5) we mainly used case folding (i.e. we converted all characters to lower case).

2. The preprocessed text is tokenized at word level.
3. Every token is projected onto a hash-value consisting of very few bits (e.g. 4 bits). A simple algorithm could calculate the MD5 value [17] for each token while only using the first n bits. Of course, custom and hence more efficient projection methods could be used when runtime is critical.
4. The generated bit values are appended to a bit string, in the order their corresponding token appears in the document. This bit string is the document's MiLe fingerprint.

MiLe fingerprints are relatively short and can be seen as a lossy compressed version of the document as each token of the input text is mapped to a part of the resulting fingerprint while the order in which tokens occur is preserved. As a result, MiLe fingerprints can be used to locate the exact position of matching parts in the original documents without having to have access to these documents. If stop wording is part of the preprocessing MiLe can still be used to give a good estimate as to where reuse has occurred.

Generating MiLe Fingerprints for Object-Based Documents. The generation of a MiLe fingerprint for an object-based document works quite similar as for a text-based document. In the following, we describe the generation of a MiLe fingerprint using a PowerPoint presentation as example. However, the presented algorithm can be applied to other types of object-based documents as long as the underlying content is in some form ordered and can be accessed. There are three main differences to the text-based version that need to be addressed when generating MiLe fingerprints for object-based documents:

1. The preprocessing
2. The order of objects
3. The object feature used for fingerprinting

For preprocessing, the object-document is decomposed into modular objects, that means all grouped elements in the presentation are "un-grouped" until they reach a modular state. The text elements are preprocessed like in the text-based version of MiLe.

While the order of slides in a presentation is given by default, objects on a slide have no obvious order. However, since MiLe is order preserving two identical slides need to be processed in the exact same order. There are different possibilities to determine the order of objects including the position of an object (i.e. its coordinates), its layer or - what we make use of - a given ID. This ID is unique for all objects on a slide. During the preprocessing of a PowerPoint document the non-textual objects on a slide are ordered by their ID.

The last difference to the text-based version of MiLe is how objects find entrance into the fingerprint. Texts are usually divided into tokens (i.e. words) and each token is used as feature for the generation of the fingerprint. The same applies for the text fragments of object-based documents. However, for a non-text object there are various features that could be used for fingerprinting. Possibilities include its shape, area, width and height, color or combinations of the above.

These work well for basic objects like lines, arrows or geometric shapes. However, for images or even more complex objects the named features are not distinctive enough. In those cases we export a scaled image of the object as feature.

The features are then processed in the given order the same way as in the text-based version of MiLe to generate the fingerprint of an object-based document.

4.2 Containment Calculation

Once the fingerprints of two documents have been created, reuse between these documents can be detected, measured and localized without further access to the documents' contents.

To determine the resemblance of documents A and B, their MiLe fingerprints are treated as strings and a basic string matching algorithm is applied:

1. Shingles are extracted from B's fingerprint and stored in a lookup table. Here, a token corresponds to the bit length chosen during fingerprint creation. The shingle length corresponds to the minimal length m a match has to have at least. This parameter also greatly affects the probability of collisions: With a bit length of four and a shingle size of five the size of a comparison unit will be 20 bits.
2. An integer used for counting matches is initialized.
3. Shingles (using the same shingle length as above) are extracted from A's fingerprint. Each shingle is, in the order of appearance, compared to the list of shingles extracted for B.
4. If B contains the shingle, the match counter is incremented with regard to the previous shingle. The counter is incremented by one, if B did contain the previous shingle, as this means that two consecutive shingles and hence $m+1$ tokens matched. The counter is incremented by m if B did not contain the previous shingle: Here an individual shingle (m tokens) matched. [1]

To obtain the containment of A in B the value of the resulting match counter c has to be divided by the length of A's fingerprint (number of tokens):

$$C(A, B) = \frac{c}{N_A - m + 1} \qquad (2)$$

Hence, the calculation is not based on the number of matching shingles but on the number of matching tokens (i.e. words) which improves the accuracy. As each document always consists of roughly as many shingles as tokens the divisor in equation 2 is in both cases almost identical. The dividend on the other hand can differ greatly, depending on the shingle size and the distribution of matches.

4.3 Using MiLe on Large Corpora

MiLe's runtime behavior is similar to that of state of the art approaches like k-gram for the one-to-one comparison of document fingerprints. However, mostly

---

[1] For further refinement one can keep track of the shingles that have been matched and delete them from the list of B's shingles.

this is not the main use case. What is usually needed is an efficient way to compare one input document to a large scale corpus. One scenario could be a plagiarism detection system that offers customers the possibility to upload an input document that is then checked against all stored documents. In this section we will describe how to use inverse indexes to store MiLe fingerprints that allow for efficiently processing such queries. A naïve approach would be to build a lookup table using the fingerprint's shingles as keys, thereby generating keys of the size of MiLe's comparison unit (cp. Section 4.2). While in this setting we would still benefit from the more accurate resemblance calculations and the robustness against small changes (see Section 4.4), we now have a storage consumption that is equal to that of k-gram and, if we additionally store the complete MiLe fingerprint, even higher. The easiest way of reducing the storage requirements is to not insert a document pointer for every comparison unit. This is similar to the subset selection approach of 0 mod p, Winnowing or Hailstorm. If we only store a document pointer for every o^{th} shingle (we call o the overleap factor) we reduce the storage requirements by a factor of o. To still benefit from the contiguity of the content we change the resemblance calculation algorithm as follows (m describes the minimal match length, o the overleap factor):

1. Create MiLe fingerprint for the input document that is to be compared to the corpus and initialize a counter c_i for each document D_i in the corpus.
2. For each shingle (i.e. comparison unit) in the document's fingerprint lookup the shingle in the hash-table.
   (a) If it is not found, continue with the next shingle.
   (b) If a match was found for a document D_i and the previous shingle for D_i was not a match (note, that previous in this case refers to the oth predecessor) then increment c_i by $m + w \cdot (o-1)$. Here w can be used to parameterize the percentage of how many of the overleaped tokens will be marked as matching (see below).
   (c) If the previous shingle for document D_i was also a match, increment c_i by the overleap factor o.
3. To obtain the containment the resulting match counters c_i have to be divided by the length of the corresponding fingerprints (cp. Section 4.2).

The idea behind these incrementing steps is that if a match was the first in a series there is a certain probability that the previous $o - 1$ tokens are also matches but were not matched because of the overleap. As we cannot quantify this probability we assume that it is 50% therefore setting $w = 0.5$ and hence adding $0.5(o-1)$. If the match is not the first in a series we act on the assumption that the tokens in between are also matches and therefore increment the counter by o. This strategy is comparable with the bridging strategy proposed in [9]. However, Hamid et al. still weigh all shingles equally and thus do not take the contiguity of the underlying texts fully into account. If the overleap factor is less or equal to the minimal match size, the missing steps between two matches can be easily obtained out of the keys of two consecutive matches. This can be used to refine the containment calculation if necessary. For some use cases, for example, when the exact position of where reuse has taken place is relevant the complete MiLe fingerprint has to be stored alongside the inverted index. However, as the space needed to store the MiLe fingerprint is constant and since usually low bit rates can be used, the overleap factor approach still yields good compression rates as seen in Section 5.

4.4 Properties of MiLe

The two dominant parameters of the MiLe approach are the bit length b for fingerprint creation and the minimal match length m. The size of a MiLe fingerprint for a document A with $|A|$ tokens is $|A| \cdot b/8$ bytes. The size of MiLe fingerprints can therefore be controlled directly through adjusting b.

When working with very low bit sizes (such as $b = 2$) the minimal match length m has to be increased in order to avoid accidental collisions. This can be regarded as a strictness factor, as MiLe ignores all matches of less than m tokens. If a bigger bit size is used, a smaller m can be used accordingly. Since the bit size has to be chosen before creating the fingerprints it cannot be adjusted afterwards[2]. The minimal match length on the other hand can be adjusted for each resemblance calculation, thereby it is possible to adapt MiLe for a specific use case without recalculating fingerprints.

k-gram is often criticized for its lack of flexibility and - mainly for bigger window sizes - sensitivity to small changes. The MiLe fingerprint provides for a certain kind of robustness against small changes. It can be quantified as a function of the ordered common tokens in two compared sequences. The probability that two sequences are matched by MiLe is

$$pr_{match} = \frac{1}{2^{b(m-c)}} \quad 0 \leq c \leq m \qquad (3)$$

where c is the number of common tokens of two sequences in the respective order, b the bit size and m the minimal match length. Thus the more tokens in two sequences already match, the higher the probability that these sequences will be matched although they do not overlap completely. The steepness of this increase is determined by the chosen bit size. $c = m$ constitutes a regular match.

How to choose b and m very much depends on the use case at hand. From the evaluations conducted (see Section 5) we can conclude that the size of the comparison unit $(b*m)$ should be in the range of a bit size which is sufficient for algorithms like k-gram or winnowing on the given corpus. In use cases where the basic MiLe algorithm is applicable it is preferable to use very low bit rates (e.g. $b = 3$) as this yields the highest compression rates. However, this means that the containment calculation has to be conducted in a stricter mode (larger m). On the other hand, if used with an inverted index (see Section 4.3) the dominant factor in respect to storage consumption is the number of document pointers stored per document. Hence the bit size can be increased to allow for a smaller minimal match size.

---
[2] Actually, it is possible to downgrade MiLe fingerprints, i.e. create the 4-bit MiLe fingerprint out of the 5-bit fingerprint.

A simple statistical analysis, under the assumption that words are equally distributed, suggests that with a comparison unit of 20 bits it is possible to handle a corpus consisting of one million documents each consisting of 10,000 words. Under these assumptions, when comparing an input document to the entire corpus, we can expect less than 2000 documents where the containment calculation is off by more than 5% due to collisions originating from a too small comparison unit. Note, that in this model the probability for collisions grows linear with the number of documents in the corpus, i.e. if the number of documents in the corpus is doubled, you should expect twice as many documents with an error of more than 5% in the containment calculation.

5 Evaluation

To evaluate MiLe and compare it to existing approaches two corpora have been used. An annotated subset of the TREC newswire corpus created and used by Seo and Croft [19] for text-based documents and a corpus which resulted from the evaluation of the LIS.KOM framework (see [12] and [13] for details) for object-based documents. We compare the results of MiLe with the results of k-gram quality wise. K-gram is generally seen as benchmark and none of the selection algorithms based on k-gram performs equally well. Neither Hash-breaking nor DCT fingerprinting have reached the quality of k-gram either. To show that MiLe can compete in terms of storage consumption we additionally evaluated 0 mod p and winnowing with different configurations and compared the fingerprint sizes on the TREC corpus.

5.1 Annotated TREC Corpus

The TREC newswire corpus is a large corpus consisting of news stories of several big American newspapers and news agencies like Wall Street Journal, LA Times, Financial Times or Associated Press. We use a small manually annotated subset of it. We have chosen this corpus as it has been specifically created for the evaluation of reuse detection methods.

Evaluation Setting. The annotated TREC corpus consists of 600 document pairs manually categorized into six categories. The corpus was originally created by Seo and Croft to evaluate their DCT fingerprinting approach against other existing approaches [19]. Three levels of reuse are distinguished, which when applying an asymmetric containment measure, result in six different categories. The categories used are named:

1. Most / Most (C1): Most of the text of document A is reused covering most of the text of document B
2. Most / Considerable (C2): Most of the text from document A is reused in B covering a considerable amount of document B
3. Most / Partial (C3): Most of the text of document A is reused in B, covering only a small part of document B

4. Considerable / Considerable (C4) (as above)
5. Considerable / Partial (C5) (as above)
6. Partial / Partial (C6) (as above)

The thresholds for manual categorization were at 0.80 containment for most, 0.50 for considerable and 0.10 for partial. Since the corpus did not contain document pairs with no reuse and hence the partial threshold would be ineffectual for automatic classification, we added a seventh category with documents that have no resemblance. We have added 100 document pairs for category 7.

The evaluation of a reuse detection approach can now be treated as a categorization problem and thus quality measures like precision and recall can be applied. We decided to use a ten fold cross-validation approach on the given 700 document pairs. We used the Weka framework for our tests and the F1 measure as harmonic mean of precision and recall as measure. We averaged the results over ten runs to reduce statistical variations. We used the two containment measures for each document pair as the only features for Weka's tree based J48 classifier.

Results. We have compared MiLe's performance to that of k-gram, 0 mod p and winnowing. Table 1 contains an excerpt from the results. For k-gram, winnowing and 0 mod p 16 bit fingerprints were used, as the performance stalls at that point. However bit sizes down to 13 bits produce more or less acceptable results. The standard deviation of the average F1 value over the ten runs is given in parentheses. MiLe was evaluated in the two modi described in Section 4: the basic algorithm and the extended version for large corpora with a given overleap factor o. We included the best configurations for 0 mod p and winnowing and found that shingle sizes of only 2 and 3 produce the best results. Note that the fingerprint sizes given in table 1 assume that the fingerprints are stored directly. When using an inverted index the fingerprint size would depend upon the size used for a document pointer. The tendency suggested by the results can however be converted directly to the number of document pointers needed per document.

With only 2 bits, basic MiLe produces slightly better results than 0 mod 4 while producing a fingerprint that is only half the size. Even when assuming 13 bit fingerprints for 0 mod p (which comes at the cost of quality) MiLe would still outperform 0 mod 4 in terms of storage consumption. As expected, with increasing bit rates MiLe's results increase quality wise and from 4 bits on MiLe's results even get better than k-gram's. Still the storage consumption is comparable to that of 0 mod p and winnowing.

When considering large corpora the overleap factor described in Section 4.3 allows MiLe to use an inverted index. If an overleap factor equal to the minimal match size is used the storage space needed per document is equal to that of a basic MiLe fingerprint. The quality decrease on the other hand is still low enough as for MiLe to produce better results with less storage consumption than 0 mod p or winnowing.

Table 1. Performance of fingerprinting techniques on annotated TREC newswire collection. MiLe is divided into the basic algorithm (Section 4.2) and MiLe in large corpora settings (Section 4.3). The fingerprint sizes are given in bytes.

Approach	C1	C2	C3	C4	C5	C6	C7	F1 (std)	Size
2-gram	0.954	0.859	0.909	0.833	0.818	0.940	0.994	**0.901** (0.012)	600
3-gram	0.930	0.838	0.880	0.826	0.749	0.895	0.992	**0.873** (0.009)	600
0 mod 4, k=2	0.901	0.716	0.817	0.713	0.628	0.908	0.995	**0.811** (0.010)	150
0 mod 6, k=2	0.902	0.701	0.760	0.673	0.526	0.875	0.986	**0.775** (0.013)	100
winnowing									
k=2, w=4	0.905	0.781	0.871	0.778	0.735	0.909	0.995	**0.853** (0.011)	240
k=3, w=6	0.882	0.758	0.853	0.783	0.682	0.876	0.993	**0.832** (0.010)	171
MiLe									
b=2, m=8	0.915	0.853	0.854	0.781	0.594	0.772	0.959	**0.818** (0.010)	75
b=3, m=5	0.928	0.864	0.837	0.818	0.712	0.886	0.984	**0.861** (0.010)	113
b=4, m=4	0.925	0.890	0.894	0.802	0.734	0.937	0.998	**0.883** (0.014)	150
b=5, m=4	0.926	0.905	0.896	0.871	0.813	0.957	1.0	**0.910** (0.010)	188
MiLe									
b=3, m=5, o=6	0.924	0.796	0.824	0.755	0.554	0.833	0.982	**0.810** (0.019)	94
b=4, m=5, o=4	0.904	0.844	0.900	0.797	0.736	0.896	0.992	**0.867** (0.013)	188
b=4, m=5, o=5	0.913	0.774	0.850	0.751	0.670	0.900	0.995	**0.836** (0.014)	150

5.2 LIS.KOM Corpus

The LIS.KOM framework supports, among others, the automatic capturing of structured relations emerging from reuse processes conducted on documents. During the evaluation of the framework reuse relations between PowerPoint documents have been captured. These relations reflect the reuse of PowerPoint documents and include near-duplicates as well as partial reuse. The collected relations have been manually categorized with regards to their validity. The LIS.KOM framework seldom captures invalid relations. However, while PowerPoint documents are reused because of their contents most of the time, sometimes a document is reused because of its template or structure. These relations are captured by the LIS.KOM framework but are worthless for most - if not all - utilization scenarios. Thus it is desirable to sort these out automatically.

Evaluation Setting. The object-based LIS.KOM corpus consists of 290 relations connecting 367 different PowerPoint documents. 244 of the relations have been categorized as *valid* whereas 46 relations have been categorized as *template* or *invalid* relations. In most cases documents connected by a non-valid relation do not overlap as much as valid relations do. Thus it is feasible to apply fingerprinting techniques to automatically determine the validity of a given relation. A simple categorization problem with two categories results where precision and recall can be applied. For this evaluation we compared the object-based version of MiLe with a straightforward adaptation of k-gram for object-based documents. We applied a ten fold cross-validation using the containment measures

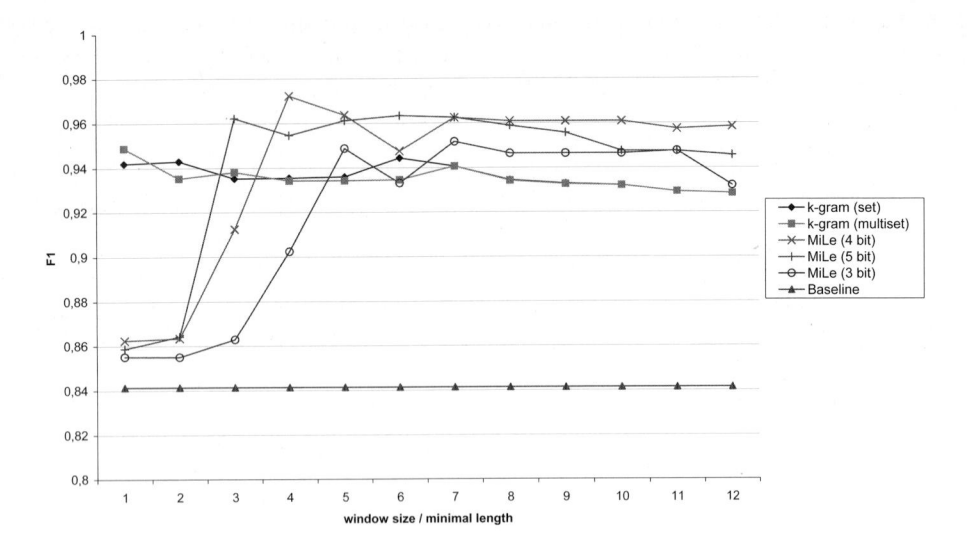

Fig. 1. Comparison of MiLe and k-gram for object-based documents

for each relation as features for optimizing the containment thresholds on the training sets. Due to the given distribution of categories a baseline algorithm which categorizes each relation as *valid* reaches a quality of already 84.1%.

Results. Figure 1 shows the results for the evaluation of MiLe and k-gram on the LIS.KOM corpus. It is evident, that for bit sizes of 4 or 5, MiLe performs significantly better than the adapted k-gram. Even when using MiLe with a bit size of 3, the algorithm performs better than k-gram for values of $m \geq 7$. The categorization quality of both algorithms is comparatively stable for many different parameterizations. The storage consumption of MiLe is for all bit sizes significantly smaller than that of k-gram (as shown in Section 5.1), especially when using MiLe with 3 bits. Both approaches are able to raise the given baseline considerably. The optimal configuration of MiLe reaches a categorization quality of 97,2% for the F1 value. This is the case for a configuration of MiLe with bit size 4 and minimal match length 4, which is a configuration very similar to the optimal one on the TREC corpus. For both algorithms, the optimal thresholds for the calculated containment reside between 10 and 30 percent in most configurations. However, the stricter the configuration, i.e. the bigger the window size or minimal match length respectively, the smaller the optimal threshold which the containment has to pass for a relation to be counted as valid.

6 Conclusions

In this paper we propose MiLe, a fingerprinting approach for detecting local reuse, which is a current and relevant topic of research and can be applied to support Technology Enhanced Learning in various ways. MiLe can be used to detect text reuse as well as reuse between object-based documents (e.g. PowerPoint presentations). We have evaluated the performance of our approach for both cases, the former on an annotated subset of the TREC newswire collection, which was specifically designed for this purpose, and the latter on the LIS.KOM corpus. Our results show that MiLe is not only able to produce better results than k-gram - which is generally used as benchmark for local reuse detection - but that it can also compete with selection approaches like 0 mod p or winnowing in terms of storage consumption. MiLe's runtime performance is comparable to that of the k-gram based selection algorithms when using an inverted index as described in Section 4.3. As the evaluation has shown, the overleap factor allows for compression rates better than those achieved by 0 mod p or winnowing, while still producing better results.

So far the MiLe approach is promising, as evaluations have shown good results, especially quality wise. We have proposed an inverted index structure that allows MiLe to be used on large corpora. However, so far MiLe has only been evaluated on comparably small corpora, so that future work has to include an evaluation of MiLe on a large corpus. This should also be used to empirically validate the claims made in Section 4.4 on how to choose MiLe's parameters in order not to generate too many collisions. Beyond that, future work will include in-depth research on the exploitation of the flexibility provided by the full length MiLe fingerprints, as this is one of the interesting factors that distinguishes MiLe from other approaches.

References

1. Barrón-Cede, A., Rosso, P.: On automatic plagiarism detection based on n-grams comparison. In: ECIR 2009: Proceedings of the 31th European Conference on IR Research on Advances in Information Retrieval, pp. 696–700. Springer, Heidelberg (2009)
2. Brin, S., Davis, J., García-Molina, H.: Copy detection mechanisms for digital documents. In: SIGMOD 2005: Proceedings of the 1995 ACM SIGMOD international conference on Management of data, pp. 398–409. ACM, New York (1995)
3. Broder, A.Z.: On the resemblance and containment of documents. In: SEQUENCES 1997: Proceedings of the Compression and Complexity of Sequences 1997, Washington, DC, USA, p. 21. IEEE Computer Society, Los Alamitos (1997)
4. Broder, A.Z.: Identifying and filtering near-duplicate documents. In: COM 2000: Proceedings of the 11th Annual Symposium on Combinatorial Pattern Matching, London, UK, pp. 1–10. Springer, Heidelberg (2000)
5. Broder, A.Z., Glassman, S.C., Manasse, M.S., Zweig, G.: Syntactic clustering of the web. In: Proceedings of the Sixth International World Wide Web Conference (WWW6), pp. 1157–1166 (1997)
6. Steven Burrows, S., Tahaghoghi, M.M., Zobel, J.: Efficient plagiarism detection for large code repositories. Softw. Pract. Exper. 37(2), 151–175 (2007)
7. Charikar, M.S.: Similarity estimation techniques from rounding algorithms. In: STOC 2002: Proceedings of the thiry-fourth annual ACM symposium on Theory of computing, pp. 380–388. ACM Press, New York (2002)

8. Clough, P., Gaizauskas, R., Piao, S.S.L., Wilks, Y.: METER: MEasuring TExt Reuse. In: Proceedings of the 40th Anniversary Meeting for the Association for Computational Linguistics (ACL 2002), Philadelphia, pp. 152–159 (July 2002)
9. Hamid, O.A., Behzadi, B., Christoph, S., Henzinger, M.: Detecting the origin of text segments efficiently. In: WWW 2009: Proceedings of the 18th international conference on World wide web, pp. 61–70. ACM, New York (2009)
10. Kim, J.W., Selçuk Candan, K., Tatemura, J.: Efficient overlap and content reuse detection in blogs and online news articles. In: 18th International World Wide Web Conference (April 2009)
11. Klerkx, J., Verbert, K., Duval, E.: Visualizing reuse: More than meets the eye. In: Proceedings of the 6th International Conference on Knowledge Management, I-KNOW 2006, Graz, Austria, pp. 489–497 (September 2006)
12. Lehmann, L., Hildebrandt, T., Rensing, C., Steinmetz, R.: Capture, management and utilization of lifecycle information for learning resources. IEEE Transactions on Learning Technologies 1(1), 75–87 (2008)
13. Lehmann, L., Mittelbach, A., Rensing, C., Steinmetz, R.: Capture of lifecycle information in office applications. International Journal of Technology Enhanced Learning 2, 41–57 (2010)
14. Lyon, C., Malcolm, J., Dickerson, B.: Detecting short passages of similar text in large document collections. In: Lee, L., Harman, D. (eds.) Proceedings of the 2001 Conference on Empirical Methods in Natural Language Processing, Pittsburg, PA USA, pp. 118–125 (2001)
15. Manber, U.: Finding similar files in a large file system. In: WTEC 1994: Proceedings of the USENIX Winter 1994 Technical Conference on USENIX Winter 1994 Technical Conference, p. 2. USENIX Association, Berkeley (1994)
16. Metzler, D., Bernstein, Y., Croft, B.W., Moffat, A., Zobel, J.: Similarity measures for tracking information flow. In: CIKM 2005: Proceedings of the 14th ACM international conference on Information and knowledge management, pp. 517–524. ACM, New York (2005)
17. Rivest, R.: The md5 message-digest algorithm (1992)
18. Schleimer, S., Wilkerson, D.S., Aiken, A.: Winnowing: Local algorithms for document fingerprinting. In: Proceedings of SIGMOD 2003, San Diego, CA. ACM Press, New York (June 2003)
19. Seo, J., Bruce Croft, W.: Local text reuse detection. In: Proceedings of SIGIR '08, Singapore, July 2008, ACM Press, New York (2008)
20. Syropoulos, A.: Mathematics of multisets. In: WMP 2000: Proceedings of the Workshop on Multiset Processing, London, UK, pp. 347–358. Springer, Heidelberg (2000)
21. Verbert, K., Ochoa, X., Duval, E.: The alocom framework: Towards scalable content reuse. Journal of Digital Information, 9 (2008)
22. Wise, M.J.: Running karp-rabin matching and greedy string tiling. Technical report, Basser Department of Computer Science - The University of Sydney (1993)

Developing and Validating a Rigorous and Relevant Model of VLE Success: A Learner Perspective

Daniel Müller[1] and Stefan Strohmeier[2]

[1] IMC, Altenkesseler Str. 17 D3,
66115 Saarbrücken, Germany
[2] Chair for Management Information Systems, Saarland University,
Postfach 151150, 66041 Saarbrücken, Germany
`daniel.mueller@im-c.de`, `s.strohmeier@mis.uni-saarland.de`

Abstract. Design characteristics constitute a promising approach to support researchers and practitioners in designing, selecting, and evaluating Virtual Learning Environments in order to prevent costly misconceptions in every phase of the software application process. Hence, the current paper aims at providing a rigorous and relevant model for assessing the success of Virtual Learning Environments so that researchers and practitioners will be enabled to a) better understand particular information- and system-related success drivers, b) systematically evaluate Virtual Learning Environments, and c) have a means for management interventions, task prioritizations as well as effective and efficient resource allocation.

Keywords: DeLone and McLean IS Success Model, Evaluation Method for TEL, System- and Information-Related Design Characteristics, Virtual Learning Environments.

1 Introduction

At present rigorous and relevant approaches for the development, implementation and improvement of Virtual Learning Environments (VLE) are needed "to improve the understanding and communication of educational needs among all stakeholders" [23], ranging from researchers to practitioners [26]. In so doing, rigorous approaches are characterized by sound foundations (e.g. theoretically-based models and/or survey instrument) and methodologies, whereas their relevant counterparts stand out due to their reply of practice-oriented business needs (e.g. "which design characteristics may support systems/course designers in developing, implementing and improving successful VLE") [26]. Thereby, it is of great importance to investigate the drivers or determinants of VLE success to assist system, and course designers in building, and operating systems that are useful and accepted by the learners. However, a specific theory of successful VLE is missing at present as existing approaches are mostly focusing on information systems (IS) in general. Amongst them the DeLone and McLean IS Success Model (ISSM) which constitutes the most prominent approach [20, 21]. Contrary to the Technology Acceptance Model (TAM), which does not propose concrete system design guidelines [43, 62, 64, 69], the ISSM identifies and provides general qualities which are thought to enhance user satisfaction, the use of, and the (perceived) net benefit(s) (NB) of using a VLE [20, 21]. However, being a general approach, the main disadvantage of the ISSM is that specific VLE-related success drivers cannot be directly derived from the model itself. Rather, the ISSM offers insights into the process of how general qualities, namely system- and information quality, influence the final success [20, 21]. Hence, the ISSM offers a general and "useful framework for organizing IS success measurements" [46] which can and should be adapted to the VLE context [21, 46]. Yet, beside more general recommendations for the selection of success measures [52], a widely accepted set of measures contingent on VLE in particular lacks currently. Consequently, the main purpose of this paper is to derive a rigorous and relevant research model for assessing the success of VLE from a learner perspective [26]. A positive side effect of installing such a rigorous and relevant research model is seen in its potential to reduce significantly the number of measures applied for VLE success assessment so far, that research results may be better compared and findings better validated [21]. In so doing, the paper firstly provides more insights into design characteristics as a promising means for designing, selecting, and evaluating VLE (chapter 2.1). Beyond, a comprehensive literature review on empirical work relevant to design characteristics contingent on VLE is presented in order to underline the urgent need for developing and validating a rigorous and relevant research model for assessing VLE success. (chapter 2.2). Secondly, a research model is developed (chapter 3), which then is operationalized, conceptually validated, and tested pilotly (chapter 4). Thirdly, corresponding results will be presented (chapter 5). Particularly attention is paid to the results relevant to the measurement model as this study is limited to the development and validation of the survey instrument, and thus does not focus on testing corresponding hypotheses. Finally, the main findings will be summarized (chapter 6).

2 Foundations

The subsequent chapter now provides more insights into the concept of design characteristics relevant to the ISSM, which subsequently are exemplarily illustrated by means of particular information- and system-related design characteristics contingent on VLE. Beyond, a comprehensive literature review on relevant work to ISSM-related design characteristics contingent on VLE is presented to underline the need for developing and validating a rigorous and relevant research model for assessing VLE success.

2.1 Design Characteristics of VLE

According to [57], VLE are systems for the administrative and didactical support of learning processes in higher education and vocational training settings. An ideal-typical architecture of such systems encompasses an administrative database, a content database as well as an administrative, analytical, communicational, authoring as well as learning process management (i.e. flow control) component. Depending on the kind of flow control component one can distinguish between linear, adaptable, and adaptive VLE (AVLE) [5, 57]. Thereby, a holistic approach of VLE is pursued, i.e. VLE are understood to show full administrative and didactical functionalities which refer to learning materials in particular (i.e. courses). This means that VLE are understood to show an inevitable symbiosis of system functionalities and learning materials. The VLE in turn can be either designed, selected and/or evaluated based on so-called design characteristics. These design characteristics, which are either referred to as system characteristics within the technology acceptance literature [18, 62] or as quality characteristics within the user satisfaction literature [20, 21] are those salient properties "of a system that can help individuals develop favorable (or unfavorable) perceptions regarding the usefulness or ease of use of a system" [62], and thus constitute crucial levers to positively influence user acceptance and system success [18, 20, 21, 62]. According to [20, 21, 43, 62, 69], design characteristics can be broadly categorized into system-, information-, and service-related design characteristics. Whereas system-related design characteristics are understood as a set of properties referring to VLE core functionalities as such, information-related design characteristics are understood as a set of properties which refers to learning materials inherent to VLE in particular (i.e. course content). Hence, as distinct from the aforementioned IT artifacts which are considered to be appropriate for design characteristics research, service-related design characteristics, however, are understood as a set of properties which refers to more human-related VLE success drivers (e.g. end-user support), and consequently does not visibly constitute characteristics of the VLE itself. Therefore, service-related design characteristics are beyond the scope of this paper. Moreover, based on the findings of [43, 62, 69], and in accordance with a systematical review and derivation of system- and information-related design characteristics contingent on VLE [42], it is suggested that system-related design characteristics such as flexibility, learning-process support and interactivity, amongst others, positively influence ISSM- as well as TAM-specific dependent variables such as user satisfaction [20, 21], perceived ease of use (PEOU), respectively its antecedents, as well as the behavioural intention (BI) to use the VLE, the final use [62] of the VLE and the (perceived) NBs [21, 51] of using a VLE. Similarly, information-related design characteristics such as relevancy, understandability and consistency, amongst others, are assumed to influence equally the aforementioned dependent variables, whereas PEOU is replaced by the TAM-specific dependent variable perceived usefulness (PU) of applying the VLE.

2.2 Literature Review on Design Characteristics Contingent on VLE Success

Based on the promising impact of design characteristics on VLE adoption, and success [18, 20, 21, 62], the subsequent elaboration now provides a comprehensive literature review on empirical work relevant to rigorous, i.e. theoretically founded, design characteristics contingent on VLE success in order to underline the urgent need for developing and validating a rigorous as well as relevant research model for assessing VLE success from a learner perspective. With a more particular view to specific results, Table 1 describes the main findings separated into the underlying theory used, the postulated hypotheses (and results) as well as the applied data analysis method. Firstly, as preconditioned, all studies show a theoretical, i.e. rigorous [26], foundation, either in the shape of TAM [10, 28, 32, 39, 47, 50, 59], the ISSM [36], or amalgamations of both research streams [48, 49, 65, 71]. Often, these foundations are of central importance for the derivation of design characteristics.

Table 1. Studies concerning rigorous design characteristics contingent on VLE success

Study	Theory	Hypothesis and Result	Method of Analysis
[10]	TAM	System Quality - BI (0.13*)	SEM
[28]	TAM	Relevance – PU/NB (0.61***)	SEM
[32]	TAM	Content Quality – PU/NB (0.15***) Course Attributes – PU/NB (-0.06*)	Regression Analysis
[36]	ISSM	Information Quality - Satisfaction (0.42**) Information Quality – BI (0.33**) System Quality - Satisfaction (0.18*)	SEM
[39]	TAM	Interactivity and Control - PU (0.233*)	SEM
[47]	TAM	System Functionality – PU/NB (0.147*) System Interactivity – PU/NB (0.379*) System Response – PU/NB (0.208*)	SEM
[48]	TAM/ISSM	Information Quality – PU/NB (0.36***) Information Quality - BI (0.24**) System Quality - BI (0.28**)	SEM
[49]	TAM/ISSM	Information Quality - Satisfaction (0.41**) System Quality - Satisfaction (0.27**)	SEM
[50]	TAM	Flexibility – PU/NB (0.57**) Flexibility - Satisfaction (0.35**)	SEM
[59]	TAM	System Adaptability - PU (0.659*)	Regression Analysis
[65]	TAM/ISSM	Information Quality – PU/NB (0.5*) System Quality – PU/NB (-0.18)	SEM
[71]	TAM/ISSM	Information Quality - Satisfaction (0.42***) System Quality - Satisfaction (0.17*)	SEM

BI=Behavioural Intention; NB=(Perceived)Net Benefit; PU=Perceived Usefulness.
*$p<0,05$; **$p<0,01$; ***$p<0,001$.

For instance, the frequently detectable combination of information quality and system quality as relevant design characteristics [36, 48, 49, 65, 71] is a direct result of the ISSM used for founding the corresponding studies. On the contrary, the design characteristics used in studies with an exclusive focus on TAM [10, 28, 32, 39, 47, 50, 59] mostly lack a properly patterned derivation as they are altogether considered to be external variables to the core TAM constructs [62]. However, to better understand particular associations postulated in the ISSM, one needs these TAM studies as they comprehensively elaborate the influence of particular design characteristics on target variables such as PU which simultaneously may be used for the ISSM inherent dependent variable NB as both are understood as "the extent to which a person believes that using an IT will enhance his or her [job] performance" [21, 51, 62]. Secondly, the design characteristics identified are of fairly different granularities, since quite coarse-granular, global characteristics such as system quality [36, 48, 49, 65, 71], and rather medium-granular, more specific characteristics such as flexibility [50] can be differentiated. Fine-granular, really detailed, design characteristics however could not be found. Hence, the postulated hypotheses (and results) are mainly limited to either coarse-, or medium-grained design characteristics. Hence, none of the ISSM-based studies evaluated particular, i.e. more medium- and/or fine-granular, design characteristics derived from the two major categories system quality and information quality so far. Thus, the findings bear witness to rigorous but not relevant design characteristics

[26], particularly significant for decision makers, IT staff (e.g. system designer/implementer), or course designers. Thirdly, the predominant method of analysis was found to be structural equation modeling (SEM) [10, 28, 36, 39, 47, 48, 49, 50, 65, 71]. However, only one study fully exploited the whole potential of this kind of analysis by proofing particular interdependencies between specific information- and system-related design characteristics [39]. Thus, beyond focusing on the confirmation of particular research hypotheses, future work should also more concentrate on exploring undiscovered interrelationships among design characteristics.

3 Theoretical Model

As a rigorous, and relevant research model for measuring VLE success from a learner perspective is missing at present (Chapter 2.2), the subsequent elaboration therefore presents such a research model which core principles are patterned according to the extended ISSM [21, 51] as well as the integrated research model of [69]. The ISSM was chosen as a sound starting point as it already constitutes a rigorous basis for VLE success measurement (chapter 2.2). Beyond, many validated measures for the proposed core success dimensions such as system quality, information quality, usage, user satisfaction as well as (perceived) NBs (chapter 2.2) already exist which consequently might foster the rigorousness of the proposed research model [26]. Regarding the relevance of our research model, 11 medium-granular system-related design characteristics were derived by means of a comprehensive expert Delphi approach [42] based on the ISSM success dimension system quality [21]. For the purpose of this study, five of them were considered due to the experts' rated impact on VLE success as well as their assumed ability to explain high levels of system quality variance (Tab. 2). Beyond, in order to incorporate the learner perspective equally, an additional end-user oriented Delphi study was conducted according to the same principles as the expert Delphi study mentioned above. This study revealed VLE flexibility to be the most important system-related design characteristic from a learner point of view, whereas the remaining set of system-related design characteristics almost entirely was in accordance with the experts' statements. Hence, flexibility was incorporated into the research model as an important end-user-centric system-related VLE design characteristic too (Tab. 2):

Furthermore, based on the ISSM success dimension information quality [21] 7 medium-granular information-related design characteristics were derived by means of a comprehensive expert Delphi approach [42], whereas four of them were considered according to the same principles taken as a basis for the selection of expert-centric system-related VLE design characteristics (Tab. 3). Beyond, information relevance was incorporated into the research model too as the end-user oriented Delphi study revealed it to be the most important information-related VLE design characteristic (Tab. 3). Equally to system-related VLE design characteristics, the remaining set of information-related design characteristics almost entirely was in accordance with the experts' statements. Finally, beside system quality and information quality, respectively their particular sub-dimensions (Tab. 2, and 3), Table 4 depicts three further ISSM core constructs which were incorporated into the research model.

Table 2. Systems-Related Design Characteristics of VLE: Constructs and Definitions

Construct	Definition	Adapted from
System Quality	System quality measures the desired characteristics which refer to the specific properties of the VLE itself.	[21]
Flexible	VLE are *flexible* if they allow system- as well as learner-driven adjustments (e.g. system-based navigation support vs. learner-based control) of the learning process, respectively its inherent learning activities and/or materials, according to learner-based (e.g. prior, respectively current knowledge, and/or oriented towards particular learning goals/tasks to be achieved in a specific subject domain, etc.) and/or contextual (e.g. mobile vs. stationary device, etc.) information.	[69]
Learning-Process-Supportive	VLE are *learning-process-supportive* if they support the provision of (further) learning activities and/or materials with their inherent information (e.g. activity description and/or instruction, etc.) according to the learners' current status in the unit of learning, and help the learners to coordinate audit dates, group meetings, etc.	own-developed
Interactive	VLE are *interactive* if they allow for learner-system- (e.g. taking self-tests, uploading assignments, etc.), learner-learner-, and/or learner-teacher-communication and/or collaboration (e.g. via audio/video conference, blackboard, chat, forum, etc.).	[45]
Appealing	VLE are *appealing* if their graphical user interface has a pleasant appearance.	[38]
Transparent	VLE are *transparent* if they allow the learners to keep an eye on their own and/or other learners' learning history (i.e. completed and/or passed learning activities of a unit of learning) and current status in the learning process.	own-developed
Structured	VLE are *structured* if learners can quickly detect the allocated information (e.g. learning resources such as learning materials, collaboration services, assessment items, system-generated information such as user guidance, feedback, etc.) in, respectively can easily navigate the graphical user interface.	[30]

Table 3. Information-Related Design Characteristics of VLE: Constructs and Definitions

Construct	Definition	Adapted from
Information Quality	Information quality measures the desired characteristics which refer to the learning materials provided by the VLE.	[21]
Relevant	The information provided by VLE is *relevant* if the learning materials applied improve learners' knowledge in a specific subject domain as they are either based on prior, respectively current knowledge in, and/or are oriented towards particular learning goals/tasks of a specific subject domain.	[8, 38]
Understandable	The information provided by VLE is *understandable* if the words, sentences, and abbreviations applied within the learning materials are clear in meaning (e.g. by use of definitions), easy to comprehend and easy to read.	[10, 13, 28, 30, 38, 48, 49, 66, 67]
Consistent	The information provided by VLE is *consistent* if the learning materials themselves are without contradictions, coherent and presented in a logical order.	[28]
Credible	The information provided by VLE is *credible* if they originate from an trustworthy source (e.g. teacher, certified and/or reputable organizations, etc.).	own-developed
Challenging	The information provided by VLE is *challenging* if the learning materials contain difficult but interesting tasks which stimulate learners' curiosity to solve them.	own-developed

Table 4. Further ISSM Constructs and their Definitions

Construct	Definition	Adapted from
Net Benefits	Net benefits capture the balance of positive and negative impacts of the VLE and its inherent learning resources (e.g. learning materials, collaboration services, etc.) on the learners.	[21]
Use	Learner's real use of a VLE.	[62]
Satisfaction	Learners' opinion of the VLE and its inherent learning resources (e.g. learning materials, collaboration services, etc.).	[21]

Based on the associations postulated by the ISSM as well as on the six additional system-, and five additional information-related sub-dimensions, a research model is proposed which assumes that system quality, information quality, respectively their corresponding sub-dimensions, are linked to a VLE's use and user satisfaction. Beyond, it is proposed that these success dimensions in turn influence the (perceived) VLE NBs. In so doing, chapter 5 presents corresponding results which are, however, limited to the measurement model as this study is limited to the development and validation of the survey instrument, and thus does not focus on testing corresponding hypotheses.

4 Method

As survey-based approaches are the dominant method for data gathering purposes in VLE adoption and success research at present [42], the above-mentioned approach was applied to pilot test the research model.

4.1 Measurement and Conceptual Validation

The survey instrument development was patterned according to [1, 7, 14, 17, 40, 70] which ensured the survey (constructs) to be rigorously developed and validated according to the recommendations postulated by [56], namely, content/construct validity, and reliability by means of a pretest as well as a pilot study using previously utilized survey instruments. Thereby, in line with [14, 21, 29, 55] groups of items were compiled from validated instruments to represent each construct. Beyond, the wording of each item was modified to fit the VLE context. In so doing, appropriate item writing principles were considered [22].

Table 5. Item Placement Ratios

Construct	No. of Items	IPR
System Quality: Flexible	8	94
System Quality: Learning-Process-Supportive	3	88
System Quality: Interactive	3	96
System Quality: Appealing	3	100
System Quality: Transparent	4	100
System Quality: Structured	3	96
Information Quality: Relevant	3	96
Information Quality: Understandable	3	96
Information Quality: Consistent	3	96
Information Quality: Credible	3	100
Information Quality: Challenging	3	100
Total	39	97

In case there were no items for hitherto unknown constructs such as learning-process-supportive, transparent, consistent, credible, and challenging (chapter 3.1), special attention was paid to their comprehensive development. Hence, the authors followed prominent guidelines of scale development procedures [14] and conducted an end-user-oriented focus group [54] with nine students (two Bachelor and seven Master students), all of them experienced in the research topic, the use of VLE, and the procedure of focus groups. Since all constructs under consideration (chapter 3.1) were modeled using reflective indicators, i.e. all items are considered to be replaceable reflections of the underlying constructs [6, 68], the deployment of a focus group helped us in providing item wordings that effectively conveyed our intent to the survey respondent [15, 41]. Thus, all items to be developed were based on their underlying construct definitions to ensure high levels of reliability [14]. To ensure content validity, i.e. the degree to which the item pools reflected all relevant facets of their underlying constructs [61], the item pools were reviewed by six VLE experts (two PHD students, two Master students, one Bachelor student and one secretary, all of them experienced in the research topic and the use of VLE for at least one year) with a particular view to item relevancy, and wording. To ensure construct validity, a card-sorting approach similar to [17, 29, 40] was conducted. However, this approach was limited to the sub-constructs of system, and information quality (Tab. 2, and 3) for the following reasons: Firstly, most of these items were new developed, reworded, or contextualized to VLE system types. Secondly, a sorting of all items (Tab. 6) was considered to be not feasible for the judges. In so doing, another eight VLE experts (four PHD students, two Master students, one Bachelor student and one secretary, all of them experienced in the research topic and the use of VLE for at least one year) had to assign 39 items to 11 well-defined target constructs (chapter 3.1). To better carve out the consistency of the experts' assignments, the item placement ratio (IPR) was applied. As one can see in Table 5, the IPR, i.e. the percentage to which all experts assigned the initial set of items unequivocally to the intended target constructs [40], revealed the following: firstly, as more than half of the judges assigned each item to the adequate construct, all constructs proved to have face validity [61]. Moreover, as all items were consistently assigned to one particular construct (Tab. 5: Overall IPR = 97%), all constructs were also considered to demonstrate convergent validity with their constructs, and discriminant validity with other constructs [61]. Finally, as almost all constructs showed highest degrees of "correct" item placements (Tab. 5), the survey instrument was considered to have a high potential for good reliability scores [40]. With a view to the inter-rater reliability in particular, i.e. the level of the experts' agreement in assigning items to the intended target constructs, Cohen's Kappa [16] with scores above the recommended level of 0.65 [60] proved the card-sorting procedure to be satisfying.

Hereafter, a preliminary survey questionnaire was drafted which was pretested prior to the pilot test (chapter 4.2) by another eight VLE experts (four PDH students, two Master students, one professor and one secretary, all of them experienced in the research topic and the use of VLE for at least one year) to ensure an easy-to-understand item wording as well as an easy-to-understand questionnaire structure (objective and scope of the survey included) [7]. Each item was measured on a 5-point, Likert-type rating scale, ranging from 1 (strongly disagree) to 5 (strongly agree). In contrast, the final use was measured by the average amount of minutes spent on the VLE each day. The specified items, organized by construct, are shown in Table 6.

4.2 Setting and Procedure

The context of the survey instrument was the success of VLE in higher education settings. Thus, in order to pilot test the instrument prior to deploying it in the field, the survey was tested pilotly with a group of 20 MIS students who participated as test subjects. In so doing, students were asked to refer to their VLE which was used for learning delivery purposes during an ERP course in the winter term 2009/2010 at Saarland University/Germany. The main objective of this pilot test was to confirm the results of the card-sorting procedure (chapter 4.1), and gathering additional feedback from the participating end-users. Thereby, the quite small sample size of 20 students were, and is still, not considered to prevent our research model to show sufficiently high statistical power to validate the measurement model (chapter 5).

5 Results

The research model was tested pilotly, and analyzed using partial least squares (PLS), a SEM technique that is well suited for highly complex predictive models [4, 11]. PLS was most appropriate given the large number of constructs that resulted when extending and adapting the ISSM to the VLE context. Beyond, [12] noted that PLS requires minimal restrictions in terms of distributional assumptions and sample size which makes PLS the ideal method for pilot testing the survey instrument. Thereby, smartPLS was used for the analysis. In so doing, all constructs under consideration were modeled using reflective indicators as this approach considers indicators to be replaceable reflections of the underlying constructs [6, 68] which in turn makes the ongoing refinement of the survey instrument highly convenient as only items have to be changed, not the underlying construct definitions. Hence, the final survey instrument to be tested pilotly included 53 items representing 16 constructs which were exhaustively defined in chapter 3. In so doing, the analysis of the measurement model included the estimation of the construct reliability as well as the convergent and discriminant validity of the instrument items. Table 6 lists the remaining set of 44 items representing 16 survey constructs which appeared to be the current result of this pilot test. Thereby, Cronbach's Alpha (CA) was found to be almost entirely above the recommended level of 0.70 [7, 44], indicating adequate construct reliability [44]. The only exception was found to be transparent (CA=0,68) which therefore should be slightly modified in the ongoing research process as low inter-item correlations indicate that not the entire set of items systematically reflects the "appropriate" construct domain, and thus is producing slightly tendencies of unreliability [14].

Similarly to CA, the Composite Reliability (CR) of all constructs equally demonstrated to be above the recommended levels of at least 0.70 [7, 44], equally indicating adequate construct reliability [44]. Furthermore, the Average Variance Extracted (AVE) of all constructs showed levels above the recommended limit values of at least 0.5 [24] so that a satisfying construct reliability could be entirely approved. At the same time, the corresponding AVE values confirmed the survey items to have adequate convergent validity [24]. Furthermore, the discriminant validity of the survey items was found to be satisfactory as the square root of the AVE for almost each construct was larger than the correlations of that construct with all other constructs in the research model (Fornell-Larcker criterion) [24]. The sole exception was found to be interactive which correlated quite highly with understandable (0,90) so that these two constructs will be trialed once again in the ongoing research process. Discriminant and convergent validity were further confirmed as the remaining set of survey items (Tab. 6) demonstrated loadings above 0.50 on their associated factors [56], and the item loadings within each associated factor were found to be higher than those across constructs. Based on this criterion, nine items (flexible = six items; learning-process-supportive, interactive, transparent = one item) were not included in the current survey instrument (Tab. 6). Surprisingly, none of these items were deletion candidates during the card-sorting procedure. One possible reason might have been that the VLE under consideration did not support particular functionalities which were reflected by the deletion candidates. Hence, the current item pool will be revised and further developed in the ongoing validation phase of this research project to ensure universal applicability of the item pool whereas the generally recommended minimum of three items per construct will be targeted [29]. In so doing, the use of reflective indicators makes the ongoing refinement of the survey instrument highly convenient [6, 68]. Finally, based on the current item pool, the significance of the item loadings was analyzed using a bootstrapping procedure with 100 samples. Fortunately, almost all loadings were significant at the 0.001 level.

Table 6. Survey Items and Measurement Properties

Construct	Item	Adapted from	Mean	St. dev.
System Quality AVE = 0.86 CA = 0.92 CR = 0.95	In terms of system quality, I would rate the VLE highly.		2,90	0,99
	Overall, the VLE is of high quality.	[69]	2,90	0,89
	Overall, I would give the quality of the VLE a high rating.		2,75	1,04
Flexible AVE = 0.80 CA = 0.75 CR = 0.89	The VLE allows me to adjust the learning sequence according to my personal needs.	[39, 47]	2,65	0,96
	The VLE allows me to select the learning materials I consider appropriate.	[39, 47]	3,30	1,14
Learning-Process-Supportive AVE = 0.79 CA = 0.74 CR = 0.88	The VLE allows me to coordinate learning-supportive activities (here: audit dates, group meetings, etc.).	*own-developed*	2,55	1,32
	The VLE supports the provision of additional information per learning activity (here: activity description and/or instruction, etc.).		2,45	1,02
Interactive AVE = 0.77 CA = 0.72 CR = 0.87	The VLE allows me to interact with my teacher (e.g. via audio/video conference, blackboard, chat, forum, etc.).	[39, 47, 58]	3,80	3,55
	The VLE allows me to interact with my fellow students (e.g. via audio/video conference, blackboard, chat, forum, etc.).	[39, 47, 58]	0,98	1,02
Appealing AVE = 0.82 CA = 0.89 CR = 0.93	The commands within the VLE's graphical user interface are well-depicted by buttons and symbols.	[28]	2,65	0,96
	The layout of the VLE's graphical user interface is friendly.	[10, 13, 48]	2,90	1,26
	The VLE has an attractive graphical user interface.	[25]	2,70	1,23

Table 6. (*continued*)

Construct	Item	Source	Mean	SD
Transparent AVE = 0.61 CA = 0.68 CR = 0.82	The VLE allows me to keep an eye on my learning history (here: my completed/passed learning activities of this course).		2,65	1,31
	The VLE allows me to keep an eye on my current status in this course.	[39]	2,65	1,11
	The VLE allows me to keep an eye on my remaining learning activities of this course.		2,80	1,12
Structured AVE = 0.73 CA = 0.82 CR = 0.89	The organization of learning materials in the VLE's graphical user interface is clear.	[28, 36, 47, 48, 49]	3,00	0,77
	It is easy to find the learning materials in the VLE's graphical user interface.	[48]	2,70	0,95
	It is easy to navigate the VLE's graphical user interface.	[10, 13, 38]	2,95	0,92
Information Quality AVE = 0.92 CA = 0.95 CR = 0.97	Overall, I would give the learning materials provided by the VLE high marks.		3,25	1,04
	Overall, I would give the learning materials provided by the VLE a high rating in terms of quality.	[69]	3,30	0,90
	In general, the VLE provides me with high-quality learning materials.		3,10	0,94
Relevant AVE = 0.88 CA = 0.94 CR = 0.96	The learning materials exactly fit my current knowledge-level in this subject domain.	[28, 36, 49, 59, 67]	2,50	0,97
	The learning materials exactly fit my personal learning goals/tasks in this subject domain.	[8, 36, 49, 66, 67]	2,55	1,32
	The learning materials improve my knowledge in this subject domain.	[59]	3,40	1,02
Understandable AVE = 0.77 CA = 0.85 CR = 0.91	The words, sentences, and abbreviations applied within the learning materials are clear in meaning (e.g. by use of definitions).	[28, 30, 38, 48, 49]	3,15	1,24
	The words, sentences, and abbreviations applied within the learning materials are easy to understand.	[13, 28, 30, 38, 48, 49, 67]	3,20	1,12
	The words, sentences, and abbreviations applied within the learning materials are easy to read.	*own-developed*	3,30	1,19
Consistent AVE = 0.76 CA = 0.85 CR = 0.91	The learning materials are without contradictions (e.g. consistent use of defined terms).		3,10	1,04
	The learning materials are coherent.	*own-developed*	3,25	0,70
	The learning materials are presented in a logical order.		3,35	1,06
Credible AVE = 0.84 CA = 0.91 CR = 0.94	I trust in the learning materials' originator (e.g. teacher, professional institution/organization).		3,35	1,35
	The learning materials' originator (e.g. teacher, professional institution/organization) is an (officially) approved source of information.	*own-developed*	3,50	1,12
	The learning materials' originator (e.g. teacher, professional institution/organization) has a good reputation.		3,30	1,19
Challenging AVE = 0.71 CA = 0.79 CR = 0.88	The tasks contained (with)in the learning materials arouse my curiosity.	[39]	3,25	0,83
	The tasks contained (with)in the learning materials arouse my ambition.	*own-developed*	3,20	1,03
	The tasks contained (with)in the learning materials are appropriately tricky.	*own-developed*	3,35	0,96

Table 6. (*continued*)

Net Benefits AVE = 0.95 CA = 0.97 CR = 0.98	Using the VLE improves my performance in my study.		2,55	1,02
	Using the VLE in my study increases my productivity.	[17, 62]	2,55	1,16
	Using the VLE enhances my effectiveness in my study.		2,45	1,07
Use AVE = 1.0 CA = 1.0 CR = 1.0	On average, how much time do you spend on the VLE each day?	[62]	10,15	13,75
User Satisfaction AVE = 0.66 CA = 0.83 CR = 0.89	Overall, the learning materials I get from the VLE are very satisfying.		3,40	0,92
	I am very satisfied with the learning materials I receive from the VLE.	[69]	3,25	0,77
	All things considered, I am very satisfied with the VLE.		2,95	1,02
	Overall, my interaction with the VLE is very satisfying.		3,10	0,77

AVE=Average Variance Extracted; CA=Cronbach's Alpha; CR=Composite Reliability

6 Conclusions

Within this paper, first steps in the development of a rigorous and relevant research model for assessing the success of VLE from a learner perspective were undertaken [26]. This hopefully will stimulate future research, especially quantitative studies, to reduce significantly the number of measures applied for VLE success assessment so far so that research results may be better compared and findings better validated [21]. However, as already mentioned in chapter 5, the research model and some of its constructs needs further development and validation before it can be applied in practice. Beyond, future research endeavours have to empirically validate and apply the revised research model in higher education and vocational training settings.

References

1. Aladwani, A.M., Palvia, P.C.: Developing and Validating an Instrument for Measuring User-Perceived Web Quality. Information and Management 39, 467–476 (2002)
2. Arbaugh, J.B.: Virtual Classroom Characteristics and Student Satisfaction With Internet-Based MBA Courses. Journal of Management Education 24(1), 32–54 (2000)
3. Bailey, J.E., Pearson, S.W.: Development of a Tool for Measuring and Analyzing Computer User Satisfaction. Management Science 29(5), 530–545 (1983)
4. Barclay, D., Higgins, C., Thompson, R.: The Partial Least Squares Approach to Causal Modeling, Personal Computing Adoption and Use as an Illustration. Technology Studies 2(2), 285–309 (1995)
5. Bodendorf, F.: Typologie von Systemen für die computergestützte Weiterbildung. In: Bodendorf, F., Hofmann, J. (eds.) Handbuch der Informatik: Computer in der betrieblichen Weiterbildung, vol. 15.2, pp. 63–82. Oldenbourg, Munich and Vienna (1993)
6. Bollen, K., Lennox, R.: Conventional Wisdom on Measurement: A Structural Equation Perspective. Psychological Bulletin 110(2), 305–314 (1991)
7. Lewis, B.R., Templeton, G.F., Byrd, T.A.: A Methodology for Construct Development in MIS Research. European Journal of Information Systems 14(4), 388–400 (2005)

8. Brusilovsky, P., Peylo, C.: Adaptive and Intelligent Web-based Educational Systems. International Journal of Artificial Intelligence in Education 13, 159–172 (2003)
9. Catterall, M., Maclaran, P.: Focus Groups in Marketing Research. In: Russell, W.B. (ed.) Handbook of Qualitative Research Methods in Marketing, pp. 255–267. Edward Elgar, Cheltenham (2006)
10. Chang, S.-C., Tung, F.-C.: An Empirical Investigation of Students' Behavioural Intentions to Use the Online Learning Course Websites. British Journal of Educational Technology 39(1), 71–83 (2008)
11. Chin, W.W.: Issues and Opinions on Structural Equation Modeling. MIS Quarterly 22(1), 7–16 (1998)
12. Chin, W.W., Marcolin, B.L., Newsted, P.: A Partial Least Squares Latent Variable Modeling Approach for Measuring Interaction Effects: Results from a Monte Carlo Simulation Study and an Electronic-Mail Emotion/Adoption Study. Information Systems Research 14, 189–217 (2003)
13. Chiu, C.-M., Hsu, M.-H., Sun, S.-Y., Lin, T.-C., Sun, P.-C.: Usability, Quality, Value and E-Learning Continuance Decisions. Computers & Education 45, 399–416 (2005)
14. Churchill, G.A.: A Paradigm for Developing Better Measures of Marketing Constructs. Journal of Marketing Research 16, 64–73 (1979)
15. Clark, L.A., Watson, D.: Constructing Validity: Basic Issues in Objective Scale Development. Psychological Assessment 7(3), 309–319 (1995)
16. Cohen, J.A.: A Coefficient of Agreement for Nominal Scales. Educational and Psychological Measurement 20, 37–46 (1960)
17. Davis, F.D.: Perceived Usefulness, Perceived Ease of Use, and User Acceptance of Information Technology. MIS Quarterly 13(3), 319–340 (1989)
18. Davis, F.D.: User Acceptance of Information Technology: Systems Characteristics, User Perception and Behavioral Impact. International Journal of Man-Machine-Studies 38, 475–487 (1993)
19. Davis, F.D., Bagozzi, R., Warshaw, P.: User Acceptance of Computer Technology: A Comparison of Two Theoretical Models. Management Science 35(8), 982–1003 (1989)
20. DeLone, W.H., McLean, E.R.: Information Systems Success: The Quest for the Dependent Variable. Information Systems Research 3(1), 60–95 (1992)
21. DeLone, W.H., McLean, E.R.: The DeLone and McLean Model of Information Systems Success: A Ten-Year Update. Journal of Management Information Systems 19(4), 9–30 (2003)
22. Dillman, D.A.: Internet, Mail, and Mixed-Mode Surveys: The Tailored Design Method. John Wiley & Sons, New York (2008)
23. European Conference on Technology Enhanced Learning, Sustaining TEL: From Innovation to Learning and Practice (2010), http://www.ectel2010.org/conference
24. Fornell, C., Larcker, D.F.: Evaluating Structural Equation Models with Unobservable Variables and Measurement Error. Journal of Marketing Research 18, 39–50 (1981)
25. Fu, F.-L., Chou, H.-G., Yu, S.-C.: Activate Interaction Relationships Between Students Acceptance Behavior and E-Learning. In: Dong, G., Lin, X., Wang, W., Yang, Y., Yu, J.X. (eds.) APWeb/WAIM 2007. LNCS, vol. 4505, pp. 670–677. Springer, Heidelberg (2007)
26. Hevner, A.R., March, S.T., Park, J., Ram, S.: Design Science in Information Systems Research. MIS Quarterly 28(1), 75–105 (2004)
27. Hoever, K.M., Steiner, C.M.: Adaptive Learning Environments: A Requirements Analysis in Business Settings. International Journal of Advanced Corporate Learning 2(3), 27–33 (2009)
28. Hong, W., Thong, J.Y.L., Wong, W.-M., Tam, K.-Y.: Determinants of User Acceptance of Digital Libraries: An Empirical Examination of Individual Differences and System Characteristics. Journal of Management Information Systems 18(3), 97–124 (2001-2002)

29. Kankanhalli, A., Tan, B.C.Y., Wei, K.-K.: Contributing Knowledge to Electronic Knowledge Repositories: An Empirical Investigation. MIS Quarterly 29(1), 113–143 (2005)
30. Lee, G.T., Dahlan, N., Ramayah, T., Karia, N., Hasmi Abu Hassan Asaari, M.: Impact of Interface Characteristics on Digital Libraries Usage. Malaysian Online Journal of Instructional Technology 2(1), 1–9 (2005)
31. Lee, Y., Kozar, K.A., Larsen, K.: The Technology Acceptance Model: Past, Present, and Future. Communications of the Association for Information Systems 12(50), 752–780 (2003)
32. Lee, Y.-C.: An Empirical Investigation into Factors Influencing the Adoption of an E-Learning System. Online Information Review 30(5), 517–541 (2006)
33. Liaw, S.-S., Chang, W.-C., Hung, W.-H., Huang, H.-M.: Attitudes toward Search Engines as a Learning Assisted Tool: Approach of Liaw and Huang's Research Model. Computers in Human Behavior 22, 177–190 (2006)
34. Liaw, S.-S., Huang, H.-M.: An Investigation of User Attitudes toward Search Engines as an Information Retrieval Tool. Computers in Human Behavior 19, 751–765 (2003)
35. Lin, C.Y.Y.: Human Resource Management in Taiwan: A Future Perspective. International Journal of Human Resource Management 8(1), 29–43 (1997)
36. Lin, H.-F.: Measuring Online Learning Systems Success: Applying the Updated DeLone and McLean Model. Cyber Psychology & Behavior 10(6), 817–820 (2007)
37. Lin, H.-F., Lee, G.-G.: Determinants of Success for Online Communities: An Empirical Study. Behaviour & Information Technology 25(6), 479–488 (2006)
38. Lindgaard, G.: Usability Testing and System Evaluation: A Guide for Designing Useful Computer Systems. Chapman & Hall, London (1994)
39. Martínez-Torres, M.R., Toral Marín, S.L., Barrero García, F., Gallardo Váquez, S., Arias Oliva, M., Torres, T.: A Technological Acceptance of E-Learning Tools Used in Practical and Laboratory Teaching, According to the European Higher Education Area. Behaviour & Information Technology 27(6), 495–505 (2008)
40. Moore, G.C., Benbasat, I.: Development of an Instrument to Measure the Perceptions of Adopting and Information Technology Innovation. Information Systems Research 2(3), 192–222 (1991)
41. Morgan, D.L.: Focus Groups as Qualitative Research, 2nd edn. Sage Publications, Thousand Oaks (1997)
42. Mueller, D., Strohmeier, S.: Design Characteristics of (Adaptive) Virtual Learning Environments: Literature Review and Expert Study (accepted). In: 3rd European Academic Workshop on Electronic Human Resource Management (2010)
43. Mueller, D., Zimmermann, V.: A Learner-Centred Design, Implementation, and Evaluation Approach of Learning Environments to Foster Acceptance. International Journal of Advanced Corporate Learning 2(3), 50–57 (2009)
44. Nunnally, J.C.: Psychometric Theory. McGraw-Hill, New York (1978)
45. Palloff, R.M., Pratt, K.: Building Learning Communities in Cyberspace: Effective Strategies for the Online Classroom. Jossey-Bass, San Francisco (1999)
46. Petter, S., DeLone, W., McLean, E.: Measuring Information Systems Success: Models, Dimensions, Measures, and Interrelationships. European Journal of Information Systems 17, 236–263 (2008)
47. Pituch, K.A., Lee, Y.-K.: The Influence of System Characteristics on E-Learning Use. Computers & Education 47, 222–244 (2006)
48. Poelmans, S., Wessa, P., Mills, K., Bloemen, E., Doom, C.: Usability and Acceptance of E-Learning in Statistics Education Based on the Compendium Platform. In: International Conference of Education, Research and Innovation (ICERI 2008), pp. 1–10 (2008)
49. Roca, J.C., Chiu, C.-M., Martínez, F.J.: Understanding E-Learning Continuance Intention: An Extension of the Technology Acceptance Model. International Journal of Human-Computer Studies 64, 683–696 (2006)

50. Sahin, I., Shelley, M.: Considering Students' Perceptions: The Distance Education Student Satisfaction Model. Educational Technology & Society 11(3), 216–223 (2008)
51. Seddon, P.B.: A Respecification and Extension of the DeLone and McLean Model of IS Success. Information Systems Research 8(3), 240–253 (1997)
52. Seddon, P.B., Staples, S., Patnayakuni, R., Bowtell, M.: Dimensions of Information Success. Communication of the Association for Information Success 2, 2–39 (1999)
53. Specht, M., Burgos, D.: Modeling Adaptive Educational Methods with IMS Learning Design, pp. 1–13 (2007), http://jime.open.ac.uk/2007/08
54. Stewart, D.W., Shamdasani, P.N., Rook, D.W.: Focus Groups: Theory and Practice, 2nd edn. Sage Publications, Thousand Oaks (2007)
55. Stone, E.F.: Research Methods in Organizational Behavior. Goodyear, Santa Monica (1978)
56. Straub, D.W.: Validating Instruments in MIS Research. MIS Quarterly 13(2), 147–169 (1989)
57. Strohmeier, S.: Informationssysteme im Personalmanagement: Architektur – Funktionalität – Anwendung. Vieweg+Teubner, Wiesbaden (2008)
58. Sun, P.-C., Tsai, R.J., Finger, G., Chen, Y.-Y., Yeh, D.: What Drives a Successful E-Learning? An Empirical Investigation of the Critical Factors Influencing Learner Satisfaction. Computers & Education 50, 1183–1202 (2008)
59. Tobing, V., Hamzah, M., Sura, S., Amin, H.: Assessing the Acceptability of Adaptive E-Learning System. In: 5th International Conference on eLearning for Knowledge-Based Society, pp. 1–10 (2008)
60. Todd, P.A., Benbasat, I.: An Experimental Investigation of the Impact of Computer Based Decision Aids on the Process of Preferential Choice, Working Paper, School of Business, Queen's University, Kingston, Ontario (1989)
61. Urbach, N., Smolnik, S., Riempp, G.: Development and Validation of a Model for Assessing the Success of Employee Portals. In: 17th European Conference on Information Systems, pp. 1–13 (2009)
62. Venkatesh, V., Bala, H.: Technology Acceptance Model 3 and a Research Agenda on Interventions. Decision Sciences 39(2), 273–315 (2008)
63. Venkatesh, V., Davis, F.D.: A Theoretical Extension of the Technology Acceptance Model: Four Longitudinal Field Studies. Management Science 46(2), 186–204 (2000)
64. Venkatesh, V., Morris, M., Davis, G., Davis, F.: User Acceptance of Information Technology: Toward a Unified View. MIS Quarterly 24(3), 425–478 (2003)
65. Wang, W.-T., Wang, C.-C.: An Empirical Study of Instructor Adoption of Web-Based Learning Systems. Computers & Education 53, 761–774 (2009)
66. Wang, Y.-S.: Assessment of Learner Satisfaction with Asynchronous Electronic Learning Systems. Information & Management 41, 75–86 (2003)
67. Wang, Y.-S., Wang, H.-Y., Shee, D.Y.: Measuring E-learning Systems Success in an Organizational Context: Scale Development and Validation. Computers in Human Behavior 23, 1792–1808 (2007)
68. Weiber, R., Mühlhaus, D.: Strukturgleichungsmodellierung: Eine anwendungsorientierte Einführung in die Kausalanalyse mit Hilfe von AMOS. In: SmartPLS und SPSS. Springer, Heidelberg (2010)
69. Wixom, B.H., Todd, P.A.: A Theoretical Integration of User Satisfaction and Technology Acceptance. Information Systems Research 16(1), 85–102 (2005)
70. Yang, Z., Cai, S., Zhou, Z., Zhou, N.: Development and Validation of an Instrument to Measure User Perceived Service Quality of Information Presenting Web Portals. Information and Management 42, 575–589 (2005)
71. Yeung, P., Jordan, E.: The Continued Usage of Business E-Learning Courses in Hong Kong Corporations. Education and Information Technologies 12(3), 175–188 (2007)

The Design of Teacher Assistance Tools in an Exploratory Learning Environment for Mathematics Generalisation

Darren Pearce-Lazard, Alexandra Poulovassilis, and Eirini Geraniou

London Knowledge Lab
{darrenp,ap}@dcs.bbk.ac.uk, e.geraniou@ioe.ac.uk

Abstract. The MiGen project is designing and developing an intelligent, exploratory environment to support 11–14-year-old students in their learning of algebraic generalisation. Deployed within the classroom, the system is also providing tools to assist teachers in monitoring students' activities and progress. This paper describes the architectural design of these Teacher Assistance tools and gives a detailed description of one such tool, focussing in particular on the technologies and approaches chosen to implement the necessary functionality given the context of the project.

Keywords: Exploratory Learning, Mathematics Generalisation, Teacher Assistance Tools, Intelligent Support.

1 Introduction

The MiGen project is co-designing, developing and evaluating with teachers and teacher educators a pedagogical and technical environment for improving 11–14-year-old students' learning of algebraic generalisation[1]. The idea of 'seeing the general through the particular' is a powerful way of introducing students to generalisation [1]. In MiGen, we are adopting a constructionist approach [2], allowing students to create and manipulate patterns and algebraic expressions and to perceive the relationships between them. Following [3], MiGen is based on the premise that learners build knowledge structures particularly well in situations where they are engaged in constructing public entities — in our context, these are patterns and expressions that they will share with other students. The MiGen system acts as a mediator of social interaction between students, and also between the teacher and the students, through which shared mathematical expressions are constructed and observed. The system provides not only a means by which students construct their own problem space but also a communicative function through which mathematical interpretations are made explicit and can be discussed with others.

There has been little previous work on supporting students in a constructionist context (e.g. [4,5,6]) while, conversely, it has been argued that considerable guidance is required to ensure learning in such contexts [7]. The exploratory nature of our learning environment requires that personalised feedback be provided to students by the system

---

[1] See http://www.migen.org/ for details of the project's aims and background.

during their construction process. Also, since students are undertaking loosely-defined rather than structured tasks, teachers need to be assisted in monitoring their students' actions and progress by appropriate visualisation and notification tools [8]. The aim of these tools is to assist teachers in developing teaching strategies, informing them of students' progress, the appearance of common misconceptions, students who may be disengaged from the task and students who may be in difficulty. This will allow teachers to support learners in a personalised way, informing the teacher's own interventions in encouraging students to reflect on their constructions, on the feedback the system is giving them, on working towards specific goals, and in communicating and sharing their constructions with others.

In [9], we described the conceptual model and architecture of the MiGen system as a whole. Here, we focus specifically on the design of the teacher assistance tools, motivating and describing their architectural design and giving a detailed description of one such tool. The paper is structured as follows. Section 2 gives a brief overview of the MiGen system and the overall system architecture to the level of detail necessary for this paper. Section 3 describes the architectural design of the teacher assistance tools, and gives a detailed description of the Student Tracking tool in particular. In Section 4 we discuss how this will be extended in the coming months with additional tools and the evaluation activities that we are planning.

To our knowledge, this work is the first targeted at visualising students' progress through constructionist learning tasks and at notifying teachers of students' attainment of specific landmarks as they are undertaking their constructions. We discuss the novelty and contribution of our work further in Section 4.

2 The MiGen System Context and Architecture

The MiGen system will be deployed within the classroom. During a lesson, students work on mathematics generalisation problems as selected by their teacher and presented to them by the system. While this is happening, the teacher may wish to view real-time representations of the students' activities and progress. At other times, teachers may also wish to access historical information about their students' progress as maintained by the system.

MiGen comprises a number of tools, which we describe here to the level of detail necessary for this paper. We refer the reader to the cited references for more details of some of these tools.

At the heart of the system is the **eXpresser**, a mathematical microworld [10,11] which supports students in undertaking mathematics generalisation tasks. As part of a possibly larger activity sequence (see the Activity Tool below), students are asked to construct 'generalised patterns' using the eXpresser. Figure 1a and Figure 1b show two instances of an example pattern. The eXpresser supports students not only in their construction of the pattern but also in deriving expressions (rules) underpinning the pattern, e.g. the number of green tiles required (light grey) given the number of red tiles (dark grey).

The eXpresser microworld gives a lot of freedom to students, who may construct their patterns in a variety of ways for the same task. For example, if a student has constructed their pattern using a series of 'C' shapes as illustrated in Figure 1c, they may derive an expression such as $5r + 3$ for the number of green tiles, where r is the number of red tiles. A range of other possible constructions that students may follow are shown in the remaining diagrams of Figure 1 which also show that the form of the resulting expressions (all of which are equivalent to $5r + 3$ of course) can vary widely. If r is a variable, all of these constructions are *general* and changing the current value of r will lead to the pattern changing appropriately too.

Figure 2 shows the eXpresser user interface. Students use building blocks that they construct from square unit tiles in order to make their patterns, which they can subsequently colour. During their construction, they make use of numbers which they can subsequently 'unlock' to turn them into variables, thus generalising their pattern. Both locked and unlocked numbers can be used in expressions. We refer the reader to [12] for further details of the eXpresser.

Microworlds are designed to provide opportunities for learners to develop complex cognitive skills rather than just knowledge of concepts in the subject domain [10,11]. The tasks that students are usually asked to undertake are open-ended in nature, have multiple possible solutions, and encourage students to explore the construction environment and follow a variety of construction strategies. [13] describes MiGen's multi-layer learner model which, as well as modelling the attainment of concepts in the subject domain, also includes a 'layer' of knowledge comprising microworld-specific concepts that operationalise the concepts of the subject domain, as well as encompassing the affordances of the microworld itself.

In MiGen, tasks are designed to contextualise students' interaction with the eXpresser, including specific learning objectives that the learner should achieve as they undertake a task e.g. 'find a general expression to colour your pattern' — see Figure 2(G).

As a student interacts with the eXpresser, so a series of *landmarks* are automatically inferred by the system, which are then notified to the teacher via the Teacher Assistance tools (see below). There are two categories of landmark:

Task-independent (TI) landmarks occur when the system detects that specific actions or sequences of actions have been undertaken by a student e.g. 'student has placed a tile on the canvas', 'student has made a building block', 'student has unlocked a number'. The detection of TI landmarks is not dependent on knowledge specific to the task that the student is working on.

In contrast, *task-dependent* (TD) landmarks require intelligent reasoning to be applied to combinations of actions (this is done by the eGeneraliser — see below). TD landmarks require access to knowledge about the task and their detection may have a degree of uncertainty associated with it. Examples of TD landmarks are: 'student has made a plausible building block' (requires knowledge of the set of possible solutions to a task), 'student has unlocked too many numbers' (requires knowledge about how many variables a task needs), 'student has coloured their pattern generally' (requires reasoning on the student's expression).

The **Activity Tool** presents students with activity sequences targeting mathematics generalisation, as designed by the designer or teacher. These activity sequences include phases such as introduction to an exploratory learning task, undertaking a task using the

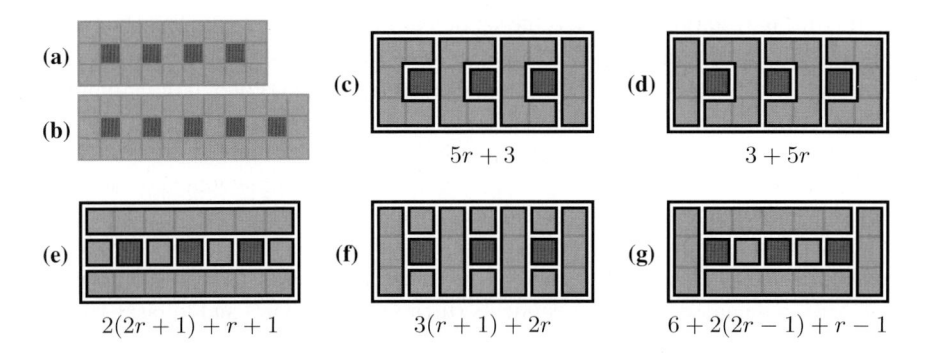

Fig. 1. (a)–(b) Instances of an example pattern and (c)–(g) several possible general constructions where each expression specifies the number of green tiles in terms of r, the number of red tiles

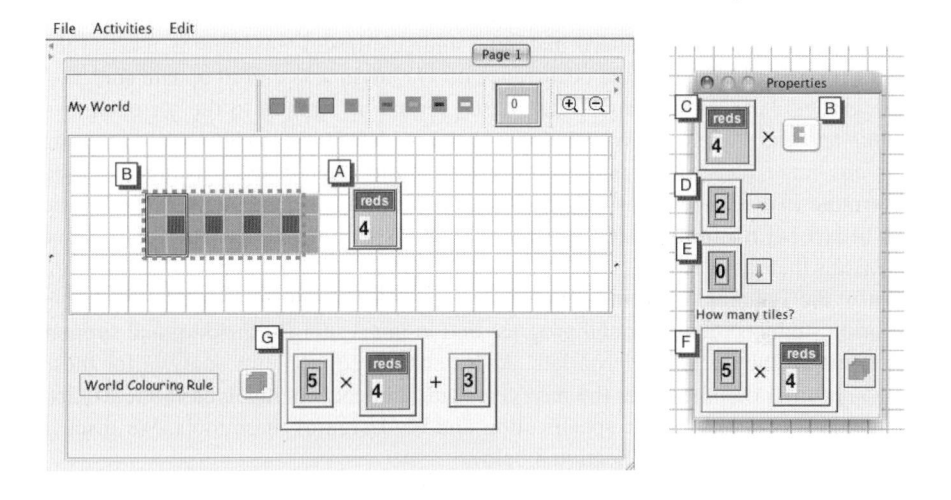

Fig. 2. Constructing a pattern in the eXpresser and describing it with a rule. Letters highlight the main features: (A) An 'unlocked' number that acts like a variable is given the name 'reds' and signifies the number of red (dark grey) tiles in the pattern. (B) Building block to be repeated to make a pattern. (C) Number of repetitions (in this case, the value of the variable 'reds'). (D,E) Number of grid squares to translate B to the right and down after each repetition. (F) Units of colour required to paint the pattern. (G) General expression that gives the total number of units of colour required to paint the whole pattern.

eXpresser, reflecting on a task, and sharing and discussing their constructions and rules with other students.

A **Task Design Tool** is planned for the near future. This will allow the designer or teacher to describe new maths generalisation tasks, and to input into the system a set of possible solutions for them, i.e. possible constructions and associated expressions. Currently, the set of possible solutions for a task is input into the system by the research team using the eXpresser.

Part of the description of a task is the set of learning objectives supported by the task, as selected by the designer/teacher from the total set of learning objectives supported by the system. Currently, such information describing tasks is entered directly into the MiGen database by the research team.

The total set of learning objectives supported by the system, and also the total set of landmarks that are detectable by the system, are easily extensible with new ones as the system is being developed and extended over time.

The **eGeneraliser** is a suite of intelligent components which take as their input information from the eXpresser as students are undertaking tasks, as well as information in the MiGen database relating to students (their learner model) and to tasks (the task description and the set of possible solutions). These intelligent components infer the occurrence of TD landmarks, generate real-time feedback for students (e.g. prompts to help students engage with a task, improve their solutions, generalise their solutions), and also update students' learner models during, and at the end of, each student's usage of the eXpresser tool.

A hybrid of case-based, pattern matching and rule-based reasoning is used in the eGeneraliser in order to infer the occurrence of TD landmarks and to update students' learner models [14]. For example, case-based reasoning applied to the set of known solutions and the student's own solution is used to determine if appropriate building blocks are being constructed and used correctly, while rule-based reasoning is used to determine if the student has coloured their pattern in a general way. We refer the reader to [15,14] for further details of the eGeneraliser components and the inference mechanisms that they employ.

Finally, the **Teacher Assistance Tools** is a suite of tools aiming to assist the teacher in monitoring students' activities and progress and in intervening with additional support for students as she decides appropriate. An extensive requirements analysis for these tools has been undertaken over the past year with the teachers involved in the MiGen project, and this is driving the specification and co-design of these tools. We discuss these tools in greater detail in Section 3 below.

The overall MiGen system has the client-server architecture illustrated in Figure 3. The 'ball-and-socket' notation indicates a component which provides an API (the ball) and the components that use this — the socket(s). For example, the eGeneraliser Information Layer provides an API which is used by the eGeneraliser User Interface. The client software is executed on each student's and teacher's computer, while the server software is executed on one server computer. The architecture is based on Representational State Transfer (REST) [16], for the reasons discussed in detail in [9], including simplicity of installation and operation of the system by schools, scalability, and ease of performance tuning. In particular we use Restlet, a lightweight Java REST framework[2].

As students interact with the Activity Tool and with the eXpresser, these tools' User Interface components update the data structures managed by their corresponding Information Layer components. These components in turn post information about students' actions to the MiGen Server, including the occurrence of TI landmarks. The MiGen Server stores a timestamp with each instance of a TI landmark. The MiGen server stores

---

[2] See http://www.restlet.org/

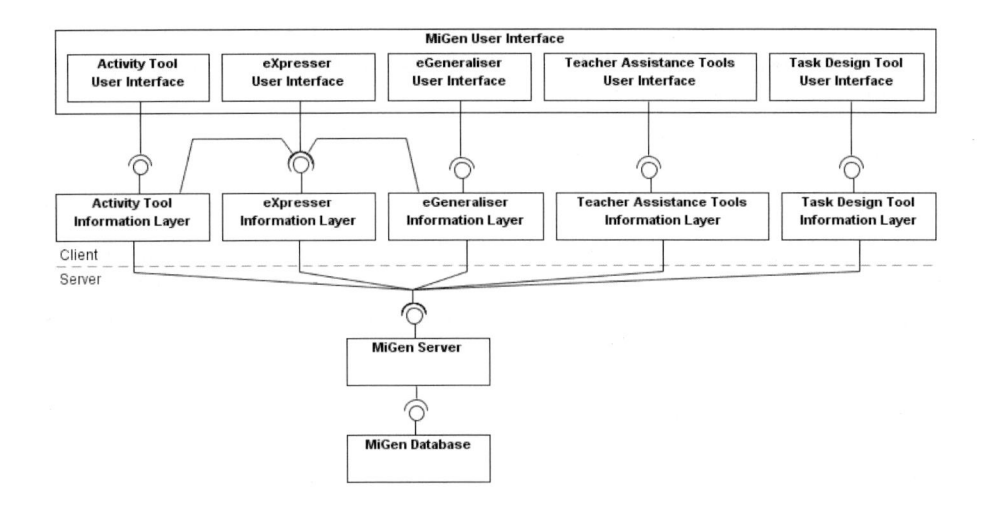

Fig. 3. MiGen system architecture

all its data in the MiGen database which is implemented in JavaDB, a lightweight 100% Java SQL-compliant RDBMS.

The eGeneraliser Information Layer 'listens' to updates in the eXpresser Information Layer and from time to time infers the occurrence of a new TD landmark for this particular student, which it posts to the MiGen Server. It may also generate updates to the student's learner model which it similarly posts to the MiGen Server. It may also generate feedback messages appropriate for the student, which it displays to the student through the eGeneraliser UI and also posts to the MiGen Server. The MiGen Server stores a timestamp with each instance of a TD landmark, learner model update and feedback message.

The Teacher Assistance tools subscribe to the MiGen Server to be notified of the occurrence of TI and TD landmarks; more generally, they may subscribe to be notified of the occurrence of other updates as well e.g. to students' learner models. At present, the Teacher Assistance tools do not generate any information updates of their own and so do no posting to the MiGen Server — this may change in future versions of the system.

3 The MiGen Teacher Assistance Tools

The Teacher Assistance tools derive their information from the MiGen database, via the MiGen Server. This information includes:

- log data relating to students' activities and constructions, as posted to the MiGen Server by the Activity tool and the eXpresser Information Layers;
- TI landmarks detected by the Activity tool and the eXpresser as students interact with these;
- TD landmarks inferred by the eGeneraliser;

- data posted to the MiGen Server by the eGeneraliser relating to updates that it has made to a student's learner model and feedback that it has generated for a student;
- the students' learner models; and
- the task descriptions and possible solutions.

Within any RESTful architecture such as the one implemented for MiGen, all data resources within the system are made available via their own unique URL and are addressable using this URL. For example, the occurrences of task landmarks are located at URLs of the form:

```
/UserSets/<id1>/ExpresserModels/<id2>/TaskLandmarkSet/TaskLandmarkOccurrences/
```

on the MiGen Server, where each `<id>` identifies a particular entity within the preceding collection of entities. For example, `/UserSets/` is the collection of all UserSets defined within the database and `/UserSets/4` is the UserSet within this collection with id '4'.

This URL demonstrates various entities defined within the MiGen database:

- There are a number of UserSets defined, with each UserSet representing a collection of MiGen users. Such a set can (and frequently does) consist of just a single user. However, in collaborative activities a pair of students (or possibly more) will be co-located at the same computer and the UserSet will consist of all of them. In this way, the intelligent support within the system is actually provided to whatever the population of each UserSet is. In principle, this could conceivably even be an entire class (including the teacher). It is a topic of future work to determine how learner modelling information obtained from multi-person UserSets can be used to populate the learner models of the individual students that comprise that set.
- Each UserSet can create an arbitrary number of ExpresserModels, with one ExpresserModel being created by each invocation of the eXpresser.
- Each ExpresserModel is associated with a TaskLandmarkSet which in turn comprises of a set of timestamped occurrences of landmarks.

As task landmarks are generated, the relevant components of the system post these occurrences to URLs of the above form. The MiGen Server then updates the database appropriately. Any such update to the database can also lead to the notification of all components of the architecture that have previously registered their interest in this data resource. In particular, the Teacher Assistance tools register their interest in URLs of this form, as well as other data resources, and the architecture ensures that these tools are notified when the data resources change. This includes notification of additions, deletions and updates.

Figure 4 shows a UML Sequence Diagram illustrating this process involving both TI landmarks (from the eXpresser) and TD landmarks (detected by the eGeneraliser). As the User(Set) manipulates their constructions and expressions using the eXpresser User Interface, the underlying eXpresser Information Layer is updated (message ①). These events are posted to the MiGen Server ② (which in turn stores the data in the MiGen database). The eXpresser Information Layer also notifies the eGeneraliser Information Layer of the user's actions so that it can appropriately process them ③. The eXpresser Information Layer is also responsible for posting task-independent landmarks to the MiGen Server ④. The server notifies the Teacher Assistance Information Layer (⑤)

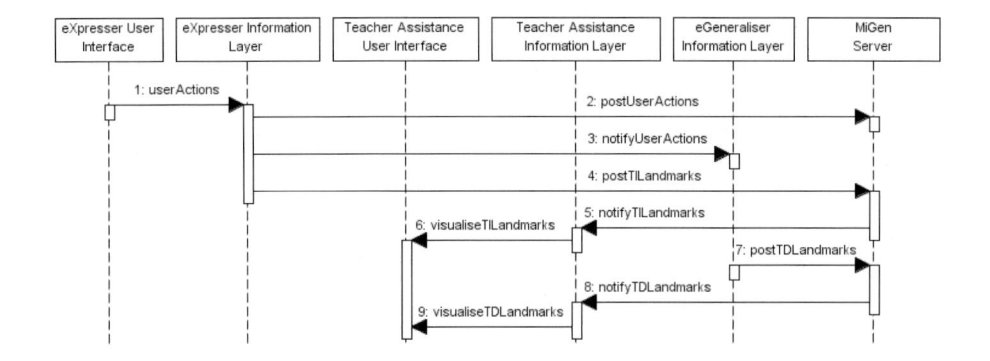

Fig. 4. UML sequence diagram demonstrating how the teacher assistance tools receive information about the occurrence of task-dependent (TD) and task-independent (TI) landmarks

which in turn updates its user interface ⑥. While task-independent landmarks occur directly and immediately from students' actions within the eXpresser, task-dependent landmarks are detected after the appropriate reasoning is applied within the eGeneraliser Information Layer, based on the actions of the user within the eXpresser so far. At various times therefore, the eGeneraliser Information Layer posts task-dependent landmarks to the MiGen Server (message ⑦). Since the Teacher Assistance Information Layer has registered interest (in this example) in receiving all landmark information, it is therefore notified ⑧ and the new landmark information is then used to update the visualisations within the Teacher Assistance User Interface ⑨.

Although this example pertains to the communication of task landmarks from the eXpresser and eGeneraliser to the Teacher Assistance tools, this pattern of messages also extends straightforwardly to landmark occurrences that are also posted by the Activity Tool to the server and that Teacher Assistance tools may also register to be notified of. This communication pattern therefore provides a general architectural template for supporting all of the information requirements of the Teacher Assistance tools in the MiGen system.

3.1 The Student Tracking Tool

So far, we have co-designed with teachers and implemented one of the envisaged suite of Teacher Assistance tools — the Student Tracking tool. This tool provides teachers with information about individual students' attainment of TI and TD landmarks as they are undertaking a task using the eXpresser in the classroom, so that the teacher can follow students' progress on this task and intervene as she decides is appropriate in order to provide guidance and set new goals for individual students.

Figure 5 shows a screenshot of the Student Tracking tool. Each row shown represents the progress of the student named on the far left. Each column corresponds to a landmark as labelled at the bottom of the screenshot (we list the full set of TI and TD landmarks in Appendix A). A coloured cell indicates that a particular landmark has occurred for a particular student. The occurrence count is provided in the cell itself. The

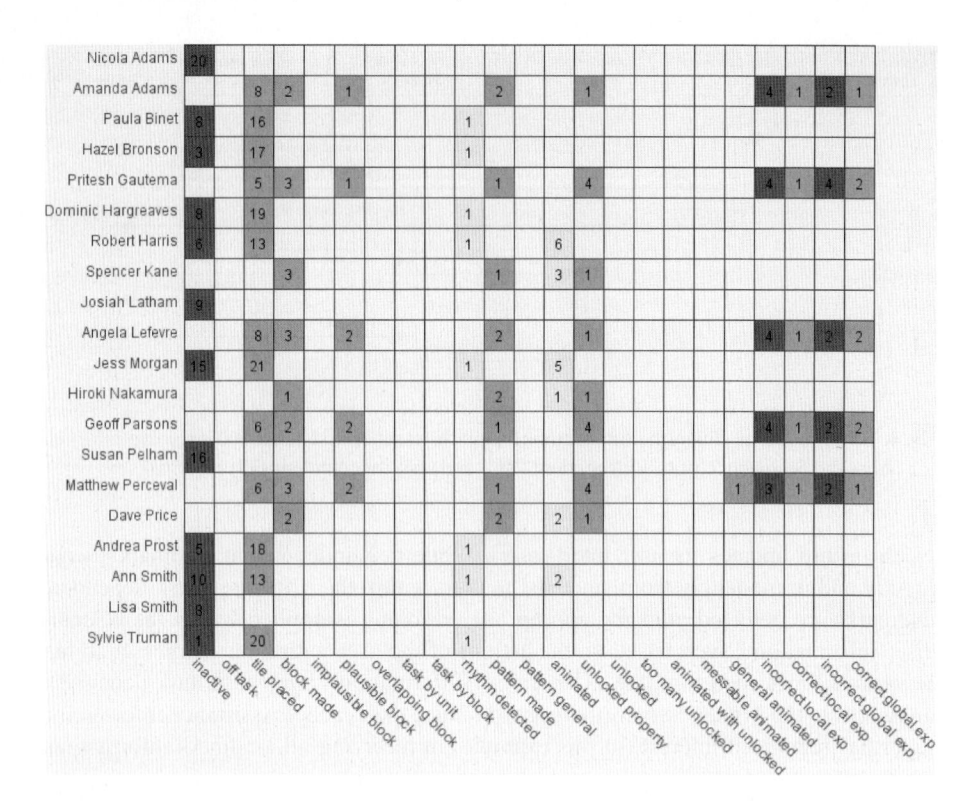

Fig. 5. The Student Tracking User Interface showing the number of times each landmark has occurred for each student during the current task. Student names are listed in alphabetical order by last name. Landmarks are listed in order of expected first occurrence. See Table 1 for an explanation of the colours used. See Appendix A for an explanation of each landmark.

Table 1. Types of task landmark. The first column colours correspond to those used in Figure 5.

Colour	Type	Description
Green (mid-grey)	Positive	The occurrence of such a landmark indicates that the actions of the student are in line with what would be expected from constructive interaction with the system.
Red (dark-grey)	Negative	The occurrence of such a landmark is regarded as an obstruction to constructive use of the system. For example, the student being off-task or inactive.
Yellow (light-grey)	Neutral	The occurrence of such a landmark indicates that the student is showing some understanding of how to use the system but it is not quite on the right (or wrong) track. For example, the student has constructed their pattern using repetitions of individual unit tiles, rather than a larger building block (this is the 'rhythm detected' landmark).

colouring of the cells indicates whether the landmark is regarded as being 'positive', 'negative' or 'neutral', as described in Table 1.

From Figure 5, it is immediately apparent that several users have been inactive at some point during their interaction with the system. However, many of these users have achieved other positive and/or neutral landmarks. For example, Ann Smith did have some periods of inactivity but she has also started placing tiles. She has also attempted to 'animate' her construction (this allows her to test out its generality by applying her expression to several instances of the pattern, as generated automatically by the system), even though she has not yet unlocked any numbers so as to in fact generalise her expression. All of these indicate to the teacher that Ann is having problems using the system, understanding the task or both. Lisa Smith, on the other hand, has just been inactive. Patterns of landmark occurrences such as these can assist the teacher in making decisions about which students need help the most.

In contrast to Ann and Lisa, we see that Angela Lefevre is progressing well with the task: she has placed tiles, made a plausible building block, built a pattern using this block and has unlocked one of its properties. She had problems specifying a correct local expression (this is an expression for the number of tiles of a particular colour in a specific pattern) and also with specifying the global expression correctly (this is the expression for the number of tiles of a particular colour in the construction overall). However, crucially, she has not yet animated her construction to test out its generality. The teacher can therefore use this information to remind her to try animating her construction. Angela would then see whether she has built it generally. This demonstrates therefore that not only can this representation show the teacher who needs help the most but can also provide more subtle information which can be used to ask students thought-provoking questions or further facilitate them on their way to successful completion of the task.

The data shown in Figure 5 is simulated user interaction data, semi-automatically generated by the authors in order to test the Student Tracking tool. Classroom-based activities are planned for the near future in order to evaluate the tool in context in collaboration with our teacher partners. For these trials, we are also planning to provide an additional visualisation within the Student Tracking tool which does not aggregate the total number of occurrences of each landmark but which instead presents the individual landmark occurrences for a student in the order in which they occur. This timeline-driven view will use the same data as the aggregated view shown above, but will tell a more detailed 'story' about the way in which a student has interacted with the system in undertaking the task. We show this additional view in Figure 6. This view shows the sequential occurrence of each landmark for a group of students during their interaction with the task. Each landmark (coloured as before) is positioned in relation to the time at which the landmark occurred (with time increasing upwards). Taking Ann Smith as an example once again, this representation shows that, initially, Ann seemed to be disengaged from the task: she clicked on the animate button a couple of times despite her canvas being empty and then proceeded to place a handful of tiles. At this stage, the system detected that she was inactive for a while. If the teacher had viewed this representation at that point, she could have intervened and encouraged Ann to try placing

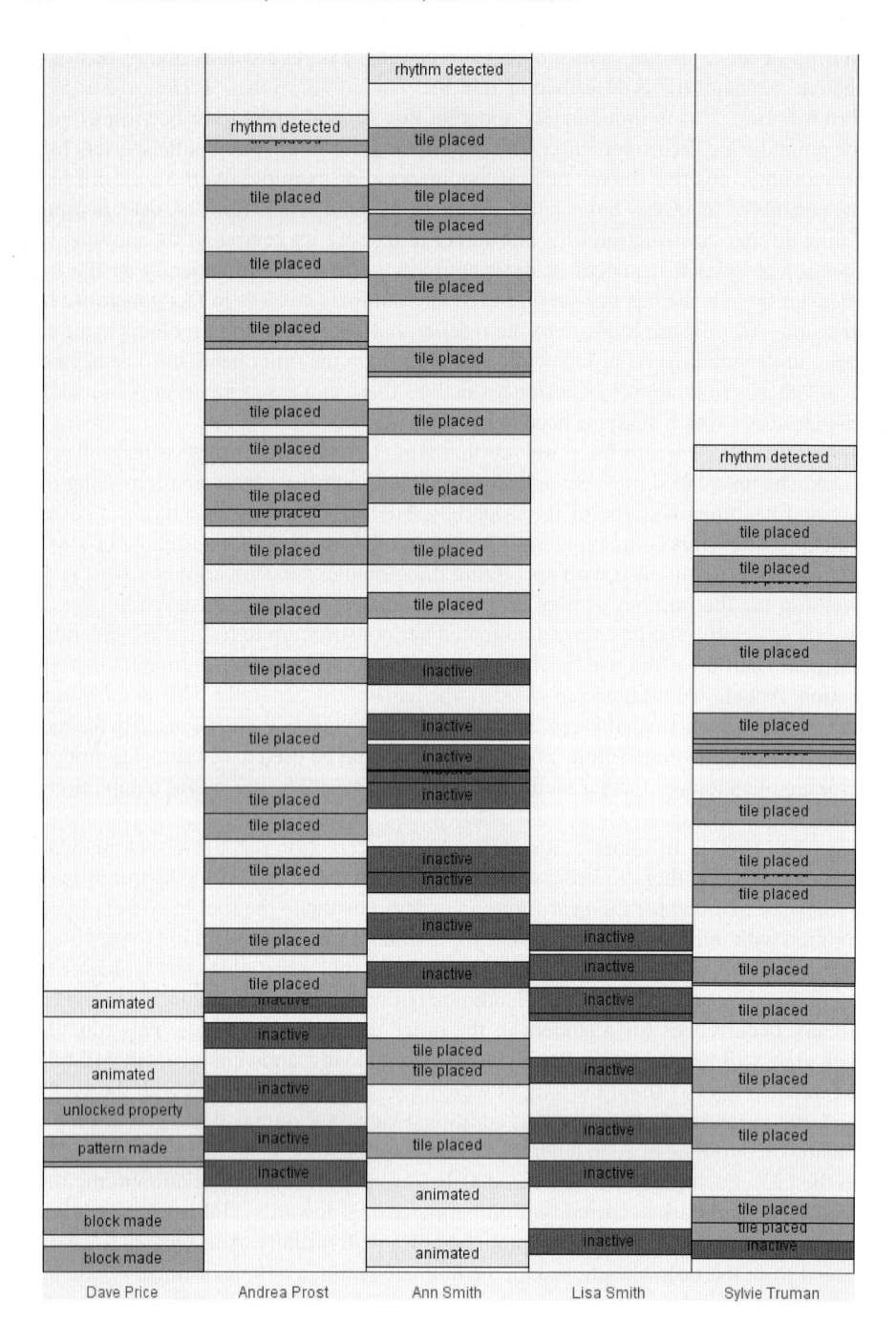

Fig. 6. A portion of the Landmark Timeline User Interface showing when landmarks occur for each user. This is a different view of the same data used in Figure 5. As before, the meaning of the colours is explained in Table 1.

single tiles to construct the pattern. She would then be able to see that Ann subsequently followed her advice and the system detected rhythm in Ann's placement of the tiles.

4 Discussion and Conclusions

In this paper we have described the architectural design of the Teacher Assistance tools of the MiGen system, an intelligent exploratory enviroment aiming to support 11–14-year-old students in their learning of algebraic generalisation. MiGen's Teacher Assistance tools aim to provide information to teachers about their students' activities and progress as they use the eXpresser and Activity tools, assisting them in the detection of students who may be experiencing difficulties, alerting them to students who seem to be demonstrating misconceptions and to those who may benefit from further, more challenging tasks. In general, the tools aim to allow the teacher to effectively facilitate the students' productive interaction with the system. The architectural design of the Teacher Assistance tools we have presented in this paper is generic and is applicable to the whole suite of such tools that are planned for development in the MiGen project in the coming months. We have given a detailed description of one such tool — the Student Tracking Tool. Several MiGen system components are used to infer the occurrence of task-independent and task-dependent landmarks of relevance to the teacher as students undertake tasks using the eXpresser microworld, and this information is presented in real-time to the teacher by the Student Tracking Tool.

To our knowledge, ours is the first work targeted at notifying the teacher about students' attainment of landmarks during constructionist learning tasks. There has of course been much work in developing tools that assist teachers' instructionist role, but to our knowledge there are no other tools that assist teachers in tracking their students' progress during constructionist learning. The work closest to ours is that of [17] which uses Web log data generated by course management systems to help instructors be aware of students' activities in distance learning classes; [18] which presents tools for helping teachers understand students' behaviour in adaptive tutorials through post-analysis of the system's data logs; [19] which presents tools for teachers to visualise students' progress through simulation-based practical work sessions; and [20] which provides awareness information to teachers so as to support their moderation of multiple e-discussions.

[17] uses techniques from information visualisation to represent multidimensional student tracking data, and our Student Tracking tool has a similar representation to their visualisations. However, they do not focus on detecting and visualising the occurrence of landmarks in open-ended constructionist learning tasks but rather on visualising students' social and behavioural aspects, their progress with respect to the course schedule, and their performance on quizzes and assignments and the level of knowledge achieved for each domain concept of the course. We refer the reader to that paper for an extensive review of other work in visualisation of data collected by course management systems, some of which also uses data mining and intelligent techniques to analyse student data and generate feedback to users — though, again, none of this earlier work focusses on constructionist learning. [18] adopts a hybrid approach whereby part of the data mining effort is teacher-driven and part is automated, but like much other work in educational

data mining it does not focus on monitoring students' ongoing progress through constructionist learning tasks. [19] composes a practical work session from a sequence of simulation-based problems (analogous to our eXpresser tasks undertaken within activity sequences); however, there are explicit conditions on simulation states that evaluate to correct/incorrect and there are explicit requests by learners for validation of conditions, neither of which is the case with our more open-ended constructionist learning tasks in MiGen.

A first version of the Student Tracking tool has been designed and implemented. The next phases of work on this tool will be one final iteration of its functionality and user interface with our teacher collaborators, followed by deployment and evaluation within full classroom-based activities. In particular, we wish to determine to what extent our expectations about how teachers will use the Student Tracking tool, as described in Section 3.1, are borne out in a practical classroom setting. How extensively will teachers consult the Student Tracking visualisation as their students are undertaking an eXpresser task? Will they find all the landmarks helpful or just a subset of them? Is the differentiation of landmarks into positive, neutral and negative helpful? How will teachers balance their use of the aggregated Student Tracking view and the more detailed timeline-based view? Will the tool allow teachers to easily spot students who may be disengaged from a task, students who may be in difficulty, the occurrence of common trends and misconceptions? We will gather data relating to these key questions by (a) observing our partner teachers in the classroom as they conduct lessons using MiGen, and (b) conducting post-lesson interviews with teachers.

We are also planning two further teacher assistance tools, the Student Progress Tool and the Classroom Dynamics tool. The Student Progress Tool will provide teachers with longer-term information about learning objectives that their students have attained, as recorded within the students' learner models. [13] discusses in detail MiGen's multi-level learner model and the process by which this is updated as students undertake tasks. In brief, at the lowest level, the Task Short Term Model contains information about a student's construction strategies and attainment of particular Task Learning Objectives (LOs) during one task instance. The occurrence of task landmarks provides evidence for the attainment of Task LOs, as encapsulated within a set of declarative rules co-designed with teachers, which are applied by the eGeneraliser to the landmark occurrences and the current Task Short Term Model as a student is undertaking a task. The Task Long Term Model contains aggregated information about a student's strategies and achievement of Task LOs during multiple attempts at a particular task. The students' Microworld Long Term Model contains aggregated information about the students' attainment of LOs across all tasks undertaken. Finally, the student's Domain Long Term Model contains information about the students' attainment of LOs as relating to the subject domain of mathematics generalisation. When a student finishes an instance of a task using the eXpresser, their Task Long Term Model, Microworld Long Term Model and Domain Long Term Model are updated by additional rule-based components within the eGeneraliser which successively infer updates to each higher 'layer' of the learner model based on the current values of this layer and the values of the layer below it. There are explicit correspondences between task LOs and domain LOs built into the system. For example, the task LO 'identify variants and invariants of constructions and expressions' corresponds to the domain LO 'identify variants and invariants' as extracted from the U.K. Maths National Curriculum. The Student Progress Tool will provide teachers with a visual overview of students' degree of attainment of task LOs and domain LOs over students' longer-term interaction with the eXpresser.

The Classroom Dynamics (CD) tool will provide a visual overview of students' locations in the classroom and their progress with respect to ongoing individual and collaborative activities. The CD tool will support the teacher in selecting to view and monitor different aspects of this information and in using this to inform her choice of interventions, including choices of how best to group students together for collaborative activities on the basis of their individual work and progress.

Acknowledgements. The MiGen project is funded by the ESRC/EPSRC Technology-Enhanced Learning programme (RES-139-25-0381). We thank the other members of the MiGen team for our ongoing stimulating collaborative research on the project.

References

1. Mason, J., Graham, A., Johnston-Wilder, S.: Developing Thinking in Algebra. Paul Chapman Publishing, Boca Raton (2005)
2. Harel, I., Papert, S. (eds.): Constructionism. Ablex Publishing Corporation, Norwood (1991)
3. Noss, R., Hoyles, C.: Windows on Mathematical Meanings. Kluwer Academic Publishers, The Netherlands (1996)
4. Lesh, R., Kelly, A.E.: A constructivist model for redesigning AI tutors in mathematics. In: Laborde, J. (ed.) Intelligent learning environments: The case of geometry. Springer, New York (1996)
5. Kynigos, C.: Insights into pupils' and teachers' activities in pupil-controlled problem-solving situations. In: Information Technology and Mathematics Problem Solving: Research in Contexts of Practice, pp. 219–238. Springer, Heidelberg (1992)
6. Hoyles, C., Sutherland, R.: Logo Mathematics in the Classroom. Routledge, London (1989)
7. Kirscher, P., Sweller, J., Clark, R.E.: Why minimal guidance during instruction does not work: An analysis of the failure of constructivist, discovery, problem-based, experiental and inquiry-based learning. Educational Psychologist 41(2), 75–86 (2006)
8. Mavrikis, M., Geraniou, E., Noss, R., Hoyles, C.: Revisiting pedagogic strategies for supporting students' learning in mathematical microworlds. In: Proceedings of the International Workshop on Intelligent Support for Exploratory Environments at EC-TEL 2008 (2008)
9. Pearce, D., Poulovassilis, A.: The conceptual and architectural design of a system supporting exploratory learning of mathematics generalisation. In: Proceedings of the 4th European Conference on Technology Enhanced Learning (EC-TEL), Nice, France, pp. 22–36 (2009)
10. Thompson, P.W.: Mathematical microworlds and intelligent computer-assisted instruction. In: Artificial intelligence and instruction: Applications and methods, Boston, MA, pp. 83–109. Addison-Wesley Longman Publishing Co., Inc., Redwood City (1987)
11. Hoyles, C.: Microworlds/schoolworlds: The transformation of an innovation. In: Keitel, C., Ruthven, K. (eds.) Learning from computers: mathematics education and technology, pp. 1–17. Springer, Berlin (1993)
12. Noss, R., Hoyles, C., Mavrikis, M., Geraniou, E., Gutierrez-Santos, S., Pearce, D.: Broadening the sense of 'dynamic': a microworld to support students' mathematical generalisation. The International Journal on Mathematics Education (ZDM) 41(4), 493–503 (2009)

13. Mavrikis, M., Gutierrez-Santos, S., Pearce-Lazard, D., Poulovassilis, A., Magoulas, G.: Learner modelling in microworlds: conceptual model and architecture in MiGen. Technical Report BBKCS-10-04, Birkbeck College, University of London (April 2010), http://www.dcs.bbk.ac.uk//research/techreps/2010/
14. Gutierrez-Santos, S., Cocea, M., Magoulas, G.: A case-based reasoning approach to provide adaptive feedback in microworlds. In: Proceedings of Intelligent Tutoring Systems, ITS 2010 (to appear, 2010)
15. Cocea, M., Gutierrez-Santos, S., Magoulas, G.: Challenges for intelligent support in exploratory learning: the case of ShapeBuilder. In: Proceedings of the International Workshop on Intelligent Support for Exploratory Environments at EC-TEL 2008 (2008)
16. Fielding, R.T.: Representational State Transfer (REST) (Chapter 5). In: Architectural styles and the design of network-based software architectures. University of California, Irvine. PhD Thesis (2000)
17. Mazza, R., Dimitrova, V.: CourseVis: A graphical student monitoring tool for supporting instructors in web-based distance courses. International Journal of Man-Machine Studies 65(2), 125–139 (2007)
18. Ben-Naim, D., Marcus, N., Bain, M.: Visualization and analysis of student interactions in an exploratory learning environment. In: Proceedings of the 1st International Workshop on Intelligent Support for Exploratory Environments (part of ECTEL 2008) (2008)
19. Gueraud, V., Adam, J.M., Lejeune, A., Dubois, M., Mandran, N.: Teachers need support too: Formid-observer, a flexible environment for supervising simulation-based learning situations. In: Proceedings of the 2nd International Workshop on Intelligent Support for Exploratory Environments (part of AIED 2009), pp. 19–28 (2009)
20. Wichmann, A., Giemza, A., Krauß, M., Hoppe, H.U.: Effects of awareness support on moderating multiple parallel e-discussions. In: Proceedings of the 8th International Conference on Computer Supported Collaborative Learning (CSCL 2009), Rhodes, Greece, pp. 646–650 (June 2009)

A Description of Landmarks

The table below provides a description of all the landmarks ordered as in Figure 5 and indicates whether they are task-independent (TI) or task-dependent (TD).

Landmark Name	TI/TD	Description
inactive	TI	The student has not been interacting with the system for some period of time.
off task	TD	The student is interacting with the system but is off-task.
block made	TI	The student has created a building block out of existing tiles/blocks/patterns.
tile placed	TI	The student has placed a single unit tile on the canvas.
implausible block	TD	The student has created an implausible building block which is unlikely to lead to a solution.
plausible block	TD	The student has created a plausible building block which could lead to a solution.

Landmark Name	TI/TD	Description
overlapping block	TD	The student has made a building block that will lead to overlaps when it is used.
task by unit	TD	The student has constructed the task pattern with unit tiles and some structure has been detected.
task by block	TD	The student has constructed the task pattern by creating a block and repeating it.
rhythm detected	TD	The student has placed unit tiles and some rhythm has been detected.
pattern made	TI	The student has made a pattern out of some of their existing tiles or building blocks.
pattern general	TD	The student has created a pattern and coloured it generally.
animated	TI	The student has clicked on the 'animate' button regardless of the content of their canvas.
unlocked property	TI	The student has unlocked a number within the property list of a constructed pattern.
unlocked	TI	The student has unlocked a number anywhere in their model.
too many unlocked	TD	The student has unlocked too many numbers for this particular task.
animated with unlocked	TI	The student has clicked on the 'animate' button and some numbers are currently unlocked.
messable animated	TD	The student has animated their construction but it is not general — it can be 'messed up'.
general animated	TD	The student has animated their construction and it is general.
incorrect local exp	TD	The student has created an incorrect expression for one of their patterns.
correct local exp	TD	The student has created a correct expression for one of their patterns.
incorrect global exp	TD	The student has created an incorrect expression for the construction overall.
correct global exp	TD	The student has created a correct expression for the construction overall.

Representing the Spaces When Planning Learning Flows

Mar Pérez-Sanagustín, Davinia Hernández-Leo, Raúl Nieves, and Josep Blat

ICT Department, Universitat Pompeu Fabra, C/Roc Boronat 138, 08018 Barcelona, Spain
{mar.perez,davinia.hernandez,raul.nieves,josep.blat}@upf.edu.com

Abstract. Collaboration scripts formulate flows of orchestrated groups and learning activities. When these scripts are computationally supported they are called Computer-Supported Collaborative Learning scripts. Several modeling languages have been proposed to computationally represent the scripts so that they can be interpreted by learning environments. In this paper we address how the definition of these scripts can be influenced by the impact of the space characteristics, including the electronic and non-electronic devices available to support the learning activities. The use of portable and electronic devices is increasing the importance of the role of educational spaces, which become an agent able to shape users' interactions and, therefore, the way collaboration and learning is produced. This paper introduces a model that enables the specification of the space as a conditioning factor in the design and enactment of scripting processes. Two real scenarios and a web-based prototype application for the design of learning spaces illustrate the value of the proposed model.

Keywords: CSCL, space model, scripting processes.

1 Introduction

Orchestration is the term used in the Computer Supported Collaborative Learning (CSCL) field to define the process of organizing a flow of interrelated activities and group hierarchies for stimulating group interactions that potentially produce fruitful learning [4]. Scripts are proposed in this context as a way to guide and support these orchestration processes [5]. When these interactions are technologically mediated these scripts are called Computer Supported Collaborative Learning Scripts (or CSCL scripts). CSCL scripts can be automatically interpreted by learning environments. This automation facilitates the orchestration processes by computationally guiding students along the sequence of activities (indicating groups, resources and tools needed to conduct the activities) and, therefore, reducing the coordination efforts of teachers and students [17].

Different approaches and tools have been developed for technologically supporting CSCL scripts [8, 9, 10, 12, 18, 19, 20]. However, in the last few years, the infusion of portable and interactive devices has opened up new opportunities for collaborative learning that these approaches are not able to capture. The anywhere and everywhere capabilities of these technologies put the space as a central factor that can shape users' interactions by enabling or inhibiting learning [3, 7, 21, 23]. Whether the elements of the learning environment are portable or not, electronic or not, sharable or not conditions the way students are distributed over the space and how they interact by affecting not only the orchestration processes but also the way in which the learning flow is defined. In this context, space and its elements become essential factors that should be considered during the whole cycle of the scripting process: the edition, the instantiation and the enactment. New formalization efforts for integrating the space as a factor in the scripting process definition are required.

This paper presents a conceptual model of the space. This model defines the space elements that condition the design and enactment of a CSCL script design process when applied to blended learning contexts (where online, technology supported, and face to face (f2f) activities are combined in a given space [19]). The objective is to enable the design of a complete, abstract and portable description of the main space elements to support the integration of the space as part of a scripting process definition. Therefore, the aim of this paper is twofold: (1) to describe and discuss the main elements of the space model we developed and (2) to present an example of two real learning settings in which a system based on the model would help in the design of the space involved in the collaborative script applied.

This paper is structured as follows. Section 2 discusses the main aspects of the literature on learning spaces and educational technology that motivate this work. In section 3, the conceptual model of the space is presented by defining the requirements it should fulfill and by describing its main elements. Section 4 presents two real learning scenarios in which the space plays a crucial role for the script definition. In the same section, an application prototype based on the ideas of the model is used to represent the spaces intervening in both experiences. Finally, both representations serve as a basis for discussing the requirements that the model overcomes. In the end, section 5 presents the conclusions and future work lines derived from the proposal.

2 Motivation

This work has been mainly influenced by contributions in two fields: research on learning spaces and studies in educational technology aiming at computationally supporting the organization of collaborative learning flows. This section presents the main concepts of these fields that inspired the model definition.

2.1 The Influence of Space in Learning

Research on learning spaces studies highlight the influence of the physical space in learning practices. The physical space is considered a changing agent that has an impact on learning: it affects how one learns and how one teaches. Space can shape users' interactions and activate collaborative learning [3, 7]. Whether physical or virtual, the space becomes a determining contextual factor in blended learning scenarios by enabling or inhibiting learning [23]. Diana Oblinger states in her book "Learning Spaces", "*a particular space can bring people together; it can encourage exploration, collaboration, and discussion. Or, space can carry an unspoken message of silence and disconnectedness*" [22].

Since the first schools appeared, the space influences the teaching methods and the way we learn. However, the introduction of information technologies (IT) in education brings new possibilities to educations that are transforming learning experiences [22, 23]. In this context, the space becomes still more important and relevant in the learning environments and an essential factor altering the learning design processes. Computational artifacts have moved from being conceived as a means of distance communication to be an element embedded in the educational setting that can increase the possibilities of f2f experiences [26]. To understand how the integration of technology in learning environments can benefit learning it is necessary to understand the relationship between the space, the technological devices and the learning activities that can be carried out. Temple says, " (…) *Technological change is said to be affecting the nature of learning itself, as well as the ways in which it takes place (…)*" [27]. For example, Dix et al. consider or support the idea that "*devices are situated and embedded within a space and their interaction is mediated through this space*" [1].

A study by Milne [21] proposes six categories organized into three clusters for classifying learning technologies as a first step to understanding how they relate to the physical space design. The first cluster is called **Virtual technologies** and refers to technologies not tied to particular physical hardware. In this group we find the first two categories: (1) technologies to support **online presence**, either through real-time interaction or asynchronous personal repositories (Skype, Flickr...) and (2) **online resources** that provide access to resources that are public, not personal, in nature; for example, databases or digital libraries. The third, fourth and fifth categories are clustered into those technologies that include a specific physical instantiation and are named **Installed appliances**: (3) **media representations systems** or devices that allow playback of media of different formats (DVD player or slide-to-video unit), (4) **remote interaction systems** such as web cameras or videoconferencing systems that allow real-time interaction and (5) **room-scale peripherals** referring to those devices for supporting group interacting such as interactive displays or room schedule displays. And the third cluster stands for **Mobile devices** and corresponds to (6) **Personal information and communication devices** such as PDAs, smart phones, Table PCs or iPods. We make use of this categorization to define in our model the different types of elements that can be found in a learning space and affect learning practices.

Besides, other researchers highlight the importance of the affordance of technology as something that influences the way in which educational strategies are carried out in educational settings [16, 26]. Affordance is defined by Kirschner as "*the perceived properties of a thing in reference to a user that influences how it is used*". Hence, in a learning context it is crucial not only to understand what the potential of the technology embedded into the learning setting is but also how people use it for supporting collaboration.

2.2 Technology for Structuring Learning Flows

Some researchers in educational technology have put their efforts into studying ways to computationally represent learning flows for facilitating orchestration tasks. In particular, CSCL scripts are seen as a mechanism for reducing the coordination efforts of teachers and students when orchestrating a collaborative activity [17]. One of the best-established modeling languages used for representing learning flows is IMS Learning Design (IMS LD) [13, 19]. This specification supports the use of a wide range of pedagogies in online learning. IMS LD specifies what activities have to be performed by learners and teachers to attain the learning objectives. With IMS LD, the formal design of a teaching-learning process is modeled through what is called a Unit of Learning (UoL). A UoL can be distributed and interpreted with runtime systems conforming to this specification. In a UoL electronic resources and tools can be modeled within a learning flow using the IMS LD *environment* element. *Environments* contain references to the *learning objects* (resources) and *services* (tools such as chat or forums) needed to carry out a particular activity. However, *environments* are only devoted to specify the supporting resources and tools within a virtual space but they are not meant to model physical elements of the learning setting.

Some specialized tools for collaborative learning have been specially designed based on IMS LD specification. Collage, for example, is an authoring tool which helps users when creating their own collaborative Learning Designs in IMS LD using existing patterns, called Collaborative Learning Flow Patterns (CLFP). These patterns represent the broadly accepted techniques used to structure the flow of types of learning activities involved in collaborative learning situations [12].

Other approaches have been developed for computationally supporting collaborative learning flows. In another paper by Miao et al. (2005), a CSCL scripting language and a conceptual framework for this modeling language is presented. They perform an analysis of the IMS LD specification and outline its main limitations for CSCL scripting. Finally, they propose a new specification that is able to capture the main elements of CL practices [20]. A study by Kobbe et al. (2007) proposes a generic framework for the specification of collaboration scripts. It provides a list of components necessary for describing a script that is independent of its particular implementation in a computer-supported learning environment, addressing concerns from both research and practices [17]. In the same line, Harrer and Hoppe created a modeling language for collaborative scripts called MoCoLADe (Model for Collaborative Learning Activity Design) [8]. This language was developed as a visual language for the edition of collaborative learning scenarios and integrated as a plugin into another application called FreeStyler. Since this visual editing tool cannot be integrated into any other learning engine to be interpreted, the proposal incorporates the option of exporting graphical models into IMS-LD documents. In this way, they can be interpreted and reused by LD players or editors. All these approaches propose good solutions for capturing the necessities for computationally represent CSCL scripts. Nonetheless, these solutions lack consideration of the physical space as a factor conditioning the edition and enactment of a script.

Summarizing, technology enhances current learning spaces by transforming, extending and offering new possibilities for collaborative learning practices. To reflect on the affordances of the technology-enhanced spaces and their limitations whilst designing a collaborative experience means reflecting on the new opportunities that technology offers for generating innovative learning practices. New approaches categorizing and specifying space elements conditioning learners' interactions and affecting teaching and learning design processes, compatible with the current learning specifications are required for supporting designers and practitioners in a reflective process for conceiving innovative learning scenarios. Furthermore, we contend that, a conceptual model specifying and categorizing the space components might be a first approach towards a deeper understanding of how technology-enhanced spaces offer new learning opportunities which would not be possible without technology. Therefore, we need a model sufficiently expressive to facilitate teachers and designers modeling, managing and graphically representing any learning space according to their particular educational needs. Furthermore, we need this model to be interoperable and compatible with existing specifications for facilitating the spaces' reuse.

3 Modeling the Space

This section introduces a conceptual model of the space following a schema similar to the structure adopted by [18] when presenting IMS LD. Firstly, we present the requirements that this model aims to fulfill according to the needs specified in the previous section and secondly, we introduce each of the elements that compose it.

3.1 Objectives of the Space Model

The objective of the space conceptual model is to provide a framework of elements that can describe any physical learning space in a formal way. More specifically, the space model and its compliant implementations aim to meet the following requirements:

- R1. Completeness: This conceptual model must be able to describe any type of physical learning space. The model should be also able to describe the usage of the elements composing the physical space and their arrangement.
- R2. Graphical: All the components defined in the model should be able to be graphically represented.
- R2. Flexibility: The components defined in the model should be flexibly managed and defined. These elements should be able to be moved and located in different areas according to the learning necessities and their usage defined. In addition, the designer should be able to accommodate the different components according to the needs of the actual learning space context.
- R3. Personalization: The model must be able to provide different abstract visualizations for the different users involved in the experience according to the interactions they can perform with the different components.
- R4. Interoperability: The space model must support interoperability with other specifications.
- R5. Compatibility: The space model should be compatible with other existing specifications.
- R6. Reusability: The space model should allow isolating the components of the space and the space itself to be used in other learning situations and other contexts.

3.2 The Space Conceptual Model

Figure 1 expresses the conceptual space model as a set of UML classes and a definition of the vocabulary used. This UML representation provides a view of the overall conceptual model in an abstract way for understanding the main components and their relations [25].

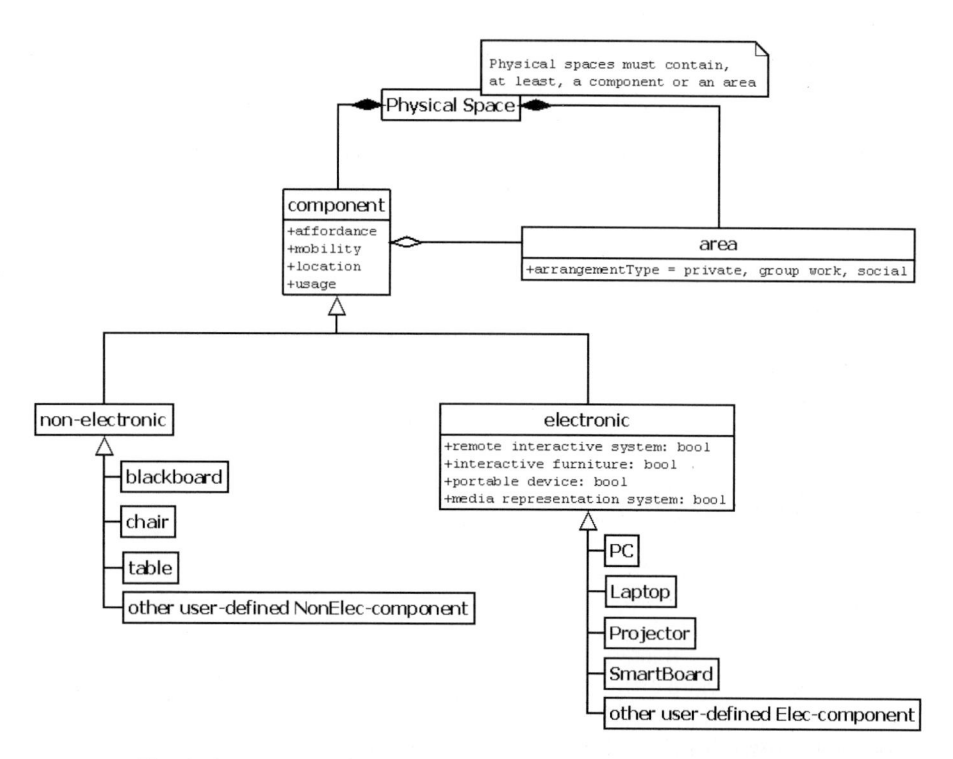

Fig. 1. Components of the space conceptual model and their relationship

Physical spaces are defined by a set of components that users can be physically in contact with, touch and manipulate. Chairs or pencils are examples of physical components. Physical space can also be composed of areas (e.g. a section of a classroom). These spaces cannot exist if there is not an area or a component associated with it. It is possible to model a physical space without components but it has to include at least one area (e.g. in a drama lesson, the teacher separates the classroom into an area for acting and another one for the audience, which is necessary for orchestrating the practice). In the same way, a physical space can be defined without areas but then, it has to include at least one component (e.g. for having an online meeting, a conference room has to be equipped by, at least, a PC or a laptop with internet connection).

Areas are sections of the physical space composed by a set of physical components and associated to a particular type of task determined by the learning designer. This relationship between areas and the physical space is expressed in the UML representation as a composition. An area cannot exist if it is not associated to an existing physical space and, if the space is deleted, the areas that it contains are also deleted. An area is the *place* where the actions occur and where the interactions between students with the components have an educational meaning. Depending on the arrangement of the components belonging to an area, their nature and their affordance some interactions are triggered. Depending on the interactions elicited by this arrangement the areas can be divided into: *private*, *group work* or *social* areas.

- *Private working area*: A type of area reserved for individual or private task. The components composing this type of areas should have been defined with an individual usage.
- *Group work area*: A type of area reserved for working in groups. The components of these types of areas should have a collective usage or provide facilities supporting communication, collaboration or coordination purposes.
- *Social area*: A type of area conceived as a *place* for socialization. The components in this area are focused on supporting the students in sharing their experiences. The main difference with respect to the *work area* has to do with the affordances of the tools that they include and the purpose of the activity. In a social area, it is not necessary to include technology for supporting a particular type of collaboration or learning objective, whereas in a work group area, technology must be used as a mechanism for scaffolding collaboration.

The components are the more atomic elements of the space with independent meaning. **Components** of the physical space are classified depending on their nature into two main groups: *electronic* and *non-electronic*. All components have a set of characteristics defined as attributes that can modify the way in which an activity is carried out. Each component is defined by its *affordance* that indicates whether the component is used by a group of persons (collective), only one person (individual) or both. A component is also characterized by its *mobility* (if it can be easily moved or not). A PC, for example, is more difficult to move than a laptop, which can condition the way in which the space is arranged for a particular activity. A component is also defined by its *usage*, which is determined by the learning practitioner or the necessities of the learning activity being carried out (if it will be used for a brainstorming activity, or negotiation, or document sharing or information visualization...). In some cases, components can have *location* attributes that define their position in the space (X, Y, Z). This location attribute is especially interesting for those activities that make use of portable devices such as PDAs or mobile phones.

Non-electronic components are the type of components that are typically found in learning or working areas and are neither electronic nor interactive. The model defines the three more typical elements found in a learning scenario: *blackboards*, *chairs* and *tables*. It is also specified a component to be defined by the learning designer depending on the learning activity. For example, in a science lab, there would be defined tests tubes or microscopes.

Electronic components are defined as components with electronic properties that allow the user to interact individually with it or with other students. These types of components have been especially designed for allowing the users individual interactions with the same component and as a medium for triggering interactions among groups of users. The model fixes as common components found in a learning environment a *PC*, a *laptop*, a *projector* and a *smart board*. Other *non-defined* electronic objects such as a tabletop or a TV can be included by the practitioner depending on the learning context. Electronic components can be described according to their nature:

- *Remote interactive systems*: these systems are focused on providing the user with a system for establishing remote connections with users in other spaces (e.g. webcam).

- *Interactive furniture*: understood as the classical elements, typically found in an educational environment, which are technologically enhanced by extending their interactive properties. This type of furniture is specially created for reacting to the users' actions and triggering interactions related with some learning aspects (e.g., noise sensitive table [6]). Interactive in this context refers to the properties of the furniture to react differently according to the user actions by changing their behavior.
- *Portable devices:* electronic components that can be easily transported. These types of objects can be seen as elements with characteristics in between remote interactive systems and interactive furniture (e.g., mobile phones).
- *Media representation systems*: devices that allow media representation (e.g., projectors).

Some devices can be described using a combination of the previous attributes. For example, a PC allows remote interactions and is also a media representation system for a little group of students. The way in which a collaborative activity is carried out undoubtedly has an impact depending on whether the devices are used for supporting online presence or users' interactions and the usage proposed by the practitioner.

4 Considering the Space in Two Collaborative Learning Situations

This section is divided into three subsections. The first subsection presents two real learning situations already carried out in which the space where they took place was relevant for the application of a Jigsaw-based script. The second subsection introduces a web-based application developed according to the space model and shows its use to represent the two spaces taking part in both scenarios. At the same time, this prototype aims at being a first approach for allowing the user to define a representation of learning spaces integrated into a scripting design process. Finally, the third subsection discusses how the two scenarios and their representations provide a first evaluation effort to understand whether the aspects defined by the model enable the modeling of two different spaces' characteristics and satisfy the targeted requirements.

4.1 Two Real Learning Situations: The Same Activity But in Two Different Spaces

Each year, the authors of this paper take part as teachers in an e-Learning seminar at the Autonomous University of Barcelona. One of the activities prepared for this seminar consists in making the students reflect about the future of educational technologies. With this purpose, the teachers propose the reading of the "Horizon Report" [14, 15] of the corresponding year. Since this document is divided in three parts (1 year or less, 2 to 3 years and 4 to 5 years), teachers organize a Jigsaw activity for collaborative working on the different sections of the paper [2, 11]. The activity is divided into three different phases: (1) an individual activity in which each student reads one of the parts randomly assigned by the teacher, (2) an expert group phase in which students having read the same part prepare a poster with the main ideas of this part and

(3) a jigsaw group phase in which experts in different parts are joined together to explain the poster to the rest of the group members.

The first academic year that this experience was carried out, the activity took place in a room including two different areas: an area with three rows of tables with PCs facing a blackboard and with a screen projector, and a second area with three separated round tables for working in groups. Due to the arrangement of the space, the teachers organized the second and third parts of the activity in the following manner. Students accessed and read their assigned report parts from the PCs but for the expert group phase, each group was allocated to one of the tables situated in the work group area and worked together on their poster. For the jigsaw group phase, students rotated through the different tables listening to the explanation of their colleagues using posters. In each rotation one of the owners of the poster had to stay at their table to explain it to the students coming to the table.

The second academic year, the activity took place in another classroom. The room was composed of a set of aligned tables with PCs in rows facing the blackboard with a projector without any appropriate place for working in groups. In this case, the teachers decided to assign one of the rows of tables to each expert group for the poster preparation. However, due to the difficulty for the students moving from one table to another the jigsaw activity was modified. Each of the expert groups presented their poster in front of the whole collective class, without forming jigsaw groups and rotating from one poster to another. One of the groups decided to prepare a presentation (instead of a poster) and presented it using the projector. This turned out to be a good idea because the posters of the other two expert groups were difficult to read from the tables. In this situation the differentiation between electronic and non-electronic component is important, for example, having an electronic portable projector totally changed the arrangement of the students in the classroom and the possibilities of presenting their work and the classroom organization. Students were located in front of the projector, which has to be located in a unique place in the classroom (ie. with a plug in source and a screen).

These two situations show how the enactment of an activity with the same learning flow is modified because of the space characteristics in which it takes place. In the first situation, the arrangement of the space elements permits the movement of the students around the class facilitating the interaction between the different expert groups. On the contrary, the classroom arrangement of the second situation constrains the students' movements limiting the classmates' interactions and then, forcing the learning flow to be changed. Moreover, if the teachers had considered the arrangement of the classroom when designing the activity they may have planned in the second situation to ask students to create the posters with the PC instead of on paper so that they could be shown on the projector.

4.2 Supporting the Space Design

The web-based application prototype has been developed according to the space model defined in section 3. The prototype provides the user with a graphical interface in which the different elements and components are directly manipulated.

Figure 2 shows an overview of the main functionalities. In the center, there is a blank sheet where the user can design graphically the learning spaces involved in the activity. In an upper menu there are represented, as an example, the three activities of the learning flow: individual, expert groups and jigsaw groups. The user can generate one representation of the activity spaces for each of the phases in the learning flow.

On the right hand of the interface the user can choose to represent a physical space. Notice that, in the same phase there can be involved different spaces at the same time. The space type is represented as a dark gray rectangle or a square in the central sheet of the interface. Clicking on the space, the user can define the number of areas forming the space and select whether the area is for private or group work or an area with socialization purposes. The user can drag and drop components to the space. The components are classified into electronic and non–electronic typologies. For each component included in the space, the user can specify its usage; add a title for describing the object and select whether it is going to serve as a collective or individual support. In the case of being a physical component, the user could select which of the areas defined in the space (if the areas have been defined) it belongs to.

Figure 3 and 4 represents the classroom where the activity was carried out in the first situation for the first and second phases, respectively. In the first phase, students occupied the left hand side of the classroom for reading individually their section of the Horizon Report. The same space was used for the expert and jigsaw phases in the learning flow. On the right-hand of the space we can distinguish the three areas defined as *work group*. Each area contains a set of chairs and a table defined as a collective support and assigned to a particular group in its *usage* (1 year or less, 2-3 years and 4-5 years – sections of the "Horizon Report"). Although the classroom includes a projector, its usage is not been defined because it is not used as support for this experience.

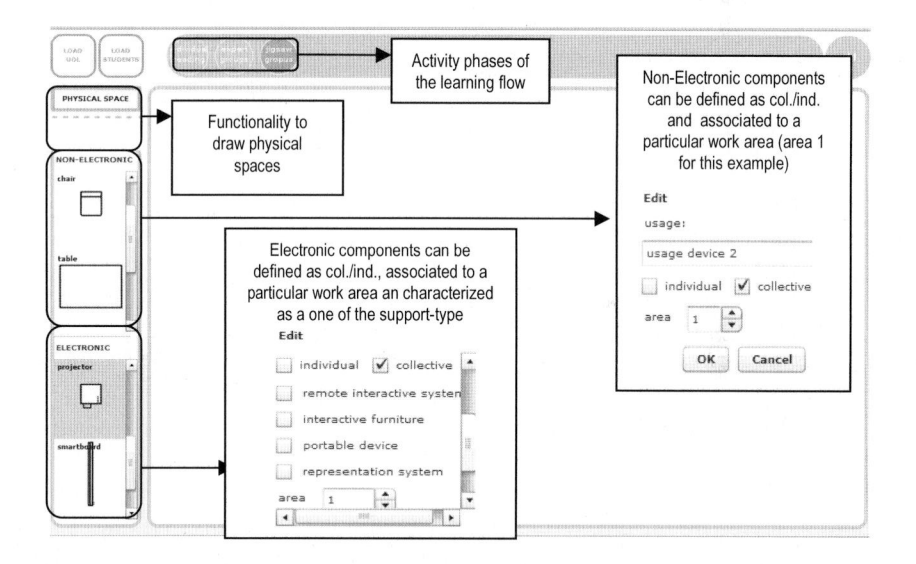

Fig. 2. General interface of the web-based prototype including the functionalities needed to represent the elements and their characteristics defined by the space model

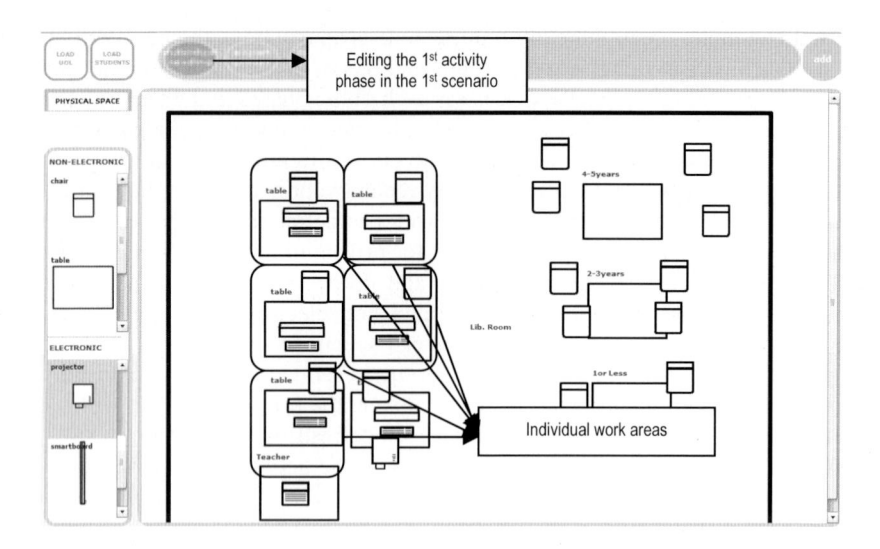

Fig. 3. Representation of the space for the learning flow in the first phase of the first learning situation

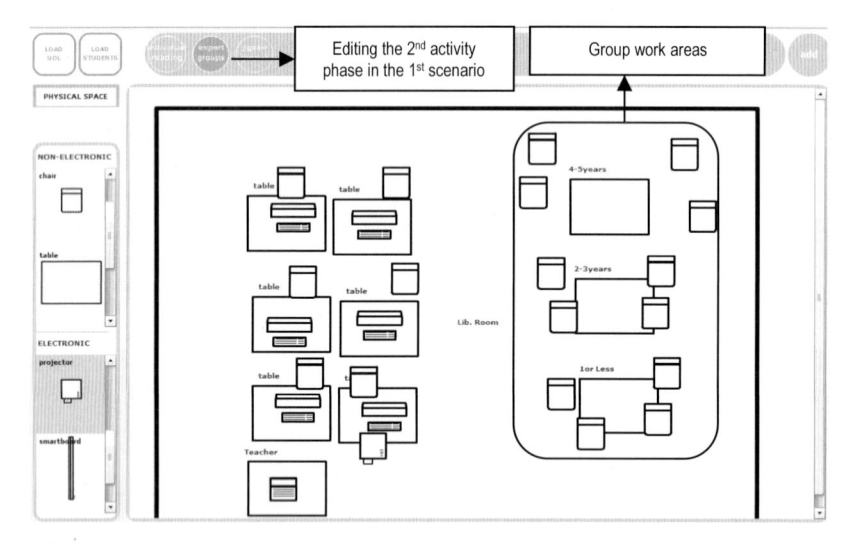

Fig. 4. Representation of the space for the learning flow in the second phase of the first learning situation

Figure 5 represents the classroom for the second situation. In this case, the space is divided into four areas. Three work group areas corresponding to the three expert groups defined for the activity. These areas are composed of a set of aligned tables with computers defined as *work group*. The tables are also defined as a collective support. The forth area corresponds to the place in front of the projector used for the

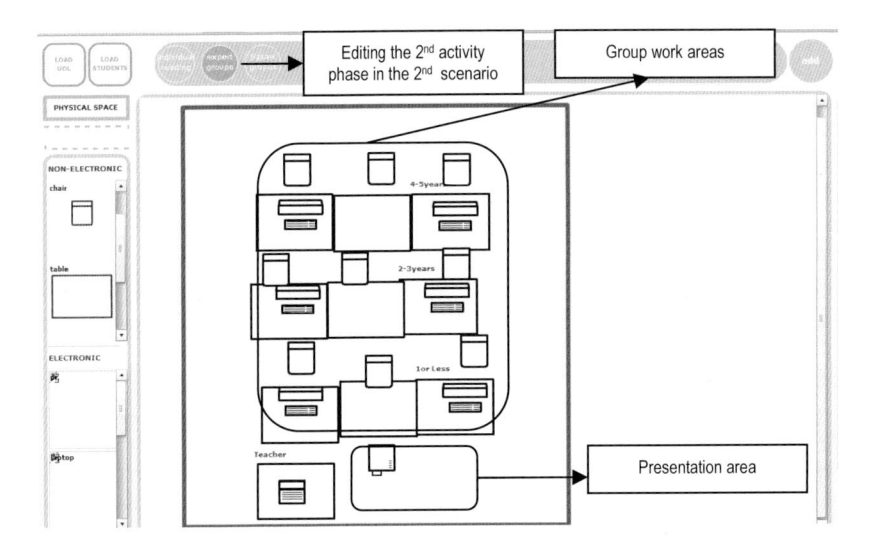

Fig. 5. Representation of the space for learning flow in the second learning situation

poster presentation and this is what differentiates this situation from the previous one. This area includes the laptop of the teacher and the projector. In this case, both elements are characterized as *representation system* support because it served one of the groups for presenting their work.

In both cases, for the first individual activity, students accessed a Learning Management System (LMS) to download the corresponding part of the Horizon Report. The LMS system could be seen as a virtual space that complements the physical space. However, the representation of these virtual spaces is out of the scope of this work because they are already considered by existing specifications for the description of activity flows, such as IMS LD.

4.3 Discussion

The analysis of the resulting space representations for the two experiences presented above provides a first evaluation of the space model. This analysis is structured in this subsection around the requirements for the model formulated in section 2.

With regard to the completeness requirement, we have shown that the model provides the elements and attributes needed to define the main characteristics of two real learning situations. On one hand, defining the usage of the components in the space allows for particularizing their learning purpose according to each situation. On the other hand, the definition of the space components arrangement enables modeling the particularities of two different spaces that make use of similar devices.

All the components have been graphically represented in the web-based application prototype presented. Although many different representations can be built from the elements in the model, this implementation is a first approach for showing that they are abstract enough and representative so as to be graphically represented. Future designs would help gain a deeper analysis of this requirement.

The two examples show that the model proposed is flexible enough for managing and particularizing the characteristics of the different components. On one hand, the components are characterized by a *usage* defined by the teacher, which makes it possible to particularize how a component is employed in a concrete learning scenario. On the other hand, the components have *location* attributes that enable the user to accommodate them according to the learning needs and characteristics of the actual situation. Moreover, the spaces designed for a phase of the learning flow can be re-used for another phase (e.g. phases 2 and 3 of the two situations).

The "Load UOL" bottom in the prototype interface shown in Fig. 4 is planned to enable importing IMS LD units determining the flow of activities (in the examples the phases of the Jigsaw) and the virtual spaces supporting the activities. The physical spaces design with our tool would complement the design of the unit of learning. This approach could be also implemented with other related specifications thus facilitating interoperability and compatibility. The space specification will be included as a new resource type to be referenced in the *environment* element of the IMS LD specification.

The tool currently being prototyped is devoted to teachers but a viewer of classroom configurations for students is also going to be developed. This viewer would show students the spaces personalized according to their roles and the associated activities. It is clear that further efforts in the development of tools and their implementation in educational situations are necessary in order to provide more evidence showing the full potential of the model in terms of their targeted requisites.

Although the two experiences analyzed describe a type of activity that is normally carried out in a "traditional" classroom (using the projector and the different classroom areas), the space is shown as a relevant factor influencing the final learning design. Besides, it is worth noticing that if the devices intervening in the design also include an interactive table and a Smart Board, the influence of the space in the learning design is expected to be even stronger.

5 Conclusions and Future Work

The Space Model presented in this paper is a first effort towards the formalization of the learning spaces to support its integration as a part of scripting design processes. The aim is to provide a complete and flexible model for graphically representing and personalizing any learning space compatible and interoperable with other specifications. Because of its recent development, it is still too early to provide evidence and strong conclusions about the effects of using the model. However, this first approach raises several questions and aspects that could be pursued in future work.

Firstly, to what extent does the space model serve for representing the characteristics of real educational scenarios? This paper has presented a preliminary evaluation of the model by analyzing its potential for representing two different real learning spaces. However, other experiences involving the use of interactive devices such as touch screens or Smart Boards are planned for the next courses to understand the capabilities of the space model to express the diversity of spaces involved in different learning scenarios.

Another line of work is the binding or computational representation of the space model so that it can be integrated in units of learning packages and interpreted by learning environments (players). Currently, we are preparing an XSD document of the space model from which we could extract XML representations of learning spaces. In parallel, we are also implementing a web-based application to validate these XML files according to the model. The idea is to use the web-based prototype presented in this manuscript to obtain an XML file representing the space that could be validated automatically by the web-based application. As mentioned above, we are also working on the integration of this space definition into a Unit of Learning represented with the IMS LD specification. In relation to this point, we have already included in the current version of the web-based prototype, a section for representing the students in class and organizing them in relation to the space and other constraints imposed by the learning flow, as proposed in [24].

From a more theoretical point of view, we are currently carrying out a study on the relationship established between the affordance of the different space elements and the learning events that they support (reflection, exploration, debate, experimentation...). In that way, it may be possible to relate particular sets of technological usages to a particular space affordance for helping practitioners in finding the most appropriate space for supporting particular learning objectives.

Finally, this work aims at reflecting on how important it is to consider the space as a factor conditioning the learning experiences of the future, in which the use of interactive devices such as a tabletop or mobile devices will be natural. This paper is also an attempt to show how necessary the space formalization efforts are to systematically understand the different usages and methods that include traditional and new devices in educational settings. We contend that this model deserves further research in order to understand what the implications in learning and teaching processes are.

Acknowledgements. This work has been partially funded by the Learn 3 project, (TIN2008-05163/TSI). The authors would also especially like to thank Patricia Santos and Javier Salinas and other members of the GTI research group for their support and ideas.

References

1. Dix, A., Rodden, T., Davies, N., Trevor, J., Friday, A., Palfreyman, K.: Exploiting Space and Location as a Design Framework for Interactive Mobile Systems. ACM Transactions on Computer-Human Interaction 7(3), 285–321 (2000)
2. Aronson, E., Blaney, N., Stephan, C., Sikes, J., Snapp, M.: The jigsaw classroom. Improving academic achievement: impact of psychological factors on education, pp. 213–224. Emerald Groups Pub. Ltd., London (2002)
3. Ciolfi, L.: Understanding spaces as places: extending interaction design paradigms. Cognition, Technology & Work 6(1), 37–40 (2004)
4. Dillenbourg, P., Fischer, F.: Basics of Computer-Supported Collaborative Learning, Zeitschrift für Berufs- und Wirtschaftspadagogik 21, 111–130 (2007)
5. Dillenbourg, P., Hong, F.: The mechanics of CSCL macro scripts. International Journal of Computer-Supported Collaborative Learning 3, 5–23 (2008)
6. Dillenbourg, P., Huang, J., Cherubini, M.: Interactive Artifacts and Furniture Supporting Collaborative Work and Learning. Springer Science + Business Media, LCC, NY (2009)

7. Gee, J.P.: Semiotic social spaces and affinity spaces: from The Age of Mythology to today's schools. In: Barton, D., Tusting, K. (eds.) Beyond Communities of Practice: Language, Power and Social Context, pp. 214–232. Cambridge University Press, Cambridge (2005)
8. Harrer, A., Hoppe, H.U.: Visual Modeling of Collaborative Learning Processes:Uses, Desired Properties, and Approaches. In: Botturi, L., Stubbs, T. (eds.) Handbook of Visual Languages for Instructional Design. Theories and Practices, Informational Science Reference, Hersey, PA, pp. 281–298 (2008)
9. Hernández-Leo, D., Asensio-Pérez, J.I., Dimitriadis, Y.: Computational Representation of Collaborative Learning Flow Patterns using IMS Learning Design. Journal of Educational Technology and Society 8(4), 75–89 (2005)
10. Villasclaras-Fernández, E.D., Hernández-Gonzalo, J.A., Hernández-Leo, D., Asensio-Pérez, J.I., Dimitriadis, Y., Martínez-Monés, A.: InstanceCollage: a tool for the particularization of IMS-LD scripts. Educational Technology & Society 12(3), 56–70 (2008)
11. Hernández-Leo, D., Villasclaras-Fernández, E.D., Asensio-Pérez, J.I., Dimitriadis, Y.: Generating CSCL scripts: From a conceptual model of pattern languages to the design of real scripts. In: Goodyear, P., Retalis, S. (eds.) E-learning Design Patterns Book (in press)
12. Hernández-Leo, D., Villasclaras-Fernández, E.D., Jorrín-Abellán, I.M., Asensio-Pérez, J.I., Dimitriadis, Y., Ruiz-Requies, I., Rubia-Avi, B.: Collage, a Collaborative Learning Design Editor Based on Patterns Special Issue on Learning Design 9(1), 58–71 (2006)
13. IMS Learning Design Best Practice and Implementation Guide, http://www.imsglobal.org/learningdesign/ldv1p0/imsld_bestv1p0.html
14. Johnson, L., Levine, A., Smith, R.: Horizon Report 2009. The New Media Consortium, Austin (2009)
15. Johnson, L., Smith, R., Levine, A., Haywood, K.: Horizon Report 2010. The New Media Consortium, Austin (2010)
16. Kirschner, P.: Can we support CSCL? Educational, social and technological affordances for learning. In: Kirschner, P. (ed.) Three worlds of CSCL: Can we support CSCL, Heerlen, The Netherlands, pp. 7–47 (2002)
17. Kobbe, L., Weinberger, A., Dillenbourg, P., Harrer, A., Hämäläinen, R., Häkkinen, P., Fischer, F.: Specifying computer-supported collaboration scripts. International Journal of Computer-Supported Collaborative Learning 2(2), 211–224 (2007)
18. Koper, R., Olivier, B.: Representing the Learning Design of Units of Learning. Educational Technology & Society 7(3), 97–111 (2004)
19. Koper, R., Tattersall, C.: Learning Design: A Handbook on Modeling and Delivering Networked Education and Training. Springer, Heidelberg (2005)
20. Miao, Y., Hoeksema, K., Hoppe, H.U., Harrer, A.: CSCL scripts: modeling features and potential use. In: CSCL 2005: Proceedings of the 2005 conference on Computer support for collaborative learning, pp. 423–432. International Society of the Learning Sciences (2005)
21. Milne, A.J.: Designing Blended Learning Space to the Student Experience. In: Oblinger, D. (ed.) Learning Spaces, EDUCAUSE, pp. 11.1–11.14 (2006), Available electronically at http://www.educause.edu/LearningSpaces
22. Oblinger, D.G.: Space as a change agent. In: Oblinger, D. (ed.) Learning Spaces, EDUCAUSE, pp. 1.1–1.4 (2006), Available electronically at http://www.educause.edu/LearningSpaces
23. Oblinger, D.: Leading the transition from classrooms to learning spaces. EDUCAUSE, Quarterly 28(1), 14–18 (2005)

24. Pérez-Sanagustín, M., Burgos, J., Henández-Leo, D., Blat, J.: Considering the intrinsic constraints for groups management of TAPPS & Jigsaw CLFPs. In: Proceedings of International Conference on Intelligent Networking and Collaborative Systems (INCoS 2009), Barcelona, Spain, November 4-6, pp. 317–322 (2009)
25. Rumbaugh, J., Jacobson, I., Booch, G.: The Unified Modeling Language Reference Manual. Addison-Wesley, Reading (2004)
26. Suthers, D.D.: Technology affordances for intersubjective learning: A thematic agenda for CSCL. In: Proceedings of the 2005 conference on Computer support for collaborative learning: learning 2005: the next 10 years!, Taipei, China, May 30 - June 4, p. 671 (2005)
27. Temple, P., Fillippakou, O.: Learning spaces for the 21 st century. Higher Education Academy, London (2007)

Studying the Factors Influencing Automatic User Task Detection on the Computer Desktop

Andreas S. Rath[1], Didier Devaurs[2], and Stefanie N. Lindstaedt[1,3]

[1] Know-Center GmbH., Inffeldgasse 21A, 8010 Graz
{arath,slind}@know-center.at
http://www.know-center.at
[2] CNRS; LAAS; 7 avenue du colonel Roche, F-31077 Toulouse, France and
Université de Toulouse; UPS, INSA, INP, ISAE; LAAS; F-31077 Toulouse, France
devaurs@laas.fr
http://www.laas.fr
[3] Knowledge Management Institute,
Graz University of Technology, Inffeldgasse 21A, 8010 Graz
http://www.kmi.tugraz.at.at

Abstract. Supporting learning activities during work has gained momentum for organizations since work-integrated learning (WIL) has been shown to increase productivity of knowledge workers. WIL aims at fostering learning at the workplace, during work, for enhancing task performance. A key challenge for enabling task-specific, contextualized, personalized learning and work support is to automatically detect the user's task. In this paper we utilize our ontology-based user task detection approach for studying the factors influencing task detection performance. We describe three laboratory experiments we have performed in two domains including over 40 users and more than 500 recorded task executions. The insights gained from our evaluation are: (i) the J48 decision tree and Naïve Bayes classifiers perform best, (ii) six features can be isolated, which provide good classification accuracy, (iii) knowledge-intensive tasks can be classified as well as routine tasks and (iv) a classifier trained by experts on standardized tasks can be used to classify users' personal tasks.

1 Introduction

Learning activities frequently occur within work processes [5]. The *work-integrated learning (WIL)* paradigm [14,23] takes these observations seriously and sees learning as a dimension of work. One goal of WIL is to foster learning during work in order to enhance task performance. For assisting the learner in this kind of learning situation her *user profile* [6,25], her interests [7], her competencies [11], and her *user context* [12,19,27] are utilized to improve the quality of support mechanisms. If her current task is automatically detected, the user can be supported with task specific learning and work material such as the retrieval of learning objects [4] or suggestions on course material, links, documents, or topical experts [12]. Hence it is important to know and understand what the user is working on or is trying to achieve. The user context includes all information that can be used to characterize the user's current situation [2] which also includes the user's current task. Automatic user task detection is an important challenge in the area of user context detection [18]. The classical approach is to model task detection as a machine learning problem. However, the main focus has been so far on using only text-based features and switching sequences [3,8,9,15,16,21,22], which do not rely on ontology-based user context models. A recent exception is our *ontology-based user task detection* approach [18] for which we have already shown that it improves the task detection accuracy compared to the existing task detection approaches SWISH [16], Dyonipos [8] and TaskPredictor 1 [22].

In this paper, we utilize our ontology-based user task detection approach in order to unveil which features and classifiers are showing a high automatic task detection performance across three independent datasets. More specifically, our main objective is to study the factors influencing the performance of task detection: (i) the used learning algorithm, (ii) the features chosen for constructing the training instances, (iii) the kind of tasks to be classified and (iv) the method chosen for training the learning algorithms. Confronted with the lack of standard datasets and of controlled user studies in the task detection field, we have designed and run three laboratory experiments with multiple users from two different domains, for collecting task detection datasets.

Studying the influence of the type of tasks to be classified is important for increasing our understanding of the *"task detection phenomenon"* itself. Can any kind of task be classified? Can we expect similar performance when classifying routine tasks and knowledge-intensive tasks? Studying the influence of the training method on the performance of classifiers can help to address the classical *"cold start problem"*. Can a classifier, trained on standard tasks performed by experts, be used to classify users' personal tasks? The importance of studying the influence of the learning algorithm and of the chosen features lies in the fact that, in a productive scenario, it is not possible to use all available algorithms and features, because of the resulting computational cost. Our goal is to find a combination of features and classifiers that achieves good results on a standard desktop computer.

The rest of the paper is organized as follows. First, we outline our approach for recording and modeling the user context, based on our user interaction context ontology. Second, we present our ontology-based user task detection approach and our methodology for evaluating its performance. Third, we describe our three experiments and the gathered datasets. Fourth, we detail the results of our evaluation, based on the influencing factors previously mentioned. Finally, we draw our conclusions and present some future work.

2 User Interaction Context Detection

Our view of the *"user context"* goes along with Dey's definition that context is *"any information that can be used to characterize the situation of entities that are considered relevant to the interaction between a user and an application, including the user and the application themselves"* [2]. We refine Dey's perspective by focusing on the *user interaction context* that we define as *"all interactions of the user with resources, applications and the operating system on the computer desktop"* [18].

A model is needed for storing the user context data in a machine processable form. Various context model approaches have been proposed, such as key-value models, markup scheme models, graphical models, object oriented models, logic-based models, or ontology-based models [24]. However, the ontology-based approach has been advocated as being the most promising one [1,24] mainly because of its dynamicity, expressiveness and extensibility. We have defined a user interaction context ontology (UICO) [18] which represents the user interaction context through 88 concepts, 215 datatype and 57 objecttype properties. It is modeled in the *ontology web language* (OWL)[1], a W3C standard for modeling ontologies widely accepted in the Semantic Web community. The majority of concepts represents the types of user interactions and the types of resources. The high number of datatype properties represent data and metadata about resources and application user interface elements the user interacted with. The objecttype properties relate (i) the user interactions with resources, (ii) resources with other resources or parts of resources and (iii) user interactions with themselves for modeling the aggregation of user interactions. The highly connected UICO is therefore naturally enabling both: (i) a variety of context-aware applications and (ii) *"mining"* activities for in-depth analyzes of user characteristics, actions, preferences, interests, goals, etc. For a detailed description of the UICO we refer to [17,18].

2.1 Automatic Population of the User Interaction Context Ontology

Context observation mechanisms are used to capture the behavior of the user while working on her computer desktop, i.e. performing tasks. Low-level operating system and application events initiated by the user while interacting with her desktop, are recorded by context observers. The data about the occurred events is then sent as an XML stream to the context capturing framework for discovering resources and for aggregating events (single user interactions) to event blocks (continuous sequence of user interactions on the same resource). This is similar to the contextual attention metadata approach [27] and to context observation in general [15,18,21,22].

Context observers, also referred to as context sensors, are programs, macros and plug-ins that record the user's interactions on the computer desktop. We developed a broad range of context sensors for standard office applications and the operating system Microsoft Windows (XP, Vista and 7). A complete list of sensors is given in [17]. The sensed contextual data sent by the context sensors is used as a basis for automatically populating the UICO. Automatic population here means an autonomous instantiation of concepts and creation of properties between concept instances of the UICO based on the observed and the automatically inferred user interaction context. The automatic population exploits the structure of user interface elements of standard office applications and preserves data types and relationships through a combination of rule-based, information extraction and supervised learning techniques. We also use our knowledge discovery framework, the KnowMiner [10] to perform named entity recognition of persons, locations and organizations as well as for extracting data and metadata of various resource types. Hence, the UICO is a much richer representation of the user interaction context than is typically stored in attention metadata sensor streams [27] since it preserves relationships that otherwise are lost.

---

[1] http://www.w3.org/2004/OWL/

This rich representation of the user interaction context is exploited for machine-learning based task detection as described in the next section. At this point we would like to note that a rule-based aggregation of user actions into tasks might be a reasonable approach for highly-structured tasks, such as administrative or routine tasks, but this is obviously not appropriate for tasks that involve a certain freedom and creativity in their execution, e.g. for knowledge-intensive tasks such as "Planning a journey" or "Writing a research paper". To handle such unstructured tasks the idea is to automatically extract a task from the information available in the ontology by means of machine learning techniques. Once detected, these tasks will also populate the ontology.

3 User Task Detection

Here, by task detection we mean *task class detection* also referred to as *task classification*, as opposed to *task switch detection*. Task switch detection involves predicting when the user switches from one task to another [16,21]. Task classification deals with the challenge of classifying usage data from user task execution into task classes or task types. Automatic task detection is classically modeled as a machine learning problem, and more precisely a classification problem. This method is used to recognize Web based tasks [9], tasks within emails [3,22] or tasks from the complete user's computer desktop [8,15,16,21,22].

Classically, solving this classification problem is based on the following steps: (i) The user context data is captured by system and application sensors. (ii) Features, i.e. parts of this data, are chosen to build classification training instances, which is done at the task level. (iii) To obtain valid inputs for machine learning algorithms, these features are first transformed into attributes [26]. This transformation may include data preprocessing operations, such as removing stopwords [8,15] and application specific terms [16], or constructing word vectors. (iv) Attribute selection [8,22] (optional step) is performed to select the best discriminative attributes. (v) Finally, classification/learning algorithms are trained and tested.

Beyond this well-accepted procedure, two major limitations within the user task detection field still have to be addressed. First, the focus of the previously mentioned approaches so far has been on using only text-based features and switching sequences, which do not rely on sophisticated models. Second, standard datasets for the evaluation of task detection approaches are still missing, as well as a representative number of controlled user studies. We address this point in the next section. Regarding the first limitation, it has been recently shown that using an ontology-based context model can increase the performance of automatic task detection [18]. This new approach has been named *ontology-based user task detection*. We extend this work, and study in detail the influence of using an ontology-based user interaction context model on task detection.

3.1 Ontology-Based User Task Detection

As mentioned previously, performing task detection consists in training machine learning algorithms on classes corresponding to task models. This means that each training instance presented to the machine learning algorithms represents a task that has to

Action Category	All Categories	Content Category
- task duration - EB duration - mean EB duration - median EB duration - mean time between EBs - median time between EBs - number of Es per EBs - action element of E - action type of E - letter input keys - number input keys - navigation input keys - control input keys - application interactions - resource interactions - EB resource interactions - used resource interactions - included resource interactions - referenced resource interactions - resource type interactions - semantic type	**Application Category** - window title - application name - raw event source - accessibility object name - accessibility object description - accessibility object role - accessibility object role description - accessibility object value - accessibility object help - accessibility object help topic **Switching Sequence Category** - application switch - E type switch - E level resource switch - E and EB resource switch - E and EB resource type switch	- content of EB - content in focus - user input **Ontology Structure Category** - concept instances - datatype properties - objecttype properties **Resource Category** - resource content - used resource content - used resource URI - used resource metadata - referenced resource content - referenced resource URI - included resource content - included resource URI E = event EB = event-block

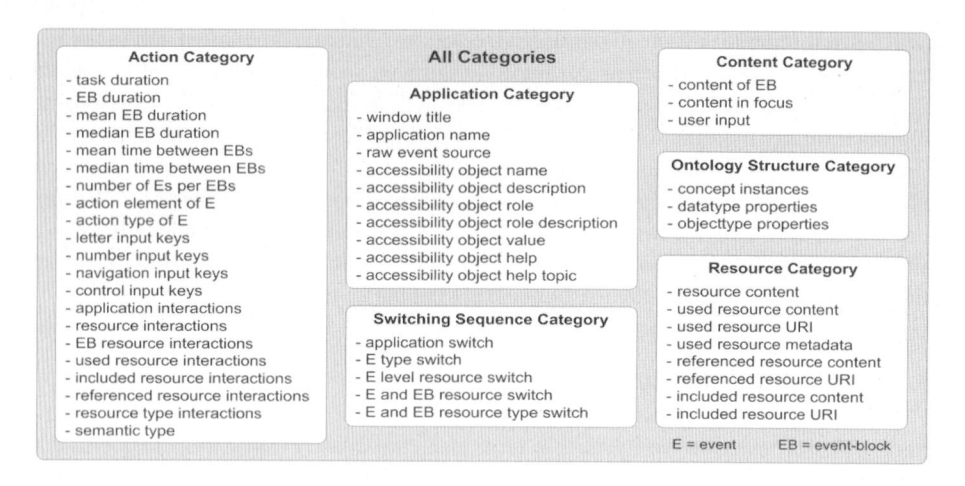

Fig. 1. Overview of all features (and their respective feature categories) engineered from our User Interaction Context Ontology (UICO)

be "labeled". Thus, training instances have to be built from features and feature combinations derived from the user context data at the task level. In our ontology-based approach, this means deriving features from the data associated with a Task concept.

Based on our UICO, we have engineered 50 features for constructing the training instances (see Figure 1). They are grouped in six categories: (i) *action*, (ii) *application*, (iii) *content*, (iv) *ontology structure*, (v) *resource* and (vi) *switching sequences*. The *action category* represents the user interactions and contains features about the interactions with applications [8], resources types, resources, key input types (navigational keys, letters, numbers), the number of events (E) and event blocks (EB), the duration of the event blocks, and the time intervals between event blocks. The *application category* contains the classical *window title* feature [8,15,16,21], the application name feature [8] and the newly introduced accessibility objects features. The *content category* consists of features representing the content of task-related resources, the content in focus and the text input of the user. The *ontology structure category* contains features representing the number of instances of concepts and the number of datatype and objecttype relations used per task. The *resource category* includes the complete contents and URIs [22] of the used, referenced and included resources, as well as a feature that combines all the metadata about the used resources in a 'bag of words'. The *switching sequences category* comprises features about switches between applications, resources, event types and resource types.

We use the machine learning toolkit Weka [26] for parts of the feature engineering and classification processes. The following steps are performed to preprocess the content of text-based features (in this sequence): (i) remove end of line characters, (ii) remove markups, e.g. \&lg and ![CDATA, (iii) remove all characters but letters, (iv) remove German and English stopwords, (v) remove words shorter than three characters. For numeric features, we apply the Weka PKIDiscretize filter to replace discrete values by intervals. We transform text-based features into vectors of words with the StringToWordVector function of Weka.

3.2 Methodology for Performance Evaluation

In all our task detection experiments, we use learning algorithms considered as classical in the text classification area. Besides, we study their performance with the same evaluation methodology, to ensure the comparability of results across the different experiment's datasets. In all our experiments, the following parameters are varied in order to evaluate their influence on the task detection performance: (i) the learning algorithm, (ii) the set of used features and (iii) the number of attributes generated from the features. Furthermore, the set of used features is varied by including (i) each feature individually, (ii) each feature category individually, (iii) all feature categories or (iv) the *Top k* best performing single features, with $k \in \{2, 3, 4, 5, 6, 7, 8, 9, 10, 15, 20\}$.

The evaluated learning algorithms are: Naïve Bayes (NB), Linear Support Vector Machine (SVM) with cost parameter $c \in \{2^{-5}, 2^{-3}, 2^{-1}, 2^0, 2^1, 2^3, 2^5, 2^8, 2^{10}\}$, J48 decision tree (J48), and k-Nearest Neighbor (KNN-k) with $k \in \{1, 5, 10, 35\}$. The different values for the number of neighbors k are introduced in order to explore the task detection performance with different decision boundaries. The values of the cost parameter for the SVM are borrowed from the libSVM practical guide[2]. The Weka machine learning library [26] and the Weka integration of the libSVM[3] provide the necessary tool set to evaluate these algorithms based on standard classification evaluation measures [26], such as accuracy, precision, recall and f1-measure.

For each learning algorithm $l \in L$, each feature category $\phi \in \Phi$ and each feature $f \in F$, the g attributes having the highest *Information Gain* value (IG) are selected. Information gain attribute selection is used because (i) it is one of the fastest and most popular algorithms in the text classification field, and (ii) "pre-evaluations" with more advanced attribute selection methods showed little improvement. As values for g, 50 different measure points are used for analyzing the required number of attributes for high task detection accuracy values. Half of them are equally distributed over the available number of attributes with an upper bound of 5000. The other half is defined by $G = \{3, 5, 10, 25, 50, 75, 100, 125, 150, 175, 200, 250, 300, 500, 750, 1000, 1500, 2000, 2500, 3000, 3500, 4000, 5000, 7500, 10000\}$, the upper bound being 10000 or the maximum number of attributes available, whichever is less. The choice of these specific measuring points is motivated by two reasons. First, previous evaluations of task detection performance reported that good results were achieved with a low number of attributes (about 200-300) [8,15,22], and hence we put a special focus on similar numbers of attributes. Second, we also want to investigate the influence of using higher numbers of attributes on task classification.

Two methods are used for evaluating the learning algorithms. First, a stratified 10-fold cross-validation is performed: statistical values for each fold are computed, as well as the mean and standard deviation of each value across the folds. Second, a training and test set evaluation is performed. The training and test sets are constructed based on the specific research question investigated in each experiment (see next section). The training set and test set instances are strictly parted (i.e. constructed and preprocessed independently) to avoid any bias. Each learning algorithm is then trained on the training set and evaluated on the test set.

---

[2] http://www.csie.ntu.edu.tw/~cjlin/libsvm/
[3] http://www.cs.iastate.edu/~yasser/wlsvm/

We use two different techniques for isolating the best features or feature combinations, as well as the best classifiers: (i) *dominance matrices* and (ii) *paired t-tests*. Similar cross-datasets comparison methods have been proposed for evaluating learning algorithms on text categorization [28] and for evaluating hierarchical clustering algorithms on multiple document datasets [29]. The feature (resp. classifier) dominance matrix computes how often a feature or feature combination (resp. a classifier) outperforms another one. We say that a feature/feature combination (resp. classifier) outperforms another one if one of the following conditions (tested in this order) is satisfied: (i) higher accuracy (ii) higher micro precision, (iii) higher micro recall, (iv) lower number of attributes. We perform paired t-tests to study the statistic significance of the results achieved by the classifiers, based on: (i) their accuracy and (ii) the micro f-measures. We perform the paired t-tests at three different significance levels ($\alpha = 0.005, \alpha = 0.01$ and $\alpha = 0.5$) using the *Apache Commons Mathematics Library*[4].

4 Experiments

4.1 Related Work and Datasets

In *SWISH* [16] about four hours of real usage data observed from a single user was recorded, which gave five different tasks. In Dyonipos [8] about 140 tasks were collected from one user. The dataset used for evaluating TaskPredictor 1 [22] contains 177 tasks performed by two users, and the one used for evaluating TaskPredictor 2 [21] contains 304 tasks performed by two users (user 1: 299 tasks, user 2: 5 tasks). These datasets show several limitations for studying task detection and drawing conclusions about the performance of classifiers and features. Besides the small number of users, and the fact that each dataset relates to only one domain, a more critical issue is that no task classes were defined prior to the data collection and that the gathered tasks were labeled only afterwards and not by the user. An exception is an experiment performed in the APOSDLE project [15], in which business task classes such as *market analysis*, *product design and specification*, *find and contact suppliers*, *contract placement* and *triggering production* were predefined. But again this experiment was limited to one user and one domain. This is because of the poorness of these datasets that we decided to perform several experiments in laboratory settings, with multiple users from different domains, and with several predefined task classes. The experiments are only briefly described here because of space limitations. Further details about the design and settings of the experiments can be found in [17].

4.2 First Laboratory Study

The initial objective of *Task Experiment 1* was to study the influence on task detection of the computer environment in which tasks were performed. Users had to execute similar tasks both in a controlled environment, namely on a single laboratory computer, and on their personal workstations. 14 probands, within the working domain of the Know-Center GmbH, participated in the experiment, which produced 218 tasks. Additional

---

[4] http://commons.apache.org/math/

tasks were performed by one of the users, who was playing the role of the expert, which increased the total number of tasks to 271. The idea was to also evaluate the performance of a classifier trained only on tasks performed by the expert. The experiment was exploratory, the comparison was *within subjects* and the manipulations were targeting (i) the computer environment, (ii) the type of task (standard vs. personal and routine vs. knowledge-intensive) and (iii) the task class.

The first manipulation was achieved by varying the work environment, i.e. the computer desktop environment in which the participants performed their tasks. The first environment was a *laboratory computer* on which a set of standard software used in the company was installed. The second one was the company's *personal workstations* of the users, with their personal desktop settings and with access to their personal files, folders, bookmarks, emails, etc. All participants performed the same set of tasks in both environments, but half of them started on the laboratory computer, and the others started on their personal workstations. All assignments of the users were randomized.

The second manipulation was based on the task type. The two dichotomies we introduced between task types were: (i) *routine task* vs. *knowledge-intensive task* and (ii) *standard task* vs. *personal task*. A "standard task" is a task executed by the user on behalf of a *persona* (i.e. an artificial person) that we named "Bill Adams", as opposed to a "personal task" which is performed by the user for herself. All participants performed each task both in a standard and in a personal way, and the fact of starting with the standard or the personal task was randomly chosen.

The third manipulation resulted from the choice of studying five task classes, chosen by the users as being typical of their domain. Three of them were considered as **routine tasks** (*Filling in the official journey form* (55 tasks), *Filling in the cost recompense form* (45 tasks), *Creating an application for leave* (51 tasks)) and the other two as **knowledge-intensive tasks** (*Planning an official journey* (52 tasks), *Organizing a project meeting* (15 tasks)). The figures in the brackets represent the number of task executions for each task recorded in the experiment. The order in which the users had to execute the tasks was randomly generated.

4.3 Second Laboratory Study

Task Experiment 2 was designed similarly to *Task Experiment 1*, but was performed in another domain and with different task classes. 10 probands from the Computer Science Department of the Graz University of Technology participated in the experiment, which produced 134 tasks. Seven task classes were studied which resulted in the following recorded dataset: four were considered as **routine tasks** (*Registering for an exam* (19 tasks), *Finding course dates* (20 tasks), *Reserving a book from the university library* (20 tasks), *Registering for a course* (17 tasks)) and the other three as **knowledge-intensive tasks** (*Programming an algorithm* (20 tasks), *Preparing a scientific talk* (19 tasks), *Planning a study trip* (19 tasks)).

4.4 Third Laboratory Study

Task Experiment 3 was designed to study the possibility of classifying knowledge-intensive tasks and to evaluate the influence of the task type (analytic or synthetic) on task detection. The task classes we used were borrowed from the *CommonKADS* knowledge-intensive task classification [20]. 18 probands from the Computer Science Department of the Graz University of Technology participated in the experiment, which produced 132 tasks. The experiment was *within subjects*. The first manipulation was achieved by varying the type of the knowledge-intensive task, namely *analytic task* or *synthetic task*, as defined by the *CommonKADS* task classification. The second manipulation was performed by varying the subtypes of analytic and synthetic task classes. Recording the user interaction context for these task classes led to the following dataset:

Analytic tasks: *Classification*: "Classify a list of computer science terms to hardware and software" (17 tasks), *Diagnosis*: "Find the origin of a malfunction in a computer program" (15 tasks), *Assessment*: "Assess whether a student has to pay tuition fees based on her/his application" (19 tasks), *Prediction*: "Predict the questions of an exam based on historical data" (16 tasks).

Synthetic tasks: *Design*: "Create a simple conceptual design for the software of an elevator system" (18 tasks), *Assignment*: "Assign students to study groups led by study assistants" (16 tasks), *Planning*: "Plan a software project for the development of a document management system" (16 tasks), *Scheduling*: "Create a schedule for the design and development of an electronic library book lending system" (15 tasks).

5 Evaluation of Task Detection Performance

Globally over the three datasets, the different task instances could be classified with a high accuracy, by using the stratified 10-fold cross-validation method. The levels of accuracy achieved were 88.55% for Dataset 1, 94.84% for Dataset 2 and 86.43% for Dataset 3 (see Table 1). However it is important to note that these high accuracy levels were reached by finding, for each dataset, the best task detection setting among all possible settings, obtained by varying the classifier, the set of used features and the number of attributes. Even though the best results were generally achieved by considering the set of all 50 features or a combination of the best performing features, there was not one setting that could perform best across experiments. Exploring all possible settings for reaching high accuracy levels is obviously not realistic within a productive scenario. Thus, with the idea of trying to reduce the space of possible task detection settings in mind, we will now analyze individually each factor that can have an influence on task detection.

5.1 Influence of the Task Type

Standard Tasks vs. Personal Tasks. A "standard task" is a task executed by the user on behalf of a *persona*, as opposed to a "personal task" which is performed by the user for herself. By having several users executing the same standard task, very similar task instances were expected, all those instances having a common *specific goal* (e.g. "Planning the trip of Bill Adams to EC-TEL 2010") contrary to personal tasks. Thus, it could seem easier to detect standard tasks than personal tasks. We evaluated this in Task Experiments 1 and 2, by trying to classify standard task instances (among 5 task classes)

Table 1. Overview of all task detection performance results of the three laboratory experiments

Evaluations	Exp. 1	Exp. 2	Exp. 3
Stratified 10-Fold Cross-Validation			
Detection of the Task Model (5/7/8 Classes)	88.55%	94.84%	86.43%
Routine vs. Knowledge-Intensive Tasks (2 Classes)	94.94%	100.00%	-
Routine Tasks (4 Classes)	-	94.64%	-
Knowledge-Intensive Tasks (3 Classes)	-	100.00%	-
Standard Tasks (5/7 Classes)	88.41%	98.57%	-
Personal Tasks (5/7 Classes)	86.00%	94.05%	-
Analytic vs. Synthetic Tasks (2 Classes)	-	-	94.73%
Analytic Tasks (4 Classes)	-	-	97.14%
Synthetic (4 Classes)	-	-	85.24%
Train/Test Set Evaluation			
Personal Tasks based on Standard Task (5/7 Classes)	77.14%	92.42%	-

or personal task instances (among 7 task classes) independently, using the stratified 10-fold cross-validation method. We found only a small difference in the achieved accuracy values, of about 3.5% in favor of standard tasks.

In Task Experiments 1 and 2, we also evaluated the performance of task detection while training the classifiers on standard task instances and testing them on personal task instances. We obtained the accuracy values of 77.14% and 92.42% respectively, with 5 and 7 task classes respectively involved. These results suggest that training on task instances sharing a common specific goal is sufficient for classifying personal task instances. These results are also strongly supported by the facts that (i) the datasets of Tasks Experiments 1 and 2 included 218 task instances (113 standard / 105 personal) and 134 task instances (68 standard / 66 personal) respectively, (ii) Tasks Experiments 1 and 2 involved 14 and 10 users respectively and (iii) these experiments were performed in two different domains. The conclusion we can draw from this result is that a classifier trained by a group of experts on standard tasks performs well while classifying personal tasks performed by users.

Routine Tasks vs. Knowledge-Intensive Tasks. In Experiments 1 and 2, we investigated the possibility of distinguishing routine tasks from knowledge-intensive tasks. We evaluated our learning algorithms on this two-class classification problem, by using the stratified 10-fold cross-validation method. We reached the accuracy levels of 94.94% and 100% for Tasks Experiments 1 and 2 respectively. This shows that task instances could easily be classified between routine tasks and knowledge-intensive tasks.

It could seem easier to detect routine tasks than knowledge-intensive tasks, since the latter involve more freedom and should produce very different task instances. We evaluated this in Task Experiment 2, by trying to classify routine task instances (among 4 task classes) or knowledge-intensive task instances (among 3 task classes) independently, using the stratified 10-fold cross-validation method. The accuracy achieved was of 94.64% for routine tasks and 100% for knowledge-intensive tasks. However this last result is not well supported for two reasons: (i) this was only a three-class classification problem and (ii) the task classes involved were too different such that it was too easy for the classifiers to find distinguishing features to train on. Even though the accuracy value itself is controversial, this result shows that knowledge-intensive tasks could be detected as well as routine tasks.

Analytic Tasks vs. Synthetic Tasks. Task Experiment 3 was designed to understand better what kinds of knowledge-intensive tasks could be detected. We used the dichotomy between analytic and synthetic tasks, as defined in the *CommonKADS* classification for knowledge-intensive tasks [20]. We first studied the two-class classification problem consisting in distinguishing analytic tasks from synthetic tasks, by using the stratified 10-fold cross-validation method. We obtained an accuracy of 94.73%, showing that these two classes could easily be distinguished.

We also studied the detectability of various task classes of each type (analytic vs. synthetic), by trying to classify analytic task instances (among 4 task classes) or synthetic task instances (among 4 task classes) independently, using the stratified 10-fold cross-validation method. The accuracy achieved was 97.14% for analytic tasks and 85.24% for synthetic tasks. Again this shows that knowledge-intensive tasks can be well classified by our approach.

5.2 Influence of Context Features and Feature Categories

Based on the evaluations performed on our three datasets, we can study the stability of the performance achieved by each feature and each feature category (see Table 1). By computing a dominance matrix for each experiment (based on how often a feature/feature category outperforms the others) a ranking of the features/feature categories can be obtained. An overview of the results, for the top 22 features/feature categories is presented in Table 2. Those are the features/feature categories that appear in the top 15 ranking produced by at least one dataset.

Several interesting insights are provided by Table 2. First, the good representation of features and feature categories engineered based on our ontology clearly signals the positive influence on the task detection performance of adopting our UICO approach. Second, the best results are achieved by the *Application Category* and by the combination of all 50 features (*All Categories*). The fact that the *Application Category* performs slightly better also shows that it is not true that: "The more features are considered, the better the achieved classification accuracy is". Third, the single features achieving the best results are the *accessibility object name* and the *window title*. Besides, the standard deviation of the *accessibility object name* feature is one of the lowest, which indicates the good stability of its performance across datasets. The fact that the *accessibility object name* feature, which is specific to our UICO approach, performs slightly better than the well-known *window title* feature also signals the benefits of making use of the features derived from the accessibility objects. Accessibility objects are associated with graphical user interface elements of applications, such as application windows and controls[5]. For example the `acc.object.name` value of the close button of a Microsoft

---

[5] http://msdn.microsoft.com/accessibility

Table 2. Computation of the ranking of the features and feature categories. The global ranking R_G is given by the average μ_R of the rankings of the features/feature categories for all the task detection evaluations shown in Table 1 based on the three datasets (R_1, R_2 and R_3) and by the standard deviation δ_R in case of a draw.

R_G	Feature / Feature Category	R_1	R_2	R_3	μ_R	δ_R^2	δ_R
1	Application Category	1	2	2	1.67	0.33	0.58
2	All Categories	3	1	1	1.67	1.33	1.15
3	accessibility object name	4	4	3	3.67	0.33	0.58
4	window title	2	3	6	3.67	4.33	2.08
5	Resource Category	6	7	4	5.67	2.33	1.53
6	used resource metadata	9	6	5	6.67	4.33	2.08
7	accessibility object value	5	12	8	8.33	12.33	3.51
8	Action Category	13	5	7	8.33	17.33	4.16
9	datatype properties	8	9	10	9.00	1.00	1.00
10	Ontology Structure Category	10	8	11	9.67	2.33	1.53
11	Switching Sequences Category	20	11	9	13.33	34.33	5.86
12	accessibility object role	15	15	15	15.00	0.00	0.00
13	resource type interactions	19	10	16	15.00	21.00	4.58
14	Content Category	7	27	12	15.33	108.33	10.41
15	application interactions	21	16	13	16.67	16.33	4.04
16	concept instances	22	14	14	16.67	21.33	4.62
17	resource interaction	31	13	15	19.67	97.33	9.87
18	content of EB	11	28	21	20.00	73.00	8.54
19	content in focus	12	30	18	20.00	84.00	9.17
20	accessibility object role description	14	25	30	23.00	67.00	8.19
21	used resource interaction	32	15	22	23.00	73.00	8.54
22	resource content	15	35	23	24.33	101.33	10.07

Windows command window is "Close" and the `acc.obj.description` is "Closes the window". Fourth, if we reduce this table by considering only the features that appear in the top 15 rankings produced by the three datasets, we can isolate what we consider as being the best performing features: the *accessibility object name* feature, the *window title* feature, the *used resource metadata* feature, the *accessibility object value* feature, the *datatype properties* feature and the *accessibility object role* feature. Because of the low standard deviation values associated with them, the performance of these six features also proves to be stable across datasets. It is again worth noting that four of these features are new and specific to our UICO approach.

5.3 Influence of the Classifier

By using all the evaluations performed on our three datasets, we can analyze the stability of the performance achieved by each classifier (Naïve Bayes, Linear Support Vector Machine, J48 decision tree and k-Nearest Neighbor). By computing a dominance matrix for each experiment (based on how often a classifier outperforms the others) a ranking of the classifiers can be obtained. An overview of the results is presented in Table 3. The J48 classifier obtains the first rank and the lowest standard deviation. This indicates that

Table 3. Computation of the ranking of the classifiers. The global ranking R_G is given by the average μ_R of the classifier performances for all the task detection evaluations shown in Table 1 based on the three datasets (R_1, R_2 and R_3). The standard deviation δ_R is also given.

R_G	Classifier	R_1	R_2	R_3	μ_R	δ_R^2	δ_R
1	J48	2	2	1	1.67	0.33	0.51
2	NB	1	1	5	2.33	5.33	2.04
3	KNN-5	4	5	2	3.67	2.33	1.5
4	KNN-35	6	4	3	4.33	2.33	0.69
5	KNN-1	5	6	4	5.00	1.00	1.00
6	KNN-10	7	3	6	5.33	4.33	1.58
7	SVM	3	7	7	5.67	5.33	0.77

it is the most stable across datasets. The Naïve Bayes algorithm performs best on the first two datasets, but poorly on the third one, involving only knowledge-intensive tasks. It seems that Naïve Bayes cannot deal with the creative freedom inherent to knowledge-intensive tasks. The Linear Support Vector Machine classifier performs rather well on the first dataset, but is the worst on the two other datasets. The k-Nearest Neighbor algorithm shows rather constant results, but performs slightly better on the third dataset. Knowing that both Naïve Bayes and Linear Support Vector Machine are linear classifiers, the fact that they perform rather badly on the third dataset, contrary to J48 and k-Nearest Neighbor, might indicate that the decision boundary is non-linear in this case.

From the paired t-tests computed based on the classifiers achieved accuracy, we can derive partial orders of these classifiers, for each dataset. For Tasks Experiments 1, 2 and 3 the resulting partial orders are $\{J48, NB\} \gg \{KNN\text{-}1, KNN\text{-}5, KNN\text{-}10, KNN\text{-}35\} \gg \{SVM\}$, $\{NB\} \gg \{J48, KNN\text{-}1, KNN\text{-}5, KNN\text{-}10, KNN\text{-}35\} \gg \{SVM\}$ and $\{J48\} \gg \{NB, KNN\text{-}1, KNN\text{-}5, KNN\text{-}10, KNN\text{-}35\} \gg \{SVM\}$ with $\gg$ indicating a statistical significance on a $\alpha = 0.005$ level. The J48 decision tree and Naïve Bayes classifiers globally outperform the k-Nearest Neighbor and Linear Support Vector Machine learners, which supports the result given in Table 3. Furthermore, the paired t-tests we computed based on the micro f-measures, and which we omit here because of space limitations, are similar and confirm this result.

5.4 Comparison with Related Work

The most popular features identified for having a high discriminative power among tasks are the `window title` feature [8,16,22], the `file path/web page url` feature [22], and the `content in focus` feature [8]. In our findings we confirm the feature choice of these approaches and compare them to novel context features and feature categories introduced by our approach (see Figure 1).

In terms of attributes used for training the machine learning algorithms an interval of 200-300 attributes is suggested to be sufficient by [8,22]. Our results confirm that only a small ratio of attributes are required to successfully identify tasks. The best overall accuracies were obtained on the interval between 100-500 attributes. The results that led to this interval cannot be presented here because of space limitation.

In the task detection experiments reported in [15] the SVM learning algorithm was mentioned as the one with the highest achieved accuracy. In [8] the good performance of the SVM learning algorithm was confirmed and the high accuracy achieved by the KNN learner highlighted. On our datasets the SVM showed the worst accuracy and f-measures. The good performance of the KNN learner can be confirmed. In contrast with [8] the Naïve Bayes learner performed very well across our experiment's datasets.

5.5 Discussion

The *generalizability to other tasks and domains* of the results obtained by this research work is limited because (i) only two domains with (ii) selected tasks were studied and (iii) only a sample of experts of the domain were involved in the experiments. However, this research work successfully discovered novel features and feature categories as well as classifiers that showed a stable and high task detection performance. Further experiments in other domains with other tasks and users are required in order to generalize.

The method for *finding the best possible detectability of tasks* for the UICO approach, comprising the evaluation of the feature categories, single performing features and *Top k* best performing single features, is limited from a theoretical point of view, in the sense that not all combinations of the 50 features were studied. However, from a practical point of view it is not reasonable to compute all possible feature combinations of 50 features, which would represent $2^{50} - 1 \approx 1.13 * 10^{15}$ combinations. In our research we have reduced the number of possible combinations by suggesting a set of six features. Finding a good combination of features for specific tasks of a domain is what we consider as fine tuning task classification. Besides, we believe that there is no unique feature combination performing well for all settings.

We have tested four types of classifiers: Naïve Bayes, k-Nearest Neighbors, Linear Support Vector Machines and J48 decision trees. However, *there are many more classifiers* in the area of machine learning that could prove to show a good applicability to the task detection problem.

6 Conclusion and Future Work

We have performed three laboratory experiments for evaluating the influence on our ontology-based user task detection approach of the following factors: (i) the used classifier, (ii) the selected features, (iii) the task type and (iv) the method chosen for training the classifiers. We have gained several insights from our evaluation. First, the J48 decision tree and Naïve Bayes classifiers provide a better classification accuracy than other classifiers, in our three experiments. Second, we have isolated six features that present a good discriminative power for classifying tasks, which is stable across datasets. Third, even though it could seem easier to classify routine tasks, our experiments show that knowledge intensive tasks can be classified as well as routine tasks. Fourth, we have shown that a classifier trained by a group of experts on standardized tasks performs well while classifying personal tasks performed by users.

Our goal is to find a combination of classifiers and features that achieves good results on a standard desktop computer. In future work we will investigate in combining unsupervised learning mechanisms for identifying boundaries in the user interaction context data based on the discovered context features and applying the J48 decision tree and Naïve Bayes learning algorithms for classifying these clusters to task classes. Open questions we will address are (i) in which intervals should a clustering take place, (ii) are the context features that worked well in supervised learning also applicable in an unsupervised learning setting and (iii) develop a real-time task detection application respecting the computational power available on standard desktop computers. Accurate automatic task detection will allow a more reliable construction of fine-grained user profiles about the user's interests, competencies, learning goals and knowledge indicating events, extending what we have already shown in [13].

Acknowledgments

The Know-Center is funded within the Austrian COMET Program - Competence Centers for Excellent Technologies - under the auspices of the Austrian Federal Ministry of Transport, Innovation and Technology, the Austrian Federal Ministry of Economy, Family and Youth and by the State of Styria. COMET is managed by the Austrian Research Promotion Agency FFG.

References

1. Baldauf, M., Dustdar, S., Rosenberg, F.: A survey on context-aware systems. International Journal of Ad Hoc and Ubiquitous Computing 2(4), 263–277 (2007)
2. Dey, A.K., Abowd, G.D., Salber, D.: A conceptual framework and a toolkit for supporting the rapid prototyping of context-aware applications. Human Computer Interaction 16(2), 97–166 (2001)
3. Dredze, M., Lau, T., Kushmerick, N.: Automatically classifying emails into activities. In: Proc. IUI 2006, pp. 70–77 (2006)
4. Duval, E., Hodgins, W.: A LOM research agenda. In: Proc. WWW 2003, pp. 1–9 (2003)
5. Eraut, M.: Informal learning in the workplace. Studies in Continuing Education 26(2), 247–273 (2004)
6. Fischer, G.: User modeling in human-computer interaction. User Modeling and User-Adapted Interaction 11(1-2), 65–86 (2001)
7. Goecks, J., Shavlik, J.: Learning users' interests by unobtrusively observing their normal behavior. In: Proc. IUI 2000, pp. 129–132 (2000)
8. Granitzer, M., Kröll, M., Seifert, C., Rath, A.S., Weber, N., Dietzel, O., Lindstaedt, S.N.: Analysis of machine learning techniques for context extraction. In: Proc. ICDIM 2008, pp. 233–240 (2008)
9. Gutschmidt, A., Cap, C.H., Nerdinger, F.W.: Paving the path to automatic user task identification. In: Workshop on Common Sense Knowledge and Goal-Oriented Interfaces, IUI 2008 (2008)
10. Klieber, W., Sabol, V., Muhr, M., Kern, R., Öttl, G., Granitzer, M.: Knowledge discovery using the KnowMiner framework. In: Proc. IADIS 2009 (2009)
11. Ley, T., Ulbrich, A., Scheir, P., Lindstaedt, S.N., Kump, B., Albert, D.: Modelling competencies for supporting work-integrated learning in knowledge work. Journal of Knowledge Management 12(6), 31–47 (2008)

12. Lindstaedt, S.N., Ley, T., Scheir, P., Ulbrich, A.: Applying scruffy methods to enable work-integrated learning. European Journal of the Informatics Professional 9(3), 44–50 (2008)
13. Lindstaedt, S.N., Beham, G., Kump, B., Ley, T.: Getting to know your user - unobtrusive user model maintenance within work-integrated learning environments. In: Cress, U., Dimitrova, V., Specht, M. (eds.) EC-TEL 2009. LNCS, vol. 5794, pp. 73–87. Springer, Heidelberg (2009)
14. Lindstaedt, S.N., Scheir, P., Lokaiczyk, R., Kump, B., Beham, G., Pammer, V.: Knowledge services for work-integrated learning. In: Dillenbourg, P., Specht, M. (eds.) EC-TEL 2008. LNCS, vol. 5192, pp. 234–244. Springer, Heidelberg (2008)
15. Lokaiczyk, R., Faatz, A., Beckhaus, A., Goertz, M.: Enhancing just-in-time e-learning through machine learning on desktop context sensors. In: Kokinov, B., Richardson, D.C., Roth-Berghofer, T.R., Vieu, L. (eds.) CONTEXT 2007. LNCS (LNAI), vol. 4635, pp. 330–341. Springer, Heidelberg (2007)
16. Oliver, N., Smith, G., Thakkar, C., Surendran, A.C.: SWISH: semantic analysis of window titles and switching history. In: Proc. IUI 2006, pp. 194–201 (2006)
17. Rath, A.S.: User Interaction Context - Studying and Enhancing Automatic User Task Detection on the Computer Desktop via an Ontology-based User Interaction Context Model. Ph.D. thesis, Graz University of Technology (2010)
18. Rath, A.S., Devaurs, D., Lindstaedt, S.N.: UICO: an ontology-based user interaction context model for automatic task detection on the computer desktop. In: Workshop on Context, Information and Ontologies, ESWC 2009 (2009)
19. Schmidt, A.: Impact of context-awareness on the architecture of e-learning solutions. In: Architecture Solutions for E-Learning Systems, ch. 16, pp. 306–319. Information Science Reference, IGI Publishing (2007)
20. Schreiber, G., Akkermans, H., Anjewierden, A., Dehoog, R., Shadbolt, N., Vandevelde, W., Wielinga, B.: Knowledge Engineering and Management: The CommonKADS Methodology. The MIT Press, Cambridge (1999)
21. Shen, J., Irvine, J., Bao, X., Goodman, M., Kolibaba, S., Tran, A., Carl, F., Kirschner, B., Stumpf, S., Dietterich, T.G.: Detecting and correcting user activity switches: algorithms and interfaces. In: Proc. IUI 2009, pp. 117–126 (2009)
22. Shen, J., Li, L., Dietterich, T.G., Herlocker, J.L.: A hybrid learning system for recognizing user tasks from desktop activities and email messages. In: Proc. IUI 2006, pp. 86–92 (2006)
23. Smith, P.J.: Workplace Learning and Flexible Delivery. Review of Educational Research 73(1), 53–88 (2003)
24. Strang, T., Linnhoff-Popien, C.: A context modeling survey. In: Workshop on Advanced Context Modelling, Reasoning and Management, UbiComp 2004 (2004)
25. Ulbrich, A., Scheir, P., Lindstaedt, S.N., Görtz, M.: A context-model for supporting work-integrated learning. In: Nejdl, W., Tochtermann, K. (eds.) EC-TEL 2006. LNCS, vol. 4227, pp. 525–530. Springer, Heidelberg (2006)
26. Witten, I.H., Frank, E.: Data Mining: Practical Machine Learning Tools and Techniques, 2nd edn. Morgan Kaufmann, San Francisco (2005)
27. Wolpers, M., Najjar, J., Verbert, K., Duval, E.: Actual usage: the attention metadata approach. Educational Technology & Society 10(3), 106–121 (2007)
28. Yang, Y., Liu, X.: A re-examination of text categorization methods. In: Proc. SIGIR 1999, pp. 42–49 (1999)
29. Zhao, Y., Karypis, G., Fayyad, U.: Hierarchical clustering algorithms for document datasets. Data Mining and Knowledge Discovery 10(2), 141–168 (2005)

Learning 2.0
Promoting Innovation in Formal Education and Training in Europe

Christine Redecker[*] and Yves Punie

Institute for Prospective Technological Studies (IPTS),
European Commission, Joint Research Centre,
Edificio Expo, C/Inca Garcilaso 3,
41092 Seville, Spain
{Christine.Redecker,Yves.Punie}@ec.europa.eu

Abstract. Take up of Web 2.0 applications in formal Education and Training is still in an experimental phase and scientific evidence on Learning 2.0 practices in schools and universities is scarce. To gather more insights on the current use and potential impact of Learning 2.0, IPTS conducted an exploratory study on the use of social media applications in formal Education and Training to enhance learning activities and promote innovation and inclusion. The study employed a triangulation of research methodologies, drawing on a literature review, a collection of 250 cases, 16 in-depth case studies and an expert workshop. This article presents and discusses the main findings of this study. The evidence gathered suggests, among others, that Learning 2.0 approaches require and facilitate technological, pedagogical and organisational innovation and can thus contribute to the modernisation of European Education and Training institutions deemed necessary for facing the challenges of the 21st century.

Keywords: Learning 2.0, Web 2.0, social media, learning communities, school education, teacher training, innovation, inclusion, modernization.

1 Introduction

Over the last few years, "Web 2.0" or "social media" applications have seen unprecedented take up, changing the way people access, manage and exchange knowledge, and the way they connect and interact [1]. This trend is accompanied by the emergence of structurally different learning styles, especially among young people. From an educator's point of view, social media applications are extremely versatile and offer flexible and dynamic learning opportunities that are often more appealing and engaging than traditional learning arrangements. They have therefore considerable potential for supporting and facilitating learning processes.

However, as social media is a recent phenomenon, take up in formal Education and Training (E&T) is still in an experimental phase. While the internet in general and

---

[*] The views expressed in this article are purely those of the authors and may not in any circumstances be regarded as stating an official position of the European Commission.

social media in particular are being used outside E&T institutions to supplement, complement and enhance learning and training [2, 3], very little evidence is available on the ways in which social media are used within formal E&T.

To gather evidence on the current use of social media applications in formal E&T and to assess their potential for promoting innovation and inclusion, the Institute of Prospective Technological Studies (IPTS)[1], in collaboration with the European Commission DG Education and Culture, launched a research project in 2008 on "Learning 2.0 – the Impact of Web 2.0 Innovations on Education and Training in Europe". This project – and its twin study on informal learning [4] – collect a vast resource of evidence using different sources and strategies, and synthesizing evidence generated along different research lines using triangulation. The methodological framework for the assessment included desk-based research using available studies, reports and statistics [5]; a stakeholder consultation combined with an assessment of cases documented in the research literature, which served to set up a database of 250 Learning 2.0 projects [6]; the in-depth study of 16 promising cases: a set of 8 cases promoting innovation [7], and a set of 8 cases targeting groups at risk of exclusion [8]; and a validation workshop in which 20 external experts reviewed the research results [9]. All findings are synthesized in a final report [10].

This article will discuss, based on the findings of the research project and in the light of recent evidence on the use of social media outside formal E&T, the potential of Learning 2.0 for promoting innovation in formal E&T. It will present general tendencies concerning the take-up of social media (Section 2) and the emerging changes in learning patterns and styles (Section 3). The current landscape of Learning 2.0 in Europe, as it emerges from the study, will be outlined and major impact areas will be pointed out (Section 4). Eight Learning 2.0 cases will be discussed, with a view to identifying areas for innovation in E&T (Section 5). Some of the more salient challenges to the deployment of social medial in formal E&T, as they emerge from the research, are presented in Section 6, and finally, Section 7 outlines the key findings of the study.

2 Learning via the Internet and Social Media Outside Formal E&T

The internet has become an important source of information for significant parts of the European population [2]: 60% of the EU27 population (aged 16 to 74) uses the internet at least once a week; 48% uses it every day; 51% use it for finding information about goods and services; 33% for seeking health-related information; and 31% for reading online newspapers and magazines. In 2009, an average of 31% of the EU27 population (aged 16 to 74) already used the internet for seeking information with the purpose of learning, up 8% from 2007. This figure shows little variation across Member States, ranging between 20% and 50% in the majority of European countries.

These data indicate that outside formal E&T, the internet is being used widely, all across Europe, also for learning purposes. This finding is confirmed by the recent

---

[1] The Institute for Prospective Technological Studies (IPTS) is one of the seven research institutes that make up the European Commission's Joint Research Centre.

OECD evaluation of PISA data [3]. However, only 5% of Europeans use the internet for doing online courses, with little variation across EU Member States [2], Additionally, while more than 80% of 15 year-olds in most OECD countries use computers frequently at home, the majority do not use them at school [3].

With the emergence of social media applications, which encourage more active and interactive internet usage, informal learning, based on knowledge exchange and online collaboration is further strengthened [4]. Eurostat data, collected in 2008, confirm that many Europeans are making use of the opportunities offered by social media to facilitate communication and knowledge exchange [11]: 35% of the EU27 population (ranging from 23% in Bulgaria to 50% in Finland) and 57% of those using the internet (ranging from 33% in Ireland to 75% in Portugal), used it for "advanced communication services", i.e. writing or reading blogs, posting messages, instant messaging, telephone/video calls. This figure rises to 73% of the group aged 16 to 24 as a whole and to 83% of the internet users of this age group. Instant messaging (35% of all internet users and 67% of those aged 16 to 24); online networking activities (26% and 50%); reading weblogs (25% and 39%); and internet telephoning (26% and 35%) range highest.

Young people's internet use is focused on communication, information and entertainment: according to OECD data [3], more than 60% of students aged 15 frequently use their computers for e-mail or chatting (69%) and looking up information about people, things or ideas on the Internet (61%). 58% of young people use the internet to download music, 54% to play games, 41% to download software and 37% to collaborate with a group or team. Young people see the internet as an opportunity to learn from others, engage with people in similar situations and also as a direct source of expert support [12].

Another trend supporting the use of social media for knowledge exchange, information and learning purposes is reflected in the high usage of internet sites and services to exchange audiovisual content. In 2009, 61% of European internet users and 81% of internet users aged 16 to 24 used the internet for leisure activities related to obtaining and sharing audiovisual content, e.g. downloading/playing music, films and/or games (67% of internet users, 78% of those 16 to 24); listening to web radios or watching web television (43% of internet users, 65% of those aged 16-24), or uploading and sharing self-created content (19% of internet users, 32% aged 16 to 24).

Given that social media applications and services have only recently become available, these high usage rates indicate a surprisingly rapid take up among large parts of the European population.

3 Changing Learning Styles

Various studies indicate that young people who grew up surrounded by digital media tend to display significantly different learning styles from previous generations. Several terms have been used to describe this generation of learners, such as "Digital Natives" [12, 13], "The Digital Generation"[14], "Net Generation" [15], "Millenials" [16], "New Millennium Learners" [17] or even "Neomillennial Learners" [18, 19]. They have also been dubbed "The Instant Messaging Generation" [20], "The Gamer Generation" [21] for the obvious reference to video games, or even "Homo zappiens" [22] for their ability to control different sources of digital information simultaneously.

While not all young people display the "typical" properties of NML and there are profound discrepancies between different OECD or EU countries and within different countries, reflecting prevailing digital divides (cf. [17]), there is a general consensus among researchers that learning styles have been changing in parallel with the growing use of technology in daily life, and that these changes become particularly apparent when looking at young people, i.e. those who are typically students in upper secondary and tertiary education. Young people (aged 16-24) are the most frequent internet users [14]: 73% of them use the internet every day [2] and, for example, in the UK, 75% of them claim they could not live without the internet [12].

Learning styles in this cohort are shaped by the ubiquity, accessibility and ease of use of digital resources [16, 23]. Young people are continuously connected with their peers and "always on" [12, 15]. They select and appropriate technologies for their own personal learning needs, mixing and matching different tools and capitalising on social networks [24].

Compared to previous generations of learners, they tend to think more visually and in a non-linear manner; they practice multitasking and give preference to multimedia environments [16, 18, 19]. In learning environments they are easily bored, need a variety of stimuli not to get distracted, are impatient and expect instant feedback and rewards [18]. They are social, team-spirited and engaged, goal-oriented and pragmatic [15, 23].

In parallel with changing living and learning patterns, the skills and competences needed in a knowledge society have also changed significantly. To come to terms with the information overload of the digital era, learners (need to) employ learning strategies that involve searching, sieving, managing, re-combining, validating and contextualizing information [25]. Thus, three sets of transversal skills become more and more important [25-27]: (1) reflective, critical and evaluation skills; (2) collaboration and communication skills [28] and (3) innovation, creativity, and learning to learn.

Social media are a paradigm example of internet applications that promote these key competences and, at the same time, require, reflect and respond to young people's learning styles. Furthermore, as there is evidence of the fact that the use of technology in primary and secondary schools can enhance student motivation [29] and performance [3], using social media in formal E&T appears to be a promising strategy for facilitating and improving learning opportunities. While Learning 2.0 is not yet common practice in formal E&T, some institutions are experimenting with social media tools, as will be shown in the next section.

4 The Landscape of Learning 2.0

To better understand the current use of social media in formal E&T, 250 cases, all over Europe were gathered in a database [6]. This case collection exemplifies and illustrates the diversity and scope of Learning 2.0 approaches in formal E&T in Europe and yields some valuable insights on ways in which social media are and can be employed in formal E&T to promote innovative learning and teaching approaches. In particular, the collection provides evidence on educational settings; user groups; tools used; objectives targeted and activities carried out (Section 4.1) and indicates key impact areas of Learning 2.0 (Section 4.2).

It has to be noted, however, that this sample of initiatives is by no means representative of the Learning 2.0 landscape in Education and Training and is biased by the research focus; the collection method (drawing on a literature review and stakeholder consultation); and the fact that, due to the novelty of Learning 2.0, only very few trials had been documented and assessed at the time of data collection. Furthermore, since data collection took place in 2008 and the Learning 2.0 landscape is rapidly evolving, some of the cases are no longer active or have changed focus and approach.

4.1 The Learning 2.0 Case Collection

Due to the focus of the data collection, the case collection contains a sample of initiatives that are mainly set in formal E&T and aim to prepare students for degrees and certifications (194 cases, 82% of cases). However, a number of Learning 2.0 cases taking place in non-formal (41 cases, 17% of cases) and informal learning contexts (47 cases, 20% of cases) are also included.

The sample includes a good distribution of educational settings: higher education institutions (40%), secondary schools (39%), vocational training institutions (15% on tertiary level; 17% on secondary level) and primary schools (27%), and, to a lesser extent, adult training centres (13%). More than one third of all Learning 2.0 takes place in more than one institution and 15% of all cases report that they address more than one type of learning in parallel. These findings suggest that Learning 2.0 practices are currently being explored as means to overcome the traditional division between different education settings and transcend institutional barriers.

The primary users of Learning 2.0 applications are students (78% of cases) and their teachers/trainers (39%). However the sample shows that social media tools are also being used to open up formal E&T to hard(er)-to-reach groups (35%) and third parties (36% of cases), including parents (9%), external experts (14%), and the general public (12%). Adult learners (11%) are less targeted and involved in the Learning 2.0 initiatives gathered for this study. It should be noted that 40% of the initiatives target more than one user group simultaneously. This result seems to confirm that Learning 2.0 strategies lend themselves to opening up institutional learning to the outside world, to bridging different learning contexts and to involving different actors.

The collection of cases gathered shows that blogs (41%) and social networking (40%) applications are the most frequently applied tools. They are followed by discussion platforms (29%), wikis (29%), and photo- and video-sharing services (23%). Podcasts and vodcasts (14%), folksonomies and/or social tagging (13%), and virtual realities (5%) are less frequently used. Other tools include a wide variety of applications ranging from dedicated tools for E&T, like Learning Management Systems (e.g. Moodle), Virtual Learning Environments, and ePortfolios, to more generic ones including serious games, microblogging applications (e.g. Twitter) and voice-over-IP applications (e.g. Skype).

The objectives, and the activities which aim to achieve them, are many and varied. The three most frequently named objectives are: (1) developing new ways of learning using social software tools (68% of all cases), (2) improving collaboration amongst actors (57%) and increasing the motivation and thus the participation of learners in the Learning 2.0 experience (49%). Further objectives addressed by Learning 2.0 activities comprise the improvement of (peer) support for learning (30%), accessibility of learning (24%), learning results (24%), self-directed learning activities and skills (24%), the connection of learners with society (21%), and personalisation (15%) and management of learning (13%). Almost 90% of cases address multiple objectives through the application of social media applications in learning and teaching in Education and Training.

Concerning the way in which social media tools are employed, most of the cases are predominantly multi-activity based (70%). The majority of cases target complex, innovative and integrated activities, like creating and sharing knowledge (73%) or collaborating and interacting (67%). Basic activities, like accessing and delivering information (25% and 10% respectively), are far less frequently mentioned and seem to be subsidiary to the main focus of the case activity. Only 10% of all entries include activities such as assessment, evaluation and accreditation.

4.2 Key Impact Areas of Learning 2.0

The case collection provides a snapshot of a rich and diverse landscape. The take up of social media for learning is a multidimensional and dynamic phenomenon, undergoing constant evolution, which makes it difficult to model all activities that emerge in this area in a common framework. However, at the same time, some common and differentiating features become visible when we look at the landscape as it set out by the case collection.

Considering the 250 case descriptions [6] and drawing on research evidence [5], five general approaches to using social media in formal educational settings can be discerned. Although these different perspectives are partly overlapping and often jointly targeted, each dimension indicates different strategies and objectives related to using social media in E&T (see Figure 1).

1. (L) Learning: In many cases, social media tools are used as scaffolds to implement pedagogical strategies intended to support, facilitate, enhance and improve learning processes. As the cases gathered illustrate, Learning 2.0 is very versatile in accommodating diverse learning needs and preferences by addressing different sensory channels; supplying more engaging (multimedia) learning environments [30, 31]; enabling personalised ways of retrieving, managing and transforming information [32, 33]; equipping learners and teachers with a variety of adaptable tools [34]; and integrating students into collaborative networks that facilitate the joint production of content and offer peer support and assistance [35]. They thus allow for the implementation of learning strategies that are tailored to each learner's individual preferences, interests and needs and provide learning environments which are better suited to accommodating individual differences, supporting differentiation in heterogeneous learner groups.

2. (A) Achieving: Learning 2.0 approaches can be used as a means to make learning more effective and increase academic achievement [36-40]. Social media supply learners and teachers with a wide variety of didactical and methodological tools that can be fitted to the respective learning objectives and to the individuals' needs with a positive effect on their performance and achievement [40]. Research evidence gathered from some of the cases studied suggests that Learning 2.0 strategies can successfully be used to enhance individual motivation [31], improve learner participation and foster social and learning skills [41]. They can further contribute to the development of problem-solving and higher order cognitive skills like reflection and metacognition [42], increase self-directed learning skills and enable individuals to better develop and realize their personal potential [38].

3. (N) Networking: In many cases, often in addition to other objectives, social media applications are used as communication and networking tools among students or teachers and between students and teachers [43-46]. The examples studied demonstrate that social networking tools (1) support the exchange of knowledge and material [34]; (2) facilitate community building, providing teachers and learners with social environments that offer assistance and (emotional) support [47]; and (3) provide platforms for collaboration, allowing teachers and learners to jointly develop (educational) content [34].

4. (D) Embracing Diversity: In a number of cases, social media applications are used as a means of integrating learning into a wider community, reaching out to virtually meet people from other age-groups and socio-cultural backgrounds, linking to experts, researchers or practitioners in a certain field of study and thus opening up alternative channels for gaining knowledge and enhancing skills. In this perspective, Learning 2.0 enables students to broaden their horizons, and collaborate across borders, language barriers, and institutional walls [48], thus anchoring their learning experiences in a rich world of diverse cultures, traditions, languages and opinions.

5. (S) Opening up to Society: Many educational institutions appropriate social media as an opportunity for facilitating access by current and prospective students to information, making institutional processes more transparent and facilitating the distribution of educational material [43-45]. In some cases, social media tools are used to encourage the involvement of third parties like parents, prospective future employers or external experts; or to promote inter-institutional cooperation [49].

Together these five approaches to Learning 2.0 give rise to new areas for innovation in learning, to innovative lands for Learning, or "iLANDS" (Figure 1). These different uses of social media indicate that Learning 2.0 approaches can facilitate innovation in E&T in a variety of ways. Technological innovation is fostered, across all fields, by making new tools available and re-shaping the use of available tools though different educational uses. Organisational innovation can be supported in particular by using social media to open up E&T institutions to society and to allow

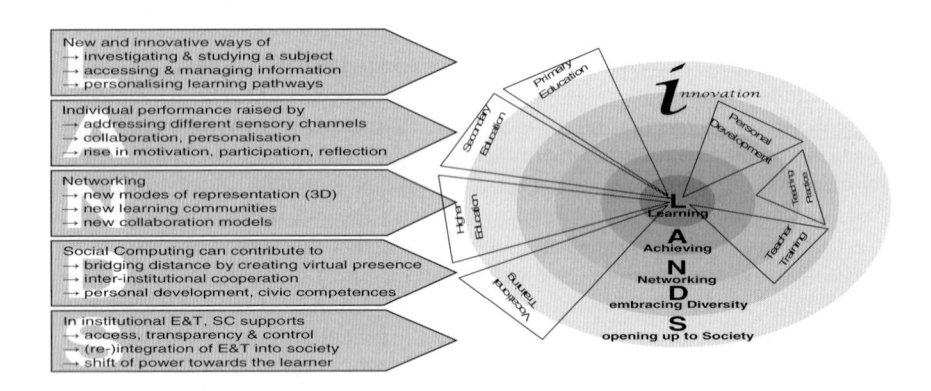

Fig. 1. iLANDS for innovation in learning

for learner and teacher collaboration across geographic and institutional boundaries. Most significantly, however, Learning 2.0 approaches facilitate pedagogical innovation by enabling the implementation of pedagogical approaches and strategies that put the learner at the centre of the learning process and promote collaboration, self-regulated learning and personalization and can contribute to empowering the learner.

5 Learning 2.0 Practices for Facilitating Innovation in E&T

To validate and refine these findings, eight cases were selected for in-depth study with a view to assessing *how* Learning 2.0 approaches facilitate innovation in formal E&T [7]. Another set of eight cases, that cannot be discussed in depth here, was selected to assess how Learning 2.0 approaches can promote inclusion (cf. [8]). The main objective of the case assessment was to provide evidence on good practice, to identify success factors and obstacles, and to reach a better understanding of the innovative potential of Learning 2.0. The cases were selected from the database on the basis of their richness and variety and also the extent to which they could be comprehensively assessed. Data collection included key informant interviews; user surveys with the aid of a self-administered questionnaire; automated data collection from the platforms and services used; and, where possible, observation and focus groups.

5.1 Case Overview

The cases selected for in-depth study address a variety of audiences and learning objectives. *Welker's Wikinomics* is a collaborative online learning environment which supports classroom teaching in a secondary school in Zurich, Switzerland. *SecondReiff* was a project at the RWTH Aachen University in Germany which used a 3D space in the virtual world SecondLife for the study of architecture. *Protovoulia* is a Greek 'umbrella' site for innovative online services for teachers and pupils in Greek primary and secondary schools. *Web 2.0 Knowledge Management at IBM* is an example of workplace learning, combining a variety of social media tools. *KooL* employs an integrated, collaborative online environment for English language learning at a vocational school for glass professionals in Rheinbach, Germany. The Elektro-Technologie-Zentrum *(ETZ)* Stuttgart *online community* uses an online learning platform that has been enhanced step-by-step with additional tools and features. *LeMill* is a web-service for the exchange of learning resources and materials among teachers. *Nettilukio*, an online upper secondary school, offers a comprehensive study programme for the Finnish University entrance qualification, using a learning platform, virtual classroom technology, wikis and blogs.[2]

As displayed in Table 1, the in-depth analysis of these cases identified several areas in which Learning 2.0 approaches facilitate the pedagogical, technological and organisational innovation in formal E&T deemed necessary to modernize E&T [50].

---

[2] Cf. Welker's Wikinomics: http://welkerswikinomics.wetpaint.com, Protovoulia: http://www.protovoulia.org/en/prwtovoulia.htm, IBM Knowledge Management: www.ibm.com/software/de/web20/, KooL: http://www.rheinfit.de/GlassProfessionals.htm, ETZ: http://community.etz-stuttgart.de, LeMill: http://lemill.net; Nettilukio: http://www.nettilukio.fi/fi/sisalto/nettilukio/06_in_english?n:selres=765612

Table 1. Overview of the Case Assessment (adapted from [7])

Case Contribution to Overall Findings '++' = strong contribution; '+' = moderate contribution; empty cells indicate no contribution	Welker's	SecondReiff	Protovoulia	IBM	KooL	ELKOnet	LeMill	Nettilukio
Technological Innovation								
Trend towards embedded or integrated solutions	+		++	++	++	++		
Near-future trends: Virtual worlds, mash-ups, integration		++		++				
Organisational Innovation								
New interfaces between formal & informal environments	++	+	++		+	+	+	+
Opening E&T organisations towards society	+		++	++	++			
Promoting institutional flexibility and openness	+		++		+		+	+
Pedagogical Innovation								
New ways of collaborative creation and exchange	++	++	++	++	++	+	++	+
New forms of communication among learners & teachers	++	++	++	++	+	++	++	++
More personalized and learner-centred environments	++	++	+	++	+			++
New forms of blended learning scenarios	++	++	++	+	++	+		++
Motivational advantages; learner's sense of ownership	++	++	+	++	++	+		+

5.2 Technological Innovation

As the appropriation of social media tools for learning purposes is advancing, certain trends indicating technological innovation in E&T are becoming apparent:

Trend towards embedded or integrated solutions vs. isolated tools: In most of the cases studied, a trend from the use of isolated tools (e.g. stand-alone wikis or blogs) towards integrated solutions (e.g. blogs and wikis embedded in learning management systems) was visible. The developmental line of social media in educational settings seems to go from more unstructured and creative tools in the past towards more structured and organised environments, which is also a current trend for social media applications in general. Some disadvantages of isolated tools could be detected and some additional advantages of integrated solutions can be reported, concerning e.g. navigation processes and data transfer.

Virtual worlds and mash-ups are trends for the near future; the extended integration of external social communities and tools is emerging: Two of the cases studied already use virtual worlds. In the SecondReiff project, SecondLife is used as the main learning environment and at IBM, virtual worlds are used within the context of research and experimental development. Another trend expected for the near future is that there will be flexible individual combinations of functions from different applications (mash-ups). Several project managers of different case studies plan to improve their initiatives by integrating external social communities like Facebook and content of other external social media environments like del.icio.us, Flickr or YouTube. The latter tools are seen as especially rich resource databases for learning material that could be integrated into different teaching and learning scenarios.

5.3 Organisational Innovation

The cases studied demonstrate that the implementation of Learning 2.0 strategies both requires and facilitates organisational innovation.

New interfaces emerge between different learning environments and settings: The case assessment shows that, in many cases, the limitations of formal learning were transcended when the classroom was extended to become a virtual learning environment, accessible at all times and places. However, they also show that, to ensure the sustainability of these new virtual learning spaces, interfaces between different learning settings need to be well-defined; the tools employed must be fitted to learners' needs and course requirements; and assessment and certification issues need to be addressed. E&T organisations need to be open to adapting their institutional framework to these changes and must actively engage in embedding Learning 2.0 in their organisational structure and culture.

Opening E&T organisations up to society: In several of the cases, it was outlined that social media tools can be used effectively to open windows from the closed environment of formal E&T to the outside world, allowing learners to pursue new ways of accessing information and gaining knowledge, and linking the subject content back to real life experiences. This impact can be transferred from the project to the institutional level by implementing similar tools and elements in the organisation as a whole.

Promoting institutional flexibility and openness: Learning 2.0 projects can help E&T institutions to implement more open and dynamic structures and can support changes in organisational culture. The cases studied indicate that successful experiences with Learning 2.0 projects within an educational organisation tend to lead to more heterarchical management processes, which further improve organisational flexibility.

5.4 Pedagogical Innovation

The main strength and the greatest innovation potential of Learning 2.0 lies in facilitating pedagogical innovation, i.e. in transforming learning and teaching approaches in such a way that learning goals can better be addressed and achieved. In particular, Learning 2.0 facilitates pedagogical innovation by giving rise to:

New ways of collaborative creation and exchange of learning content and metadata: Learning content is not delivered in a top-down approach as in traditional (e-)Learning environments, but generated, modified, commented and rated by the learners themselves. Different kinds of user-generated content (text, pictures, sound, videos, etc.) can be combined, allowing for creative and diverse forms of expression.

New forms of communication among learners and teachers/trainers: The different social media tools each come with new forms of communication between users. Some tools explicitly promote new communication structures and processes (e.g. virtual classrooms and meetings), while for others, new communication structures are an accompanying phenomenon (e.g. commenting in blogs, self-presentation and user-tagging in communities, commenting and rating in content-sharing tools).

More personalized and learner-centred environments; individual documentation of competencies; e-portfolios; personal learning plans and learning diaries: Social media tools support self-presentation and thereby put more focus on the individual learner than traditional web-based learning management systems. Social media tools support a more playful and experimental approach to learning, allowing learners to present themselves and their insights in original ways. Personal blogs can be used as individual homepages, which can be used for setting up learning plans and diaries, for showcasing work and documenting competences, and as a personal repository, containing all links and resources frequently consulted for learning and leisure.

New forms of blended learning scenarios (formal/informal; classroom/distance; intra-/extra-institutional; mixed learning scenarios and pedagogical approaches): By its very nature, social media support informal learning processes. Consequently, in the eight cases studied, more informal aspects of learning are integrated into a formal learning situation. Social media tools can offer new ways for blended learning, implementing mixed classroom/home learning scenarios. They also support new pedagogical approaches.

Motivational advantages through active, enjoyable, discovery-based learning approaches and learners' sense of ownership of produced content: Social media tools support more active learning processes and support the learner's sense of ownership of content, which in turn encourages motivation. In all eight case studies, motivational aspects have been stressed by the project organisers and most learners have reported high motivation. A moderating variable has been the digital literacy of the user. Low digital literacy is related to low motivation to use new ICT-based tools.

6 Challenges, Barriers and Bottlenecks

The following technical, pedagogical and organisational bottlenecks were identified in both the study and at the expert workshop [9], which may hinder the full deployment of Learning 2.0 in E&T institutions in Europe:

Inclusion & equity: There is evidence that the introduction of digital technologies in homes and schools can serve to reinforce and reproduce existing inequalities in the education system [3, 51, 52]. Accessibility constitutes a major obstacle to equal opportunities and remains a key problem for inclusion. Differences in the necessary competences and skills, which are correlated with students' economic, cultural and social capital, affect students' opportunities to benefit from technology use in schools, and account for a "second digital divide" [3]. Additionally, differences in familiarity with social media in particular, may constitute another type of barrier, leading to a possible "participation divide" [53]. Therefore, to benefit from the advantages of Learning 2.0, equal access to these tools and the necessary skills for using them resourcefully have to be ensured.

Advanced digital competence: Learning 2.0 strategies require the confident and critical use of ICT and an informed and critical attitude towards interactive media and digital information – especially concerning its safety, security and reliability. Adolescents particularly often lack these skills [46, 52, 54]. Teachers need assistance in supplying their students with the necessary advanced digital skills to safely use social media environments [46].

Safety and privacy concerns: Social media raises important issues in relation to identity, trust, reputation and privacy [46, 52, 54]. The risks arising from using open online environments are a bottleneck for deploying the full range of social media approaches in educational institutions. Particular risks associated with the uncritical use of social networking services by adolescents and young adults arise in connection with self-destructive behaviour, cyberbullying and online grooming. Additionally, advertising and spamming might pose a threat to the use of social media with younger learners [52, 55]. Educators need to make sure that the identity of their learners is protected; that rules for conduct are implemented and adhered to; and that intellectual property rights are respected.

Special needs: While supporting different learning paces and cognitive styles, thus generally empowering learners, Learning 2.0 also risks creating and increasing difficulties for students with physical or cognitive disabilities [56], or special learning needs [57]. For example, text-based collaboration and knowledge building activities with wikis and blogs can disadvantage dyslectic students [57]. However, in these cases, due to the richness of social media, alternative tools can be chosen that accommodate these differences and mediate the inclusion of learners with special needs [56].

Pedagogical skills: Educators' confidence in and experiences with social media services is one of the main barriers to exploiting them within E&T [46, 58]. Also at university level, lecturers' lack of appropriate competencies is seen as one of the reasons for delay in deployment of the opportunities offered by social media [59]. The integration of technology in classroom teaching is hampered by the absence of incentives to use technology and get involved in innovation; the dominant culture in the teaching profession; a lack of personal experience with technology-enhanced teaching; and a lack of vision [17]. A recent online survey of teachers in Europe, which had almost 10,000 responses, indicates that while 62% of teachers declare having received training in innovative pedagogies, only 36% have received training in how to use ICT in the classroom [60]. Initial teacher training and continuous professional development and support must be put in place to assist teachers and trainers in seizing the opportunities offered by social media.

Uncertainty: Social media is a recent phenomenon that underlies continuous change and transformation. As a consequence, many key issues relevant for sustained deployment of Learning 2.0 in E&T have not yet been addressed or solved adequately. In particular, uncertainties arise concerning the future development and availability of current applications and services; the reliability of user-produced content; suitable assessment and certification strategies; and valid pedagogical concepts and methods for learning with social media [43, 46].

Requirements for institutional change: The appropriation of social media in formal education requires schools to re-evaluate their role in society as knowledge providers. New ways to support teachers, learners and administrators are needed, which will challenge existing power structures. Resistance to change may cause E&T institutions not to take an active role in deploying promising Learning 2.0 strategies.

7 Conclusions

Learning 2.0 both requires and facilitates technological, pedagogical and organisational innovation in formal E&T.

Learning 2.0 strategies give rise to *technological innovation* in E&T by making new tools available and re-shaping the use of available tools though different educational uses. The deployment of Learning 2.0 in formal E&T can furthermore contribute to fostering *organisational innovation*. Social media allows E&T institutions to create learning environments that are transparent and open to society, accessible at all times and places and accommodate all individuals involved in and affected by formal E&T. Social media also enables educational institutions to intensify their collaboration with other organisations, across borders, language barriers, and sectors. Learning 2.0 can thus contribute to making educational organisations more dynamic, flexible and open.

Most importantly, however, Learning 2.0 promotes *pedagogical innovation* by encouraging teaching and learning processes that are based on personalization, self-directed learning and collaboration. Social media increase the accessibility and availability of learning content; provide new formats for knowledge dissemination, acquisition and management; allow for the production of dynamic learning resources and environments of high quality and interoperability; embed learning in more engaging and activating multimedia environments; and equip learners and teachers with versatile tools for knowledge exchange and collaboration.

However, to seize the opportunities offered by Learning 2.0, technological change has to go hand in hand with changes in teaching methods and organizational processes. Additionally, barriers to access must be removed for all learners. Digital competences in general and the ability to competently and critically use social media in particular need to be fostered. E&T institutions need to provide an adequate infrastructure and actively support the implementation of Learning 2.0; teachers need to be equipped with the necessary skills and privacy and security concerns must be addressed.

References

1. Ala-Mutka, K., Broster, D., Cachia, R., Centeno, C., Feijóo, C., Haché, A., Kluzer, S., Lindmark, S., Lusoli, W., Misuraca, G., Pascu, C., Punie, Y., Valverde, J.-A.: The Impact of Social Computing on the EU Information Society and Economy. In: European Commission - Joint Research Centre - Institute for Prospective Technological Studies, Seville (2009)
2. EUROSTAT: i2010 Benchmarking indicators 2009 (2010)
3. OECD-CERI: Are the New Millennium Learners Making the Grade? Technology Use and Educational Performance in PISA. Centre for Educational Research and Innovation. OECD (2010)
4. Ala-Mutka, K.: Learning in Informal Online Networks and Communities. European Commission - Joint Research Centre - Institute for Prospective Technological Studies, Seville (2010)

5. Redecker, C.: Review of Learning 2.0 Practices: Study on the Impact of Web 2.0 Innovations on Education and Training in Europe. European Commission - Joint Research Center -Institute for Porspective Technological Studies, Seville (2009)
6. Redecker, C.: Learning 2.0: Case Database. European Commission - Joint Research Center -Institute for Porspective Technological Studies, Seville (2009)
7. Heid, S., Fischer, T., Kugemann, W.F.: Good Practices for Learning 2.0: Promoting Innovation. An In-depth Study of Eight Learning 2.0 Cases. European Commission - Joint Research Center -Institute for Porspective Technological Studies, Seville (2009)
8. Cullen, J., Cullen, C., Hayward, D., Maes, V.: Good Practices for Learning 2.0: Promoting Inclusion. An In-depth Study of Eight Learning 2.0 Cases. European Commission - Joint Research Center -Institute for Porspective Technological Studies, Seville (2009)
9. Ala-Mutka, K., Bacigalupo, M., Kluzer, S., Pascu, C., Punie, Y., Redecker, C.: Learning 2.0: The Impact of Web2.0 Innovation on Education and Training in Europe. European Commission - Joint Research Centre - Institute for Prospective Technological Studies, Seville (2009)
10. Redecker, C., Ala-Mutka, K., Bacigalupo, M., Ferrari, A., Punie, Y.: Learning 2.0: The Impact of Web 2.0 Innovations on Education and Training in Europe. Final Report. European Commission - Joint Research Center -Institute for Porspective Technological Studies, Seville (2009)
11. EUROSTAT: Computers and the Internet in households and enterprises. Special module 2008: Individuals - Use of advanced services (2009)
12. Hulme, M.: Life Support: Young people's needs in a digital age. YouthNet Report (2009)
13. Prensky, M.: Digital Natives. Digital Immigrants On the Horizon 9 (2001)
14. European Commission: EU Youth Report 2009. European Commission, Brussels (2009)
15. Olbinger, D.G., Olbinger, J.L.: Educating the Net Generation. Educause (2005)
16. Pedró, F.: The New Millennium Learners: Challenging our Views on ICT and Learning. OECD-CERI (2006)
17. OECD-CERI: New Millennium Learners. Initial findings on the effects of digital technologies on school-age learners. In: OECD/CERI International Conference "Learning in the 21st Century: Research, Innovation and Policy" OECD (2008)
18. Baird, D.E., Fisher, M.: Neomillennial User Experience Design Strategies: Utilizing Social Networking Media to Support "Always On" Learning Styles. Journal of Educational Technology Systems 34, 5–32 (2006)
19. Dede, C.: 7-12: Planning for Neomillennial Learning Styles. Educause Quarterly 28, 7–12 (2005)
20. Lenhart, A., Rainie, L., Lewis, O.: Teenage Life Online: The Rise of Instant-Message Generation and the Internet's Impact on Friendship and Family Relationships. Pew Internet and American Life Project, Washington, D.C (2001)
21. Carstens, A., Beck, J.: Get Ready for the Gamer Generation. TechTrends 49, 22–25 (2005)
22. Veen, W.: A New Force for Change: Homo Zappiens. The Learning Citizen 7, 5–7 (2003)
23. Lam, I., Ritzen, M.: Tools and Pedagogies that Fit the Ne(x)t Generation of Students. In: EDEN Annual Conference, Lisbon, Portugal (2008)
24. Conole, G., de Laat, M., Dillon, T., Darby, J.: Disruptive technologies, pedagogical innovation: What's new Findings from an in-depth study of students' use and perception of technology. Computers & Education 50, 511–524 (2008)
25. Siemens, G.: Knowing Knowledge (2006)
26. European Council: Recommendation of the European Parliament and the Council of 18 December 2006 on key competences for lifelong learning. European Council, Brussels (2006)

27. Owen, M., Grant, L., Sayers, S., Facer, K.: Social software and learning. Futurelab Opening Education Reports (2006)
28. Rudd, T., Sutch, D., Facer, K.: Towards new learning networks. Futurelab Opening Education Reports (2006)
29. Balanskat, A.: Study of the impact of technology in primary schools. Synthesis report. STEPS project. EUN, Brussels (2009)
30. Witte, S.: That's Online Writing, Not Boring School Writing: Writing with Blogs and the Talkback Project. Journal of Adolescent & Adult Literacy 51, 92–96 (2007)
31. De Freitas, S.: Learning in Immersive Worlds. A review of game-based learning. JISC e-Learning Programme (2007)
32. Vuorikari, R.: Folksonomies, Social Bookmarking and Tagging: State-of-the-Art. European Schoolnet and Insight observatory for new technologies and education (2007)
33. Baggetun, R., Barbara, W.: Self-Regulated Learning and Open Writing. European Journal of Education 41, 453–472 (2006)
34. Porto, S.: Disrupting the Technological Culture: A Faculty Perspective on the Impact of Web 2.0 in Online Education Practices. In: EDEN Annual Conference, Lisbon, Portugal (2008)
35. Laat, M.d.: Networked Learning. University of Southampton. Politieacademie - Police Academy of the Netherlands. PhD Thesis (2007)
36. Chang, C.K., Chen, G.D., Li, L.Y.: Constructing a community of practice to improve coursework activity. Computers & Education 50, 235–247 (2008)
37. Edirisingha, P., Salmon, G.: Pedagogical Models for Podcasts in Higher Education. In: EDEN Annual Conference, Naples, Italy (2007)
38. Evans, C.: The effectiveness of m-learning in the form of podcast revision lectures in higher education. Computers & Education 50, 491–498 (2008)
39. Cramer, K.M., Collins, K.R., Snider, D., Fawcett, G.: The virtual lecture hall: utilisation, effectiveness and student perceptions. British Journal of Educational Technology 38, 106–115 (2007)
40. Deal, A.: Podcasting. A Teaching with Technology White Paper. Teaching with Technology. Educause (2007)
41. Langhorst, E.: The Dixie Clicks: How a Blog about the Civil War Turned into a Runaway Hit. School Library Journal 52, 46–48 (2006)
42. Barth, M.: From e-Learning to the Acquirement of Competencies: Wiki-based Knowledge Management and Complex Problem Solving. In: EDEN Annual Conference, Naples, Italy (2007)
43. Franklin, T., van Harmelen, M.: Web 2.0 for Content for Learning and Teaching in Higher Education (2007)
44. Suhonen, M., Uimonen, J.: Media Centre for e-Learning - An Application for Implementing Effective and High Quality Learning. In: EDEN Annual Conference, Naples, Italy (2007)
45. Calvani, A., Bonaiuti, G., Fini, A., Ranieri, M.: Towards e-Learning 2.0: New Paths for Informal Learning and Lifelong Learning - an Application with Personal Learning Environments. In: EDEN Annual Conference, Naples, Italy (2007)
46. Childnet International: Young People and Social Networking Services. Childnet International Research Report (2008)
47. Keegan, H.: Social Software for Virtual Mobility: An Online Community of Practice-Based Learners. In: EDEN Annual Conference, Naples, Italy (2007)

48. Kuru, S., Nawojczyk, M., Niglas, K., Butkeviciene, E., Soylu, A.: Facilitating Cross-Border Self-directed Collaborative Learning: The iCamp Case. In: EDEN Annual Conference, Naples, Italy (2007)
49. Hodgkinson-Williams, C., Slay, H., Siebörger, I.: Developing communities of practice within and outside higher education institutions. British Journal of Educational Technology 39, 433–442 (2008)
50. European Commission: The use of ICT to support innovation and lifelong learning for all - A report on progress. Commission Staff Working Document (2008)
51. Green, H., Facer, K., Rudd, T., Dillon, P., Humphreys, P.: Personalisation and Digital Technologies. Futurelab Opening Education Report (2005)
52. Davies, T., Cranston, P.: Youth Work and Social Networking. Final Research Report. The National Youth Agency (2008)
53. Hargittai, E., Walejko, G.: The Participation Divide: Content Creation and Sharing in the Digital Age. Information. Communication & Society 11, 239–256 (2008)
54. Byron, T.: Safer Children in a Digital World. The Report of the Byron Review. Byron Review – Children and New Technology (2008)
55. Fielder, A., Gardner, W., Nairn, A., Pitt, J.: Fair Game? Assessing commercial activity on children's favourite websites and online environment. National Consumer Council and Childnet International (2007)
56. Bühler, C.: Fisseler: Accessible E-Learning and Educational Technology - Extending Learning Opportunities for People with Disabilities. In: International Conference of Interactive computer aided learning: EPortofolio and Quality in e-Learning (ICL 2007), Villach, Austria (2007)
57. Woodfine, B.P., Nunes, M.B., Wright, D.J.: Text-based synchronous e-learning and dyslexia: Not necessarily the perfect match! Computers & Education 50, 703–717 (2008)
58. European Commission: Learning, Innovation and ICT. In: Lessons learned by the ICT cluster Education & Training 2010 (2010)
59. Blin, F., Munro, M.: Why hasn't technology disrupted academics' teaching practices Understanding resistance to change through the lens of activity theory. Computers & Education 50, 475–490 (2008)
60. Cachia, R., Farrari, A., Kearney, C., Punie, Y., Van den Berghe, W., Wastiau, P.: Creativity in Schools in Europe: A Survey of Teachers. European Commission - Joint Research Center - Institute for Prospective Technological Studies, Seville (2009)

Extended Explicit Semantic Analysis for Calculating Semantic Relatedness of Web Resources

Philipp Scholl, Doreen Böhnstedt, Renato Domínguez García,
Christoph Rensing, and Ralf Steinmetz

Multimedia Communications Lab (KOM)
Technische Universität Darmstadt
Rundeturmstr. 10, 64283 Darmstadt, Germany
{scholl,boehnstedt,renato,rensing,ralf.steinmetz}@kom.tu-darmstadt.de
http://www.kom.tu-darmstadt.de

Abstract. Finding semantically similar documents is a common task in Recommender Systems. Explicit Semantic Analysis (ESA) is an approach to calculate semantic relatedness between terms or documents based on similarities to documents of a reference corpus. Here, usually Wikipedia is applied as reference corpus. We propose enhancements to ESA (called Extended Explicit Semantic Analysis) that make use of further semantic properties of Wikipedia like article link structure and categorization, thus utilizing the additional semantic information that is included in Wikipedia. We show how we apply this approach to recommendation of web resource fragments in a resource–based learning scenario for self–directed, on–task learning with web resources.

Keywords: Explicit Semantic Analysis, Semantic Relatedness, Wikipedia, Reference Corpus, Recommendation.

1 Introduction and Motivation

A common task in Information Retrieval is finding documents that are similar to a given document. *Similarity* in this context has been usually determined as a measure of term overlap that occurs in these documents [1]. However, in recent work, a more high–level measure called *semantic relatedness* that abstracts from the terminology used and aims towards a more semantic dimension, where the similarity between *concepts* of the underlying documents is taken into account.

This is especially useful as humans tend to focus the similarity of documents in concepts rather than in terms. Especially in domains where users need to find similar documents but do not exactly know the terminology, abstracting from terminology towards a more semantic measure can be applied.

One of those domains is the domain of Technology Enhanced Learning (TEL), where different audiences with different levels of knowledge exists. For example, novices tend to be not aware of terminology of the domain they are learning, whereas experts are able to communicate in a brief manner using the professional terminology. Further, in different stages of achieved expertise, different aspects of learning materials are important, giving either a broad overview or rather a very narrow scope of the learning domain.

Thus, for applications in TEL that support retrieval and recommendation of documents, being able to find semantically related documents is an essential task.

1.1 Crokodil

The scenario we address with this work is a research prototype for supporting self–directed, resource–based learning with web resources, *Crokodil* (a project based on ELWMS.KOM [2]). As the importance of the World Wide Web as a major source for knowledge acquisition has been growing steadily in the last decade, both specifically designed learning materials (e.g. information contained in Web Based Trainings or tutorials) and web resources that are not specifically intended to be used for learning (e.g. user generated content in blogs, wikis or forums) are available at a large scale.

Crokodil supports learners in finding, collecting and organizing these learning materials in a so–called *Knowledge Network* (KN). These KN are based on Semantic Networks [3], that represent knowledge in a graphical notation consisting of nodes and relations. In *Crokodil*, the learning materials are stored as nodes in the KN. A peculiarity is that often only a part of a web resource is relevant for the information needs of a learner. *Crokodil* allows saving only the needed fragments, furthermore called *snippets*.

A major challenge is supporting learners using *Crokodil* in finding learning materials that are relevant for their current information needs. Therefore, we propose a *recommender system* that helps learners finding related content from other learners by recommending snippets that are semantically related to those they recently added to their KN.

1.2 Snippets

In a user study [4], we evaluated — among other research questions — how learners select relevant content. The lab study served to examine how learners can be supported in organizing their learning processes with web resources by setting goals. During the study, participants were asked to collect learning materials from web resources, learn with the assembled information and take a performance test afterwards. The participants were instructed to collect the information from the web resources that they deemed to be relevant for their learning tasks, allowing them to select content in the *desired granularity*. Thus, we collected 1357 different snippets from 104 participants.

For comparing the properties of snippets with "normal" bookmarked web pages (as these serve a similar goal), we randomly crawled Delicious[1], a social bookmarking service that allows storing relevant URLs online, for a comparison corpus. We downloaded 1004 HTML pages thereof and, after stripping HTML–specific content like markup, compared them to the snippets gained from our study.

---
[1] http://delicious.com

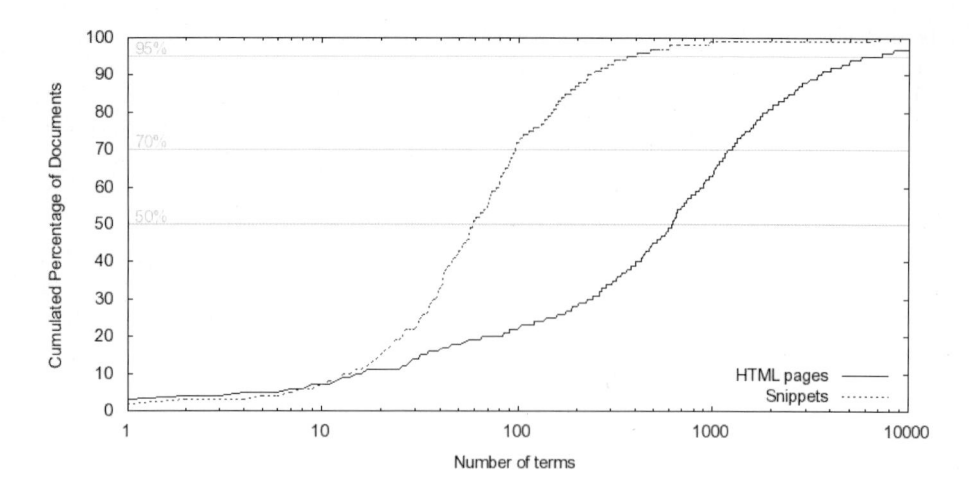

Fig. 1. Cumulated term counts of snippets in comparison with term counts of full web pages

The results (see fig. 1) show, that snippets differ from whole web resources in some accords:

- They mostly deal with a specific, well–defined domain, covering only one subject. Web pages, however, usually cover a lot more information.
- On average, snippets consist of 120 terms, whereas web pages consist of about 1600 terms.
- 70% of snippets are smaller than 100 terms, 70% of web pages are smaller than 1000 terms.

Based on observations in this analysis of snippets, we state the requirements an approach should have in order to generate content–based recommendations:

- In short snippets, there are only few significant terms. A larger context is not available, thus the algorithm will have to abstract from the term level.
- The algorithm should be stable and provide good results, no matter how long the different snippets are.
- The snippets may be about any topic. Thus, the algorithm should be able to infer over any generic knowledge domain.
- Learners should be able to inspect *why* two snippets are regarded as being semantically related. This allows the learners to analyze if the recommended item is really relevant in their current learning situation.

The remainder of this paper is organized as follows: in section 2, we give an overview of related work, map it with our requirements, and present the foundation of our work, Explicit Semantic Analysis (ESA). In section 3, we introduce our extensions to the basic ESA approach. Selected evaluations of our approach are presented in section 4. Eventually, we conclude in section 5 and give an outline for next steps and open issues.

2 Related Work

Most approaches to compare documents apply the vector space model (VSM) [1] in combination with the cosine similarity for calculating document similarity. Thus, approaches based on VSM have in common to quantify the syntactic overlap. Documents are represented by high–dimensional feature vectors derived from the terms used in the document. The similarity between two documents is modeled by the angle between the representing vectors. However, as the vectors are entirely based on syntactical features, i.e. the term occurrences in the document, VSM is not applicable in cases of documents that are semantically related but have little term overlap.

Further, in some scenarios similarity should not be expressed over terms but over the meaning of a document. For example, different documents written for or by differing audiences (e.g. beginners vs. experts) may be written using a different terminology, e.g. using synonyms or hypernyms. Although these documents describe the same semantic concepts, the term–based similarity will be rather low. This is called the *vocabulary gap* [5].

Therefore, there is a need to abstract from the terms used in a document towards a more semantic representation, meaning that similarity is not to be expressed via common terminology, but rather by usage of terminology in a common semantic context. As *similarity* is a term that is not really applicable to the semantic dimension, the term usually preferred is *semantic relatedness* [6]. In this work, we use the term *similarity* when a term–based measure is applied and *relatedness*, when a semantic measure is applied.

As semantic relatedness is a measure that is — at least — difficult to calculate with only the documents to compare, related approaches usually utilize additional information by employing *reference corpora* in order to provide additional general knowledge. In related work, many different corpora have been used. Most provide structured access to semantic properties of terms (e.g. WordNet, Roget's Thesaurus), whereas other corpora, like Wikipedia, represent the underlying semantics inherently in the documents they contain.

One of the most popular reference corpora is WordNet [7], a broad coverage lexical network of English words. WordNet provides networks of synsets that contain terms like nouns, verbs, adjectives and adverbs, each representing a lexical concept. The synsets are interlinked with a variety of relations (e.g. denoting homonymy, synonymy, etc.). Jiang and Conrath [8] combine an approach using WordNet with corpus statistics. They merge a content–based, node–centric information content approach with a node–distance, edge–centric approach and apply those to the WordNet noun synsets. According to [6], this approach performs better than others they compared. Another popular data source that has been used for calculating semantic relatedness is Roget's Thesaurus. Jarmasz and Szpakowicz [9] use it as a base to calculate *semantic distance* between terms based on the path length in the thesaurus graph. They convert the distance to semantic similarity by subtracting the path length from the maximum possible path length.

However, both corpora are well–structured and have to be manually serviced by experts. Roget's Thesaurus, for example, dates from 1805 (with an edition from 1911 in the public domain). Although general terminology is contained, the Thesaurus cannot keep up with the rapid evolution of knowledge nowadays.

Another approach that has gained momentum in the last years is Latent Semantic Analysis (LSA) [10]. LSA is an approach that uses a custom corpus of documents to abstract from the terminology used and derives inherent semantic concepts. So, with LSA, different terms that are used as synonyms or are cooccurring often are mapped into a single concept. Further, by mapping terms, the overall corpus dimensions may be reduced significantly, thus transforming the search space. This projection and reduction is achieved by applying a singular value decomposition on a corpus matrix and then truncating the least significant values. LSA, although being a stable approach that performs well, has some limitations regarding our requirements stated in section 1. First, the approach needs to be given the dimensions to reduce. This heavily depends on the topics of the documents that are present in the scenario. Second, the resulting concepts are sets of terms and are not easily readable by humans. Thus, we refrain from applying it to our scenario.

In recent research, the collaboratively edited, open encyclopedia Wikipedia has been increasingly used for information retrieval related tasks (e.g. [11], [12] and [13]). This is due to the sheer amount of articles available (over 1 Mio articles in the German version as of 2010), with each article representing a distinct *concept*. Additionally, Wikipedia provides further semantic information about the concepts described in articles, most notably links to related articles (*article links*) and a (mostly hierarchical) category structure (*category links*). Another criterion that makes use of Wikipedia for information retrieval suitable is that it is constantly updated to the current state of knowledge, e.g. new articles are added and old ones are adjusted accordingly.

WikiRelate! [11] is an approach that computes semantic relatedness between terms. Given two terms to analyze, WikiRelate! searches the Wikipedia article names (called *lemmata*) for the terms and calculates the distances between found articles based on the articles' contents and the category structure of Wikipedia. As it only supports computation of semantic relatedness between terms, this approach is not applicable to documents.

Kaiser et al. [14] introduce *conceptual contexts* of documents as linkage graphs that represents the document and its relations. Basically, they map the documents to compare to Wikipedia articles and apply a weighting function that determines the article's relatedness to neighbouring articles based on in– and outgoing article links. After removing all concepts that are only loosely related, they calculate the relatedness measure of the documents by computing the similarity of the graphs.

2.1 Explicit Semantic Analysis

A promising approach to calculating semantic relatedness named *Explicit Semantic Analysis (ESA)* [15] has been proposed by Gabrilovich and Markovitch.

Here, documents are not represented by occurring terms but by their similarity to concepts derived from Wikipedia articles. ESA is based on the assumption that in Wikipedia an article corresponds to a semantically distinct concept. Thus, by comparing documents to all articles in a Wikipedia corpus that has been pre–processed by tokenization, stemming, stop word removal and a term weight metric, a vector is obtained that contains a similarity value to each of the articles. This vector, called *semantic interpretation vectors*, abstracts from the actual term occurrences and thus represents a semantic dimension of that document. A major advantage of ESA is that semantic relatedness can be calculated for terms and documents alike, providing good and stable results for both modes [15].

Formally, the document collection is represented as a $n \times m$ Matrix M (called *semantic interpreter*), where n is the number of articles and m the number of occurring terms in the corpus. M contains (normalized) *tf–idf* document vectors of the articles. *tf–idf* is a commonly used measure of relevance of a term in relation to a corpus D, where the *term frequency* tf of term t_i for each document $d_j \in D$ and the *inverse document frequency* idf of all occurrences of term t_i are taken into account. For calculating the similarity between the document and the corpus, the *cosine similarity measure* (1) is employed. Analogously, two documents represented as semantic interpretation vectors can be easily compared by using cosine similarity again.

$$sim(d_i, d_j) = \cos(\phi) = \frac{d_i \cdot d_j}{|d_i| * |d_j|} \quad (1)$$

Gabrilovich and Markovitch show that ESA outperforms other approaches like WikiRelate!, WordNet, Roget's Thesaurus and LSA [15]. Kaiser et al. [14] see ESA as a competitor to their approach using conceptual contexts, but they do not compare their approach to ESA.

Although ESA is commonly used with Wikipedia as reference corpus, it is not necessarily restricted to it. In theory, all textual corpora that follow the structure of providing unique documents (i.e. covering different topics) could be applied. Gabrilovich and Markovitch [15] apply ESA to a corpus derived from the Open Directory Project themselves, mapping concepts to the categories of the directory. Notably, Anderka and Stein [16] dismiss the hypothesis that the reference corpus needs to be semantically well–structured, i.e. semantic concepts are only described by one document. They show that ESA with the Reuters newswire corpus and even random corpora may achieve comparable results to ESA with Wikipedia. Still, as Wikipedia provides distinct semantic concepts as labels (i.e. the lemmata of the articles), it is better for humans to interpret and understand the relatedness between documents.

In general, ESA fulfills the requirements as a foundation for our recommendation algorithm stated in section 1. ESA can cope with documents of arbitrary size, has the backing of a broad knowledge base (i.e. Wikipedia) and performs well compared to other approaches. Still, it leaves space for improvements, especially as far as utilization of additional semantic information from the Wikipedia corpus goes. Thus, in the next section, we will present our adjustments to ESA.

3 Our Approach

As described above, Explicit Semantic Analysis (ESA) only makes use of the article information that Wikipedia contains, i.e. only analyzes the term → article allocation. However, Wikipedia provides a wealth of semantic information, namely the links between articles and the categorization structure of articles. ESA neglects this available information completely.

Thus, we introduce *eXtended Explicit Semantic Analysis* (XESA), an approach that semantically enriches the interpretation vectors obtained from ESA, which has been described in section 2. In detail, we present three different approaches to extending ESA, one utilizing the article link graph of Wikipedia, one using the category structure and one approach that combines those two. We expect these approaches to perform better than ESA, as they enrich ESA by additional semantic information.

However, before presenting the XESA extensions, we revisit ESA formalizing our approach to implementing it:

- First, we preprocess a Wikipedia dump[2] (in our work we use the dump of the German Wikipedia from June 2009) with stemming, stop–word removal, *tf–idf* calculation and normalization.
- Then, we aggregate all article vectors into the semantic interpreter matrix M with the shape $n \times m$, where n is the number of articles and m the number of terms.
- For each document d that is to be compared, the same preprocessing steps have to be executed, so that we receive the document vector v_d with the form $1 \times m$, where m is the number of terms.
- As all document vectors are normalized, we get the interpretation vector i_{esa} that represents the cosine similarity of v_d with all article vectors of M simply by applying the inner product (2) with transposed M.
- Finally, the result is the interpretation vector i_{esa} with the dimensions $1 \times n$.

$$i_{esa} = v_d \cdot M^T \qquad (2)$$

This interpretation vector i_{esa} is the foundation for all further approaches. The basic idea is to enrich this interpretation vector with additional information derived from semantic information that can be extracted from the Wikipedia corpus.

3.1 Utilization of the Article Graph

On average, Wikipedia articles link to 30 other articles. These links can be interpreted as semantic relationships to other concepts. For example, the German article for *General Relativity* links to other articles *Space*, *Time* and *Gravitation*. Thus, there is an obvious generic relatedness to the concepts expressed by these article links.

---

[2] Available from http://dumps.wikimedia.org/

The overall article linkage graph of Wikipedia can be represented as the adjacency matrix $A_{Articlegraph}$ of dimensions $n \times n$, where n is the number of articles. If an article a_i links to a_j, the respective cell in the matrix is set to 1, otherwise it is set to zero, resulting in a sparse matrix.

$$A_{Articlegraph_{i,j}} = \begin{cases} 1 & \text{if } a_i \text{ contains a link to } a_j \\ 0 & \text{otherwise} \end{cases} \quad (3)$$

Initially, we intended to include weights that decrease with the linkage distance of articles on indirect links, e.g. if a_i links to a_j and a_j links to a_k, that a value greater than 0 (but less than 1) is inserted into $A_{Articlegraph_{i,k}}$. Yet, preliminary tests showed that the semantic relatedness between articles linked by second degree is already very low, thus it would only raise computation overhead without contributing to the result. Therefore, we refrained from adding this weighted distance measure.

As articles never contain a reference to themselves, the adjacency matrix has to be added to the identity matrix $I_{|articles|}$ so that the diagonals are not 0. Otherwise, there is the possibility that already computed information is lost. Further, a weight factor w is introduced that determines how strong the influence of the article graph is on the original i_{esa}. On multiplication of the semantic interpreter from ESA with the resulting matrix (4), the relevant semantic information already present in i_{esa} is reinforced.

$$i_{xesa:ag1} = i_{esa} * (w * A_{Articlegraph} + I_{|articles|}), w \in [0..1] \quad (4)$$

Performance–wise, the article graph extension poses the challenge that the complete interpretation vector has to be multiplied with a large matrix again. Additionally, we observed i_{esa} to usually contain only few similarity values that are significant and lots of values that are really small. Thus, for boosting efficiency of calculation, we introduce the function `selectBestN` that truncates i_{esa} after the first best N similarity values. This has the effect that the second matrix multiplication is more efficient to be calculated because i_{esa} is sparsely filled with values > 0. Thus, we define a second approach that reduces the overall calculation complexity by only taking the N highest similarity values into account (5).

$$i_{xesa:ag2} = i_{esa} + \texttt{selectBestN}(i_{esa}) * (w * A_{Articlegraph}), w \in [0..1] \quad (5)$$

A challenge, though, is finding an appropriate N that speeds up calculation without deteriorating the quality of the result too much. This will be dealt with empirically in section 4.

3.2 Utilization of Category Information

The category structure of the German Wikipedia contains approximately 80.000 categories with 920.000 articles categorized (approximately 87% of all articles).

Besides adminstrative categories and categories that group different articles by properties of the underlying concepts (e.g. *list of German authors by birth year*), there are categories that provide semantic information. These categories represent groupings by semantic properties and express mostly *is–a* relations.

Similar to [17], we append information that encodes category affiliation to the interpretation vector i_{esa}. Therefore, we create the matrix C with the dimensions $n \times m$, where n is the number of articles and m the number of categories (6). On multiplying i_{esa} with C, the result is the vector c_{cat} that encodes information about articles and categories (7).

$$C_{i,j} = \begin{cases} 1 & \text{if article } a_i \text{ links to category } c_j \\ 0 & \text{otherwise} \end{cases} \qquad (6)$$

$$c_{cat} = i_{esa} * C \qquad (7)$$

$$i_{xesa:cat} = (i_{esa}, c_{cat}) \qquad (8)$$

Finally, c_{cat} is appended to i_{esa}. In (8), this is expressed by the appending operator ",". Thus, this operation changes the dimensions of the vector i_{esa} by appending the category vector dimensions. Analogue to the approach using the article graph, this calculation is inefficient if all non–zero values are kept; thus, we apply the above–mentioned `selectBestN` to i_{esa} again, resulting with (9).

$$i_{xesa:cat} = (i_{esa}, \texttt{selectBestN}(i_{esa}) * C) \qquad (9)$$

3.3 Combination of Article Graph and Category Extensions

Finally, the article link and category extensions to ESA can be applied in combination. This is rather straight–forward, instead of i_{esa} the result of the article graph extension $i_{xesa:ag1}$ is used (10).

$$i_{xesa:combination} = (i_{xesa:ag1}, \texttt{selectBestN}(i_{xesa:ag1}) * C) \qquad (10)$$

We include this approach just for sake of completeness, as the efficiency of this extension is not adequate as will be seen in section 4.

4 Evaluation

In this section, we present an evaluation that compares ESA to our different XESA variants.

4.1 The Snippet Corpus

In order to evaluate XESA, we needed an evaluation corpus that fulfills several requirements:

- In our experiments, we applied the German Wikipedia. Thus, the evaluation corpus should consist of German documents.
- Documents in the evaluation corpus should conform to our snippet definition, i.e. documents should contain between 20 and 200 terms.
- Documents in the evaluation corpus should honour our scenario of resource–based learning with web resources. That is, they should contain a narrow scope of topics and be basically appropriate to answer special information needs.
- Documents should contain different topics and have different scopes, i.e. should not only represent narrow factual knowledge but also contain opinions and overview information.

Because we did not find an appropriate available set of documents that met our requirements, we built a small corpus in a user study [18] with eight participants. The participants were asked to research answers to a catalogue of ten questions using only fragments of web resources. For each question they were to find five snippets that (partially) contained the answer to this question. Further, they were instructed to restrict the snippets' length to 20 to 200 terms. This was not a fixed requirement though, if needed, the participants were allowed to collect larger web resource fragments.

In order to conform to the fourth requirement named above, the questions were formulated so that five different types of questions were asked with two questions per type. We identified the following question types as relevant for our scenario:

- *Opinions*, e.g. "Is the term *Dark Ages* justified?"
- *Facts*, e.g. "What is the FTAA?"
- *Related snippets* to a common topic, e.g. "Find examples for internet slang!"
- *Homonyms*, e.g. "What are Puma, Jaguar, Panther, Tiger and Leopard?"
- *Broad topics*, e.g. "Find information about the evolution of man!"

After having collected the answers, duplicate answers and answers from the same sources were discarded. Finally, the evaluation corpus D consisted of 282 snippets (a short summary is available in table 1) that were labeled with their question types and manually split into groups of different semantic concepts. Because, as expected, homonyms and broad topics showed to be consisting of snippets with different meaning, we got 14 different semantic groups.

Table 1. Short summary of evaluation corpus

Size of corpus	282 documents
Average length of snippets	95 terms
Minimal length	5 terms
Maximum length	756 terms
Standard deviation	71.3 terms

4.2 Evaluation Methodology

For evaluating XESA, we applied a methodology similar to [19] that is used to evaluate search engine rankings. Basically, a semantic relatedness value is calculated for each snippet document $q \in D$ with all $d \in D \setminus q$. The result is a list that is ranked by decreasing relatedness. We define that q and a compared document d_k at rank k are semantically related (i.e. $r_k = 1$) if they are in the same semantic group D_q (11), i.e. they handle the same semantic concept.

$$r_k = \begin{cases} 1 & \text{if } q \text{ and } d_k \in D_q \\ 0 & \text{otherwise} \end{cases} \tag{11}$$

Further, *precision at rank* (12) and *recall at rank* (13) are used to calculate the *average precision* (14) over one relatedness comparison for different recall values. Eventually, all pair–wise comparisons are averaged and the average precision is plotted against recall. One measure that expresses the quality of these results is the *break–even point* [20], the point where precision equals recall (and, as presented in our plots, the interpolated precision–recall curve crosses $f(r) = r$, i.e. the angle bisector of the first quadrant).

$$precision(k) = \frac{1}{k} \sum_{1 \leq i \leq k} r_i \tag{12}$$

$$recall(k) = \frac{1}{|D_q|} \sum_{1 \leq i \leq k} r_i \tag{13}$$

$$\text{average precision} = \frac{1}{|D_q|} \sum_{1 \leq k \leq |D|} r_k * precision(k) \tag{14}$$

For ESA (fig. 2), the break–even point is at 0.575, the mean average precision is 0.595 with standard deviation 0.252.

4.3 Empirical Evaluation of selectBestN and Article Graph Weight

As described in section 3, we introduced the function `selectBestN` that discards all i_{esa} values but the n best values for better calculation performance. After some preliminary experiments, we decided to compare the XESA variant using the article graph ($i_{xesa:ag2}$) using three different values, i.e. $n \in (10, 25, 100)$.

The results in fig. 3 show that the article graph extension performs best with $n = 25$. This is consistent with the results we got using the other extensions as well, so, in the following, we only present results that were computed with $n = 25$.

Further, the article graph weight w used with all XESA article graph extensions was tested with $w \in (0.25, 0.5, 0.75)$. In our experiments, there was no difference between using the weights 0.5 and 0.75. Therefore, we will use $w = 0.5$ in all presented results.

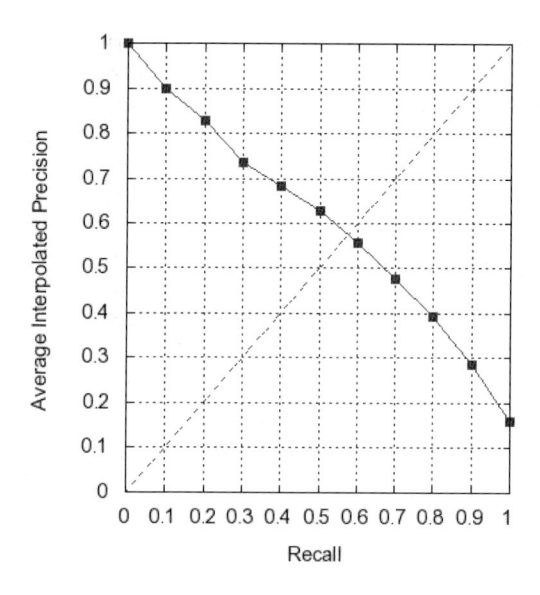

Fig. 2. The precision–recall diagram for basic ESA with the break–even point where $f(r) = r$

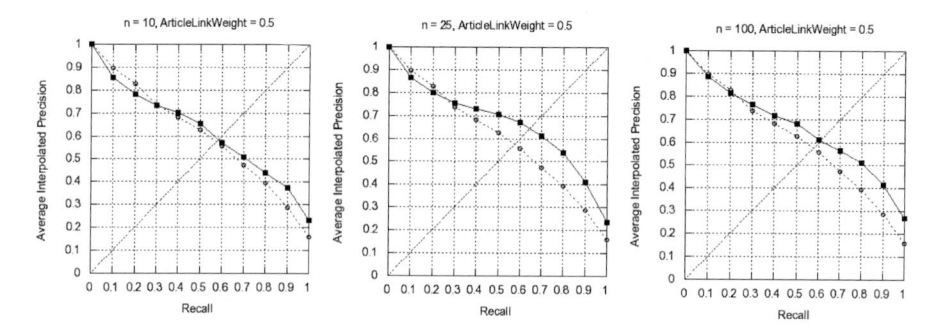

Fig. 3. Calculating the relatedness using the article graph extension with $n \in (10, 25, 100)$

4.4 Comparison of ESA with XESA

In this section, we compare results of the different XESA variants presented in section 3.

The precision–recall diagrams of all XESA variants presented in section 3 using the selectBestN–parameter n with 25 and the link article graph weight w as 0.5 are displayed in fig. 4. This plot shows that both article link graph extensions perform best, significantly surpassing ESA results by 7%, whereas the category extension still outperforms ESA by 5.4% but cannot measure up to the article graph variants. Both variants combined, however, are not able to

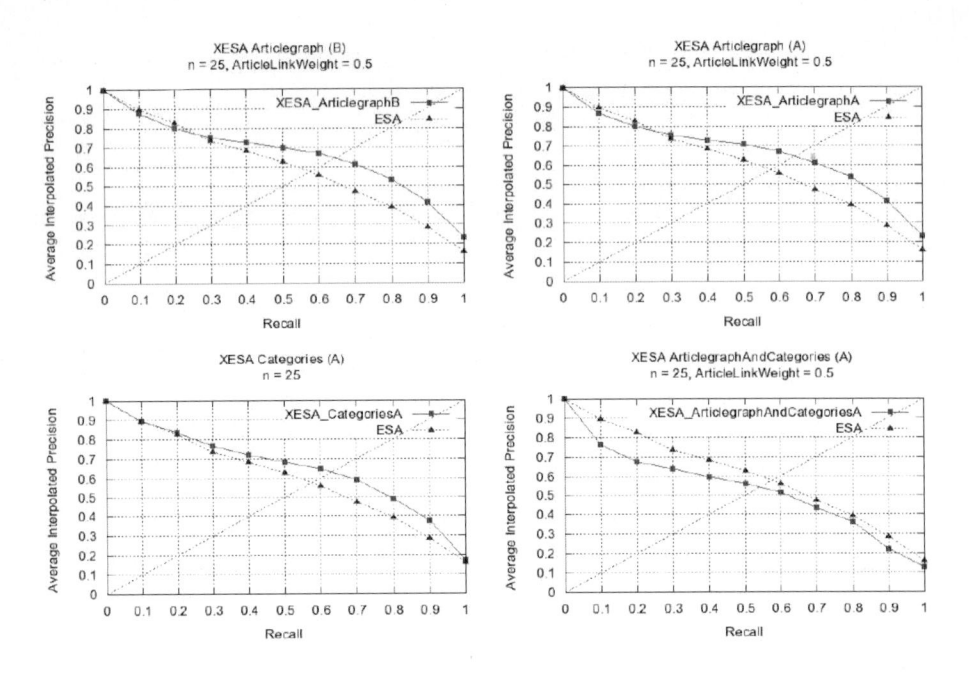

Fig. 4. Precision–Recall Plots of all XESA variants

Table 2. Summary of XESA's results (best are marked bold)

Approach	Break–even Point	Mean Average Precision	Standard Deviation
ESA	0.575	0.595	**0.252**
XESA$_{xesa:ag1}$	0.644	0.654	0.286
XESA$_{xesa:ag2}$	**0.645**	**0.657**	0.284
XESA$_{cat}$	0.629	0.646	0.274
XESA$_{combined}$	0.539	0.515	0.301

even achieve the performance of the basic ESA approach. Detailed results are additionally displayed in table 2.

These results show that the semantical information that can be derived from the Wikipedia article graph and the categories is beneficial for computing the semantic relatedness between documents. We think that the article graph variants of XESA perform best because they represent a specific relatedness between concepts. By linking articles, the human editors wanted to express closeness of the underlying concepts. While being linked, some context of this relation can also be found in the linking article as well. For example, the article *General Relativity* links to the article *Space* and shares terminology with that article. Thus, by adding information about the relation, semantic information already known is strengthened by this connection. Categories, however, provide an organizational, top–down view on the concepts. While they provide semantic information about the grouping of articles, they are already abstracted from the specific concept itself. Therefore, the results of XESA's category variant improve ESA but still cannot measure up to the article graph variants.

Further, we presume that the results of the XESA combination variant are worse than ESA's results, because a multiplicatory effect comes into effect. By multiplying the interpretation vectors of different semantic dimensions in that approach, there seems to occur a semantic diversification, i.e. the interpretation vector $i_{xesa:combination}$ is enriched by semantic information based on heterogeneous sources (article graph and categories). Thus, noise is added and the specifity of the semantic dimensions is decreased significantly.

As expected, the 14 semantic groups of the corpus proved to perform differently based on their abstraction. For example, snippets containing fact knowledge in a narrow topic are more easily related than broad topics, because certain terms are common in that group. XESA showed to outperform ESA in recognizing the semantic relatedness between documents in the groups that use different terminology.

Additionally to the evaluation presented here, we compared XESA to ESA in regards of semantic relatedness of single terms. We performed some tests with a corpus created from ratings of the perceived relatedness of 65 term pairs [21]. XESA's results were not significantly different from the same evaluation using ESA. We think that this scenario does not benefit from our approach of semantically enriching the resulting interpretation vector, because the context that is given by additional terms in documents is necessary to exploit the semantic information contained in Wikipedia. Presumably, additional information seemed to add noise to the interpretation vectors that degraded our results.

5 Conclusions and Further Work

In this paper, we presented a scenario of resource–based learning using web resources. We briefly described our research prototype *Crokodil* that aims to support this self–directed way of learning and proposed a recommendation mechanism based on several requirements. We analyzed related work on the basis of these requirements, identifying the approach Explicit Semantic Analysis (ESA) as a foundation for enhancement. We described three approaches of semantically enriching the interpretation vectors obtained by ESA based on Wikipedia article links and categories. Eventually, we evaluated these extensions, subsumed under the name eXtended Explicit Semantic Analysis (XESA), and showed that the extension based on the article link graph, outperforms ESA by 7% on a corpus of snippets. We infer that ESA, albeit a stable and well–performing approach, can be enhanced by using semantic information contained in Wikipedia.

In future work, we will focus on the recommendation engine that provides semantically related content. An open question is, whether and how learners benefit from the offering of unknown, but related, snippets. We think that an interesting research question will be, whether learners profit more from strongly related snippets or weakly related snippets. This requires further evaluations in an open self–directed learning setting. Further, we want to pursue the question whether Wikipedia lemmata — the titles of the articles — may serve as human–readable topical hints respectively tags for learners. Further we believe that taking into account the relevance of links between articles will improve the article graph extension. For example, *General Relativity* links to *Baltimore*, which is less relevant than the link to *Spacetime*.

A valuable extension to *Crokodil* would be to recommend snippets in other languages that represent the same concepts. As Wikipedia provides inter–language links between articles about the same concepts, this seems to be feasible.

Acknowledgments. This work was supported by funds from the German Federal Ministry of Education and Research under the mark 01 PF 08015 A and from the European Social Fund of the European Union (ESF). The responsibility for the contents of this publication lies with the authors.

References

1. Baeza-Yates, R., Ribeiro-Neto, B.: Modern Information Retrieval. Addison-Wesley, Reading (1999)
2. Böhnstedt, D., Scholl, P., Benz, B., Rensing, C., Steinmetz, R., Schmitz, B.: Einsatz persönlicher Wissensnetze im Ressourcen–basierten Lernen. In: Seehusen, S., Lucke, U., Fischer, S. (eds.) DeLFI 2008: 6. e–Learning Fachtagung Informatik, Köllen, Bonn, Gesellschaft für Informatik. LNI, vol. P–132, pp. 113–124 (September 2008)
3. Sowa, J.F.: Semantic Networks. In: Shapiro, S.C. (ed.) Encyclopedia of Artificial Intelligence, vol. 2, pp. 1493–1511. John Wiley, New York (1992)
4. Scholl, P., Benz, B.F., Böhnstedt, D., Rensing, C., Schmitz, B., Steinmetz, R.: Implementation and Evaluation of a Tool for setting Goals in self-regulated Learning with Web Resources. In: Cress, U., Dimitrova, V., Specht, M. (eds.) EC-TEL 2009. LNCS, vol. 5794, Springer, Heidelberg (2009)
5. Zesch, T., Müller, C., Gurevych, I.: Extracting lexical semantic knowledge from Wikipedia and Wiktionary. In: Proceedings of the Conference on Language Resources and Evaluation, LREC (2008)
6. Budanitsky, A., Hirst, G.: Evaluating Wordnet-based measures of lexical semantic relatedness. Computational Linguistics 32(1), 13–47 (2006)
7. Fellbaum, C.: Wordnet: An Electronic Lexical Database. MIT Press, Cambridge (1998)
8. Jiang, J.J., Conrath, D.W.: Semantic similarity based on corpus statistics and lexical taxonomy. In: Proceedings of International Conference Research on Computational Linguistics, ROCLING X (1997)
9. Jarmasz, M., Szpakowicz, S.: Rogets thesaurus and semantic similarity. In: Recent Advances in Natural Language Processing III: Selected Papers from RANLP, p. 111 (2004)
10. Deerwester, S., Dumais, S.T., Furnas, G.W., Landauer, T.K., Harshman, R.: Indexing by Latent Semantic Analysis. Journal of the American society for information science 41(6), 391–407 (1990)
11. Strube, M., Ponzetto, S.P.: Wikirelate! Computing semantic relatedness using Wikipedia. In: Proceedings of the National Conference on Artificial Intelligence, vol. 21, p. 1419. AAAI Press, MIT Press, Menlo Park, Cambridge (2006)

12. Milne, D., Witten, I.H.: Learning to link with Wikipedia. In: CIKM 2008: Proceeding of the 17th ACM conference on Information and knowledge management, pp. 509–518. ACM, New York (2008)
13. Zesch, T., Gurevych, I.: Analysis of the Wikipedia category graph for NLP applications. In: Proceedings of the TextGraphs-2 Workshop (NAACL-HLT 2007), pp. 1–8 (2007)
14. Kaiser, F., Schwarz, H., Jakob, M.: Using Wikipedia-based conceptual contexts to calculate document similarity. In: International Conference on the Digital Society, pp. 322–327 (2009)
15. Gabrilovich, E., Markovitch, S.: Computing semantic relatedness using Wikipedia-based explicit semantic analysis. In: Proceedings of the 20th International Joint Conference on Artificial Intelligence, pp. 6–12 (2007)
16. Anderka, M., Stein, B.: The ESA retrieval model revisited. In: Proceedings of the 32nd international ACM SIGIR conference on Research and development in information retrieval, pp. 670–671. ACM, New York (2009)
17. Gabrilovich, E., Markovitch, S.: Overcoming the brittleness bottleneck using Wikipedia: Enhancing text categorization with encyclopedic knowledge. In: Proceedings of the Twenty–First National Conference on Artificial Intelligence, pp. 1301–1306. American Association for Artificial Intelligence Press, AAAI, Menlo Park (2006)
18. Grimm, J.: Berechnung semantischer Ähnlichkeit kleiner Textfragmente mittels Wikipedia. Master thesis, Technische Universität Darmstadt (September 2009)
19. Chakrabarti, S.: Mining the Web: discovering knowledge from hypertext data. Morgan Kaufmann Publishing, San Francisco (2003)
20. Yang, Y.: An evaluation of statistical approaches to text categorization. Information Retrieval 1(1), 69–90 (1999)
21. Gurevych, I.: Using the structure of a conceptual network in computing semantic relatedness. In: Dale, R., Wong, K.-F., Su, J., Kwong, O.Y. (eds.) IJCNLP 2005. LNCS (LNAI), vol. 3651, pp. 767–778. Springer, Heidelberg (2005)

Leveraging Semantic Technologies for Harmonization of Individual and Organizational Learning

Melody Siadaty[1,2], Jelena Jovanović[3], Dragan Gašević[2,1],
Zoran Jeremić[3], and Teresa Holocher-Ertl[4]

[1] School of Interactive Arts and Technology, Simon Fraser University, Canada
[2] School of Computing and Information Systems, Athabasca University, Canada
[3] FON, School of Business Administration, University of Belgrade, Belgrade, Serbia
[4] Centre for Social Innovation/Technology and Knowledge, Vienna, Austria

Abstract. For a successful learning organization, it is of crucial importance to have successful methods for stimulation and sharing of working and learning activities of their employees. However, there are two important challenges to be addressed: i) combination of individual and organizational incentives that motivate employees to take part in knowledge building and sharing activities; and ii) structuring of learning and knowledge building activities and their outcomes in a representation that can assure unambiguous knowledge sharing. To address these challenges, we propose a framework of individual and organizational factors for knowledge sharing and a set of ontologies that provides a systematic and interlinked representation of concepts of individual and organizational learning. On top of these proposals, we developed and here present a software solution, which has been evaluated through a case study conducted in a large enterprise context.

Keywords: Knowledge Sharing, Organizational Learning, Ontologies, Harmonization.

1 Introduction

Goal-oriented and self-directed learning are the predominant forms of adult learning, especially in workplace settings [12] [14]. Even though learning goals are typically personally defined, they are highly influenced by the overall organizational expectations and goals, as well as goals of the colleagues a person closely collaborates with (e.g., teammates). In addition, learning goals are not preset and immutable. Instead, they tend to change during the learning process, i.e., to evolve through an individual's interactions with others, and their participation in knowledge building and sharing activities [14]. To make these activities beneficial both for individuals and organizations they work for, employees should be assisted in the cyclic process of (re-)thinking, defining and attaining their learning goals. This process often involves making use of and contributing to the organization's collective knowledge, where contributions come in diverse forms such as reflections; annotations (e.g., comments and ratings) of existing resources; and exchange of ideas and problem solutions within the organization's social network.

Learning is not an isolated process, but highly social and community centered [22]. It is about building and maintaining networks through connecting with other, contributing knowledge to the network and making use of knowledge shared by other members. Knowledge sharing has been recognized as the critical part of this process, especially in workplace learning settings [26]. By sharing their knowledge as well as using the knowledge shared by others and building on top of it, individuals can improve both their own knowledge and contribute to the collective organizational knowledge, thus, supporting their individual learning goals as well as organizational expectations. For example, an individual's knowledge of a certain topic can be improved by considering and further reflecting on reviews, comments, and suggestions obtained from peers. This requires that individuals first externalize their knowledge and share it with others. However, in practice, this is not happening as learning experiences are very rarely written down and shared [26], whilst well documented learning experiences could serve as very valuable knowledge objects that could help novices in a certain domain area in setting, refining and/or attaining their learning goals.

It is very important to indicate that individuals' contributions often originate from different systems and tools. For them to be effectively used as a part of the shared organizational knowledge, they have to be structured, organized and well annotated, so that they can be (re-)discovered and (re-)used inside organizations or publicly. Social technologies already provide means that motivate individuals (and partly organizations) to collaboratively build and share knowledge on the Web. However, they suffer from the problems of ambiguity in shared meanings and the lack of semantics (e.g., as simple as synonyms), the lack of coherent categorization schemas, and the needed time and size of the community in which they will be used [16]. Moreover, current social technologies are not or are very little context-aware and thus, it is very hard to provide a systematic harmonization of personal learning experiences with others in organizations. To address these challenges, here, we propose the use of semantic technologies. The core part of our solution is *a set of ontologies* (Sect. 4) that brings in a structure and attaches the explicit (i.e. machine-'consumable') semantics to the knowledge shared by individuals. Ontologies also add explicit semantics to the data about individuals' knowledge building and sharing activities and allow for seamless integration of this data. Finally, ontologies allow for unambiguous representation of individual and organizational goals and can facilitate the task of bringing these in line (e.g., by enabling automatic detection of how close they are to each other and generating appropriate feedback to both individuals and organizations).

While semantic technologies offer promises of better data management and sharing, it would be naïve to expect that the technology alone will solve the problem [19]. Knowledge sharing often does not happen spontaneously and there are numerous inhibitors of this process (discussed in Sect. 2). Thus, individuals need to be motivated to learn, to share knowledge and, in doing so, to follow the organization's norms and goals. This is most easily achieved when the individual and organization's goals are harmonized [17]. Additionally, adult learners need to be free to direct themselves [12]. Hence, the organization should just point the directions and expectations and not impose the behavioral/work models. The individuals should have the freedom to follow the provided suggestions or to choose their own ways of accomplishing the "negotiated" learning goals. To address these challenges and investigate them, in this paper, we present two services – Personal Learning and Knowledge Management (PLKM) and Organizational Learning and Knowledge Management (OLKM) – that we are developing to facilitate and foster learning and knowledge sharing activities both from personal (PLKM) and organizational (OLKM) perspectives. The former service allows individuals to easily share their knowledge and to dynamically reflect about, define and adapt their learning goals, taking the learning goals of their peers and the organization into consideration [14]. PLKM facilitates all these activities irrespective of the application an employee is using in the given moment. The latter service (OLKM) allows organizations to (re-)define policies related to knowledge sharing and more importantly to receive and review the feedback about employees' knowledge building and sharing activities as well as integrate the newly learned knowledge into official organizational norms.

2   A Framework for Knowledge Sharing within an Organization

Successful knowledge sharing within an organization depends on the synergy of three main groups of factors [19]:

- Individual: motivation of individual employees to capture, disseminate, and apply existing and newly generated knowledge;
- Organizational: organizational structures that facilitate transparent knowledge flows; a well-communicated and open organizational culture; the organization's goals that clearly communicate the benefits of knowledge sharing practices; managers who lead by example and provide clear feedback;
- Technical: software solutions that allow for seamless and ubiquitous knowledge sharing, and facilitate knowledge discovery, (re-)use, and (re-)combination (mash-ups).

Accordingly, in this section, we look at different kinds of individual-level incentives and inhibitors for knowledge sharing within an organization and how they can be addressed by appropriate combination of organizational and technical factors. In this way, we identify a set of factors that we want our tools to support, thus establishing a framework that directs our work on technical developments.

One major inhibitor of knowledge sharing is employees' fear that by sharing their knowledge, they will turn it into a common good and thus lose their expert power and distinctiveness compared to others [8]. By increasing the visibility of the individuals' expertise, organizations can counteract the feeling of losing expert power through the sharing of knowledge. We identify this as Factor 1. Receiving organizational recognition, positive feedback on the knowledge shared, or feedback on how the knowledge being shared has helped colleagues or the company, often improves one's knowledge sharing self-efficacy [26]. This individual's self-perception of competency, credibility, and confidence within organizational contexts, also known as organization-based self-esteem [18], increases the likelihood that the individual will share his/her knowledge with others (see also Factor 9).

According to Hall [9], people are more willing to share their knowledge if they believe that doing so is useful, i.e., if they feel that their act of sharing knowledge will be appreciated by the community and that their knowledge will actually be beneficial for the community members. This feeling can be induced by providing individuals with feedback about the usage of the knowledge they imparted with the organization, so that they can have continuous awareness of their contribution to the shared knowledge. We refer to this as Factor 2.

Related to the previous issue, low awareness of the value that the knowledge possessed by an individual could have for others, is also cited as one of inhibitors for knowledge sharing. This issue is marked as Factor 3 in our framework. This awareness could be raised by having virtual message boards where everyone can post the kinds of knowledge he/she might need, so that people who possess organizationally relevant knowledge easily recognize that their knowledge is needed and would be appreciated by others. In addition, by annotating these posts with the topics specific to the knowledge domain, the task of identifying relevant knowledge sources (either knowledge objects or people) can be significantly automated (e.g., in the manner done by Aadwark, http://vark.com/).

Trust is often seen as a necessary precondition for knowledge sharing. This quintessential element of organizational culture refers to employees' trust that others do not misuse their knowledge, as well as trust that the knowledge being shared is accurate and credible. The feeling of trust in the quality of content can be improved by encouraging employees to comment upon and/or rate knowledge objects they consumed. In other words, validation of content is done by the community. We refer to this practice as Factor 4. It would enable others to make more informed decisions when choosing knowledge objects. Additionally, it can invoke positive competitiveness in individuals, motivating them to put more effort in externalizing knowledge, so that their contribution is higher rated. It has been shown [25] that the consumption of shared knowledge, influences knowledge donating in a positive sense – the more shared knowledge a person makes use of, the more he or she is willing to also donate knowledge to others. Therefore, by increasing trust in the knowledge being shared and thus boosting its usage, an organization implicitly makes a positive impact on knowledge "donation" as well.

The feeling of trust among the members of a community often results from shared vision [24] (e.g., common goals) and shared language [7] (e.g., similar jargon and terminology). Accordingly, knowledge sharing can be enhanced through *emergent domain vocabularies* – domain vocabularies initially defined by the organization, but also evolve to accommodate the terminology used by the given community (e.g., a project team). This is Factor 5 in our framework and can be technically supported through approaches for merging domain ontologies and collaborative tags [23].

Studies have found that organizational attitudes including job satisfaction and organizational commitment also foster knowledge sharing [6]. In particular, affective commitment, which is related to an individual's identification and involvement with the organization, is found to be especially relevant for knowledge sharing [25]. Harmonization of personal and organizational goals (Factor 6) can lead to higher affective commitment, and thus positively influence employees' knowledge sharing attitudes and activities.

It is also important for an organization to explicitly state its expectations and norms regarding knowledge sharing activities as well as to link knowledge sharing to company goals and values [15]. We recognize such an approach as Factor 7. This is particularly important as it was shown (e.g., in [11]) that the more time and effort employees perceive as necessary to codify knowledge in order to share it, the less likely they are to engage in knowledge sharing activities. The organization's expectations regarding knowledge sharing activities are sometimes further emphasized by considering the employees' participation in knowledge sharing activities as a criterion of their performance evaluations (Factor 8). Hence, employees are expected to document valuable knowledge, share it, as well as use others' knowledge; all of which to be considered part of their performance evaluation. This kind of incentive targets employees' extrinsic motivation. However, the organization can also target intrinsic motivation by stimulating perceived competence (i.e., the feeling of being competent enough to do a certain task), perceived autonomy and relatedness (i.e., the feeling of belonging and being connected with others) [20]. We refer to this practice of stimulating intrinsic motivation as Factor 9.

Having identified some important factors that affect knowledge sharing within an organization, in the following sections, we introduce concrete software solutions (services and ontologies) that we are developing to address some of the challenges these factors impose.

3 Services for Individual and Organizational Learning

This section introduces two services that, built on the underlying ontologies (described in Sect. 4), support knowledge sharing activities within an organization. By providing a ubiquitous and seamless sharing platform (i.e. facilitating the technical factors), the Personal Learning and Knowledge Management and Organizational Learning and Knowledge Management services, respectively aim at stimulating individual and organizational factors that affect successful sharing of knowledge in workplace environments. A summary of these factors can be seen in Table 1.

Table 1. Factors affecting knowledge sharing supported by our proposed software solutions

Factor	Description	Nature (incentive/inhibitor)	How this factor is addressed with the proposed software solutions
1	Fear of losing "expert power"	inhibitor	PLKM – visibility levels
2	Awareness of utility of the shared knowledge	incentive	PLKM - Feedback forms, OLKM - emerging vocabularies/ organzational goals
3	Low awareness of the value of one's knowledge for others	inhibitor	PLKM - sharing problems and requests for help and/or advice
4	Misuse of the shared knowledge	inhibitor	PLKM – quality of the shared knowledge
5	Having a shared vision and language	incentive	OLKM – adding collaborative tags to domain ontologies
6	Job satisfaction/ organizational commitment	incentive	OLKM and PLKM – Harmonization of personal and organizational goals
7	Organizational expectations and norms on knowledge sharing	incentive	OLKM - emerging vocabularies/ organizational goals
8	Individuals' extrinsic motivation	incentive	OLKM - emerging vocabularies/ organizational goals, knowledge profiles (initially defined via OLKM), represented in feedback forms (provided by PLKM)
9	Individuals' intrinsic motivation	incentive	PLKM – feedback regarding shared knowledge and sharing activities

3.1 Personal Learning and Knowledge Management (PLKM)

The Personal Learning and Knowledge Management (PLKM) service provides an environment for individuals where they can manage cycles of their learning process within their daily work activities in an organization. Specifically, they can create and share their learning goals; participate in learning and knowledge building activities to achieve these goals; share and document about their learning experiences within accomplished activities, thus contributing to the collective knowledge in their organization; and further refine and nurture their personal learning goals. It is important to notice that PLKM is a ubiquitous software service that can be invoked from any Web-based application. It aggregates individuals' distributed data, scattered in different systems by leveraging the Linked Data principles [2] and our ontologies (Sect. 4).

Managing Personal Learning Goals. A learning process is typically initiated by allowing individuals to define their personal learning goals, harmonized with the goals of the organization they belong to. Both personal and organizational learning goals are represented as sets of competences, and modeled via the Competence ontology (Sect. 4). Considering that defining a commonly accepted characterization of the term "competence" has been subject of much debate within the research community [21], here we briefly mention that within the scope of this research competence is considered to be an individual's skill related to a certain domain topic (e.g. being able to design a car seat using the CATIA software), and leave the rest of this discussion out of the scope of this paper. Following this definition, we initially relied upon the updated version of Bloom's taxonomy [3], but are open to its further modifications based on the specific needs and requirements of the organization, and the context in which it has to be used. Domain topics describe the domain in-use represented via the respective domain ontology (Sect. 4). Contrary to conventional competence-based approaches (e.g. [5]), the personal learning goals are not limited to a set of predefined organizational goals; they are dynamic, can continuously evolve and change during knowledge processes. To further support harmonization of individual and organizational goals, and thus address Factor 6, this module of PLKM allows individuals to define their goals based not only on their personal goals, but to browse and select from the available learning goals in the organization, reflecting organizational expectations/goals and the learning goals of their colleagues. For instance, individuals may want to gain certain competences to be able to better perform the tasks they are responsible for within a project (based on their organizational roles), or they may wish to acquire those competences that would make them eligible for a certain promotion (organizational expectations), or they want to achieve a set of competences that a competent co-worker has. Further, individuals have an option to track their progress with respect to the defined learning goals (Fig. 1).

Let's Share! – Engaging in Knowledge Building and Sharing Activities. Having defined their personal learning goals, individuals engage in learning and knowledge building activities toward achieving their goals. PLKM supports individuals in picking the proper activities by recommending them a set of activities, along with relevant recommended knowledge objects to perform those activities. Those recommendations are based on a set of contextual criteria like an individual's profile and usage behavior and experiences of previous learners in achieving similar goals. This functionality of

PLKM is out of the scope of this paper and we do not get into details of how this recommendation is performed and represented to individuals.

Learning and knowledge building activities can happen in different systems and applications that individuals interact with during their daily work activities. Utilizing social-bookmarking approaches, the Let's Share! module of PLKM provides individuals with an easy-to-use sharing tool which is easily accessible from diverse applications users interact with. Being ubiquitously present and available, individuals use Let's Share! whenever they intend to document their learning efforts and also to share their learning experiences and the knowledge gained or produced. Additionally, Let's Share! allows users to explicitly define the visibility level of the knowledge being shared, be it learning goals, activities or experiences, thus addressing Factor 1.

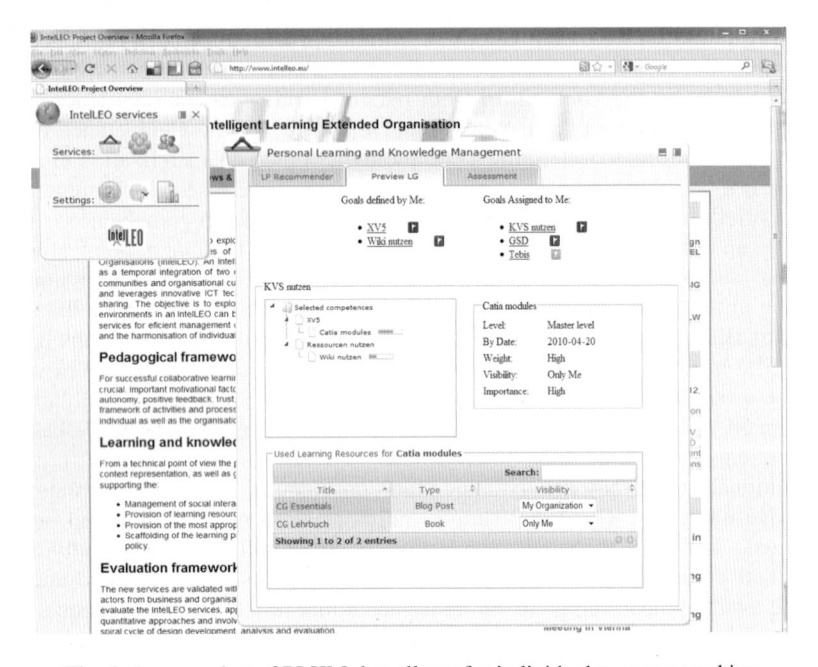

Fig. 1. A screenshot of PLKM that allows for individual progress tracking

On the other hand, Let's Share! also enables users to get notified on the usage of their shared knowledge by providing individuals with (periodic) visual indicators illustrating the quantity and quality (e.g. average 'crowd's opinion' on a shared knowledge item) of the knowledge that they have shared and, the shared knowledge that they have used. Addressing Factors 2 and 4, this utility of the PLKM leads to further motivating individuals in sharing their knowledge and thus, contributing to the collective knowledge of the organization.

3.2 Organizational Learning and Knowledge Management (OLKM)

The OLKM service establishes the framework where organizational goals and norms are reflected. The two main modules of this service are discussed in the following.

Managing Organizational Learning Goals. By allowing for the definition of organizational goals, OLKM builds the structure around which individuals can define their personal learning goals (addressing Factor 6 together with PLKM). In addition to organizational goals explicitly defined by managers in terms of competences (Sect. 3.1), this module of OLKM allows for the discovery of emerging learning goals which can be learned from personal learning goals defined and shared by individuals and harmonized with organizational goals. If some personal goals are frequently being defined by members of an organization, the managers might consider them as 'emerging' organizational goals. As can be seen, organizational goals are also dynamic and can evolve via the contributions of the community members.

Applying Organizational Rules and Expectations. OLKM also provides managers with tools where they can set organizational rules and configurations such as visibility of goals or learning activities, or rules applied for achieving certain promotions. Such regulations further affect the way individuals conduct their learning processes within the organization, intensifying the harmonization of their personal goals with organizational goals and expectations. This module of OLKM allows managers to provide individuals, who had shared their personal learning goals, with feedback on the above mentioned "emerging" organizational goals, making this utility of OLKM threefolded: i) by providing feedback to individuals on the usage of their knowledge sharing activities, it supports Factor 2, ii) it makes it explicit to employees that their knowledge sharing activities are recognized and valued by the organization, and thus worth devoting time and energy (Factor 7) and iii) it targets individuals' intrinsic motivation for knowledge sharing by giving them the feeling of being competent in contributing to the organization's goals and objectives (Factor 9).

The same process with the individual-organizational goals happens when individuals comment on and annotate their shared knowledge. Domain vocabularies of an organization are initially defined by the managers-in-charge, via this module of OLKM (and modeled via domain ontologies). However, there might be some terminologies among the employees which are not initially modeled in the organization's domain ontologies, but frequently reflected in the annotations that individuals use to comment on or tag different shared knowledge objects or activities. Similar to frequently defined personal learning goals, managers also get notified about these collaborative tags via this component and decide whether to add them to the existing vocabulary of the organization, thus supporting Factors 2, 5, 7 and 9. Here, we are using an approach to evolving ontologies based on tag clouds [23].

Additionally, this component provides organizational managers with a tool where they can create knowledge sharing profiles (e.g. ranging from 'total consumer' to 'total donator'), which are used in accordance with visual feedback indicators already discussed in PLKM. Based on individuals' level of participation in knowledge sharing activities, captured and modeled via the respective underlying ontologies, e.g. User model, Workflow and Competence ontologies (see Sect. 4), they will receive (periodic) notifications of their knowledge sharing profiles. These notifications are represented by the Let's Share! module in PLKM, while the initial configuration of the profiles is set through this module of OLKM (thus, supporting Factor 6). Such type of feedback can also, intrinsically, motivate individuals to contribute to knowledge sharing activities (Factor 9).

We explained that PLKM allows users to have control over their shared data and set the visibility level of their sharing activities at the individual level. However, each organization might have certain rules and policies in terms of sharing organizational knowledge. To address this issue, OLKM enables managers to set access rights for the knowledge being shared, e.g. prohibiting sharing of certain types of activities or knowledge objects used in the context of a certain organizational objective. Thus, this module of OLKM assures that individuals' knowledge sharing process is compliant with the organization's culture, rules and norms, leading to higher levels of organizational commitment (supporting Factor 6).

4 Ontologies for Knowledge Sharing

The services presented in the previous section rely on a set of ontologies that provides a common model for data representation and exchange. Since we have developed this set of ontologies within the IntelLEO project (http://intelleo.eu/), we named them IntelLEO ontologies and use this term to refer to them throughout the paper.

4.1 Ontologies for Knowledge Sharing

IntelLEO ontologies are relevant for the presented services as they enable formal representation, storage and seamless exchange of data about:

- individuals' interactions with different and often heterogeneous systems, tools and services they use in their daily work and learning activities; that is, the ontologies serve as a common, machine-interpretable, high-level interaction data model;
- individual's learning experiences (i.e., learning activities and their context), knowledge being shared as well as different kinds of annotations (tags, comments, ratings and the like) that capture either personal or community reflections on the content/knowledge being shared;
- personal learning goals, on one hand, and organizational goals and expectations, on the other.

In addition, the flexibility offered by ontologies as a knowledge representation technique allows for seamless integration of individual knowledge into the collective knowledge of the organization. In particular, one of the main advantages that ontologies offer is the easy integration of knowledge from different, often dispersed sources [2]. Hence, they are an excellent means for integrating individuals' knowledge into shared, organizational knowledge.

As discussed in Sect. 2, previous research in the knowledge sharing domain has shown that both employees and managers can benefit from feedback about knowledge building and sharing activities within the organization. The structure and semantics that ontologies add to the captured and stored interaction data provide an excellent basis for the creation of such feedback. Hence, PLKM and OLKM services leverage this feature of ontologies to offer individuals and managers with relevant feedback and thus further stimulate knowledge sharing activities.

Finally, domain-specific ontologies can be used to annotate semantically different kinds of knowledge being shared, undertaken or planned learning activities, content that was used or produced. The advantage of semantic annotation (i.e., annotation using concepts from an appropriate, topic-specific ontology) over the popular tag-based annotations is that ontology concepts have unambiguously defined semantic accessible to both humans and machines. It also allows for semantic interlinking (i.e., connecting based on meaning) of diverse kinds of components of a learning process (e.g., activities, content, knowledge, people). Thus, by leveraging semantic annotations, advanced search, discovery and recommendation services can be provided to end users.

4.2 IntelLEO Ontologies – A Brief Overview

IntelLEO ontologies have been developed through a combined top-down (review of existing work in the field) and bottom-up (requirements elicitation) approach. Since a common and even recommended practice in ontology engineering is to reuse existing ontologies whenever possible (instead of re-inventing new ones) [2], when designing the IntelLEO ontologies we heavily relied on the ontologies already available and in use. Specifically, we leveraged widely accepted and used ontologies for modeling people and online communities (FOAF, http://xmlns.com/foaf/0.1 and SIOC, http://rdfs.org/sioc/spec/), ontologies for content annotation (DC, http://purl.org/dc/terms/ and CommonTag, http://www.common-tag.org/), as well as some of the ontologies of the LOCO framework (http://jelenajovanovic.net/LOCO-Analyst/loco.html) for modeling characteristics of learning situations. Also in accordance with ontology engineering best practices, all the IntelLEO ontologies are designed with modularity and flexibility in mind so that they can be easily reused and extended. Here we present just some snippets of these ontologies aimed at illustrating how they support the PLKM and OLKM services.

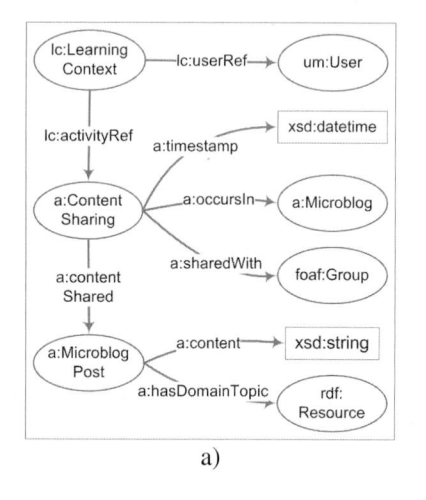

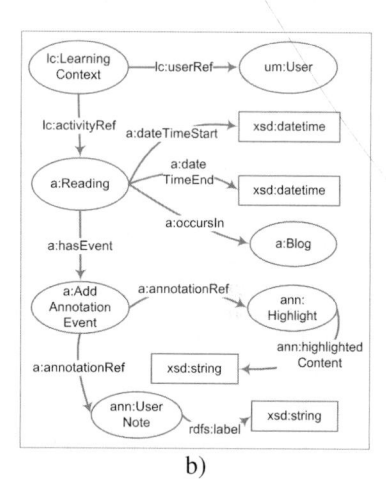

Fig. 2. Using ontologies to represent the context of (a) content sharing activity; (b) content annotation event

Fig. 2a[1] illustrates how we represent data about an individual's content sharing activity. This activity, as any other learning activity, occurs within a specific learning context, where learning context is defined as a specific learning situation characterized by the learning activity that was performed, the learning content that was used and/or produced, and the learner(s) involved [10]. In the particular case depicted in Fig. 2a, learning context characterizes a situation where an individual shared a microblog post with a group (e.g., his team-mates); the post is annotated with one or more domain topics (i.e., topic from appropriate domain ontologies). The time and the online environment where the sharing activity occurred are captured as well. Another example (Fig. 2b) illustrates how we use ontologies to represent data about content annotation (which is again a kind of knowledge sharing). In this case, learning context characterizes a situation when an individual, while reading a blog post, highlights certain parts and adds his comments to it.

Finally, Fig. 3 illustrates how individual and organizational goals are represented and how they relate to each other. In the upper part of the figure is a representation of a task, which is a part of the project an individual works on. The task has its prerequisites expressed in terms of the required competence and the required level of that competence. In the bottom part of the figure is an individual's learning goal represented through target competence and target level of that competence. This goal stems from the missing prerequisites for accomplishing the task and can be either self-defined (um:PersonalLearningGoal) or set by a manager (um:AssignedLearningGoal). Project, competence and competence level are "in the middle", linking the individual and organizational goals/perspectives.

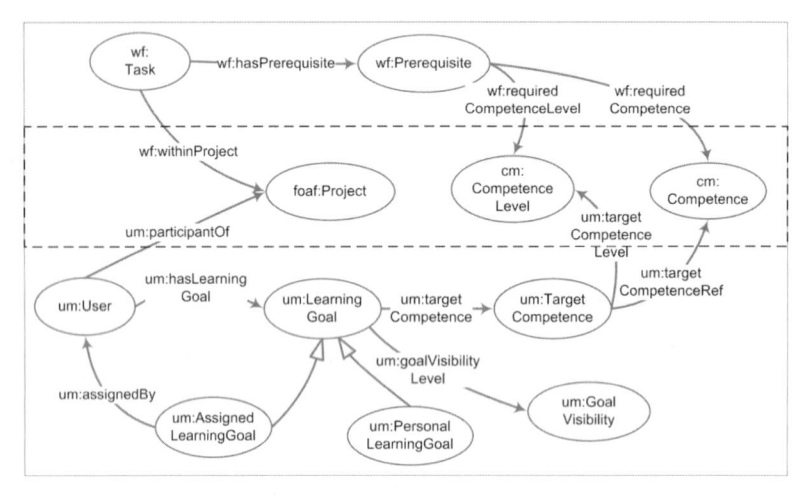

Fig. 3. Representation of personal and organizational goals using concepts and properties from the User Model (um), Competence (cm) and Workflow (wf) ontologies

---

[1] To avoid the clutter, we do not present all the concepts and properties that are used for describing elements of a learning context. The same applies for the other two figures.

5 Case Study

We have conducted an evaluation of the early prototypes of our services within three very different application cases. In this section, however, due to page limits, we introduce only one of these application cases. The aim of this section is to express how our proposed services can be used to address contextual factors affecting knowledge building and sharing activities inside real-life business cases, thus here we demonstrate these services assuming their full functionalities. More thorough evaluations, based on more advanced functionalities of the services, will be conducted by the end of July 2010.

Enterprise A[2] is a large enterprise in the automotive industry. Within this organization, a small business unit needs to implement an innovative approach to collaborative learning and knowledge building processes.. The dynamic and competitive nature of this enterprise makes managing the knowledge process very challenging, especially for its newcomer employees. As there is no institutional education program for the type of job undertaken by the business unit, the most important source of expert knowledge are peers and the knowledge pool generated by related projects. Newcomers have to familiarize themselves with organizational policies and administrative regulations, cautiously create their learning goals, in line with organizational goals, pursue learning and knowledge building activities and continuously refine and adjust their learning goals. On the other hand, more experienced employees are less concerned about getting started with creating and pursuing their learning goals. They are already familiar with the big picture of how things happen in Enterprise A, and involved in rather time-constrained projects. What matters more for these individuals is to be able to find the "how-to"s for different problems that they face, as efficiently as possible. Typical in design environments, there is no preset solution for every problem, instead, such "how-to"s are mostly based upon other individuals' experiences. Thus, having a rich set of "how-to"s within the enterprise requires all employees to actively participate in sharing their knowledge and experiences with the rest of the enterprise. A major concern in contributing to the collective knowledge of the organization, however, is the motivation of employees to spend their most scarce resource (i.e. time) on codifying their experiences to be shared (currently they are only shared via informal, face-to face meetings). To this end, gaining a superior reputation among other colleagues and even managers, is an important factor that can motivate individuals within the competitive environment of Enterprise A to expose their expertise, compensating for the time-consuming task of codifying the conducted activity or experience into something shareable. In this way, by sharing their experience, the individuals would not only contribute to the collective knowledge of the organization, but they would have a chance to improve their skill profiles to "problem-solvers", while making their expertise visible among their peers and the management.

IPR issues are also of high concern for both groups of individuals. Due to the very competitive nature of Enterprise A, all the knowledge within the organization, from organizational objectives to shared experiences of individuals, is strictly protected and distributable only if compatible with organization's complicated privacy policies. This makes most of the employees preferring to avoid the challenging task of sharing

---

[2] Due to privacy and IPR rights, at the moment we refer to this enterprise as Enterprise A.

knowledge when facing the trade-off between getting involved with verifying organizational policies and gaining some potential reputations within the enterprise.

The project involved five employees with different experience levels and from different sub-departments in the requirements elicitation via explorative interviews and focus groups, and two project champions in the evaluation of early prototypes. By involving those employees in this stage of evaluation, we identified the following situations in which the presented services were considered important and useful for the organization under study: The personal learning goal management module of the PLKM software allowed newcomers of Enterprise A to easily initiate and attain their learning and knowledge sharing processes. As this module is a light-weight semantic-enabled widget, it can be embedded in any web-based application that individuals use in their daily work activities, and thus does not put the burden of "learning to work with yet another tool" on them. By means of this module, the newcomers had access to the set of organizational goals and could see a full description on each goal reflecting organizational norms and expectations about it (N.B. it is assumed that the initial set of organizational objectives are previously added to the system via the OLKM software, by a manager of the enterprise). Here, users also see the prerequisite competences for achieving each goal and can accordingly adjust their personal learning goals.

It was also noted that, to keep pace with the dynamic changes of the business unit's tasks and expertise, the more experienced employees can individually share new learning goals and competences via the Let's Share! module. This allows for a continual adaption and advancement of the departments' learning goals and competence development. Let's Share! of PLKM along with OLKM made knowledge sharing become a very handy activity for the employees of Enterprise A. First of all, OLKM aids with clarifying the access-rights applying to the knowledge object/activity to be shared: the visibility levels that individuals can set for the knowledge object /activity that they want to share, is already filtered based on the access-rights set by the managers via OLKM, thus individuals merely set the visibility level that they desired to assign to this knowledge and did not have to be concerned about violating any organizational privacy rights. Second, this module is context-aware[3], thus it (automatically) gathers all the contextual information about the knowledge object or activity to be shared, e.g. the personal learning goal (and the respectively harmonized-with organizational objective) plus the project/task this knowledge has been used within and the competence-profile of the user sharing it (of course, if the user wishes to share his/her profile). Thus it makes the time-consuming task of codifying the knowledge as easy as bookmarking a web-resource. Only a small number of employees produce external web-resources, but the documentation and externalization of knowledge and experiences is mainly based on the internal wiki-systems as well as the organization's Intranet. Thus, our services help to share internal resources that are relevant for colleagues. Finally, the feedback provided by Let's Share! offers individuals with visual indicators on i) how good knowledge-consumers or donators they are and the status of their "skill-profile" based on the criteria set by managers via the OLKM component, and ii) comments and annotations on their shared knowledge, reflecting how others think about their knowledge sharing activities, thus affecting individuals' intrinsic motivation to further participate in knowledge sharing activities.

---

[3] Due to the page limit, we do not discuss the concept of "context", or how it is captured here.

6 Related Work

Improving knowledge sharing within an organization has been the subject of several research efforts recently, both from the technological and organizational standpoints. The challenge is to ensure that knowledge sharing is provided within an organizational context during everyday working process and in working environment.

The APOSDLE EU project aims at enhancing knowledge workers' productivity by supporting informal self-directed work-integrated learning in the context of their everyday work processes [13]. The applied knowledge creation and sharing approach was based on the reuse of the existing (organizational) knowledge objects (KOs). Additionally, KOs created during everyday work processes could be tagged, stored and made available for later (re-)use by other employees. Collaboration among employees is supported through tools allowing for communication and sharing of the documents being discussed and marking relevant parts within these documents. It also offers a space for joint creation and annotation of documents that support the explanation and further discussion of the concepts being examined.

The TENCompetence Foundation, established to sustain the results of the TEN-Competence EU project, aims to support and foster lifelong learning through an integrated open source software infrastructure [5]. This infrastructure provides users with functionalities for creation, storage, search, retrieval, reuse, sharing and quality rating of knowledge resources. A particularly interesting tool integrated into this infrastructure is GroupMe! [1]. It combines Web 2.0 and Semantic Web technologies to provide a personalized content management in a group (social networking) context. By leveraging Semantic Web technologies, it also allows for integration and sharing of resources relevant for a group of users.

Within the ACTIVE EU project, semantic technologies are used for addressing three particular requirements of knowledge workers: the need to share information easily and effectively; the need to prioritize information relevant to the current task; and the need to reuse and share information [27]. Specifically, the approach applied in ACTIVE is to combine formal and informal knowledge, i.e. it investigates how to provide easier sharing of information through combining the ease-of-use of folksonomies with the richness of formal ontologies.

The MATURE EU project examines how: informal knowledge is developed in organizations, networks and communities of practice to develop and support the exchange of knowledge with support of social software tools [4]. MATURE Knowledge Services are composite software services concerned with knowledge entities (people, content and semantic structures). They enable people to add or improve knowledge contained in knowledge entities or to discover knowledge based on the available knowledge entities and their relationships.

While all the described projects target knowledge sharing within organizational settings, most of their efforts are put on solving problems of sharing information easily and effectively, and providing tools for knowledge creation, storage, search, retrieval, reuse and sharing. However, less attention is paid to the problem of motivating users for knowledge sharing. In our work we try to go a step further by analyzing incentives and disincentives for knowledge sharing within organizations and propose appropriate software solutions to support it.

7 Conclusion

As our initial evaluation through the case study demonstrates there is a positive attitude towards the proposed software solution (Sect. 3) for harmonization of personal and organizational learning by levering the framework for individual and organizational incentives introduced in Sect. 2 and ontologies introduced in Sect. 4. While these results are encouraging, it is the major direction of our future work to provide more rigorous evaluation of the overall approach. There have been employees involved in the current user studies, but the number is not very large as it is difficult to get access to those employees. So, in general, we want to increase the number of participants involved in the studied enterprise. In that evaluation, it will be our major goal to investigate how our software solution supports the perceived value of the factors outlined in Sect. 2. While qualitative methods like initial questionnaires including open questions and follow-up semi-structured interviews will help to reveal important details about individual, organizational and technical factors that influence the acceptance and usage of the developed services, it is a challenging task to identify data collection methods which will allow for collecting data about more objective variables. In the first iteration planned for the laboratory setting in the studied enterprise A, we plan to ask their employees to complete a few tasks, and then analyze logs produced in completing those tasks, which will help to evaluate the learnability and usability of the services, revealing problems, design ideas, and design gaps.. Moreover, it is our plan to conduct similar evaluations in an SME, university and professional certification organizations. One important goal will be to compare how different organizational cultures influence knowledge sharing. Our final objective is to evaluate how the proposed framework can be extended to allow for knowledge sharing in an inter-organizational context.

From the semantic technologies perspective, it is clear that many details are not provided primarily due to the space constraint of this paper. In our future publications, we are going to report on these issues and provide formalization of our approach. Moreover, evaluation of the used semantic technologies from both the standard information retrieval and usability perspectives will be in the core of our work.

Acknowledgments. This publication was partially supported/co-funded by the European Community/European Union under the Information and Communication Technologies theme of the 7th Framework Program for R&D. This document does not represent the opinion of the European Community, and the European Community is not responsible for any use that might be made of its content.

References

1. Abel, F., Frank, M., Henze, N., Krause, D., Plappert, D., Siehndel, P.: GroupMe! - Where Semantic Web meets Web 2.0. In: Proc. of 6th Int'l. Semantic Web Conf., pp. 871–878 (2007)
2. Allemang, D., Hendler, J.: Semantic Web for the Working Ontologist: Effective Modeling in RDFS and OWL. Morgan Kaufmann, San Francisco (2008)
3. Anderson, L.W., Krathwohl, D.R., et al.: A Taxonomy for Learning, Teaching, and Assessing: A Revision of Bloom's Taxonomy of Educational Objectives. Allyn & Bacon, Boston (2000)

4. Attwell, G., Barnes, S.A., Bimrose, J., Brown, A.: Maturing Learning: Mashup Personal Learning Environments. In: Proc. of the First International Workshop on Mashup Personal Learning Environments, Maastricht, The Netherlands (2008)
5. Berlanga, A.J., Sloep, P., Kester, L., Brouns, F., Van Rosmalen, P., Koper, R.: Ad hoc transient communities: towards fostering knowledge sharing in learning networks. International Journal of Learning Technology 3(4), 443–458 (2008)
6. de Vries, R.E., van den Hooff, B., de Ridder, J.A.: Explaining knowledge sharing: The role of team communication styles, job satisfaction, and performance beliefs. Communication Research 33(2), 115–135 (2006)
7. Dougherty, D.: Interpretive barriers to successful product innovation in large firms. Organization Science 3, 179–202 (1992)
8. Gupta, A.K., Govindarajan, V.: Knowledge management's social dimension: Lessons from Nucor Steel. Management Review 42(1), 71–80 (2000)
9. Hall, H.: Input-friendliness: Motivating knowledge sharing across intranets. Journal of Information Science 27(3), 139–146 (2001)
10. Jovanovic, J., Gaševic, D., Brooks, C., Devedžic, V., Hatala, M., Eap, T., Richards, G.: Using Semantic Web Technologies for the Analysis of Learning Content. IEEE Internet Computing 11(5), 16–25 (2007)
11. Kankanhalli, A., Tan, B.C.Y., Wei, K.K.: Contributing knowledge to electronic knowledge repositories: An empirical investigation. MIS Quarterly 29(1), 113–143 (2005)
12. Lieb, S.: Principles of Adult Learning, VISION (1991), http://honolulu.hawaii.edu/intranet/committees/FacDevCom/guidebk/teachtip/adults-2.htm
13. Lindstaedt, S., Mayer, H.: A Storyboard of the APOSDLE Vision. In: Nejdl, W., Tochtermann, K. (eds.) EC-TEL 2006. LNCS, vol. 4227, pp. 628–633. Springer, Heidelberg (2006)
14. Littlejohn, A., Margaryan, A, and Milligan, C.: Charting collective knowledge: Supporting self-regulated learning in the workplace. In. Proc. of the 9th IEEE International Conference on Advanced Learning Technologies, 208-212. (2009)
15. Mcdermott, R., O'Dell, C.: Overcoming cultural barriers to sharing knowledge. Journal of Knowledge Management 5(1), 76-85 (2001)
16. Mikroyannidis, A.: Toward a Social Semantic Web. Computer 40(11), 113–115 (2007)
17. Pata, K.: Revising the framework of knowledge ecologies: how activity patterns define learning spaces? In: Educational Social Software for Context-Aware Learning: Collaborative Methods & Human Interaction, pp. 241–267. IGI, Hershey (2009)
18. Pierce, J.L., Gardner, D.G.: Self-esteem within the work and organizational context: A review of the organization-based self-esteem literature. J. of Management 30, 591–622 (2004)
19. Riege, A.: Three-dozen knowledge-sharing barriers managers must consider. Journal of Knowledge Management 9(3), 18–35 (2005)
20. Ryan, R.M., Deci, E.L.: Self-determination theory and the facilitation of intrinsic motivation, social development, and well-being. American Psychologist 55, 68–78 (2000)
21. Sampson, D., Fytros, D.: Competence Models in Technology-enhanced Competence-based Learning. In: International Handbook on Information Technologies for Education and Training, 2nd edn. Springer, Heidelberg (2008)
22. Siemens, G.: Connectivism: Learning as Network-Creation (2005), http://www.astd.org/LC/2005/1105_seimens.htm

23. Torniai, C., Jovanović, J., Bateman, S., Gašević, D., Hatala, M.: Leveraging Folksonomies for Ontology Evolution in E-learning Environments. In: Proc. of the 2nd IEEE International Conference on Semantic Computing, Santa Clara, CA, USA, pp. 206–215 (2008)
24. Tsai, W., Ghoshal, S.: Social capital and value creation: The role of intrafirm networks. Academy of Management Journal 41, 464–476 (1998)
25. van den Hooff, B., de Ridder, J.A.: Knowledge sharing in context: the influence of organizational commitment, communication climate and CMC use on knowledge sharing. Journal of Knowledge Management 8(6), 117–130 (2004)
26. Wang, S., Noe, R.A.: Knowledge sharing: A review and directions for future research. Human Resource Management Review 20(2), 115–131 (2010)
27. Warren, P., Kings, N., Thurlow, I., et al.: Improving knowledge worker productivity – the ACTIVE integrated approach. BT Technology Journal 26(2) (2009)

Learning from Erroneous Examples: When and How Do Students Benefit from Them?

Dimitra Tsovaltzi, Erica Melis, Bruce M. McLaren, Ann-Kristin Meyer,
Michael Dietrich, and George Goguadze

DFKI GmbH, German Research Centre for Artificial Intelligence, Stuhlsatzenhausweg 3
(Building D3 2) D-66123 Saarbrücken Germany
Dimitra.Tsovaltzi@dfki.de

Abstract. We investigate whether *erroneous examples* in the domain of fractions can help students learn from common errors of other students presented in a computer-based system. Presenting the errors of others could spare students the embarrassment and demotivation of confronting their own errors. We conducted lab and school studies with students of different grade levels to measure the effects of learning with erroneous examples. We report results that compare the learning gains of three conditions: a control condition, an experimental condition in which students were presented with erroneous examples without help, and an experimental condition in which students were provided with additional error detection and correction help. Our results indicate significant metacognitive learning gains of erroneous examples for lower-grade students, as well as cognitive and conceptual learning gains for higher-grade students when additional help is provided with the erroneous examples, but not for middle-grade students.

Keywords: Erroneous examples, empirical studies, fractions misconceptions, adaptive learning, metacognition.

1 Introduction

Erroneous examples are worked solutions that include one or more errors that the student is asked to detect and/or correct. Technology opens new possibilities of instruction with erroneous examples. For example, erroneous examples can be presented in a variety of ways, with different kinds of feedback, diverse tutorial strategies and sequencing of learning material. Adapting such features to the needs of individual students can contribute to better learning. A domain that seems to need alternative ways of instruction is fractions. There is evidence that students', but also preservice teachers' understanding of fractions is frequently underdeveloped [1] and misconceptions lead to poor performance in fraction problems [2].

However, erroneous examples have been scarcely investigated or used in mathematics teaching, particularly not in the context of technology enhanced learning (TEL). On the contrary, *correct* worked examples have been shown by studies in science learning to benefit students in learning mathematics and science problem solving [3], [4], [5], and [6]. A reason behind the reluctance to use erroneous examples comes from the fact that many mathematics teachers are sceptical about discussing errors in the classroom [7]. Teachers are cautious of exposing students to errors in fear that it could lead to incorrect solutions being assimilated by students, and often believe any discussion of errors should be avoided. As a consequence, the questions remain open on (i) if erroneous examples are beneficial for learning and (ii) how they should be presented.

The little theoretical work and empirical research on erroneous examples in mathematics has provided some evidence that studying errors can promote student learning of mathematics [8], [9], [10], [11], [12]. For example, Borasi argues that mathematics education could benefit from the discussion of errors by encouraging critical thinking about mathematical concepts, by providing new problem solving opportunities, and by motivating reflection and inquiry. Moreover, the highly-publicised TIMSS studies [13] showed that Japanese math students outperformed their counterparts in most of the western world. The key curriculum difference cited was that Japanese educators present and discuss incorrect solutions and ask students to locate and correct errors.

Siegler and colleagues conducted a controlled comparison of correct and incorrect examples [14], [15]. They investigated whether self-explaining both correct and incorrect examples is more beneficial than self-explaining correct examples only. They found that when students studied and self-explained *both* correct and incorrect examples they learned better. They hypothesised that self-explanation of correct and erroneous examples strengthened correct strategies and weakened incorrect problem solving strategies, respectively. Grosse and Renkl studied whether explaining both correct and incorrect examples makes a difference to learning and whether highlighting errors helps students learn from those errors [16]. Their empirical studies (in which no help or feedback was provided) showed some learning benefit of erroneous examples, but unlike the less ambiguous Siegler et al results, the benefit they uncovered was only for learners with strong prior knowledge and for far transfer. Research in other domains, such as medical education, has demonstrated the benefits of erroneous examples in combination with elaborate feedback in the acquisition of problem-solving schemata [17].

2 Theoretical Background and Design

We take the earlier controlled studies further by investigating erroneous examples in the context of Technology-Enhanced learning with ActiveMath, a web-based system for mathematics [18]. Our ultimate goal is to develop micro and macroadaptation for the presentation of erroneous examples for individual students since the benefit of erroneous examples may depend on individual skills, grade level, etc. Microadaptation refers to the teaching strategy, or step-by-step feedback, inside an erroneous example based on the student's performance. Macroadaptation refers to the choice of task for the student, as well as the frequency and sequence of the presentation of erroneous examples. In this paper, we focus on the empirical results that inform our work on the adaptive technology. In contrast to the Siegler studies, we are interested in the interaction of students' study of erroneous examples and the situational and learner characteristics. Extending the work of Grosse and Renkl, we investigate erroneous examples with and adaptive error-detection and error-correction help in the context of TEL. This novel design relies on the intelligent technology of ActiveMath.

Our primary rationale for including error detection and correction help in the empirical studies is that students are not accustomed to working with and learning from erroneous examples in mathematics. Thus, they may not have the required skills to review, analyse, and reflect upon such examples. Taking this strand and providing additional help, we also extend the work of Kopp and colleagues in medical education [17] for mathematics education.

We believe that learning from errors can help students develop (or enhance) their critical thinking, error detection, and error awareness skills. This conjecture stems from various foundational elements, most of which are supported, at least partially, by past research. To begin with, a student can learn important error detection and correction skills by studying erroneous examples, something that is not possible with correct examples and difficult with unsupported problem solving. Moreover, erroneous examples may weaken students' incorrect strategies, as opposed to worked examples that strengthen correct strategies [14]. Additionally, similar to worked examples, erroneous examples do not ask a student to perform as in problem solving, but provide a worked-out solution that includes one or more errors. They could, in effect, reduce extraneous cognitive load in comparison to problem solving [19] while increasing germane cognitive load in the sense of creating cognitive conflict situations. Erroneous examples may, further, guide the learner toward a learning orientation rather than a performance orientation, especially in combination with help that increases student's understanding and, hence, their involvement in the learning process [14].

With regard to the possible drawbacks of erroneous examples, we hypothesise that a student is less likely to exhibit the feared 'conditioned response' of behaviourist theory [20] when studying errors that the student has not made him/herself and thus has not (necessarily) internalised. On the contrary, students may benefit from erroneous examples when they encounter them at the right time and in the right way. For example, rewarding the student for error detection may lead to annotations of these errors in memory such that they will be avoided in subsequent retrieval. At the same time, a student is unlikely to be demotivated by studying common errors in the domain, made by others, as when emphasising errors the student has made him/herself. Some of our preliminary work has already demonstrated the motivational potential of erroneous examples [21]. In the course of our investigation of erroneous examples, we aim to answer the following research questions:

When:

1. Do advanced students, in terms of grade level, gain more from erroneous examples than less advanced students?

How:

2. Can students' cognitive skills, conceptual understanding, and transfer abilities improve through the study of erroneous examples?
3. Does work with erroneous examples help to improve the metacognitive competencies of error detection, error awareness and error correction?

Based on this, our hypothesis is that presenting erroneous examples to students will give them the opportunity to find and react to errors in a way that will lead to deeper, more conceptual learning and better error-detection (i.e., metacogntive) skills. This, in turn, will help them improve their cognitive skills and will promote transfer. We further hypothesise that the effect of erroneous examples depends on whether students are supported in finding and correcting the error and on when and how they are introduced to the students. We present our design of erroneous examples and the studies we conducted to address these questions in the context of TEL.

2.1 Design of Erroneous Examples in ActiveMath

Erroneous examples, as well as standard fraction, exercises are online in ActiveMath. Their presentation is through a tutorial strategy, which defines when and how to provide

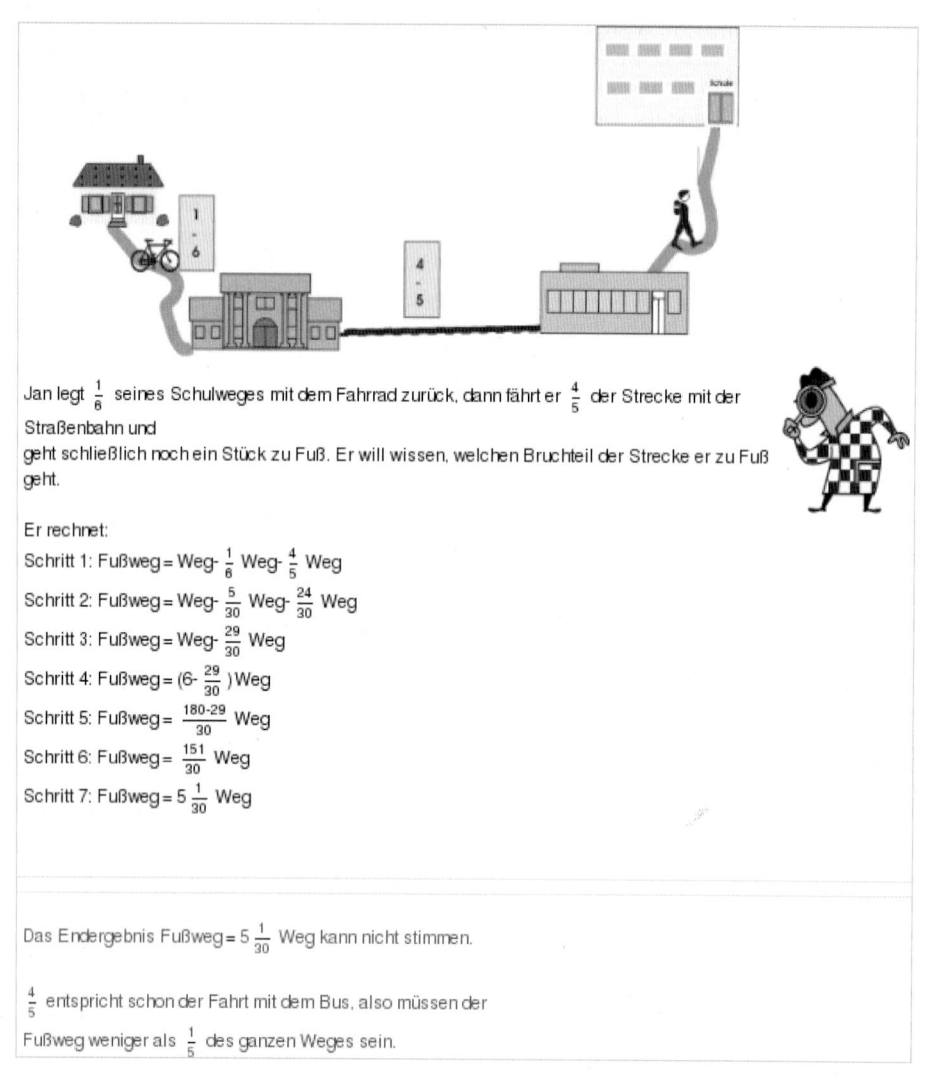

Jan legt $\frac{1}{6}$ seines Schulweges mit dem Fahrrad zurück, dann fährt er $\frac{4}{5}$ der Strecke mit der Straßenbahn und
geht schließlich noch ein Stück zu Fuß. Er will wissen, welchen Bruchteil der Strecke er zu Fuß geht.

Er rechnet:

Schritt 1: Fußweg = Weg- $\frac{1}{6}$ Weg- $\frac{4}{5}$ Weg

Schritt 2: Fußweg = Weg- $\frac{5}{30}$ Weg- $\frac{24}{30}$ Weg

Schritt 3: Fußweg = Weg- $\frac{29}{30}$ Weg

Schritt 4: Fußweg = (6- $\frac{29}{30}$) Weg

Schritt 5: Fußweg = $\frac{180-29}{30}$ Weg

Schritt 6: Fußweg = $\frac{151}{30}$ Weg

Schritt 7: Fußweg = $5\frac{1}{30}$ Weg

Das Endergebnis Fußweg = $5\frac{1}{30}$ Weg kann nicht stimmen.

$\frac{4}{5}$ entspricht schon der Fahrt mit dem Bus, also müssen der Fußweg weniger als $\frac{1}{5}$ des ganzen Weges sein.

Fig. 1. An Online Erroneous Example and the error-awareness and detection (EAD) feedback (bottom)

help, signal correct and wrong answers, give answers away, show previous steps of the students, etc. Erroneous examples in ActiveMath include instances of typical errors students make, which address standard problems students face with rule-application, or errors that target common misconceptions and deal with more fundamental conceptual understanding in fractions.

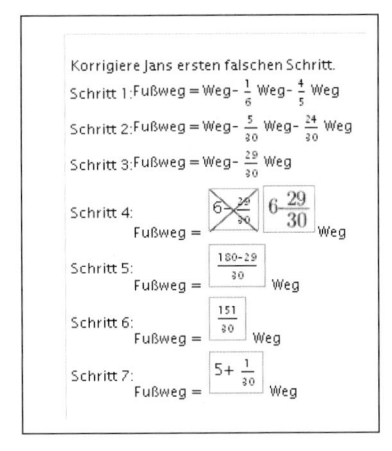

Erroneous examples consist of two phases: error detection and error correction. Fig. 1 displays the task presented in the first phase. Its translation is: "Jan rides his bike for 1/6 of the path to school, then drives with the tram 4/5 of the path and finally walks the rest of the path. He wants to know what fraction of the path he walks. He calculates:…" The steps of the erroneous solutions are presented as choices in a multiple-choice question (MCQ) and students have to select the erroneous step. After completing this phase, the student is prompted to correct the error, as shown in Fig. 2 ("Correct Jan's first wrong step").

Fig. 2. Error-correction Phase

2.2 Feedback Design

Based on pilot studies [23], we designed feedback for helping students understand and correct the errors. There are four types of unsolicited feedback: minimal feedback, error-awareness and detection (EAD) feedback, self-explanation feedback and error-correction scaffolds. (i) Minimal feedback consists of flag feedback (checks for correct and crosses for incorrect answers) along with a text indication. (ii) EAD feedback (bottom of Fig. 1) focuses on supporting the meta-cognitive skills of error detection and awareness and appears on the screen

"Why is the 4th step wrong?"
- because the length is 6*path (due to 1/6)
- because the entire length is 5*6=30*path
- because the entire length is 1*path
- I don't know.

"How can you represent the whole path?"
- With 100
- With 1*path
- I don't know.

Fig. 3. "Why" and "How" MCQs

after the student has indicated having read the task. As an example, the English translation of the EAD feedback in Fig. 1 is: "The result, walking distance=5 1/30, cannot be correct. Travel with the bus is already 4/5 of the total distance, so the walking distance must be less than 1/5." (iii) Self-explanation feedback (Fig. 3) is presented in the form of MCQs. It aims to help students understand and reason about the error through "why" and "how" questions. (iv) Error-correction scaffolds prepare the student for correcting the error in the second phase and also have the form of MCQs. The choices in the MCQs are related to different misconceptions or typical errors. By addressing such misconceptions and errors, MCQs are meant to prepare the students for correcting the error in Phase 2. Students receive minimal feedback on their choices, and eventually the correct answer. MCQs are nested (2 to 5 layers). If a student chooses the right answer at the two top-level MCQs (the "why" and "how" questions), then the next levels, the error-correction MCQs, will be skipped.

In the second, error-correction, phase the chosen step is crossed out, and an additional editable box is provided for correcting the error (cf. Fig. 2). After that error-specific feedback is provided, e.g., *"You forgot to expand the numerators"*, along with the correct solution. Here, we allow students only one attempt in order to avoid overlap with problem-solving exercises and to be able to assign learning effects to erroneous examples.

3 Studies

To assess the learning effects of erroneous examples at different grade levels and settings, we conducted lab studies with 6th, 7th and 8th-graders and school studies with 9th and 10th-graders. The participants came from both urban and suburban German schools. We first explain the general aspects of our experimental design that are common to all studies and discuss the particulars of each of the studies and the results in the following sections.

General Design. All studies used three conditions. The control condition, No-Erroneous-Examples (NOEE), included standard fraction problems of the form 3/4+5/7 with minimal feedback and the correct solution, but no erroneous examples. The experimental condition Erroneous-Examples-With-Help (EEWH) included standard exercises, and erroneous examples with provision of help (EAD, error detection/correction MCQs, and error-specific help). The condition Erroneous-Examples-Without-Help (EEWOH) included standard exercises, and erroneous examples but without additional help. The design included a pre-questionnaire, a pretest, a familiarisation, an intervention, a posttest and a post-questionnaire. The pre and posttests were counterbalanced.

3.1 6th-Grade Lab Study

Twenty-three paid volunteers in the 6th-grade participated in this study, distributed as follows: EEWH=8, EEWOH=7, NOEE=8. They had just completed a course on fractions at school. The mean of their term-grade in mathematics across conditions was 2.04 (SD=.88) (best=1 vs. fail=6), so the participants were generally good students. There was no significant difference in the means of the pretest among conditions (p=.8). The experiment was completed in one session with breaks.

3.1.1 Materials
In the intervention, both groups solved six sequences of three items: standard exercise - standard exercise - erroneous example. These sequences trained skills that are typical fraction topics taught at school, e.g. fraction addition/subtraction with like

denominators and with unlike denominators, addition of whole numbers with fractions, as well as word problems but no modelling, which would require students to use fraction operators to represent the word problems.

The posttest consisted of similar problems, and a transfer problem (which was a four-fraction addition, as opposed to the maximum of three in the intervention). Finally, three erroneous examples which included three open conceptual questions each on error detection and awareness were part of the posttest. The questions were of the kind "Why can Oliver's solution not be correct?", "What mistake did Oliver make?", "Why did Oliver make this mistake? What did he not understand about fractions?" These questions were designed to test students' error detection skills as well as their understanding of basic fraction principles. For example, the mistake Oliver made was that he added the denominators 6 and 8 in the exercise 7/6+5/8. The answer to the question about what Oliver did not understand would be "That if one adds the denominators 6 and 8, one gets 14ths, to which 6ths and 8ths cannot be transformed.", which addresses the basic concept of common denominators.

3.1.2 Results: 6th-Grade Lab Study

The results for the erroneous examples scores follow our hypotheses, although they were mostly insignificant. The EEWH condition scored highest in almost all scores. For all these scores, EEWOH came second, followed by NOEE. The big variances between conditions were only significant for correcting the error (EE-correct) in the erroneous examples. Nevertheless, we ran an ANOVA for that score, since the group size is almost the same across conditions, which means that ANOVA can produce robust results. The condition showed no significant effect in the ANOVA, there was a significant difference when comparing EEWH and NOEE for finding the error in the planned tests (Helmert contrasts) ($p=.044$, $d=1.39$). Another quite big difference was between EEWH and NOEE for the total erroneous example score ($p=.065$, $d=1.20$), which includes correcting the error and answering conceptual questions. These learning gains related to erroneous examples did not transfer to the cognitive skills where the differences between pretest and posttest are minimal in either direction for all conditions and there was a ceiling effect both in the pretest ($M=84.1$, $SD=19.3$) and the posttest ($M=84.4$, $SD=15.8$). This might be due to the high prior knowledge level of the participants.

Table 1. Descriptive Statistics: Lab Study 6th-Grade

Score	Condition Subscore	EEWH mean(sd)%	EEWOH mean(sd)%	NOEE mean(sd)%
Cognitive Skills	Pretest	80.2(26.7)	85.7(17.8)	86.5(12.5)
	Post-pre-diff	-2.1(33.6)	1.2(21.7)^	2.1(23.9)+
Metacognitive Skills (EE)	EE-find	91.7(15.4)+	76.2(31.7)^	66.5(35.6)
	EE-correct	80.2(12.5)+	75.0(21.0)^	68.7(25.9)
	EE-ConQuest*	64.6(25.5)+	60.2(33.3)^	41.7(21.2)
	EE-total	75.3(16.8)+	67.9(27.5)^	54.7(23.0)
	Total-time-on-postEE	16.9(6.2)^	13.8(5.5)+	18.0(5.1)
Transfer	Transfer	75.0(46.2)+	71.4(48.8)	75.0(46.3)^

Note: +=best, ^=middle learning gains, *= also conceptual skill

As we did not have access to the term grades of the participants before the experiment, the conditions were not balanced in that respect. Therefore, we analysed the data with the term-grade but also with the pretest score as covariates, to capture the possible influence of previous math and fraction knowledge, respectively, on the learning effects. With this analysis, there is a main effect for erroneous examples in answering conceptual questions ($p=.036$, $d=1.01$), and in the total erroneous examples score ($p=.028$, $d=3.3$), when comparing the two erroneous example conditions with the control. The same scores were also significantly higher for EEWH vs. NOEE ($p=.022$, $d=1.11$/ $p=.008$, $d=1.32$) respectively). Additionally, the difference for finding the error was significantly higher for EEWH vs. NOEE ($p=.029$, $d=1.06$).

Discussion: 6th Grade. We found significant differences in the scores for erroneous examples, which means that erroneous examples, in general, and the additional help, in particular, supported better the metacognitive skills. The higher performance in the conceptual questions related to understanding the error also indicates better conceptual understanding for the erroneous examples conditions and for the help condition. However, we had no evidence that studying erroneous examples had an effect on standard cognitive skills, where the students already had a very high level.

3.2 Lab Study: 7th and 8th Grade

Twenty-four students in the 7th and 8th-grade took part, eight in each of the three conditions. 7th and 8th-graders are similarly advanced beyond 6th-graders in their understanding of fractions, according to our expert teachers. They have had more opportunity to practice, but often retain their misconceptions in fractions. The mean of their term grade in mathematics was a little lower ($M=2.8$, $SD=1.2$) compared to the 6th grade, but still at the upper-level of the grading scale. The pretest mean difference was not significant between conditions ($p=.8$). Consistent with the judgments of the expert teachers, there was no significant difference in the scores of the 7th compared to the 8th grade ($p=.896$). Participants completed all experimental phases in one session with breaks in between.

3.2.1 Materials
7th and 8th-graders worked with the same materials as the 6th-gradres but also solved modelling exercises that were not used in the 6th-grade, since such exercises are not typically encountered in German schools in this grade. An example of a modelling exercise is: "Eva invited her friends to her birthday party. They drank 8 3/7 bottles of apple juice as well as 1 5/6 bottles of lemonade. How many bottles did they drink all together?" The expected modelling in this exercise is: 8 3/7 + 1 5/6. In total, there were seven sequences of exercises in this study. A modelling exercise also testing transfer was added to the posttest. By including such fraction modelling, we aimed to induce and measure conceptual understanding.

3.2.2 Results: 7th-8th-Grade Lab Study
As a whole, the results do not support our hypotheses for the 7th and 8th-grade. All differences in scores are small and not significant. NOEE scored better in almost all scores, apart from the conceptual questions, where EEWOH did best. EEWOH was also second best in finding the error and in the total erroneous examples score. EEWH

came second in the cognitive skills, correcting the error, transfer exercises, and modelling. The standard deviation for all scores except for improvement on cognitive skills was highest for EEWH. Since the group size is the same across conditions, the results of the ANOVA can be considered robust although Levene's test was significant for finding the error ($p=.018$), conceptual questions ($p=.000$) and for the total score on erroneous examples ($p=.000$). The only statistically significant score in the ANOVA test was the time spent on the posttest erroneous examples ($F(2, 21) =5.59$, $p=.011$, $n^2=.22$), where NOEE spent significantly more time than the erroneous-examples conditions together ($p=.009$, $d=-1.18$) and EEWH alone ($p=.003$, $d=-1.45$). Moreover, the term-grade is a significant covariate on answering conceptual questions ($F(1,21)=4.49$, $p=.047$, $n^2=.18$) and quite big for the total erroneous examples score ($F(1,21)=4.03$, $p=.059$, $n^2=.06$) which in both cases decreases the difference between the control and the erroneous example conditions that originally scored worse. There is also a significant effect of the condition for the time spent on erroneous examples ($F(2,21)=5.28$, $p=.014$, $n^2=.35$) when term-grade is considered as covariate.

Table 2. Descriptive Statistics: Lab Study 7th-8th-Grade

Score	Condition Subscore	EEWH mean(sd)%	EEWOH mean(sd)%	NOEE mean(sd)%
Cognitive Skills	Pretest	73.7(26.7)	71.2(19.7)	77.9(12.4)
	Post-pre-diff	2.4(24.4)^	-4.3(26.6)	6.9 (17.9)+
Metacognitive Skills (EE)	EE-find	68.7(34.7)	75.0(13.4)^	90.6(12.9)+
	EE-correct	57.8(26.7)^	54.7(21.1)	65.6(20.8)+
	EE-ConQuest*	55.2(46.5)	62.5(12.6)+	61.5(19.4)^
	EE-total	59.3(37.1)	63.7(11.9)^	69.8(15.0)+
	Total-time-on-postEE	8.1(4.3)+	11.5(4.2)^	15.5(4.8)
Transfer	Transfer	45.2(45.8)^	38.0(36.0)	67.3(28.5)+
Conc. Underst.	Modelling	36.4(42.2)^	19.8(35.0)	40.8(48.6)+

Note: +=best, ^=middle learning gains, *= also conceptual skill

An important result in this study is a significant difference in the scores for finding and correcting the error in ($t(23)=4.89$, $p<.001$, $r=.71$). The standard deviation for the two metacognitive competencies is comparable, but the mean for correcting is more than 0.5 point lower than for finding the error ($M=3.12$, $SD=.95$ for finding, $M=2.54$, $SD=.99$ for correction), which means that a significant number of participants was able to find the error but not correct it. This is also true when comparing separate conditions, where the difference between finding and correcting the error in EEWOH and EEWH is significant, but it is a stronger effect in EEWOH ($t(7)=6.56$, $p<.001$, $r=.92$), who could correct about 1/3 of the mistakes they found, and much less in the EEWH ($t(7)=4.19$, $p=.001$, $r=.85$), who could correct 1/2 of the mistakes they found. The same phenomenon occurred even with students who could solve exercises, but could not correct errors of the same type. For example, most students could add fractions with unlike denominators, but could not correct related errors.

Discussion: 7th-8th-Grade. An explanation for the fact that the erroneous examples conditions, and especially the EEWH condition, did not perform better in the metacognitive skills of erroneous examples, for which they were trained, is the little time they spent on erroneous examples in the posttest. Moreover, the long session might have overloaded the students and especially the ones in the EEWH condition whose sessions last long (two and a half hours) because of the help provided. The possible resulting fatigue might be the reason why they did not spent more time on erroneous examples in the posttest.

A plausible interpretation for the fact that the term grade is a significant covariate for answering conceptual questions, but not for cognitive skills is that a higher level of prior math knowledge is required to process new conceptual knowledge. This high-level knowledge is not necessary to deal with trained cognitive skills, which can be done by using well-practice solutions steps (algorithmically). The difference between finding and correcting the error may mean that although students know the correct rules for performing operations on fractions and can recognise errors that violate these rules, they still have knowledge gaps that surface when asked to correct the error.

3.3 School Study: 9th-10th-Grade

In order to test the use of erroneous examples outside the lab we conducted school studies. The school studies tested students from two different schools, one urban and one suburban, of yet a higher level (9th and 10th-grade). Our expert teachers advised that these students typically still exhibit common fractions misconceptions. However, 9th and 10th-graders have, on average, an overall higher math knowledge. Since we found that math knowledge (term grade) has a covariating effect on conceptual understanding, we wanted to see if erroneous examples would have a better effect with these higher grade students.

Forty-three students completed the study, distributed as follows: EEWH=14, EEWOH=18, NOEE=11. The difference in the pretest was not significant either between 9th and 10th grade ($p=.12$), or between conditions ($p=.7$). They completed the experiment on two days separated by a week. Many students did not attend school on the second experimental day, which led to the unbalanced conditions.

3.3.1 Materials

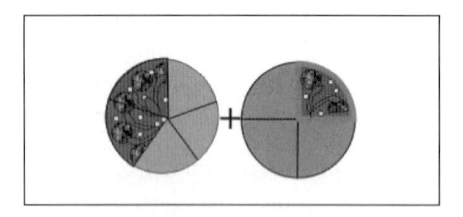

Fig. 4. Pizza representation of fraction problem 3/5+1/4

To emphasise conceptual learning and avoid a ceiling effect in this study we shifted from the traditional school fraction curriculum and included more conceptual exercises to address the basic principles for fractions. For instance, we used the principles of "addition as increasing", "subtraction as decreasing", and "part of a whole" [22]. In effect, we reorganised the materials to reflect this shift and also added one sequence to train the basic concept "part of a whole". Thus, we incorporated conceptual errors on top of the rule-application errors which were the focus of the previous lab studies. We also changed the order of presentation of the erroneous examples in the intervention; a sequence here consisted of standard exercise – erroneous examples – standard exercise, to test whether giving students the opportunity to train a bit after the erroneous examples would make a difference. Furthermore, we adjusted the pretest and posttest exercises to test these concepts and added a transfer exercise for fraction subtraction and two that asked students to transform a fraction operation represented with pizzas into a numerical fraction representation. For example, the task in Fig. 4 had to be represented as 3/5+1/4, a standard kind of exercise done at schools.

3.3.2 Results: School Study 9th- and 10th-Grade

The results of the school studies supported our hypotheses. The participants in the EEWH condition scored higher in most scores used as measures of learning. There is no clear second place that varies between EEWOH and NOEE. Although the variances tend to be high, they are mostly comparable between conditions, allowing for analysis of variance. The biggest differences were in favour of EEWH for the modelling exercises in total ($F(2,39)=3.11$, $p=.056$, $n^2=.14$), and for modelling the basic concept "part of a whole" alone which just missed significance ($F(2,39)=3.20$, $p=.051$, $n^2=.14$), and the transfer exercises (cf. Table 3) which was not significant. Conceptual understanding gave results with very high variance. Still, EEWH scored significantly higher than NOEE ($p=.016$, $d=1.28$) in modelling "part of a whole", which was trained, and even lower than in the pretest for the same concept. However, NOEE scored higher for modelling "relative part of" that was not trained during intervention, but was meant to test transfer from the more general concept "part of a whole". EEWOH scored very low in both concepts.

Table 3. Descriptive Statistics School Studies 9th, 10th-Grade

Score	Condition Subscore	EEWH mean(sd)%	EEWOH mean(sd)%	NOEE mean(sd)%
Cognitive Skills	Pretest	75.99(11.9)	64.3(20.6)	61.3(12.7)
	Diff-post-pre-total	9.3(13.8)+	2.0(24.5)	6.3(22.5)^
	Transform-total	21.5(22.9)+	8.23(32.2)^	1.6(48.7)
Metacognitive Skills (EE)	EE-find	53.6(27.5)+	47.2(27.0)	52.3(28.4)^
	EE-correct	30.4(28.0)+	15.3(24.5)	27.3(32.5)^
	EE-ConQuest*	46.4(20.3)^	48.2(25.3)+	41.7(29.3)
	EE-total	44.6(20.9)+	41.4(22.9)	40.9(26.8)^
	Total-time-on-EE	7.6(7.9)	5.8(3.3)+	6.2(3.5)^
Transfer	Add-subtr-total	30.4(36.9)+	16.7(34.3)	18.2(25.2)^
	Conc-transf-total*	49.4(36.8)+	31.9(30.0)	34.9(32.0)^
	Transfer-total	39.88(22.6)+	24.3(26.8)	26.5(28.6)^
Conceptual Understanding	Part-of-whole	21.4(42.9)+	-5.6(62.8)^	-30.7(38.5)
	Addition-as-incr	69.6(41.8)+	62.5(47.2)^	45.5(52.2)
	Subtr-as-decreas	50.0(51.9)+	25.0(42.9)	27.3(46.7)^
	Rel-part-of	28.6(46.9)^	8.3(25.7)	31.8(46.2)+
	Modelling-total	56.7(33.0)+	32.6(25.6)	33.5(29.9)^

Note: +=best, ^=middle learning gains, *=also conceptual skill

Moreover, the cognitive skills in the taught exercises increased more for EEWH that had a variance of about 10% lower than the other two conditions. EEWH reached the mean of 85.2 ($SD=14.9$) in the posttest and surpassed the other two conditions by almost 20%. This difference in the posttest was also significant, as measured by an ANOVA ($F(2,39)= 5.42$, $p=.008$, $n^2=.13$). Similarly, for the transformation exercises, EEWH scored a mean of 88.0 ($SD=20.99$) in the posttest and significantly better than the other conditions ($F(2,39)= 3.48$, $p=.04$, $n^2=.15$). The planned Helmert contrasts indicated significant main effects of erroneous examples (EEWH and EEWOH conditions) for modelling the concept "part of a whole" ($p=.038$, $d=0.63$). For the conditions EEWH and NOEE, there was a significant higher performance of EEWH in modelling "part of a whole" ($p=.016$, $d=1.28$) and almost for modelling in general ($p=.056$, $d=0.74$). The condition EEWH did significantly better than EEWOH in modelling in general ($p=.026$, $d=0.81$).

We also tested the possible covariating effect of the pretest-total. The pretest score was meant to indicate significant differences based on the prior fraction knowledge. Interestingly, the pretest scores have a covariating effect on learning for the taught cognitive skills ($F(1,39)=21.56$, $p=.000$, $n^2=.36$) and for the transformation skills ($F(1,39)=9.52$, $p=.004$, $n^2=.22$) separately. Taking this effect into account turns both of these scores into significant effects (taught cognitive skills, $F(2,39)=3.46$, $p=.041$, $n^2=.14$ and transformation skills $F(2,39)=3.45$, $p=.042$, $n^2=.13$), as well as for modelling the concept "part of whole" ($F(2,39)=3.96$, $p=.027$, $n^2=.17$). Through a closer look with help of the planned contrasts, a main effect of erroneous examples can be seen (EEWH and EEWOH conditions) for modelling the concept "part of a whole" ($p=.04$, $d=0.67$). For the conditions EEWH and NOEE, there was a significantly higher performance of EEWH in the transformation exercises ($p=.015$, $d=0.8$) and modelling "part of a whole" ($p=.007$, $d=0.9$) and almost for taught cognitive skills ($p=.058$, $d=0.62$). The condition EEWH only did significantly better than EEWOH in the taught cognitive skills ($p=.019$, $d=0.77$), but differences were also quite big in the transformation exercises ($p=.085$, $d=0.56$), and in modelling in general ($p=.061$, $d=0.61$). An additional interesting result is that EEWH condition spent significantly more time-on-task ($p=.037$, $d=0.68$) than any of the other two, but even more than NOEE ($p=.016$, $d=0.79$).

Moreover, although we did not find any significant difference between conditions in metacognitive skills, we again found that significantly more students across conditions could find the error in the posttest erroneous examples than correct it $t(42)=8.84$, $p=.000<.001$, $r=.81$.

The above results for the 9th and 10th-grade are by and large robust, however the variance was significantly big for transformation ($p=.003$), where EEWH has a much smaller variance than any of the other two conditions. This difference, in combination with the different sample sizes, might make the results for this score unreliable.

Discussion: 9th- and 10th-Grade School Study. The most striking result is that erroneous examples with help had a significant effect for the taught cognitive skills over erroneous examples without help and an almost significant effect over no erroneous examples. The source of this might be the higher math knowledge of the more advanced students (9th- and 10th-grade). Confronting the students with more conceptual exercises on fractions may have contributed to this result, too.

Moreover, our results indicated a beneficial use of erroneous examples as a whole for the conceptual exercises dealing with modelling. The high variance in modelling the basic concepts tested in this experiment indicates that some students could understand the principle behind them and had no problems applying them, whereas others were just confused. This effect is particularly high for the EEWOH in modelling "part of a whole", as well as not for modelling "relative part of" that was not taught at all during intervention, but was meant to test transfer from the more general concept "part of a whole". Both of these concepts seem to have been particularly confusing for EEWOH. The higher variance and the negative learning effect in "part of a whole" for EEWOH may mean that this condition was confused by being asked to represent the difficult concept "part of a whole" explicitly and conceptually (as opposed to the standard school algorithmic approach). Since they received no help, they could not recover from the confusion at all, unlike EEWH, and scored badly both in this trained concept ("part of a whole"), and in the transfer concept ("relative part of"). A possible explanation for the high learning effect of EEWH but also the high variance is that they had the chance to practice the basic concept "part of a whole" in the way taught by the erroneous examples with additional support. This resulted in scoring better at the relevant exercise, and relatively high in transferring from this concept to "relative part of", but might have still confused students who rely on purely procedural/algorithmic solutions. NOEE managed to score better than EEWOH as they just used the standard algorithmic strategy taught at school without necessarily having a deeper understanding of the concept.

4 General Discussion

In our studies with different levels of students we had some consistent results but also some results that reveal a difference in how erroneous examples with error detection and correction help can influence mathematics learning.

We found that more advanced students (9th and 10th-grade) benefit from erroneous examples with help in terms of cognitive skills (including standard problem solving) in general, as opposed to erroneous examples without help or no use of erroneous examples at all. Although this was not the case for either of the two less advanced levels that we tested, it might have been an artefact of the very high prior fraction knowledge of the particular participants (6th, 7th, and 8th-grade). Moreover, we had some sources of evidence that deep conceptual understanding is influenced by erroneous examples with additional error detection and correction help. Such evidence includes the better performance of the EEWH over the NOEE condition at the conceptual questions in the 6th-grade, as well as the higher scores in modelling "part of a whole" for EEWH vs. NOEE and in modelling as a whole for EEWH vs. EEWOH (both for the 9th and 10th-grade). The higher grades (9th, 10th) also received more intervention materials aiming at conceptual understanding. The difference in conceptual understanding between EEWH and EEWOH for the same grade levels might have also instigated the respective difference in cognitive skills. Additionally, we found that erroneous examples can also influence the metacognitive skill of error detection for lower-grade (6th-grade) but highly competent students. There is a possible twofold explanation for this. First, these students, who have just learned fractions can handle the demanding erroneous examples because the cognitive skills and domain knowledge that erroneous examples presuppose is readily available to them. Second, there is room for improving their error-detection significantly as they have not yet applied much what they have learned to make errors themselves and, hence, practice error-detection on their own errors.

Overall, we found some main effects for erroneous examples for the less advanced 6th-grade (metacognitive skills) and the more advanced 9th and 10th-grade (conceptual understanding), but most effects were for erroneous examples with help. This is consistent with the results of Kopp and colleagues [17] in the medical domain in terms of the benefit of erroneous examples with help, although the domains differ a lot and a comparison is tenuous. We also found that the use of erroneous examples without help might be worse than no use of erroneous examples for conceptual and transfer skills, which is not reliably true for metacognitive skills. As a whole, the inconsistent performance observed in the school study with regard to the modelling might mean that there was a conflict between the standard procedural way fractions are taught at school and the conceptual way our erroneous examples deal with them. This effect might be stronger for EEWOH who are left confused, due to the lack of guidance. More familiarity with erroneous examples and the conceptual strategy might counterbalance this confusion, especially when combined with provision of help. Siegler [14] has suggested that requests for explanation of correct and incorrect strategies lead to a period of "cognitive ferment" (p. 51) and only later do they cause the development of correct strategies and the ability to self-explain. He attributes this delay to a state of increased uncertainty and variability. Another possible explanation for the lack of transfer between the taught concept ("part of a whole") and the untaught concept ("relative part of") might be that the theoretically subordinate category of "relative part of" is actually not cognitively subordinate, and hence there is no transfer between the two basic concepts in terms of learning.

Our results do not support the use of erroneous examples with or without help for medium-advanced students (7th and 8th-grade), where prior knowledge seems to play a crucial role. A reason for that might be the combination of the high grade level but also the high competence (term grade and pretest scores) which the participants had and was not the case for the 9th and 10th-grade.

An interesting mismatch between the competencies of finding and correcting the error across conditions is evident in our results. This mismatch persisted in all our studies independent of student level or material design, and it was significant in our studies with the two higher grade students (7th-8th and 9th-10th-grades). Ohlsson [24] has described this phenomenon as dissociation between declarative and practical knowledge. It is intriguing that in our school studies with 9th and 10th-graders, students' cognitive skills did improve through erroneous examples, despite the fact that their ability to find errors developed significantly more than that of correcting errors. This might show that the competence of correcting typical errors is not necessary for monitoring, correcting, or avoiding one's own errors. That is consistent with Ohlsson's argument, that when the competency for finding errors is active, it functions as a self-correction mechanism that, given enough learning opportunities, can lead to a reduction of performance errors. However, it is a new finding in comparison to previous research in erroneous examples that has not differentiated between the competencies of finding and correcting errors. In our case, it seems like erroneous examples with error-detection and error-correction help that specifically train finding errors and explaining them might offer the required learning opportunities without the need to develop the error-correction skill. The contribution of such help is also in line with the theoretical work by van Gog and her colleagues [25] who have advocated its use in the context of worked examples as a way for promoting conceptual understanding.

Regarding the presentation of erroneous examples, we have at least a first indication that they are more beneficial when presented after the students have been confronted with standard exercises and followed again by standard exercises, since we only found a significant improvement at tasks other than erroneous examples when this order of presentation was used. A potential explanation is that this gives students the opportunity to review the material before working with erroneous examples that might also increase the perceived relevance of erroneous examples, as well as to practice what they have learned after the presentation of the erroneous examples.

In general, although our results show room for further improvement in the students' understanding of fractions, they still reveal a good trend for erroneous examples as an instructional method that can help students in this demanding domain, in particular for more advanced students (higher grade) who have had fractions in the past, but also for students just having learned fractions. They also indicate that previous results on the benefits of self-explaining correct and incorrect examples by Siegler and colleagues in water displacement and mathematical equality problems [14], [15] and Grosse and Renkl in probability problems [16] are transferable to online erroneous examples in the fraction domain.

4.1 Open Questions

A question that remains open is how less and medium advanced students (6th, 7th, and 8th-grade) can be helped to improve their cognitive skills using erroneous examples. A practical measure here, in terms of our design of online erroneous examples, may be to allow students to explicitly request more help. It is likely that they will use this extra feature if they feel uncertain about their answer, thus overcoming a possible shortcoming of our design of online erroneous examples which assumes that if students can answer the basic "why" and "how" process-oriented MCQs they do not need error detection and correction help; MCQs dealing with this issue are skipped in that case. However, this might be too coarse an indicator for when and how much help is needed. Moreover, it underestimates the difficulty students have with applying rules.

The materials and instructional design might also need adaptations. For instance, the results might be clearer if we enrich our conceptual exercises and test more whether errors that reveal lack of conceptual understanding are not used. We want to elaborate more on such conceptual exercises since the standard fraction exercises practiced at school might be too simple to be able to influence students' performance alone through process-oriented help, as we have observed in our studies with the less-advanced and medium-advanced students and is also hypothesised from a theoretical perspective by [25]. A good start would be to try to replicate our results for the advanced students (9th and 10th-grade) using the new more conceptual materials with the other grade levels. A more representative sample in terms of prior math and fraction knowledge is also a prerequisite for this test. Furthermore, the replication of the results would help rule out the possibility that the materials alone and not the level made the difference in our results. Moreover, due to the big variances in the study with 9th and 10th grades and the unequal group sizes we are already planning to collect additional data points to be able to draw even more reliable conclusions.

Finally, we want to test whether the order of presentation really plays a significant role, by using the more conceptual material and varying the order of presentation between different conditions.

Acknowledgments. This work was supported by the DFG - Deutsche Forschungsgemeinschaft under the ALoE project ME 1136/7.

References

1. Jones Newton, K.: An Extensive Analysis of Preservice Teachers' Knowledge of Fractions. American Educational Research Journal 45(4), 1080–1110 (2008)
2. Stafylidou, S., Vosniadou, S.: The development of students' understanding of the numerical values of fractions. Learning and Instruction 14, 503–518 (2004)
3. McLaren, B.M., Lim, S.J., Koedinger, K.R.: When and how often should worked examples be given to students? New results and a summary of the current state of research. In: Love, B.C., McRae, K., Sloutsky, V.M. (eds.) Proceedings of the 30th Annual Conference of the Cognitive Science Society, pp. 2176–2181. Cognitive Science Society (2008)
4. Paas, F.G., van Merrienboerg, J.J.G.: Variability of worked examples and transfer of geometrical problem-solving skills: A cognitive-load approach. Journal of Educational Psychology 86(1), 122–133 (1994)
5. Renkl, A.: Learning from worked-out examples: A study on individual differences. Cognitive Science 21, 1–29 (1997)
6. Trafton, J.G., Reiser, B.J.: The contribution of studying examples and solving problems. In: Proceedings of the Fifteenth Annual Conference of the Cognitive Science Society (1993)
7. Tsamir, P., Tirosh, D.: In-service mathematics teachers' views or errors in the classroom. In: International Symposium: Elementary Mathematics Teaching, Prague (August 2003)
8. Borasi, R.: Capitalising on errors as "springboards for inquiry": A teaching experiment. Journal for Research in Mathematics Education 25(2), 166–208 (1994)
9. Müller, A.: Aus eignen und fremden Fehlern lernen. Praxis der Naturwissenschaften 52(1), 18–21 (2003)
10. Oser, F., Hascher, T.: Lernen aus Fehlern - Zur Psychologie des negativen Wissens. Schriftenreihe zum Projekt: Lernen Menschen aus Fehlern? Zur Entwicklung einer Fehlerkultur in der Schule, Pädagogisches Institut der Universität Freiburg (1997)
11. Seidel, T., Prenzel, M.: Mit Fehlern umgehen - Zum Lernen motivieren. Praxis der Naturwissenschaften 52(1), 30–34 (2003)
12. Strecker, C.: Aus Fehlern lernen und verwandte Themen, http://www.blk.mat.uni-bayreuth.de/material/db/33/fehler.pdf
13. OECD: International report PISA plus (2001)
14. Siegler, R.S.: Microgenetic studies of self-explanation. In: Granott, N., Parziale, J. (eds.) Microdevelopment, Transition Processes in Development and Learning, pp. 31–58. Cambridge University Press, Cambridge (2002)
15. Siegler, R.S., Chen, Z.: Differentiation and integration: Guiding principles for analyzing cognitive change. Developmental Science 11, 433–448 (2008)
16. Grosse, C.S., Renkl, A.: Finding and fixing errors in worked examples: Can this foster learning outcomes? Learning and Instruction 17, 612–634 (2007)
17. Kopp, V., Stark, R., Fischer, M.R.: Fostering diagnostic knowledge through computer-supported, case-based worked examples: effects of erroneous examples and feedback. Medical Education 42, 823–829 (2008)
18. Melis, E., Goguadze, G., Homik, M., Libbrecht, P., Ullrich, C., Winterstein, S.: Semantic-aware components and services in ActiveMath. British Journal of Educational Technology. Special Issue: Semantic Web for E-learning 37(3), 405–423 (2006)

19. Paas, F.G., Renkl, A., Sweller, J.: Cognitive load theory and instructional design: Recent developments. Educational Psychologist 38, 1–4 (2003)
20. Skinner, B.F.: The behavior of organisms: An experimental analysis. Appleton-Century, New York (1938)
21. Melis, E.: Design of erroneous examples for ActiveMath. In: Bredeweg, B., Looi, C.-K., McCalla, G., Breuker, J. (eds.) 12th International Conference on Artificial Intelligence in Education. Supporting Learning Through Intelligent and Socially Informed Technology (AIED 2005), vol. 125, pp. 451–458. IOS Press, Amsterdam (2005)
22. Malle, G.: Grundvorstellungen zu Bruchzahlen. Mathematik Lehren 123, 4–8 (2004)
23. Tsovaltzi, D., Melis, E., McLaren, B.M., Dietrich, M., Goguadze, G., Meyer, A.-K.: Erroneous Examples: A Preliminary Investigation into Learning Benefits. In: Cress, U., Dimitrova, V., Specht, M. (eds.) EC-TEL 2009. LNCS, vol. 5794, pp. 688–693. Springer, Heidelberg (2009)
24. Ohlsson, S.: Learning from Performance Errors. Psychological Review 103(2), 241–262 (1996)
25. van Gog, T., Pass, F., van Merrienboerg, J.J.G.: Process-Oriented Worked Examples: Improving Transfer Performance Through Enhanced Understanding. Instructional Science 32, 83–98 (2004)

Enhancing the Learning Process: Qualitative Validation of an Informal Learning Support System Consisting of a Knowledge Discovery and a Social Learning Component

Eline Westerhout[1], Paola Monachesi[1], Thomas Markus[1], and Vlad Posea[2]

[1] Utrecht University, Utrecht Institute of Linguistics OTS,
Janskerkhof 13a, 3512 BL Utrecht, The Netherlands
[2] "Politehnica" University of Bucharest,
Department of Computer Science and Engineering,
313 Splaiul Independentei, Bucharest, Romania

Abstract. In a Lifelong Learning context, learners often rely on informal learning materials to access and process information. There is a growing interest in accessing educational material on the social web. We have created a system that facilitates learners and tutors in accessing informal knowledge sources in the context of a learning task and describe the results of a summative and formative evaluation of this system. The system consists of a knowledge discovery component and a social learning component. The evaluation shows that with our system informal resources can successfully enhance the learning process within a Lifelong Learning context. The knowledge discovery component assists the learner in identifying relevant concepts, discovering relations between concepts, and mastering the correct vocabulary. In addition the social learning component offers relevant and trusted documents and contacts on the basis of a learner's social network.

Keywords: informal learning, knowledge discovery, social learning, social search, validation, lifelong learning.

1 Introduction

In a Lifelong Learning context, learners access and process information in an autonomous way. Very often they rely on informal learning materials, that is, on (non-)textual content available through the web which is uploaded and accepted by the community of learners and not necessarily by a content provider of an institution. Social media are also becoming increasingly relevant in the informal learning context with learners using them not only in their free time but also for educational tasks. Institutions such as MIT, Berkeley and Stanford employ YouTube to post videos of their lectures. Their channels have been accessed more than one million times and have between 30 and 60 thousand members. However, the social aspects of these sites are not fully explored for learning purposes but the figures illustrate that there is a growing interest in accessing educational material on the social web.

One of the objectives of the Language Technologies for Lifelong Learning (LTfLL) project[1], is to create services that facilitate learners and tutors in accessing informal knowledge sources in the context of a learning task. To this end, an inFormal Learning Support System (iFLSS) is being developed which allows the stakeholders (i.e. tutors and learners) to identify, retrieve and exchange learning material. The iFLSS exploits the intrinsic features of social media applications, that is, their resources, the tags used to label them and the networks of users. More specifically, the system sustains informal learning by means of a knowledge discovery component which is based on an ontology enhanced with the vocabulary of the community of practice (CoP) expressed by the tags used and by a social search component that retrieves relevant material on the basis of the tags and users belonging to the CoP. Communication is facilitated through the use of social networks and new communities of learners can be established through the recommendations provided by the system.

In this paper, we focus on the results of a summative and formative evaluation of the iFLSS after providing an overview of its technical features. We have carried out a scenario-based evaluation of the system and its various components. We have employed questionnaires to assess the contribution of the iFLSS to the learning process while interviews have provided more detailed feedback on the use of the system and suggestions on possible ways to improve it.

2 State of the Art

The iFLSS relies on Web 2.0 technology to develop appropriate solutions for current learning problems. Several authors are exploring similar possibilities. In [1], social bookmarking and wisdom of the crowd are analyzed as being useful for the needs of researchers and learners. They conclude that Web 2.0 offers a large number of technologies that can be used for learning. The authors state that we must not build tools because we have the technology, but because learners need them. The social web features are exploited in learning environments in the European Mupple and TenCompetence projects. In [2], the authors describe an environment that allows for the creation of personal learning environments using mash-ups of existing web services. ReMashed [3] is a more recent application based on recommendations from the content of social networking applications like Delicious or Slideshare. There are not many contributions in the eLearning context with respect to social search but there is a driving force in industry that contributes to the fast development of this area. Aardvark[2] Mahalo[3], and Google Social[4] are just a few of the most important social search applications recently developed. Aardvark identifies a user from the searcher's social network

---

[1] http://www.ltfll-project.org
[2] http://vark.com/
[3] http://www.mahalo.com
[4] http://www.google.com/s2/search/social

to answer a query while Google Social identifies the best users and resources from their network and Mahalo allows users to build search answers.

The iFLSS, like the learning environments previously discussed, exploits the intrinsic features of social media applications. Its theoretical foundations are laid in [4], who views the knowledge building process as a mutual construction of individual and social knowledge, seeking a balance between the Acquisition (individual) and the Participation (social) Metaphor. In his view, knowledge is a socially mediated product. Individuals develop personal representations and beliefs from their own perspectives, but they also do so on the basis of socio-cultural knowledge building, shared language and external representations. These personal representations and beliefs are extended through social interaction, communication, discussion, clarification and negotiation, which occur in conversations. Learners, therefore, build knowledge collaboratively and then internalize it in a personal knowledge building process. This internalization also follows Vygotsky's ideas [5]. As a result, learners become skilled members of a Community of Practice (CoP) [6], mastering the learning domain speech genre [7]. Bakhtin's view is that an expert is a person who handles such a speech genre. In order to do this the expert has to master the appropriate vocabulary. However, experts should also be able to build a discourse (i.e. to act in society), therefore we should also be able to detect an expert with respect to his role in the CoP, that is a central figure who can often create a bridge across different communities. CoPs in real life use social networks on the Internet to exchange information and to communicate. Therefore, we assume in the iFLSS that the role of experts in a community is captured by the artifacts they produce on these social networks on the Internet. The use of ontologies in the iFLSS, is also related to Bakhtin's view [7], since they provide a formalization of the knowledge of a domain approved by experts.

3 The inFormal Learning Support System

Learners use search engines such as Google to acquire new knowledge by locating relevant resources and answers to questions [8]. However, it is not always easy to identify the most appropriate learning materials on the web. In order to assist learners we have developed an inFormal Learning Support System (iFLSS) that aims at solving two problems.

The first problem is due to the fact that learners, when they are new to a domain, do not know how the relevant concepts are related to each other. In addition, they do not always master the technical vocabulary necessary to carry out successful searches. The knowledge discovery component of the iFLSS (section 3.1) assists learners by providing insights in the conceptual representation of their domain of investigation. In this way, the system supports them in their knowledge discovery process. A second problem is that learners often have difficulty deciding which resources are the most appropriate ones in the context of a given learning task and whether they come from a trusted source. Standard search engines are based only on textual information and lack an explicit social dimension that can help solve these shortcomings. Social media applications

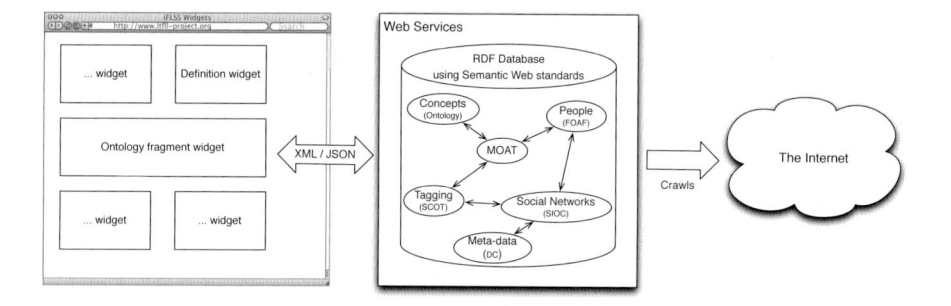

Fig. 1. iFLSS architecture overview

such as Delicious[5], Slideshare[6] or YouTube[7] can be employed to add this social dimension to search since they contain relevant social information in the form of tags, networks of users, user profiles and documents. In addition, learners can benefit from guidance and thus they might profit from finding appropriate people (i.e peers) in their extended social network that can help them. The social learning component of the iFLSS (section 3.2) supports the learner by offering search services based on the social networks of the learners.

Figure 1 depicts an overview of the overall architecture of the iFLSS. The backend web services are built on solid Semantic Web technologies which support lexicalised domain ontologies and large amounts of learning objects, users and meta-data through existing modeling standards. The user interface of the iFLSS is implemented using widgets that respect the W3C widget standard and that can be deployed in popular social networking or learning applications like Moodle or Elgg. In the rest of this section, we provide a more detailed overview of the technical features of the components and how the crawled informal learning data has been automatically converted into semantically interpretable RDF.

3.1 Knowledge Discovery

The knowledge discovery component of the iFLSS puts the concepts the learner is trying to acquire into perspective, guiding him in discovering relations and new concepts and in finding relevant learning materials. To this end, the service relies heavily on a domain ontology, which can be browsed by the learner to identify the main concepts in a domain, the relations among them and relevant resources (texts, videos, slides) that are associated with these concepts.

Ontologies can play an important role in the learning process within e-learning applications since they provide a formalization of the knowledge of a domain as approved by an expert. In addition, they can facilitate (multilingual) retrieval and reuse of content as well as mediate access to various sources of knowledge [9]. However, they also present some obvious shortcomings since they are often

---
[5] http://www.delicious.com
[6] http://www.slideshare.net
[7] http://www.youtube.com

static representations that model the knowledge of the domain at a given point in time. In addition, they might be incomplete or might not correspond to the representation of the domain knowledge available to the learner as expressed through public utterances on the social web. The vocabulary of the learners – especially novices – might be different from that of domain experts and could be more sensitive to evolving terminology or less specialized terms.

To overcome these problems, we have developed a methodology to enrich existing domain ontologies automatically with a personalized conceptualization and domain specific terms that maximally overlap with the learner's current perspective. The existing concepts in the ontology trigger the identification of new related concepts from the tags assigned by users in the social media applications, such as Delicious. The enriched ontology includes in this way the vocabulary of the learner's community of practice within the structure proposed by the expert. It is thus possible to reduce the gap between a domain expert's view and that of the learner.

In our case, we have enriched the LT4eL domain ontology on computing that was developed in the Language Technology for e-learning project[8]. It contains 1002 domain concepts, 169 concepts from OntoWordNet and 105 concepts from DOLCE Ultralite. The connection between tags and concepts is established by means of language-specific lexicons, where each lexicon specifies one or more lexicalizations for each concept. Tags are extracted from social media applications by means of a crawler. Similarity measures are employed to identify whether the tags are new lexicalisations of existing concepts from the LT4eL domain ontology. If the tags do not match an existing concept, we attempt to identify relations among the existing ontology concepts and the new concepts derived from the tags by relying on a background ontology, such as DBpedia [10]. Several heuristics are employed to discover taxonomic relations, synonyms and new relations explicitly coded in DBpedia. Ambiguities are resolved through an appropriate disambiguation algorithm. We refer to [11] and [12] for a more detailed description.

Figure 2 shows the interface of the knowledge discovery system. The ontology is displayed as a graph and depicts the concepts and their relations to each other, allowing thus for an understanding of the meaning of the concepts. However, in many cases this seems to be insufficient [13] and, therefore, the definition of a concept (extracted from Wikipedia) is shown when the learner selects it. We distinguish between concepts coming from an expert-validated domain ontology (blue concepts: *object-oriented programming language*, *JavaScript*, *HTML*, *scripting language*) and concepts that have been automatically added (green concepts: *CSS*, *DOM*, *JQuery*, *Ajax*, *JSON*). This transparency in the origin of concepts supports the learner in balancing completeness with correctness and relevancy. Search is triggered either by clicking a concept or by making a query: a list of documents extracted from Delicious best matching that concept is retrieved. The five most frequently used tags for each of the documents are displayed when the learner goes with the mouse over the document titles.

---

[8] http://www.lt4el.eu

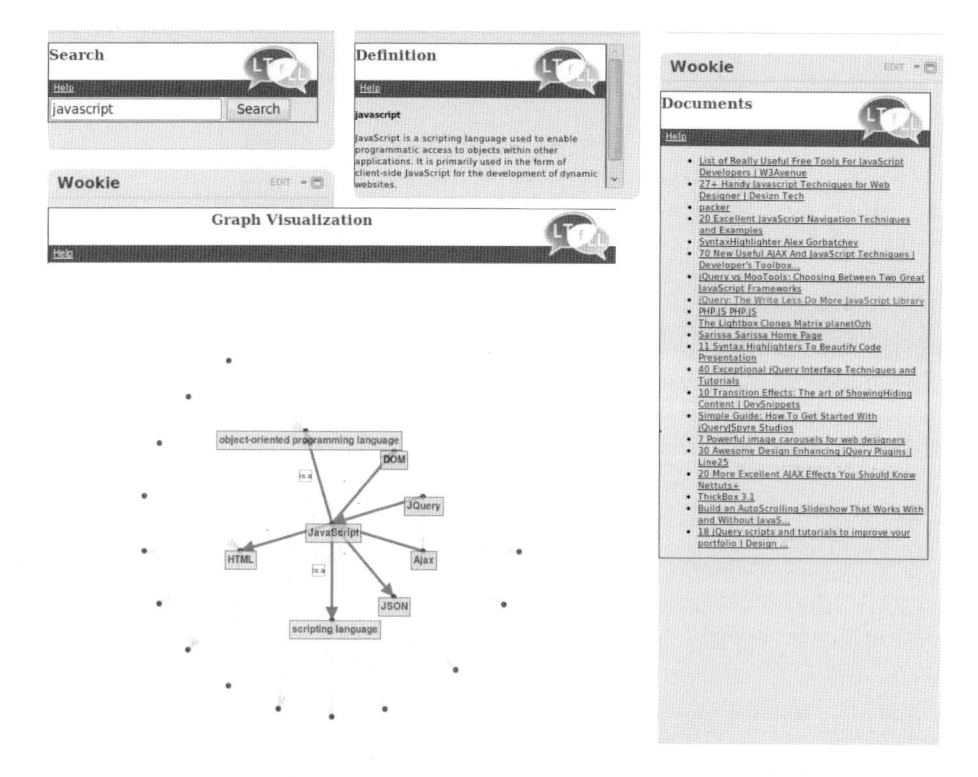

Fig. 2. The knowledge discovery component

3.2 Social Learning

The knowledge discovery component supports the learner in identifying relevant documents for his learning task. However, he still does not have the necessary means to assess whether the documents retrieved are appropriate for his task and whether they should be trusted. The social learning component of the iFLSS assists the learner in solving these problems by relying on data coming from social media applications and information about the learner's social network. Resources that have been tagged or uploaded by members of the learner's social network are retrieved. In this way, the suggested resources are associated with the name of a peer who is known to the learner and whom the learner trusts and knows already how to contact. The connection between the peers makes our recommendations valuable to the learner and adds a trust dimension to the materials retrieved. In addition, the social search can be used to create connections between learners and possible tutors. The social media tutors are different from the face to face tutors, since they offer assistance mostly by means of the documents posted (blog articles, bookmarks, presentations) and they offer less or none direct assistance.

A learner may use several social media applications on a daily basis. In order to provide valuable feedback on the content of these networks we have developed

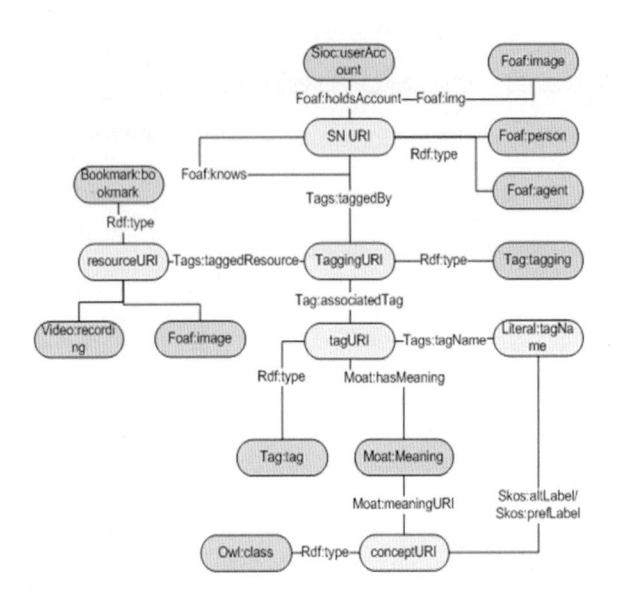

Fig. 3. The semantic vocabularies describing learning resources and activities

a tool that indexes the social relations as well as the learning resources from these social networks. The monitoring tool looks at the learner's network at two levels – the level of peers and the level of the peers' contacts. It extracts information about users and resources and converts these data into semantic data using vocabularies that describe activities performed on the web (SIOC[9]), tagging ontologies (Tagging[10], MOAT[11]), relations between people (FOAF[12]) and resource types (Video[13], SIOC, Dublin Core[14], FOAF). Figure 3 specifies how these semantic vocabularies together describe the learning resources and activities. The semantic data obtained from the monitoring tool are used to provide three types of learning services: search, recommendation and profiling. The data model is further explained in [14].

The search service returns relevant information from the social network of the learner (such as slides, videos, bookmarks) on the basis of a search query. The search is tag-based, which means that it uses the tags assigned by the community to describe the content. The FolkRank algorithm [15] (similar to PageRank) has been used for ranking the documents. To decide on the importance of a resource, this algorithm investigates the importance of the person who created or bookmarked it and the popularity of its tags.

---

[9] http://sioc-project.org/
[10] http://scot-project.org/
[11] http://moat-project.org/
[12] http://www.foaf-project.org/
[13] http://digitalbazaar.com/media/video
[14] http://dublincore.org/

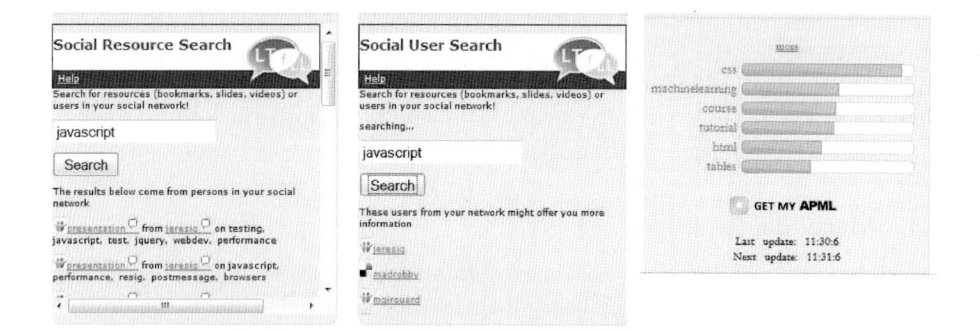

Fig. 4. The social learning component of the iFLSS

Profiling a learner means identifying a series of topics that are interesting for the learner and his networks and generating a list containing these concepts and their importance for the learner. Using this list a learner can rapidly check which are the main concepts addressed in his network. Also, by looking at the profile of a peer, a learner can see immediately if there are common interests they can relate upon. For profiling, we have developed a tool that generates an APML file (Attention Profile Markup Language)[15].

The interface of the social learning component (figure 4) is composed of three different parts: the resource search, the user search and the profiling widget. The resource search shows bookmarks, videos and presentations belonging to peers or friends of peers according to a given query. The resources are presented together with a link, the tags that are used to define them and the name of the peers who recommended them. The user search returns the names and links to the profiles of the peers with the most similar profile to the search query. The profiling widget shows a list of the most important tags used by the learner and his peers together with their importance. The widgets also show the sources of the peers and resources by indicating the logos of the social networking applications where they can be found.

4 Qualitative Validation

The validation aims to show how the functionalities offered by the iFLSS can enhance the learning process of learners. A scenario-based evaluation was adopted, which means that the software was validated within the context of a realistic learning task. The software and the learning process were evaluated using a questionnaire containing summative questions (e.g. Is the learning process more effective when our software is used?, Is the software time-saving?, How does it contribute to the quality of the learning process?). In addition to the summative questionnaires, interviews were conducted with small groups of learners in which a number of summative and formative questions were discussed. While the

---

[15] http://apml.areyoupayingattention.com

summative evaluation focused on the contribution of the services to the learning process, the formative evaluation provided feedback on the use of the system and yielded suggestions on how to improve it (e.g. Is the system easy to use? How could we improve the interface?). The results of both the summative and the formative evaluation of the services are presented in this paper.

4.1 Methods

Participants. The system has been validated with 19 students, which were divided into two groups on the basis of their prior knowledge about the domain. The first group contained 12 first year Arts students without any knowledge about the validation domain ('novice learners'). The other group consisted of 7 third year Computer Science students, who already had some knowledge about the validation domain, but still could improve their level of knowledge ('advanced learners'). The interviews with the students after the experiment revealed that for the novice learners most concepts addressed in the scenario were completely new, while the advanced learners already knew some of them.

Setting. The topic addressed in the scenario is the creation of a website to present results from a research project. The domain is slightly different for the novice and advanced learners; the novices' scenario is about basic website development (HTML, CSS), while the scenario of the advanced learners focuses on dynamic website development (JavaScript, JQuery, AJAX). Since the tutor does not have time to support his learners, he recommends them to use the iFLSS. The learners first use the knowledge discovery part of the iFLSS to discover which techniques and tools may be useful for creating their website. They identify relevant concepts and get acquainted with the domain by looking at relations, reading definitions, and consulting documents that explain how to build a website. Even though the knowledge discovery component allows the learner to acquire the basic information about what is needed for building a website, they still have some practical questions to get really started and have difficulties to identify the most relevant documents for their task. Therefore, they use the social network based component of the iFLSS to search for documents that have been created or recommended within their network. They are connected to their tutor on Delicious, SlideShare and YouTube and have in this way access to the experts and expertise in his network. The fact that experts bookmarked a learning object, provides the learner with information on its quality and reliability, since learners would not expect experts to bookmark documents of low quality. Furthermore, the social search enables the learners to find people in their network that can support them. The learners can easily see what the main interests are within their networks (i.e. learner and direct contacts) by looking at the APML profile, which modifies as time goes by and terms are added to the network.

Evaluation measures. The learners expressed their level of agreement on a number of statements using five point Likert scale items. The statements focused on several aspects of the system, such as the effectiveness of learning, the contribution to the learning process, and the usability of the system. The average scores and standard deviations are used to indicate the opinions of the learners on these aspects. Since the statistical power is often low (i.e. below 80%) due to the small sample sizes of the groups with novice and advanced learners (respectively 12 and 7), it is not always possible to draw statistical conclusions. When the statistical power was high enough, a paired t-test has been employed to compare the responses of the same learners to different questions whereas an unpaired t-test has been used to provide insights in differences between the novice and advanced learners. The system will be tested with a larger group of learners in the next evaluation round.

The issues raised in the answers to the open questions and the interviews have been examined as well to get better insights in the motivations of the learners.

4.2 Results

Evaluating the iFLSS. The main result of the evaluation is that both components of the iFLSS support the learners in their learning process, which can be seen in table 1. The knowledge discovery component was considered very useful for getting acquainted with a domain, since it helps the learner to easily discover how concepts are related to each other and what they mean. The documents retrieved enabled them to find appropriate documents on the concepts. The advanced learners appreciated this component more than the novice learners ($t(17) = -1.966$, $p<0.10$). The social learning component of the iFLSS was appreciated as well. The possibility to retrieve learning materials from the tutors network and to identify relevant people for a domain were perceived as supporting the learning process. The advanced learners are again more positive than the novice learners ($t(17) = -2.736$, $p<0.05$). The success of the social learning service strongly depends on the quality and size of the network, and thus on the willingness of tutors to use it. The novice learners were more skeptical in this respect, which may be related to the fact that they are mainly first year bachelor students, who have less contact with their tutors than the third year students. The fact that the learners would recommend both components to other learners also reveals that the learners are positive on the relevance of the system for their learning process. Again, the advanced learners are significantly more positive than the novice learners for both components ($t(17) = -2.57$, $p<0.05$ and $t(17) = -2.49$, $p<0.05$).

The remainder of this section focusses on the evaluation of the two components of the iFLSS – the knowledge discovery component and the social learning component.

Evaluating the Knowledge Discovery Component. The ontology fragment constitutes the core of the knowledge discovery component while the definitions and learning materials offer the learner additional support by providing extra information on the selected concept.

Table 1. Evaluating the inFormal Learning Support System

Component	Mean	Stdev
Useful for the learners' studies		
Knowledge discovery	4.26	0.56
Social learning	4.11	0.46
Recommend to other learners		
Knowledge discovery	4.16	0.50
Social learning	3.79	0.78

Ontology Fragment and Browsing. The concept browsing functionality assists the learner in finding out which concepts are semantically related and in which way. This information can then be used in several ways (e.g. to define a specific search query, to find out how known terms are related to each other, or to discover new related concepts). A potential problem related to the browsing functionality is that the amount of information shown in the fragment can be distracting when a learner is new to a domain.

Table 2. Evaluating the ontology fragment

ID	Statement	Learners	Mean	Stdev
1	'The related concepts in the ontology fragment improved my understanding of the topic.'	Novice	3.75	0.45
		Advanced	4	0.58
		All	3.84	0.5
2	'Concept browsing would be useful for my studies.'	Novice	4	0.74
		Advanced	4.57	0.53
		All	4.21	0.71

Table 2 shows that the ontology fragment assisted the learners in completing the task from the scenario (statement 1). Learners are even more positive on the usefulness of the ontology for their own studies (statement 1 vs. statement 2, $t(18) = -2.348$, $p<0.05$): both the novice and the advanced learners agreed that concept browsing would be useful, the advanced learners being even significantly more positive than the novice learners ($t(17) = -1.784$, $p<0.10$).

Definitions and Documents. An evaluation of a previous version of the system showed that novice learners appreciated the documents more than the ontology fragment [13]. Wikipedia definitions were therefore included in the current version to assist the learners in this respect. The interviews revealed that the definitions play an important role in the learning strategy of the learners. The learners used them to decide which concepts from the ontology should be explored in more detail.

Entering a query or clicking a concept triggered the search for documents bookmarked in Delicious. Although the learners considered the Delicious documents relevant for the task (table 3, statement 4), they expected them to be less useful for their own studies for three reasons. A first problem concerns the type of documents, which are often highly practical (e.g. tutorials or examples of code). Although this is very useful for building websites, in other domains one may need more in-depth information. The second problem is related to the difficulty level of the learning materials: the learners wondered whether it would be possible to include an indicator in this respect. As a last problem, some learners remarked that, although most documents are relevant, some of them are only slightly related to the query. This is due to using a tag-based search method, in which documents are selected on the basis of the tags that have been assigned to them and not on the basis of the content of the documents.

Table 3. Evaluating the definitions, the learning materials, and the tags

ID	Statement	Learners	Mean	Stdev
3	'The definitions of the concepts provide valuable information that is relevant for the task.'	Novice	4.25	0.62
		Advanced	4.57	0.79
		All	4.37	0.68
4	'The documents retrieved are relevant for the task.'	Novice	3.58	0.67
		Advanced	4	1
		All	3.74	0.81
5	'The tags shown in the document list for each of the documents provide valuable information that is relevant for the task.'	Novice	4	0.95
		Advanced	4.33	0.82
		All	4.11	0.90

The tags helped the learners to decide on the relevance of the documents (table 3, statement 5). The interviews revealed that the main strategy for deciding on the relevance of the learning materials was first looking at the title, then checking the tags, and eventually opening the documents. The added value of the tags over the titles is that they show on which topic(s) the document focuses. They can also provide information on the type of document, since tags like 'tutorial' are very common.

Evaluating the Social Learning Component. The knowledge discovery component thus assists the learners in getting acquainted with a domain and finding out which terms are relevant. However, the learners still encounter difficulties in selecting the most appropriate documents and would therefore like to know whether there are people that can provide them support. The social learning component, described in section 3.2, can be employed for this. The elements of this component are searching for peers and learning materials in the context of a learner's network, and showing the APML profile. We focused on the evaluation of the search for peers and learning materials. The experiment leader was the tutor and all learners were connected to this person on SlideShare, Delicious and YouTube. The APML profile reflects in this scenario the interests of the tutor, since the learners did not use their own networks but were only connected to this person. The learners were asked to indicate how the APML profiles could be used to support their learning process.

Relevance and Reliability of the Peers. The learners could use information provided by the system itself (i.e. by looking at the tags belonging to a person) and go to the profile pages from the peers on SlideShare, Delicious, or YouTube to assess the relevance of the recommended people. For 63.2% of the learners, it was not straightforward to assess whether a person was relevant on the basis of the information provided by the system (table 4). The interviews revealed that many learners used the profile pages of the persons to decide on their relevance. Providing more information on the expertise of the learner in the system would help the learner.

Table 4. Assessing relevance and reliability of the recommended peers

ID	Statement	Learners	Mean	Stdev
6	'The feedback provided by the system made it easy to judge whether the people are relevant.'	Novice	3.67	0.49
		Advanced	3.43	0.98
		All	3.58	0.69

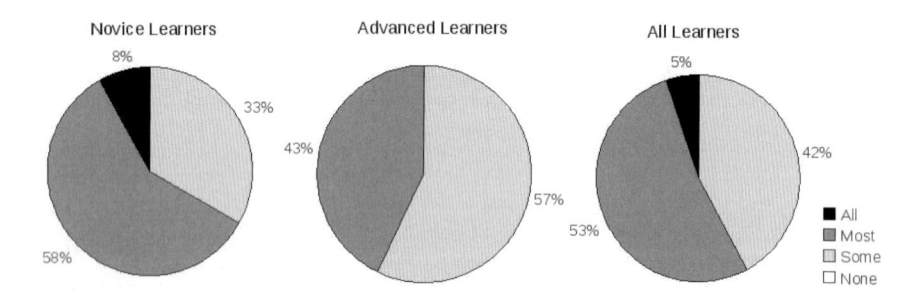

Fig. 5. Relevance of the recommended peers

Using the information provided by the system and the profile pages from the peers, the learners were able to figure out which people are relevant. Figure 5 shows that all learners agreed that the social learning system recommends at least some relevant people, although there are differences with respect to the amount of people considered relevant by the novice and advanced learners.

Relevance and Reliability of the Learning Materials. The quality and relevance of the learning materials proposed by the social learning component were judged positively by the learners (table 5). The interviews revealed that the learners considered them more relevant for the learning process than the documents retrieved with the knowledge discovery component. The learners used both the tags and the information on the peers who bookmarked or uploaded the documents to assess the relevance of the learning materials. The peer information added a trust dimension to the results. The feedback of the system to decide on the reliability of the learning materials is significantly higher judged by the advanced learners than by the novice learners (statement 8, $t(17) = -2.62$, $p<0.05$).

Table 5. Assessing relevance and reliability of the learning materials retrieved

ID	Statement	Learners	Mean	Stdev
7	'The documents retrieved are relevant for the task.'	Novice	3.83	0.72
		Advanced	4.29	0.76
		All	4.00	0.75
8	'The social network information helped me to judge the reliability of documents.'	Novice	3.42	0.67
		Advanced	4.14	0.38
		All	3.68	0.67

Some novice learners preferred the documents from their own tutor (i.e. a direct contact) above the results from non-direct contacts (peers of peers), since knowing the tutor personally made it more probable for them that a document is relevant. The advanced learners had no problems in this respect. The learners judged the documents retrieved as being relevant (table 5, statement 7) and indicated in the interviews that they preferred them above the results obtained with the knowledge discovery component, since they are more trusted and more relevant.

4.3 Discussion

The learners were positive about the relevance of the iFLSS for their studies, but provided several suggestions for improvement as well. The most important issue mentioned in the interviews is that they preferred the documents of the social learning component over the results obtained with the knowledge discovery component. The learning materials from the social network were judged as more trusted and more relevant, because they have been extracted from the network of the learner. We plan to integrate this suggestion in the next version of the system, in which we want to enable social network based search through the ontology. The results of the knowledge discovery component can be provided when the network does not contain (enough) resources on a topic.

Some learners found it challenging to decide on the reliability of peers and documents on the basis of the feedback provided by the iFLSS. A possible solution suggested during one of the interviews is to show the APML profiles of the peers as mouse-over (e.g. as cloud tags) to give the learner a quick and compact impression of their area(s) of expertise. However, we need to investigate to which extent the reliability information remains necessary when the learners use the system during an extended period of time. It might be the case that positive experiences with the system (i.e. it recommends relevant peers) make the current situation, in which the reliability of the peers can be derived from the profiles, sufficient for the learners.

The informal learning resources are described by a number of tags which have been assigned to them by the users of the social networks. As soon as many learners have bookmarked a document, the wisdom of the crowd ensures that the tags reflect the content of the document. However, as we noticed in the knowledge discovery component, it is possible that a document has been frequently tagged with a term that is discussed in a small part of the document, while the document focuses on a different concept. As a consequence, documents on related topics are often retrieved as well. Since developing a ranking method for documents was not one of our main goals, the current search is based on a simple algorithm. However, the results indicate that we need to implement a more sophisticated ranking algorithm that takes this aspect into account to improve on the ranking.

5 Conclusions and Future Work

The evaluation of the iFLSS has shown that informal resources can be successfully used to enhance the learning process within an eLearning context when appropriate technologies are used. The ontology browsing service and the definitions from the knowledge discovery component are especially relevant when a learner is new to a domain. This component assists the learner then in identifying relevant concepts, discovering relations between concepts, and mastering the correct vocabulary. The social network based search employs the social network of the learner to provide him with relevant and trusted documents and to suggest contacts that have knowledge on the topic of his query.

We plan to integrate the knowledge discovery and social learning components further by enabling the learner to search for documents and peers within his network on the basis of the ontology. In this way, the strong features of the two components will be combined, which will result in an enhanced system. We also want to develop services that can retrieve formal learning materials and academic learning materials (e.g. from Cite-U-Like or Google Scholar) in addition to the social media resources to make the system suitable for different tasks. We plan to validate the integrated and extended version of the system at the end of this year with a larger sample of learners over a longer period of time, making it possible to draw stronger conclusions.

The widget-based implementation of the iFLSS allows the learner to select the combination of widgets that best supports his learning task contributing thus to a more personalized learning experience. Furthermore, it permits an easy integration of the services into existing systems, like Moodle or Elgg.

References

1. Ullrich, C., Borau, K., Luo, H., Tan, X., Shen, L., Shen, R.: Why web 2.0 is good for learning and for research. In: Proceeding of the 17th international conference on World Wide Web - WWW 2008, p. 705. ACM Press, New York (2008)
2. Wild, F., Mödritscher, F., Sigurdarson, S.: Designing for Change: Mash-Up Personal Learning Environments. eLearning Papers 9, 1–15 (2008)
3. Drachsler, H., Rutledge, L., Van Rosmalen, P., Hummel, H., Peccu, D., Arts, T., Hutten, E., Koper, R.: ReMashed - An Usability Study of a Recommender System for Mash-Ups for Learning. International Journal of Emerging Technologies in Learning (iJET) 5(S1), 1–8 (2010)

4. Stahl, G.: Group Cognition: Computer Support for Collaborative Knowledge Building. The MIT Press, Cambridge (2006)
5. Vygotsky, L.: Mind and society: The development of higher mental processes. Harvard University Press, Cambridge (1978)
6. Lave, J., Wenger, E.: Situated learning: Legitimate peripheral participation. Cambridge University Press, Cambridge (1991)
7. Bakhtin, M., Emerson, C., Holquist, M.: Speech genres and other late essays. University of Texas Press, Austin (1986)
8. Kuiper, E., Volman, M., Terwel, J.: Students' use of web literacy skills and strategies: Searching, reading and evaluating web information. Information Research: An International Electronic Journal 13(3), 13–13 (2008)
9. Monachesi, P., Simov, K., Mossel, E., Osenova, P., Lemnitzer, L.: What ontologies can do for eLearning. In: Proceedings of the International Conference on Interactive Mobile and Computer Aided Learning, IMCL 2008. (2008)
10. Auer, S., Bizer, C., Kobilarov, G., Lehmann, J., Cyganiak, R., Ives, Z.: Dbpedia: A nucleus for a web of open data. In: The Semantic Web, pp. 722–735 (2008)
11. Monachesi, P., Markus, T.: Using social media for ontology enrichment. In: The Semantic Web: Research and Applications. Springer, Heidelberg (2010) (in press)
12. Monachesi, P., Markus, T.: Socially driven ontology enrichment for eLearning. In: Proceedings of the Language Resources and Evaluation Conference, LREC 2010 (2010) (in press)
13. Monachesi, P., Markus, T., Mossel, E.: Ontology enrichment with social tags for elearning. In: Cress, U., Dimitrova, V., Specht, M. (eds.) EC-TEL 2009. LNCS, vol. 5794, pp. 385–390. Springer, Heidelberg (2009)
14. Posea, V.: Bringing the Social Semantic Web to the Personal Learning Environment. In: Proceedings of the 10th IEEE International Conference on Advanced Learning Technologies (2010)
15. Hotho, A., Jäschke, R., Schmitz, C., Stumme, G.: Information Retrieval in Folksonomies: Search and Ranking. In: Sure, Y., Domingue, J. (eds.) ESWC 2006. LNCS, vol. 4011, pp. 411–426. Springer, Heidelberg (2006)

Pattern-Mediated Knowledge Exchange in Non-Governmental Organizations

Franziska Arnold[1], Johannes Moskaliuk[2], Till Schümmer[3], and Ulrike Cress[1]

[1] Knowledge Media Research Center, Konrad-Adenauer Straße 40,
72072 Tuebingen, Germany
[2] University of Tuebingen, Konrad-Adenauer Straße 40,
72072 Tuebingen, Germany
[3] FernUniversität in Hagen, Universitätsstraße 1,
58084 Hagen, Germany
{f.arnold,j.moskaliuk,u.cress}@iwm-kmrc.de,
till.schuemmer@fernuni-hagen.de

Abstract. Non-governmental organizations often face the challenge that practical knowledge cannot easily be transferred between practitioners with different degrees of expertise, as there is no way of directly observing good practice, and practical knowledge often only exists in implicit form. In this paper, we describe how patterns may be used to support sharing practical knowledge, and based on the co-evolution model by Cress and Kimmerle, we provide a theoretical framework for describing how an exchange of practical knowledge takes place. We present the results of a case study that supports the efficiency of patterns. Patterns facilitate the exchange of good practice by leading to more explicit and understandable descriptions.

Keywords: Knowledge Exchange, Practical Knowledge, Collaborative Knowledge Building, Patterns, Non-Governmental Organizations.

1 Introduction

Non-governmental organizations (NGOs) are organizations that pursue charitable, humanitarian, or cultural objectives, but are not funded by any government. They are social communities with important social functions, and typically a large number of people who work for an NGO are volunteers [4]. Like other organizations, NGOs are under pressure to use their financial and staff resources efficiently and to improve their own practices constantly. An exchange and reflection of good practice is crucial for raising the occupational qualification of their personnel to the required level and to work successfully [4,11].

Knowledge of good practice is in most cases implicit and not easy to externalize, because it is based on experienced work routines which are often carried out unconsciously [10]. For this reason, it is difficult for practitioners to ensure an efficient exchange of practical knowledge. A process of reflecting of one's own practice and of advancing practical knowledge will need to be assisted by the NGO itself. So the main question of this paper is: how can practitioners be supported by providing conditions for an exchange of their practical knowledge?

In this paper, we will present a theoretical framework for describing how a computer-supported exchange of practical knowledge takes place. Referring to this, we assume that patterns facilitate the exchange of practical knowledge by making implicit knowledge explicit. In this regard, we will discuss the results of a case study on the application of the pattern concept. Our research takes place within the research project PATONGO (Patterns and Tools for Non-Governmental Organizations). The aim of PATONGO is to investigate and optimize the web-based exchange of good practices and to develop a common knowledge base using Web 2.0 technologies[1].

2 Theoretical Background

2.1 Exchange of Practical Knowledge

Generally, the larger part of practical knowledge will consist of implicit knowledge about sequences of action [10]. The *externalization* of such practical knowledge is laborious, because practitioners have to be aware of their individual sequences of action. From their own concrete knowledge, they will have to draw general conclusions, which can then be presented as abstract knowledge, and transfer that to other cases. Moreover, *internalization* processes are also a complex procedure and not easy to perform in the everyday working life of people working in the field. They will have to transfer information from an abstract level to a very specific and concrete situation, in order to make it adaptive. Both externalization and internalization are indispensible components of what constitutes collaborative knowledge building.

Sharing knowledge and consequential collaborative knowledge building (especially in an online context like the project PATONGO) are complex procedures. In this regard we will present the co-evolution model as a theoretical framework. It explicates the interaction between individual knowledge and collaborative knowledge building by using of a common knowledge base.

Co-Evolution of Knowledge. The co-evolution model by Cress and Kimmerle [3] has borrowed a perspective from Luhmann's sociological systems theory [8]. The model makes a distinction between two systems: the cognitive and the social system and considers the exchange of knowledge as an interplay between the cognitive and social system. Both systems interact by externalization and internalization. The social system is defined through the communication that occurs within an internet platform. People may change an artefact; they may collaboratively reflect their individual knowledge and tell of their own practice. Thus, collaborative knowledge building by Web 2.0 technologies takes place. These technologies, for example in the form of wikis, allow jointly editing articles on practical knowledge in the common encyclopedia, which is intended within the project PATONGO.

For the cognitive system, the mental effort that is required for externalization leads to deeper individual processing and clarification of the respective piece of knowledge. This will improve the individual's knowledge. The process of internalization will lead

---

[1] The co-operation partners include: FernUniversität Hagen, EKD (Evangelische Kirche in Deutschland, i.e. mainline Lutheran Protestant Church in Germany) and the Knowledge Media Research Center at Tuebingen.

to individual learning through inter-individual knowledge transfer, as people have to process information and integrate it into their own individual knowledge. So processes of externalization and internalization will lead to a mutual development of the practical knowledge of the practitioner, and of the collective knowledge base created by all practitioners. Cress and Kimmerle use the term co-evolution for this interaction between the cognitive and the social system [3].

2.2 Patterns for Sharing Practical Knowledge and Case Study

When experts are confronted with a problem, they will resort to solutions which have proved in the past that they work under conditions with similar problems. The invariant aspects of this solution structure, abstract fragments of individual cases, can be considered as a mental pattern. This unchangeable structure is based on specific problem situations, and the result of repeatedly applying a procedure of abstracting single experiences. Knowledge of this structure distinguishes an expert from a novice [7]. But often such practical knowledge is only available in implicit form. This means that experts may resort to this knowledge, but are not aware of the problem-solution pair. The aim of the pattern approach is to reduce these complications by externalizing practical knowledge and allocating this knowledge to others.

Based on examples of good practice, patterns collect the know-how of experienced practitioners, including invariant components of recurring problems and their successful solution within work routines [1]. This means that a pattern describes a frequent problem "and then describes the core of the solution to that problem, in such a way that you can use this solution a million times over, without ever doing the same way twice" [1, p. x]. So patterns of successful solutions are used as samples for solving recurrent problems in similar contexts, and they make it possible to externalize implicit knowledge by providing structures to fill in. They support the co-evolution of a user's practical knowledge and of the common knowledge base, as they provide the stage for successful communication between these two systems.

The pattern concept is derived from architecture and based on Christopher Alexander's idea to collect samples of good practice as problem-solving examples for their purpose of designing houses and streets by the respective communities [1]. The concept of a 'good practice collection' has been already implemented, e.g., in the fields of object-oriented software development [6,12]. Assuming that using patterns for describing complex software problems leads to improved externalization of knowledge, it seems to be a good idea to share and reflect practical knowledge by using patterns as well.

The documentation of practical knowledge in terms of patterns has been described in an increasing number of contexts, but in many cases only based on some inductive theoretical justification of their potential. Only few, not very systematic studies exist reviewing the practical implementation of patterns in a specific field. Although some practical derivations of a pattern concept exist, and it is plausible that the pattern approach is efficient, there is no theoretical framework so far and no empirical evidence of the mode of operation of patterns. What has been missing so far is an explicitly cognitive point of view at the pattern approach and its practical implementation in different fields.

Patterns from a Cognitive Point of View. Writers are guided, during the act of composing their texts, by distinctive processes of thinking, like rhetorical considerations, their own long-term memory, and individual writing processes. The main difficulty of such a writing process is becoming aware of one's own rhetorical situation. Relating to the exchange of practical knowledge, the authors of good practice descriptions will first have to become aware of their own knowledge, in order to be able to externalize it effectively. But retrieving information from the implicit part of one's own long-term memory is a difficult process. For this reason there is a need for "finding the cue that will let retrieve a network of useful knowledge" [5, p. 371]. We assume that patterns can support these awareness processes by preparing structures for reflecting and scrutinizing one's own actions and behaviors. But to be able to do that, writers have to reorganize the retrieved information, because it contains an individual structure and may in this form not match what readers need. Authors of good practice descriptions have to review and edit their practical knowledge in such a way that this knowledge may be adapted by other practitioners. In this context, research on representational guidance has shown that people will process represented material in a more intense way if they get it in the form of graphs or matrices, instead of an unstructured text [13,14]. And, in turn, applied to the pattern concept, representational guidance would imply that the inherent structure of patterns will guide and support practitioners when they write down their own good practice.

Flower and Hayes often observed a coherent underlying structure behind the writing process, although the writers themselves believed that their writing processes were disorganized and chaotic [5]. These results seem to be evidence for the existence of "patterns in mind". According to Kohls and Scheiter, patterns may exist in the form of mental representations [7]. Such "patterns in mind" will include a problem-solving schema, which activates adequate solution structures when a known problem is recognized. So patterns can serve as a structure for problem-solving. Problem-solving processes are actions aimed at achieving some target state. Individuals who solve a problem will arrive at their destination by passing different sub-goals and recalling the required knowledge from memory in order to solve a current problem by analogy to an example [2,9]. In the same fashion, patterns may support finding the best possible way of solving the problem. They act as an operator to proceed from one sub-goal to the next one, and may be considered as analogies and worked examples [14].

Case Study. Patterns provide an adequate structure that can improve systematic descriptions of experiences and behavior. From this point of view, we expect that patterns will facilitate the externalization of practical knowledge and lead to a more comprehensible and adaptive description of good practices. To test this hypothesis, we performed a qualitative case study with ten vicars in the middle of their apprenticeship of becoming pastors, and compared two conditions (blank sheet of paper and structured pattern in a wiki) of a good practice description.

The participants were asked to describe two different good practices of their ecclesiastical daily work. At the beginning, they were requested to write down the first good practice description in the form of an unstructured pen and paper version. After each participant had described a project, they received a description of some good practice from another vicar and acted as a reviewer. In this second round, the vicars were asked to highlight all those points of the description which they did not understand (requests). After that, in the third and last round, each vicar was confronted with a new, previously unknown description of a good practice and had to criticize constructively and highlight those areas which they thought could be improved by their own ideas and experiences (suggestions for improvement).

The second good practice which each of the vicars was asked to report was meant to be written down in the form of a structured pattern (provided in a wiki). The cycle of writing down the own description and reading descriptions from two other vicars was similar to the first good practice description in the pen and paper condition. On the line of this procedure each vicar wrote two good practice descriptions. So the study realizes a within-subject design with repeated measures (without pattern vs. with pattern).

A good project description has to be complete, understandable and adaptive to other situations. We determined the quality of the written practice descriptions by analyzing the comments of vicars who had read and reviewed the project description. These comments may be understood as a form of feedback from experienced peers and as a valid evaluation of the quality of the respective practices. On average, there were significantly more *requests* concerning the description of good practices if this was written down in blank sheets of paper ($M=9.2$, $SD=4.36$) than in the structured patterns ($M=2.0$, $SD=2.33$, $t(9)=4.72$, $p=.001$). This can be seen as evidence for the assumption that practices described by patterns offered a more explicit and more understandable structure to practitioners with some routine than practices described without the support of patterns. The results of *suggestions for improvement* were along the same lines: in contrast to the patterns ($M=0.3$, $SD=0.48$), the paper versions received significantly more *suggestions for improvement* by the vicars ($M=2.3$, $SD=1.7$, $t(9)=3.72$, $p=.005$). What was frequently criticized was a missing categorization of information and unavailable recommendations on what should be done. In contrast to that, the patterns seemed to include all the required information in their categories for a good practice description. This indicates that patterns lead to fewer requests and suggestions for improvement because of their inherent structure, which guides both the author and the reader of the good practice description.

3 Conclusion

These results lead to the assumption that an explicit structure, as provided by a pattern, will facilitate an effective description of one's own practical knowledge and, in this way, enable a successful exchange of knowledge within a decentralized NGO. Patterns seem to support the difficult process of becoming aware of one's own knowledge, and guide authors in writing down their implicit knowledge. This may lead to deeper elaboration and reflection of their own practice, which will, in turn, be improved. So an NGO may save precious resources by using patterns. Good practice descriptions can serve as a collection of tested, successful solutions of recurrent problems in work routines.

Acknowledgement. This research was founded by the German Federal Ministry of Education and Research, the European Social Fund and the European Union (support code 01PF08005A).

References

1. Alexander, C., Ishikawa, S., Silverstein, M.: A Pattern Language: Towns, Building, Construction. Oxford University Press, Oxford (1977)
2. Anderson, J.R.: The Architecture of Cognition. Harvard University Press, Cambridge (1983)
3. Cress, U., Kimmerle, J.: A Systemic and Cognitive View on Collaboration Knowledge Building with Wikis. International Journal of Computer-Supported Collaborative Learning 3, 105–122 (2008)
4. Edwards, M.: Organizational Learning in Non-Governmental Organizations: What have we learned? Public. Admin. Develop. 17, 235–250 (1997)
5. Flower, L., Hayes, J.R.: A Cognitive Process Theory of Writing. Coll. Compos. Commun. 32(4), 365–387 (1981)
6. Gamma, E., Helm, R., Jonson, R., Vlissides, J.: Design Patterns: Elements of Reusable Object-Oriented Software. Addison-Wesley, Reading (1995)
7. Kohls, C., Scheiter, K.: The Psychology of Patterns. In: Proceedings of the 2008 Conference on Pattern Languages of Programs (PLoP). ACM, Nashville (2008)
8. Luhmann, N.: Social Systems. Stanford University Press, Stanford (1995)
9. Newell, A., Simon, H.A.: Human Problem Solving. Prentice Hall, Englewood Cliffs (1972)
10. Polanyi, M.: The Tacit Dimension, Doubleday, Garden City (1966)
11. Schümmer, T., Mühlpfordt, M., Haake, J.: Computer Supported Reflection of Good Practice. Paper submitted to CRIWG 2010 (2010)
12. Schümmer, T., Lukosch, S.: Patterns for Computer-Mediated Interaction. John Wiley & Sons Ltd., Chichester (2007)
13. Suthers, D., Hundhausen, C.: An Experimental Study of the Effects of Representational Guidance on Collaborative Learning Processes. The Journal of the Learning Science 12(2), 183–218 (2003)
14. Wodzicki, K., Moskaliuk, J., Cress, U.: Patterns for Social Practices: A psychological Perspective. In: Kohls, C., Wedekind, J. (eds.) Investigations of E-learning Patterns: Context Factors, Problems and Solutions, IGI Global, Hershey (in press)

Modelling a Stakeholder Community via a Social Platform: The Case of TELeurope.eu

Noaa Barak[1], Daniel Burgos[1,2], Anthony Fisher Camilleri[3], Fred de Vries[4], Marcus Specht[4], and Caroline Windrum[5]

[1] Atos Origin, Albarracín 25, Madrid 28037, Spain
[2] International University of La Rioja. G.V. Rey Juan Carlos I, 41, Logroño 26002, Spain
[3] Scienter, Via Val d'Aposa 3, Bologna, Italy
[4] Open University of the Netherlands
[5] University of Nottingham, UK
{noaa.barak,daniel.burgos}@atosresearch.eu

Abstract. Past attempts at creating stakeholder networks for specific fields of research or industrial sectors have shown to be a resource-consuming and time-consuming process, which requires continuous monitoring and political efforts, as well as the trial-and-error deployment of technological tools. Still, these networks are thought to be an efficient and essential communication instrument for addressing challenges and building capacities. The EU FP7 STELLAR Network of Excellence has the mission of establishing a network for Technology Enhanced Learning (TEL) stakeholders, and has decided to do so via an online social community called TELeurope. In this paper we provide an overview of some relevant experience in establishing collaborative networks in the fields of business sciences, learning networks and communities of practice and reflect on our experience thus far with TELeurope.

Keywords: stakeholder network, social networks, STELLAR, TELeurope, Technology-Enhanced Learning, community of practice, virtual community.

1 Introduction and Background

Stakeholder networks are becoming a popular tool to facilitate dialogue in a thematic field or sector, with the aim of reaching a network-wide approach for resolving problems and addressing challenges. Svendsen and Laberge [1] define a stakeholder network as "a web of groups, organisations and/or individuals who come together to address a complex and shared cross-boundary problem, issue or opportunity". Past experiences in establishing such networks, have fostered the development of theories and models to cope with three main challenges of establishing an effective stakeholder network: 1) identification of stakeholders, 2) network management, and 3) engagement. Nowadays, when reflecting on the establishment of a new stakeholder network, these three challenges have to be addressed, in view of the possibilities of using social software and web-based collaborative tools. In this regard, we draw out perspectives from three fields: business sciences [1], Learning Networks [2] [3] and communities of practice [4], [5].

With regards to the business sciences view, the literature lists cases in which corporations were forced to establish a stakeholder network by challenges which posed a barrier to their activity and had to be resolved through interactions with stakeholders [1]. A recent paradigm shift is described in which the approach towards stakeholder networks is becoming less *organisation-centric* and more *network-focused*. The *organisation-centric* approach, trying to manage and control stakeholders and inviting them to the network based on their potential influence, tends to result in short-term relationships, mostly focused on yielding benefits for the organiser, rather than to the overall network. In contrast, according to the *network-focused* approach, the initiating organisation is a symbiotic part of the environment and its sustainability depends on the well-being of its stakeholders. This approach yields a *multi-stakeholder network*, rather than a bilateral connection.

With regards to the learning network view [2][3], we highlight the key requirements to facilitate exchange and participation in a learning network: 1) facilities for members to create, search, get/access and study, 2) governance by community policies, 3) instruments to manage, change and apply policies, 4) high level of dialogue, interaction and collaboration, 5) an explicit exchange reward system which is consistent with self-organization principles, and 6) a right balance between usability for the participants and flexibility/complexity.

Finally, a Community of Practice (CoP) is describes as "a group of professionals who share a common interest for a domain or a specific topic. They meet on a regular basis, face-to-face or online... They share their daily practice... and generate new insights and understanding of their profession." [4]. Although a somewhat homogenous group this can be considered as a special case of a stakeholder network.

2 The STELLAR Stakeholder Network

STELLAR is a Network of Excellence, funded by the European Commission, with the aim of unifying the diverse community of TEL in Europe. STELLAR is motivated by "the need for European research on TEL to build upon, synergize and extend the valuable work we have started by significantly building capacity in TEL research within Europe" [6]. As preparation, the authors of this paper have researched and mapped the TEL research community in Europe [7], and then drafted the terms of reference and the theoretical structure of the stakeholder network [8]. December 2009 saw the official launch of the STELLAR stakeholder network via a stakeholder panel held at the Online Educa Berlin conference (OEB), and the initiation of an ELGG-based [9] social platform branded by the name TELeurope.eu [10].

2.1 Mapping TEL Stakeholders in Europe

Our findings in relation to the map of TEL stakeholder are out of the scope of this paper and are reported in [11]; however our methodology is relevant to the understanding of the convening process of the network. Rather than simply categorising stakeholders, a framework was developed whereby each stakeholder is classified according to their membership within sub-groups of a set of groups. The characteristics of each sub-group were described in terms of their overall position and interest in

TEL, as well as in terms of their needs and possible interest in the instruments making up the STELLAR project. The measurement of stakeholders' alliance potential was based upon work done by the World Bank [12]. The purpose of defining this indicator is to allow the network coordinators to identify how members might be most appropriately rallied in the pursuit of a particular initiative.

2.2 Description of the STELLAR Stakeholder Network

Three key principles have shaped the development of the STELLAR network: 1) openness: to welcome all those with interests in technology enhanced learning whether as researchers, practitioners, designers or users. 2) Collaboration; the Network has to bring together different perspectives and interests in order to increase cohesion and reduce fragmentation in TEL at the European level. 3) Sustainability. To this end, the most important decision taken as a result of this strategy has been the branding of the online community as "TELeurope.eu": designed to be a visible and recognisable brand within the European TEL Community. Choosing to separate TELeurope from the main STELLAR brand is expected to strengthen the sustainability of the network and ease the connection with other initiatives in the field.

TELeurope provides a number of benefits to potential members: 1) networking opportunities and being part of a larger community of shared interests, 2) increasing the visibility of personal profiles, 3) receiving news of projects, events, promotional opportunities, leading developments in TEL and other communications, 4) access to resources such as reports and 'grey' literature , 5) access to expert discussions and opinions, and 6) opportunities for funding, collaboration and employment. At the more collective level, the community could potentially benefit from : 7) collective lobbying power, 8) access to test beds on a regional scale, 9) expert reviews, 10) EU-wide TEL research presence, and 11) a "neutral zone" to discuss field related matters; a way of reducing barriers between research, innovation, policy and practice; and contributing to the development of the research agenda related to TEL.

The first set of benefits might be viewed as offering immediate or direct forms of interaction between stakeholders; however, the second set of benefits will take time to evolve, emerging out of the growing sense of community identity.

Based on these principles and previous analysis, we have pre-structured TELeurope with the aim of containing three main groups: 1) Stakeholder advisory board, 2) Network of Networks, and 3) Research and innovation. In addition, members will be able to freely create their own groups. In practice, over a period of four months, over 300 individuals have created an account on the TELeurope platform and have mainly used the service to enable the creation of their own groups. In total, 17 groups were created. In most cases, these were linked to existing TEL research projects and conferences looking for the involvement of others in the community, or were linked to specific STELLAR activities. Some activity outside of TELeurope has been taking place with regards to the Stakeholder Advisory Board; however the other two main groups are lagging behind.

3 Analysis

STELLAR aims at establishing a *multi-stakeholder network*, which will bridge the gaps between communities and disciplines in TEL. However, some of its actions while convening the network can be perceived as promoting a unidirectional flow of information, accommodating the needs of STELLAR, but less the needs and interests of TEL stakeholders. It has identified stakeholders and events based on their popularity and influence, as perceived by STELLAR, and these were targeted as the first invitees to join the network. Similarly, in a preliminary list of use cases drafted by STELLAR members [8], 8 out of 13 use cases (over 60%) involved STELLAR members; this is a bias towards the initiator of the network. Yet, examples to the contrary exist: an extended list of use-cases is currently underway, intentionally highlighting networking between non-STELLAR members. Additionally, at the Online Educa Berlin (Dec 2009) a group of stakeholders were invited to attend a stakeholder panel in which they were asked to reflect on the purpose of the network.

We have consciously chosen to make the TELeurope community open for all persons of interest, upon the completion of a simple registration process and confirmation of an email address. However, it seems that, despite this *network centric* approach, stakeholders are lacking a strong incentive to become engaged in the community, and instructions from the convenor´s side are not readily acted upon. Furthermore, the establishment of TELeurope did not take into consideration existing processes and best practices of establishing a stakeholder network, from the three perspectives presented previously and so it has not been successful in clearly communicating some of the key features of the network to its members.

With regards to usability, complexity and flexibility, TELeurope has to be balanced. Members make extensive use of the group creating function, thus demonstrating the network's flexibility. However, several aspects need to be improved, such as the lack of support for specific use-cases, an unintuitive interface and the provision of basic features common to many social networks.

At the moment, an awareness service ("dashboard") presents recent activities on the platform, as well as site announcements, but it cannot yet be configured to comply with members' preferences. When compared to the main collaborative features in communities of practice [4], it is evident that TELeurope is still lacking some advanced services to foster social interactions and awareness.

Table 1. TELeurope's compliance with the requirements for participation and exchange of information

Requirement	Realisation in TELeurope
Facilities to create, search, get/access and study	Supported through: create and join groups, participate in discussion, upload and download files, post messages on "the wire", search members and content
Governance by community policies	Monitoring is performed by the moderators and focuses on removing spammers; it does not reflect policy
Instruments to manage, change and apply the different policies	Unavailable as a community activity
High level of dialogue, interaction and collaboration	There is not much interaction yet; needs to be stimulated and supported by the STELLAR project
An explicit exchange reward system	A general plan has been outlined and different metrics have been discussed [8], not yet implemented.
Balance between usability and flexibility/complexity	Customisable homepage and profiles are available; however data on usability is scarce and it is hard to assess the balance. Basic information and tutorials are not available.

Finally, table 1 presents TELeurope´s compliance with the basic requirement for exchange and participation [2]. Although TELeurope offers some of the functionalities mentioned, it is still failing when it comes to the application of policies and a reward mechanism. The lack of statistics on user engagement makes it difficult to maintain a balance between usability and flexibility of the system.

4 Discussion and Conclusions

In this paper, we relate to views and experiences coming from Business, Learning Networks and Communities of Practice, however none is entirely adequate to the special case of a web-based stakeholder network dedicated to research.

After one year of activity, and four months since the launch of TELeurope, the STELLAR stakeholder network is experiencing a tension between an organisation-centric and a system-whole approach. On the one hand, the network is defined as a *multi-stakeholder* network, aimed at providing benefits to the TEL field as a whole, rather than to STELLAR or a specific group of stakeholders inside the network. On the other hand, activities so far have had an *organisation-centric* feel – trying to demonstrate STELLAR's achievements more than the actual progress on facilitating interdisciplinary dialogue. In order to achieve its goals, TELeurope should take a step towards a more *network-focused* view, possibly by applying participatory design.

The authors of this paper intend to continue using TELeurope as a case-study through which they hope to draft a theoretical basis to support similar networks, highlighting both the organisational and the technical aspects.

Acknowledgements. This paper was supported by the STELLAR Network of Excellence (FP7, ref. 231913), and the Spanish national project TELMA (www.ines.org.es/telma, TSI-020110-2009-85). The authors wish to thank their collaborators in STELLAR, with a special mention to Dr. Marie Joubert of the University of Bristol, UK.

References

[1] Svendsen, A.C., Laberge, M.: Convening Stakeholder Networks: A New Way of Thinking, Being and Engaging. JCC 19, 91–104 (2005)
[2] Hummel, H., Tattersall, C., Burgos, D., Brouns, F., Kurvers, H., Koper, R.: Critical Facilities for Active Participation in Learning Networks. IJWBC 2(1) (2005)
[3] Koper, R., Pannekeet, K., Hendriks, M., Hummel, H.: Building communities for the exchange of learning objects: theoretical foundations and requirements. ALT-J. 12(1), 21–35 (2004)
[4] El Helou, S., Raffier Möller, M.D., Daele, A., Gillet, D.: Social Software for Supporting Interaction in a Community of Practice Dedicated to e-Learning. In: Workshop on Social Networking in Organizations, CSCW (2008)
[5] Burgos, D.: The structure and behavior of virtual communities engaged in informal learning about e-learning standards (Estudio de la estructura y del comportamiento de las comunidades virtuales de aprendizaje no formal sobre estandarización del e-learning). Doctoral dissertation, European University of Madrid, Villaviciosa de Odón, Madrid, Spain (2006)

[6] STELLAR: The network of excellence for Technology Enhanced Learning (project reference: 231913), http://www.stellarnet.eu/
[7] Camilleri, A., Barak, N., de Vries, F., Joubert, M., Specht, M., Windrum, C., Persico, D., Kraker, P.: Report of the process of establishing a Stakeholder Panel. STELLAR Deliverable 5.1 (2009)
[8] Barak, N., Burgos, D., Specht, M., De Vries, F., Windrum, C., Camilleri, A., Lindstaedt, S., Persico, D.: Report on Guidelines and Monitoring tools-metrics. STELLAR Deliverable 5.2 (2009)
[9] ELGG, http://elgg.org/
[10] TELeurope, http://teleurope.eu/
[11] Camilleri, A., Barak, N., Burgos, D., Ullmann, T.D.: Engaging the community in multidisciplinary TEL research: a case-study on networking in Europe. EDEN (2010)
[12] World Bank. Policy Toolkit for Strengthening Healthcare Reform (2000), http://info.worldbank.org/etools/docs/library/48545/RD1.PDF.pdf (last accessed July 2009)

Scenario-Based Multi-User Virtual Environments: Productive Failure and the Impact of Structure on Learning

Shannon Kennedy-Clark, Michael J. Jacobson, and Peter Reimann

Centre for Research on Computer Supported Learning and Cognition,
Faculty of Education and Social Work
University of Sydney, Sydney, Australia
{shannon.kennedy-clark,michael.jacobson,
peter.reimann}@sydney.edu.au
http://sydney.edu.au/education_social_work/coco/

Abstract. The purpose of this paper is provide an overview of a study designed to investigate the impact of structure on learning activities designed for developing scientific inquiry skills in a scenario-based multi-user virtual environment. The research will compare the results of participants exposed to high-structure and low-structure initial activities. Participants will be 150 year nine high school students who will be studying inquiry learning as part of their set curriculum. Students will complete pre, mid and posttests. The research will focus on the use of *Virtual Singapura*, a scenario-based multi-user environment, in a classroom environment.

Keywords: Multi-user virtual environment, productive failure, scenario-based learning, inquiry learning, learning theories.

1 Introduction

Multi-User Virtual Environments (MUVEs) have been the focus of a growing number of research studies, and with this growth the possibilities for using this technology in a learning space have become increasingly plausible as the technology becomes more accessible. In recent years MUVEs have been used in a diverse range of virtual classrooms and learning spaces both in secondary and tertiary institutions [1-3]. Several studies have involved replicating a classroom to facilitate virtual lecture and tutorial groups [4], other studies have provided learners with a quest-like learning experience wherein learners need to use inquiry skills to solve problems [5] and others still have combined in-world activities with real world mentoring [5, 6]. Given the diverse range of applications of MUVE technology it is necessary to clarify the location of this research within this field. This paper will focus on the use of a scenario-based MUVE in a high school science inquiry unit of study.

In this study, the focus is not on rapid delivery, 'just in time' learning or speeding up of the learning process through using technology in the classroom. Instead, the study is underpinned by the notion of 'slow learning' derived from the slow food movement. So rather than focusing on speed, the study focuses on using and designing MUVE technology for a pace of learning that allows learners to absorb and enjoy the learning benefits when using a rich and dynamic learning environment.

The data collection for this study commenced with a pilot with pre-service teachers in March and will conclude in August 2010 following the collection of data from a secondary school.

1.1 Scenario-Based Multi-User Environments

A MUVE is a virtual environment derived from game technology that has the following five criteria: an avatar that represents the participant; a 3D virtual environment; the ability to interact with artefacts (objects) and agents (in-world characters); communication functions (e.g. chat) and, in some instances, the ability to communicate with intelligent agents and, finally, a 'real world' context that is created to provide an authentic experience.

As with most computer games, a scenario-based MUVE is underpinned by a narrative that forms the learning experience. The benefit of using a scenario-based MUVE in an educational space is that learners can interact with an environment that they may not be able to access or experience in a traditional classroom setting.

1.2 Productive Failure

PF provides an alternative approach to how structure is used in a learning activity. PF is a learning strategy that suggests by exposing learners to a low-structure problem that greater learning is achieved when students are then presented with subsequent structured and unstructured activities [7, 8]. While students may fail in the initial low-structure encounter they are supported with a structured activity in the second phase of the treatment. This paper suggests that it is the placement of the low-structure activity in the initial encounter that results in greater learning than highly structured learning experiences.

2 Background

The ability to solve a diverse range of complex and ill-defined problems is a requirement of many learning and workplace situations. However, learners are often taught how to solve inquiry problems through the use of highly structured activities and are not afforded opportunities to engage in process such as defining the problem, creating hypotheses and testing these hypotheses without the accompanying structure.

The benefits of using worked examples and highly structured problem solving activities extends only to problems that are similar – indicating that through highly structured activities general problem solving skills are not acquired [9]. The restriction created by the use of the sequence of high to low-structured activities and the lack of opportunities provided to learners to engage in inquiry problem solving activities can impair a learner in developing appropriate skills as the structures constrain the learner to a narrow problem solving scope. Gaining an understanding of a productive failure treatment should provide insight into why reducing structure in an initial engagement with a problem can result in greater understanding and improved learning outcomes [7].

Reducing the degree of structure in the initial activity in a sequence of inquiry activities in a MUVE is learning strategy that provides an alternative to the guided inquiry approach that underpins MUVEs such as *Quest Atlantis* and *River City*. A guided inquiry sequence commences with highly structured activities that guide a learner through the virtual space and then fades the structure out of a learning domain as the learner progresses through the activities [5]. This research proposes that a treatment that uses the opposite arrangement - beginning with a low-structure activity - may also provide benefits for the learners.

The extent of structure is the focus of the research as using a productive failure treatment in an initial encounter presents a gap in the research field in terms of the learner processes and the learner experience. At present, research into the use of productive failure in initial activities is limited to several studies; however, the results of the studies indicate that there is a significant difference between participants in a productive failure treatment and participants in the control condition, suggesting that there is substance to the premise of reducing structure in initial inquiry activities [7, 8]. This research will focus on the initial stage of a productive failure cycle within the domain of inquiry.

3 Method

3.1 Participants and Procedure

The participants for the study are a cohort of 150 ninth-grade students of above average ability drawn from six general science classes at a selective government high school. The science classes are taught by six different teachers across the timetable. Students were selected from this school in order to provide a homogeneous level of academic ability. The students were selected for the high-school on the basis of their academic performance. While there is a range of abilities within the year cohort, the students tend to be high academic achievers that perform well on state and national tests. The school was also selected due to its technical capabilities. The school had sufficient bandwidth and computers to allow for two classes of approximately thirty students to work in pairs.

The trial will run over eight 40 minute lessons, table 1 provides and overview of the study schedule. The first two classes will be a pre-test and introduction to the virtual world. Students will develop their avatars and be placed in teams. It is important during this stage of the study that no teaching of inquiry skills be undertaken as this pre-teaching may impact upon how students engage with the inquiry activities within the virtual space.

Table 1. Productive Failure in a Virtual World research design

Class	Class1/2	Class 3	Class 4	Class 5	Class 6/7/8
Productive Failure	Pre test Orientation	Low-structure	High-structure	Low-structure	Post test Interviews Assessments
High Structure	Pre test Orientation	High-structure	High-structure	Low-structure	Post test Interviews Assessments

The virtual world and activities will be run in classes three, four and five. Class six will be a post-test and a discussion. Class seven will be a far transfer assessment wherein students will complete a paper-based historical inquiry activity on the *Tollund Man*. The purpose of this activity is to ascertain whether or not students can transfer their inquiry skills to a different style of activity external to the virtual world and to see if there is a difference between the productive failure and non productive failure groups. Class eight will be team presentations. Students will present their findings to the class. This will be a reflective task that is designed to see how students critically evaluate their experimental design and again to see if there is a difference in perspectives between the productive failure and non productive failure groups.

Classroom teachers will run the sessions so that students will be familiar with the teaching style and classroom environment. Researchers will provide technical support during the classes. Teachers will be provided with lessons plans and materials to try to standardize the way in which the study is run.

Three of the classes will be given the productive failure activities and three of the classes will be given the non productive failure activities. This will prevent students from comparing materials during the class. Students will be assigned a partner during the trial. All 'in world' activities will be completed with a partner. Pre and post tests will be completed individually.

3.2 Materials

Virtual Singapura. The virtual environment that will be utilised in this research project is *Virtual Singapura*. *Virtual Singapura* was developed in Singapore as part of a collaborative project between researchers at Singapore Learning Sciences Laboratory (National Institute of Education) and faculty in Computer Engineering and in Art, Design, and Media at Nanyang Technological University[1].

The story or scenario for the virtual world lends itself to the trial of productive failure in a scientific inquiry domain. *Virtual Singapura* is set in 19th century Singapore and is based on historical information about several disease epidemics during that period. The students are transported back in time to help the Governor of Singapore, Sir Andrew Clarke, and the citizens of the city try and solve the problem of what is causing the illnesses and to develop appropriate inquiry skills such as defining the scope of the problem; identification of research variables; establishing and testing hypothesis and presentation of findings. In order to create an authentic learning experience, 19th century artefacts from Singapore have been included in the environment. These artefacts include historical 3D buildings and agents that represent different ethnic groups in Singapore at the time such as Chinese, Malay, Indian, westerners, and historic period photographs.

The school will be required to download the client software onto the computers. Students will be provided with logins and passwords. The virtual world has a control environment and five experimental conditions. Students will assign themselves an avatar. The avatar can be controlled by using the arrow keys on the laptop. Students can use the chat functions to talk to their partner. Students select various artefacts in world by moving the mouse pointer to the artifact and selecting the artifact. An

---

[1] Virtual Singapura is located at http://155.69.101.53/wiki/index.php/Main_Page#Introduction

information window will appear on the right of the screen. Students can talk to agents in world by moving near the agent, the agent will recognize that a student is nearby and will respond with a salutation. Students can also right-click on the agent to access a list of prepared questions.

Paper-Based Activities. Students will be provided with paper-based activities to work through while in the virtual world. The pre and post tests will also be paper-based. The far transfer activity will be paper-based.

Camtasia. Camtasia will be used to record screen shots and audio recordings. Camtasia can also record video images however as the participants will be under 18 we will not use this application. The audio recording should provide a rich source of process data. From analyzing this data it should be evident if there is a difference between the two groups in terms of how they engage with the virtual problems.

Pilot. A pilot study was run in March 2010 with 28 pre-service teachers at the University of Sydney. The pilot tested the design of the learning activities. Participants were required to complete a post pilot questionnaire. The results of the study showed that the introduction to the MUVE, the tools and the problem needed to be clarified before the student trial (table 2).

Table 2. Pre-service teachers' understanding of the introduction, scenario and problem

Area	Clear	Not Clear	Suggested improvements
Clarity of introduction	71.4%	28.6%	Audio introduction, shorter, explanation of tools, and tool bars, improved navigation
Clarity of virtual scenario	82.1%	17.9%	More detail, explanation of control and experimental conditions, more understanding of navigation
Clarity of problem to be solved	60.7%	39.3%	More detail of problem needed, better understanding of functions like bug catchers, hard to move between worlds
N = 28			

4 Final Comments

Research into productive failure is still in its preliminary stages. While several studies have shown significant differences between productive failure and non productive failure treatments, as yet this concept has not been applied to a MUVE. The notion of 'slow' learning has informed this research in that the use of the MUVE is seen as an experience that is meant to be savored and enjoyed by students rather than speeding up the learning process, hence allowing for greater reflection and absorption on the learning experience. As research into the use of MUVE technology has not yet shown significant evidence of transfer of skills, the combining of the technology and productive failure should provide insight into how best to design virtual learning experiences in order to facilitate the acquisition of inquiry skills.

Acknowledgments. The Centre for Computer Supported Cognition and Learning at the University of Sydney would like to acknowledge Singapore Learning Sciences Laboratory Nanyang Technological University for their ongoing support in the use of *Virtual Singapura*.

References

1. Barab, S.A., et al.: Making Learning Fun: Quest Atlantis, A Game Without Guns. Educational Technology, Research and Development 53(1), 86–107 (2005)
2. Dalgarno, B., Lee, M.: What are the learning affordances of 3-D virtual environments? British Journal of Educational Technology 41(1), 10–32 (2010)
3. Jacobson, M.J., et al.: An Intelligent Agent Augmented Multi-User Virtual Environment for Learning Science Inquiry: Preliminary Research Findings. In: 2008 American Educational Association Conference, New York (2008)
4. de Freitas, S., et al.: Learning as immersive experiences: Using the four-dimensional framework for designing and evaluating immersive learning experiences in a virtual world. British Journal of Educational Technology 41(1), 69–85 (2010)
5. Ketelhut, D.J., et al.: A multi-user virtual environment for building higher order inquiry skills in science. In: American Educational Research Association, San Francisco, CA (2006)
6. Shaffer, D.W.: Epistemic frames for epistemic games. Computers and Education 46(3), 223–234 (2006)
7. Kapur, M.: Productive Failure. Cognition and Instruction 26(3), 379–424 (2008)
8. Kapur, M., Kinzer, C.K.: Productive Failure in CSCL Groups. International Journal of Computer-Supported Learning 4(1), 21–46 (2009)
9. Sweller, J., Cooper, G.A.: The use of worked examples as a substitute for problem solving in learning algebra. Cognition and Instruction 2(1), 59–89 (1985)

Experimentation and Results for Calibrating Automatic Diagnosis Belief Linked to Problem Solving Modalities: A Case Study in Electricity

Sandra Michelet, Vanda Luengo, Jean-Michel Adam, and Nadine Mandran

Laboratoire Informatique de Grenoble (LIG), Bâtiment ENSE3
961 rue de la Houille Blanche – BP 46 – 38402 Grenoble cedex – France
{Sandra.Michelet,Vanda.Luengo,Jean-Michel.Adam,
Nadine.Mandran}@imag.fr

Abstract. Learners increasingly work with virtual laboratories that provide various activities and tools, including sophisticated modeling and simulation systems. The learning environments have to combine traces to establish the most precise diagnosis possible on the learner's activity. This paper presents a diagnosis tool, called DiagElec, establishing a diagnosis on the learner's activity. DiagElec integrates a notion of belief, which is related to the modalities in the generated diagnoses. To analyze our model, we have carried out a two-phase experiment, first with learners and then with teachers. From the corpus of diagnosis done by the teachers, we are looking for the emergence of a model of human behavior to recalibrate the degree of belief defined into the diagnosis rules.

Keywords: Adaptive diagnosis, problem solving modality, open environments.

1 Introduction

Over the recent decade, virtual laboratories provide the students and the teachers with access to sophisticated modeling and simulation systems. "The goal is to develop sound and flexible environments that support all the students", p.388 [1]. Despite these research actions and the availability of the systems, the majority of these kinds of environment do not integrate automatic diagnosis. Indeed, the diversity of the proposed tools modifies the automatic diagnosis. We are researching the factors to be taken into account for an automatic diagnosis.

Our implemented diagnosis model (*DiagElec*) takes into account some essential factors to calculate an adapted diagnosis and feedback for an open environment allowing students to solve electricity problems. In order to evaluate these factors, we did an experiment with learners to collect traces and with teachers who proposed diagnoses from the learners' traces.

In this paper we focus our work on the problem solving modality (PSM) factor. We call modality each computer tool or manner (interface) provided to the learner to do a pedagogical activity. In our paper we study this PSM factor by analyzing diagnoses contexts. A diagnosis context is a set of collected traces coming from a combination of modalities (traces coming from one or more computer tools). In addition, as DiagElec takes into account the PSM factor in its algorithm, we try to find a model from the experimental data, which allows us to calibrate the belief associated to each modality and each type of knowledge.

2 Taking into Account the PSM Factor

From a theoretical point of view, we can consider each PSM as a semiotic register defined by Duval as "A representation system which has its own meaning and functioning constraints"[1] [2]. Indeed, in new platforms such SCY [3], which proposes inquiry activities, some semiotic registers could be combined with a pedagogical activity. In this example the system provides several PSMs such as a simulation, a text editor, or a graph editor, according to the requested task. With each PSM the student uses the associated semiotic register. From the tutoring system point of view, the combination of some PSM needs to take into account the adaptation dimension related to the implication of several semiotic registers. Thus, this variety of PSM modifies the diagnosis: information about the learner activity comes from different sources with different meanings and need to be combined.

TEL systems with several PSMs and automatic diagnosis exist, such as Cabri-Euclide [4] in the geometry proof domain or Andes [5] in physics. In these systems it is not possible to have an association of some contradictory PSMs to compute the diagnosis. In the Cabri-Euclide example the student can construct the geometry figure and write statements to do a geometry proof, but the system does not allow inconsistencies between the figure and the statements: if the student proposes an inconsistent statement, the system produces a feedback to the student and the diagnosis is only based on the proposed statements.

We are interested in designing a diagnosis that is able to take into account several traces coming from different PSMs and is also able to manage possible contradictions between them. In previous experimentations [6], we observed that with this kind of open environment, the students can produce traces showing contradictions. In these situations, and if we would like totake into account all PSM, the system has to decide which PSM is more credible.

3 Model of PSM and Belief in DiagElec

Our open environment provides MCQ, formulations, and a microworld called TPElec[2]. The domain application is electricity; our microworld allows the student to manipulate electric circuits with basic components. The proposed problems were built on the model of scientific reasoning.

By taking into account meta-data problems (for example, its statement and its characteristics) and by enriching the rough traces generated from each PSM using a model of the domain, we obtain traces which will be used for the diagnosis.

DiagElec models knowledge, skills, and errors about electricity (DC circuits). DiagElec is written in Prolog language. In relation to the formulation traces, we do

---
[1] The original reference is translated by us.
[2] Tpelec.imag.fr.

not analyze directly the formulations given in natural language by the learner. We translate each formulation into Prolog facts. So the diagnosis done by DiagElec is semiautomatic.

The diagnosis provided by DiagElec is a vector composed of a set of couples (Detected element, Degree of belief). In our tool, every knowledge, skill and error is modeled by a *Code* with the following format: [Letter-Number] where *Letter* ∈ {k, s, e}, k, s, e correspond respectively to Knowledge, Skills and Error; *Number* is the id.

DiagElec integrates the concept of uncertainty by associating a degree of belief to each knowledge element modeled. This degree of belief is between 1 and 4, where 1 means less degree of belief and 4 means more degree of belief.

For example, *D(L1,P2,TPElec)* = {(k11,3), (e7,2), (s6,4), (s21,1)} the vector corresponding to the diagnosis of the learning activity of learner L1, for the problem named P2, and the diagnosis is based on traces coming from the microworld TPElec. In this case k11 was detected with a degree of belief of 3. *D(L1,P2,TPElecForm)*= {(k11,3),(e7,2),(e2,1),(s21,1)} is a diagnosis vector for the same learner, the same problem, but for another diagnosis context (TPElec and formulation). The different algorithm steps are showed in the next figure, which will explain in next paragraphs.

---

1. Initialization of the considered δ context, and of the α weights associated with each PSM composing δ context.

2. For a learner L, ∀ i∈ [1,N$_δ$], ∀ M ⊂ δ, computation of the elementary diagnosis vectors D(F$_i$(L,P,M)):

   - Application of the diagnosis rules unified with context δ and with the associated modalities
   - Output : D(F$_i$(L,P,M)) *a vector of couples (detected element, degree of belief)*

3. Computation of D(L,P,δ) from the N$_δ$ diagnosis vectors D(F$_i$(L,P,M)) resulting from step 2 :

   - ⊎: Union of the D(F$_i$(L,P,M)) vectors with adjustment of the degree of belief proportionally to the α weight affected to M in the δ context.
   - Output : D(L,P, δ) the diagnosis vector for the learning activity of learner L, based on the δ context

---

Fig. 1. Main steps of the DiagElec algorithm for a specific context

We call M, F, and T the Prolog facts, which respectively are linked to answer from MCQ (M), formulation in natural language (F) and manipulations of electric components with the TPElec microworld (T). We can combine these three information sources into the following **7 distinct diagnosis contexts**. We name δ this diagnosis context. The DiagElec algorithm takes the productions of the learner in chronological order and computes the diagnosis vector corresponding to δ context. We call D(L,P,δ) the resulting diagnosis vector calculated from the productions of learner L solving problem P with the tools composing δ context, like the examples presented. We call F$_i$(L,P,M) the elementary productions (Prolog facts) of learner L for the solving problem P with the modality M, and D(F$_i$(L,P,M)) the diagnosis vector for this production. The computation of D(L,P,δ) is described as follows:

$$D(L, P, \delta) = \biguplus_{i=1}^{N_\delta} D(F_i(L, P, M)), \forall M \subset \delta$$

where N_δ is the total number or facts corresponding to the productions of learner L in the δ context for problem P. The symbol ⊎ corresponds to the union of the elementary vectors, with an adjustment of the degree of belief proportionally to the α weights associated with the PSMs of the δ context.

4 Experimentation

The experiment was done in two steps. The first one, involving 60 learners, was the gathering of the traces produced by the learners' activity. The second one was realized with three teachers[3] who were asked to diagnose the learners' productions. We selected, with a protocol related to hypothesis of our research, 18 learners, and we showed their productions to the teachers according to the 7 contexts. Each teacher had to identify the learners' knowledge, skills and errors, and to give a degree of belief for each detected element.

For each learner, problem and diagnosis context, we obtained 4 diagnosis vectors, one from each expert. We name our human experts E_1, E_2, E_3 and E_4. From these 4 vectors, for each detected element, we have extracted the degrees of belief given by each expert, assigning the value 0 for the expert(s) who did not detect this element. We obtain belief vectors associated to each detected element: 4 values corresponding to the given degrees of belief. For example, Belief(L,P2,TPElec,k7) = {2, 0, 1, 3} means that the degrees of belief for knowledge k7, for the activity of learner L on the problem P2 with the TPElec modality (diagnosis context), are respectively 2 for E_1, 1 for E_3, 3 for DiagElec, and was not detected by E_2. For this experiment, we have obtained 19901 belief vectors.

From the belief vectors, we have computed, the human convergence (hc) established using the following formula: $hc = \sqrt{d1^2 + d2^2 + d3^2}/3$ (d1, d2 and d3 are the differences between the teachers' degrees of belief). We consider that there is *total human convergence* if hc = 0, *partial convergence* if $0 < hc \leq 0.5$ and *human divergence* otherwise. The 0.5 value corresponds to the case of two teachers giving the same degree of belief, and the third giving a different value with a difference of 1.

5 Results

From our 19901 belief vectors, we have removed, all the vectors corresponding to detections done only by DiagElec (belief vector of type {0,0,0,a}, a≠0). We obtain 18306 vectors (Fig. 2). Human experts are mainly in agreement (72.13%). However this agreement seems to be related to the diagnosis context: for the *formulation* context (F) we have a lower convergence rate (56.3%), because natural language is often ambiguous. With only MCQs (M) there is 100% a total human convergence, obviously, no interpretation of the learner's answer is needed. The best convergence (79.8%) corresponds to the PSM combining the TPElec microworld and MCQs.

---

[3] Their work is supported by the French National Institute of Educational Research (INRP).

Problem solving modalities	Number	Total Human Convergence		Partial Human Convergence		Human Divergence	
		Number	%	Number	%	Number	%
M	118	118	100,0%	0	0,0%	0	0,0%
F	1963	1105	56,3%	450	22,9%	408	20,8%
T	1599	1102	68,9%	414	25,9%	83	5,2%
M+F	3750	2918	77,8%	438	11,7%	394	10,5%
M+T	2913	2324	79,8%	463	15,9%	126	4,3%
F+T	3095	1907	61,6%	803	25,9%	385	12,4%
M+F+T	4868	3730	76,6%	767	15,8%	371	7,6%
TOTAL	18306	13204	72,13%	3335	18,22%	1767	9,65%

Fig. 2. Human convergence according to the diagnosis context

In a second phase [7] we kept only the vectors corresponding to a total human convergence. We focused on the number of elements detected by the teachers, according to the different modalities (except modality MCQ only (M) which does not need interpretation from the teacher). We applied an ANOVA in order to measure the effect of the interaction between detected elements and PSMs, on the degree of belief given by the human experts. The *ANOVA shows a significant effect of the modalities* (F=294,6, df(5,132), p<0.001) and the diagnosed elements (F=174,7, df (2,13068), p<0.001) on the degree of belief, and their interaction on the degree of belief is also significant (F=38,8, df(10,13068), p<0.001).

Our analysis was done for only total human convergence and with the hypothesis that *the degrees of belief given by DiagElec are similar to those given by the human experts*. This hypothesis was tested according to each type of detected element and each diagnostic context. Because the human experts are in total convergence, we represent them by a meta-expert. For each hypothesis, did an analysis of variance tending to reject the hypothesis in each case (p<0.0001).

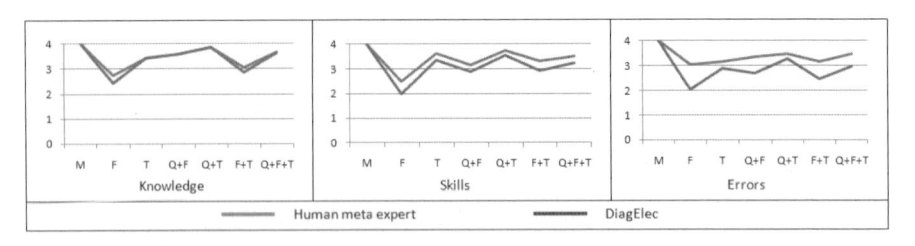

Fig. 3. Degree of belief comparison between DiagElec and the human meta-expert

This figure (Fig 3) shows the comparison between the degrees of belief given by DiagElec and those given by the meta-expert for each diagnosis context. We can observe that an adjustment of the degree of belief given by DiagElec is needed and this degree will be different according to the type of the detected elements.

6 Conclusion

Our experimentation shows that in order to do a better diagnosis, a degree of belief must be taken into account with PSM factor. By the computation of traces coming from various modalities, provided from the learner activity, a finer automatic diagnosis can be done. We can know which types of diagnosis elements are better detected in accordance to the diagnosis context. So we have a better view of the contribution of each PSM in the final diagnosis. Moreover, in the case of a contradiction between the learner's productions coming from different PSMs, the collected data helped us to better know how to define the weight to be assigned to each one, with the goal to do the best adaptive diagnosis and feedback as possible [8]. We plan another experiment with more teachers in order to validate our automatic diagnosis and to do an automatic adjustment of the degree of belief by a data mining process.

References

1. Woolf, B.P.: Building Intelligent Interactive tutors: student-centered strategies for revolutionizing e-learning. Elsevier, Burlington (2009)
2. Duval, R.: Registres de représentation sémiotique et fonctionnement cognitif de la pensée. Annales de didactique et de sciences cognitives (1991)
3. d'Ham, C., Marzin, P., Wajeman, C.: SCY-Science Created by You: an online environment for inquired-based and design-based learning. In: First Workshop on the S-Team European Project (2009)
4. Luengo, V.: Some didactical and epistemological considerations in the design of educational software: the Cabri-Euclide example. International Journal of Computers for Mathematical Learning 10, 1–29 (2005)
5. VanLehn, K., Lynch, C., Schulze, K., Shapiro, J.A., Shelby, R., Taylor, L., Treacy, D., Weinstein, A., Wintersgill, M.: The Andes Physics Tutoring System: Lessons Learned. International Journal of Artificial Intelligence and Education 15(3) (2005)
6. Michelet, S., Adam, J.M., Luengo, V.: Adaptive learning scenarios for detection of misconceptions about electricity and remediation. In: International Journal of Emerging Technologies in Learning, EBSCO, vol. 2(1) (2007)
7. Michelet, S., Luengo, V., Adam, J.M., Mandran, N.: How to take into account different problem solving modalities for doing a diagnosis? In: International Conference on Intelligent Tutoring Systems, Pittsburg, USA (2010)
8. Keenoy, K., Levene, M., De Freitas, S.: Personalised Trails: How machines can learn to adapt their behaviour to suit individual learners. Technology Enhanced Learning, Special on Trails in Education, Sense 1, 33–58 (2007)

Exploring Mediums of Pedagogical Support in an across Contexts Mobile Learning Activity

Jalal Nouri, Johan Eliasson, Fredrik Rutz, and Robert Ramberg

Department of Computer and System Sciences,
Stockholm University, Stockholm, Sweden
{jalal,je,rutz,robban}@dsv.su.se

Abstract. The possibility to step out of the classroom for learning in authentic contexts, that which earlier have been studied in abstract terms in the classroom context, can be an enormous asset to the educational system. A successful realization of this possibility relies, however, on that the designed mobile learning activities provide the pedagogical support learning requires. In this exploratory study, we aim to present findings on how learners can be supported in a mobile learning activity by utilizing resources available in educational settings such as teachers, mobile technology, and the possibility to cross contexts.

Keywords: Pedagogical Support, Mobile Learning, Learning Context, Conversational Framework, Learning Activity Design.

1 Introduction

By taking advantage of mobile technology, new learning opportunities emerges that removes the barriers of traditional instruction, and enables us to bring learners to otherwise remote and authentic contexts for physically engaging learning activities [1]. However, bringing children outside the classroom to engaging physical activities does not result in a desired learning outcome per se. From a socio-cultural point of view, appropriate assistance (i.e. scaffolding) needs to be provided in order to develop higher levels of understanding [2]. In line with this, a growing body of productive research work has been conducted on the notion of scaffolding in educational settings. These approaches have, to large extent, either emphasized teachers scaffolding functions in conventional classrooms with their physical constraints, or more recently on computer-based environments where teachers are not present [3]. More recently, in the mobile learning field, the scope of the consideration has to a high degree been limited to scaffolding possibilities of the mobile technology, such as in [4]. With this exploratory study, we aim to present findings on how learners can be supported in these new contexts with all available means, technology and other support included, seen from a general pedagogical activity design perspective. We present a mobile learning activity study and demonstrate the roles the mobile technology, teachers, and pre- and post activities, can play in supporting essential learning processes depicted by the Conversational Framework.

2 Conversational Framework

The Conversational Framework is grounded on conceptions of how humans learn and can be mapped onto the traditions of constructivism and socio-cultural learning [5]. With a basis on a synthesis of the main principles of the aforementioned learning traditions, and on findings from empirical research on formal learning, it represents a general account of what it takes to learn and outlines the minimal requirements needed to fully support a formal learning process [5]. The central ground of these requirements is the dialogue between the learner and the knowledgeable others.

Regarding the value of the framework, Laurillard [5] argues that it provides a way of checking that a learning activity design is sufficiently rich to support what it takes for students to learn. The framework also provides a technology-neutral way of stating learning needs based on the claim that learning does not change significantly with the incorporation of technology. It rather gives rise to the opportunity to analyze how we can support the framework with technological tools, and gives a map of the kind of opportunities a teacher and an activity must offer the learners [5]. In addition to the above motivations, the reasons we use the Conversational Framework in this paper are three-folded: 1.) it supports collaborative and conversational approaches to learning which is in line with our study; 2.) it is grounded on empirical research on student learning [5]; and 3.) it is proposed to be suitable for mobile learning [5, 6].

In order to facilitate the analysis of if a given learning activity is providing the needed support, Laurillard [5] recommends the use of the following checklist:

1. access explanations and presentations of the theory, ideas or concepts?
2. ask questions about their understanding of the theory, etc, by providing the opportunity for answers from the teacher, or their peers?
3. offer their own ideas and conceptual understanding, by providing comment on them from the teacher, or their peers?
4. use their theoretical understanding to achieve a clear task goal by adapting their actions in the light of their understanding, or in response to comments or feedback?
5. repeat practice, by providing feedback on actions that enables them to improve performance?
6. repeat practice, by enabling them to share their trial actions with peers, for comparison and comment?
7. reflect on the experience of the goal-action-feedback cycle, by offering repeated practice at achieving the task goal?
8. discuss and debate their ideas with other learners?
9. reflect on their experience, by having to articulate or produce their ideas, reports, designs, performances, etc. for presentation to their peers?
10. reflect on their experience, by having to articulate or produce their ideas, reports, designs, performances, etc. for presentation to their teachers?

List 1. The Conversational Framework Checklist [5]

3 The MULLE Study

The MULLE (Math edUcation and pLayful LEarning) study was held in the autumn of 2009 and aimed at fifth-grade children practicing the area concept, across indoors and outdoors contexts, collaboratively, concretely, physically, and playfully. The children worked in two groups of three children each in four sub-activities: two indoors introductory activities, an outdoor field activity, and an indoors debriefing activity. Two teachers were available during all activities.

The two introductory activities aimed at giving the children hands on experience with the mobile phones used in the outdoor activity, and introducing the scenario to let the children come prepared to the outdoor activity with a representation of the tasks. The scenario for the outdoor activity of MULLE was that an imaginary, almost extinct, species needed to be relocated from the local wild animal park. The task for the children was to see to that the new enclosures for the animals had the right measurements. Measuring large enclosures required the children to use our mobile software application, which measures the distance between two mobile devices using GPS.

The outdoor activity started outside the school. After a short introduction they were told to follow the instructions on the master device which told them to go to a meadow on the other side of the woods. In the small field, they were introduced to the first task and asked to guess the area of two small rectangles marked by plastic cones. The rectangles had different length and width but were both 12 m^2. Each group had prepared one 1x1 meters cardboard square to measure the areas. After a completed task they would send the answer to receive a new task. When they had guessed and calculated the areas correctly they received a message on the master device to go to the big field for the second task. In the big field, they were asked first to guess and then to measure the area of the large rectangle. The large rectangle had cones to mark the corners and an area of 4000 m^2. The student groups measured the rectangle by measuring each side of it using the mobile devices. The third and last task was to go to another field nearby and to create their own rectangle of 4000 m^2. The activity ended with the children showing their own area to one of the teachers.

The scenario for the debriefing activity was that the children were to design the plan of an amusement park. The area of the park was known in advance, the children were to calculate appropriate length and width, and to draw the plan using pen and paper. Similarly, they were to place attractions and service facilities, each with a certain area, in the amusement park they had created. The purpose of the debriefing activity was to let the children repeat the tasks performed outdoors, but this time in more abstract terms, aided with the concrete experiences gained outdoors.

4 Method

The study presented here examined how the learners were pedagogically supported by the designed activities in regard of the aspects of support the Conversational Framework puts forward. The empirical data was collected through audio- and video recordings so as to capture both speech and actions. A microphone was attached to each student and four researchers recorded the activities with cameras from both long and short distance. The total amount of video and audio data was approximately 6 hours.

The collected data was then divided between three researchers into three parts, introduction data, outdoor activity data, and debriefing data. Each researcher analyzed respective part by searching for episodes in which the interactions could be mapped onto the Conversational Framework Checklist (see List 1). An example of such an interaction is a teacher presenting a concept to a student (item 1 in List 1). This analysis resulted in a detailed picture of the interactions supported by the activity. In the next step of the analysis the selections of interactions, with a mapping relation to List 1, were re-analyzed by one of the researchers, thus a certain degree of intra-rater reliability is attained, and furthermore categorized according to the elements of the Checklist (see List 1). This analysis resulted in the identification of four sources of support; mobile technology support, teacher support, introduction activity support, and debriefing activity support. Each source of support was further identified to support the learners in different ways and have been categorized accordingly.

5 Results

The result of our analysis produced a map of the supportive roles the activity components could play successfully (see Fig. 1). Labels in natural language are used to refer to the categories of support and the mapping relations to the Checklist (see List 1) are presented for each category. However, due to the limitations of this short paper a full presentation of the analyzed data is not possible.

Introduction	Outdoor activity		Debriefing
	Mobile technology	Teachers	
Task representation support (1, 2, 3, 4, 8, 9, 10)	Simple feedback (1, 3)	Rich feedback (1, 2, 3, 4, 5)	Repetition support (4, 5, 6, 7)
Technical skill support (5, 6)	Task instructions (4)	Reflection support (1, 2, 3, 4, 5, 10)	Discussion support (1, 2, 3, 8, 9, 10)
	Clues (1, 5)	Collaboration support (facilitator of 1, 2, 3, 4, 6, 8, 9)	Reflection support (7, 9, 10)
	Repetition support (7)	Task adaptation (1, 5)	

Fig. 1. The supportive roles and their mapping to the Checklist (see List 1)

5.1 Introduction

In the first part of the introduction the teacher introduced the task structure of the outdoor field activity and the students asked questions and were provided with answers. At the time of the outdoor field activity, we could observe that this support provided a task representation that was utilized successfully. The students referred back to the introduction at several occasions and were able to resolve arising information needs in this manner. Our impression is also that the students were sufficiently skilled in using the technology and navigate the software system, as a result of allowing them to practice using the technology beforehand. Put differently, the introduction of the task and the practice on the technology resulted in skills and understandings that contributed to increased performance and smoother learning flow in the outdoor activity without the need to attain teacher help in situ. This can be valuable in settings where there are more students, less teachers and greater physical distances between teachers and students.

5.2 Mobile Technology

As a source of support, the mobile technology was identified to offer four distinct categories of support according to the Checklist (see List 1). During the outdoor activity, we could observe that the children expressed satisfaction after receiving feedback on the answers the provided the device. The feedback, and the confirmation of the task approach, also resulted in that the students successfully took a similar approach at new similar tasks, being confident of its validity and hence able to do adjustments and improve the approach. In addition, the mobile device could provide task instructions, offer clues that were utilized in situations where information needs arise, and propose opportunities for repetition of tasks. As such, the mobile technology could play a significant role, and could pose as a complement to the teacher when information needs arise.

5.3 Teachers

The teachers available in the field could, contrary to the capacity of the mobile device, analyze the childrens behaviors and conversations, and as such, provide adaptive feedback, adjust and adapt the task, regulate the collaboration and foster reflection by asking relevant questions connected to the conversational threads of the children.

The help from a more knowledgeable person was an influential factor that resulted in the continuation of the learning process, not only for the learner the teacher had a dialog with but also for the other group members that became more involved by knowing which next step to take. An adapted dialogical conversation of this kind is currently beyond the capacity of the technology.

5.4 Debriefing

The debriefing activity task was constructed to be an abstract metaphorical representation of the outdoor task; the two tasks had the same underlying mathematical structure and were objects of practice for the same mathematical concepts. While the outdoor activity task facilitated situated learning and physical manipulation on concrete objects, the debriefing task involved the abstract versions of these objects, motivated abstract thinking, and enabled both repetition and transfer from concrete to abstract, from outdoor activity to classroom activity. It opened up a possibility to utilize the concrete experience gained in the outdoor activity as an aid to understand the abstract material. In addition, the debriefing activity supported elaborated discussions and reflections to a much higher extent than the outdoor activity. Noticeable is that the debriefing activity supported all of the Checklists (see List 1) ten pedagogical elements and consequently, to a certain degree, compensated for pedagogical needs that potentially were not met in the previous activities

6 Conclusions and Future Work

A successful realization of the possibility to learn in authentic contexts relies on that the designed mobile learning activities provide the pedagogical support learning requires. The aim of this study was to investigate how teachers, mobile technology, and activity structures such as introduction and debriefing can act as mediums of support in a mobile learning activity. Our results indicated that each of these components could provide support to the learners.

It is worthwhile to emphasize the importance of outdoor mobile learning activities to be fun, engaging and motivational. Equally important is nevertheless to recognize that they may not be pedagogically supportive enough on its own accord and that classroom activities can bridge the shortcomings and follow up learning processes in a meaningful way. A natural progression which the results of this study call attention to is further analyses of how we, from a Conversational Framework point of view, can design well-orchestrated activities and processes that support learning, where technology is one medium amongst other.

References

1. Sharples, M., Taylor, J., Vavoula, G.: A Theory of Learning for the Mobile Age. In: Andrews, R., Haythornthwaite, C. (eds.) The Handbook of E-learning Research, pp. 221–247. Sage, London (2007)
2. Wood, D., Bruner, J.S., Ross, G.: The role of tutoring and problem solving. Journ. of Child Psychology and Psychiatry 17, 89–100 (1976)
3. McLoughlin, C.: Scaffolding: Applications to learning in technology supported environments. In: Collis, B., Oliver, R. (eds.) Proc. of World Conference on Educational Multimedia, Hypermedia and Telecommunications, pp. 1826–1831 (1999)
4. Chen, S., Kao, T., Sheu, J.: A mobile learning system for scaffolding bird watching learning. Journal of Computer Assisted Learning (19), 347–359 (2003)
5. Laurillard, D.: Pedagogical forms for mobile learning: framing research questions. In: Pachler, N. (ed.) Mobile Learning: towards a research agenda, pp. 153–175. WLE Centre IoE, London (2007)
6. Pachler, N., Bachmair, B., Cook, J., Kress, G.: Mobile Learning: Structure, Agency, Practices. Springer, New York (2010)

Overview and Preliminary Results of Using PolyCAFe for Collaboration Analysis and Feedback Generation

Traian Rebedea, Mihai Dascalu, Stefan Trausan-Matu,
Dan Banica, Alexandru Gartner, Costin Chiru, and Dan Mihaila

"Politehnica" University of Bucharest, Department of Computer Science and Engineering,
313 Splaiul Independetei, Bucharest, Romania
{traian.rebedea,mihai.dascalu,stefan.trausan,costin.chiru,
dan.mihaila}@cs.pub.ro, dan.banica@cti.pub.ro,
alexandru.gartner@gmail.com

Abstract. Although Computer-Supported Collaborative Learning (CSCL) advocates the use of instant messaging and discussion forums for collaboration between learners, there is a scarcity of tools for leveraging the information in this kind of conversations. Thus, these technologies are primarily used for communication and, once the conversation is over, the raw data is rarely manually analyzed by tutors, teachers and other learners. This paper presents a methodology and a system that can be used for providing feedback and support to learners and tutors that are involved in tasks that make use of chats and forums. In order to achieve this objective, PolyCAFe employs Natural Language Processing and Social Network Analysis techniques to discover polyphony and inter-animation in textual collaborations. To evaluate the proposed approach and the designed system a first validation experiment has been performed and the results are discussed and analyzed in the end of the paper.

Keywords: CSCL, Natural Language Processing, Polyphony, Collaboration, Feedback, Assessment.

1 Introduction

Recent years showed an explosion of the interest in collaborative and social computer applications and platforms on the web. This makes the use of such tools very common, not only for general communication but also for informal and even formal learning. Moreover, Computer-Supported Collaborative Learning (CSCL) is not only a fashionable approach. It is also based on a totally different paradigm [1], based on dialogism and the social-cultural ideas of Bakhtin [2] and Vygotsky [3], which appeared decades before the invention of the computer.

In recent years, several CSCL applications appeared that used different kinds of web communication and collaboration tools and environments like forums, chats, blogs, wikis etc. However, no system is really providing complex analysis and feedback facilities on chat and forum discussions in order to be useful for learners and tutors. There are at least two factors that explain this situation. The first factor is that, even if dialogism [2] is considered as a fundamental paradigm of CSCL [1], extremely few software implementations started from it [4, 5]. The second factor is related to the fact that the majority of collaborations in CSCL are based on the exchange of text messages. Thus, another problem arises from the fact that current Natural Language Processing (NLP) systems are far from providing reliable text understanding systems. Moreover, in CSCL chats and forums there are usually more than two participants, a case which is generally ignored in most NLP theories developed for conversation analysis [5].

The PolyCAFe system (**Pol**yphonic **C**onversation **A**nalysis and **Fe**edback generation) is integrating dialogistic polyphony [4, 5] with Social Network Analysis [6] and NLP [5, 6]. It was developed as one of the modules of the Language Technologies for Lifelong Learning project (http://www.ltfll-project.org). As the automatic analysis of conversations is a difficult task, PolyCAFe combines approaches from previous systems that analyze chat and/or forums that use TF-IDF [7], Latent Semantic Analysis – LSA [8], Social Network Analysis [7], WordNet [7, 8], plus the TagHelper environment [9]. PolyCAFe provides abstraction and feedback services for supporting both learners and tutors that are involved in assignments that make use of chat or forum conversations. The services are packed into web widgets that can be easily integrated into other web applications. An online version of the system with all the widgets is available at the following address: http://ltfll-lin.code.ro/ltfll/wp5/.

The paper continues with a section that describes the architecture, technologies and main functionality of PolyCAFe. Section 3 provides a short overview of the web widgets developed to support and deliver the feedback. The validation methodology, the experiment and the most relevant results are presented in section 4. The paper ends with conclusions and improvements for the second version of the system.

2 The PolyCAFe Framework

In order to analyze a chat or forum and provide feedback on content (utterances), participants and collaboration, the system is structured on several layers: NLP pipe (spelling correction, stemmer, tokenizer, POS tagger, NP chunker), semantic sub-layer (linguistic ontology, LSA), analysis (metrics derived from Page's essay grading techniques [6] and readability evaluation), advanced NLP and discourse analysis techniques (the identification of speech acts, lexical chains, adjacency pairs, co-references, discussion threads) that are used for discovering interactions among the participants, Social Network Analysis, Collaboration and Polyphony sub-layer uses these interactions and, by combining them with advanced discourse structures, looks for convergence and divergence and polyphonic inter-animation.

A key role in the analysis is played by the *integration of results* from all previous sub-layers in order to offer textual and graphical *feedback* and a *grade proposal* for each participant of a chat or forum discussion.

Before evaluating the actual content, the analysis process assesses each utterance based on two sets of surface measures: readability and metrics derived from the initial studies of Page's essay grading techniques [10]. Readability analysis is used for understanding the complexity of the text in terms of reading ease with high impact on comprehension, retention, reading speed and persistence. On the other hand, the metrics derived from Page's essay grading techniques cover the following only from a quantitative perspective: fluency, spelling, diction and utterance structure. These metrics are very important because of the actual way of obtaining them: starting from trins (intrinsic variables used in manual evaluation), proxes (computer approximations of interest) are selected for obtaining a good reflection of the grading process, therefore ensuring a high correlation between manual and automatic assessment.

LSA has a key role in the analysis and is used for measuring the similarity between concepts and between utterances. The LSA training process has some particularities: firstly, the documents that are part of the corpus used in the supervised learning process are chats with the similar topics of discussion and all of them are in the same domain; these chats are segmented upon participants (each participant has an inner consequence) and a fixed window of maximum allowed terms per document. Secondly, each word is tagged with its corresponding Part of Speech Tag and verbs are reduced to their stem because all forms induce very similar actions. General aspects regarding LSA involve the use of TF-IDF (term frequency, inverse document frequency) and setting the number of maximum dimensions of the projection after SVD is performed to a predefined value of 300. Also, in order to reduce the actual impact of repetitions of words in the same utterance, the logarithm function is applied on the number of actual encounters. Another role for LSA is topics determination which is done by assessing the similarity between a concept and the chat's semantic vector obtained by summing up all utterance vectors.

A different perspective is focused on speech acts and argumentation acts which are determined using cue-words, cue-phrases and an extended pattern search that includes the power of regular expressions, but is improved to consider synonyms and other semantic information, plus the utterance-based structure of chat conversations [5]. The last separated module is focused on implicit links determination using repetitions, lexical chains based on WordNet, LSA similar concepts / utterances and heuristics based on speech acts.

All previous modules and factors are integrated in the grading process where two grades are obtained: one for each utterance which combines the quantitative approach (length in characters of words after stop words elimination and stemming, logarithmic number of occurrences) with the qualitative one (similarity with the entire discussion, with a set of predefined topics to be covered); the second mark addresses the current thread evolution and uses all identified speech acts and interactions by adding at the current level of discussion the mark multiplied by a preset coefficient.

The entire process of grading participants is centered on the conversation graph built upon explicit and previously identified implicit links and the social networks analysis metrics applied to this graph. Because the number of participants per chat is small, the following factors specific to graph theory are computed for determining the most competitive and involved participant in the discussion: degree, centrality (closeness centrality, graph centrality, eigen–values) and user ranking similar to the well known Google PageRank algorithm.

In addition, threads are identified using specific graph algorithms. In the current implementation, algorithms for depth-first search and strongly connected components are used, but in order to reduce the length of the discussion threads and to filter out implicit links the computation of the bridges of the graph, plus the maximum flow and minimal cuts are considered for the next version of the system.

Collaboration is also measured under multiple perspectives: the quantitative one is based on social cohesion between all SNA metrics, percentage of interactions (both explicit and implicit) between different speakers related to the overall chat; the qualitative approach introduces the notion of 'gain' under personal evolution (links to previous personal utterances) and collaborative building with transfer of knowledge, ideas or concepts. In this process LSA is used for assessing the actual transfer, impact and correlation between two utterances, the previously described utterance mark is used as a starting point and gain expresses a cumulative projection of previous utterances of the same thread.

3 The PolyCAFe Services and Widgets

As we wanted to offer learners and tutors as much control over the system and its functionalities, PolyCAFe was implemented as an online platform that decouples the processing from the interface. The processing is done using web services whose results are displayed in web widgets that respect the Widgets 1.0 requirements drafts elaborated by the W3C. The widgets can be deployed in any application that supports the widget container Wookie (http://incubator.apache.org/wookie/). Several important web platforms (e.g. Wordpress, Elgg) already have plug-ins that are used to integrate Wookie.

Using this strategy five web widgets were designed to provide feedback and support for each conversation to students and tutors that are using Elgg as a Personal Learning Environment:

- Textual feedback on the whole conversation (based both on content and collaboration);
- Textual feedback for each participant of the conversation;
- Feedback and indicators computed at the utterance level (e.g. speech acts, importance of an utterance, etc.);
- An improved graphical visualization for a conversation designed for studying inter-animation;
- A semantic search widget for a discussion.

4 Preliminary Validation Results

A first validation experiment has been run at the "Politehnica" University of Bucharest in order to determine the pedagogical effectiveness, efficiency and relevance of the results delivered by the system, plus user satisfaction. It involved 9 students, 5 tutors and the teacher of the Human-Computer Interaction course from the Computer Science department. A previous validation experiment is described in [11].

The experiment consisted of an assignment that the students needed to solve in English by debating using a chat environment called ConcertChat. Then, the assignments were uploaded by the tutors to PolyCAFe and the results were visible to both students and tutors. All the students have been at the first usage of PolyCAFe, and only two of the tutors had used it prior to the validation experiment. Therefore, the collected data and viewpoints are those of users unfamiliar with the system. We have used a think-aloud protocol during the usage of the software, plus private notes taken by each user. A similar approach was used for tutors, but the think-aloud lasted for only 1 hour and then the tutors were asked to use the system in their spare time for evaluating the chats of the students. Afterwards, both learners and tutors had to answer a Likert scale questionnaire with over 30 questions, in order to capture their opinion about the system on the whole and each widget in particular, and then take part in a focus group.

The results are very encouraging as the tutors have validated unconditionally all the functionality of PolyCAFe, while the students have validated most of the functionality, only 5 questions being not validated or validated by only a small margin. Considering the Likert scale from 1 – lowest score (strongly disagree), to 5 – highest score (strongly agree), the 35 questions addressed to the tutors received average scores between 3.50-5.00, the most important results being that the tutors find the system relevant and useful for their activity, that the time for providing final feedback to the students is definitively reduced and the quality of the feedback is improved.

On the other side, the students have validated 28 out of 32 questions, with average scores between 3.66-5.00. The students reported in the focus group that several misleads have been found using this widgets. These errors or misleads were reported to be only minor without influencing the overall feedback, however it has been suggested to try and fix them in order to gain the full trust of the users.

Table 1. Short overview of the validation experiment results

Validation Statement	Learners Agreement	Tutors Agreement
PolyCAFe feedback is useful	1.00	1.00
PolyCAFe feedback is relevant	0.63	0.80
Conversation feedback is useful	0.78	0.80
Conversation visualisation is useful	0.89	1.00
Utterance feedback is useful	0.83	1.00
Participant feedback is useful	0.78	1.00
Search conversation is useful	0.61	1.00

The validation results show that both tutors and learners consider that the feedback and facilities offered by PolyCAFe are useful and relevant. However, some of the widgets (and the associated feedback) should be improved: the conversation and participant feedback, plus the search conversation results. The most important suggestions from the students were to explain using tool-tips how each feedback item is computed (this statement might be explainable due to the fact they are senior Computer Science students), to repair the misleads and to change the scale in the participant feedback widget. All the results of this validation round are going to be used for the second version of the system due at the end of 2010.

5 Conclusions and Further Work

This paper introduces PolyCAFe, a web-based system that analyzes collaborative chat conversations and discussion forums in order to provide feedback and support to students and tutors engaged in these activities. To achieve this task, it makes use of NLP and SNA techniques, together with a novel approach based on polyphony, inter-animation and collaboration. The system has been used and validated in a formal context, although this situation also arises naturally in an informal one, especially in communities of practice. The transferability of this approach is of great interest as the system should be used in other contexts as well. There are two distinct aspects that are partially inter-related: language and domain transferability. In order to use PolyCAFe for another language, the modules of the NLP pipe must be available and integrated in the system. Moreover, a corpus of general text documents and a specific one related to the domain of the discussion is needed.

Acknowledgments. The research presented in this paper was partially performed under the FP7 EU STREP project LTfLL.

References

1. Koschmann, T.: Toward a dialogic theory of learning: Bakhtin's contribution to learning in settings of collaboration. In: Hoadley, C., Roschelle, J. (eds.) Proccedings of the Computer Supported Collaborative Learning (CSCL 1999), Palo Alto, CA, pp. 308–313 (1999)
2. Bakhtin, M., Emerson, C. (Trans.): Problems of Dostoevsky's poetics. University of Minnesota Press, Minneapolis (1984)
3. Vygotsky, L.: Mind in society. Harvard University Press, Cambridge (1978)
4. Trausan-Matu, S., Rebedea, T.: Polyphonic Inter-Animation of Voices in VMT. In: Stahl, G. (ed.) Studying Virtual Math Teams, Boston, MA, pp. 451–473. Springer, US (2009)
5. Trausan-Matu, S., Rebedea, T.: A Polyphonic Model and System for Inter-animation Analysis in Chat Conversations with Multiple Participants. In: Gelbukh, A. (ed.) CICLing 2010. LNCS, vol. 6008, pp. 354–363. Springer, Heidelberg (2010)
6. Dascalu, M., Trausan-Matu, S., Dessus, P.: Utterances Assessment in Chat Conversations. Research in Computing Science, Special Issue on Natural Language Processing and its Applications, Mexico 46, 323–334 (2010)
7. Adams, P.H., Martell, C.H.: Topic detection and extraction in chat. In: Proceedings of the 2008 IEEE International Conference on Semantic Computing, pp. 581–588 (2008)
8. Dong, A.: Concept formation as knowledge accumulation: A computational linguistics study. Artif. Intell. Eng. Des. Anal. Manuf. 20(1), 35–53 (2006)
9. Rose, C.P., Wang, Y.C., Cui, Y., Arguello, J., Stegmann, K., Weinberger, A., Fischer, F.: Analyzing Collaborative Learning Processes Automatically: Exploiting the Advances of Computational Linguistics in Computer-Supported Collaborative Learning. International Journal of Computer Supported Collaborative Learning (2007)
10. Eastman, J.K., Owens Swift, C.: Enhancing collaborative learning: discussion boards and chat rooms as project communication tools. Business Communication Quarterly 65(3), 29+.Eluminate (2002)
11. Rebedea, T., Trausan-Matu, S.: Computer-assisted evaluation of CSCL chat conversations. In: Proceedings of the 9th International Conference on Computer Supported Collaborative Learning, vol. 2, pp. 183–185 (2009)

A Framework for the Domain-Independent Collection of Attention Metadata

Maren Scheffel, Martin Friedrich, Katja Niemann,
Uwe Kirschenmann, and Martin Wolpers

Fraunhofer Institute for Applied Information Technology,
Schloss Birlinghoven, 53754 Sankt Augustin, Germany
{maren.scheffel,martin.friedrich,katja.niemann,
uwe.kirschenmann,martin.wolpers}@fit.fraunhofer.de
http://www.fit.fraunhofer.de

Abstract. We present a simple and extendible framework to collect attention metadata and store them for further analysis. Currently, several metadata collectors have been implemented but the framework allows the easy integration of further data collectors. Analysis results, e.g. recommendations or fostering of self-reflection, can then support the user in her learning.

Keywords: attention metadata, framework architecture, recommendation.

1 Introduction

Today, learners spend significant amounts of time on continuously managing digital information that is either found or provided. In consequence, learning is severely hampered through the continuous distractions of provided content that simply increases the cognitive load of learners beyond meaningful states. The information provision is basically controlled by the information coming into the cognitive system. The critical element is the attention that enables the utilization of this type of processes. Making the important information more salient thus directs cognitive resources to the most valuable and critical learning material. Furthermore, by capturing indicators for attention, supportive learning tools become possible, e.g. by enabling support for reflective learning [1].

Recent learning environments are highly specialized to support the user in specific tasks in specific environments. Task and environment independence are not addressed with these applications. Hence, the applications only insufficiently tailor their support to the needs of the learner. Furthermore, through relying on information about the user collected from the system internally, all other information about the learner is neglected. In consequence, when the learner changes the learning environment, only such information about the learner is transferred that is created using user profiling standards like PAPI [2]. These standards do not provide means to describe all aspects of the user. Therefore, we have taken a different approach by collecting contextualized attention metadata

(CAM) [3] on the system level, thereby capturing all interaction of the learner with the systems she uses. In this paper, we present a general framework and infrastructure for collecting and processing CAM records. In section 2 we present related work, focussing on frameworks with related functionality. Section 3 then deals with the functionalities of our framework and describes different wrappers as well as different CAM bindings. Before concluding our work in section 5, we will point out several ways of analysis of the collected CAM in section 4.

2 Related Work

Similar to our proposed framework, Broisin and Vidal [4] present a framework to track and share attention metadata using web services based on web technologies. Using a service-based approach simplifies the integration of existing tools into the framework and facilitates the generation of attention metadata on different environments. Since their framework uses Attention.XML, it records that an action was executed but does not distinguish between different action types. Without this distinction, however, it is much too general to generate recommendations or statistics for self-reflected learning, thereby contrasting our approach significantly.

The duine framework [5] provides a set of software libraries allowing developers to integrate prediction engines into a specific domain. The services range from collecting data to recommending items. The generic structure of the framework allows the definition of profile models for users, items or additional information which is required to generate recommendations. Even though the duine framework gives a very generic approach to adapt and integrate recommendations, in contrast to our approach, it does not focus on a specific data format which makes a cross domain analysis of data almost infeasible.

Lehmann et al. [6] introduce the LIS.KOM framework to capture, manage and utilize lifecycle information for learning resources. Similar to our approach the authors develop plug-ins to gather content change information within specific tools. Even though the framework is architecturally closely related to our work, it focuses on documents and their relations instead of user actions.

3 Framework

Since none of the presented frameworks suites our needs, we build our own framework for collecting and analyzing attention metadata. In the following section we describe the flexible and extendible framework, the wrapper library for collecting attention metadata and the evolution of the CAM schema.

3.1 Functionality

The functionality of the framework is delivered through several components. The user's interactions with the applications on her computer are collected by so called wrappers (see section 3.2). All user actions monitored in that way get converted into datasets conforming to the CAM schema and are forwarded to a central framework instance which in turn feeds the data to a database for storage and later analysis.

In a first version of the framework we mainly focused on its local application. The user was provided with a graphical user interface to manually edit the settings of the framework such as choosing the location of the CAM store. By now we have improved the framework by following a service-oriented approach (SOA). To connect the wrappers and the centralized framework instance we wrapped the framework into a web service. Using a web service-oriented approach allows us to extract processes from applications to a set of separate services. In addition, this leads to a loose coupling of the single modules and improves the interoperability, reusability and scalability of the services as well as the extensibility of the framework. New wrappers can now easily be integrated into the existing structure as single wrappers only need a web service call to access the framework and store the collected CAM into the database. To provide a user interface for starting and stopping the collection of CAM we built a separate application to invoke the storage procedure of the web service. Moreover, we achieved database independence by using JPA annotations and by integrating several database libraries for different database systems such as MySQL, PostgreSQL or HSQLDB.

Another advantage of the service-oriented approach is the further decoupling of the framework from local systems which allows applying the framework on the server side. It is therefore possible to integrate the framework into server side applications like web portals as it is currently being done in the European projects ROLE[1] and OpenScout[2]. Integrating the framework into several portals allows cross domain analysis because the collected usage metadata is stored using a unifying metadata schema. A very important aspect when calculating cross domain analyses is to respect privacy issues, e.g. anonymization of the collected CAM. In its current implementation, privacy and security remain open issues to be addressed at a later stage.

3.2 Wrappers

To gather CAM from tools and applications that the user is working with, so called metadata wrappers need to be developed and plugged into the framework. Currently, a wrapper library is being developed that can easily be extended and adapted by external programmers. Since the wrappers connect to the framework, they only need to deal with the specific requirements of the tools but not with the processing and storage of the data. We already built wrappers to gather usage metadata from the interaction with the file system, the email tools Mozilla Thunderbird and Office Outlook as well as the instant messaging tool Skype. These tools cover a broad range of different actions comprising desktop browsing as well as communication behaviour. This data provides a good starting point for possible analyses like self-reflection or recommendation.

---

[1] http://www.role-project.eu/
[2] http://www.openscout.net/

The user's desktop browsing is tracked using an adapted version of the user activity logger [7] where the events of opening and closing of applications and files are recorded. To keep track of a user's interaction with e-mail clients three different wrappers are offered. The adapted version of the Adapted Dragontalk [8] plug-in is used for monitoring user interactions with Mozilla products. All events concerning the Thunderbird interface, e.g. opening an e-mail, creating a new folder or moving an e-mail to another folder, are recorded. The wrapper for Outlook is realized as a COM log-in project [9] and monitors similar actions. For monitoring the users' communication behaviour with the instant messaging tool Skype, a listener that connects the Skype4Java API has been developed. The development of these wrappers raised new demands on the CAM schema, which are discussed in the next section.

3.3 CAM Bindings

We use the contextualized attention metadata (CAM) schema which is derived from the AttentionXML schema to store recorded observations. A full description of the CAM schema can be found in [3] while the core elements are depicted in figure 1. As observations in CAM are focused on the user, the top element *group* is the representation for each user. For every application used, the *group* has a *feed*, and for each digital object used by an application, each *feed* has an *item*. Whenever an object is accessed, information about this *event* is captured. The *event*, in turn, can have several sub-elements that contain further information, such as *context*, *actionType* or *relatedData*. The CAM schema is developed to describe as many types of attention metadata as possible. Therefore, CAM records of a user do not merely describe the user's foci of attention but rather her entire computer usage behaviour.

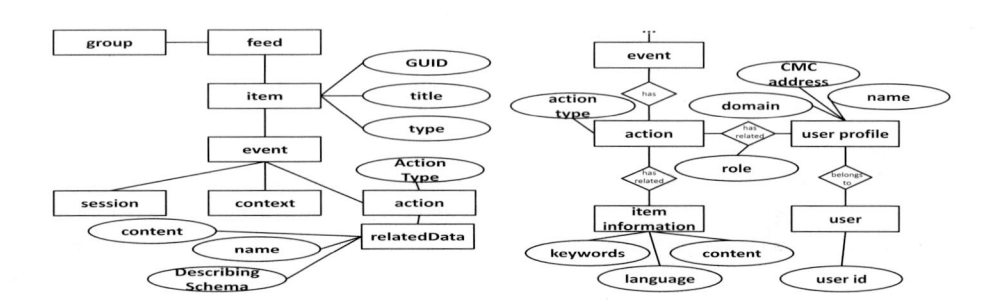

Fig. 1. CAM core elements

Fig. 2. Extended CAM schema

As the CAM schema is originally based on XML, we first used its XML binding. Due to performance reasons we now store the data in a relational database and have also extended our schema to store action related data about the users and the items involved as shown in Figure 2.

Because of its hierarchical structure, the XML binding does not represent the so called user action object (UAO) information which specifies observations where users execute actions on objects directly and does not allow flexibility for other data representations depending on the specific application either. We therefore defined an RDF binding for CAM [10] to enable reasoning over CAM representations, e.g. for recommendation purposes. In order to be able to represent information that extends the RDF typical structure of subject property object, we follow a more complex approach by forming a conceptual triangle of the user, the resource and the events with two-way relations between each two elements. Our motivation to create an RDF binding for CAM was that querying and reasoning as well as the extension from other vocabularies are easier to do. Monitoring systems can make observations in parallel and independently from each other. Finally, the CAM RDF binding allows flexible and extensible CAM representations, fit to the intended use of the data, e.g. analysis, recommendation etc.

4 Possible Analyses

The collected CAM instances enable new services that conduct sophisticated analysis beyond application boundaries to support the user. One possible service supports the user through query expansion and result re-ranking. Assuming a student, Lisa, is working on her desktop and communicates with a friend using Skype. They are talking about the next exam and use keywords like "Java", "search algorithms" and "programming". Then Lisa uses a search engine to find new learning objects on the web using the search query "Java", the system now proposes to also add the term "programming" to the query to increase the quality of the search results due to Lisa's learning needs. Additionally, the system re-ranks the result list from the external search engine according to Lisa's actual context. Here, learning objects related to search algorithms would be presented first.

Monitoring the user also enables the extraction of typical behavioural patterns of the user. Assuming Lisa typically starts Skype, Firefox and Outlook together after system startup, one day Lisa starts her system and launches only Firefox and Skype, the system now asks her "Should I automatically start Outlook as well?". Otherwise Lisa would start working and at the lunch break a colleague might ask her about an e-mail he sent her that she did not receive due to the fact that her e-mail client was not active.

Furthermore, studies have shown that self-monitoring and self-evaluation of one's own behaviour support the successful acquisition of skills and a better understanding of the things studied [11]. The collection and analyses of CAM can also be used to visualize the user's activities on the computer and therefore enable self-reflection. Lisa could become aware of the fact that she spent more time looking at emails and chatting via Skype with friends instead of focusing on the currently more important task of exam preparation.

5 Conclusion

In this paper we presented a simple and extendible framework to record observations and store them as contextualized attention metadata as this allows continuous observation of actions carried out by the user with applications on digital objects. It is so far possible to integrate new CAM collectors and to store the collected data in different formats. Data analyses can then be used for recommendations, the support of self-reflection or finding of behavioural patterns of the user. After getting positive feedback from a small group of test users we are encouraged to continue our work and extend the framework with more wrappers and analysis applications and to evaluate it on a larger scale.

References

1. Schmitz, H.-C., Scheffel, M., Friedrich, M., Jahn, M., Niemann, K., Wolpers, M.: CAMera for PLE. In: Cress, U., Dimitrova, V., Specht, M. (eds.) EC-TEL 2009. LNCS, vol. 5794, pp. 507–520. Springer, Heidelberg (2009)
2. Standard for Information Technology – Public and Private Information (PAPI) for Learners (PAPI Learner). IEEE Learning Technology Standardization Committee (LTSC) Version 8, draft, CEN-WSLT (2001), http://www.cen-ltso.net/main.aspx?put=230
3. Wolpers, M., Najjar, J., Verbert, K., Duval, E.: Tracking Actual Usage: the Attention Metadata Approach. Educational Technology and Society 10(3), 106–121 (2007)
4. Broisin, J., Vidal, P.: From a specific tracking framework to an open and standardized attention environment based on Attention.XML. In: Duval, E., Klamma, R., Wolpers, M. (eds.) EC-TEL 2007. LNCS, vol. 4753, pp. 1–13. Springer, Heidelberg (2007)
5. van Setten, M.: Supporting People in Finding Information: Hybrid Recommender Systems and Goal-Based Structuring. PhD Thesis (2005)
6. Lehmann, L., Hildebrandt, T., Rensing, C., Steinmetz, R.: Capture, Management and Utilization of Lifecycle Information for Learning Resources. IEEE Transactions on Learning Technologies 1(1), 75–87 (2008)
7. User Activity Logger, http://pas.kbs.uni-hannover.de/
8. Adapted Dragontalk, http://www.l3s.de/~chernov/pas/Documentation/Dragontalk/thunderbird_documentation
9. COM log-in project, http://www.add-in-express.com/add-in-net/com-addins.php
10. Muñoz-Merino, P.J., Delgado Cloos, C., Muñoz-Organero, M., Wolpers, M., Friedrich, M.: An Approach for the Personalization of Exercises based on Contextualized Attention Metadata and Semantic Web Technologies. In: Jemni, M., et al. (eds.) Proc. of the 10th IEEE ICALT, pp. 89–91. IEEE Computer Society, Los Alamitos (2010)
11. Kitsantas, A.: Self-monitoring and attribution influences on self-regulated learning of motoric skills. Paper presented at the annual meeting of the American Educational Research Association (1997)

Who Students Interact With? A Social Network Analysis Perspective on the Use of Twitter in Language Learning

Carsten Ullrich[1], Kerstin Borau[1], and Karen Stepanyan[2]

[1] Shanghai Jiao Tong University, Shanghai, China
[2] Buckinghamshire New University, High Wycombe, United Kingdom
ullrich_c@sjtu.edu.cn, kerstinborau@mail.onlinesjtu.com,
karen.stepanyan@bucks.ac.uk

Abstract. This paper reports student interaction patterns and self-reported results of using Twitter microblogging environment. The study employs longitudinal probabilistic social network analysis (SNA) to identify the patterns and trends of network dynamics. It is building on earlier works that explore associations of student achievement records with the observed network measures. It integrates gender as an additional variable and reports some relation with interaction patterns. Additionally, the paper reports the results of a questionnaire that enables further discussion on the communication patterns.

Keywords: microblogging, social network analysis, social networking, collaborative learning.

1 Introduction and Background

Microblogging platforms have acquired a considerable attention of educational practitioners and researchers [1]. Twitter is one of the microblogging services that enable users to post brief messages and communicate with other users. This paper summarises an empirical study that evaluates the use of Twitter as part of a foreign language learning course. It, namely, [a] analyses the interaction of participants (both learners and teachers) by using SNA techniques and [b] evaluates the self-reported use of microblogging – developing a coherent argument on the prevalent patterns of student communication.

The literature is unequivocal on the central role of student interaction for effective learning. Despite the growing body of e-learning research, the studies of online interaction are often incomprehensive due to limitation of the employed research methods and the complexity of the field in general. SNA is one of the methods that have a great potential for revealing and quantifying indistinct interaction patterns. Hence, the use of SNA is considered beneficial for developing our understanding of online practices of teaching and learning [2]. This paper extends the earlier conducted study [3, 4] that analysed the use of Twitter for second language learning. This study introduces the gender variable and attempts to identify its association to network measures of student interaction. The rationale for this research is to identify interaction patterns that can inform educational designers, practitioners and technologists by shedding light on the dynamics of participant interaction within a microblogging environment.

2 Description of the Study and Research Methods

Twitter was introduced at the distant college of Shanghai Jiao Tong University, China (Online-SJTU). This microblogging service was used as part of an English course for native speakers of Chinese. The participants created a new, personal Twitter account. Students were prompted to become "follow"/"befriend" the instructor as well as their peers. Since each Twitter user receives the messages of his/her friends, each student who followed the instruction would receive the messages of fellow students and of the instructor. The students were then told to post at least seven microblogging messages a week and to read the incoming messages of their fellow students. In order to increase Twitter participation, we introduced a grading scheme in which the student use of Twitter contributed up to 20% of their final grade. Each week, student updates were counted and scores assigned. The score did only depend on the number of messages. Students received the full score of five points when more than 20 updates a week were posted.

The methodology of this study integrates analysis of the interaction network and the collected questionnaire data. The study, first, employs SNA techniques that are commonly used for analysing human interaction and relationships between individuals, groups and communities [5, 6]. The evaluation and monitoring of student communication using SNA techniques can shed light on the levels of cohesion within the group of learners and identify disadvantaged participants [2, 7]. The application of SNA can identify hidden factors that may affect student participation, open collaboration and personal development. The use of SNA in educational research can become a valuable and a fundamental resource for understanding student interaction and participation, subsequently leading to improvement of teaching techniques and tools [8].

This study employs application of probabilistic longitudinal SNA techniques that enable reporting identified patterns with statistical precision. The techniques used in the analyses in of this study were drawn from conceptual works on SNA. The previous study identified preferences of students to interact with participants of similar achievement scores. At the same time the study indicated a popularity of participants with higher scores [4]. This study is aiming to identify whether there are network interaction patterns that are associated with participant gender. Furthermore, this study evaluates quantitative data of using Twitter and discusses the results within the context of this study.

2.1 Data Overview and Operationalisation

The data used in this study constitutes the messages posted by the participants within the Twitter microblogging environment. These messages were posted in a public domain, hence, visible to the peers, teachers and the general public. Students were able to communicate with one another by using the communication conventions widely used within the selected microblogging environment. In case a message was addressed to a specific peer, it was therefore possible to identify the addressee. The messages posted by one participant (actor i) to another (actor j) are defined as a directed tie (from i to j; i→j) only when there are more than three messages posted in total. The interaction was observed throughout a period of 56 days. Out of total 5256 messages, posted by 108 participants, 1266 directed messages and 87 interacting participants were considered in

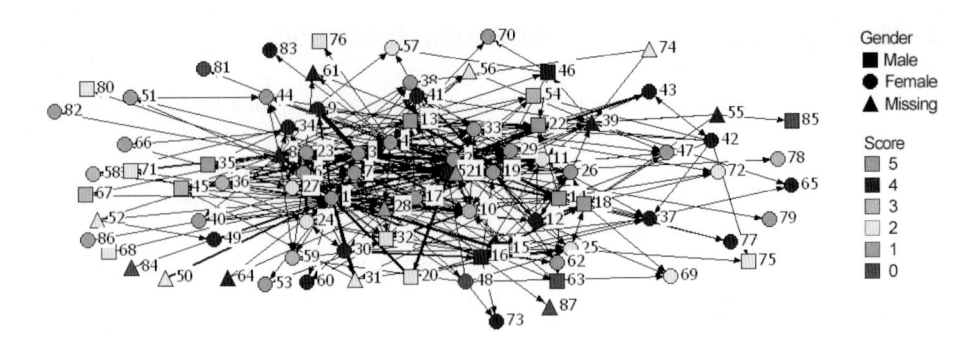

Fig. 1. Overall interaction network. Ties with greater weight denote intensity of interaction.

the study. The network of participant interaction that includes all the exchanged messaged is presented in Fig. 1. The diagram and the measure of density (d=0.16) indicates that the participants were relatively well connected.

The network data was then divided into three equally timed waves (i.e. segment of communication data) for further longitudinal network analysis. Despite having the timestamp of each communicated message, this segmentation of data was required before processing in SIENA 3.17. Furthermore, the overall valued network was dichotomised to include only the communication with a threshold of at least three exchanged messaged. The dichotomised waves are presented in Fig 2.

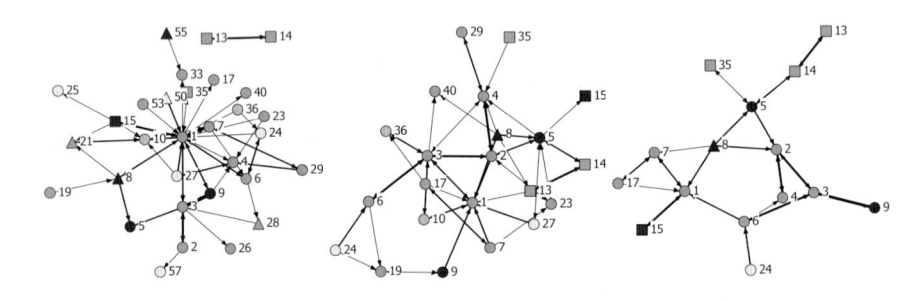

Fig. 2. Networks of intensive interaction in three consecutive stages of the course

At the end of the lecture, as part of their homework students were asked to fill out a bilingual questionnaire (English/Chinese) about their usage of and opinion on Twitter. A total of 96 students completed the questionnaire. Of these, 82 students claimed to have used Twitter at least once. Since this paper investigates the effects of usage of Twitter, we excluded the 14 questionnaires of the students who never used Twitter from the analysis. Most participants (62 = 75%) of the students who completed the survey were female, 25% (=20) were male. Half of the participants were aged 20-25 (=42), 40% (=33) were aged 25-30, and 10% (=7) over 30.

3 Data Analysis

This study employs stochastic SNA models for capturing regularities with statistical accuracy. This section conjecture and test a set of hypothesis (Table 1), that are derived from the research literature that discusses social interaction patterns in relation to network theories. This approach allows testing whether common interaction patters are also prevalent in an online learning environment that employs microblogging. Furthermore, the results enable a discussion the benefits of employing SNA in online learning research.

Table 1. Research hypotheses, parameters and conditions

Hypotheses	Null Hypotheses
H1: (Homophily effect) Same gender participants tend to interact among themselves. (Actor Level)	$H8_0$: *Same Gender <= 0;* at $\alpha<0.05$
H2: (Indegree popularity effect) Participant gender is related to his/her acquired attention. (Actor Level)	$H9_0$: *Gender Covariate-alter = 0;* at $\alpha<0.05$
H3: (Outdegree popularity effect) Participant gender is related to his/her outreach. (Actor Level)	$H10_0$: *Gender Covariate-ego = 0;* at $\alpha<0.05$

To evaluate the dynamics of the developed network, a set of concepts for addressing issues related to the formation and evolution of social networks have been selected, namely *homophily (actor level) and reciprocity (dyadic level)*. The analysis was conducted by using dynamic actor-driven models defined and evaluated with SIENA (v. 3.17) software jointly with the StOCNET graphical interface package [9, 10]. Based on the conjectured hypotheses a number of models were defined. The models determine the sets of probabilistic tests.

Network Dynamics in Relation to Gender: Models 1-4 are drawn for testing the hypotheses around the conjectured homophily and popularity effects in relation to participant gender. This approach is similar to the earlier discussed study [4] that revealed an association of student scores with the number of replies students get and the people they communicate with. This approach may indicate whether gender is, in any way, related to the prominent interaction patterns. The results of the estimation tests (Table 2) allow us to comment on network parameters with at least 95% confidence interval. The significant results are marked with an asterisk. A negative value of outdegree density is consistent in all the models. This pattern indicates a tendency for exhibiting a selective approach in reaching out other participants. Similarly, reciprocity is identified as a prominent pattern within the observed network. The parameters of reciprocity are positive and statistically significant suggesting a tendency towards reciprocation of initiated communication.

The estimation results, conducted under Model 1, indicate a positive and significant (0.50) value for the Same Gender covariate. Hence, the $H1_0$ can be rejected – suggesting an existence of gender homophily effect within the network. Furthermore, the model design allows us to report that female participants tend to interact with other females. However, there are a number of constraints that that need to be taken into account when interpreting the results. Firstly, while some of the results are statistically significant the values are very close to the acceptable barrier of $\alpha < 0.05$. Additionally, the distribution of sexes among the registered participants was not equal and most importantly, the gender information was partially missing. While SIENA software allows the use of missing data and adjusts computations accordingly [11], the paper restrains further generalisation. Models 2-4 test the existence of popularity effects based on participant gender. It is apparent from Table 2 that none of the parameters (i.e. Gender Ego or Gender Alter) indicate statistical significance. Hence, $H2_0$ and $H3_0$ cannot be rejected. In other words, it is impossible to report on the existence of participant popularity effect with due statistical precision. Hence, no assumptions can be made on whether certain gender can be related to the behaviour of initiating or attracting communication from other participants.

Table 2. Estimation results: testing for gender effects

Network Effects	Network Dynamics	Model 1	Model 2	Model 3	Model 4
Out-degree and Reciprocity	Outdegree (density)	-5.56 (0.28)*	-5.3 (0.24)*	-5.61 (0.29)*	-5.61 (0.26)*
	Reciprocity	5.04 (0.39)*	5.08 (0.39)*	5.03 (0.38)*	5.01 (0.36)*
H1:Homophily	Same Gender	0.50 (0.23)*	-	0.58 (0.27)*	0.61 (0.27)*
H2: Popularity	Gender Ego (Outdegree)	-	-0.06 (0.21)	-0.24 (0.18)	-0.12 (0.24)
H3:Popularity	Gender Alter (Indegree)	-	-0.08 (0.16)	-	-0.15 (0.18)

Self-Reported Communication Results: The communication patterns were analyzed by six questions (see Figure 3). The first two questions inquired whether the students used Twitter updates to communicate with their classmates and teacher, respectively. 22% (=18 students) and 16% (=13 students) stated that they never used Twitter for such communication. The log data of the actual updates confirms this data: 22 students posted less than 4 updates during the grading period (recall that Twitter was introduced two weeks before the grading period started). However, about 80% sometimes or often used Twitter for communication in class. Given number of 4552 updates, Twitter indeed has stimulated active communication.

According to the analysis and the questionnaire results the chosen approach in using microblogging offered realistic opportunities for reading and writing. One third of the students stated that they often replied to updates of their classmates. More than half (56%) sometimes and only 14% never replied to updates. The updates confirm this data. However, only about 8% of the updates contained the "@" symbol. Given that not everyone was familiar with this syntax and that often dialogues arouse among

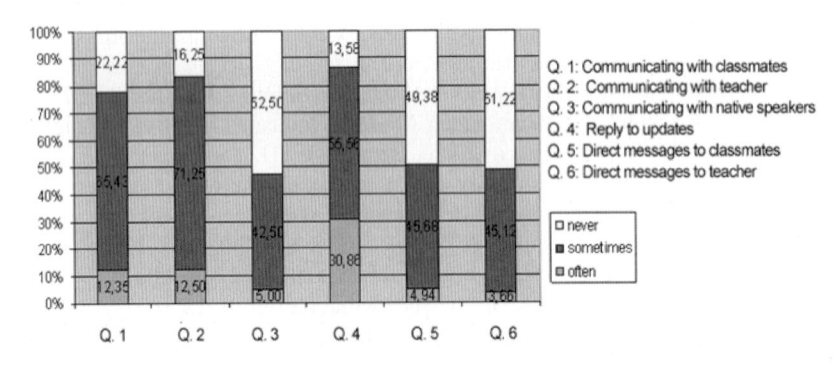

Fig. 3. Self-reported communication patters

common themes the number of replies could be considerably higher. Direct messages were used much less often. Half of the students claim that they never sent any direct message neither to their classmates nor to their teacher. Twitter does not offer a way to access the number of direct message sent to or received by a given user.

4 Conclusions

This study examines participant interaction within a microblogging environment and reports the prevalent network patterns. The probabilistic approach to the network analysis allows reporting the results with statistical precision. The results indicate: [a] a significant homophily effect – a preference of participants to interact with peers of the same gender; [b] no significant evidence of popularity effect in relation to gender; [c] self-reported inclination to reply to initiated posts; and [d] self-reported tendency towards public communication. Employing SNA techniques and questionnaire data, this study attempts to identify interaction patterns that may not otherwise be immediately evident. It raises points for consideration when integrating microblogging services to teaching and learning.

References

1. Ullrich, C., Borau, K., Luo, H., Tan, X., Shen, L., Shen, R.: Why web 2.0 is good for learning and for research: principles and prototypes (2008)
2. Haythornthwaite, C.: Social Network Methods and Measures for Examining E-learning. Social Networks (2005)
3. Borau, K., Ullrich, C., Feng, J., Shen, R.: Microblogging for Language Learning: Using Twitter to Train Communicative and Cultural Competence, p. 87 (2009)
4. Stepanyan, K., Borau, K., Ullrich, C.: A Social Network Analysis Perspective on Student Interaction Within the Twitter Microblogging Environment. In: The 10th IEEE International Conference on Advanced Learning Technologies, Sousse, Tunisia (2010)
5. Wellman, B., Berkowitz, S.D.: Social structures: A Network Approach. Elsevier Science & Technology Books (1997)
6. Wasserman, S., Faust, K.: Social Network Analysis: Methods and Applications. Cambridge University Press, Cambridge (1994)
7. Reffay, C., Chanier, T.: How social network analysis can help to measure cohesion in collaborative distance-learning, Designing for change in networked learning environments. In: Proceedings of the International Conference on Computer Support for Collaborative Learning, pp. 343–352 (2003)
8. Martínez, A., Dimitriadis, Y., Rubia, B., Gómez, E., De la Fuente, P.: Combining qualitative evaluation and social network analysis for the study of classroom social interactions. Computers & Education 41, 353–368 (2003)
9. Snijders, T.A.B.: The Statistical Evaluation of Social Network Dynamics. Sociological Methodology 31, 361–395 (2001)
10. Steglich, C., Snijders, T.A.B., West, P.: Applying SIENA: An Illustrative Analysis of the Coevolution of Adolescents' Friendship Networks, Taste in Music, and Alcohol Consumption. Methodology 2, 48–56 (2006)
11. Snijders, T.A.B., Steglich, C.E.G., Schweinberger, M., Huisman, M.: Manual for SIENA, version 3. University of Groningen, Groningen (2006)

Conditions and Effects of Teacher Collaboration within a Blended Professional Development Program for Technology Integration

Albena Todorova[1] and Thomas Osburg[2]

[1] University of Munich (LMU), Psychology of Excellence in Business and Education, Martiusstr. 4, 80802 Munich, Germany
[2] Intel Corp., CAG Europe, Dornacher Str. 1, 85622 Feldkirchen, Germany
albena.todorova@psy.lmu.de, thomas.osburg@intel.com

Abstract. Research on professional development (PD) for teachers in technology integration indicates that collaboration is among the key elements contributing for developing relevant competencies and adopting new teaching practices. This paper examines collaboration between teachers within the large-scale PD program "Intel Teach – Advanced Online" in Germany. The external evaluation of the program provides evidence regarding teachers' teamwork, their use of the collaboration tools of the online platform, the effects of teachers' collaboration on their learning and the conditions for collaboration. The findings revealed a strong impact of effective collaboration on individual gains from participation in the program. It was however found that in the conditions of school internal training, teachers showed clear preference for face-to-face interactions, than for using the provided online collaboration tools.

Keywords: Collaborative Learning, Online Collaboration Tools, Online Platform, Teacher Professional Development.

1 Introduction

Research on professional development for teachers in technology integration indicates that collaboration is among the key elements contributing for developing relevant competencies and adopting new teaching practices [1],[2],[3]. Collaborative problem solving was one of the eight design principles for effective professional development in technology use identified a decade ago by Hawley & Valli [2] in their meta-analysis of the literature on the topic. More recently the benefits of participating in professional learning communities are emphasized [3],[4]. This line of research is supported by findings that the successful integration of technology in the classroom is influenced to a large extent by external support, access to up-to-date resources and participation in a community of teachers working with technology, rather than being solely dependent on the technical skills of teachers [5].

Alongside school-based communities facilitating collaboration between teachers, the endorsement of Web 2.0 technologies has brought about web-based communities of practice and computer-supported environments for collaboration, based on the advantages of different types of communication, various media support and the opportunity for extending a community to incorporate a large number of participants with different experiences, knowledge and backgrounds. However, research reveals that in most cases teachers work in isolation during their everyday work [6]. The dynamics between online communities, everyday interaction with colleagues in school and individual work poses the question what opportunities are really used by teachers and what can be facilitated through professional development to use the full potential of collaboration for supporting knowledge sharing, integration and generation, and for transforming teaching practices toward more learner-centered instruction. This paper examines collaboration between teachers within the large-scale professional development program "Intel® Teach – Advanced Online" in Germany and discusses the findings from the program evaluation regarding teacher collaboration.

2 Intel® Teach - Advanced Online

The teacher professional development program Intel Teach - Advanced Online is a program within the Intel® Education Initiative of Intel Corp. towards advancing education through the use of technology. One of the main components of the initiative is the Intel® Teach Program - a professional development program aimed at training classroom teachers to effectively integrate technology in instruction to enhance student learning. The program provides a portfolio of courses targeting different aspects of integrating technology in classroom teaching, including classroom software productivity tools and student-centered approaches to learning; integrating technology into existing classroom curricula; using online tools to enhance students' higher order thinking skills; and advancing teachers' methodological skills. The program discussed in this paper - Intel Teach - Advanced Online, was one of these offerings, which was developed and introduced in Germany and subsequently localized in several other countries. A new version of the program preserving the general design and content, but supported by a Moodle-based online platform has recently replaced the previous version and is in the process of localization in further countries. The new program in Germany is being currently implemented as Intel® Lehren Interaktiv (http://www.intel-interaktiv.de/).

The concept for Intel Teach - Advanced Online was developed by the Academy for Teacher Training and Staff Management in Dillingen (Akademie für Lehrerfortbildung und Personalfuehrung, ALP) belonging to the Ministry of Education in Bavaria, Germany. The academy assured that the content of the program matched the curricula in all federal states and fostered the cooperation with various public education institutes. The course is based on a blended learning format of face-to-face meetings and individual and collaborative learning supported by an online platform, which enables self-paced on-the-job professional development. Participants in the program are guided and assisted in the training process by mentors.

A typical course of the program is initiated by an interested teacher, who receives training to become mentor and presents the program to his or her colleagues in the school. Teachers, who decide to participate in the program form one or more groups. Supported by the mentor they choose a pedagogical approach or technology tool to learn about, and subsequently work collaboratively to develop a unit plan, implement it in their classroom practice, evaluate it and enhance it for further use. This pedagogical framework is called 'Learning Path.' All steps in the process are supported and directed through the online platform of the program, which includes several main areas to suit personalized needs at a particular time: areas for work with the learning path and areas with resources, collaborative tools, additional information and online support.

In order to complete the chosen learning path, teachers work collaboratively using the online tools to plan and design curriculum and they can use for their classes the tools and resources provided on the platform. The online environment of the program and the embedded tools for collaboration enable teachers' joint work, solving problems and sharing knowledge, expertise, and materials. These include tools, such as messaging, wiki, document sharing, chat, calendar, forum, online-questionnaire and quiz tool, server for documents, container for documents, and RSS. Every tool had a description on how to be used and on how to embed it in the school-internal training and collaboration with colleagues. In the new version of the platform, online collaboration is organized in a similar way, however it is supported in a more intuitive way, based on the Moodle functionality with an integrated e-Portfolio system.

In the course of participating in the professional development program, every group of teachers chose a leader for contact with the mentor and to function as administrator for the Group tool on the online platform for registering the new group, adding members, etc. Online information about the steps involved in the professional development program drove the organization of individual learning and teamwork. Additionally the platform offered training materials for team building and provided a schema for organization of the teamwork as guidelines for teachers in their work on a Learning Path. The suggested phases included individual learning from materials on the online platform about theoretical frameworks and teaching methods, and team meetings, during which teachers go through the process of choosing a Learning Path and developing and implementing a lesson unit. The provided schema for structuring the team meetings provided guidelines for the learning process, however, teachers were not obliged to follow it. They could choose how long to spend on their project, whether to work on only one Learning Path or to learn simultaneously about further methods and technology tools, within their group or even with other groups of teachers. They were also able to access the online platform and collaboration tools both from school and from home.

3 Findings Related to Teachers' Collaboration

A systematic external evaluation of the implementation of Intel Teach - Advanced Online in Germany was conducted by the Institute for Media and Educational Technology in the University of Augsburg in the period from 2005 to 2008 [6], [7]. Data has been collected through an online, self-report end-of-training survey of teachers who completed the program in two phases. 4633 surveys filled by teachers were collected from January 2005 till April 2007, and 403 surveys from May till October 2007 (total n=5036). Additional self-report surveys have been filled by mentors (n=152) online, and by teachers (n=418) and university students (n=67) at the educational fair Didacta 2006. For determining the conditions of implementation in the different federal states, online questionnaire have been filled by regional mentors of the program (n=14). In 2007 case studies of schools (n=16) in four federal states in Germany have been conducted through interviews and group discussions for examining the sustainability of the program and the factors for its successful implementation.

Overall, the evaluation findings as reported by the external evaluators in detail elsewhere [7], showed that the program had a highly positive impact on teachers' competencies for integrating technology in their teaching within student-centered learning scenarios, as well as on teachers' attitudes toward technology and practices of classroom technology integration. The evaluation data provides evidence for teachers' teamwork during the program and their use of the collaboration tools of the online platform. Furthermore, analysis of the findings reveals the impact of teachers' collaboration on their learning and on the effectiveness of the program. In additions, the evaluation sheds light on the conditions for collaboration in the participating schools.

Collaboration between Teachers. Regarding the participation in collaborative teams, most of the teachers worked with three or more colleagues in an average of twelve hours, in comparison to spending on the average 16 hours in individual learning and 10 hours in implementation of the developed unit in the classroom. Particularly high satisfaction with the collaborative activities was expressed by teachers who worked in a team with colleagues from the same discipline. The majority of the participating teachers (90%) considered teamwork important for their work in school. Teams in the program usually consisted of four or more teachers. In smaller schools the number of teachers in a group was higher, which can be related to the findings that teachers in smaller schools work together more often than teachers in larger schools.

Despite the functions embedded in the online platform to support between-school teams through online communication and collaboration, such interactions were not realized due to the implementation of the program Intel Teach – Advanced Online as a school internal training in 83% of the cases. Therefore is it not surprising that the online collaboration tools were not always used. Less than half of the teachers (48%) reported that the online-tools "planner/scheduler" and "messages" supported the teamwork. Same observations were made for the online-tools "forum", "notes", "whiteboard", "server for documents". As interviews and group-discussions (84 teachers were involved) showed, teamwork was based on face-to-face activities. The online-tools for teamwork thus were not essential for the functioning of the team and scarcely used. However, the overall feedback about collaboration within the program was positive. The majority of teachers reported that the teamwork with their colleagues worked out well and that the atmosphere in their team was good.

Effects of Collaboration on Outcomes. The analysis of the evaluation data showed a strong impact of effective collaboration on individual gains from participation in the program. When collaborative work with other teachers was successful, teachers reported higher gains compared to the cases in which the collaboration did not work well (Fig. 1).

More than two-third of the teachers (65,4%) report increased readiness for collaborative work and learning after the program. However, relatively few teachers admit to have started collaborating in different forms as result of the professional development or that they intend to do in future. The reason is that they had already participated in

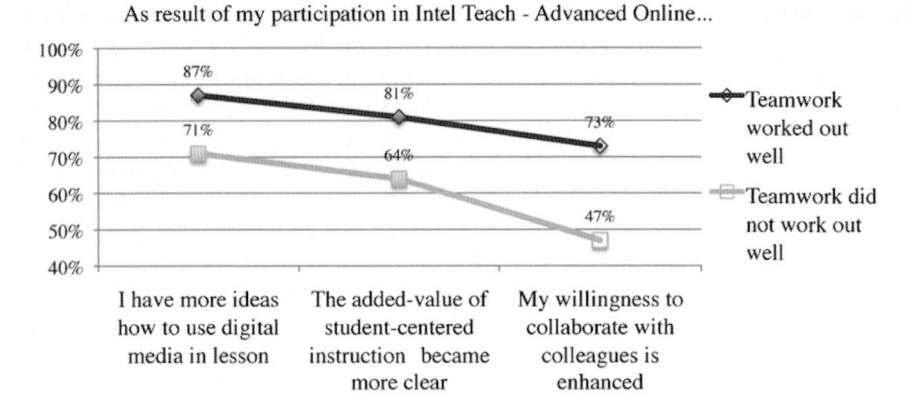

Fig. 1. Significance of Effective Collaboration for Successful Participation in Intel® Teach - Advanced Online

collaborative activities before the program. Particularly high percentage of teachers had already collaborated with colleagues in order to prepare their classes or had taught interdisciplinary. Over two-thirds of the teachers reported collaborating with other teachers more often as result of their participation in the program.

Conditions for Teacher Collaboration. The support from the school leadership was a significant moderator of the influence of various factors on the outcomes of the program. Absence of support was associated with poor technical and time resources, disadvantageous school climate and collaboration, and with less prior experience with integrating technology in class. Evidence from the case studies however, revealed that teachers worked in generally supportive school environment with mostly good collaborative work and with support from the school leadership. The majority of participants described staff relations, cooperation between colleagues, and support by the school management as good. Teachers considered it as rewarding when their teamwork functioned in close cooperation with their colleagues, and an intensive exchange of ideas took place.

Teamwork was also affected by the organization of the engagement with the professional development offering. For instance, teachers appreciated strict times of meetings, to which all team-members, and additionally the mentors were present. For this purpose in some cases teachers used the times scheduled for meetings of teachers of their discipline. Although teachers with positive experience from the collaboration with their colleagues benefited more from the program, this was not only related to their readiness and competencies for collaboration, but was also related to the provision of time for teamwork by the school. Here the role of the school leadership is central, and it needs to support the objectives of the program and to recognize the involvement of the tutors and the teachers.

4 Conclusion and Implications

The external evaluation of the program Intel Teach Advanced Online showed that collaborative professional development for teachers in integrating technology in class could be successfully realized through a blended-learning offering. However, in the conditions of school internal training, teachers show clear preference for the face-to-face interactions, rather than using online collaboration tools. It is not clear whether a different form of implementation or organization of the professional development process would facilitate more intensive and productive use of online collaborative tools, or whether it would have advantages over face-to-face collaboration.

At individual school level it was shown that successful in-school implementation of the advanced course was facilitated when the school mentor supported and supervised participating colleagues and structured the advanced course according to the needs and requirements of the participants. The outcomes from the program were also enhanced when cooperation in the team worked well and also provided for firmly agreed dates in the school on which several teams got together and where the school mentor was present to offer targeted support. Blended-learning in this relation has an advantage, as such long-term collaboration between teachers in a team is supported by face-to-face meetings.

Collaborative learning seems to be an important component of successful professional development, particularly effective teamwork and sharing practices with other teachers. The evaluation findings showed that during the professional development course teachers used intensively the opportunities for collaboration with other teachers. Furthermore, reports show that after receiving their certificates, more than two-thirds of the participants continued to work with their teams on other learning paths. At the same time the findings based on teachers' self-reports need to be accepted with caution. For instance, despite the teachers' reports for increased collaboration as result of the participation in the program, according to Senior Teachers, responsible for the implementation of the program on federal state level, collaboration between teaching staff had barely improved.

Despite the limited weight of the evaluation findings as evidence for the effectiveness of collaborative professional development, the experience from the implementation of Intel® Teach – Advanced Online offers an example of its application in practice and allows us to discuss some further implications. As exchange between participants of different schools was not supported, it should be considered how a requirement for networking could be incorporated into the didactic concept and facilitated by the online platform. After revision of the significance of collaboration between teachers and the influence of tutors, a different concept is implemented in the new version of the program – peer coaching. It is expected that this additional support will enhance teachers' acquisition of competencies and skills, according to their individual needs. This can also be addressed by the introduction of e-Portfolios as part of the professional development, as a mechanism to identify gaps, track development and find peers with relevant knowledge and skills for coaching and collaboration. Further possibilities for interaction between teachers and for forming a virtual community of practice or community of professional learning will contribute to the impact of the program on teaching practices and to the sustainability of the program.

References

1. Cordingley P., Bell M., Rundell B., Evans D., Curtis, A.: The impact of collaborative CPD on classroom teaching and learning. In: Research Evidence in Education Library, EPPI-Centre, Social Science Research Unit, Institute of Education, University of London, London (2003)

2. Hawley, W.D., Valli, L.: The essentials of effective professional development: A new consensus. In: Darling-Hammond, L., Sykes, G. (eds.) Teaching as the Learning Profession: handbook of policy and practice, pp. 127–150. Jossey-Bass, San Francisco (1999)
3. Vescio, V., Ross, D., Adams, A.: A review of research on the impact of professional learning communities on teaching practice and student learning. Teaching & Teacher Education 24(1), 80–91 (2008)
4. Bolam, R., McMahon, A., Stoll, L., Thomas, S., Wallace, M.: Creating and sustaining professional learning communities. Research Report Number 637. General Teaching Council for England. Department for Education and Skills, London (2005)
5. Pianfetti, E.S.: Teachers and technology: digital literacy through professional development. Language Arts 78(3), 255–262 (2001)
6. Wei, R.C., Darling-Hammond, L., Andree, A., Richardson, N., Orphanos, S.: Professional learning in the learning profession: A status report on teacher development in the United States and abroad. National Staff Development Council, Dallas, TX (2009)
7. Ganz, A., Reinmann, G.: Blended Learning in der Lehrerfortbildung - Evaluation einer Fortbildungsinitiative zum Einsatz digitaler Medien im Fachunterricht. Unterrichtswissenschaft 35(2), 169–191 (2007)
8. Häuptle, E., Florian, A., Reinmann, G.: Nachhaltigkeit von Medienprojekten in der Lehrerfortbildung. Abschlussbericht zur Evaluation des Blended Learning- Lehrerfortbildungsprogramms, Lehren – Aufbaukurs Online (Arbeitsbericht Nr. 20). Universitaet Augsburg, Augsburg (2008)

Enhancing Learning with Off-Task Social Dialogues

Jozef Tvarožek and Mária Bieliková

Faculty of Informatics and Information Technologies,
Slovak University of Technology,
Ilkovičova 3, 842 16 Bratislava, Slovakia
{jtvarozek,bielik}@fiit.stuba.sk

Abstract. In Peoplia, a socially intelligent tutoring agent helps students learn by augmenting learning opportunities with social features. The tutoring agent engages in off-task conversations with the students before and after the instructional activities, motivating them to work with the system more successfully. We describe the tutor's architecture and early experiments in the domain of middle school mathematics. Students who engaged with the socially intelligent agent liked the system more, and attained higher learning gains.

Keywords: off-task dialogues, social intelligence, motivation, problem solving.

1 Introduction

Tradeoffs between motivating students vs. providing them with actual learning experiences are still researched [1]. Various approaches for improving student's motivation and learning have been proposed: addressing emotional and affective states of students [2], narrative-centered environments with story-based learning [3,4], and adaptive web-based systems [5,6]. The affective support seems hard to realize in practice and currently remains limited [7], and since narrative-centered story-based approaches completely alter the way teaching occurs as compared to traditional classrooms or even a typical ITS interface, their use in traditional domains such as mathematics and computer science is not exactly straightforward.

In our research we attempt to improve students' motivation in learning environments with a socially intelligent agent, the tutoring friend, which addresses social aspects beyond that of an individual student [8]. In this paper, we describe the architecture of a socially intelligent tutoring agent, and report on experiments evaluating the effects of introducing the tutoring agent into a learning environment.

The social context of individual students is important in learning, and friends engage in more extensive conversations and have been found to be more supportive and critical that non-friends [9]. On the other hand, expert human teachers watch both task-oriented performance and motivational indicators [10], and various socially intelligent interaction tactics for tutoring agents to accomplish motivational goals have been proposed [11]. Major research efforts also continue to explore politeness and its role in effective tutorial dialogue, motivating students and learning [12,13,14].

Research suggests that artificial tutors are able to maintain the appearance of social intelligence without full natural language understanding, that is currently deemed intractable. In our approach, the socially intelligent agent employs a finite-state dialogue management that is able to engage in simple getting-to-know conversations, after which student is guided to structured problem solving exercises. Students that engaged with the artificial tutoring friend produced better learning outcomes.

2 The Peoplia System – Overview

Peoplia is an interactive web-based environment that helps students to learn using various types of learning opportunities that are facilitated by a socially intelligent tutoring agent, the tutoring friend [8], see Figure 1. It features pseudo-tutor assessments with free-text answering. Questions for assessments and exercises are generated by a task generator, discouraging cheating and surface learning. Peoplia is an attempt to build an integrated environment for (1) the assessments as occurring in regular classrooms, and (2) home study with self exercises; while augmenting the available learning opportunities with social features [15]. It contains generic social features such as friends management, invitations, and updating your profile.

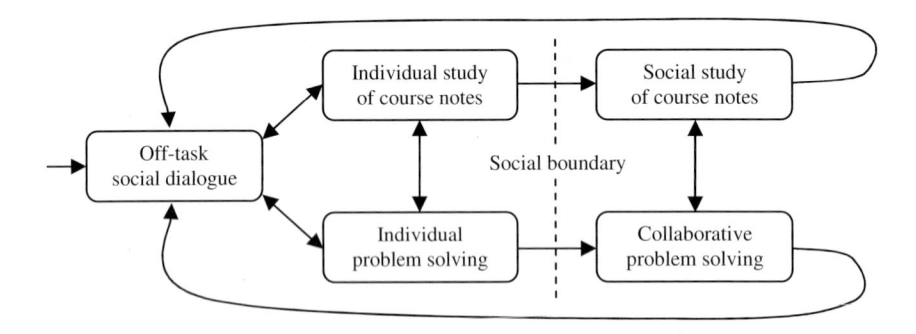

Fig. 1. Types of learning opportunities in Peoplia with admissible transitions (arrows), which are facilitated by the tutoring friend

Learning opportunities. The system (Figure 1) features two learning types: *study of course notes* and *problem solving*, that can be engaged either individually or in collaboration, i.e. four types of learning opportunities are available in total. The most traditional form of learning support, course notes (Figure 2), is used for supporting conceptually difficult domains such as theoretical computer science, for which developing a large set of pseudo-tutor problems may not be feasible or desirable. Course materials are represented in the same rich content format as problem descriptions. Transferring existing materials into this format does not require use of complex features of the format and thus requires only a small additional effort. In social mode, course materials are augmented by facilities for highlighting important concepts, and assigning sticky notes that enable to unwind a Q&A conversation.

For problem solving, students work on structured exercises that start with an initial question. Upon providing a wrong answer additional questions or scaffolding hints are administered to the student [16]. Difficulties of following these solution paths are statistically calibrated to allow for adaptive selection of tasks and a premature finish of administering a subtask that becomes too hard for the current level of student's ability.

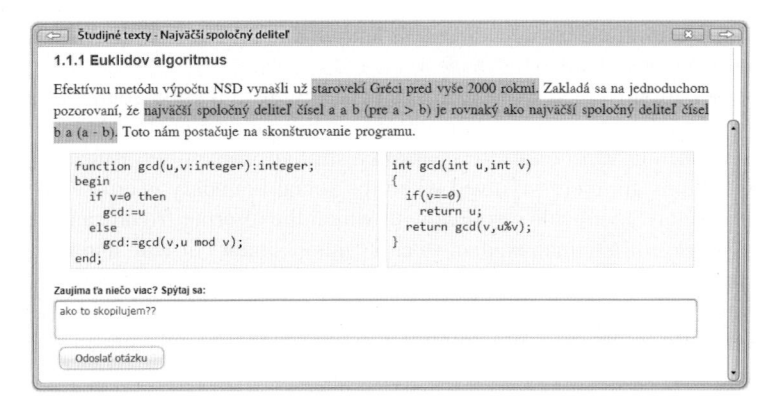

Fig. 2. Sample of course notes with highlights, sticky notes (not shown), and an option to ask for further assistance

In collaborative mode (Figure 3), individual problem solving is enhanced by synchronous collaboration features: (1) instant messaging, (2) voting for the most agreeable answer in the team, and (3) a multi-user interface version of interactive components that are specified in the question description.

Student answers are graded (matched to the predefined set specified in the problem description) by the two-stage grading process mentioned earlier. A single human grader is capable of grading answers generated by a class of 20 students without any noticeable lag in responses to the students [16].

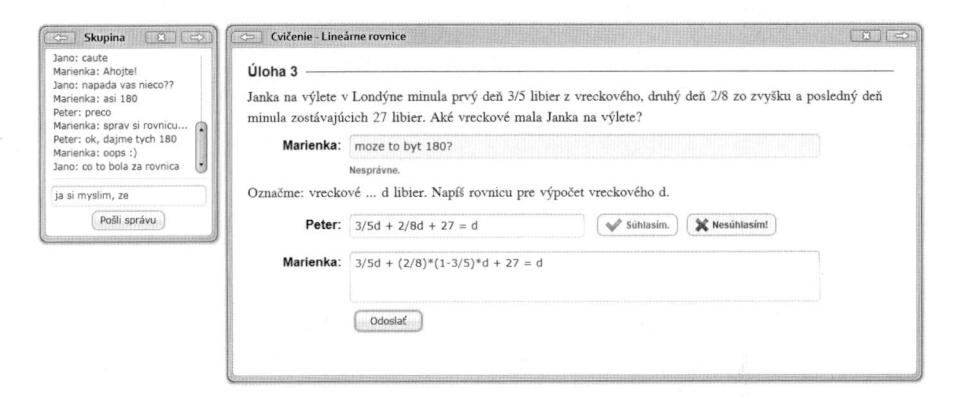

Fig. 3. Collaborative problem solving – free-text answer with voting mechanism

Social intelligence in Peoplia. The surface features of Peoplia make it a generic shell for an interactive pseudo-tutor environment, with the accent on ways that the social dimension augments the features of students' learning experience. The tutoring friend guides students to structured learning opportunities using the off-task social dialogues. Social dialogues are designed to be task-agnostic and can be scripted separately from the domain content, making it a tractable problem. Nevertheless, the tutoring friend influences the transitions between different learning activities such that the reasons for the transition become clear to the student.

Transitions are governed by rules that can recommend a good course of action for the student at any given moment. For example, when an examination is imminent, the student is advised to work on exercises from a similar problem set. Rules for facilitating the transitions get more involved when the social boundary is crossed (Figure 1), as other people are a valuable resource with which the tutoring friend can "negotiate". It is not possible for a human student to cross this boundary at will, and the transition *must* be facilitated by the tutoring friend. For example, when a student repeatedly demonstrates incompetent behavior (in terms of social/task abilities) the tutoring friend can refuse to put him in a group that would probably only impair the work of others due to his unfit behavior. On the positive end, when a student of low ability who is otherwise completely polite does seem to have hit an impasse, he might get paired up with a student of high ability who would be (through negotiations) expected to provide a very helpful hand for at least a short amount of his time.

The appearance of social intelligence in the off-task conversations is based on a finite-state dialogue manager. For the sake of experiments a dialogue manager capable to extract student's hobbies was developed (Figure 4). Dialogues were limited in length so that its "human" traits do not become readily apparent, while the tutor's dialogue capability is improved offline from dialogue transcripts by content authors.

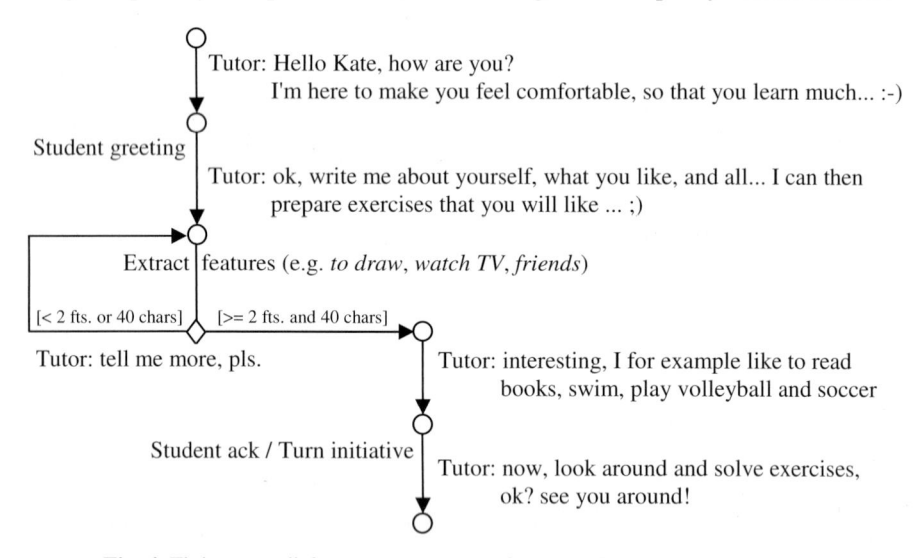

Fig. 4. Finite-state dialogue manager used for extraction of student's hobbies

Technical considerations. On the server side, data persistence works as a large write-back cache allowing for near zero database accesses for most of the clients' requests. The student environment is a rich client implemented in the Microsoft Silverlight framework and communicates with the server over the TCP layer in duplex mode, which combined with the caching functionality enables sub-100 ms latencies for common students' actions within the environment even though most of the decisions are made on the server.

3 Evaluation and Discussion

In previous experiments when middle school students were tasked to work with the system during an algebra class [8], we observed that students reveal on average 1.56 (st.dev 1.75) features about themselves in a social conversation with the tutoring friend, and only about 56% of the students engage with the tutoring agent at all.

In this paper, we analyze post hoc the learning outcomes of students that engaged vs. those that did not engage in social conversation with the tutoring friend. Total of 16 students took part in the study. They first took a pre-test, then worked for 90 minutes problem solving in Peoplia, followed by a post-test. All students used the exact same system. Table 1 summarizes the obtained test scores.

Table 1. Test scores (in percent, normalized)

	pre-test		post-test		gain	
	mean	st.dev	mean	st.dev	mean	st.dev
Not engaged	0.429	0.245	0.465	0.283	0.037	0.283
Engaged	0.439	0.273	0.562	0.284	0.123	0.192

Students that engaged in a conversation with the tutoring agent exhibited higher learning gains. The *not engaged* group showed relatively low learning gain 3.7% vs. 12.3% exhibited by the *engaged* group. This effect however may also be due to their previously higher motivation, and cannot be attributed to the conversation with the intelligent tutor alone. We need to further investigate the motivational state of students before the experiment, and examine the role the tutor can play, if any, in motivating students that were not motivated before.

In summary, students that engaged in social off-task dialogues with the tutor were more effective in solving problems correctly, and liked the system more (Table 2), suggesting that learning environments may produce higher learning gains by "being friends" with the students, providing them with socially relevant motivation.

Table 2. Students' answers statistics and questionnaire results

	Not engaged		Engaged	
	mean	st.dev	mean	st.dev
Number of tasks attempted	7.71	3.86	7.00	1.80
Number of tasks solved correctly	2.85	1.46	4.00	2.45
Questions (response scale: 1=worst, 5=best)				
1. How much did you learn in Peoplia?	2.29	1.25	3.33	0.71
2. How much did Peoplia help you on the post-test?	2.29	1.11	3.33	1.12
3. How much would you like to use Peoplia again?	3.14	1.07	4.33	1.12
4. How did you like Peoplia?	2.86	1.07	4.22	0.97

Additional research needs to be conducted to evaluate the motivational benefits of introducing a socially intelligent tutoring agent. Moreover, to provide students with more in-depth social dialogues, we currently explore the tractability of extending the conversational capabilities considerably by bootstrapping its strategy from Wizard-of-Oz data produced by human wizards during regular use by students.

Acknowledgments. This work was supported by the Scientific Grant Agency of SR, grant No. VG1/0508/09, the Cultural and Educational Grant Agency of SR, grant No. 028-025STU-4/2010, and it is a partial result of the Research & Development Operational Program for the project Support of Center of Excellence for Smart Technologies, Systems and Services II, ITMS 25240120029, co-funded by ERDF.

References

1. Boyer, K.E., Phillips, R., Wallis, M., Vouk, M., Lester, J.C.: Balancing the cognitive and motivational scaffolding in tutorial dialogue. In: Woolf, B.P., Aïmeur, E., Nkambou, R., Lajoie, S. (eds.) ITS 2008. LNCS, vol. 5091, pp. 239–249. Springer, Heidelberg (2008)
2. Craig, S.D., Graesser, A.C., Sullins, J., Gholson, B.: Affect and learning: An exploratory look into the role of affect in learning. Journal of Educational Media 29, 241–250 (2004)
3. Rowe, J.P., McQuiggan, S.W., Mott, B.W., Lester, J.C.: Motivation in narrative-centred learning environments. In: Proceedings of the Workshop on Narrative Learning Environments, AIED 2009, Marina del Rey, pp. 40–49 (2007)
4. McQuiggan, S.W., Rowe, J.P., Lee, S., Lester, J.C.: Story-based learning: The impact of narrative on learning experiences and outcomes. In: Woolf, B.P., Aïmeur, E., Nkambou, R., Lajoie, S. (eds.) ITS 2008. LNCS, vol. 5091, pp. 530–539. Springer, Heidelberg (2008)
5. Šimko, M., Barla, M., Bieliková, M.: ALEF: A Framework for Adaptive Web-based Learning 2.0. In: IFIP Advances in Information and Communication Technology Series, World Computing Congress 2010. Springer, Heidelberg (2010)
6. Barla, M., Bielikova, M., Ezzeddinne, B., et al.: On the impact of adaptive test question selection for learning efficiency. Computers & Education 55(2), 846–857 (2010)
7. Blanchard, E.G., Volfson, B., Hong, Y.J., Lajoie, S.P.: Affective Artificial Intelligent in Education: From Detection to Adaptation. In: AIED 2009. IOS Press, UK (2009)
8. Tvarožek, J., Bieliková, M.: Feasibility of a Socially Intelligent Tutor. In: Aleven, V., Kay, J., Mostow, J. (eds.) ITS 2010, Part II. LNCS, vol. 6095, pp. 423–425. Springer, Heidelberg (2010)
9. Hartup, W.: Cooperation, close relationships, and cognitive development. In: The company they keep: Friendship in childhood and adolescence, pp. 213–237. Cambridge University Press, Cambridge (1996)
10. Lepper, M., Henderlong, J.: Turning "Play" into "Work" and "Work" into "Play": 25 years of Research on Intrinsic versus Extrinsic Motivation. In: Intrinsic and extrinsic motivation: The search for optimal motivation and performance, pp. 257–307 (2000)
11. Johnson, W.L.: Interaction tactics for socially intelligent pedagogical agents. In: IUI 2003, pp. 251–253. ACM Press, New York (2003)
12. Mayer, R.E., Johnson, W.L., Shaw, E., Sandhu, S.: Constructing computer-based tutors that are socially sensitive: Politeness in educational software. Int. Journal of Human-Computer Studies. 64(1), 36–42 (2006)
13. McLaren, B.M., Lim, S., Yaron, D., Koedinger, K.R.: Can a Polite Intelligent Tutoring System Lead to Improved Learning Outside of the Lab? In: AIED 2007, pp. 331–338 (2007)
14. Wang, N., Johnson, W.L., Mayer, et al.: The politeness effect: Pedagogical agents and learning outcomes. Int. Journal of Human-Computer Studies 66, 98–112 (2008)
15. Malone, E., Crumlish, C.: Designing Social Interfaces: Principles. O'Reilly Media, Sebastopol (2009)
16. Tvarožek, J., Kravčík, M., Bieliková, M.: Towards Computerized Adaptive Assessment Based on Structured Tasks. In: Nejdl, W., Kay, J., Pu, P., Herder, E. (eds.) AH 2008. LNCS, vol. 5149, pp. 224–234. Springer, Heidelberg (2008)

Audience Interactivity as Leverage for Effective Learning in Gaming Environments for Dome Theaters

Panagiotis Apostolellis and Thanasis Daradoumis

University of the Aegean, Department of Cultural Technology and Communication,
Harilaou Trikoupi & Faonos Street, 811 00, Mytilene, Lesvos, Greece
{p.apostolellis,daradoumis}@aegean.gr

Abstract. Informal or free-choice learning has become a well-established means of disseminating knowledge to school classrooms over the last years. Various technology-enhanced public spaces, like science centers and cultural heritage museums, are nowadays equipped with state-of-the-art digital dome theaters, where groups of people (mainly children) attend educational programmes. The overwhelming majority of such 'shows' include astronomical phenomena and in few cases cultural heritage. In this paper, we investigate the potential learning benefit of integrating audience interaction with gaming environments in the immersive space of a dome theater. In order to achieve this, we examine how six factors of the Contextual Model of Learning proposed by Falk & Dierking, can be applied in an integrated schema of group interactivity and game design in immersive learning environments.

Keywords: Audience Interaction, Informal Learning, Contextual Learning, Gaming Environments, Dome Theaters.

1 Introduction

"In the digital age, learning can and must become a daylong and lifelong experience", where "education initiatives should aim to improve learning opportunities not only in schools, but also in homes, community centers, museums, and workplaces." [1]. The notion of free-choice or informal learning has become more and more popular over the last decade, especially for young children, as it was clearly urged some years ago by Mitchel Resnick. It is a standard practice nowadays for classes to visit museums in order to provide out-of-school pedagogy to students. Science centers, planetariums, cultural heritage museums are more and more equipped with digital dome theaters, where large groups of children are immersed in virtual worlds; though, in most cases as passive spectators. Hence, do these spaces exploit the available technology to its full capacity? In our opinion, there is a very promising combination of informal education practices in such immersive spaces which has been left unexplored up until now. That is their ability to allow a large number of co-located people to participate and engage in game-based learning activities. We will examine this potentiality through a brief discussion about the integration of gaming environments with audience interaction, in the contextual learning milieu of dome-equipped museums.

2 Learning in Technology-Enhanced Museums

Different learning theories have evolved over the years and applied to various educational settings. Cognitivist psychologists like Bruner, Piaget and Dewey advocated that it is through experience, exploration and active engagement that learners come to understand the world around them. This view of learning, widely known as *constructivism*, is the perfect match for the technological museum setting where young visitors are asked to interact with digital exhibits and construct knowledge [2]. Vygotsky shifted the constructivist theory one step further by emphasizing the importance of social interaction in fostering learning and, consequently, the child's development [3]. Practices stemming from these theories lead researchers (including us) to believe that the museum is a fruitful setting for contextual learning where visitors make meaning and find connection in relation to some place or situation by engaging in authentic activities [4].

2.1 Technologies for Effecting Learning

With proper exploitation of state-of-the-art technologies, these institutions can provide unique experiences by immersing visitors in virtual worlds, where they can collaborate constructively in game-based learning activities. Such technologies include interactive dome theaters with real-time capabilities, where audiences can collaboratively participate in game play. What makes these spaces unique is the potentiality to exploit the advantages of *game environments* in accordance with their *audience interaction* capabilities. Let us briefly examine in what ways these two properties have been employed in order to achieve learning in school-age children, which constitute the overwhelming majority of technology-enhanced museum visitors.

Gaming Environments. An inherent characteristic of children – and even adults – is play; we all grew up through playing with toys and exploring the world around us. This fact sets off a major flaw of the school education system, that it is boring, slow and mostly out of touch [5]. This calls for Papert's view of *constructionism*, which is built on the assumption that "children will do best by finding ('fishing') for themselves the specific knowledge they need" and that "organized or informal education can help most by making sure they are supported morally, psychologically, materially, and intellectually in their efforts" (p.139). And what is a better way to educate the 'computer and video games generation' than adopting its properties and making learning fun for students, trainers, parents and everyone involved in the learning process [6].

In accordance to such beliefs many researchers have studied the potential benefits of bringing video games in education and came up with a group of virtues that make games such good learning tools. More specifically children's interactions in the virtual worlds of games has been argued to account for increased motivation and challenge, problem-solving and decision-making skills, sociality, enjoyment and pleasure, ego gratification, creativity, and emotion [6]. All these factors contribute to an intense sense of devotion in the gaming (learning) activities encountered, which is believed to have great potential to foster learning. Other advocates of the tremendous educational potential of games emphasize that by exploring ideas in virtual worlds, players are encouraged to solve problems collaboratively, and through contextual peer-to-peer teaching participate in the creation of learning communities [7]. Adverse opinions about the educational value of games argue that they promote aggressive behavior, individualistic attitude and abstinence from other leisure activities. However, independent interviews with 7 to 14 years old children of the 'computer gaming culture' have shown that games do not interfere with other activities, and do not lead to social isolation; instead, it is with the company of friends that the majority of children enjoy most their favored leisure activity [8].

Additionally, storytelling is a key element for imparting (factual) information and falls in with the recreational character that most museums try to promote, by utilizing engaging learning games. During these games audience members are able to participate in complex social relationships and collaboratively create their own stories as they experience them [9]. However, most such endeavors include a small group of people who are physically distributed in the museum exhibitions and engage in a kind of 'treasure hunt', in order to gather information and complete a mission (e.g. [10]). This fact urged us to explore the benefits that audience interaction can bear in imparting knowledge to a large co-located group of children, immersed in gaming environments, in an interactive dome theater.

Audience Interaction. *Audience Interactivity* is a fairly new and unexplored field, and refers to the process in which a large number of co-located people engages in interacting meaningfully with the content presented to them on a large-scale display. Such practices can be usually found in science museums holding planetariums or dome theaters, which can accommodate such a large audience. No matter how rapidly such venues have proliferated over the last decade, they still lack either the infrastructure or the will to implement and evaluate such mass interaction systems.

Various methods have been tried to achieve interaction in such systems, the most prominent of which are the mass-audience polling device Cinematrix™, motion analysis techniques, and custom joypad setups. Among the very few cases in which researchers ventured to experiment with this technology as a learning tool, are two productions on science education [11] which employ Cinematrix™ paddles to selectively present information about cell biology and the brain, to an audience of 150 people situated in a planetarium. Although this work was very promising, as concluded by informal observations, there was no formal evaluation carried out to assess the efficacy of mass interaction for facilitating learning.

Other research efforts with a larger audience participating in interactive games include the work of Maynes-Aminzade et al. [12], who experimented with facilitating mass-interaction by means of motion tracking techniques and laser pointers. Although this work still does not include any formal critique methods, we agree with its conclusions that "the greatest challenge lies not in developing the technology for audience interaction, but in designing engaging activities". We have also been experimenting with this subject for the past two years, developing immersive, interactive VR productions for a digital dome, with the use of live navigation and narration. Although the used paradigms of audience interaction are fairly simple so far [13], we find that the impact they have on school-age children is intense.

The above works are indicative of the research carried out so far in the field of audience interaction. However, we believe that there is a considerable gap in this field, concerning the exploitation (and evaluation) of audience collaboration in immersive gaming environments and its potential impact on learning facilitation.

2.2 Contextual Learning in Gaming Environments with Audience Interactivity

As stated before, informal learning settings have provided fertile ground for the cultivation and evaluation of discovery, experiential, constructivist, and social constructivist learning practices. As opposed to school classrooms, they have the supreme advantage of engaging their audiences, either physically or virtually, in authentic activities which preserve their contextual attributes. That is why we propose that there are six factors of the Contextual Model of Learning, proposed by Falk and Dierking [4], which can be appropriately applied to leverage the learning efficacy of gaming environments with audience interactivity.

Motivation and Expectations. Learning in museums is facilitated when expectations about the visit are fulfilled and when intrinsically motivated individuals are attracted and reinforced. Children belonging to school classrooms which most often visit technology-enhanced museums are usually aware of the activities they will engage in, thus arrive in the venue with a positive predisposition. When their expectations are met or even better surpassed with the use of state-of-the-art technologies (like Virtual Reality, immersive projection, mass-interaction, etc.), then they tend to become more motivated to participate in the unique experience that unveils before them.

Moreover, motivation is instigated by properly exploiting the various properties of gaming environments. Technical properties of games such as interactivity, narrative and virtuality, as well as affective ones like engagement, immersion and empathy are widely believed to act as an inducement for audience participation. The affective state during which game players are totally immersed in the virtual world loosing sense of time and presence, also known as *flow* [14], is accounted for increased motivation and consequently engagement in the (learning) activities involved.

Prior Knowledge, Interests and Beliefs. Meaning making of the museum experience is framed within, and constrained by the prior knowledge, interests and beliefs of the visitors. By appropriately structuring the content of the gaming environment within the curricula of the targeted age group, these requirements can be easily met. It should be clear, though, what is the target group of the designed experience, so that teachers can prepare and motivate students in the classroom prior to the visit, as well as designers can reassure that the material presented in the game conforms to the subject taught at school. Also, the game-style format and collaborative nature of the learning activities lie within the common personal interests of most school-age children, who devote most of their leisure time in social game playing [15]. Beliefs are mainly formed at home and through interpersonal communication and vary widely, thus the content and way of presentation should be general enough to make allowances for the variety of these beliefs; a virtue that most contemporary game genres possess.

Choice and Control. Learning is ultimately achieved when individuals can exert choice over the type and pace of the content, and feel that they are in control of their own learning. This constitutes one of the huge advantages of museums compared to formal education and its strength should be exploited in the case of every "exhibit" possible. Audience interaction in dome theaters (here considered as a form of museum "exhibit") provides the paramount potential to offer choice and control to every one of the members of a virtual gaming experience. The sense of personal involvement in such mass-interactive activities shall promote audience members from passive recipients of knowledge to active participants of the learning experience.

Within-Group Sociocultural Mediation. Collaborative learning is fostered through the social interactions of group members, by virtue of deciphering information, reinforcing shared beliefs, and making meaning. Another boon of audience interaction is the potential to utilize collaborative learning techniques among audience members. Various features embedded in the gaming environment can contribute in this direction such as providing competitive activities between groups, encouraging cooperation by assigning roles and dividing labor, and designing tasks in such a way in order to enhance the sense of belonging to a (learning) community.

Facilitated Mediation by Others. Learning can be enhanced (or hindered) through the contribution of expert guides (e.g. museum educators, explainers, performers, etc.) or more skillful co-participants. By employing an interaction facilitator, who could be embodied as an avatar in the virtual gaming world (a technique also known as the "Wizard of Oz" in the field of Human-Computer Interaction), could very well serve to clarify misunderstandings, provide guidance and assistance, offer extra information, and contribute towards a smooth and unproblematic interactive learning experience. Moreover, similar assistance can be offered by more knowledgeable peers concerning either interaction-related issues (e.g. the use of interaction devices) or content-related matters (e.g. advice about the strategy used in order to tackle a specific problem).

Reinforcing Events and Experiences Outside the Museum. Knowledge and experience gained by the visit is incomplete and requires external enabling contexts (e.g. school, home, everyday life) in order to become whole and get assimilated. For this reason, the interaction log can be published and distributed to audience members as a narrative of the learning activities completed within the gaming environment. This practice will foster discussion in other milieus, allowing children-participants to relive the experience and contextualize the knowledge acquired during their visit.

3 Conclusion

Over the last decade, experiential, discovery and constructivist learning practices have found their way in technology-enhanced museums. The dome theaters that many such museums are equipped with have been solely used for the dissemination of passive experiences, mainly of astronomical phenomena and in few cases for cultural heritage. In the very few instances where audience interactivity was attempted [11, 12, 13], the provided interaction scenarios were too limited to be accounted for true cognitive learning, not to mention the complete lack of evaluation methods and empirical studies. However, there have been some attempts to assess learning in different settings of technology-enhanced museums. In such a research, which compared the impact of an interactive exhibition with two Virtual Reality programmes, findings revealed that learning was less effected in the dome theater setting [16]. This was basically attributed to the lack of direct interaction of visitors with the content, which is – in our opinion – the fundamental deficiency of such installations. Thus, we strongly believe that group interactivity in conjunction with game design in such an immersive space as a dome theater has immense potential to learning, principally for school-age children who are the usual visitors of technology-enhanced museums.

References

1. Resnick, M.: Rethinking learning in the digital age. In: Kirkman, G. (ed.) The Global Information Technology Report: Readiness for the Networked World, pp. 32–37. Oxford University Press, New York (2002)
2. Hein, G.: The constructivist museum. Journal of Education in Museums 16, 21–23 (1987)
3. Vygotsky, L.: Mind in Society: The Development of Higher Psychological Processes. Harvard University Press, Cambridge (1978)
4. Falk, J.H., Dierking, L.D.: Learning from museums: visitor experiences and the making of meaning. AltaMira Press, Walnut Creek (2000)
5. Papert, S.: The Children's Machine: Rethinking School in the Age of the Computer. Basic Books, New York (1993)
6. Prensky, M.: Digital Game-Based Learning. McGraw-Hill, New York (2001)
7. Squire, K., Jenkins, H.: Harnessing the power of games in education. Insight 3(1), 5–33 (2004)
8. Fromme, J.: Computer games as a part of children's culture. Game Studies 3(1) (2003)
9. Talin, D.: Real interactivity in interactive entertainment. In: Dodsworth Jr., C. (ed.) Digital Illusion: Entertaining the Future with High Technology, pp. 151–159. Addison-Wesley, Reading (1998)
10. Danks, M., Goodchild, M., Rodriguez-Echavarria, K., Arnold, D.B., Griffiths, R.: Interactive Storytelling and Gaming Environments for Museums: The Interactive Exhibition Project. In: Proceedings of the 2nd international conference on Technologies for e-learning and digital entertainment, Hong Kong, China, pp. 104–115 (2007)
11. Fisher, R., Vanouse, P., Dannenberg, R., Christensen, J.: Audience Interactivity: A Case Study in Three Perspectives Including Remarks about a Future Production. In: Proc. of the Sixth Biennial Symposium for Arts and Technology, New London, Connecticut (1997)
12. Maynes-Aminzade, D., Pausch, R., Seitz, S.: Techniques for interactive audience participation. In: Proceedings of the Fourth IEEE International Conference on Multimodal Interfaces, Pittsburgh, PA, USA (2002)
13. Christopoulos, D., Apostolellis, P., Onasiadis, A.: Educational Virtual Environments for Digital Dome Display Systems with Audience Participation. In: Proceedings of the 13th Pan-hellenic Conference in Informatics-Workshop in Education, Corfu, Greece, pp. 265–275 (2009)
14. Csikszentmihalyi, M.: Flow: the psychology of optimal experience. Harper, New York (1990)
15. Nielsen Interactive Entertainment: Video gamers in Europe – 2005; Research report for Interactive Software Federation of Europe (ISFE), 25 p. (2005)
16. Pujol, L., Economou, M.: Worth a Thousand Words? The Usefulness of Immersive Virtual Reality for Learning in Cultural Heritage Settings. International Journal of Architectural Computing 1(7), 157–176 (2009)

Free-Riding in Collaborative Diagrams Drawing

Furio Belgiorno, Ilaria Manno,
Giuseppina Palmieri, and Vittorio Scarano

ISISLab
Dipartimento di Informatica ed Applicazioni "R.M. Capocelli"
Università di Salerno, Fisciano (SA), Italy
{furbel,manno,palmieri,vitsca}@dia.unisa.it

Abstract. In this paper, we study the issue of free-riding in collaborative learning. Free-riding occurs when a part of the students lean on the efforts of the rest of their team and do not contribute much to the team work. It impacts negatively on performances of the whole team [1]. We present an experiment of collaborative diagram drawing (through a synchronous collaborative drawing tool, called Shared Drawing tool) in a Software Engineering course, that shows a significant equal participation and suggests that students employ some self-regulatory behaviors that results in fruitful collaboration.

1 Introduction

In collaborative learning [2], students at various performance levels work together in small groups toward a common goal and the success of one student helps other students to be successful. In general, it is assumed in the community that, when using computer-based collaborative learning, student participation is increased with respect to a similar face2face activity [3]. As a matter of fact, some research [4,5] points out that it is not always the case [6] due to poor collaboration and, among others, due to the so called "free-rider" effect: some students lean on the effort of their co-students and let the others do the work. In [1] the authors found that free-riding in student groups have a negative effect on their team performance since the free-riding behavior of some students demotivate the other students and, then, the overall team performance decreases. In [7], authors found that the use of collaborative tools increased when the students believed that their teammates were equally engaged and involved in the project (i.e. no free-rider), while in [8] authors use pair-programming to decrease the effect of free-riding.

In this paper we present our experiment of collaborative diagram drawing in a Software Engineering course. The analysis of this experiment shows a significant equal participation and suggests that students employ some self-regulatory behaviors that results in fruitful collaboration. We also describe the Shared Drawing tool, used for collaboratively drawing Use Case diagrams. The tool is part of the CoFFEE platform [9] and, as such, can be assembled with several other tools.

2 CoFFEE and the Shared Drawing Tool

CoFFEE (Collaborative Face-to-Face Educational Environment) is a suite of applications designed to support collaborative learning in classroom. The main applications of

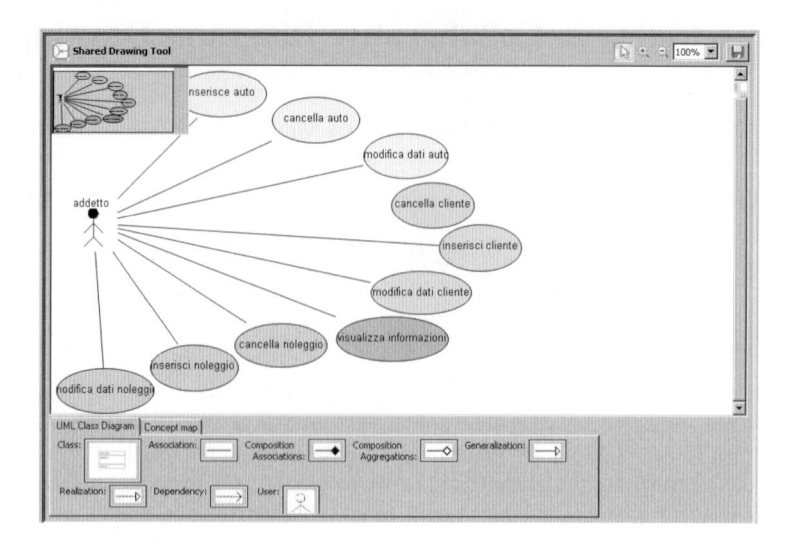

Fig. 1. SDT screenshot showing the creation of a UML diagram

the suite are the CoFFEE Controller (launched by the teacher) and the CoFFEE Discusser (launched by learners) which provide access to the collaborative tools [10].

CoFFEE has been designed also to allow the integration of new tools, and this has allowed us to develop and integrate in the platform the **Shared Drawing tool**.

The Shared Drawing Tool (SDT) supports the synchronous collaborative creation and editing of graphs: it has a shared 2-dimensional space which can be filled with variety of figures containing text (eventually) linked with arrows. The SDT provides also a direct support for creating concept maps and UML diagrams. A user can add contributions, freely move the contributions already present in the workspace, modify or delete his/her own contributions, or even other users' contributions. Contribution texts, sizes, fonts and colors can be modified at any time as long as the tool is active. The tool has two main configurable parameters: the editing policy (allowing item modifications only to the author or to everybody) and the choice of shapes and arrows to make available (they are organized in logical groups). In Fig. 1 screenshot of the SDT during the experiment described in Section 3 is shown.

3 The Experiment

The SDT has been tested in an experiment conducted in collaboration with the University of Basilicata as laboratory activity of the Software Engineering course. Our analysis concerns the effectiveness of CoFFEE in terms of support to the collaboration and in particular we want evaluate the degree of participation of the students.

The setting. The experiment involved 36 students in Computer Science of the University of Basilicata (27 Bachelor students and 9 Master students) and has been realized simulating a remote scenario (with no face2face interactions). The assigned tasks were about a software system to manage *(a)* a library, *(b)* selling and rental of films, *(c)* a car rental, *(d)* an e-commerce platform to order CDs. The tasks were similar in complexity and for each task the students were asked to provide a Use Case Diagram.

The collaboration through CoFFEE has been organized following the "'Think, Pair, Share'" method (TPS) [11] to encourage students participation. The students are organized in groups of four people, and the activity of each group has been structured in three steps: *(1)* "*think*", students work individually on the task to carry out; *(2)* "*pair*", students work in pairs on the task to carry out, eventually sharing previous results; *(3)* "*share*", students work all together to produce a final solution, eventually sharing the previous results. Each group participated in a CoFFEE session implementing the TPS method: the "think" phase was the step 1 with 4 groups of one person with the SDT; the "pair" phase was the step 2 with 2 groups of 2 persons with the SDT and the Chat; the "share" phase was the step 3 with all the 4 persons of the group and with the SDT and the Chat. At each step, the results from the previous phase are copied onto the shared workspace of the SDT.

The analysis of participation. To evaluate the degree of participation of the students we have collected and analyzed the *traces* produced by CoFFEE. The *trace* is an XML file written by the CoFFEE Controller (the server of the suite) and contains all the interactions and messages sent by students and teacher (the chat messages, the shared drawing tool actions, clients connections and disconnections and so on).

We have evaluated the participation of students in the collaborative session by using the Gini coefficient (*Gc*), a statistical measure of dispersion introduced by the statistician Corrado Gini. There are different definitions of Gini coefficient, and the one we find more useful in this context [12] refers to n discrete variables x_i for $i = 1,\ldots,n$ (in our context x_i is the number of contributions from each student i), ordered in non decreasing order, i.e. $x_i \leq x_{i+1}$ for $i = 1,\ldots,n-1$, with average $\bar{x} = \frac{1}{n}\sum_{i=1}^{n} x_i$. The definition is the following:

$$Gc = \left(\frac{2}{n^2 \cdot \bar{x}}\right) \sum_{i=1}^{n} \left(i - \frac{n+1}{2}\right) x_i$$

The Gini coefficient can range from 0 to 1: close-to-0 values indicate an equal distribution (0 corresponds to complete equality), while close-to-1 values indicate unequal distribution, (and 1 shows maximum inequality).

We have calculated the Gini coefficient on the 16 traces collected after the experiment (2 were eliminated because of technical problems that corrupted the traces, although the users were able to complete the task flawlessly). In Fig. 2 we report the Gini coefficients for all the traces, for each step and in total. Furthermore, for the steps 2 and 3 we have calculated the *Gc* for each tool (the step 1 had only one tool, the SDT). Then, in the bottom of the table, we have calculated the *Gc* mean on each step (and tool) and on the total of all the traces.

The total mean of Gini coefficients (*Gc*: 0.122) and the relative standard deviation (*st. dev.*: 0.043) indicate that the average participation among all the groups has been well balanced: indeed, the most unbalanced group (trace 7) presents a total *Gc* of (only) 0.208. Mean *Gc* values and the relative standard deviations on each step indicate that the

Trace	Step 1	Step 2			Step 3			total
		tot.	SD tool	chat tool	tot.	SD tool	Chat tool	
Trace 1	0,098	0,075	0,523	0,082	0,153	0,287	0,148	0,093
Trace 2	0,168	0,120	0,392	0,151	0,199	0,561	0,198	0,130
Trace 3	0,088	0,174	0,225	0,052	0,172	0,454	0,188	0,110
Trace 4	0,057	0,092	0,231	0,389	0,157	0,136	0,038	0,059
Trace 5	0,227	0,223	0,354	0,229	0,196	0,485	0,178	0,156
Trace 6	0,072	0,265	0,236	0,011	0,111	0,328	0,142	0,109
Trace 7	0,221	0,149	0,107	0,063	0,306	0,511	0,187	0,208
Trace 8	0,046	0,169	0,169	0,051	0,185	0,542	0,179	0,095
Trace 9	0,055	0,154	0,400	0,192	0,187	0,639	0,198	0,089
Trace 10	0,137	0,119	0,194	0,303	0,222	0,477	0,142	0,060
Trace 11	0,098	0,063	0,444	0,148	0,181	0,269	0,100	0,104
Trace 12	0,142	0,273	0,445	0,122	0,194	0,639	0,154	0,119
Trace 13	0,223	0,141	0,275	0,139	0,079	0,422	0,297	0,141
Trace 14	0,048	0,170	0,637	0,222	0,324	0,750	0,161	0,144
Trace 15	0,246	0,148	0,389	0,081	0,279	0,520	0,218	0,201
Trace 16	0,207	0,228	0,367	0,218	0,081	0,553	0,094	0,104
Mean	0,133	0,160	0,337	0,153	0,189	0,473	0,164	0,122
Dev.ST.	0,073	0,062	0,141	0,102	0,070	0,157	0,058	0,043

Fig. 2. Gini coefficients for the 16 traces. For each trace we report the Gc for each step as well as for each tool of the step. Furthermore, for each trace we report the Gc for the whole collaborative session (*total*). In the bottom we report the mean Gc on all the traces (for the steps and in total) and the standard deviation (for the steps and in total).

first step ('think') has been the most balanced (Gc: 0.133) while the third step ('share') has been the least balanced (Gc: 0.189). This consideration indicates that the individual work has been carried out by all the students with comparable efforts, while the participation in the steps 2 and 3 is a little less balanced, but with low Gc values.

Usage patterns. We have also considered the equal participation within each collaborative step (i.e. step 2 and 3), by analyzing the tool usage patterns. We show some arguments to support the statement that the students have (independently) elaborated a role strategy, where participation was (on the total) equal, but the roles within the group were well defined.

In the second step ('pair') the students were merged in pairs, with the SDT and the chat. In the SDT workspace, they found both the diagrams created (personally) in the previous step. In the third step ('share') the students worked all together with SDT and the chat and, again, they found in the SDT workspace the diagrams produced in the previous step by each pair.

First of all, as shown in Fig. 3, almost in all the traces the Gc of the SDT is larger (= uneven contributions) than the total Gc of the step. Similar results can be drawn also for step 2 (even if in step 2 students were paired). This means that, while the participation was uneven for the SDT (i.e. some student contributed more), the participation to the chat was such to "equalize" the participation on the total, as it is shown by the the lower Gc of the step (in total). It indicates that the students choose to discuss and collaborate, first, on the chat and, then, to discuss and draw, with some students that "drew" more than they chatted and some students that did the opposite. In general, it seems to indicate an automatic, implicit self-regulatory behavior of students.

As an example of the kind of pattern that we found often in the traces, we report here the analysis of a typical trace. The diagram in Fig. 4 (left) shows the cumulative distribution of successive messages sent in each tool of trace 14. In the first 11 minutes there is a peak of messages exchanged on the chat (max: 298) and no message

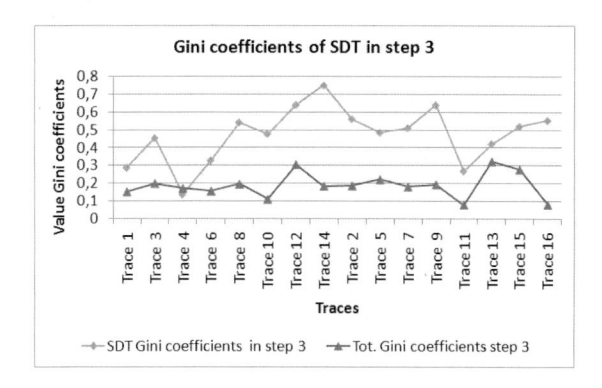

Fig. 3. For all the traces (in step 3) the SDT Gini coefficient is almost always greater than the mean Gc of the step

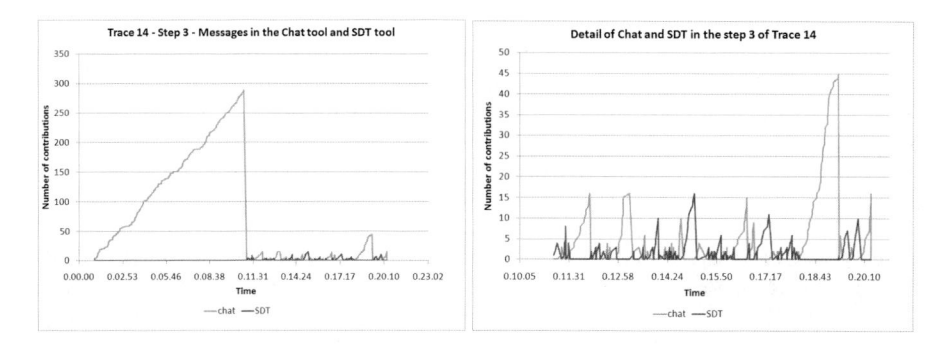

Fig. 4. (left) Cumulative distribution of messages sent on a tool without interleaving with other tool's messages; time is on the x-axis. (right) Zooming the diagram on the left after the 11-th minute.

at all sent on the SDT. In this phase the students explain each other the diagrams that they inherited from the previous step (when they were split in pairs) and organize the work to produce a final diagram. The next phase (shown, zoomed, in Fig. 4 (right)) is a sequence of activities on the chat and SDT. From the diagram, it looks almost like a self-similarity diagram, where several micro-phases of discuss-draw are realized. From this preliminary analysis a pattern seems to emerge, a spontaneous and effective behavior that allows students to coordinate the work on the diagram to be built, thus showing that the difficulties resolving conflicts found in other studies [13] are most probably addressed by the parallelism and the structure provided by CoFFEE and by the TPS methods applied. It should also be remarked that this pattern, while showing a distinction of roles, does not impact on the equal participation of students, because of the values of Gc previously shown.

4 Conclusions

We believe that the quality of the collaboration is witnessed by the fact that the students found a common pattern to self-organize the work, in a way that the load was equally shared and the task completed successfully. The CoFFEE platform and the Shared Drawing Tool proved themselves effective in ensuring higher and homogeneous contributions among users, because of its design choices (allowing parallel contributions, multiple tools to convey different information flows differently), of its flexibility (the possibility of mixing up to 5 tools in the same step), its structure (the powerful scripting mechanisms that allows to implement didactic methodologies and techniques like TPS) and its coherent and natural user interface. We would also like to stress out that the result of equal participation can be due to the combination of the TPS scheme with the previous factors. The technique Think-Pair-Share places larger personal responsibility on the student since the very beginning of the activities and, therefore, in our opinion, is also a key factor in minimizing the free-riding.

Acknowledgments. The authors gratefully acknowledge the support by Andrea Guaiana during the development of Shared Drawing tool. The authors also thank the collaboration by Ugo Erra and Giuseppe Scanniello in setting up the experiment.

References

1. Ruël, G.C., Bastiaans, N., Nauta, A.: Free-riding and team performance in project education. Technical report, Research Report 03A42, University of Groningen, Research Institute SOM (Systems, Organisations and Management) (2003)
2. Johnson, D.W., Johnson, R.T.: Learning Together and Alone: Cooperative, Competitive, and Individualistic Learning. Allyn & Bacon, Boston (1998)
3. McConnell, D.: Implementing Computer Supported Cooperative Learning. Stylus Publishing, LLC (2000)
4. Weisband, S.: Overcoming social awareness in computer-supported groups. Computer Supported Cooperative Work (CSCW) 2(4), 285–297 (1994)
5. Weisband, S.P., Schneider, S.K., Connolly, T.: Computer-mediated communication and social information: Status salience and status differences. The Academy of Management Journal 38(4), 1124–1151 (1995)
6. Salomon, G.: What does the design of effective CSCL require and how do we study its effects? SIGCUE Outlook 21(3), 62–68 (1992)
7. Maldonado, H., Lee, B., Klemmer, S.R., Pea, R.D.: Patterns of collaboration in design courses: team dynamics affect technology appropriation, artifact creation, and course performance. In: CSCL 2007: Proceedings of the 8th International conference on Computer supported collaborative learning, pp. 490–499. International Society of the Learning Sciences (2007)
8. Hazzan, O., Dubinsky, Y.: Teaching a Software Development Methodology: The Case of Extreme Programming. In: CSEET 2003: Proceedings of the 16th Conference on Software Engineering Education and Training, Washington, DC, USA, p. 176. IEEE Computer Society, Los Alamitos (2003)
9. Belgiorno, F., De Chiara, R., Manno, I., Overdijk, M., Scarano, V., van Diggelen, W.: Face to face cooperation with CoFFEE. In: Dillenbourg, P., Specht, M. (eds.) EC-TEL 2008. LNCS, vol. 5192, pp. 49–57. Springer, Heidelberg (2008)

10. De Chiara, R., Manno, I., Scarano, V.: CoFFEE: an Expandable and Rich Platform for Computer-Mediated, Face-to-Face Argumentation in Classroom. In: Educational Technologies for Teaching Argumentation Skills. Bentham eBooks (in press)
11. Holcomb, E.L.: Asking the Right Questions: Techniques for Collaboration and School Change. Corwin Press, Inc. (2001)
12. Fitze, M.: Discourse and participation in esl face-to-face and written electronic conferences. Language Learning & Technology 10(1), 67–86 (2006)
13. Smarkusky, D., Dempsey, R., Ludka, J., de Quillettes, F.: Enhancing team knowledge: instruction vs. experience. In: SIGCSE 2005: Proceedings of the 36th SIGCSE technical symposium on Computer science education, pp. 460–464. ACM, New York (2005)

Affordances of Presentations in Multi-Display Learning Spaces for Supporting Small Group Discussion

Brett Bligh and Mike Sharples

Learning Sciences Research Institute, University of Nottingham,
Exchange Building, Jubilee Campus, Wollaton Road, Nottingham, NG8 1BB, UK
{Brett.Bligh,Mike.Sharples}@nottingham.ac.uk

Abstract. Learning and teaching is often supported using presentation software to display pre-authored slides in sequence over time. We wish to consider the pedagogic implications of Multi-Display Learning Spaces (MD-LS), where multiple partitions of presented information overlay a larger area within the physical environment. We discuss the use in university teaching of the Multi-Slides plug-in for popular presentation software, along with multiple projectors, to cascade multiple slides of information simultaneously across two walls of a seminar room. We use examples derived from postgraduate teaching to argue that MD-LS allow for *enabling juxtapositions* of visual materials — such as evidence, results, conceptual frameworks and task specifications — which can be used by students and tutors as cognitive tools to promote reasoned, argumentational dialogue. We consider the spatial implications for learning, and relate MD-LS to attempts within the literature to conceive classrooms of the future.

Keywords: learning spaces, classroom of the future, multi-display systems, learning in Higher Education, spatiality of technology.

1 Introduction

Within this paper, we consider the implications of multi-display technologies for small group learning within Higher Education. We describe a Multi-Display Learning Space (MD-LS) at Nottingham, outlining how the technologies available within the space — including multiple interactive whiteboards, projected screens and software — can be used to facilitate collaboration within small group learning. We present examples, taken from postgraduate teaching, of students using *enabling juxtapositions* of visual materials to aid their learning. Throughout, our motivation is to explore what kind of Learning Space might be created by multiple information surfaces.

Common configurations of small group learning spaces more accurately reflect the pedagogies of 19th century *disciplinary education* than contemporary models of learning as a social activity [9]. We wish to explore how conceptions of human beings as "informavores" actively navigating information within their environment [7], and *spatial discovery* used as a metaphor for cognitive, constructivist models of learning [5], can be related to learners' active use of multiple shared information screens to scaffold their verbal contributions to small group learning. Research into the use of multi-display systems to support educational activities is relatively sparse, but several scenarios have been proposed by researchers. Anderson [2] envisages the future use of multi-display systems within an *iRoom* to assist in providing rich, small group work in school history lessons, used along with 3D displays, speech input and the manufacture of olfactory stimuli. Slotta [10] proposes to build the *S3 Concept Wall*, a grid of wall-mounted computer monitors displaying sections of a large computer desktop, with which learners interact using a remote from a Wii games console, to be used for activities such as co-operative concept mapping.

Two implemented systems within Higher Education have focussed on supporting teaching within large lectures. Both *Virtual MultiBoard* (VMB) [8] and *MultiPresenter* [6] take as their starting point the wish to replicate the benefits of multiple sliding blackboards in lecture theatres. Both projects use a touchscreen PC to manage the information displayed over multiple projectors, and both report similar advantages from initial evaluations: learners benefit from the contextualisation of the information which is currently the focus of teaching, while the previous materials which are retained onscreen form an information history which can be referred back to by students and lecturers. Closer to the topic of this paper, the "digital flipchart" system *PolyVision Thunder* has been used in small-scale teaching of postgraduates on an educational technology course [3]; a moveable, touch sensitive plasma screen was used to manage the imagery across a bank of projectors, promoting a high quantity of both surface and deep-type learning interactions. More recently, Bligh and Lorenz [4] have documented the teaching aspects of utilising an MD-LS in postgraduate visual arts education. This paper takes their three-tier ecology of *technology* (Multi-Display Systems), *space* (Multi-Display Learning Spaces) and *learning methodology* (Multiple Perspective Learning) as a starting point. But where Bligh and Lorenz [4] focus upon the affordances for teaching, proposing *comparative viewing* as a discipline-based methodology for authoring structured materials and documenting the *spatial scaffolding* which can be used by teachers for the purpose of directing the attention of students, here we focus on the implications for learners, demonstrating their visual use of the space in support of their verbal contributions.

2 The Multi-Display Learning Space

The Multi-Display Learning Space used here has been developed within a small seminar room, equipped with 3 interactive whiteboards and 3 other projection screens across two adjacent walls. The room also contains a ceiling-mounted "comfort monitor" and a plasma screen called the "easel". The six main display surfaces can be called upon to receive content from one of two computers, each running different software, as well as a high definition video conferencing codec. Switching the displays between input sources is accomplished using wall-based, infra-red switches. Figure 1 presents a view of the room, while Table 1 provides an overview of the systems available within the space. *Multi-Slides* can be configured to cascade PowerPoint presentations over all six display surfaces. Users can include or exclude monitors from the presentation cascade, and specify the order of the cascade across the (included) monitors. Excluded monitors can be used to display other software, for example a web browser.

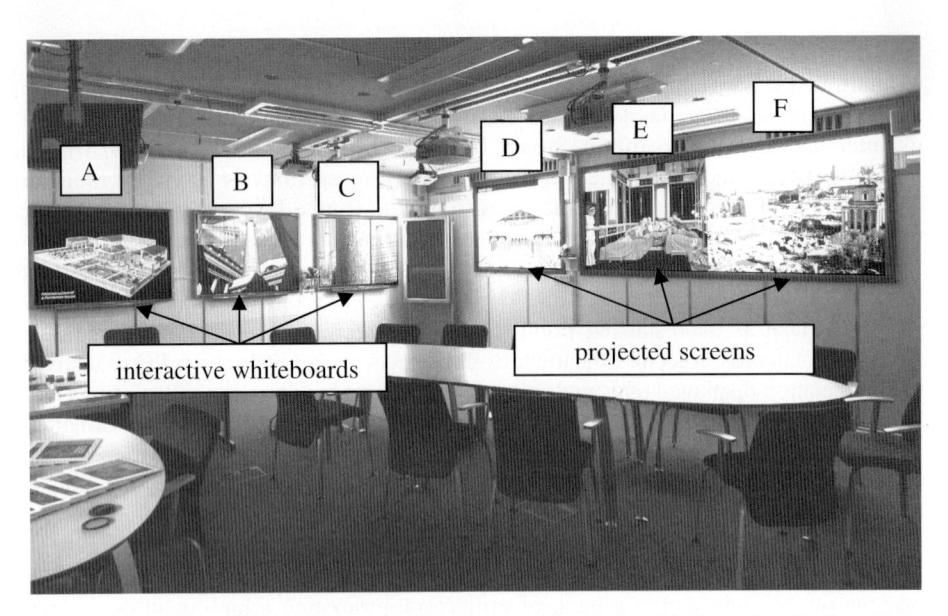

Fig. 1. A view of the Multi-Display Learning Space with six shared information displays (three interactive whiteboards and three projected screens). The moveable Thunder *easel* can be seen positioned between screens C and D. Computer 1 is housed along with keyboard, mouse and monitor at the desk in front of screen A. Computer 2 is rack-mounted and is out of shot.

Table 1. A summary of multi-display systems available in the MD-LS and their relationship to processing and display hardware

Computer	System	Description	Displays
1	Multi-Slides	PowerPoint plug-in, allows presentations to be cascaded across multiple display surfaces	A B C D E F
1	Smart Meeting Pro	Enhanced IWB system, allows several boards to be connected to the same session	A B C (D E F)
2	PolyVision Thunder Pro	Digital flipchart system, uses easel plasma screen to interact with materials displayed on additional displays	D E F + easel
Codec	Lifesize Team	Video conferencing system	B C

The variety of information sources presents challenges in terms of the furniture orientation within the room, which has been unchanged for several years. A large table which can be separated into three sections (one rectangular, the other two semi-circular), is accompanied by a variety of chairs and smaller, secondary tables. The furniture is moveable to support meetings or group work, and has occasionally been removed entirely to allow for the activities of larger groups.

3 Learning within the Multi-Display Learning Space

The space described here has mostly been used for postgraduate teaching, supporting topics such as Architecture (sustainable design), History (20th century ideologies),

Education (ICT in learning, and discourse analysis) and Classics (ancient art). For some time we have gathered data such as video-recorded observations and interviewed users of the room. Here, we document examples from Classics teaching to illustrate how the MD-LS supports learners, further contextualising those examples by discussing other disciplinary teaching sessions.

Ancient Art and its Interpreters is an MA-level, seminar-based module. The four students on the course interact with the primary evidence of displayed artworks in the seminars by offering interpretations verbally, having first prepared by reading a piece of literature (secondary evidence) prior to the session. Our intention was to create dialogue around juxtaposed groups of images, selected by the tutor to scaffold discussion. Here we discuss three ways in which the displayed imagery supported students in such dialogue: through providing *contextualised*, *complementary*, and *competing* information. We do not have space to present full transcripts here, so instead we proceed by describing the cogent elements of our examples.

3.1 Top-Down Contextualisation Using Anchor Slides

Typical linear presentations, which are constrained by the low resolution of their information surface, tend to isolate small pieces of information within slides, serving in turn to fragment the thoughts of the audience [11]. In teaching sessions within the MD-LS, on the other hand, the teacher was able to use an "anchor slide" [4] to contextualise the information on display, reinforcing conceptual links between the visually disparate information presented. An example involved the teacher using an anchor slide at F showing an aerial photograph of the ruins of a Roman grotto to contextualise images at A-E of surviving artefacts from the grotto, largely museum catalogue images. Student 2 takes a laser pointer from the tutor and uses this to direct the attention of his listeners as he speaks about the relationships between the museum artefacts on display. The student specifically laser points in the sequence F, F, F, A, F, B, F, E, F, E, A, B, E, C while discussing the original spatial relationships between the artefacts as they originally appeared in the Sperlonga grotto, and how they relate to wider elements of mythology such as the tales of the Argo.

This example demonstrates that the possibilities for contextualisation presented by the MD-LS arise as a result of the affordances of the *shared* display ecology; with multiple pieces of private information, such as paper, it would be difficult to maintain the shared dialogue, while a single shared display would have rendered it necessary to manipulate the interface *during* discussion, affecting its flow. Contextualisation has been a recurring pattern within our explorations of MD-LS. In prior work with *Thunder Pro*, student architects used maps to contextualise choices around sites for locating buildings, or building plans as contexts for both section diagrams and photographs of scale models. Similarly, History tutors have used frameworks of facts to provide a backdrop to a debate between students about the merits of two opposing strategies during the Chinese Civil War.

3.2 Complementary Information

Previous work [1] has noted the general benefits of complementary information for problem solving, based largely upon cognitive studies of CSCL scenarios. Here, we note the benefits of complementary *shared* information. In our example, student 2 has been asked to consider two narrative representations of a myth, represented by images taken from the sides and bottom of a wine vessel. Using a pen to point at the screens, the student points repeatedly between screens A, B, and C, at one point oscillating quickly between A and C to indicate a specific difference in representation. The vessel itself is discussed to use complementary strategies for presenting visual information on its surfaces, presenting slightly different images representing the stages of the myth, with the final image presented on the lower inside surface and thus available to the viewer only after the wine has been consumed.

3.3 Competing Information

The third example we present illustrates that learners are able to *contrast* competing evidence, considering its persuasiveness before further *using* it as the basis for interpretation. The arrayed visual evidence has been selected by the tutor to provide different *examples* of a style of interpretation taken from the literature, but student 4 immediately begins by distinguishing *between* the sets of evidence, going on to offer alternative interpretations of her own. Painting contexts are seen to support the conventional explanation, but the images of an "eye-cup" are taken as evidence of an opposing theory. Student 4 gestures with her hand towards D, D, F, F, D, D before leaving her seat (rarely observed in these sessions) and standing between D and F to illustrate her point to the group, clearly illustrating the extent to which she relies on alternating between views of the sets of evidence in order to construct interpretations. Once again, similar examples can be extracted from our other work. History students worked in small groups to construct lists of economic factors contributing to historical developments and then came together as a whole class, comparing their lists and subsequently debating how influential the relative factors actually were. Student architects presented design alternatives for sound barriers to encompass a building and then discussed the relative merits of each plan. Education students doing discourse analysis compared and contrasted their (juxtaposed) annotated manuscripts on the interactive whiteboards and discussed how their results related to the formal frameworks and model solutions passively displayed on the projected screens.

4 Discussion

We contend that the properties of Multi-Display Learning Spaces fit well with the visual and spatial discovery abilities of learners. While the benefits of multiple external representations, for example in textbooks, have been recognised in prior work, here we have sought to relate this to pedagogic understanding of multiple shared classroom displays. Such a configuration allows students to use the information to support themselves when speaking, and to better understand the arguments of others when listening by intersubjectively relating the gestures and attention direction of the speaker to the shared information. However, while the examples we present here show that students are able to interact with the materials from their seats, we witnessed few examples in the Classics sessions of student *movement*. MD-LS are classrooms which present particular challenges in terms of room configuration — including furniture layout and physical relations between people — which need to be investigated further.

Acknowledgments. The space discussed here and the research time of the first author were supported by the Visual Learning Lab, a Centre for Excellence in Teaching and Learning funded by HEFCE. We thank Katharina Lorenz, Associate Professor in Classical Studies at the University of Nottingham, and Duncan Peberdy and Jane Hammersley of *space2inspire*.

References

1. Ainsworth, S.: DeFT: A conceptual framework for considering learning with multiple representations. Learning and Instruction 16, 183–198 (2006)
2. Anderson, P.: The future of human-computer interaction. In: Emerging Technologies for Learning, pp. 24–31. Becta, Coventry (2008)
3. Bligh, B., Li, S.: On the use of a multiple display, in-room collaboration system to promote free response formative discussion between learners and tutors in small group seminars. In: Proceedings of INTED 2009, pp. 4863–4874. IATED, Valencia (2009)
4. Bligh, B., Lorenz, K.: The Rhetoric of Multi-Display Learning Spaces: exploratory experiences in visual art disciplines. Seminar.net: International Journal of Media, Technology & Lifelong Learning 6(1) (2010)
5. Dix, A.: Paths and Patches: Patterns of Geognosy and Gnosis. In: Turner, P., Turner, S., Davenport, E. (eds.) Exploration of Space, Technology, and Spatiality: Interdisciplinary Perspectives, pp. 1–16. Information Science Reference, Hershey (2009)
6. Lanir, J., Booth, K.S., Findlater, L.: Observing Presenters' Use of Visual Aids to Inform the Design of Classroom Presentation Software. In: Proceedings of ACM CHI 2008 Conference on Human Factors in Computing Systems, pp. 695–704. ACM Press, New York (2008)
7. Leach, M., Benyon, D.: Navigating a Speckled World: Interacting with Wireless Sensor Networks. In: Turner, P., Turner, S., Davenport, E. (eds.) Exploration of Space, Technology, and Spatiality: Interdisciplinary Perspectives, pp. 26–39. Information Science Reference, Hershey (2009)
8. Rößling, G., Trompler, C., Mühlhäuser, M., Köbler, S., Wolf, S.: Enhancing Classroom Lectures with Digital Sliding Blackboards. In: Proceedings of ITiCSE 2004, pp. 218–222. ACM Press, New York (2004)
9. Schratzenstaller, A.: The Classroom of the Past. In: Mäkitalo-Siegl, K., Zottmann, J., Kaplan, F., Fischer, F. (eds.) Classroom of the Future, pp. 15–39. Sense Publishers, Rotterdam (2010)
10. Slotta, J.: Evolving the Classrooms of the Future: The interplay of pedagogy, technology and community. In: Mäkitalo-Siegl, K., Zottmann, J., Kaplan, F., Fischer, F. (eds.) Classroom of the Future, pp. 215–242. Sense Publishers, Rotterdam (2010)
11. Tufte, E.: Beautiful Evidence. Graphics Press LLC, Cheshire (2006)

Recommending Learning Objects According to a Teachers' Contex Model

Jorge Bozo, Rosa Alarcón, and Sebastian Iribarra

Department of Computer Science
Pontificia Universidad Católica de Chile
Santiago - Chile
{jorge.bozo,ralarcon,seiribar}@uc.cl

Abstract. Several online repositories make available learning resources known as Learning Objects (LOs), and tasks such as identifying useful metadata, diminishing the annotation effort, and facilitating LOs discovery and retrieval, remain still as open challenges. Advanced searching techniques such as recommending systems have been studied to address these issues, though mainly focused on *students*. We focus on *teachers* and exploit their context in order to identify metadata that describes LOs content. Teachers' profiles consider also such metadata in a hybrid approach for recommending LOs to teachers and instructors.

1 Introduction

Learning Objects can be considered as small instruction pieces, or building blocks, that can be shared, re-used in other contexts, and combined in bigger instruction blocks [7]. LOs have been the focus of intensive research due to its promise of allowing a massive scale industry where standards for creating and annotating digital content facilitate sharing and reuse, diminishing its creation cost. The proposal is appealing but it has not been as successful as expected. One of the reasons may be SCORM (Shareable Content Object Reference Model) [2], which is a collection of technical standards and specifications for Web-based e-Learning systems, including standards for the metadata (IEEE-LOM), structure, repositories, and infrastructure for LOs management. The systems that conform SCORM are costly, heavyweight and highly complex [6]; IEEE-LOM metadata is complex and ambiguous, it requires a lot of effort and expertise, raising annotation cost [7]; most importantly, it lacks support for representing pedagogical concerns such as the learning needs and goals that they attend [9].

An alternative approach aims for a more open and lightweight strategy where informal, user-based taxonomies annotate LOs with tags, or by supporting organized collections administered by communities of teachers [6] with or without metadata. The idea is appealing but the lack of consensus in the metadata and its meaning difficults the integration of LOs repositories and the provision of federated searches limiting the search scope. Furthermore, it fails to acknowledge the needs and practices followed by teachers and instructors, particularly from primary and secondary education which are highly regulated. Pedagogical tools such as curricula, lesson plans, rubrics and so on, are resources and terminology extensively used by teachers and instructors but are notably absent in both heavyweight and lightweight approaches [6].

These limitations are relevant for LOs search. LOs are stored in centralized repositories that host various items ranging from hundreds to millions of objects [10]. A repository either contain LOs and their associated metadata, or only the metadata and a referral to the actual object location or to a hosting web site where additional search could be required, making LOs discovery a cumbersome task. In this paper we address the problem of LOs search by means of a recommender system. We present a metadata model that reduces the annotation effort by considering information relatively stable and familiar to teachers, in order to define a teachers' context . The metadata is used to annotate both, the content and teachers' profiles and serve as the basis for implementing a hybrid recommender system. Our goal is to focus on *teachers* as content producers and searchers. When teachers search LOs they do so with a goal in mind and within the context of their own praxis, future work will extend such ontology with metadata such as teaching style, and by providing backwards compatibility with IEEE-LOM.

2 Recommender Systems in e-Learning

Learning resources can be found also in-the-wild [6] by searching open content through Web searchers such as Google or Yahoo, or even in public sites such as Wikipedia, Youtube, iTunes or the MIT Open Courseware. The problem with these approaches is not the lack of resources but the over abundance of material and the lack of acknowledgment of existing institutional cultures and practices [6]. Teachers and instructors, particularly in primary and secondary education, conform a community of practice that share a common (or similar) terminology, tools and skills. This property is intuitively reflected in stable LOs repositories such as, MERLOT (www.merlot.org) which contains more than 20.000 resources and provides a resources classification based on pedagogical attributes such as, assignment, assessment, case study, practice, and so on.

Recommender systems in education have been studied as a means for supporting users in finding appropiate resources, among other tasks [4]. In general, recommender systems techniques are classified as *content-based*, *collaborative filter* or a *hybrid* of both approaches. Content-based techniques recommends similar items according to the history of user preferences regarding certain item's properties. Collaborative filter considers the preferences of users with similar profiles (clusters) [1,12]. However, recommender systems in education are quite different than recommender systems of goods or services, because they must consider not only the learners/teachers preferences for certain material, but also how this material may help them to achieve their goals. For instance, the SMART project [4] recommends items considering pedagogical characteristics such as previous knowledge along with learner's interests. Nadoslki et al. [8] evaluate an ontology-based strategy for modeling the learner's profile versus a lightweight (peer-rates) approach and find that the ontology-based technique is costly but more accurate. Manouselis [5] proposes a classic neighbourhood-based collaborative filtering algorithm for recommending LOs that considers multi-dimensional ratings on LOs, provided by the teachers (peer-rates); and a nice review of the area can be found in Manouselis [4]. In this paper we propose a hybrid approach where teachers context is modeled in an ontology that serves as the basis for the LOs metadata and the teachers' profile. A collaborative filter technique based on the ontology is also presented.

3 A Contextual Model for Annotating Metadata

Although there is no consensus on the definition of *what* a LO is, there is a wide recognition of the relevance of metadata as a key component for describing its characteristics, so that basic tasks such as searching and sequencing can take place. As mentioned before, the IEEE-LOM (IEEE LO *Metadata*) is a standard for annotating LOs; it comprehends 60 attributes grouped into nine categories such as, general content, life cycle, meta-metadata, technical characteristics, educational usage, rights, relations, annotation and classication. IEEE-LOM has been criticized because of its complexity, unfamiliar vocabulary, its lack of pedagogical information that makes hard for teachers to find it useful, and its ambiguity [6,7]. Alternative metadata models have been proposed, for instance, Sarirete [11] considers e-learning communities of practice and proposes an ontology including concepts such as actors with roles and profiles, competencies, knowledge, activity, internal and external environment. The ontology, however, is also too detailed and specialized (e.g. activity includes 28 concepts) rising annotation cost.

Manouselis [4] differentiates Technology Enhanced Learning (TEL) context in macro and micro-context. Macro-context comprises the educational setting, its elements are quite stable and present in teacher's everyday life. Let us consider, the Chilean[1] curriculum as seen in Figure 1. Rectangles represent concepts and arcs the relationships among them. The dotted rectangle comprises the concepts of the *curriculum* domain.

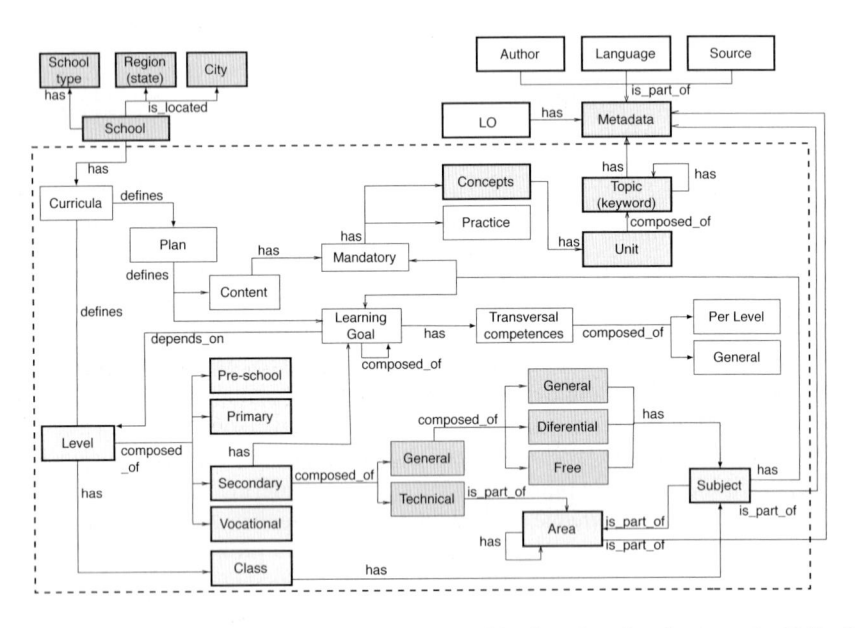

Fig. 1. A conceptual model of the curriculum as used in the educational system in Chile. The model serves as the basis for the LOs metadata.

---

[1] http://www.curriculum-mineduc.cl/curriculum/
marcos-curriculares/educacion-regular

Table 1. Values for factors f_k

k	f_k	User Profile
1	0,50	Level
2	1,00	Subject
3	0,75	Area
4	0,20	Region
5	0,03	City
6	0,03	School type
7	0,03	School

The curriculum comprises a study *plan* and the *curricula* which is a collection of educational *levels* and *classes* (i.e. student groups). A class has assigned *subjects* (e.g. physics) that belong to a curricular *area* or sub-area, and must satisfy specific *learning goals* (i.e. competences) and sub-goals according to the corresponding educational level. Subjects are taught using *content* that may be *mandatory* or optional (not shown in the figure), intended for developing *practical* skills or acquiring *conceptual* knowledge. Concepts are organized into thematic *units* (e.g. dynamic forces) and *topics* (e.g. force vectors). Learning goals attend *transversal competencies* that are a general or correspond to an educational level. Other sources of contextual information may include the institution itself (e.g. the school). Since institutions are stable, the effort of collecting such information is manageable. Teachers typically are assigned to a particular level, area or subjects, although there may be some mobility among these concepts.

4 Using the Contextual Model in a Recommender System

In content-based recommendation, users must evaluate items in order to declare its interest so that similarity with other items can be established. In collaborative filtering, suggestions will be generated for items that have been favored by people (users) with similar preferences (weighting of items). Similarity between users is measured on the basis of a vector of "closed neighbors". For "new" items, the recommendation is based on the combination of items known to the nearest neighbors [12]. We follow a hybrid approach including both a collaborative filter and content-based filter.

The information used for generating recommendations comprehends the LO *metadata*, the teacher's *profiles*, the LO *evaluations* and the *statistics* on the LO usage.

1. *LO metadata*: The LO metadata is based on the curricular context, that is, *author*, *title*, educational *level*, *area*, *concept*, *unit*, *topic*, and *subject*.
2. *Teacher profile*: Profiles are based on user clustering, where clusters are defined by similarity. Teachers have associated a *base profile* that comprehends the elements as educational *level*, *subject*, *area*, *region*, *city*, *school type* and *school*.
3. *Evaluation*: A LO can have one or more evaluations made by different users. The evaluation $e_\mathcal{U}$ represents user satisfaction in the range from 1(very unsatisfied) to 7 (very satisfied) as rated by the user $\mathcal{U}$.
4. *Statistics*: Dynamic information regarding an item LO_i such as the number of downloads (D_i), evaluations (E_i) made for the LO, the evaluations average (P_i) and the date of the last actualization (F_i).

Since teachers have a *base profile*, profiles may coincide in one or more of the profile metadata, forming clusters of similar *base profiles*. The calculation of the similarity (*base profile* similarity), for a new user in comparison with the users already registered allows to determine the cluster of the new user. The similarity between user profiles $\mathcal{U}$ and $\mathcal{V}$, is calculated as follows. Assume that $\mathcal{U} = \langle u_1, ..., u_7 \rangle$ and $\mathcal{V} = \langle v_1, ..., v_7 \rangle$.

Then the similarity is given by the expression $S(\mathcal{U}, \mathcal{V}) = \sum_{k=1}^{7} c_k \cdot f_k$, where $c_k = 1$ if $u_k = v_k$, and $c_k = 0$ in other case, and the values of the factors f_k are determined according to Table 1.

Recommendation algorithms distinguish *new users* from *regular users* (with a history in the system). In both cases, the recommendation considers the LO usage statistics and the evaluations done by the users to the LOs. The followed process include 4 stages described below.

Pre-load Correlation: For a user A that has interacted with the system (downloaded and evaluated LOs), we calculate the coefficients R_{Aj} (*Pearson* correlation) for each of the n users in A's cluster. These calculations determines which users are the most similar in the cluster in order to generate recommendations based on what was positively evaluated by their closest neighbors.

New users: User with no record of preferences (new) are assigned to a cluster based on a similitude S calculations. For this cluster, we consider the information of the LO usage statistics generated by the users in the cluster. Since the user is new, no *Pearson* correlation is calculated.

Users with history: For a user A with history, we analyze the information of the n users ($B_1, B_2, ..., B_n$) in A's cluster that have some degree of similaraty with it. For this sub-cluster, the *Pearson* coefficients are recalculated.

Ranking LOs lists: A set of recommended LOs is also ranked internally, thus, an order criterion is established for the set $\mathcal{C}$ of m recommended items, we consider the total number of LO downloads (D_i), evaluations (E_i), evaluation average (P_i) the date of the last LO update (F_i), and the relationship between downloads and evaluations $f_i = \frac{E_i}{D_i}$.

In a general purpose recommender system, all users are treated equally, we raise two important and distinctive diferences between a *base user profile* and a *preferences profile*. To validate the effects of this difference we tested the algorithms using the Catalog RED (*Digital Educational Resources*) repository provided by the Chilean government, which contains information about the school. The teachers were provided by SIMCE (www.simce.cl), consisting on more than 2.500 schools, and more than 20.000 teachers. This information was used to create *base profile* and to define the similarity matrix of *base profile*.

5 Conclusions and Future Work

Platforms aimed at training and education generate virtual shared spaces for learning, foster the development of interactive teaching/learning activities and opens the opportunity to various actors in the education field to participate, interact and collaborate. Recommender systems integrated in these environments may promote authors and empower users. An author's reputation will often depend directly on the number of times that his or her LOs appear in the recommendations made to other users. Reputation, the generalized reciprocity and the interest of the community may be the motivation behind the contribution of knowledge within the communities of users that are generated around these platforms [3].

Recommender systems can be used as a means to face the over abundance of resources available in the Web, by acknowledging the goals of specific communities of practice such as teachers if the recommender algorithms consider the community properties and values. Most of the research on recommender systems in education do not consider the context of the user who is asking for content. For example, roles such as *student* and *teacher* are ignored and the possibility of specializing the recommendation is lost. Nadolski et al. [8] evaluate the effects of using an ontology that models user preferences and finds that an ontology-based strategy is more accurate although is costly and complex. Other researchers [6] aim for a light-weight approach when faced with the complexity of IEEE-LOM metadata. We aim for an intermediate approach where an ontology is used as the basis for a hybrid recommender, but represents (partially) the context of teachers; users are familiar with the terms and meaning of the ontology and since information is mainly stable, it may require less effort from the users to annotate LOs. Our results so far are experimental, our next step consists on applying the implemented algorithm in the LOs repository provided by catalog *RED* and create the schools and teachers provided by SIMCE.

References

1. Felfernig, A., Burke, R.: Constraint-based recommender systems: technologies and research issues. In: Fensel, D., Werthner, H. (eds.) ICEC. ACM International Conference Proceeding Series, vol. 342, p. 3. ACM, New York (2008)
2. Learning Systems Architecture Lab Carnegie Mellon University. The SCORM Best Practices Guide for Content Developers (2004)
3. Ma, M., Agarwal, R.: Through a glass darkly: Information technology design, identity verification, and knowledge contribution in online communities. Information Systems Research 18(1), 42–67 (2007)
4. Manouselis, N., Drachsler, H., Vuorikari, R., Hummel, H., Koper, R.: A sneak preview to the chapter recommender systems in technology enhanced learning. In: Proceedings of the 3rd International Workshop on Social Information Retrieval for TEL, p. 535 (2009)
5. Manouselis, N., Vuorikari, R., Assche, F.V.: Simulated analysis of maut collaborative filtering for learning object recommendation. In: Proceedings of the Workshop on Social Information Retrieval in Technology-Enhanced Learning (SIRTEL 2007), Crete, Greece (2007)
6. Millard, D., Howard, Y., McSweeney, P., Arrebola, M., Borthwick, K., Varella, S.: Phantom tasks and invisible rubric: The challenges of remixing learning objects in the wild (October 2009)
7. Motelet, O.: Improving Learning-Object Metadata Usage during Lesson Authoring. PhD thesis, Universidad de Chile (October 2007)
8. Nadolski, R., van den Berg, B., Berlanga, A., Drachsler, H., Hummel, H., Koper, R., Sloep, P.: Simulating light-weight personalised recommender systems in learning networks: A case for pedagogy-oriented and rating-based hybrid recommendation strategies. Journal of Artificial Societies and Social Simulation 12(1), 4 (2009)
9. Nitto, E.D., Mainetti, L., Monga, M., Sbattella, L., Tedesco, R.: Supporting interoperability and reusability of learning objects: The virtual campus approach. Educational Technology & Society 9(2), 33–50 (2006)
10. Ochoa, X., Duval, E.: Quantitative analysis of learning object repositories. IEEE Transactions on Learning Technologies 2(3), 226–238 (2009)
11. Sarirete, A., Chikh, A., Berkani, L.: Ontocope: Ontology for communities of practice of e-learning. In: Dillenbourg, P., Specht, M. (eds.) EC-TEL 2008. LNCS, vol. 5192, pp. 395–400. Springer, Heidelberg (2008)
12. Segaran, T.: Programming Collective Intelligence: Building Smart Web 2.0 Applications. O'Reilly Media, Inc., Sebastopol (2007)

Preferences in Multiple-View Open Learner Models

Susan Bull, Inderdip Gakhal, Daniel Grundy, Matthew Johnson,
Andrew Mabbott, and Jing Xu

Electronic, Electrical and Computer Engineering, University of Birmingham, U.K.

Abstract. Educational systems that model the user enable personalisation. Systems that open the model to the user to prompt reflection are increasingly common. These often offer a single view of the model. We introduce multiple-view open learner models, and show the varied preferences for model presentation.

1 Introduction

Adaptive learning environments create a model of a user's understanding inferred from their actions (e.g. problem solving, answers, navigation). Typically, the aim is to achieve an accurate learner model to enable personalisation. Such adaptation may include choice of material; tasks, exercises or difficulty of problems; method of presentation. The underlying model will often not be in a suitable form for learner scrutiny. However, it has been suggested that learner models be opened to the user they represent, to: promote reflection; give greater responsibility for decisions in learning; support navigation; encourage formative or self-assessment [1]. These are commonly referred to as 'open learner models' (OLM). Models have been presented in a variety of ways, from skill meter overviews ([2],[3],[4]) to structured views, including conceptual graphs [5], Bayesian networks [6] and hierarchical trees [7]. Thus an OLM, whether simple or complex, allows the user to view inferences about their knowledge in an *understandable form*. It has been found that users may attend to different model information depending on whether it is presented in a way they prefer [8]. We therefore investigate whether there may be different preferences for model view with six multiple-view OLMs, with different subject areas and different target users.

2 Six Multiple-View Open Learner Models

OLMs may be fully integrated into a learning environment or may be independent of a larger system with the aim of promoting metacognitive skills such as planning, reflection, self-monitoring; and facilitate learner independence. Here the learner maintains control over choices in their learning, completing tasks and accessing the model as required. They then undertake appropriate study away from the system according to the information in their OLM. Such models are termed 'independent OLMs'. We introduce systems of the latter type, where interactions aim to help the user understand their knowledge state so they can identify their learning needs for themselves. Fig. 1 shows the differences in the structure of the model views for each system.

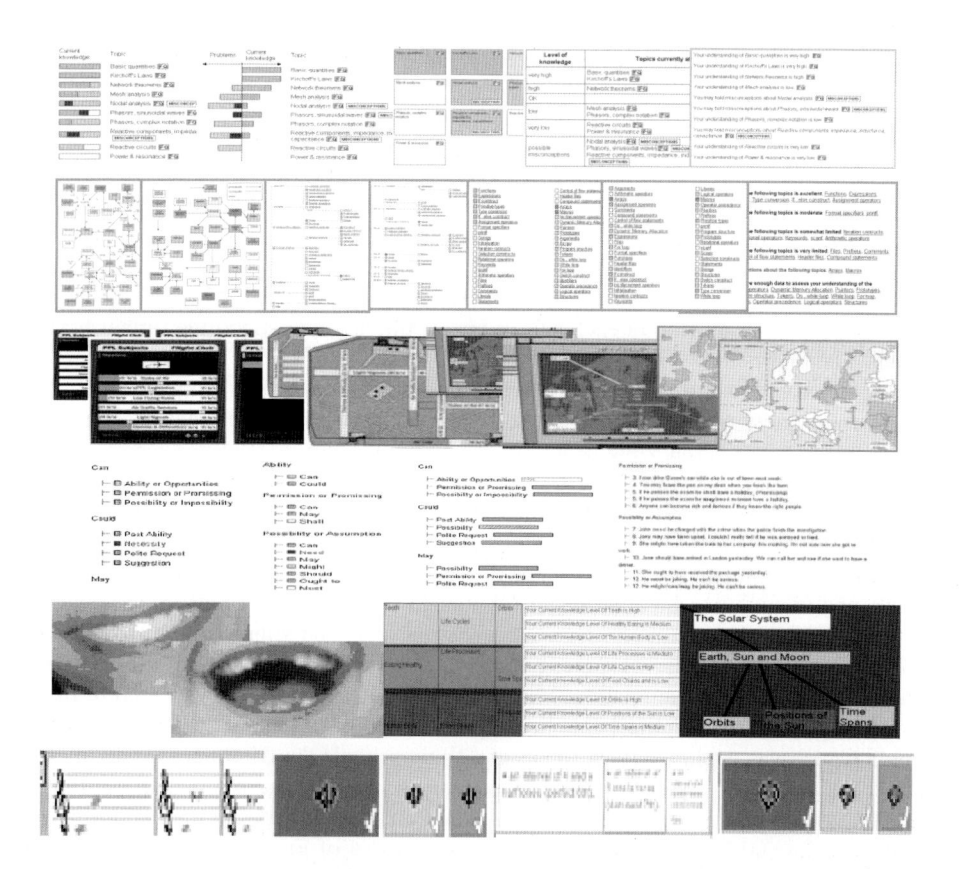

Fig. 1. OLM views: OLMlets, Flexi-OLM, Flight Club2, OLMLA, Point of View, MusicaLM

1. *OLMlets* is domain-independent, for easy adoption into a range of university courses. Use in most courses is voluntary, and 2/3 of students use it across courses in which it is available. Fig. 1 (top) shows the structure of the views: skill meters give knowledge level of topics, including extent of misconceptions; a similar graphical view, but with positive information about knowledge on one side of an axis, and negative information (not known, misconceptions) on the other; boxes around topic names with colour showing knowledge; table with knowledge in ranked order; text summary of knowledge. A statement of misconceptions can be obtained (e.g. "You may believe that resistance is reactive" in a 1st year electrical circuits course). We use data from 22 courses, comprising 812 learner models. Most courses were 1 term.

2. *Flexi-OLM* (Fig. 1 row 2) was deployed for 2 terms in a university C programming course. 65 of the 135 students registered used Flexi-OLM. Given the more structured underlying model (possible because of a specific domain), most views are more complex than OLMlets. Each shows the same basic information (level of understanding by colour of nodes, descriptions of misconceptions - e.g. "you may believe that division of two integer values can give a floating point result"), but with some variation due to the nature of the specific views (e.g. information about relationships

between concepts). The detailed views are in the form of maps (concept and prerequisite relationships), and tree structures (hierarchy of related concepts and lecture structure). List views (ranked, alphabetical), and a ranked text summary, are simpler.

3. *Flight Club2* Trainees studying for their Private Pilot's Licence must complete 7 ground exams by independent learning alongside practical flight training. The content of ground examinations will often not match current practical training. Flight Club2 (Fig. 1 row 3) was designed to take advantage of the potential for OLMs to help users identify their learning needs. Each of the 4 OLM views has a simple (s) and detailed (d) presentation (an intermediate level of detail compared to OLMlets/Flexi-OLM). The simple views are first in each pair in Fig. 1; the more detailed give further breakdown. The first pair is skill meters. The meters move from the left departures board to the right arrivals board once knowledge has reached that required to pass the exam. The runway view is similar: runways fill with colour as knowledge increases, but the layout reflects the aerial view of an airport, with crosspoints relating to prerequisite knowledge. The radar view depicts knowledge by distance of aircraft from the airport (centre of screen). Aircraft move inside the airport perimeter once knowledge reaches an examinable standard. The map view shows theoretical airspace boundaries. Each segment represents a topic, with colour to show level: green for excellent; yellow for weak, and various intermediate stages (similar to OLMlets boxes and coloured nodes of Flexi-OLM). The detailed views are accessed from the simple ones, and include breakdowns of knowledge of topics and preparation time estimates until the trainee is likely to be ready for examination. Misconception statements can be accessed from all views (e.g. "the size of the radar beam grows proportionately with antenna size"). Flight Club2 was deployed for 4 weeks in a flight school. The 50 trainees studying for ground examinations were invited to volunteer, 43 of whom participated. An initial session was scheduled, and 28 users also logged on again at times of their choosing.

4. *OLMLA* (OLM for Language Awareness - row 4 of Fig. 1) has an intermediate level of complexity (between OLMlets/Flexi-OLM). It is designed for advanced language users such as non-native English speakers studying at English-speaking universities. Despite their advanced level, such students can still have problems which become particularly important in their academic writing. OLMLA is currently implemented for modal verbs. There are 4 OLM views: alphabetical index (verbs listed alphabetically with coloured nodes indicating skill level, and representations for any function for which a verb is used incorrectly); language function (verbs listed according to functions of use, also using coloured nodes to portray knowledge, and verbs used inaccurately); items showing knowledge or skill level (skill meters, including functions for which the verb is incorrectly used); example sentences which could be generated by the user according to their learner model (including more than one representation if a user is inconsistent in rule use). Expert equivalents are also available for direct comparison. OLMLA was evaluated in a lab setting with 15 engineering MSc student volunteers, who were non-native speakers of English. Interactions lasted about 40 minutes. Users were instructed to use the system as best suited them.

5. *Point of View* was designed for 10-11 year-olds learning science subjects (Earth, Sun, Moon; Health & Teeth; Food Chains & Life Cycles). Point of View has 9 topics in 3 areas and, as in the other OLMs, misconceptions are modelled (e.g. confusing predators and prey). Fig. 1 row 5 shows excerpts from the 4 model views: picture, ranked according to knowledge, text, hierarchy. Each view displays the 3 levels of

knowledge. In the text, this is indicated by 'high', 'medium', 'low'. In the ranked list, knowledge is shown by gold, silver and bronze, with subtopics in ranked position within the overall topic. The hierarchy also uses gold, silver and bronze to indicate knowledge, but integrated into a simple hierarchy. Here colours relate to each level (topic/subtopics) of the subjects modelled. The picture views relate to the topic being studied; e.g. in 'health and teeth', healthy teeth indicate stronger knowledge than the mouth with missing teeth. Text misconceptions descriptions are available in each view. Users were 12 primary school pupils. Evaluation took place in 2 20 minute sessions, separated by a week, so total interaction time for each child was 40 minutes.

6. *MusicaLM* aims to help learners of basic music theory formatively assess their understanding of intervals and basic chords. There are 4 topics (accidentals, basic intervals, rare intervals and basic triad chords), which together contain 18 concepts. The OLM presents examples of beliefs the learner may hold in 4 forms. As the model is built from the last 3 inferences for each concept, there may be up to 3 conflicting beliefs presented together in the learner model (most recent on the left). In the bottom row of Fig. 1, the first view is music notation: the notes give a musical example of the inferred belief. The second is the music notation's complement in audio: the music (audio) view plays the music sequence to the learner, as if played on the piano. The third is the text view (e.g. a description of how the harmony is built, and the name of the inferred concept). The fourth view is spoken word: this is the aural complement to the text view (the information in the text view is spoken to the learner). Similar to some of the above OLMs, colour is used to identify how each belief compares to that which an expert would hold (expert beliefs can also be viewed, for comparison). MusicaLM was evaluated with 15 adult volunteers in 30 minute sessions.

3 Results and Discussion

Results. Table 1 shows number of model inspections in each system (combining totals for all views) to illustrate the scale of use, which can be compared to the number of users. It also gives percentagges of use of each view for each system, for comparison across systems. In the OLMs used alongside university courses there were many model accesses. In the lab studies, mean model viewings (after initial familiarisation) were lower. Lowest were viewings by Flight Club2 users. In OLMlets, most students used the skill meters, with accesses accounting for 80% of viewings. 10% used the graph (often in combination with skill meters), but there was little use of other views - though those who did use them, used them frequently. In Flexi-OLM preferences were more diverse. The lecture view (a tree structure) was the most commonly used, while the other tree (hierarchy) was used to a lesser extent (at a similar level to the text statements of knowledge). The map views (concept map and prerequisites) were used less, as was the alphabetical index, a list view. In contrast, the ranked list was used second most frequently. Viewings in OLMLA were evenly split, with each view attracting around 1/4 of accesses. Some users had a specific preference; others used more than one view. In Flight Club2, the more detailed model views are accessed through the simple ones. Therefore, the fact that the simple views were accessed more frequently, does not necessarily mean they were found more useful. The skill meters and runway are both forms of skill meter. The combined total simple viewings of skill meters and runway are 21%, with a combined total of 9% for the two detailed versions. For the simple views, this is similar to the map (19%) and radar (23%), suggesting different preferences amongst trainees, or trainees regularly using more than one simple view. However, the detailed map and radar views were used a little more frequently than the detailed skill meter/runway combined. Point of View accesses had a similar pattern to OLMLA, but only 3 of the 4 views sharing similar usage, and one accessed to a lesser extent. MusicaLM also revealed a range of preferences. Music notation (domain-specific) was consulted most frequently (50%), though music audio (the other domain-specific view) was consulted third most frequently (of 4).

Table 1. Number of users and inspections (total, mean) of the OLMs, and inspections of views

OLM	OLMlets	Flexi-OLM	Flight C 2	OLMLA	Point of V	MusicaLM
Users	810 (22 courses)	65	43	15	12	15
Total	59737	5163	439	266	265	380
Mean	74 (per model)	79	10	18	22	25
	80 sk m	12 hier	11 sk m-s	21 sk m	15 hier	50 notation
	10 graph	35 lecture	4 sk m-d	29 index	29 ranked	18 audio
	4 boxes	8 concept m	10 runway-s	25 func	27 text	26 text
	3 table-rank	5 prereq	5 runway-d	25 example	29 picture	6 spoken
	3 text	5 index	19 map-s			
		22 ranked	13 map-d			
		11 text	23 radar-s			
			14 radar-d			

Discussion. We here consider different methods of presenting the OLM to help users benefit from effects such as improved self-assessment skills [3], as they may pay attention to different information depending on whether the OLM is presented in a form they prefer [8]. Earlier work with Flexi-OLM and OLMlets suggested the utility of multiple OLM views in a university setting. We have here explored this further with fuller deployments of these OLMs, a deployment with trainee pilots, and lab-based studies with an additional 3 OLMs. The results show that across a variety of systems, although not always evenly divided, user preferences for model views differ. It is less important which views were preferred where the split was uneven, than the fact that there were a range of preferences that included the generally less commonly accessed views. This applies with both children and adults; with adults in independent learning and taught course contexts; with OLMs having different levels of complexity and methods of model externalisation; and OLMs in different subjects.

There was greater access to the OLMs deployed in courses. In both OLMlets and Flexi-OLM, there were stronger preferences for some of the views, and particularly for the OLMlets skill meters. However, users were also using the skill meters in combination with other views (especially graph); and some users used the skill meters rarely, having other preferences. The lecture hierarchy was used the most in Flexi-OLM, though the difference between choices was less strong than in OLMlets. The above suggests that, while some views may suit more students, they are not always the preferred method of accessing information and, indeed, even those who use the more popular views, do not necessarily use only those views.

When considering the lab-based studies of OLMLA and Point of View, the spread of use of views was more even – particularly with OLMLA. This may be because these were experimental scenarios, so users did not have the same motivation to use the OLMs for learning. Alternatively, the OLMLA views, although showing the same information, display it from slightly different perspectives. Consultation of a greater range of views might be considered more useful by learners. In Point of View, 3 of the 4 views were equally used, 27-29% of inspections, with the 4th used for only 15% of inspections. The more complex hierarchy was less frequently used, suggesting that children found the simpler views easier. In MusicaLM the differences were larger, though still indicating variation in preferences - but a domain-dependent view (music notation) appeared particularly useful, being consulted for half the model inspections.

Flight Club2 had an initial scheduled session, and remained available for 4 weeks. 65% of trainees logged in at least one additional time. However, inspections of the model were lowest with Flight Club 2. This might be expected compared to OLMlets and Flexi-OLM, because these were deployed for longer. However, it is not clear why inspections were lower than in the lab-based studies. It may be because these were highly motivated users, learning entirely independently. Trainees were used to taking control of their learning, and were perhaps more proficient at self-assessment. Having viewed their model, they may not need to return to check their changing knowledge.

It would be interesting to consider whether greater access to a view is due to more users, or a view being more heavily used by a small group. However, as our specific concern is to support users with different preferences, the important point is that different views were accessed by learners. At this stage we recommend OLM designers consider multiple views, so learners may use the views that *they* find easier, and may use them in combination. We suggest this is particularly important in independent OLMs where externalisation of the model aims to prompt reflection and facilitate learner independence, but it may also be helpful in other integrated OLM contexts.

References

1. Bull, S., Kay, J.: Student Models that Invite the Learner. In: The SMILI Open Learner Modelling Framework. Int. J. Artificial Intelligence in Education, vol. 17(2), pp. 89–120 (2007)
2. Weber, G., Brusilovsky, P.: ELM-ART: An Adaptive Versatile System for Web-based Instruction. Int. J. Artificial Intelligence in Education 12, 351–384 (2001)
3. Mitrovic, A., Martin, B.: Evaluating the Effect of Open Student Models on Self-Assessment. Int. J. Artificial Intelligence in Education 17(2), 121–144 (2007)
4. Corbett, A.T., Anderson, J.: Knowledge Tracing: Modeling the Acquisition of Procedural Knowledge. User Modeling and User-Adapted Interaction 4, 253–278 (1995)
5. Dimitrova, V.: StyLE-OLM: Interactive Open Learner Modelling. Int. J. Artificial Intelligence in Education 13(1), 35–78 (2003)
6. Zapata-Rivera, J.-D., Greer, J.E.: Externalising Learner Modelling Representations. In: Workshop on External Representations, AIED 2001, San Antonio, Texas, pp. 71–76 (2001)
7. Kay, J.: Learner Know Thyself: Student Models to Give Learner Control and Responsibility. In: Int. Conference on Computers in Education, AACE, Charlottesville, pp. 17–24 (1997)
8. Bull, S., Cooke, N., Mabbott, A.: Visual Attention in Open Learner Model Presentations. In: Conati, C., McCoy, K., Paliouras, G. (eds.) UM 2007. LNCS (LNAI), vol. 4511, pp. 177–186. Springer, Heidelberg (2007)

Supporting Free Collaboration and Process-Based Scripts in PoEML

Manuel Caeiro-Rodríguez, Luis Anido-Rifón, and Roberto Perez-Rodriguez

University of Vigo, Vigo 36310, Spain
Manuel.Caeiro@det.uvigo.es

Abstract. This paper introduces a modeling language to facilitate the development of e-learning solutions in accordance with different pedagogical approaches, focusing specially in the support of collaborative learning settings. Usually, e-learning systems are very dependent on the technology, that determine or constrain the pedagogical approach that can be used. *Educational Modeling Languages* (EMLs) have been proposed to solve this problem. Typically, they are process-based modeling languages that support the computational modeling of educational units in accordance with different pedagogical approaches. Nevertheless, this solution is very complex as the language needs to cover many issues. The introduced language is named as PoEML: *Perspective-oriented Educational Modeling Language* and it follows a separation of concerns approach to simplify such complexity.

1 Introduction

From our point of view, a main goal in e-learning systems should be to provide a "one-size-fits-all" solution, namely: a solution that supports different pedagogical approaches. *Educational Modeling languages* (EMLs) [1,2,3] have been proposed as a modeling solution to enable the achievement of such a goal. The main idea underlying these languages is to separate the pedagogical and computational issues involved in e-learning systems. EMLs are intended to support the computational modeling of educational units (e.g. a course, a lesson, a lab practice, a collaborative seminar) independently of the pedagogical approach. Then, the obtained models are processed by software systems that are able to support the "enactment" of the educational units. In this way, as long as the EML supports the modeling of the variety of pedagogies a "one-size-fits-all" e-learning solution is provided. Nevertheless, this is not a simple goal [4] [5] [6]. Firstly, EMLs need a great expressive power to support the computational modeling of educational units independently of the pedagogical approach. This expressive power is translated into a huge number of elements, relationships and behaviors required by the variety of pedagogical alternatives. Secondly, EMLs should enable the authoring and delivering of educational units in a simple way by common teachers not experts in these technologies. A key requirement at this point is to support pre-defined adaptations and non-expected changes during the delivery of educational units. Finally, EMLs should promote the reuse of the models of educational units in order to facilitate the development of great-scale learning solutions.

In our previous research we have been working towards the achievement of a powerful EML providing a great expressive power while satisfying reusability, adaptability and flexibility requirements. As a result of such a work we produced the *Perspective-oriented EML* (PoEML) [7] [8] based on a *separation-of-concerns* approach. Separation of concerns is a long standing idea that simply means that a large problem is easier to manage if it can be broken down into pieces. Following this approach, concerns involved in educational units are arranged in separated parts of the language. In conjunction the language is very expresive and as long as each part can be changed or modified in a separated way it is facilitated the reuse, adaptation and flexibility of the models of educational units.

Nevertheless, a main problem in the PoEML proposal remains to be solved: its use by non-expert users to create models of educational units and to manage their delivering. This paper focus on this topic. In this paper it is shown how the language supports different pedagogical approaches. Particularly, it is shown how it can be used to support different collaborative learning scenarios ranging from free collaboration to process-based scripts.

2 Supporting Free Collaboration and Process-Based Scripts

In general, collaborative educational units may involve different levels of coordination. Usually, two extreme approaches are distinguished that have been the center of a heated discussion [9] [10] [11]. On the one hand, there are normative models that try to structure collaboration by restricting the tasks to be performed. On the other hand, there are those advocating that collaborative systems should take flexibility to the extreme, leaving the coordination to the users and simple mediating in the interaction (i.e. supporting communication and co-operation). During the last years several attempts have attempted to conciliate and integrate these two extreme positions, arguing that both kinds of activities are *"seamlessly meshed and blended in the course of real world"* [11] [12]. More specifically, Bernstein [11] identifies four categories of approaches to support coordination from highly unstructured to highly structured:

- *Context*. It involves the more flexible and simple coordination solution as the system only supports communication and co-operation functionalities. Participants are responsible for the coordination.
- *Awareness*. It involves the notification to certain participants of what is happening in the collaboration and what other participants are doing or have done (e.g. teachers are notified of certain events produced by learners).
- *Constraints*. Participants are provided with constraints about how goals can be achieved. The constraints limit the participants' work. These constraints can correspond to ill-defined plans that have not been completely specified [13]. For example, in a lab practice teachers provide the main deadlines to obtain a solution, but learners can work freely while satisfying them.

- *Directions*. Participants are provided with strict instructions about what they have to do[1]. There are several issues that can be arranged for the provision of directions:
  - Restricting the activities that can/must be performed. Activities can be enabled and disabled in accordance with a established order.
  - Performing the assignment of participants to specific activities. For example, a group of learners perform a lab task and each member of the group is assigned to a sub-task. In addition, it should also be supported the assignment of participants to groups.
  - Supporting the transfer of information between activities. Data from one activity may be transferred from another activity or from an external artifact or application.

Next sections introduce the modeling of an educational unit considering these four levels of coordination. Firstly it only takes into account the more basic support (providing context), then the other levels are introduced step by step. This example is about a lab practice that requires the performance of a simulation program in GPSS (a simulation programming language). This lab practice has been inspired by a degree course provided by the Department of Informatics Engineering of the University of Coimbra.

2.1 Providing Context

The lab practice can be proposed by simply supporting the context required to perform it. In PoEML this can be modeled as an ES whose goal is to perform the GPSS program. The participants involved in the practice are a couple of learners that are assigned in a free way (the participant assignment does not appear in the next code as it is modeled in the parent ES). The ES involves an environment that contains some artifacts (e.g. simulation data, statistical tables, a programming environment, and a simulator). Nothing more is specified. As a result, participants can collaborate freely coordinating themselves with out any specific support.

2.2 Awareness

The simulation practice can include some awareness to facilitate participants' coordination. For example, both learners are notified when: (i) a change is produced in the program and documentation and (ii) when a simulation takes more than 2 hours.

PoEML enables to model this behavior using *AwSs*. To do it, we need to know the events that are going to be captured, namely: (i) *write* event in the artifacts and (ii) *init-sim* and *finish-sim* events in the *simulator*. The following code contains the *AwSs learners-awareness*. It identifies the recipient of the awareness,

---

[1] In any case, these directions have not to be interpreted as static plans. It is possible to consider different alternatives for the same plan where a single path can be selected in accordance with the features of participants or their previous results [14] [15].

the role *learner* and is made up by two *AwSs*. The *artifact-awareness AwS* indicates the capture of *write* events over artifacts *program* and *documentation*. The *simulator-awareness AwS* includes a composite event capture made up by the event operators *sequence* and *temporal-aggregation* over the events *init-sim* and *finish-sim*. This composition enables to detect if an *init-sim* is produced and a *finish-sim* event is not produced in the next 2 hours.

```
<AwS id="learners-awareness">
  <sink role="learner"/>
  <AwS id="artifact-awareness">
    <event-capture event="write"/>
    <source>
      <on artifact="program"/>
      <on artifact="documentation"/>
    </source>
  </AwS>
  <AwS id="simulator-awareness">
    <event-capture>
      <sequence>
        <event-capture event="init-sim"/>
        <temporal-aggregation period="2h" count="0">
          <event-capture event="finish-sim"/>
        </temporal-aggregation>
      </sequence>
    </event-capture>
    <source>
      <on service="simulator"/>
    </source>
  </AwS>
</AwS>
```

2.3 Constraints

A greater coordination support can be provided by considering some constraints and suggestions to perform the task. In the simulation practice the following constraints are proposed: (i) the practice has to be finished not later than 4 weeks after it is started; (ii) learners cannot perform more than 10 simulations. PoEML supports the modeling of these constraints using the elements of the *Temporal, Awareness* and *Interaction* packages. The first constraint can be easily established introducing a temporal constraint on the simulation practice ES. Meanwhile, the second constraint is modeled using *InSs* made up by an *AwS* to detect when 10 simulations has been performed and an operation invocation to disable the simulations.

2.4 Directions

The directions coordination solution involves the provision of detailed instructions. In the simulation practice this is achieved by decomposing it into five sub-activities: (i) Analysis and Design; (ii) Basic Coding; (iii) Random Numbers coding; (iv) Interface Coding; and (v) Validation and Documentation. In this way, learners have a support to organize their work. PoEML supports this decomposition into phases through the *Functional* perspective. It simply involves the specification of the five sub-goals and the corresponding composition relationships. Further coordination support could be provided by considering the transfer of artifacts between activities, the assignment of concrete participants to activities or the establishment of a execution order. PoEML enables the modeling of these issues by assigning each sub-goal to a *Sub-ES* and by using the elements of the *Social*, *Informational* and *Process* packages, respectively.

3 Conclusions

This paper introduces an EML based on the *separation-of-concerns* approach: PoEML. The paper devotes a special attention to the support of the variety of collaboration scenarios that can be considered in the support of educational units. This is a complex design problem involving many different human interaction contexts and schemes. In this way this paper argues agains the critics of some authors to this kind of modeling languages. Dillenbourg [16,17] signaled that *CSCL scripts* will not be successful as they are very specific and it is very difficult to apply them in the real practice. The design trade-off is obvious. Except for a few tasks, it is difficult and "expensive" to create models of collaborative educational units. Anyway, the EML approach has many advantages. EMLs are proposed to support the design, communication and execution of models of educational units, facilitating and promoting their reuse. As a result, educational units (and in general e-learning solutions) have not to be modeled completely from the scratch. By the contrary, they can be developed as living entities that can be created (in a simple way), grow (e.g. providing more precise specifications) and evolve (e.g. introducing alternative plans) during their life-time. In addition, it has been shown as PoEML can be used to model not just CSCL Scripts, but also free collaboration scenarios. Moreover, it is possible to go from one to the other by introducing changes and modifications in the model.

Acknowledgements

This work is supported by *Universidade de Vigo*, under program contract 08VIA08, *Xunta de Galicia* under grant INCITE09E2R322090ES, eContentplus programme ECP 2007 EDU 417008 (www.aspect-project.org), a multiannual Community programme to make digital content in Europe more accessible, usable and exploitable, and *Ministerio de Industria, Turismo y Comercio* under grant TSI-020110-2009-170 (GAMETEL. Simulaciones y juegos educativos adaptados a cada usuario y a mltiples dispositivos).

References

1. Rawlings, A., van Rosmalen, P., Koper, R., Rodrguez-Artacho, M., Lefrere, P.: Survey of educational modeling languages(EMLs). Technical report, CEN/ISSS WS/LT Learning Technology Workshop (2002)
2. Vignollet, L., David, J.P., Ferraris, C., Martel, C., Lejeune, A.: Comparing educational modeling languages on a case study. In: ICALT 2006: Proceedings of the Sixth IEEE International Conference on Advanced Learning Technologies, Washington, DC, USA, pp. 1149–1151. IEEE Computer Society, Los Alamitos (2006)
3. Koper, R.: Modelling units of study from a pedagogical perspective. the pedagogical metamodel behind EML. Technical report, Open University of the Netherlands (2001)
4. Bailey, C., Fill, K., Zalfan, M.T., Davis, H.C., Conole, G.: Panning for gold: Designing pedagogically-inspired learning nuggets. In: Koper, R., Tattersal, C., Burgos, D. (eds.) Current Research on IMS Learning Design. OpenUniversiteit Nederland, pp. 49–60 (2005)
5. Neumann, S., Klebl, M., Griffiths, D., Hernandez-Leo, D., de la Fuente-Valentin, L., Hummel, H., Brouns, F., Derntl, M., Oberhuemer, P.: Report of the results of an IMS learning design expert workshop (2009)
6. Derntl, M., Neumann, S., Oberhuemer, P.: Report on the standardized description of instructional models (2009)
7. Caeiro, M., Llamas, M., Anido, L.: PoEML: A Separation-of-Concerns Proposal to Instructional Design. In: Handbook of Visual Languages for Instructional Design: Theories and Practices, pp. 185–209. Information Science Reference (November 2007)
8. Caeiro, M., Marcelino, M.J., LLamas, M., Anido, L., Mendes, A.: Supporting the modeling of flexible educational units poeml: A separation of concerns approach. Journal of Universal ComputerScience 13(7), 980–990 (2007)
9. Raposo, A.B., Pimentel, M.G., Gerosa, M.A., Fuks, H., Lucena, C.J.P.: Prescribing e-learning activities using workflow technologies. In: CSAC 2004, pp. 71–80 (2004)
10. Schmidt, K., Simone, C.: Coordination mechanisms: Towards a conceptual foundation of cscw systems design. CSCW 4(2-3), 155–200 (2000)
11. Bernstein, A.: How can cooperative work tools support dynamic group processes? bridging the specificity frontier. In: Proceedings of ACM Conference on Computer Supported Cooperative Work (2000)
12. Schmidt, K., Simone, C.: Mind the gap! towards a unified view of cscw. In: 4th Conf. on the Design of Cooperative Systems (2000)
13. Strijbos, J.W., Martens, R.L., Jochems, W.M.G.: Designing for interaction: six steps to designing computer-supported group-based learning. Computers and Education 42(4), 403–424 (2004)
14. Heinl, P., Horn, S., Jablonski, S., Neeb, J., Stein, K., Teschke, M.: A comprehensive approach to flexibility in workflow management systems. In: Prinz, D.G.W., Wolf, A.L. (eds.) Proc. of the International Joint Conference on Work Activities Coordination and Collaboration (WACC 1999), San Franciso, USA, pp. 79–89. ACM, New York (1999)
15. Cao, J., Wang, J., Law, K.H., Zhang, S., Li, M.: An interactive service customization model. Journal of Information and Software Technology (48), 280–296 (2006)
16. Dillenbourg, P.: Over-scripting CSCL: The risks of blending collaborative learning and instructional design. In: Kirschner, P.P.A. (ed.) Three Worlds of CSCL. Can We Support CSCL? Open Universiteit Nederland, Heerlen, The Netherlands, pp. 61–91 (2002)
17. Dillenbourg, P., Hong, F.: The mechanics of CSCL macro scripts. International Journal of Computer-Supported Collaborative Learning 3(1), 5–23 (2008)

A Simple E-learning System Based on Classroom Competition

Iván Cantador and José M. Conde

Departamento de Ingeniería Informática
Universidad Autónoma de Madrid
Campus de Cantoblanco, 28049 Madrid, Spain
`ivan.cantador@uam.es, jose.conde@estudiante.uam.es`

Abstract. We present an e-learning system based on online forms that allows teachers to easily organise competitions in a classroom. This system is used in a preliminary study to evaluate whether cooperative competition is positive or not in education, and to identify which are the characteristics this kind of activity should have to be no harmful for students, motivating and helping them in their learning process.

Keywords: education, e-learning, student motivation, competition, cooperation.

1 Introduction

In the literature, there is a controversy about whether the use of competition in education is positive or not [1]. There are authors who are strong supporters of its benefits, claiming that a well-organised competition challenges its participants to give their best, and thus enhances the students' motivation, self-esteem and learning [2-5]. Other authors, however, state that competition damages the learning process by forcing students to focus on goals instead of on the process itself, and also argue that the stress to which students are exposed has negative effects [6-7].

Despite this controversy, there is a more general agreement that team competition is less harmful for students, and can effectively improve their learning skills. Cooperative goals make students take better care of their responsibilities and tasks for the sake of their groups [8]. Moreover, anonymous rather than face-to-face competitions are commonly preferred [9]. A "healthy" competition is defined in [10] as a short activity where outcomes have to be trivial, and which has to be focused on the process rather than on the outcomes.

Following these principles, we propose a simple e-learning system based on online forms that allows teachers to easily organise cooperative competitions in a classroom. This system is used in a preliminary study to evaluate whether cooperative competition is positive or not in education, and to identify which characteristics this kind of activity should have to be no harmful for students, motivating and helping them in their learning process.

The rest of the paper is organised as follows. Section 2 presents the system implemented to organise cooperative competitions. Sections 3 and 4 describe the conducted case study and discuss preliminary results. Finally, Section 5 ends with some conclusions, and depicts some future research lines.

2 System Description

In order to allow teachers to organise competitive e-learning activities with little effort and no need of sound technical knowledge in Computer Science, we propose a simple Web system based on online forms automatically created with Google Docs[1].

A competition created with the system is composed of two stages. In the first stage, groups of students pose several multiple-choice questions about the last topic studied in the classroom, and submit them via online forms. The teacher is notified when new submissions are placed on the system. Then, he corrects and evaluates the received questions. Evaluated questions are sent to the student groups. In the second stage, each group is requested to answer the questions prepared by the rest of the groups, and also to evaluate their quality based on several established criteria. According to the number of questions correctly answered, and the question evaluations given by the teacher and the rest of participants, each group is assigned a score. The weights of these criteria in the scoring formula are set by the teacher. The scores of all groups are published after each round so students know how they are going in the competition. This is done through several rounds, covering different subject topics. The final score of a group is the sum of its scores in the different rounds.

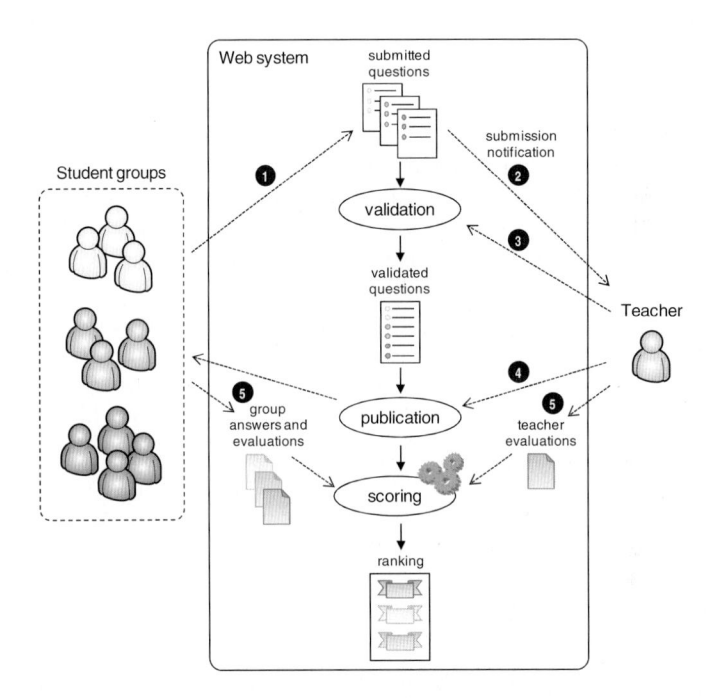

Fig. 1. Tasks conducted during a competition round: 1) question submission by student groups; 2) notification of question submissions; 3) teacher's validation of questions; 4) Web publication of questions; 5) student groups' answering and evaluation, and teacher's evaluation of questions.

---

[1] Google Docs, http://docs.google.com

The performance of participants in a contest is evaluated as follows. Let G be the groups of students who participate in the competition. The total number of groups is $|G|$. Let t be the teacher of the subject who evaluates the questions submitted by the different groups. We define $S = G \cup t$ as the set of subjects involved in the competition, i.e., the groups of students and the teacher. Let Q be the set of questions a group submits at the current round of the competition, and let $|Q|$ be the number of submitted questions per group. By $q_{g,i}$ we denote the i-th question submitted by group g. Let $eval(s,q): S \times Q \to [0,10]$ be a function that corresponds to the evaluation given by subject s to question q. Let $answ(g,q): G \times Q \to \{0,1\}$ be a function that is 1 if group g answers correctly question q, and 0 otherwise. Finally, let g_a be the active group, i.e., the group whose score we want to compute at current stage of the competition. The score obtained by group g_a is a function $score(g): G \to [0,10]$ defined as:

$$score(g_a) = \theta_{eval} \frac{1}{|Q|} \sum_{i=1}^{|Q|} eval(t, q_{g_a,i}) +$$

$$+ \theta_{diff} \left(10 - \frac{\sum_{g \neq g_a} \sum_{i=1}^{|Q|} |eval(t, q_{g_a,i}) - eval(g, q_{g_a,i})|}{|Q| \cdot (|G| - 1)} \right) +$$

$$+ \theta_{answ} \cdot 10 \cdot \frac{\sum_{g \neq g_a} \sum_{i=1}^{|Q|} answ(g_a, q_{g,i})}{|Q| \cdot (|G| - 1)}$$

where $\theta_{eval}, \theta_{diff}, \theta_{answ} \in [0,1]$, $\sum_i \theta_i = 1$, are fixed parameters that weight the influence of three factors considered on the computation of the score value: the professor's evaluation of the active group's questions, θ_{eval}, the difference between such evaluation and those provided by the rest of the groups, θ_{diff}, and the percentage of correct answers given by the active group for the questions of the rest of the groups, θ_{answ}.

The values of the fixed parameters taken in the conducted experiment were $\theta_{eval} = 0.5$, $\theta_{diff} = 0.3$, and $\theta_{answ} = 0.2$. This choice of the values assures that there are not unfair evaluations among students. Since student evaluations are compared with the teacher's evaluations, actual better student questions obtain higher evaluation values. The parameter setting also assures that there is a high probability that changes may occur in the rankings of the groups until the last round of the competition. In fact, during the contest, there were significant changes in the classification table through the rounds. Thus, almost all students felt they had the chance to win.

3 Preliminary Experiments

We conducted a study by using the proposed system in order to evaluate whether cooperative competition is positive or not in education, and which characteristics of this kind of activities are not harmful for students, motivating and helping them in their learning process. We hypothesised and empirically demonstrated that a competition in an e-learning environment can be beneficial if it is designed following a number of principles, such as having a symbolic or little value prize, a short duration, and a goal clearly set into the learning process instead of into the results.

The experiment was performed in a subject called Applied Informatics, which is taught to Chemical Engineering first year students at Universidad Autónoma de Madrid, Spain. The subject contents include theoretical and historical aspects about Computer Science, as well as a practical part involving MATLAB[2] programming. 77 students, distributed in 17 groups of between 4 and 6 members each, participated in the activity. The competition itself consisted of three two-week rounds. In each round, the student groups had to perform two tasks as described in Section 2. In the first task, they had to prepare 4 theoretical multiple-choice questions about the last topic studied in class, and submit them to the Web system. In the second task, each group was requested to answer the questions prepared by the rest of the groups, and also to evaluate their quality based on several criteria established by the teacher. The contest winners got a (symbolic) surprise gift and the congratulations from their classmates.

In order to keep track of the study, students were asked to fill in questionnaires at several points of the competition. They had to complete questionnaires after each round of the contest that were intended to measure the tasks difficulty, and the students' perception about the utility of the activity. Table 1 shows a summary of their responses.

Table 1. Some response statistics obtained from the intermediate questionnaires

Question	Answers	Percentage of responses
How useful was the last competition round for you to review/study the subject?	Useless at all/Not enough useful	6%
	Neither useless nor useful	35%
	Useful/Very useful	**59%**
How difficult was writing the questions by your group?	Very difficult/Difficult	18%
	Neither difficult nor easy	**49%**
	Easy/Very easy	33%
How difficult was answering the questions of the rest of the groups?	Very difficult/Difficult	26%
	Neither difficult nor easy	**54%**
	Easy/Very easy	20%
How difficult was evaluating the questions of the rest of the groups?	**Very difficult/Difficult**	**59%**
	Neither difficult nor easy	35%
	Easy/Very easy	6%
How much time did your group spend writing your questions in the last competition round?	Less than 30 minutes	22%
	Between 30 minutes and 1 hour	**55%**
	Between 1 and 1.5 hours	17%
How much time did your group spend answering and evaluating the questions of the rest of the groups in the last competition round?	Less than 30 minutes	3%
	Between 30 minutes and 1 hour	36%
	Between 1 and 1.5 hours	**39%**
	Between 1.5 and 2 hours	16%

---

[2] MathWorks: MATLAB and Simulink for Technical Computing, http://www.mathworks.com/

After the competition, there was a final questionnaire in which students were asked the name of their group, in order to allow measuring statistics relating each group ranking position in the contest with its provided questionnaire responses. Table 2 shows a summary of the responses provided to questions aiming to analyse the social atmosphere during the competition, and the students' motivation and enjoyment in the activity.

Table 2. Some response statistics obtained from the final

Question	Answers	Percentage of responses
How was the atmosphere in the group during the activity?	Very bad	0%
	Bad	0%
	Good	**53%**
	Very good	47%
How was the atmosphere among the groups during the activity?	Very bad	0%
	Bad	6%
	Good	**76%**
	Very good	18%
What was your main motivation during this activity?	The surprise prize	18%
	Reviewing and studying the subject	29%
	The pride of being first	**47%**
	Gaining recognition from my classmates	0%
	Other	6%
How much did you enjoy this activity?	Not at all	6%
	A little	35%
	Neither a little nor much	**41%**
	Quite	18%
	Much	0%

4 Discussion

Analysing the responses provided in the questionnaires, we can conclude that the proposed activity was beneficial for the students. 59% of the participants admitted that the activity was quite useful, since it made them to review and study the subject in advance, before the final exams. In contrast, only 29% of the participants stated in the questionnaires that their main motivation in the competition was the study of the subject. 18% of them said that the prize was their most important motivation, and, surprisingly, 47% claimed that they were putting an extra effort in the activity because of their proud of being first in the competition. We achieved our goal of designing a not too long activity. 77% of the participants spent less than 1 hour per round to write their group questions, and 81% of the participants spent less than 1.5 hours to answer and evaluate the questions of the rest of the groups. In general, students felt the activity tasks were not difficult. The percentages of students who said writing and answering questions were not difficult tasks were respectively 82% and 64%. In the question evaluation task, the percentage was much lower, 41%. The students commented to the teacher that this was due to the fact that the evaluation criteria were not clear in the first round of the competition. Most of the students agreed there was a good social atmosphere within and among the groups.

5 Conclusions and Future Work

In this paper, we have presented a simple Web system that allows teachers to easily organise competitive activities in the classroom. It has been used in a preliminary study showing that competition in education can be beneficial if it is designed following a number of principles, such as having a symbolic or little value prize, a short duration, and a goal clearly set into the learning process instead of into the results.

We have not put enough effort into the satisfaction of the students' enjoyment needs. As future work, the system based on online forms may be replaced by or enhanced with more sophisticated and attractive e-learning tools, and alternative gaming and competition schemas could be followed.

We still have to analyse how the conducted competition is related to the actual performance of the students' marks. Moreover, we have to investigate how different results (motivation, performance, etc.) would be without the competition (i.e., only with group work). These issues call for an experiment with a control group design.

Acknowledgements. This work was supported by the Spanish Ministry of Science and Innovation (TIN2008-06566-C04-02), and the Community of Madrid (S2009TIC-1542).

References

1. Johnson, D., Johnson, R.: Learning Together and Alone: Cooperative, Competitive, and Individualistic Learning. Allyn and Bacon Press, Boston (1999)
2. Fasli, M., Michalakopoulos, M.: Supporting Active Learning through Game-like Exercises. In: 5th IEEE International Conference of Advanced Learning Technologies, pp. 730–734 (2005)
3. Fulu, I.: Enhancing Learning through Competitions. School of InfoComm Technology, Ngee Ann Polytechnic (2007)
4. Verhoeff, T.: The Role of Competitions in Education. Faculty of Mathematics and Computing Science, Eidenhoven University of Technology (1999)
5. Lawrence, R.: Teaching Data Structures Using Competitive Games. IEEE Transactions on Education 47(4), 459–466 (2004)
6. Lam, S., Yim, P., Law, J., Cheung, R.: The Effects of Classroom Competition on Achievement Motivation. In: 109th Annual Conference of American Psychological Association (2001)
7. Vockell, E.: Educational Psychology: a Practical Approach. Purdue University (2004)
8. Thousand, J., Villa, A., Nevin, A.: Creativity and Collaborative Learning. Brookes Press (1994)
9. Yu, F.Y., Chang, L.J., Liu, Y.H., Chan, T.W.: Learning Preferences towards Computerised Competitive Modes. Journal of Computer-Assisted Learning 18(3), 341–350 (2002)
10. Shindler, J.: Transformative Classroom Management. Pearson Allyn & Bacon Press, Boston (2007)

Computerized Evaluation and Diagnosis of Student's Knowledge Based on Bayesian Networks

Gladys Castillo[1], Luís Descalço[1], Sandra Diogo[1], Eva Millán[2],
Paula Oliveira[1], and Batel Anjo[1]

[1] Department of Mathematics, University of Aveiro
[2] ETSI Informática, University of Málaga
`{gladys,luisd,sandra.diogo,paula.oliveira,`
`batel}@ua.pt, eva@lcc.uma.es`

Abstract. In this paper, we describe the integration and evaluation of an existing generic Bayesian student model into an existing computerized testing system within the Projecto Matemática Ensino (PmatE) of the University of Aveiro. The Bayesian student model had previously been evaluated with simulated students, but a real application was still needed. The testing system in PmatE is based in the use of Learning Objects (LO), which are question generators which essentially consist of some parameterized text and sets of parameterized "true/false" questions (at least four). These LO together with the experience of PmatE in using computerized tests with students, gives us ideal conditions for testing the described Bayesian student model with real students.

Keywords: Computerized testing, Bayesian networks, student modeling.

1 Introduction

Preventing school failure and decreasing drop out rates is a matter of concern in our society. In our modern world of competitive international markets and rapidly changing technologies, the importance of a good education and, in particular, of good mathematics skills should not be underestimated. For this reason, the identification of the causes of school failure and ways to overcome them should be a priority for educational boards and authorities.

It was on this basis that the Projecto Matemática Ensino (PmatE) [1], [2], [3] was born in the University of Aveiro. To increase the interest and success in Mathematics, computer tools and contents for several areas of knowledge (especially in Mathematics) have been developed. Since 1990, PmatE has been available in the web. It includes material and contents for all school grades and for different purposes: *formative* (evaluation, diagnosis and practice) and *competition* (via computerized tests). Every year, PmatE promotes six National Mathematical Competitions: one for each school degree, from Primary to Higher Education, and one for all school degrees in the network. More than 5000 students took part in the Network competition, and 18.000 students attended the final test in the University of Aveiro.

The goal of the research presented in this paper is improve the diagnostic capabilities of PmatE using approximate reasoning techniques. To this end, we have used a

Bayesian student model (BSM) based on Bayesian Networks (BNs) to be the diagnosis tool of computerized tests in PmatE. The BN paradigm was chosen because it has proven to be a sound methodology for the student modelling problem, and it has been used with this purpose in a number of existing applications (see [4] for a complete review). All this previous research has shown that a BSM allows for a sound and detailed evaluation of each student, at granularity level needed.

The model chosen to be integrated in PmatE was a previously developed generic BSM [4]. This model was chosen for two reasons: a) the conditional probabilities needed are automatically computed from a reduced set of parameters specified by teachers[1], and b) the model had already been evaluated with simulated students, and showed a good performance both in terms of accuracy and efficiency. Due to space restrictions, we do not include the model in this paper, the interested reader can find a detailed description in [4] and [5].

The main contributions of our work are: a) the introduction of a BSM in PmatE and a preliminary evaluation of this model with real students; and b) a real application of the work presented in [4], which was still missing. We hope that with this work we can encourage other researchers to use this BSM which is readily available to be used to provide accurate and efficient diagnosis with a minimum implementation effort.

2 Introducing a Bayesian Student Model in PmatE

For using the Bayesian student model presented in [4], we have implemented a web-based application that makes use of the learning objects (LOs) produced by PmatE. The LO are question generators which essentially consist of some parameterized text and sets of parameterized "true/false" questions.

Both the parameter instantiations and the validation of the student's answers are executed at run time. Thus, a LO is used to present a screen to the student, with some text on the top, followed by some (at least four) "true/false questions" related to that

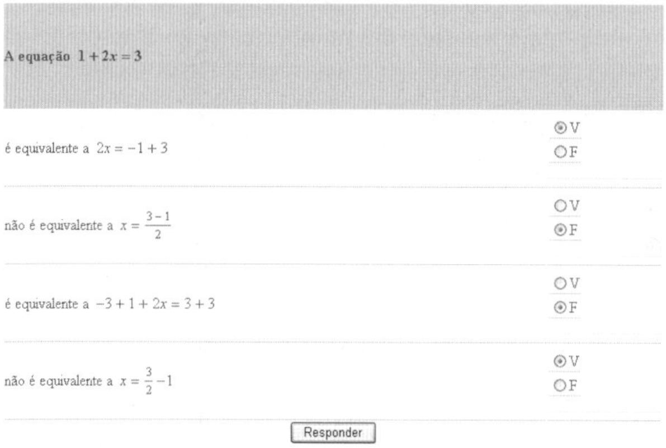

Fig. 1. An example of a question generated by a LO in PmatE

---

[1] The problem of parameter specification is usually pointed out as the bottleneck for using BN.

text. Figure 1 shows an example of a question. These readily available LO together with the experience of PmatE in using computerized tests with students, gives us ideal conditions for testing the Bayesian student model.

We have chosen the subject "1st Degree Equations" as the domain for testing our model. As indicated in the BSM used, the domain has been decomposed in topics and concepts which are the nodes for the BN representing aggregation relationships. The BSM also needs some parameters to compute the conditional probabilities needed. Such parameters are the weights that measure the relative importance of each item in the aggregated item. In our case, these parameters were provided by researchers of the PmatE team, with years of experience in modeling different mathematical domains. The structure of the BN and the weights are shown in Figure 2[2].

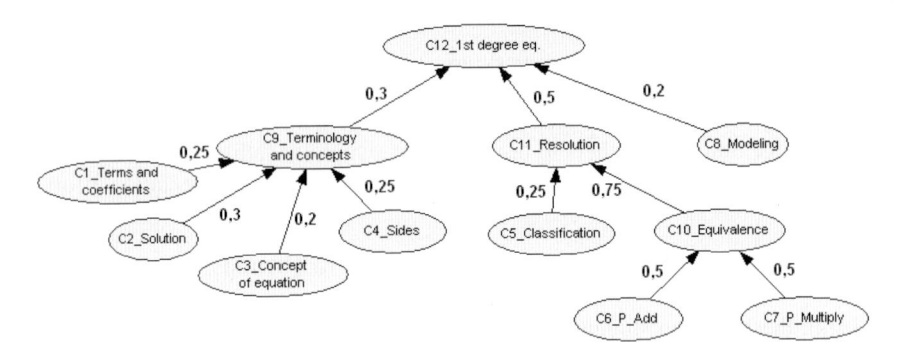

Fig. 2. BN for aggregation relationships

Now we have to define the relationships between test items and concepts. For each test item, the BSM presented in [4] needs four parameters: difficulty, discrimination, guess and slip factors. These parameters must be supplied by domain experts and are used to automatically compute the conditional probabilities needed. In our application, test items are true/false, so they have a fixed guess factor of 0.5. As for the difficulty levels, domain modelers assigned a number between 1 and 5 to each test item. In the evaluation of the approach we have assessed different values for the rest of the parameters needed by the model presented in [4] (slip and discrimination factors) to determine which combination of values provides a better adjustment between teacher's and systems evaluations.

To integrate this model in PmatE, we have implemented a web-based application using Microsoft's Visual Studio 2005 and the C# classes implementing Bayesian Networks of SMILE [6].

3 Evaluation of the Model with Real Students

The first evaluation of the proposed approach with real students[3] was performed in autum 2009. It included twenty-eight ninth-grade students (14-15 years old) in a

---

[2] All BNs have been created with GeNIe [6].
[3] The results of the evaluation of this approach with simulated students are available in [9] and [10].

public school in Figueira da Foz, Portugal[4]. Students took a computerized test composed by 14 randomized LO, thus answering to 56 randomized true/false test items. According to the percentage of correct answers (PCA), student's were assigned to proficiency levels (see Fig 3). We observe that about half of the students (46.43%) have correctly answered around 60-70% of the given test-items and assigned to the proficiency level D. The mean value of correct answers was about 74.6%.

Profic. Level	PCA Interval	% of Students
A	[90, 100]	14,29 %
B	[80, 90]	14,29 %
C	[70, 80]	17,86 %
D	[60, 70]	46,43 %
E	[50, 60]	07,14 %

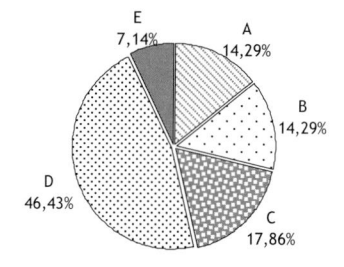

Fig. 3. Assigning students to proficiency levels, and distribution of the levels

In addition, each student also completed a paper-and-pencil test that was evaluated by the teacher. Figure 4 shows the evolution of the values for MSE of the difference between the probability estimates obtained by the BN against the estimates given by the teacher averaged over the 28 students for different slip values (from 0.01 to 0.2) and different discrimination factors (from 0.3 to 1.4).

From the results we observe that the values of the MSE are typically low (in the range of 0.11 to 0.2), and that they decrease as the slip value increases. Best fitting between expert and system's estimations are achieved for a slip value of 0.2 (average MSE 0.12). As for the discrimination index, best fit is achieved at 1.2 (average MSE 0.15). It seems that considering a high probability of slip (i.e., students fail even when having the necessary knowledge) improves the fitting. Higher values of discrimination index also seem to produce better results.

For the next analysis we use the value of the discrimination factor that provided the best results (1.2), and the best and the worse slip values (0.2 and 0.01, respectively). Figure 5 depicts the MSE values for all the students, ordered by their proficiency level (the two bars shown for each student correspond to the two different slip values). Table 1 summarizes the two main measures of location (mean, median) of the MSE values for each proficiency level. From results shown in Figure 5 and Table 1, it is clear that the best slip value is 0.2 and the best values of the MSE (mean value 0,047) are achieved for the more advanced students (i.e., those with level of proficiency A). Moreover, on average, the MSE increases as the proficiency level of the student decreases.

The results suggest that, in general, the degree of agreement between teacher's and system's estimation of student knowledge level on each topic is quite high (average MSEs between 0.1 and 0.2), and the best agreement rate is achieved for a 0.2 slip with a 1.2 discrimination factor. Also, the fit seems to be better for advanced students. As

---

[4] We thank both teachers and students for their participation.

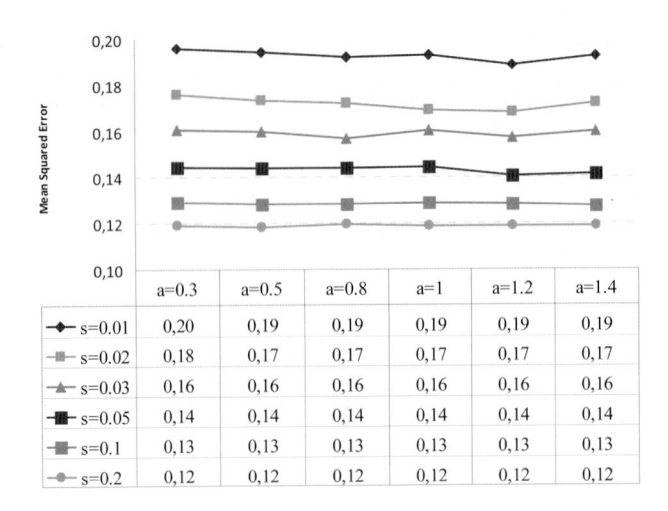

Fig. 4. Average MSE values for different slip and discrimination indexes

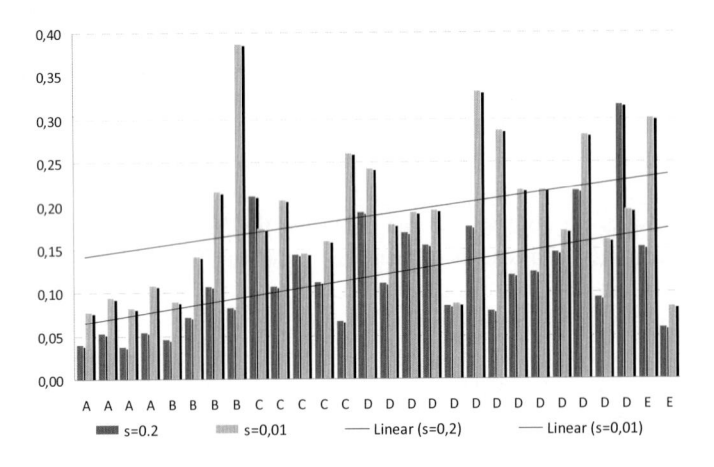

	a=0.3	a=0.5	a=0.8	a=1	a=1.2	a=1.4
s=0.01	0,20	0,19	0,19	0,19	0,19	0,19
s=0.02	0,18	0,17	0,17	0,17	0,17	0,17
s=0.03	0,16	0,16	0,16	0,16	0,16	0,16
s=0.05	0,14	0,14	0,14	0,14	0,14	0,14
s=0.1	0,13	0,13	0,13	0,13	0,13	0,13
s=0.2	0,12	0,12	0,12	0,12	0,12	0,12

Fig. 5. MSE values for different proficiency levels with trend lines for a=1.2

Table 1. Mean and median of the MSE values for different competency levels (a=1.2)

Prof. Level	n° of students	s = 0,2		s = 0,01	
		Mean	Median	Mean	Median
A	4	0,047	0,047	0,091	0,089
B	4	0,077	0,077	0,209	0,179
C	5	0,128	0,112	0,189	0,174
D	13	0,153	0,147	0,212	0,195
E	2	0,105	0,105	0,192	0,192
Average (over the 28 students)		0,119	0,109	0,189	0,185

the number of errors made by the student increases, the BN's diagnostic seems to become more sensitive to the high guessing factor. Though these first results are encouraging, further experiments with larger sets of students are needed in order to improve the quality of the diagnosis and to establish more solid conclusions.

4 Conclusions and Future Work

In this paper we have described how a predefined Bayesian student model has been integrated in an existing testing system and an encouraging but preliminary evaluation with a set of 28 students. Future work is planned in three different directions: Evaluations with larger sets of students, increased functionality and improvements of the theoretical model used.

References

[1] Projecto Matemática Ensino (PmatE), `http://pmate2.ua.pt/pmate/`
[2] Sousa, J., Batel, A., Orlando, R.: SA3C- Platform of Evaluation System and Computer Assisted Learning. WEAS Transactions on Advances in Engineering Education 2, 1–6 (2005)
[3] Pinto, J.S., Oliveira, M.P., Anjo, A.B., Vieira, S.I., Isidro, R.O., Silva, M.H.: TDmat– mathematics diagnosis evaluation test for engineering sciences students. International Journal of Mathematical Education in Science and Technology 38(3), 283–299 (2007)
[4] Millán, E., Pérez de la Cruz, J.-L.: A Bayesian Diagnostic Algorithm for Student Modeling. User Modeling and User-Adapted Interaction 12, 281–330 (2002)
[5] Millán, E., Pérez de la Cruz, J.-L., García, F.: Dynamic versus Static Student Models Based on Bayesian Networks: An Empirical Study. In: Palade, V., Howlett, R.J., Jain, L. (eds.) KES 2003. LNCS, vol. 2774, pp. 1337–1344. Springer, Heidelberg (2003)
[6] SMILE and GENIE, `http://genie.sis.pitt.edu/`
[7] Carmona, C., Millan, E., Pérez-de-la-Cruz, J.-L., Trella, M., Conejo, R.: Introducing prerequisite relations in a multi-layered Bayesian student model. In: Ardissono, L., Brna, P., Mitrović, A. (eds.) UM 2005. LNCS (LNAI), vol. 3538, pp. 347–356. Springer, Heidelberg (2005)

An Interoperable ePortfolio Tool for All

Fabrizio Giorgini

Giunti Labs, Via Portobello,
16039 Sestri Levante, Italy
f.giorgini@giuntilabs.com

Abstract. Accessible and interoperable ePortfolio system improves learning opportunities for users with disabilities by offering flexible learning paths and innovative ways of accessing information. However, most ePortfolio systems are closed systems within organisational boundaries and not accessible. This paper describes the efforts of the EU4ALL project to implement an accessible and open ePortfolio system. The result is a system that allows any user to map his learning journey from grade school to higher education and throughout their lifetime. A system where also disabled users control their own experiences, they choose what to include in their ePortfolio, how to reflect on and assess items, and with whom to share their ePortfolio.

Keywords: ePortfolio, accessibility, lifelong learning.

1 Introduction

An electronic portfolio or ePortfolio is a generic term encompassing as wide a range of types and products as there are reasons for using them. The simplest starting point is to consider an ePortfolio as an extension of the paper based-portfolio, bringing with it the obvious benefit of making a portfolio of evidence portable and shareable anywhere that you have Internet access – "the new generation of the three ring binder" *JISC My World Project Final Report, Roberts. 2006*. In fact, an ePortfolio has a much broader scope as an online collection of reflections and digital Artefacts (such as documents, images, resumés, multimedia, hyperlinks and contact information).

Learners and staff can use an ePortfolio to demonstrate their learning, skills and development and record their achievements over time to a selected audience. "ePortfolios ... are personal online spaces for students to access services and store work. They will become ever more useful as learners grow up and start moving between different types of learning and different institutions" *Secretary of State for Education and Skills, UK, January 2006*.

They have the potential to provide a central, linking role between the more rigid, institution-led learning management system and the learners' social online spaces. An ePortfolio is an ideal tool for meeting the needs of established and emerging pedagogy and approaches to learning.

In educational communities across the world the idea that anyone has an electronic portfolio is catching on. ePortfolios should provide a vehicle in which learners can present their achievements and they facilitate many useful processes, within organisations, within educational and other market sectors, and also across organisations and sectors.

As the use of ePortfolio systems grows we are likely to see many cross-organisation and cross sector frameworks of use that facilitate lifelong and "lifewide" learning.

Many of the benefits of ePortfolios lie in their potential to carry evidence of learning across organisational boundaries. They are of most benefit if they are interoperable across different lifelong contexts. Unfortunately most of the existing ePortfolio systems use proprietary formats and do not provide any import/export facility so that the use of a specific portfolio is limited to just one organisational or personal context. In addition, the accessibility of such systems is often a mirage and in many cases they represent an additional barrier for users with disabilities instead of improving learning opportunities for them by offering flexible learning paths and innovative ways of accessing information.

2 Accessibility Challenge for ePortfolios

There has been a lot of work done over the two decades in making computers and software systems or applications accessible to disabled people whatever operating system or software tools are employed [1,2]. The current best practice here needs to be adopted in the development of ePortfolio systems and their interfaces in particular. However there are particular issues for ePortfolios for which there is no current established best practice. The central issue is that an ePortfolio is essentially a one author to many readers environment. Thus accessibility in web-based authoring tools as well as content is vital if accessibility is to be achieved in an ePortfolio.

With ePortfolios come some key principles:

- A shift in the focus of eLearning pedagogies from those where content is centrally distributed towards systems having a greater level of learner participation and learner/user authoring of material. This can include collaborative document review.
- A focus on inclusivity. ePortfolios are touted to be an important element in lifelong and life-wide learning programs. Though evaluation of their use in practice is at an early stage there is a widespread belief that a major benefit will come with their use by hitherto disadvantaged and excluded persons and communities.

There are also efforts throughout the world to ensure persons are not excluded from the use of eLearning and other systems by virtue of their preferred or required computer access mechanism. In some countries this includes legislation that requires that nobody is unreasonably excluded (examples are [3], [4] and [5]). Much effort has been already addressed to ways to make content and content delivery systems accessible to all. This work includes W3C/WAI Web Content Accessibility Guidelines [6], IMS Accessibility for LIP [7] and ISO/IEC Access For All [8].

Unfortunately there is currently little awareness in the communities implementing ePortfolio for integrating the concept in planned educational schemes of what the issues with making ePortfolio systems and content accessible are. Perhaps partly because people have heard of the work mentioned above that addresses how to make content accessible many people believe that ePortfolio content, systems and use will be easily made accessible for all and that widespread inclusivity can extend to all without any extra work. This is not the case and the reasons for that are:

- when content and content delivery alone is made accessible it is possible to focus resources (financial, design etc.) at the point of production. Small changes at this point can have great effect when content or interface reaches the user. With ePortfolio content and systems, responsibility to address and possibility to address many issues moves from this central point to the many and various individual users and the media and authoring tools. Given the great variety of media, tools and interfaces it is more difficult to address the accessibility issue properly.
- When persons with specific access requirements of authoring tools work in environments where authoring is shared it places severe demands on the media representations. In particular the requirement is that the media and the way it is used support "round-tripping". That is a document may need to be edited at different times by persons with very different access requirements and the representation and process need to support that. Current common media formats and the way each is commonly used are not up to that task.
- It has been argued [9] that the technical work even just on making content alone accessible has limitations and needs to take account of broad contextual factors to be effective.

The next paragraph is dedicated to describe how the accessibility and interoperability challenges have been faced in the proposed ePortfolio solution.

3 An ePortfolio for All

The proposed solution to the problems and challenges presented above is an accessible ePortfolio system developed in the European Project EU4ALL (European Unified Approach for Accessible Lifelong Learning) [10] which provides simple and powerful tools for collecting, planning, demonstrating and sharing individual growth, preferences, achievements and performance over time and organizations. It also allows to customize visualization of the ePortfolio to be shared for supporting personal learning paths, professional development or applying for a job.

The ePortfolio system (Fig. 1 shows a screenshot of the tool) implements the W3C/WCAG 1.0 level AA guidelines for providing the users with an accessible web-based graphical user interface which empowers learners to record, edit and share things like competencies, interests, goals, achievements, reflections, current and planned personal and organisational development activities, personal media and content etc.

The ePortfolio system is also used to store and exchange the learner's "access for all" personal needs and preferences for digital delivery.

The ePortfolio system is entirely based on international standards like IMS ePortfolio [11] IMS Learner Information Package (IMS LIP) [12], IMS Content Packaging (IMS CP) [13] and implements the new ISO/IEC 24751-2 standard for the definition of the accessibility preferences with respect to the use of digital contents (see Figure 2).

Fig. 1. A screenshot of the EU4ALL ePortfolio system

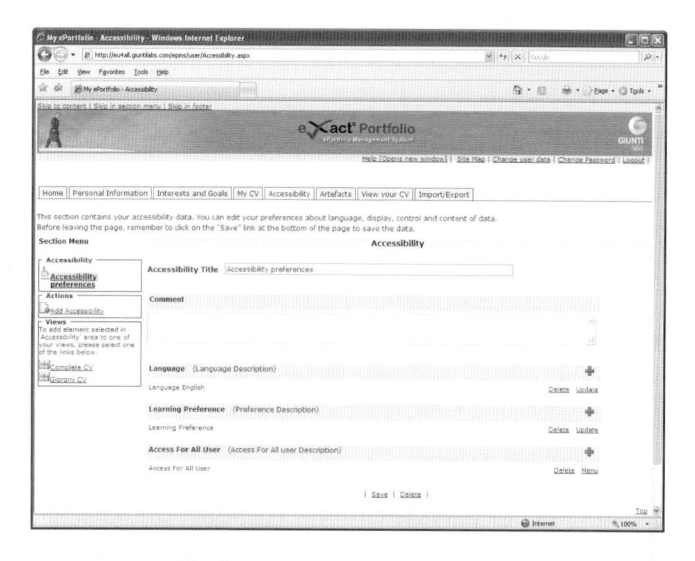

Fig. 2. The accessibility preferences

The ePortfolio system is based on a flexible and configurable architecture: it follows the SOA concept in order to support a wide range of learning and business scenarios.

The import/export functionalities implemented using web services technology potentially allow the integration with any 3rd party software solution.

In the EU4ALL project context, they allow the full integration with the project Learning Management System .LRN and Moodle; personal data, preferences, learning achievements and planning etc. can be continuously (and automatically) transferred and synchronised between the two components and eventually made available for their export (in the IMS ePortfolio format) and use in different contexts (e.g. application for a job, change of school or organisation, sharing of personal media objects or learning experiences...).

4 Conclusions

The combination of the accessible web interface developed according to the WAI/WCAG guidelines, the possibility to store the personal accessibility preferences, the services for the integration with external systems and the common ePortfolio functionalities makes the EU4ALL ePortfolio system a unique solution on the market. The system has been tested by software testers which are familiar with the different adopted standards, by some disabled users and by partners expert of usability. The first evaluation results demonstrated the almost total compliancy of the tool with the adopted standards; however, users sometimes found the terminology used to describe the ePortfolio elements too technical and suggested a more transparent use of the standards by translating, for instance, the elements that describe the usability preferences or the other ePortfolio parts in a format more familiar for them. In other words, an application profile for the IMS ePortfolio and ISO/IEC 24751-2 standards would be much appreciated.

Acknowledgements

This research has been co-funded by the European Commission within the IST integrated project EU4ALL (European Unified Approach for Assisted Lifelong Learning), grant 034778.

References

1. IMS Guidelines for Developing Accessible Learning Applications, white paper available at http://www.imsglobal.org/accessibility/accv1p0/imsacc_guidev1p0.html (accessed July 5, 2010)
2. Cooper, M.: Communications and Information Technology (C&IT) for Disabled Students. In: Powell, S. (ed.) Special Teaching in Higher Education- Successful Strategies for Access and Inclusion. Kogan Page, London (2003)
3. Needs and Disability Act 2001 (SENDA), http://www.hmso.gov.uk/acts/acts2001/20010010.htm (accessed July 5, 2010)
4. Disability Discrimination Act 1995, http://www.legislation.hmso.gov.uk/acts/acts1995/1995050.htm (accessed July 5, 2010)
5. Stanca Law, http://www.pubbliaccesso.gov.it/normative/law_20040109_n4.htm (accessed July 5, 2010)
6. WCAG, Web Content Accessibility Guidelines, http://www.w3.org/TR/WCAG10 (accessed April 19, 2010)

7. IMS ACCLIP, http://www.imsglobal.org/accessibility (accessed July 5, 2010)
8. ISO/IEC 24751-2 (2008), http://www.iso.org/iso/iso_catalogue/catalogue_tc/catalogue_detail.htm?csnumber=43603 (accessed April 19, 2010)
9. Kelly, Sloan, Phipps, Petrie, Hamilton: Forcing Standardization or Accommodating Diversity? A Framework for Applying the WCAG in the Real World. In: Proceedings of the International Cross-Disciplinary Workshop on Web Accessibility held in Chiba, near Tokyo, Japan, May 20 (2005), http://www.ukoln.ac.uk/web-focus/papers/w4a-2005/html/, http://www.w4a.info/2005/ (accessed April 19, 2010) (Special Educational)
10. EU4ALL project, http://www.eu4all-project.eu (accessed July 5, 2010)
11. IMS ePortfolio specification, http://www.imsglobal.org/ep (accessed April 19, 2010)
12. IMS Learner Information Package Specification, http://www.imsglobal.org/profiles (accessed April 19, 2010)
13. IMS Content Packaging Specification, http://www.imsglobal.org/content/packaging (accessed July 5, 2010)

Disaster Readiness through Education - Training Soft Skills to Crisis Units by Means of Serious Games in Virtual Environments

Nina Haferkamp[1] and Nicole C. Krämer[2]

[1] University of Münster, Institute of Communication Science, Bispinghof 9-14, 48143 Münster, Germany
[2] University of Duisburg-Essen, Social Psychology: Media and Communication, Forsthausweg 2, 47057 Duisburg Germany
`nina.haferkamp@uni-muenster.de`, `nicole.kraemer@uni-due.de`

Abstract. The training of soft skills in organizational settings has become very important for an effective communicative exchange between members of staff. Especially in companies where the line of communication has to be fast and unmistakable, e.g. in crisis management units, the regular training of communication skills is therefore indispensable. The DREAD-ED project proposes a technology-based teaching methodology to meet these needs. The methodology provides a serious game which enables its users to train soft skills in a virtual environment under safe conditions. The current paper presents the results of two trials conducted with crisis managers and university students.

Keywords: crisis communication, serious games, social skills.

1 Introduction

As tsunamis and earthquakes in the recent time have alarmingly demonstrated, natural disasters as well as other emergency situations such as fires are omnipresent dangers in our daily life. The advance training of emergency management personnel is therefore an important issue in reducing damage by these terrifying catastrophes. Given that disasters can vary in scope from e.g. local fires on a chemical park to large earthquakes such as the one in Haiti in winter 2010, a broad training strategy combining domain specific knowledge and social skills such as communication and decision making in groups is required [1]. These trainings of "soft skills" need to include a realistic simulation of communication in conditions of stress, fear as well as problem-solving by means of contradictory information and in the face of competing demands [2], [3], [4]. However, a regular training of social skills is either costly in terms of time and money because crisis units need 1:1 reenactments of disasters to guarantee a simulation close to reality or they are trained in traditional classroom environments, where standard operating procedures are learned from printed documents and, therefore, are far away from real crisis situations and the applied learning of social skills. Hence, both training settings only offer unsatisfactory training conditions. Nowadays with the help of new computer technologies, more flexible possibilities are given to train disaster communication. Serious games working with modern virtual environments appear to combine the engagement and realism of a simulation with the cost-effectiveness of a paper-based classroom teaching session [5]. These games are capable of simulating the general disorder of a real emergency management room and they offer various possibilities of coaching with regard to the training of soft skills and communicative behavior. Moreover, they have the advantage that all persons involved in the simulation, apart from the actual personnel taking part in the training, can be simulated. Thus, a great deal of the expense involved in running these exercises is eliminated. Against this background, the DREAD-ED (Disaster Readiness through Education) project – funded by the EU Lifelong Learning Programme – designed a serious game which provides cost-effective training and is based on the concept of experiential problem-based learning. Users of a tutor-supervised multi-user game are confronted with a fictitious natural disaster (e.g. fire at a chemical plant) whose incalculability offers the basis for various group decisions within a short period of time. The current paper describes the results of two German trials in which two different target groups with different expertise on crisis management played the game (students vs. crisis managers). Additionally, the learning outcomes were assessed.

2 The DREAD ED Game

The game places its users in a crisis management team that is dealing with an evolving emergency (e.g. a huge fire close to a chemical park). Each member is assigned a specific role that has unique abilities. These roles (e.g. leader of the team) are based on the roles of members of crisis units in reality. Between three and six people can participate in one game session [1], [6]. At the beginning of a session, the group is confronted with the disaster which is shown by means of a short television broadcast. Afterwards, four abstract six-point scales are presented to the players which represent the current game state (see fig. 1).

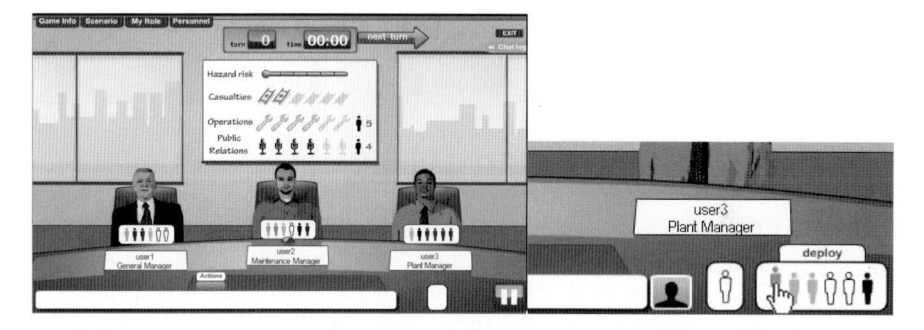

Fig. 1. Interface of the DREAD ED game

Each scale represents an individual aspect of the emergency that can vary from 1 to 6, representing 'perfect' to 'disaster.' These scales are labeled as 'Casualties', 'Hazard Risk', 'Operations', and 'Public Relations.' The 'Casualties' scale is the most important one: If it reaches its maximum, the team has lost the game. Conversely, if the team ensures that the 'Casualties' parameter does not increase, then they have completed the task successfully. Events of information that alter the game state in an unpredictable fashion are introduced after each turn in order to model the dynamically changing nature of a disaster. These injects are short television clips, radio reports, emails, short messages or telephone calls. The goal of these injects is to force the group to plan in advance for unforeseen circumstances, as well as dealing with issues of immediate importance.

The game state, that is the successful management of the disaster, can be manipulated by exchanging personnel with each other. There are nine different personnel classes (e.g. first responders, fire fighters etc.) which have a unique effect upon the game state when deployed. In addition, each player character (e.g. general manager) has a unique ability, some of which relate to particular personnel classes. Personnel classes are represented abstractly in the form of colors within the game. The goal of the game mechanic is to train effective communication with regard to the exchange of personnel with limited time available. Players have to share information about their personnel and discuss which particular personnel can be used to reduce the hazard risk of the disaster. For communication with each other, the players have to use a text chat which is comparable to ordinary chat applications such as Skype. Furthermore, a tutor who does not have a physical representation within the game supervises the game play and conducts a face-to-face discussion after the game. He/she sums up the decision-making processes during game-play together with the users and discusses weaknesses as well as strengths of the team. In order to keep this session structured, the tutor uses a field manual for interviewing the group. This field manual includes questions concerning the decisions within the game such as "How did you manage the situation that arose when xy happened? What did you do to resolve the situation?" as well as questions on the feelings of the users during game play (e. g. What were you feeling during the first leg? Was there anything that made you feel uncomfortable?). Moreover, the tutor discusses the negotiation behavior with the players by e.g. asking them whether they noticed any disagreements during discussions or whether there was a person they wanted to have more information from. Finally, the team should conclude how effectively they performed as a group in resolving the crisis in general. Next to these open questions, the participants fill in a questionnaire measuring their thoughts and opinions on the training session on a quantitative level.

3 Evaluation of the DREAD ED Game

The DREAD ED game was tested in two trials in Germany. The first trial using a beta-version of the game was conducted in June 2009. The second trial was conducted in December 2009 with the final version of the DREAD ED game. The beta-version had the same game mechanics like the final version but there were no media injects illustrating the disaster (e.g. a television report on the fire, radio reports, emails, SMS messages, and phone calls). The only information on the state of the disaster was given by the four parameters that were displayed above the avatars (see fig. 1). The final version of the game included those injects to give the players a better and more vivid impression of the catastrophe. By means of the two different versions, we could examine whether the media injects were evaluated as helpful or whether they rather handicap the game play and the learning experience. One trial lasted (including breaks) about 4 hours.

3.1 Samples

Each trial (n = 10; n_{total} = 20) had a sample of five students and five members of a German crisis unit (Mean age_{total} = 45.8; Standard Deviation = 2.11) in order guarantee that people with different expertise were able to use the game for training soft skills. The students were recruited at a large German university (Mean Age_{total} = 23.32 years, SD = 3.12).

3.2 Procedure

The trainings were subdivided into three parts: First, the tutor introduced the project, the contributing partners as well as the goals of the DREAD ED game. Next, the tutor presented the virtual learning platform and explained the features of the interface before the players tested the platform together with the tutor. We conducted four sessions with each sample. One session took about 30-45 minutes excluding breaks (some breaks were necessary to discuss problems and misunderstandings). After having tested the environment, the tutor finally conducted a feedback and debriefing session and the participants filled in a questionnaire assessing the training of soft skills, users' emotional state during game play as well as an evaluation of the gam.

3.3 Results

General Performance within the Game. The crisis unit outperformed the students in both trials. They did better in reducing the hazard risk and caused less causality than the students above all sessions. Although the crisis managers were – according to their own statements – less experienced with computer-mediated communication, their style of communication was shorter and more efficient in comparison to the communication of the students. Furthermore, their decision-making was based on more structured agreements while the students had difficulties to come to a compromise. Moreover, the crisis unit was more focused on the parameters than the students, while the latter rather tried to collect personnel of the same color without analyzing the values of the four parameters. This finally led to an increase of the causalities parameter because the students disregarded to select the specific personnel for controlling this parameter. With regard to the communicative behavior, the students stated that they felt tensed during the game, while the crisis managers reported that they "*don't care about time pressure and the development of the crisis because we are used to these problems in reality*" (male, 52 years). Quantitative data proved that students reported a higher level of "stress" (M = 3.60; SD = 1.50) in comparison to the crisis managers (M = 1.80; SD = 1.01).

Evaluation of the first Trial. The crisis managers generally pointed out that the game is a good training tool for learning a short and efficient way of communication. One of the participants (male, 29 years) stated that "*crisis units often fail because they talk too much because they are not able to distinguish important aspects from unimportant ones*". Thus, the game is – according to the crisis managers – an appropriate tool for learning effective communication because the countdown *"punishes dispensable information"* (male, 29 years). The results of the post-questionnaire underlined this evaluation. All users estimated that "effective communication" was trained most intensively ($M = 3.80$; $SD = 0.44$). The student sample additionally reported that the structuring of communication within a group can be advanced by using the game. With regard to the evaluation of the game, the crisis managers stated that losing the game is not *"painful enough"* because the whole storyline and the presentation style of the disaster *"is too far away from reality"* (male, 50 years). According to them, the visualization of a disaster by means of abstract parameters does not live up to a realistic simulation of a crisis. Quantitative data of both samples underlined that the presentation style of the scenario was evaluated as "far from reality" ($M = 3.20$; $SD = 1.10$) although the scenario itself was evaluated as "interesting" ($M = 3.00$; $SD = 1.00$). In line with this, the crisis managers as well as the students evaluated the assignment of roles to the players surprisingly negatively: The students noted that it was too difficult for them to remember the specific function of each role. Additionally, *"it was unclear how the role is related to the specific color of personnel"* (female, 24 years). The crisis managers criticized that the roles and their responsibilities do not represent real-life affordances. *"Although we have specific tasks in a real crisis management group, the DREAD ED game is not capable of displaying the diversity of responsibilities."* (male, 48 years). They recommended to delete the roles and instead of that to use anonymous names for each player. Based on these impressions, we conducted a second trial in which we tried to consider some of the remarks of the two samples.

Evaluation of the second Trial. With regard to the additional features in the final version of the game, the crisis unit evaluated media injects more positively than the students, because *"these injects are close to reality"* (2 participants). The participants stated that injects are important in order to get an understanding of the disaster situation. The students, on the other hand, reported that they did not focus that much on these injects, but rather on the personnel and the usage of the teams. *"The media injects constrained our discussion because we wanted to use the time between the turns to discuss next steps"* (female, 24 years). However, in general, quantitative data showed that the game was evaluated as less "far from reality" ($M = 2.00$; $SD = 1.23$) in comparison to the evaluation of the first trial. Another aspect that was evaluated differently by the two samples was the role of each player within the game. The crisis managers evaluated the missing of specific roles more positively than the students (Note: all participants were called users and could only be distinguished by their individual number, e.g. user1, user2). *"It was advantageous to leave out the roles due to the fact that we were all equal. This leads to a more democratized communication, in my opinion. It was not clear who of the guys had been my supervisor and this was quite good"* (male, 40 years). The students in this sample, however, remarked that they miss the nomination of a leader who assumed control over the discussion. *"Our performance would have been better if we had had a leader in our team who made the final decisions"* (female, 23 years).

4 Discussion

With regard to the training of social skills, it appears that due to its mechanics the game is able to teach an efficient exchange of information in compelling situations.

It encourages its users to critically reflect on their decisions made within the game. The comparison of emergency managers with the student sample in terms of group performance underlines how the successful use of soft skills (effective communication and group decision making) leads to success within the serious game. The crisis managers used their experiences in disaster communication to solve the game's tasks while the students, who were not experienced with communication in stressful situations, faced difficulties. The crisis unit demonstrated more efficient decision making by having short discussions and factual agreements while the communication of the students was impacted by emotions and stress. The fact that users with high experience concerning disaster communication skills were more successful in the game lends evidence to the notion that the game is able to validly train communication in stressful situations.

Acknowledgments. The DREAD ED (see http://www.dread-ed.eu) project is funded by the European Union Lifelong Learning Programme and specifically, is part of the Leonardo da Vinci subprogramme, key activity 3: "Development of ICT-based content and services".

References

[1] Linehan, C., Lawson, S., Doughty, M., Kirman, B.: There's no 'I' in Emergency Management Teams: Designing and evaluating a serious game for training emergency managers in group decision making skills. In: Proceedings of the 39th Conference of the Society for the Advancement of Games & Simulations in Education and Training, Leeds, UK, pp. 20–27 (2009)
[2] Crichton, M., Flin, R.: Training for Emergency Management: Tactical Decision Games. J. Haz. Mater. 88, 255–266 (2001)
[3] Kowalski-Trakofler, K.M., Scharf, T.: Judgment and decision making under stress: an overview for emergency managers. Int. J. Emerg. Manag. 1, 278–289 (2003)
[4] Gresham, F.M., Elliott, S.N.: Assessment and Classification of children's social skills. A review of methods and issues. S. Psy. Revi. 13, 292–301 (1984)
[5] Sanders, R.L., Rhodes, G.S.: A simulation learning approach to training first responders for radiological emergencies. In: Proceedings of the 2007 summer computer simulation conference, San Diego, California, pp. 84–91 (2007)
[6] Linehan, C., Lawson, S., Doughty, M., Kirman, B., Haferkamp, N., Krämer, N.C.: Teaching Decision Making Skills to Emergency Managers via Digital Games (submitted)

Ambient Displays and Game Design Patterns

Sebastian Kelle, Dirk Börner, Marco Kalz, and Marcus Specht

Centre for Learning Sciences and Technologies,
Open University of the Netherlands,
Valkenburgerweg 177,
6419AT Heerlen,
The Netherlands
{ske,dbn,mkl,spe}@ou.nl

Abstract. In this paper we describe a social learning game we implemented to evaluate various means of ubiquitous learning support. Making use of game design patterns it was possible to implement information channels in such a way that we could simulate ubiquitous learning support in an authentic situation. The result is a prototype game in which one person is chosen randomly to become "Mister X", and the other players have to find clues and strategies to find out who is the wanted person. In our scenario we used 3 different information channels to provide clues and compared them with respect to user appreciation and effectiveness.

Keywords: Ubiquitous Learning, Ambient Information Channel, Awareness, Game Based Learning, Game Learning Patterns.

1 Background

1.1 Ubiquitous Learning and Informational Awareness

The mobile learning paradigm [1], [2] encourages learning that is personalized, authentic, and situated [3]. Environmentally based upon this paradigm is the principle of ubiquitous learning. This concept rests upon the idea of ubiquitous computing [4], offering mobility combined with pervasive computing functionality [5]. These concepts are then orchestrated by instructional designs. Permanency, accessibility, immediacy, interactivity, situatedness, and adaptability have been identified as the main characteristics for information support in ubiquitous learning [6]. Learners need to navigate more efficiently through information and find the right information in any given context [7]. One essential aspect to implement this concept is to keep the learner continuously aware about the learning environment. Several types of awareness can be distinguished [1]: social, task, concept, workspace, knowledge, and context awareness. We suggest utilizing these types to feed information channels in the environment of the learner, which may adhere to the notion of ambience, hence contributing to a non-intrusive way of interaction, as suggested by the Ambient Information Channels (AICHE) model proposed by Specht [2].

1.2 Game Patterns

There are different ways to provide informational awareness within ubiquitous learning environments in a contextualized manner. One of the most motivating and versatile ways of doing so is the methodology of serious games (SG) and game design patterns. The discussed information channels can technically be realized as game elements, giving clues about the game's storyline or progress of opponents or collaborators. In game design, such elements are formally described as game design patterns. These can be matched with educational purposes in order to foster certain cognitive processes and sustain motivation. Similar to the Web 2.0 patterns [8], from a technical design point of view the use of such pattern has several advantages supporting reusability and interoperability [9]. A pattern consists of several data fields in which there is information on the pattern itself, its functionality, its consequences and examples. On top of that there is also information how and together with what other patterns one pattern can be combined (modulation and instantiation), or is in conflict (two patterns that cannot occur in a game without contradiction). A large repository of game design patterns derived from actual game elements has been compiled by Björk & Holopainen [10].

2 Approach

2.1 Research Objectives

The combination of a game-based and ubiquitous learning perspective forms the linkage between the theoretical concept and its implementation. While the concept of information channels is the theoretical construct we used for our basic design, the corresponding game design patterns formed the basis for the actual implementation of our prototype. In our study we focus on the following research questions: 1. Do alternations in use of different information channels influence the user activity and appreciation? And 2. Does the use of these information channels create a meaningful and productive environment to foster social collaboration?

2.2 Analysis and Design

Social, workspace, and task awareness have been identified as the awareness types they provide the most support for a social game setting where information is shared and distributed across different contexts.

Social awareness reflects how the other participants are progressing in comparison to the individual progress; we decided to implement this with a *competition pattern*. Competition can be a social concept especially when competing teams are formed. In a more fuzzy sense competition also would have a social dimension because it draws attention and creates a "motto" for social interaction. According to [10] competition is "the struggle between players or against the game system to achieve a certain goal where the performance of the players can be measured at least relatively".

Workspace awareness facilitates different types of resources supporting ubiquitous learning in a shared workspace. These resources are fed into the system and visualized using a various displays. Game elements in this case can be realized using the

Clues and *Gain Information* pattern. The clues pattern is described in [10] as "the game elements that give the players information about how the goals of the game can be reached". The *Gain Information* pattern is described as "the goal of performing actions in the game in order to be able to receive information or make deductions".

Task awareness supports the learner by facilitating and indicating the accomplishment of goals. Applying a *goal pattern* thus extends the abstract task into a concrete set of actions the participants can choose from, for reaching a goal, i.e. accomplishing the task. Being aware of the progress in accomplishing the task, individually or socially, creates an additional clue with respect to keeping up a certain momentum of motivation, which is supported by the *score pattern*, where score "is the numerical representation of the player's success in the game, often not only representing the success but also defining it" [10].

2.3 Methodology

Based on the previous analysis and the elaborated research questions a technical design has been implemented covering different design dimensions for the selected awareness types. A main point of interest was how the implementation got assimilated and perceived in a social setting simulating a ubiquitous learning environment. Furthermore the implications for its usage in a game based learning scenario were assessed experimentally.

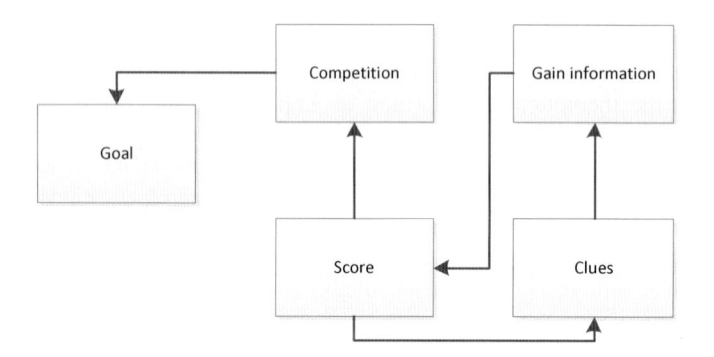

Fig. 1. Core structure of the game with patterns relevant to the awareness types

Figure 1 shows how the mentioned game patterns are interdependent. While clues could come from different sources it is noteworthy that a reflection of score would likely be a clue in itself, enabling the user to gain information, necessary to take the right decision that leads to an increased score to compete with other players and ultimately to reach the goal: to win the game. More concretely it was assessed which types of awareness are best to be targeted by which contextualized information channels: professional information was displayed in the workspace environment, while social and personal information was displayed in a social environment (see implementation section for more details). Reflecting the current score as well as the status of the game finally provided task awareness. On day one, the information clues were given via email only, on day two they were given only with information displays, and on day three we used both channels.

2.4 Implementation

The scenario selected for application of the game was at a seminar-style international meeting of PhD students of educational technology and a set of renowned instructors drawn from around Europe [11]. In this setting, the authors implemented a social learning game in which one of the participants was assigned the role as "Mr. X", and the other players needed to find out by using various clues given according to social, workspace and task awareness. These information clues were derived from a user database that was generated from a questionnaire in which the participants entered both professional and more personal (or social) characteristics and preferences like background, age, place of birth, favorite color, etc. The gathered data was then used to display clues on screens installed in the main lecture room (workspace environment), and in the entrance respectively cafeteria (personal and social environment). The data was grouped according to the different environments: "professional" information was displayed in the workspace environment, "personal" and "social" information was displayed in the personal and social environment.

The following rules were given to the participants: The game was played in several rounds. At the beginning of each round one of the participants was selected as Mr. X by random. Periodically the participants received three hints about the wanted person. These hints described Mr. X in person as well as his/her social and professional life. The task was to get information about fellow participants by getting acquainted with them and discussing who could be the wanted person. After authenticating the participants were prompted with a voting screen in which they could vote for the person they suspected to be Mr. X. The vote for the suspected person could be given by clicking on one of the person names. They were allowed to change their mind anytime and vote again as long as the current round was open. The round closed once more than 50% of all participants voted for the right person OR the wanted person was not identified after giving five times three hints. Finally, after Mr. X was revealed an according email was sent to every participant, as well as the name of Mr. X was displayed on the information displays. The score was allocated accordingly and could be found in a high score list that was also online. Alternatively, if Mr. X was not revealed within half a day, the authors stopped the round manually and declared that Mr. X had won the game. Everybody who voted for the right Mr. X got 100 points, everybody who voted for the wrong person got -50 points, Mr. X him/herself got 200 points if not revealed, and -100 points were the punishment for not voting at all.

The game was technically implemented by making use of the Google Application Engine [12] and the Adobe FLEX framework [13], facilitating the FLAR toolkit [14].

3 Results

The effectiveness of the game with respect to the prospective benefit for social interaction was monitored in two ways: the user activity (system logs) and the user response to a feedback questionnaire at the end of the event. The results of the user monitoring are shown in table 1. There were 3 days with two rounds of the game each. The user activity was highest (135 votes) on the first day, slightly slacked down during day 2 (114 votes) and picked up again on day 3 (134 votes). Within the table the number of votes is broken down into intervals throughout each round of the game. It can be read that the use of both emails and information displays created the highest dispersion of vote frequency in the according game rounds, which postulates the use of these information channels was most powerful.

Table 1. Frequency of Votes per Intervention

Intervention	Round	Frequency of votes / per time interval (20min)								
Email	I	1	4	12	19	20				
	II	27	11	21	19	1	8	2	3	2
Ambient Display	III	13	9	6	0	2	26	5		
	IV	13	4	27	10					
Both	V	11	5	5	9	10	12			
	VI	16	17	7	12	3	19	4		

In the questionnaire we had asked the participants if they preferred being sent the information clues via email or via the information displays. 66 % preferred the information displays. 63% actually preferred a combination of both information displays and emails. The game's intention was to help fostering social interaction, but only 33% of the participants thought it achieved that goal (the majority was undecided about this point). Most of the participants had the impression that the game rather helped fostering social interaction not because of specific mechanisms like "personal" or "professional" information clues, but simply by the fact that there was a game being played. In contrast to this, the questionnaire results indicate that "talking to people and pondering who could be Mr. X" influenced 44% of the participants' voting activity (the rest undecided). The dynamic voting screen (adaptive size of the name fields) had an even stronger influence (66% claimed they were influenced). The motivational power of the user authentication was only rated mediocre.

4 Conclusion

From a critical point of view the game in its current form and limited time frame has not proven to significantly enhance social collaboration. Due to the overall rising user activity it could be theorized that a growing social bond between the participants might have led to a higher incentive to play the game together, and not the other way round. Our study, however, gives indications that over a longer period of time noticeable effects possibly could be measured. We will analyse more detail of the log files to support this hypothesis. Besides the evaluation of data and feedback we could notice that people would in fact talk about the game in a cheerful way suspecting each other to be Mr. X. For the use of information channels regarding the different awareness types a strong influence was measurable for task awareness, where workspace and social awareness ranked lower. Finding ways how to implement those latter awareness types in a more efficient way will be a matter of our attention in future research.

Acknowledgments. We would like to thank the Tiroler Bildungsinstitut Grillhof for being a welcoming host who kindly supported our activities during the JTEL Winter School on Advanced Learning Technologies 2010.

References

1. Ogata, H.: Assisting Awareness in Ubiquitous Learning. In: Proceedings of the IADIS Mobile Learning 2009, Barcelona, Spain, pp. 21–27 (2009)
2. Specht, M.: Learning in a Technology Enhanced World. OCÉ, The Netherlands (2009)
3. Traxler, J.: Current State of Mobile Learning. In: Mobile Learning: Transforming the Delivery of Education and Training, p. 9. AU Press, Edmonton (2009)
4. Weiser, M.: The computer for the 21st century. Scientific American 272, 78–89 (1995)
5. Lyytinen, K., Yoo, Y.: Issues and challenges in ubiquitous computing. Communications of the ACM 45, 63–65 (2002)
6. Ogata, H., Yano, Y.: Context-aware support for computer-supported ubiquitous learning. In: Proceedings of the 2nd IEEE International Workshop on Wireless and Mobile Technologies in Education (Wmte 2004), p. 27 (2004)
7. Koole, M.: A model for framing mobile learning. Mobile Learning: Transforming the Delivery of Education and Training 25 (2009)
8. O'reilly, T.: What is web 2.0. Design patterns and business models for the next generation of software 30, 2005 (2005)
9. Agerbo, E., Cornils, A.: How to preserve the benefits of design patterns. In: Proceedings of the 13th ACM SIGPLAN conference on Object-oriented programming, systems, languages, and applications, p. 143 (1998)
10. Björk, S., Holopainen, J.: Patterns in Game Design. Charles River Media, Hingham (2004)
11. TEL Europe: JTEL Winter School on Advanced Learning Technologies 2010 (2010), http://www.teleurope.eu/pg/groups/43
12. Google App Engine - Google Code, http://code.google.com/appengine/
13. Adobe Flex, http://www.adobe.com/products/flex/
14. Saqoosha.net: Start-up guide for FLARToolkit, http://saqoosha.net/en/flartoolkit/start-up-guide/

PWGL, Towards an Open and Intelligent Learning Environment for Higher Music Education

Mika Kuuskankare[1] and Mikael Laurson[2]

[1] Centre for Music and Technology
Sibelius Academy, Finland
mkuuskan@siba.fi
http://www.siba.fi

[2] Department of Signal Processing and Acoustics
Aalto University, Finland
laurson@siba.fi
http://www.aalto.fi

Abstract. We have studied the computer based applications of composition, music theory and analysis, software synthesis, and music notation for well over two decades. The most important result of these activities is PWGL, a modern visual computer program with the emphasis on music and sound related applications.

In this paper we give a brief overview of PWGL and discuss how it could be developed into a pedagogical environment. PWGL has many advanced features that would make it ideal for developing study material in the context of music and sound. It should be of interest for both teachers and students in various levels of education.

Keywords: Educational technology, higher music education, interactivity, multimedia learning environments, human-computer interaction.

1 Introduction

The study of computer-assisted music education is still relatively young. Most of the available projects concentrate on the beginner or intermediate students. The present computer applications do not try to replace human teachers but to provide self-study environments and technological enhancement to the learning process.

There exists several computer applications, both free and commercial, that are aimed among others at music theory, ear training, and instrument tuition. One of the first music tuition systems was arguably the Piano Tutor [2] by Dannenberg. The Piano Tutor project aimed at developing an interactive multimedia tutor for beginning piano students. The more recent Digital Violin Tutor [17], in turn, addresses visualization issues by introducing a 3D animated visual feedback system. The IMUTUS system [14] provides for an interactive music tuition system for training users on traditional musical instruments (mainly targeting recorder instruction, however). The VEMUS platform [15], built upon the experiences gained during the IMUTUS project, is aimed at developing an open, interactive and networked self-practicing environment for teaching beginner students to play various wind instruments. i-Maestro [12] project develops and interactive multimedia environment for technology enhanced learning and teaching of both music theory and performance. Furthermore, Auralia and Musition by Avid Technology are examples of commercial software for ear training and music theory. They provide suites of graded exercises, tests, and automatic assessment. MiBAC is yet another example of a commercial grade software but intended especially for teaching jazz theory. Finally, LenMus (http://www.lenmus.org/) presents itself as a free and open software for learning and practicing music theory and aural skills.

Apart from LenMus most of the aforementioned programs tend to focus on one specific problem such as instrument tuition or ear training. Yet most of the systems are large software packages representing several man-years of software development. Applications that provide a full range of features, such as music notation, sound synthesis, or flexible music analytical facilities, are still scarce today. This is understandable as many of the required aspects of programs dealing with comprehensive music tuition are proven to be great challenges to model with computers.

There has been an ongoing long term research project that has concentrated in developing a modern visual music programming environment called PWGL [9]. It is primarily designed for the applications of computer assisted composition, music theory and analysis, software synthesis, and music notation. In this paper we discuss how PWGL could be developed into an advanced pedagogical environment especially for higher music education.

The rest of the paper is structured as follows. Section 2 gives a brief introduction to PWGL environment and discusses some of it's potential pedagogical applications. In Section 3 we present a fully working example prepared with the help of PWGL that aims to demonstrate its current facilities. The paper ends with some concluding remarks.

2 PWGL

PWGL is a visual environment based on OpenGL, an industry standard high performance computer graphics API that is widely used in computer-aided design, virtual reality, scientific visualization, information visualization, and video games. PWGL comprises several advanced large-scale applications, including the music notation package ENP [4], the geometric shape editor 2D-Editor [6], the software synthesizer PWGLSynth [10], and the rule-based compositional language PWGLConstraints [7].

PWGL is distributed as freeware and it runs on Macintosh OS X (10.4 or newer), and on Windows XP operating systems. PWGL been publicly available since 2006 and it is currently one of the three major composition environments. When compared to its closest counterparts, the OpenMusic of IRCAM ([1], available since 1998), and Common Music ([16], available since 1989) PWGL is still relatively new to the computer music community. Nevertheless, it has already gained wide acceptance and it is taught and used in several universities and institutions around the world. The PWGL website is located at www.siba.fi/PWGL/ providing access to all pertinent material, including the application distribution itself.

PWGL could be seen as an attempt to fill the gap between several different aspects of music tuition. It is our belief that PWGL could be established as a pedagogical tool for the academia. There have already been a considerable amount of community efforts to produce pedagogical material with the help of PWGL. For example, the composer Javier Torres Maldonado at the Conservatoire of Milan has together with his pupils produced a collection of PWGL tutorials (www.torresmaldonado.net/pedagogical_materials.html). This material is actively used in teaching during the different courses at the conservatoire. Jacopo Baboni Schilingi is a composer, the founder of the PRISMA composers group (Pedagogia e Ricerca Internazionale sui Sistemi Musicali Assistiti), and currently holds the position of composition professor at Conservatory of Montbéliard. He personally teaches several courses using PWGL and distributes his pedagogical material free of charge in the internet (www.baboni-schilingi.com/index.php?/recherches/software/). These community efforts have shown that there is both a growing interest towards PWGL and the need for an open and intelligent pedagogical tool in the field of higher music education.

3 PWGL as an Educational Platform

Although not initially designed for educational purposes, PWGL, with its considerable feature set, should prove to be an interesting platform to build on. PWGL is fully programmable and extendable and it is not tied into any specific style, methodology, genre or esthetics. We feel that there are several potential pedagogical applications to PWGL, among others: (1) music history, (2) music theory, (3) melodic and rhythmic dictates, (4) composition, harmonization, counterpoint, (5) instrument tuition, (6) ear training, and (7) musical acoustics and signal processing.

PWGL contains a versatile music notation editor that can represent music ranging from the ancient styles to the modern graphical notation of our times. Interactive and dynamic 2 or 3 dimensional graphics can be produced with the help of OpenGL. PWGL allows an automatic analysis of musical scores and visualization of the analytical information (see, [8]). By using our rule-based compositional language, it is possible to automatically compose exercises such as melodic or rhythmic dictates (cf. Percival [13]). Our software synthesizer, in turn, could be used to render ear training drills, or to teach intonation. Potentially, in the future, we could offer similar facilities in instrument tuition as the IMUTUS project by using the audio analysis facilities of our system as described in [11].

Our future work to support pedagogical applications in PWGL will mainly be focused in delivering a flexible Content Authoring Tool (CAT). CAT provides teachers with the means to create new educational material and to arrange different kinds of visual and textual components to create interactive training content, courses, syllabi etc.

Currently, PWGL provides the users with some CAT facilities but with a moderate functionality. The system consists of an in-line viewer application and a small, domain specific language DBL (Document Builder Language) that allows us to create rich documents using a combination of text, patches, and images. Our system should be extended to a full featured CAT tool that would allow the users to easily construct interactive pedagogical content. The extensions should be simple enough to be learned without programming background but also powerful enough to represent advanced learning modules. The repertoire should be extended to cover animation, video, and interactive content.

4   An Experimental Pedagogical Example

Next, we give an example of a potential educational exercise created with the help of the tools currently made available by PWGL (see Figure 1). Here, we implement an interactive counterpoint exercise. The teaching and learning traditional counterpoint is fundamental to any degree of music education. Furthermore, the rules of counterpoint are well described in several study books, such as *Gradus ad Parnassum* [3] by Johann Joseph Fux, an important Baroque era composer and music theorist.

In PWGL the whole process can be fully automated. ENP, our music notation program can be used as a user-interface component for representing the exercise and inputting the students solution. The rules of counterpoint can be expressed

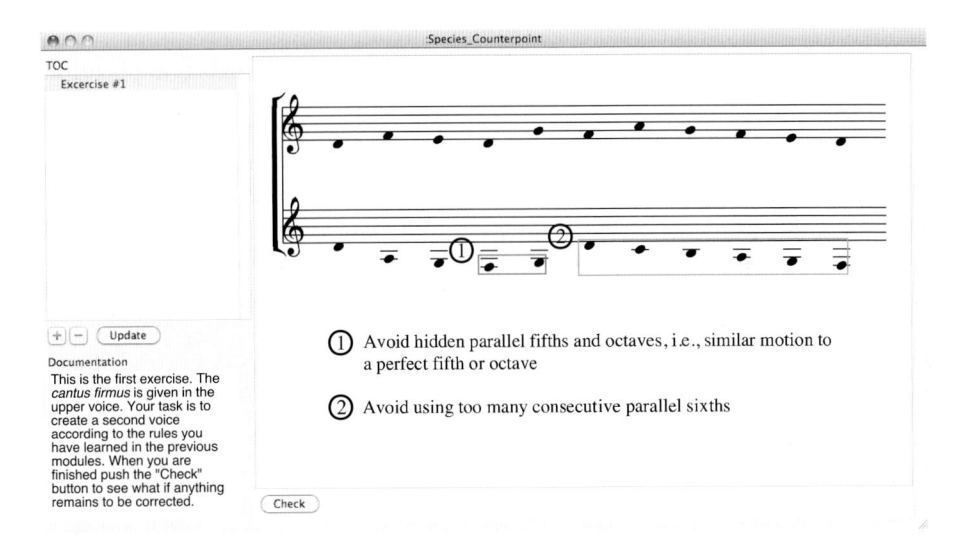

Fig. 1. An example of a pedagogical exercise created with the help of PWGL

using our rule-based music analysis system[5]. Finally, these rules can be used to generate visual clues and textual advice using the elaborate expression system provided by ENP (see [4] for examples).

The assignment shown in Figure 1 is relatively straightforward: the student is given a melodic line (*cantus firmus* as it is called using the counterpoint terminology) and he or she is required to create a second, complementing voice. At this point, the rhythms are not of importance as we use as an example the most elementary form of counterpoint called the *first species* where each note in the second part sounds against one note in the cantus firmus. Naturally, the cantus firmus would not be allowed to be modified by the student.

In our example a simple application is created that consists of a music notation editor and a push button. The music notation editor is used to input the solution. The push button is there for the students to request the software to evaluate the given solution when the student feels he or she is ready. The comments and corrections are rendered directly as a part of the music notation making it easy to relate the textual instructions with the relevant parts of the solution. Furthermore, in the lower left corner of the window a short description of the assignment is given. Here, the student can be made aware of any specific requirements or just be given some general tips on how to approach the present assignment. Above the documentation area all the different components of the study material are listed. In this example we only have one exercise but there is practically no limit as to the complexity or size of the material, be it a set of exercises or a complete year long course with multiple learning modules.

5 Conclusions

In this paper we give an overview of the potential of PWGL in the framework of computer assisted music pedagogy. PWGL already exhibits several interesting features that would make it ideal for different kinds of pedagogical applications ranging from elementary music tuition to advanced studies in composing, music theory and acoustics.

Our work dealing with music pedagogical applications of PWGL is still in its infancy. However, it is already evident that our system could prove to be a powerful system for the professional educators and students. It offers superior music notation, compositional and analytical tools, visualization devices, programmable sound, and extensibility. The level of completion of these tools and the dynamism and visual sophistication offered by PWGL is still very rare in computer applications dealing with music pedagogy.

Acknowledgments

The work of Mika Kuuskankare and Mikael Laurson has been supported by the Academy of Finland (SA 114116 and SA 122815).

References

1. Assayag, G., Rueda, C., Laurson, M., Agon, C., Delerue, O.: Computer Assisted Composition at IRCAM: From PatchWork to OpenMusic. Computer Music Journal 23(3), 59–72 (Fall 1999)
2. Dannenberg, R.B., Sanchez, M., Joseph, A., Capell, P., Joseph, R., Saul, R.: A computer-based multi-media tutor for beginning piano students. Journal of New Music Research 19, 155–173 (1990)
3. Fux, J.J.: Gradus ad Parnassum (1725)
4. Kuuskankare, M., Laurson, M.: Expressive Notation Package. Computer Music Journal 30(4), 67–79 (2006)
5. Kuuskankare, M., Laurson, M.: Survey of music analysis and visualization tools in PWGL. In: Proceedings of International Computer Music Conference, pp. 372–375 (2008)
6. Laurson, M., Kuuskankare, M.: PWGL Editors: 2D-Editor as a Case Study. In: Sound and Music Computing 2004, Paris, France (2004)
7. Laurson, M., Kuuskankare, M.: Extensible Constraint Syntax Through Score Accessors. In: Journées d'Informatique Musicale, Paris, France, pp. 27–32 (2005)
8. Laurson, M., Kuuskankare, M., Kuitunen, K.: The Visualisation of Computer-assisted Music Analysis Information in PWGL. Journal of New Music Research 37(1), 61–76 (2008)
9. Laurson, M., Kuuskankare, M., Norilo, V.: An Overview of PWGL, a Visual Programming Environment for Music. Computer Music Journal 33(1), 19–31 (2009)
10. Laurson, M., Norilo, V., Kuuskankare, M.: PWGLSynth: A Visual Synthesis Language for Virtual Instrument Design and Control. Computer Music Journal 29(3), 29–41 (Fall 2005)
11. Norilo, V., Laurson, M.: Audio analysis in PWGLSynth. In: Proceedings of Dafx 2008 Conference, Espoo, Finland, pp. 47–50 (2008)
12. Ong, B., Ng, K., Mitolo, N., Nesi, P.: i-maestro: Interactive multimedia environments for music education. In: i-Maestro 2nd Workshop on Technology Enhanced Music Education. ICSRiM - University of Leeds (2006)
13. Percival, G., Anders, T., Tzanetakis, G.: Generating Targeted Rhythmic Exercises for Music Students with Constraint Satisfaction Programming. In: Proceedings of the 2008 International Computer Music Conference, August 24-29. International Computer Music Association, Belfast (2008)
14. Raptis, S., Askenfelt, A., Fober, D., Chalamandaris, A., Schoonderwaldt, E., Letz, S., Baxevanis, A., Hansen, K.F., Orlarey, Y.: IMUTUS – an effective practicing environment for music tuition. In: Proceedings of International Computer Music Conference, pp. 383–386 (2005)
15. Tambouratzis, G., Perifanos, K., Voulgari, I., Askenfelt, A., Granqvist, S., Hansen, K.F., Orlarey, Y., Fober, D., Letz, S.: VEMUS: An integrated platform to support music tuition tasks. In: ICALT 2008: Proceedings of the 2008 Eighth IEEE International Conference on Advanced Learning Technologies, pp. 972–976. IEEE Computer Society, Washington (2008)
16. Taube, H.: Common Music: A music composition language in Common Lisp and CLOS. Computer Music Journal 15(2), 21–32 (Summer 1991)
17. Yin, J., Wang, Y., Hsu, D.: Digital violin tutor: an integrated system for beginning violin learners. In: MULTIMEDIA 2005: Proceedings of the 13th annual ACM international conference on Multimedia, pp. 976–985. ACM, New York (2005)

Vicarious Learning from Tutorial Dialogue

John Lee

Human Communication Research Centre and
School of Arts, Culture and Environment
University of Edinburgh, UK
J.Lee@ed.ac.uk

Abstract. Vicarious Learning is learning from watching others learn. We believe that this is a powerful model for computer-based learning. Learning episodes can be captured and replayed to later learners: a natural context for this is learning embedded in dialogue. This paper briefly surveys aspects of the theoretical basis of how learning may work in these contexts, and what is needed for a deeper appreciation of the mechanisms involved. A project that applies these ideas is also discussed, in which vicarious learning from tutorial group dialogue supports an online learning community that creates new learning materials as a group activity. We postulate that the resulting combination of shared activity with broader perspectives holds strong promise for online vicarious learning.

1 Introduction

The objective of this paper is to address the potential for online learning communities to exploit vicarious learning (VL), focussing on dialogue in learning. We work to understand how dialogue can facilitate VL, and develop a discussion of factors that may condition the effectiveness of such learning. A key question we address here is whether we can coherently picture the vicarious learner as a "vicarious participant" in dialogue, and how we can facilitate such participation through the appropriate use of technology.

2 Vicarious Learning and Dialogue

The idea of learning vicariously — through the experience of others — was introduced by Albert Bandura (e.g. 1986). It arises in situations where a learning experience is witnessed, *and reacted to as a learning experience*, by another learner. Because of this emphasis, vicarious learning is distinct from observational learning that arises from exposure to expert performance. A common example is the master class, where well-known teachers work with individual students in front of an audience of others, to the benefit of all. Such processes can be mediated by using communications technology to capture experiences for access by other learners at a later time (Lee 2005).

The learning process needs to be articulated and externalised if it is to be available to other learners. Dialogue with a tutor or peer learner naturally externalises learning processes, as the participants elicit explanation and clarification from each other. The centrality of dialogue in learning is also argued by Laurillard (1993) to be distinctive of higher education. VL postulates that it's possible to learn important aspects of the language, as well as the conceptual content, of a discipline through exposure to other people learning it and using it in learning. Though it is important at some stage to engage directly in dialogue and become an active user of the language, it seems clear that there is a substantial role for VL in the above sense.

Relatedly, Donald Schön (1985) claims that many professions are rooted in practice and "reflection in action", arguing that learning must be through practice, but also through dialogue with expert practitioners, who induct the learner into the forms of discourse (and hence reflection) characteristic of the profession. The design "crit" is a prototypical case of VL occurring through and around the central role of tutorial dialogue in learning.

The learner of the language of a discipline is entering a community of expert practice (cf. Wenger, 1998), also as one of a community of other learners sharing in the process. Such a community promotes a certain empathy or mutual understanding between its members, of a kind hypothesised (Cox et al., 1999) to be especially important in supporting VL. As we argue further below, empathy is perhaps at root what allows VL to work, counter to constructivist intuitions that "real" participation is indispensable for situated learning.

Hence we propose that episodes of learning mediated by dialogue can be captured and made available for the benefit of later learners. This raises issues such as: how effective dialogues can be facilitated, captured, stored and re-used, integrated into other practices, targeted to a new problem, understood by other learners — all these remain topics for research. Later we discuss two experimental approaches to putting re-use into practice.

3 Vicarious Participation in Dialogue

Students presented with VL materials are in the position of "overhearers" with respect to the original dialogue. Although Schober and Clark (1988) argue that overhearers are inevitably much impoverished in their understanding of a dialogue, Lee et al. (1998b) suggest that a closer examination shows the overhearers to have been actually rather successful in understanding dialogues, especially if able to observe them from the start.

We propose that there can be, in effect, "vicarious participation" in dialogue, such that the overhearer is able to get some of the effect of direct participation (cf. also Lee, 2005). This will depend, evidently, on the overhearer sharing significant aspects of the "common ground" shared by the participants. Schober and Clark argue that this common ground is collaboratively constructed, but clearly the construction is helped by the fact that their participants already share a great deal: the same language and the same general cultural background, etc. Similar overhearers will have a similar head start. Again, a form of empathy between participants and overhearers drives vicarious participation, so that e.g. students are likely to share more with other students than with tutors (cf. Cox et al., 1999).

3.1 Perspectives and Activity

Fox Tree and Mayer (2008) offer a somewhat related analysis, showing that overhearers pick up more when there are more "perspectives" involved in the dialogue, and arguing that this is partly why dialogue may be more effective than monologue for VL. Presumably the recognition and "uptake" of the perspectives also implies a degree of attunement between the overhearers and the original participants. This idea has a broader, perhaps more metaphorical, extension to many ways in which people's conceptualisations of a situation may relate, with potentially wide application, especially to areas such as learning (e.g. Greeno and MacWhinney, 2006). It then appears natural that one should be able to share the perspective of someone in an overheard conversation.

A key insight in the view of Schober and Clark (if by no means unique to them), is the essentially constructivist idea that activity is important in creating informational states, and that somehow this activity itself needs to be shared if effective alignment is to be achieved. The key focus of the activity in these dialogues, exchanging and sharing information and abstracting it further, is on the cognitive level of the activity. We suggest that the overhearer can engage at this level much more on a par with the direct participants and can identify with a participant closely enough to go through a very similar constructive process during the dialogue, arriving at a state almost as effectively aligned. As usual, this will only work to the extent that it is a socially grounded process.

Chi et al. (2008) introduce the "active/constructive/interactive observing hypothesis", in which learning is dependent on the degree of active engagement of the learner. They show that vicarious learning done collaboratively by pairs of vicarious learners increases engagement, compared with lone vicarious learners, producing improved learning that rivals direct tutoring. The collaborative interaction develops a constructive activity based on that of the original learner — perhaps this either strengthens "vicarious participation" (in the original learner's activity), or supplements it with a direct participation (in the observing dyad's activity) that is stimulated by the original material. Chi et al. argue that active interaction is the critical factor in learning, and that the lone vicarious learner is disadvantaged relative to the pair. A little tangential to our question concerning how vicarious learners pick up on the learning of the original learner, Chi et al.'s hypothesis does not seem to imply that vicarious uptake is in itself improved, perhaps rather that it is better exploited; but it's also possible that the observers' engagement with each other enhances their empathic engagement with the original learner. Closer analysis of alignment might help distinguish these possibilities. We propose to construe a more extended learning community that fosters, strengthens or builds on vicarious learning as an extension of the vicariously learning dyad: an opportunity for language and perhaps conceptualisations to be shared. In all such cases, empathy and social grounding seem inevitably important facilitating conditions of the relation to the original learner.

4 Approaches to Vicarious Learning Technology

There are various possible models of how vicarious learning can be put into practice. One approach is to offer specific materials as assistance to learners in situations that are identified as similar. This capitalises on a presumably maximal engagement between the learner and the original dialogue, but is expensive and complex to implement. An alternative is to put the learner in charge of identifying appropriate materials, and develop a learning community around this activity. We discuss here examples of these approaches.

In a concluded project (http://www.vicarious.ac.uk/), we investigated the use of VL in the education of speech and language therapists. An existing learning system, PATSy, provided a set of "virtual patients", including video interviews, case histories, test results, etc., which students studied as an aid to developing skills in diagnosis. Since it is often not easy to find natural situations where good learning dialogues occur frequently (Lee et al. 1998a), we adopted a methodology of using "Task-Directed Discussions" as a stimulus to dialogue, and developed a range of these for use in the PATSy situation. We built an extension to PATSy that detected points of possible intervention and then offered appropriate VL materials to assist the student, based on a theoretical characterisation of the reasoning process (Cox et al., 2005; Cox and Pang, 2007).

This approach was quite effective overall, but clearly very expensive to develop for any given domain. The second approach requires close attention to how we might exploit naturally occurring dialogues. Aside from the problem that good quality learning episodes may not occur all the time in natural learning situations, we in any case have no general way to identify such episodes, especially automatically, and especially for reuse in VL. There are many reasons for this, not least that the potential value of a dialogue to a vicarious learner is often dependent on that particular learner. Allowing the learners to identify the dialogues that they themselves find useful appears natural, but to achieve this we need to develop a means of engaging them with the material enough that they will locate and annotate the useful segments in stretches of otherwise less interesting dialogue.

We are investigating this second approach in an ongoing development we call *YouTute*. We collect naturally occurring tutorial dialogues as unedited video. Three streams are collected per tutorial (two from cameras, one from a "Smartboard"). These are later played in synchrony via a web-based interface that allows students to review the material and "edit" it by identifying segments that are of interest. These segments ("tutes") can be named, tagged, annotated and shared with other students. Students are able to see texts of relevant lecture slides, and the questions being discussed in the tutorial. The system has been deployed on several courses, is well received by students and seems to have worked especially well as a revision aid (Rabold et al. 2008). Trials have been in relatively formal aspects of computer science, where tutorials are conveniently well structured. It has yet to be trialled in other, especially less formal, subject areas such as design or the humanities. A screenshot of the system in use appears overleaf in Figure 1.

There are many differences from the VL-PATSy case, especially that the process of editing the videos and selecting "good" dialogues, which has become the responsibility of the students, has also become a shared activity. It is a form of "social networking", through which a community of students can emerge as learners who collaborate to create a new learning resource. This shared activity is also itself a learning activity, promoting reflection on the topics discussed, and re-evaluation of the original tutorial discussion. *YouTute*, we hope, allows us to enjoy many of the benefits identified by Chi et al. (2008) in the collaboration between vicarious learners. It remains to be established clearly that collaboration through an online social learning network is directly analogous to face-to-face discussion, but important elements seem to be shared. There is the added twist that our original material is not simply dialogue between a pair, but is a multi-party interaction that may involve six to eight participants. We hypothesise that greater interactivity of this kind promotes articulation and externalisation. In particular, it probably increases significantly the number of perspectives taken on the learning topic, which as we have noted is argued by Fox Tree and Mayer (2008) to be especially valuable to vicarious learners. They define "perspectives" (not necessarily in the same way as others) as the different descriptions people use for similar things, and show that dialogue promotes more perspectives than monologue. It seems clear that in a multi-party dialogue there are likely to be even more different descriptions than in the two-party situations considered by Fox Tree and Mayer. Demonstrating that this is so, and that it produces measurable effects for vicarious learners, remains work for the future, but we are optimistic.

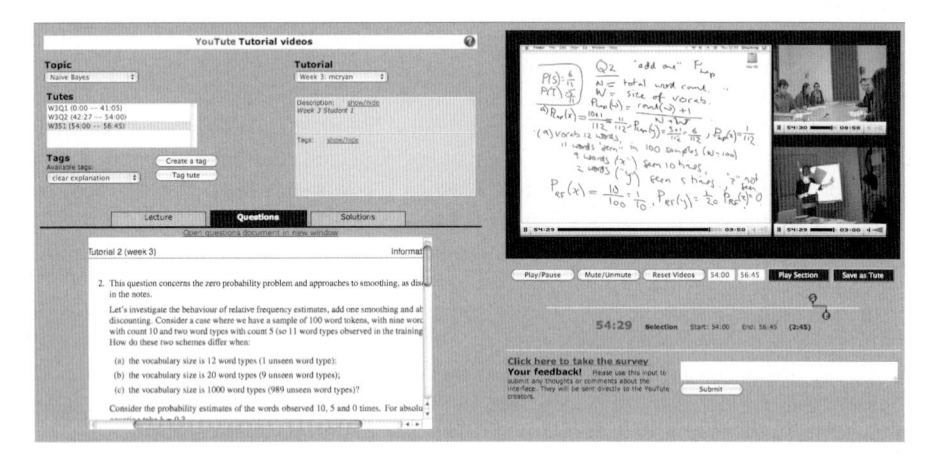

Fig. 1. *YouTute* interface

5 Conclusion

In conclusion, we suggest that we have shown good reason why vicarious learning should be expected to be a successful approach in general. We have developed aspects of the underlying theory of alignment and social grounding to underpin this claim. We have discussed two approaches to implementing it in learning technology, and propose that our *YouTute* system promises to exploit it most effectively by deploying notions of social learning, shared activity, and multiple perspectives. If we can thus combine the benefits of learners collaborating to develop a shared activity, with those of learners deriving broader cognitive stimulation from a wider range of perspectives in the material to which they are exposed, then we should see significant gains in the power and potential of vicarious learning.

Acknowledgements

The author is indebted to many collaborators for discussions of these issues over a long period. Projects were supported by the UK ESRC, and by the University of Edinburgh.

References

1. Bandura, A.: Social Foundations of Thought and Action: a social cognitive theory. Prentice Hall, Englewood Cliffs (1986)
2. Chi, M.T.H., Roy, M., Hausmann, R.G.M.: Observing Tutorial Dialogues Collaboratively: insights about human tutoring effectiveness from vicarious learning. Cognitive Science 32(2), 301–341 (2008)
3. Cox, R., McKendree, J., Tobin, R., Lee, J., Mayes, T.: Vicarious learning from dialogue and discourse: A controlled comparison. Instructional Science 27, 431–458 (1999)
4. Cox, R., Hoben, K., Howarth, B., Lee, J., Morris, J., Pang, J., Rabold, S., Varley, R.: Clinical reasoning skill acquisition: identifying learning issues and developing vicarious learning resources. In: TLRP conference, University of Warwick (2005)
5. Cox, R., Pang, J.: VL-PATSy: facilitating vicarious learning through intelligent resource provision. In: 2007 conf. on AI in Education. IOS, Amsterdam (2007)
6. Fox Tree, J.E., Mayer, S.A.: Overhearing Single and Multiple Perspectives. Discourse Processes 45, 160–179 (2008)
7. Greeno, J.G., MacWhinney, B.: Learning as Perspective Taking: Conceptual Alignment in the Classroom. In: 7th International Conference of the Learning Sciences (ICLS), Bloomington, Indiana, June 27 - July 1 (2006) (poster)
8. Laurillard, D.: Rethinking University teaching: a framework for the effective use of educational technology. Routledge, London (1993)
9. Lee, J., Dineen, F., McKendree, J.: Supporting student discussions: it isn't just talk. Education and Information Technology 3, 217–229 (1998)
10. Lee, J., McKendree, J., Dineen, F., Cox, R.: Vicarious learning: dialogue and multimodality. In: Bunt, H., et al. (eds.) Second International Conference on Cooperative Multimodal Communication, Tilburg, NL, pp. 177–180 (January 1998) (Poster abstract), http://mac-john.cogsci.ed.ac.uk/CMC98.html
11. Lee, J.: Vicarious Learning. In: Howard, C., et al. (eds.) Encyclopedia of Distance Learning. Idea Group, USA (2005)
12. Rabold, S., Anderson, S., Lee, J., Mayo, N.: YouTute: Online Social Networking for Vicarious Learning. In: ICL 2008, Villach, Austria, September 24-26 (2008)
13. Schober, M.F., Clark, H.H.: Understanding by addressees and overhearers. Cognitive Psychology 21, 211–232 (1989)
14. Schön, D.: Educating the reflective practitioner. Jossey-Bass, San Francisco (1985)
15. Wenger, E.: Communities of practice. Cambridge Univ. Press, New York (1998)

Computer-Supported Argumentation Learning: A Survey of Teachers, Researchers, and System Developers

Frank Loll[1], Oliver Scheuer[2], Bruce M. McLaren[2], and Niels Pinkwart[1]

[1] Clausthal University of Technology, Department of Informatics
{frank.loll,niels.pinkwart}@tu-clausthal.de
[2] German Research Center for Artificial Intelligence (DFKI)
{oliver.scheuer,bmclaren}@dfki.de

Abstract. Argumentation is omnipresent in our lives and therefore an important skill to learn. While classic face-to-face argumentation and debate has advantages in helping people learn to argue better, it does not scale up, limited by teacher time and availability. Computer-supported argumentation (CSA) is a viable alternative in learning to argue, currently increasing in popularity. In this paper, we present results from a survey we conducted with experts on argumentation learning systems, one which provides a glimpse on future directions.

Keywords: Argumentation, Survey, CSCL.

1 Introduction

Argumentation is omnipresent in our lives. Nevertheless, people often struggle to engage in reasoned arguments [1], making the acquisition of argumentation skills an important educational goal. Traditional face-to-face teaching methods are limited by teacher time and availability. To remedy these limitations, researchers have developed computer-based systems to facilitate the acquisition of argumentation skills.

In a detailed review of over 50 argumentation systems and methods, we surveyed the current state of the art for educational argumentation tools [2]. In addition, to better understand the decisions that have influenced the design of such systems, and to inquire into the most promising current developments and future trends, we recently conducted a web-based survey among argumentation teachers, researchers and system developers. The survey comprised four parts. First, participants were informed about the purpose of the survey, the use of the data and whether they wanted to receive the anonymized results once the analysis was completed. Second, the participants were asked about their professional background in the area of argumentation. All participants with a high degree of self-reported experience in at least one area of research, teaching and designing/developing of argumentation systems were, in the third part, asked specific multiple-choice questions about the research questions listed in section 2 below. Finally, the participants were prompted for free-text responses to open-ended questions.

The survey participants are experts in argumentation (research, teaching and developing technology). To select these experts, we collected a list of about 40 persons who we knew to have expertise through our research on the above-mentioned review article [2]. In a second step, we systematically searched through the author lists of relevant conferences (ITS, AIED, CSCL) and journals (ijCSCL) and carried out an exploratory Google search, checking home pages and publications lists, resulting in an extended list of 153 experts. We then invited the experts via e-mail to take part in the web-based survey. Participation in the survey was voluntary. As motivation we raffled an Apple iPod among all participants. In total, we received 97 responses in the (approximately) two months the questionnaire was online.

In [3] we discuss the quantitative findings of this survey. Here, we enrich these results with an analysis of the participants' free text responses.

2 Research Questions

In the survey, we were interested in the following research questions (RQ):

(1) Are visual argument representations helpful for learning and/or understanding argumentation?
(2) Can computer-supported / computer-mediated argumentation replace face-to-face argumentation?
(3) Does the formality of a domain influence the type of collaboration that is appropriate?
(4) Do argumentation researchers, teachers and system developers differ in their views on the suitability of collaboration for argument learning?
(5) Is it possible to develop automated analysis features that can effectively analyze arguments?
(6) Are there domain-specific differences that influence the suitability of automated analyses?
(7) How and when is tutorial feedback most effectively provided?

3 Results and Discussion

Our discussion is structured along three major themes, which map to the above research questions as follows: visual representation of arguments (1), individual vs. collaborative argumentation (2-4), and analysis and feedback (5-7).

3.1 Category 1: Visual Representation of Arguments

Overall, in the quantitative questions, there was a strong agreement across different domains (e.g., the law, science), that visual representations of arguments help people to gain an understanding of the topic of the argumentation (RQ 1) [3]. We asked the survey question "*Imagine that you have a software tool with graphical components representing different plausible argument moves that users can choose from. They might be able to choose from components such as claim, fact, or rebuttal and then fill in the selected shapes with text specific to their idea. Do you think such an approach would help or hinder users as they construct arguments and why?*" The positive responses to the question included reasons such as:

- Graphical representations help organize one's thoughts (e.g., *"it can facilitate the overall process in many ways, such as ... in maintaining focus on the overall process... maintaining consistency and in increasing plausibility and accuracy"*)
- They serve as an external memory aid
- They are a good support for collaborative activities
- Visually represented arguments prevent biases (e.g., *"students (...) cognitive biases prevent them from making good arguments. Diagrams can help overcome these limitations by (...) converting a memory-based cognitive operation into a more formal visual operation"*)

On the other hand, some respondents also argued against visually represented argument structures:

- Visual representations have limited expressiveness (e.g., *"research shows they feel too constricted by such systems."*)
- Visualizing arguments is artificial and only applicable to simple arguments
- Visualization may get in the way (e.g., *"experienced learners may be hindered to apply their advanced strategies"*)
- Additional visual representations may increase cognitive load

3.2 Category 2: Individual vs. Collaborative Argumentation

As our prior review revealed, one of the key differences between existing argumentation systems is the support for collaboration. In our survey, most experts agreed on the role of computers to support groups of people in conducting useful, valid arguments. However, the agreement dropped when the experts were asked if computers could *replace* face-to-face argumentation among learners (RQ 2). In addition, there was a noteworthy correlation between the formality of arguments and the role of individual learning among experts in educational argumentation (RQ 3).

In a free-text question, we asked *"Can you describe the typical process and roles that are used in arguments (or debates between parties) in your primary domain of interest?"* Here, the responses indicated that most arguments are multi-party and that argument processes are complex, involving multiple phases (e.g., preparation, engagement with clarifications, countering arguments, solution suggestions, decisions and modifications). Also, a variety of group learning modes were suggested, including:

- One participant taking a position and defending it against the others (e.g., *"students are asked to take a position regarding the controversy, to support their positions with reasons."*)
- Rotating roles
- Criticizing and modifying positions in groups
- Formation of different parties with different perspectives on the argument (e.g., *"there would be a whole-class discussion where students present both sides of the debate."*)

The survey also included a question asking *"What kinds of problems occur most frequently when your students practice argumentation collaboratively with one another?*

(As opposed to composing arguments on their own)?" Here, responses varied. Some key problems repeatedly mentioned were:

- Students biased towards their own viewpoint (e.g., *"they tend to argue by supporting their own standpoint/claim without reflecting on the connection between their standpoint/claim and the opponent's one"*)
- Agreement or disagreement problems, in particular, students agreeing too easily (e.g., *"Typically, I see students who tend to agree with one another and hesitate to disagree with someone's point of view."*)
- Student having trouble with collaborative argumentation due to a lack of argumentation skills

3.3 Category 3: Feedback Techniques

Imbuing argumentation systems with automated tutoring and feedback functionality holds promise to increase learning by adapting to individuals, groups, processes and situations. An important prerequisite for providing tutorial feedback is the ability to analyze and understand students' arguments to a sufficient extent, i.e. to identify weaknesses and to assess the quality of students' arguments in order to inform appropriate feedback. Due to the open-textured nature of arguments the development of effective analysis mechanisms is non-trivial, however. In the survey, we asked the question *"In your primary domain of interest, what are the most common mistakes made by students (or typical misconceptions) in formulating arguments on their own (i.e., individually)?"* Here, the responses show two main areas: arguments that are weak in form and structure, and problems with evidence. Related to the first area, the respondents' comments included remarks concerning

- Student's argument logic being weak overall (e.g., *"so they listed several possible arguments without real explanations or they preferred to focus on one argument only and try to articulate different aspects of this unique argument, they lacked in this case coordinating several arguments on a same topic to answer a controversial question."*)
- Student's failure to see overall, recurring patterns in arguments
- Problems with argument structures (e.g., *"Misconception of node/link ontology"*)

Related to the second area (evidence), the main problems of students (as reported on by our respondents) were

- Not recognizing the difference between evidence and claims (e.g., *"A lot of students can't distinguish between claim and argument."*)
- Not providing (enough) supporting evidence
- Not recognizing important evidence (e.g., *"Students rely too much on intuition and they work to defend their current beliefs, despite evidence and arguments to the contrary."*)
- Accepting false evidence

To what extent is the development of effective analysis mechanisms feasible (RQ 5)? Our experts showed a tendency to believe in the existence of general and recurring patterns that indicate errors and weaknesses in their domain of interest, a tendency that increases with the amount of teaching experience [3]. This finding is not surprising because it is part of a teacher's job to identify such patterns of errors and weaknesses. There was less confidence in the feasibility of defining sets of rules to *automatically* identify these patterns, and even less confidence in the feasibility of automated assessment of argument *quality*. The difficulties inherent in assessments of arguments are also clear from current and past argumentation learning systems: Tutorial support is often based on explicitly structured argument representations (e.g., argument graphs in Belvedere [4] and LARGO [5]) rather than on the more difficult task of assessing textual content. An important variable that might bear on the feasibility of automated analysis is the specific domain of interest, e.g., more formal domains might be easier to analyze due to their explicit elements and structure (RQ 6). This assumption, however, was not confirmed. Only one (statistically non-significant) tendency was identified with respect to pattern-based quality assessment. Experts from the legal domain exhibited the most skeptical stance. Interestingly, legal experts also assessed their knowledge in artificial intelligence techniques significantly higher than experts in other domains, i.e. they might have been the most aware of the difficulties of an automated quality assessment.

Another important question is when and how to react to students' errors and misconceptions (RQ 7). Obviously, the answer to the question how to react depends strongly on the specific domain, student knowledge level, and instructional goals. In the survey, we asked *"What general types of feedback do you (or would you) give to students when they make oral or written arguments in your primary domain of interest?"* Here, the answers indicate a wide spectrum of possible teacher interventions, including

- *"asking questions."*
- *"I would also ask student to consider the best arguments supporting alternative views."*
- *"I try to give them feedback that reinforces the idea that there are general principles of argument that they must strive to respect."*
- *"Individually, then, we provide careful correction of each student's analysis."*
- *"the feedback given to students is ... 'expert/human' when a learning partner reflects upon the arguments."*
- *"I might use one or more of the models of argument to draw their attention to elements that are missing or poorly connected."*
- *"Most of the feedback would be in the forms of challenges e.g ... how might somebody argue against you?"*

4 Conclusion

In this paper, we summarized the results of data collected as part of a web-based survey among experts from argumentation research, argumentation teaching and argumentation system development, particularly focusing on examples from free-text questions (cf. [3] for the quantitative data analysis). There was considerable agreement that argumentation systems are able to facilitate learning via argument visualization techniques; on the other hand, some respondents argued against graphical argument visualization. In addition, the experts agreed that computers have proven their suitability in promoting collaborative learning of argumentation. Yet, some dangers and risks of CSCL practices for argumentation learning were also mentioned, such as that students tend to agree too easily and thus not learn much. A still open issue is the future and application potential of computer-based analysis and feedback on argumentation. Here, many respondents see great potential; on the other hand, there was no agreed-upon "ideal" form of (even human) argument analysis and feedback. This points to the clear challenges that face those working on automated, computer based analysis and feedback.

Acknowledgments

We thank all respondents and pilot testers of the questionnaire. This work was supported by the German Research Foundation (DFG) under the grant "LASAD".

References

1. Kuhn, D.: The skills of argument. Cambridge University Press, Cambridge (1991)
2. Scheuer, O., Loll, F., Pinkwart, N., McLaren, B.M.: Computer-Supported Argumentation: A review of the state of the art. International Journal of Computer-Supported Collaborative Learning 5(1), 43–102 (2010)
3. Loll, F., Scheuer, O., McLaren, B.M., Pinkwart, N.: Learning to Argue Using Computers – A View from Teachers, Researchers, and System Developers. In: Aleven, V., Kay, J., Mostow, J. (eds.) ITS 2010, Part II. LNCS, vol. 6095, pp. 377–379. Springer, Heidelberg (2010)
4. Suthers, D.D., Connelly, J., Lesgold, A., Paolucci, M., Toth, E.E., Toth, J., Weiner, A.: Representational and advisory guidance for students learning scientific inquiry. In: Forbus, K.D., Feltovich, P.J. (eds.) Smart machines in education: The coming revolution in educational technology, pp. 7–35 (2001)
5. Pinkwart, N., Aleven, V., Ashley, K., Lynch, C.: Toward legal argument instruction with graph grammars and collaborative filtering techniques. In: Ikeda, M., Ashley, K.D., Chan, T.-W. (eds.) ITS 2006. LNCS, vol. 4053, pp. 227–236. Springer, Heidelberg (2006)

End-User Visual Design of Web-Based Interactive Applications Making Use of Geographical Information: The WINDMash Approach

The Nhan Luong, Patrick Etcheverry, Thierry Nodenot,
Christophe Marquesuzaà, and Philippe Lopistéguy

IUT de Bayonne - Pays Basque, LIUPPA-T2I, 2 Allée du Parc Montaury
64600 Anglet, France
{thenhan.luong,patrick.etcheverry,thierry.nodenot,
christophe.marquesuzaa,
philippe.lopisteguy}@iutbayonne.univ-pau.fr

Abstract. Visual instructional design languages currently provide notations for representing the intermediate and final results of a knowledge engineering process. This paper reports on a visual framework (called WIND - Web INteraction Design) that focuses on both designers' creativity and model executability. It only addresses Active Reading Learning Scenarios making use of localized documents (travel stories, travel guides). Our research challenge is to enable the teachers to design by themselves interaction scenarios for such a domain, avoiding any programmer intervention. The WIND framework provides a conceptual model and its associated Application Programming Interface (API). The WIND interaction scenarios are encoded as XML documents which are automatically transformed into code thanks to the provided API, thus providing designers with a real application that they can immediately assess and modify (prototyping techniques). The WIND conceptual model only provides designers with an abstract syntax and a semantics. Users of such a Domain Specific Language (DSL) need a concrete syntax. Our choice is to produce a Web-Based Mashup Environment providing designers with visual functionality.

Keywords: Interaction Design, Semantic Web, Applications of TEL in the Domain of Geography, Visual Instructional Design Languages, Technologies for Personalisation and Adaptation.

1 Introduction

Research works dedicated to Visual Instructional Design Languages (VIDL) are evolving rapidly. This article reports on our current research cycle which aims at promoting a visual language (called WIND) that focuses on both designers' creativity and model executability. The WIND language only addresses Active Reading Learning Scenarios. This specific pedagogical activity *"refers to set of high level reading, searching, problem solving and meta-cognitive skills used as readers pro-actively construct new knowledge"* [1], making use of localized documents (travel stories, travel guides) that embed a lot of geographical information about the movements of an actor within a territory. Our research challenge is to provide teachers (*user-designer*) with convenient instruments in order to design and to assess by themselves interaction scenarios for such a domain, avoiding any programmer intervention.

Our research team has developed for three years:

- a set of tools and software components for the automatic tagging of Geographical Information within textual documents. Such geographical information is composed of three complementary features: the spatial feature (SF), the temporal feature (TF) and the phenomenon feature [2]. The "spatial chain" produces an index where each SF is associated with one or more geometries. Similarly, the "temporal chain" associates TF to one or more temporal intervals and the "thematic chain" is based on well-known statistical criteria (terms frequency). Currently, two versions of such automatic chains are exploited: GeoStream [3] is a web service that can tag SF within textual documents, while πR [4] is another web service that can tag movement verbs and SF in order to find itineraries within specific textual documents (travel stories, travel guides).
- a set of tools and software components (text component, map component, calendar component) that can be parameterized and combined [5] with previous web services in order to author dedicated applications favouring active learning scenarios in relation with the discovery of a territory (see http://erozate.iutbayonne.univ-pau.fr/forbes2007/exp/ for an example). We set up two specific features of these educational applications compared with currently available web-based cartographic applications:
  1. The focus is on interaction and not on data visualization;
  2. The map is no longer the central component, neither is the text, nor the calendar: the user (learner) needs to interact from any of these components and the system should react on any of these components.

The experience gained about the production of such applications led us to initiate two complementary research actions focusing on empirical visual design approaches. The first one consists in developing a Mashup environment [6] enabling a pedagogue (teacher) to handle by him/herself the elicited modules to design and to assess his/her pedagogical application. He/She is thus able to retrieve/select travel stories or travel guides extracts, to imagine dedicated learning scenarios (how the learner may control the interaction with the application, which messages are provided to the learner) and to build the user interface (how it is organized and which interactions are available between the different parts of the interface). The second research action focuses on the design tasks required to enable a pedagogue describing how the system will diagnose the learner's behaviour while using such interactive application in order to solve a particular quiz or problem.

In this paper we shall focus on the first action but both actions should enable a teacher to easily formalize and to evaluate his/her educational ideas by using (as a learner) the automatically generated application. We therefore promote an agile design approach (evaluation step should therefore be used to check/criticize/confirm previous pedagogical choices) made possible thanks to "agile" design tools that should fully imply the end-user along the whole process by rapidly integrating his/her requirements into a technical solution.

In the next section, we present WINDMash, a web mashup environment that designers can use both to create and to assess interactive scenarios that handle geographical information. Last, discussion recalls WIND capabilities and our current works to improve the WIND framework usability.

2 WINDMash, an Environment Dedicated to the Authoring of Active Learning Scenarios for Territory Discovery

This section describes WINDMash, a mashup environment that designers can use both to create and to assess interactive scenarios that handle geographical information. WINDMash provides designers with an authoring and an execution framework that promote an agile approach to shorten as much as possible the delay between the design and the evaluation step of an interactive application. Such an approach is required now to favour end-user modelling. Let us consider a WIND application whose learning objective is to help the learners to discover prefecture around the cities that the user may highlight in the text area [1] :

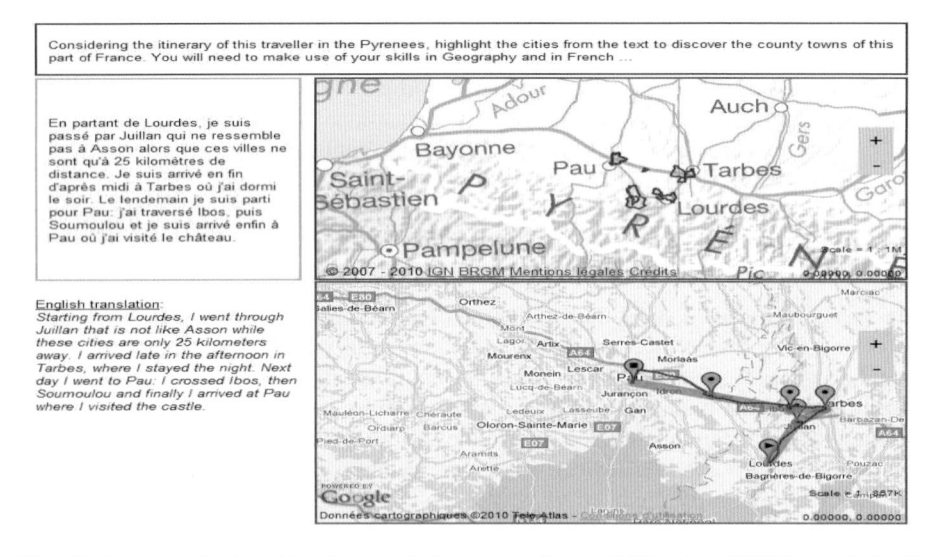

Fig. 1. An example (see http://erozate.iutbayonne.univ-pau.fr/Nhan/ectel2010/example.html) for educational purpose

We advocate that, using WINDMash, a designer (teacher) without any computer science skills can easily describe and assess such an interactive application. The instructional design process promotes three design facets (data, interface and interaction)

---

[1] Within the text, there are many words referring places, some of them are cities, others are not (e.g. the Adour river or the Ossau Valley). If the user highlights a city (e.g. the city of Lourdes), the map next zooms on the prefecture around such a city (e.g. the prefecture of Lourdes is Tarbes); in the other cases (rivers, valleys, mountains, etc.), a message is sent to the user.

in order to generate an educational web application from initially informal requirements.

2.1 The Data Facet

The data facet focuses on the information that will be provided to the learner at runtime. Starting from one or from several plain texts, the designer (teacher) may easily create a processing chain by selecting dedicated modules. This processing chain can automatically transform such input into results that can be either processed again or can be visualised with dedicated viewers: text, map, and calendar viewers (*cf.* Fig. 2). Available modules can be parameterized by the designer to reach a specific goal, enabling the designer:

- to normalize plain texts into the WIND format;
- to extract places, itineraries, etc;
- to intersect or to join previous results;
- to later visualize results with dedicated viewers to check the design process.

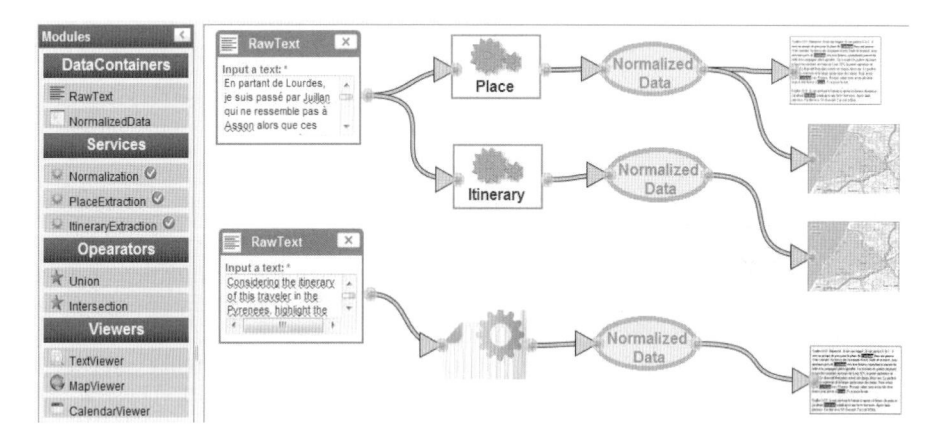

Fig. 2. Screenshot example for the data facet of the WINDMash environment

These modules are described in two ways: (1) as JSON format (see http://erozate.iutbayonne.univ-pau.fr/Nhan/windmash/modules.js) to facilitate the implementation of the environment; (2) as description texts (comprehensible by the designers) when the designers hold mouse over the modules.

2.2 The Interface Facet

The interface facet enables the designers to organize the interface of the generated application (size, position, map provider, zoom level...). The Viewers from the previous facet are concerned here. An interface containing all the Viewers is automatically generated and displayed to the designer, enabling him/her easily and rapidly define the look and feel of each Viewer. Each Viewer displays the information from the data facet and the designer may then decide where each Viewer should be presented on the screen by clicking on its header and by dragging onto a new position;

he/she can also easily resize it. Each `Viewer` has also specified characteristics. For example:

- For a `TextViewer`, the geographical words (`TextPart`) are automatically tagged by the Service modules of the data facet.
- For a `MapViewer`, the `MapParts` are automatically marked as geometries on the map layer. A point represents a location, a place; a line represents a route, a river, an itinerary; a polygon represents a region, a city, etc.
- For a `CalendarViewer`, the concerned time (`CalendarPart`)may be tagged and displayed.

2.3 The Interaction Facet

This facet allows the designer (teacher) to design the interactions between the viewers displayed in the previous facet. Currently, by default, we automatically offer some interactions between the `TextViewer`, the `MapViewer`, and the `CalendarViewer`:

- when clicking on the `TextPart`, the corresponding `MapPart` is focused and the corresponding `CalendarPart` is highlighted;
- when clicking on the `MapPart`, the corresponding `TextPart` is boldfaced and the corresponding `CalendarPart` is highlighted;
- when clicking on the `CalendarPart`, the corresponding `TextPart` is boldfaced and the corresponding `MapPart` is focused.

3 Discussion and Future Directions

In this paper, we presented WINDMash, our Mashup environment that demonstrates current capabilities of the WIND framework and its API. This environment focuses on the design of geographical applications making use of specific localized documents called "travel stories". As soon as a step is completed, the designer can execute the code which is automatically generated thanks to the WIND API. Thus, at each step of the design process (data, interface and interaction facets), it is possible to immediately visualize the design results without having to know anything about the underlying Web Mapping Services (IGN Geoportail API, Google Maps API, OpenLayers API, etc.). Of course, if, at runtime, something appears to fail, it is very easy to modify what was specified at any design step.

WINDMash can automatically extract the geographical information (place extraction, itinerary extraction) contained in such textual documents: this is the WINDMash data facet. From such information (or any inferred information from this latter information and our geographical ontology), designers can describe the interface of the application composed of Map / Text / Calendar visual components: this is the WINDMash interface facet. Our ongoing works consist in the WINDMash interaction facet. We need to focus on a visual language to describe the interactions between the visual components.

The WINDMash (see http://erozate.iutbayonne.univ-pau.fr/Nhan/windmash/) environment is currently still work in progress, according to our advances about:

- Semantic web techniques particularly for the automatic annotation of geographical information embedded in texts.

- Formal and semi-formal techniques for Human Computer Interaction: extension of the UML sequence diagram formalism to exploit both the geographical semantics captured within texts and text/map/calendar viewers available functionality; delayed reactions of the application according to decisional state-diagrams descriptions.
- Experiments of the WINDMash toolset by both pedagogues and learners. From the beginning of these works, we cooperate with teachers of several classrooms and colleges to evaluate with their pupils [7] the educational potentiality of the microworlds that we can design with the WIND framework. Teachers also help us to go further in order to be able to embed these microworlds into educational activities described in terms of learning goals and cognitive tasks needed to solve a problem, tutor goals, ...

Acknowledgements

This research is supported by the French Aquitaine Region (project n°20071104037) and the Pyrénées-Atlantiques Department (*"Pyrénées : Itinéraires Educatifs"* project).

References

1. Murray, T.: Hyperbook Features Supporting Active Reading Skills. In: Ma, Z. (ed.) Web-based Intelligent e-Learning Systems: Technologies and Applications, ch. 8, pp. 156–174. Idea Group Publishing, Hershey (2005)
2. Gaio, M., et al.: A Global Process to Access Documents' Contents from a Geographical Point of View. Journal of Visual Languages and Computing (JVLC) 19(1), 3–23 (2008)
3. Sallaberry, C., et al.: GeoStream: a Spatial Information Indexing Web Service. In: First International Opensource Geospatial Research Symposium (OGRS 2009). Springer, Nantes (2009)
4. Loustau, P., Nodenot, T., Gaio, M.: Design principles and first educational experiments of PIIR, a platform to infer geo-referenced itineraries from travel stories. International Journal of Interactive Technology and Smart Education (ITSE) 6(1), 23–39 (2009)
5. Luong, T.N., et al.: WIND: an Interaction Lightweight Programming Model for Geographical Web Applications. In: First International Opensource Geospatial Research Symposium (OGRS 2009). Springer, Nantes (2009)
6. Taivalsaari, A.: MashWare: The Futur of Web Applications. Technical Report (2009)
7. Luong, T.N., et al.: A framework to author educational interactions for geographical web applications. In: Cress, U., Dimitrova, V., Specht, M. (eds.) EC-TEL 2009. LNCS, vol. 5794, pp. 769–775. Springer, Heidelberg (2009)

Supporting Reflection in an Immersive 3D Learning Environment Based on Role-Play

Nils Malzahn, Hanno Buhmes, Sabrina Ziebarth, and H. Ulrich Hoppe

Department of computer science and applied cognitive science, University of Duisburg-Essen,
Lotharstr. 63, 47057 Duisburg, Germany
{malzahn,buhmes,ziebarth,hoppe}@collide.info

Abstract. This paper presents a framework for creating and conducting serious games. It focuses on role-playing game based learning scenarios in 3D environments. The feasibility of the presented approach is demonstrated by a training scenario for apprenticeship job interviews. Based on the assumption that reflection phases as an important part of successful learning processes are to be adequately supported, we show how phases of immersion during the role-play are connected to separate phases of reflection.

Keywords: serious gaming, role plays, metacognition.

1 Introduction

Computer games are currently one of the computer science applications with the highest amount of users. The "serious gaming" approach tries to use the attraction (i.e. the fun factor) of such media not only for entertainment purposes but also to convey serious content at the same time. Application areas for serious gaming are (among others) education and training, health care, political opinion formation and probing (cf. [1]).

Although not directly built for gaming purposes, environments like Second Life[1], a 3D world for virtualized social interaction, allow for changes of identity and role changes. Educational institutions, such as the University of Edinburgh[2], have tried to position courses in the "parallel universe" of Second Life. Unsurprisingly, success stories about content delivery oriented learning applications are still missing, as there is no clear added value in comparison to classical learning management systems or even web-based training environments. Neither 3D environments nor identity changes are of comprehensible advantage for this scenario, whereas virtual role-plays have considerable advantages over real enactment [2;3], e.g. because space and time usage may be eased, and there are more co-actors available (e.g. chat-bots). Furthermore, analysis results based on dialogue contributions and user actions that are explicitly represented in the software system may be used for learner support. A structured transcript particularly supports finding interesting situations. Thus, it enables individual or group oriented (self-) reflection.

---

[1] http://www.secondlife.com
[2] http://vue.ed.ac.uk/

These advantages led us to the design and orchestration of a scenario in the area of job interviews for apprenticeships. Role-plays clearly have an added value in the preparation phase for a successful application. However, real life role-plays have a considerable coordination overhead and the evaluation of video recordings is time-consuming. Therefore, in our approach, the role-play takes place in a virtual 3D environment and the role of the interviewer is played by a software robot.

2 Learning Environment

The 3D environment is based on the open-source Second Life clone OpenSimulator[3] (OpenSim). The server is written in C# and allows the execution of in-world scripts written in C# as well as in "Linden Scripting Language" (LSL). LSL is an interpreter language similar to JavaScript. LSL scripts are used to log actions as well as dialogues and to control the general game flow by automatically generated interventions.

2.1 Building Blocks

The XML-based Artificial Intelligence Markup Language[4] (AIML) has been designed for modeling and specifying dialogs with Eliza-like [4] chat-bots such as A.L.I.C.E.[5]. Recent studies show that chat-bots provide feasible means to improve learning results [5]. Pure AIML is restricted to text input and output. However, in many scenarios it is helpful to support a dialogue by gestures. Especially for scenarios like our job interview, timing and execution of formal interaction procedures, such as shaking hands, taking a seat etc., are relevant for the practical success of a real interview. For this reason, gestures and dialogues should be modeled in conjunction. To achieve this, we extended the original AIML grammar with tags for gestures. These gestures can be used during the dialogue by typing well-known emoticons or pressing corresponding buttons in the client interface. Emoticons are used to avoid breaks in the dialogue. Gestures are implemented as corresponding animations of the avatars. We use the Meerkat[6] viewer to access the 3D environment.

The AIML dialogues are linked to the OpenSim environment via an OpenSim Bot ("Marvin"), which has originally been developed by Pixelpark AG[7]. Marvin receives messages in the 3D environment and interprets them either as action command or as AIML dialogue snippet. Dialogue texts are processed by a slightly extended AIML library that generates the corresponding answers based on the given AIML script. Short answer delays are inserted to create the illusion of a human agent talking to the learner. Marvin logs the conversation and its topics, which are retrieved from the AIML script. Topics bundle parts of the dialogue structure. To be able to recognize gestures that are not represented by emoticons, LSL scripts are used to observe the actions conducted by the learner. These action logs may be processed for various other analyses later on.

---

[3] http://www.opensimulator.org
[4] http://docs.aitools.org/aiml/spec
[5] http://alice.pandorabots.com/
[6] http://meerkatviewer.org
[7] http://www.pixelpark.com

The analysis and reflection of the role-play is conducted using a video recording. This video is directly grabbed from the client's frame buffer during the play. It is saved in a Matroska[8] container using the widespread XVID codec. The Matroska container allows the definition of subtitles and jump marks within the video. They are used during the reflection phase to navigate within the video and highlight interesting or important interactions within the role-play video (cf. Fig. 1). Of course, the sub titles may also be used for instructions and feedback in a self-learning scenario. Generally, every AIML topic will generate a jump mark (chapter) within in the video.

Fig. 1. Screenshot of the learning video reminding the learner to be honest with the interviewer concerning school marks, as school reports were sent with the application

2.2 Architecture

The content of the sub titles and other optional (hyperlink) documents supporting the reflection phase are automatically generated by an agent framework. Specialized agents are processing specific log entries (cf. Fig. 2) from different sources as mentioned above. Log entries, analysis results and feedback instructions are exchanged via SQLSpaces [6], which is an implementation of the TupleSpace concept. This concept is based on a blackboard architecture, which has often been successfully used for natural language processing (cf. [6]).

The SQLSpaces implementation offers clients for several programming languages (e.g. C#, Java, Prolog) and a generic web service, which e.g. allows access for LSL scripts. This diversity allows for the processing of the particular analysis problems (text analysis, gesture analysis, rule based feedback generation) and export capabilities in appropriate programming paradigms. Fig. 2 sketches a cutout of the blackboard during the role-play. Agents for gesture and text analysis read and process the data contained in the TupleSpace and write new tuples with analysis results into the TupleSpace. These are used by feedback agents to generate subtitles for the video and reports for tutors or learners.

---

[8] http://www.matroska.org

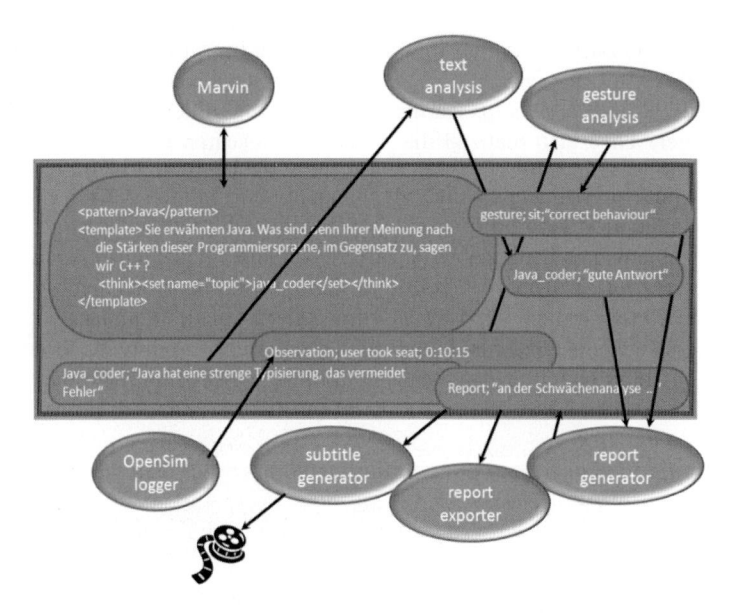

Fig. 2. Schematic overview of the TupleSpace based architecture with example data and agents

2.3 Analysis Agents

The agents work independently from each other in a data-driven process. Thus, only the available data determines the activity of the agents. This leads to a robust, flexible and adaptive framework. The analysis agents may be refined or replaced depending on domain and demand.

Since our current scenario - a job interview for apprenticeship - has many degrees of freedom concerning the possible answers of the interviewee, the answers are not evaluated with respect to their semantic correctness. It is too complex even if we would narrow down the domain, e.g. to IT-related jobs. Nonetheless, there are distinctive statements in every job interview, where the answer can be analyzed resulting into feedback consisting of general problem hints. The gesture analysis detects "missed opportunities" with respect to common rituals like greetings (handshakes, who is greeted by whom etc.). Thus, praise for correct behavior or recommendation for better performance may be shown. This is especially useful in self-learning scenarios.

3 Discussion

Many 3D based serious games try to incorporate the whole learning process within the immersive 3D environment (cf. [3;8;9;10]). Whereas we agree with Romana and Brna [3] that a "[…] careless choice in the development of a VE might defeat the learning objective […]", we disagree concerning the place for reflection. We think that an immersive situation is not well suited to support metacognitive activities and especially self-reflection in the learning process. It is plausible to assume that the strong binding of attention and reactive mindfulness connected to immersion hampers the establishment of role distance, which in turn supports self-reflection. Furthermore, the cognitive overload due to the non-trivial navigation inside of 3D environments (cf. [10]) adds to the encumbrance. In addition Roussos et al. [11] have observed that an additional 2D interfaces helps learners to sustain their interaction with the learning material longer. They also realized that tutors and researchers may participate more easily in the learning process and evaluate the performance better using the additional 2D interface.

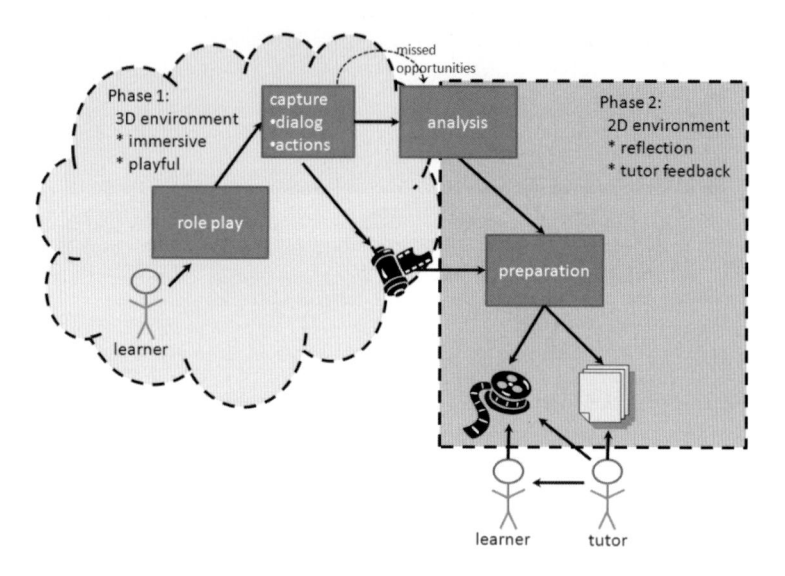

Fig. 3. Interaction of learners and tutors with the learning environment within different phases of learning

Based on these findings, we propose a change of the media setting between the gaming phase and the reflection phase. The reflection phase should take place in easier to use non immersive 2D environments like those offered by conventional desktop applications. Such an environment also offers easier access to other knowledge sources like web pages or documents in various formats and enables the exploration of multiple foci and strands. In a 2D environment with a human tutor at the learner's side, the learner may smoothly level up from Fitts [11] associative stage of learning (where the learners try to detect and smooth out errors) to the autonomous learning stage without permanent feedback by a human tutor.

Fig. 3 shows the proposed learning process and its phases in detail. The role-play takes place in the 3D environment. The reflection phase is supported with a video of the role-play from phase one. In scenarios with human tutors, the tutor may navigate to important anomalies either via the jump marks inside of the video or via hyperlinks from an overview document. This approach also allows for the repetitive replay of remarkable situations to stimulate and improve the reflection process. The video enables learner and tutor to manipulate time in a way that stimulates learning (see also [3]). Criteria for remarkable or interesting situations may either be manually searched in the transcript of the session (flexibility) or classified automatically by additional agents. Studies validating our approach are currently under development.

References

1. Zyda, M.: From visual simulation to virtual reality to games. IEEE Computer, 25–32 (2005)
2. Totty, M.: Better training through gaming. Wall Street Journal - Eastern Edition 245(80), R6-0 (2005)
3. Romano, D., Brna, P.: Presence and Reflection in Training: Support for Learning to Improve Quality Decision-Making Skills under Time Limitations. CyberPsychology & Behavior 4(2), 265–277 (2001)
4. Weizenbaum, J.: ELIZA—a computer program for the study of natural language communication between man and machine. Communications of the ACM 9(1), 36–45 (1966)
5. Kerly, A., Hall, P., Bull, S.: Bringing chatbots into education: Towards natural language negotiation of open learner models. Knowledge.-Based Systems 20(2) (2007)
6. Weinbrenner, S., Giemza, A., Hoppe, H.U.: Engineering heterogenous distributed learning environments using TupleSpaces as an architectural platform. In: Proceedings of the 7th IEEE International Conference on Advanced Learning Technologies (ICALT 2007). IEEE Computer Society, Los Alamitos (2007)
7. Erman, L., Lesser, V.R.: The HEARSAY-II speech understanding system: Integrating knowledge to resolve uncertainty. Computing Surveys 12, 213–253 (1980)
8. Backlund, P., Engström, H., Johannesson, M.: Computer Gaming and Driving Education. In: Procs. of the workshop Pedagogical Design of Educational Games affiliated to ICCE 2006 (2006)
9. Michael, D., Chen, S.: Serious games: Games that educate, train, and inform. Thomson Course Technology, Boston (2006)
10. Ojstersek, N.: Gestaltung und Betreuung virtueller Lernszenarien in Second Life. Selbstorganisiertes Lernen im Internet - Einblick in die Landschaft der webbasierten Bildungsinnovationen, Innsbruck, Wien, Bozen, pp. 296 – 300 (2008)
11. Roussos, M., Johnson, A., Leigh, M.T., Vasilakik, J., Barnes, C.: Learning and Building Together in an Immersive Virtual World. Presence 8(3), 247–263 (1999)
12. Fitts, P.M.: Perceptual-motor skill learning. In: Melton, A.W. (ed.) Category of human learning, pp. 243–285. Academic Press, New York (1964)

Facilitating Effective Exploratory Interaction: Design and Evaluation of Intelligent Support in MiGen

Manolis Mavrikis, Sergio Gutierrez-Santos, and Eirini Geraniou*

London Knowledge Lab
{m.mavrikis,sergut}@lkl.ac.uk, e.geraniou@ioe.ac.uk

Abstract. Ensuring that students' interactions with Exploratory Learning Environments are effective in terms of learning requires a significant pedagogic support from teachers. The challenge therefore is to develop intelligent systems which would be entrusted to support either the student directly when appropriate, or provide information to teachers, assisting them in their demanding role in the classroom. This paper presents the design of the tools that enable the provision of intelligent adaptive feedback in the context of eXpresser, an mathematical exploratory learning environment for 11–14 year old students. Additionally, the paper describes the metrics that are used to measure the progress in the development of the adaptive feedback interventions. These metrics provide a clear understanding of the relevance and coverage of the intelligent support provided by the system at every stage of its iterative development.

1 Introduction

Through an emphasis on learning by interaction, exploration and modelling, Exploratory Learning Environments (ELEs) have the potential to benefit teaching and learning. However, integrating ELEs in the classroom is far from a trivial process. A substantial body of research demonstrates that in order to ensure that students' interactions are effective in terms of learning, there is a need for significant pedagogic support [1,2]. However, in a classroom of 25-30 students, it is unrealistic to assume that teachers will always be able to act in accordance to their ideal role as facilitators [3].

We envisage therefore that some of the teachers' responsibilities could be usefully delegated to an intelligent system that would be entrusted to facilitate students interactions while maintaining the exploratory essence of ELEs. This does not involve intelligent support in the traditional sense where the computer typically plays the role of instructing students what is wrong and how to correct it. On the contrary, it is designed to support students throughout their interactions and aims to allow them to explore the ELE and, with the help of their teacher, develop their own solutions, reflect upon their interaction and learn. These requirements raise fundamentally different challenges than those addressed in the design of traditional intelligent tutoring systems (ITSs). Apart from the evident technical challenges, a set of these issues arise from the fact that educational theories in general and even domain-specific pedagogical strategies, particularly for ill-defined domains and tasks, are not always precise to the extent that they

---

* The authors would like to acknowledge the rest of the members of the MiGen project supported by ESRC/TLRP Grant RES-139-25-0381 (see http://www.migen.org).

can facilitate the implementation of computational support [4]. Despite the advances in the field, our understanding of how to design such systems is still limited and —as we discuss in detail in [5]— a mixture of theory and empiricism is needed that involves several cycles of development, revision, and empirical fine-tuning [4].

This paper presents the design of the tools that enable feedback provision in MiGen, a microworld-based learning environment designed to help 11–14 year old students to develop an appreciation of mathematical generalisation, which is considered one of the major routes to algebra in the UK curriculum. In addition we describe the metrics used during the formative evaluation phase to provide a measure of performance and facilitate the evaluation of the progress towards our long-term objectives.

2 Intelligent Support for eXpresser

The MiGen project revolves around the development of intelligent support for a mathematical microworld, called eXpresser. The pedagogical rationale of the project, its aims and the environment are described in detail elsewhere [6]. The eXpresser microworld is designed to support activities that require students to identify relationships that underpin figural patterns. It provides a lot of freedom to students, who are encouraged to build their own constructions and expressions in different ways. Figure 1 presents some of the main features of eXpresser. For a detailed description the interested reader is referred to [6].

To ensure that students are supported during their interaction, we enabled the microworld with a suggestion button (see Figure 1D, and an example of feedback on Figure 2). The button is disabled unless the system observes something that warrants help. Instead of providing feedback and interrupting the student, the icon changes to indicate the existence of a suggestion. The students are free to ignore these suggestions, effectively achieving not interrupting the student for something that they may not need help for.

Due to the exploratory nature of the environment students may need additional help. In the absence of natural language processing we equipped the system with a 'sentence maker'; a list of drop-down menus that allow the construction of a sentence before asking for help. This brings a double benefit. Not only does it provide the system with an indication of the nature of the student's need but also, we hypothesised, that it would provide an incentive to self-reflect since, otherwise, the help button request is not enabled. Similar sentence makers have been used successfully before but either just for self-reflection [7] or as a means of student communication [8].

Lastly, students are presented with an explicit list of tangible goals that are expected to reach in order to complete the task (see Figure 3). Related research suggests that establishing and maintaining an orientation towards task-specific goals is important [9] and that employing similar techniques affect their attitudes towards the system and towards learning in general [10]. To allow freedom to the students to interact at their own pace and also to reflect on their actions, they are responsible for checking the goal they think they have accomplished. The system provides feedback on the completion of the goal or suggestions on what to do next in order to complete it.

In [11] we present the mechanism by which students' actions are analysed, and the possible help required is diagnosed. The latter is based on actual pedagogical strategies

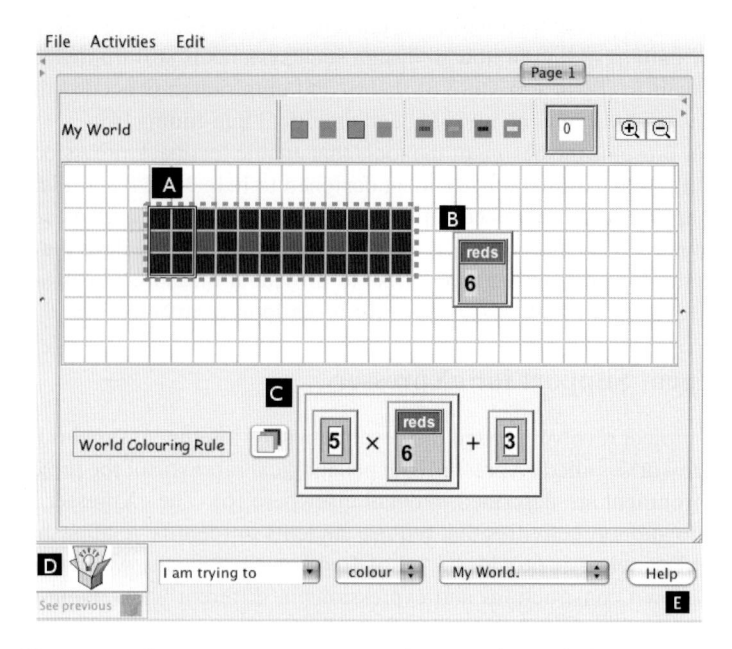

Fig. 1. In eXpresser students construct patterns paying attention to their structure and the relationships that pertain them. A building block (A) is repeated to make a pattern. A variable (B) is given the name 'reds' to represent the number of red tiles in the pattern. This variables is used in a general expression (C) that describes the total number of tiles required to surround the red tiles. Students can access suggestions (D) and request help using drop down menus (E).

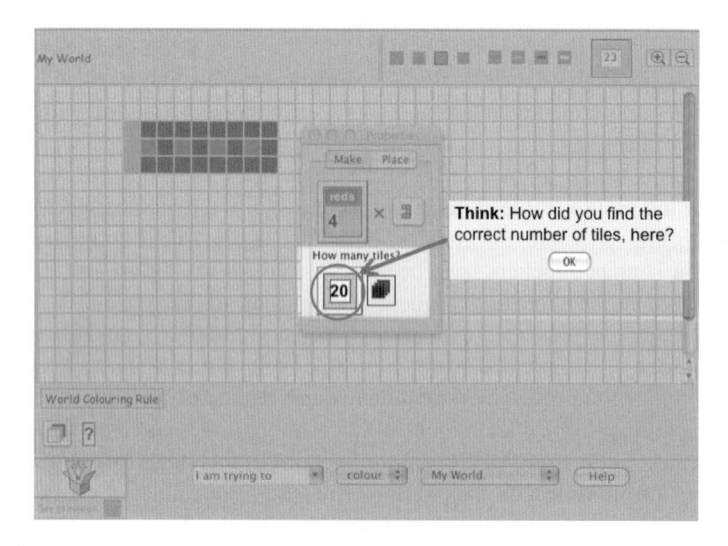

Fig. 2. An example of co-located feedback in eXpresser, designed to help students reflect on the relationships they perceive between objects but find so difficult to express

followed by the system after students have requested help. These were designed based on a theoretical account of the teachers' role (c.f. [12]) and were elaborated based on several face-to-face, wizard-of-Oz studies and focus-group sessions with teachers and teacher educators.

In brief, the pedagogical strategies followed are sequenced according to the level of specificity of the information provided. In collaboration with the teacher advisers, the reasoning mechanism is authored in such a way that after the identification of the need to follow a certain strategy, putting it into effect is adaptive to the previous help the student has received on the same issue as well as their general progress within the task. Consistent therefore with the principles of 'contingent' tutoring [9], the system gradually provides more specific help, but not more than the system's belief about the minimal help required to ensure progress.

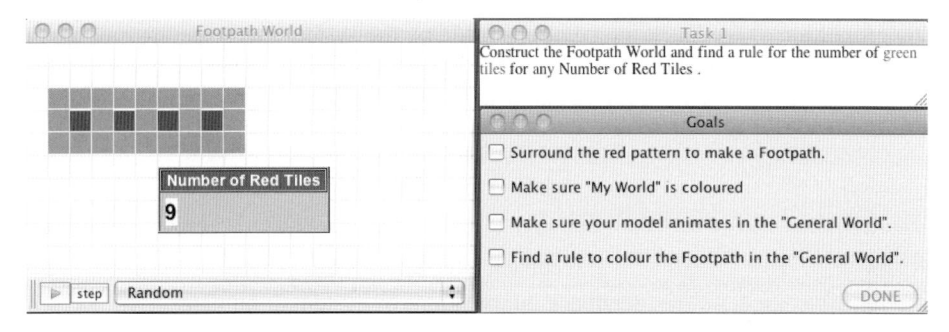

Fig. 3. A task and its goals explicitly listed. Students can check them when they consider them achieved, and the system provides appropriate feedback.

Finally, in order to encourage students to reflect on their actions, some messages are designed to interrupt their action. Even if at first this seems to compromise the principle of student control, our preliminary results suggest that these interrupting messages, which cause surprise or cognitive conflict, can help students break unproductive repetitive actions and make them think how to address the given challenge, articulate their thoughts and express them in the system.

3 Preliminary Evaluation

We have presented elsewhere our methodology for informing the design of intelligent support [5] as well as the layered technical evaluation of the various modules of the system [11]. In this section, we present the next step in our iterative process: a necessary formative evaluation phase, carried out when the intelligent subsystem is integrated but before the full system is ready to be deployed.

In this phase, we conduct field studies with small groups of students (3-6 students per group). Each student is given a computer with eXpresser running. After a familiarisation session, that includes the support functionalities, they are asked to undertake a task with the system (e.g. Figure3). The students interact with the computer in as much a realistic setting as possible (e.g. in a school classroom). One or more researchers observe the session paying special attention to the feedback provided by the system.

As the researchers are aware of the capabilities of the system, its intended use, and its limitations at each stage of the development, they can also support the students. There are four situations that may require human intervention. First, the intervention can be related to a feedback strategy that is not implemented at the given stage. Second, some feedback strategies have been identified as beyond the scope of the envisaged system, (e.g. dialogue in natural language or affective diagnosis) and are left for teachers who, supported by the system, will have their attention directed to students who seem to require help. Third, there is a need to support students when the feedback provided by the system is not relevant (e.g. not prioritised properly). Lastly, students sometimes adopt new approaches, for which support has not yet been designed.

Based on the number of interventions in each study we observe, *inter alia*, two important indicators: relevance and coverage of the feedback provided. Relevance measure the proportion of feedback interventions made by the system that were appropriate to the situation, as evaluated by subject matter experts. Feedback coverage is a measurement of the help students required that could be handled by the system.

$$relevance = \frac{\text{relevant feedback interventions by system}}{\text{feedback interventions by system}}$$

$$coverage = \frac{\text{feedback interventions by system}}{\text{feedback interventions by system or humans}}$$

4 Discussion

It is worth highlighting that these indicators are not used to qualify the system for its pedagogical purpose. This evaluation approach provides a broad understanding of the given state of the system as it progresses towards a version where it can undergo a summative evaluation. It also allows early detection of effects that are not possible to observe or investigate otherwise.

For example, in the particular setting of our latest study, the introduction of intelligent support meant that the researchers found themselves in situations where they were required to suggest to students to ask for help from the system, or to draw attention to the list of goals, that was designed to provide indirect feedback. It is our working hypothesis that the young age of the project's target group, their lack of familiarity with the innovative environment and with the support tools, together with the small-field setup did not allow for the full scale of the various help-seeking phenomena to be observed (e.g. help-abuse). One clear observation is that whenever students reached an impasse, or had problems performing the task, and felt the need for help, they did not immediately use the system's facilities. Instead, they turned to the "teachers" (i.e. the researchers taking part in the study) and asked questions or just waited silently until help was offered to them. The researchers would, at this point, first point out that the student should ask for assistance from the system. We refer to this as the "ignore computer in the presence of humans" effect, and we hypothesise that it will also be observed in classrooms where the students will be able to revert for help either to other students or to the teacher. This is in line with former research that shows that students' help-seeking behaviour is highly social behaviour and can be influenced by several factors (c.f. [13]). Our future work will therefore investigate this in more detail and look into designing appropriate metacognitive support (c.f. [14]).

References

1. Kirschner, P., Sweller, J., Clark, R.E.: Why minimal guidance during instruction does not work: An analysis of the failure of constructivist, discovery, problem-based, experiential and inquiry-based teaching. Educational Psychologist 41(2), 75–86 (2006)
2. de Jong, T., van Joolingen, W.: Discovery learning with computer simulations of conceptual domains. Review of Educational Research 68, 179–201 (1998)
3. Hoyles, C., Sutherland, R.: Logo Mathematics in the Classroom. Routledge, New York (1989)
4. Self, J.: The defining characteristics of intelligent tutoring systems research: ITSs care, precisely. International Journal of Artificial Intelligence in Education 10, 350–364 (1999)
5. Mavrikis, M., Gutierrez-Santos, S.: Not all wizards are from Oz: Iterative design of intelligent learning environments by communication capacity tapering. Computers & Education 54, 641–651 (2010)
6. Noss, R., Hoyles, C., Mavrikis, M., Geraniou, E., Gutierrez-Santos, S., Pearce, D.: Broadening the sense of 'dynamic': a microworld to support students' mathematical generalisation. Int. Journal on Mathematics Education 41(4), 493–503 (2009)
7. Aleven, V.: An effective metacognitive strategy: learning by doing and explaining with a computer-based cognitive tutor. Cognitive Science 26(2), 147–179 (2002)
8. Scardamalia, M., Bereiter, C.: Higher levels of agency for children in knowledge building: A challenge for the design of new knowledge media. J. of the Learning Sciences 1(1), 37–68 (1991)
9. Wood, H.: Help seeking, learning and contingent tutoring. Computers & Education 33(2-3) (1999)
10. Arroyo, I., Ferguson, K., Johns, J., Dragon, T., Meheranian, H., Fisher, D., Barto, A., Mahadevan, S., Woolf, B.P.: Repairing disengagement with non-invasive interventions. In: Proceeding of the 2007 conference on Artificial Intelligence in Education, pp. 195–202. IOS Press, Amsterdam (2007)
11. Gutierrez-Santos, S., Mavrikis, M., Magoulas, G.: Layered development and evaluation for intelligent support in exploratory environments: the case of microworlds. In: Aleven, V., Kay, J., Mostow, J. (eds.) Intelligent Tutoring Systems. LNCS, vol. 6094, pp. 105–114. Springer, Heidelberg (2010)
12. Geraniou, E., Mavrikis, M., Hoyles, C., Noss, R.: A learning environment to support mathematical generalisation in the classroom. In: Weigand (ed.) CERME 6, Sixth Conference of European Research in Mathematics Education (January 2009)
13. Aleven, V., Stahl, E., Schworm, S., Fischer, F., Wallace, R.: Help-seeking and help design in interactive learning environments. Review of Educational Research 77(3), 277–320 (2003)
14. Roll, I., Aleven, V., McLaren, B.M., Koedinger, K.R.: Designing for metacognition - applying cognitive tutor principles to the tutoring of help seeking. Metacognition and Learning 2(2) (2007)

GVIS: A Facility for Adaptively Mashing Up and Representing Open Learner Models

Luca Mazzola and Riccardo Mazza

University of Lugano, Faculty of Communication Sciences
Institute for Communication Technology
Via Buffi 13, CH-6904 Lugano, Switzerland
Phone: +41 58 666 4760 - Fax: +41 58 666 4647
{luca.mazzola,riccardo.mazza}@usi.ch

Abstract. In this article we present an infrastructure for creating mash up and visual representations of the user profile that combine data from different sources. We explored this approach in the context of Life Long Learning, where different platforms or services are often used to support the learning process. The system is highly configurable: data sources, data aggregations, and visualizations can be configured on the fly without changing any part of the software and have an adaptive behavior based on user's or system's characteristics. The visual profiles produced can have different graphical formats and can be bound to different data, automatically adapting to personal preferences, knowledge, and contexts. A first evaluation, conducted through a questionnaire, seems to be promising thanks to the perceived usefulness and the interest in the tool.

Keywords: Technology Enhanced Learning, Human Computer Interaction, Adaptive Presentations, Data Mashup, Open Learner Model.

1 Introduction

One of the key issues for making TEL an effective instrument for didactics is to increase the level of engagement of students with the online learning experience [1]. This is particularly important in the context of Life Long Learning (LLL), where the online learning is becoming more and more prevalent. To increase the level of engagement of learners, adaptive learning systems aim to guide learners, automatically adapting to personal preferences, prior knowledge, skills and competences, learning goals, and the personal or social context in which the experience takes place. One of the most important components of adaptive learning systems is the student model, which is in charge of keeping track of the student's knowledge and skills acquired during the learning process. In the LLL context, quite rarely learners use a single support tool, but very often companies and schools make use of different learning environments for some reasons (such as different LMS maintained by different suppliers of courses, intranet websites, custom applications). Consequently, all user information is not stored only into a specific student model system, but it is often distributed in a number of platforms used for different purposes. For this reason, there is a need to aggregate data from different tools (student models, intranet usage data, LMS data, and so on) and provide a uniform way to present these data to the interested users, preferably in visual format [2]. A specific multi-tier infrastructure was designed for this purposes. The idea was developed in the context of the GRAPPLE project [3], a research aimed at making already existing LMSes able to include adaptive contents and to share some controlled set of data about their users. Other approaches to the problem of creating personalized experience in TEL could be found under different names, such as "educational mashup" [4] or "ubiquitous and decentralized user model" [5] [6]. All these researches aim at aggregating user data from different systems, although they tackle the problem from different points of view. From the user point of view, we have to consider that a high quantity of mashed-up data might cause an overload issue [7], that becomes problematic when it distracts from the learning activity and makes the learner confused about the represented data. To limit the overload problem, the visual representations are adaptive to the role, to the context, and to the activities performed by the learner. The adaptation can help in creating more comprehensible and easier indicators. Next section briefly describes the implemented infrastructure. Then we present one adoption case, in the context of a real course and some very initial results of the evaluation we performed with learners of this course.

2 The Infrastructure

Providing modalities for opening the user profile for inspection [8] is important in the domain of LLL: the presentation of indicators of the learning process is widely accepted as one of the key points to improve participation and increase the satisfaction of participants [9]. GVIS - acronim for GRAPPLE Visualization Infrastructure Service - is an infrastructure we developed, able to extract data from different sources and enable instructional designers to easily create adaptive indicators of the learning state for learners and tutors. The user's profile is normally created on the basis of the user activities and interactions in the learning environment. Adaptive systems maintain this information in the learner (or user) models, whilst regular (not adaptive) Learning Management Systems (LMS) keep this information in form of logs, or tracking data. In the GRAPPLE adaptive system, course contents are built with respect to conceptual domain and adaptation structures, based on *concepts*, and the learner model stores, among other things, the related *knowledge level*: the measure of learner's knowledge on a specific concept. Although many LMS already provide the possibility to explore this user tracking data, in some cases the visual presentation of the information is not well suited to their users' specific needs. There are notable exceptions to this situation in the field of OLM –like OLMlets [10], in which the learner can choose between seven different representations–, but they normally rely on data from a single system they were developed with. So, we want to provide an easy way to create effective graphical presentation of arbitrary data from different and heterogeneous sources.

2.1 Adaptivity

We propose a three-tier architecture composed by a data extractor, a data aggregator, and a builder. All the levels rely on a configuration file that the *instructional designer* can change or expand in order to create graphical indicators of one or more interesting characteristics of the user profile, in form of widgets. In the current implementation, the two upper layers (aggregator and builder) can be enhanced with adaptive features. The extractor layer retrieves raw data from the sources, then the aggregator is in charge of merging and filtering data to extract more refined information. This aggregation is based on the model that the instructional designer wants to provide to the learners and reflects the didactic approach adopted in the course. With such architecture, the support to the learning process, based on adaptive profile externalization, can be reached by adapting the visualization to the specific didactic model. The adaptivity is modeled in the configuration files for both cases through a simple XML schema. This schema supports the conditional construct IF: this allows the GVIS visualization to have a different behavior with different properties. The properties can be any combination of source data values, on which a set of mathematical and logical operators can be applied. For instance, we can decide that a particular widget may show a comparison of the knowledge level of a student with the class, only if his current knowledge level is greater than a threshold value. Or we may want to show a particular widget only to the instructor of the course, not to the learners. This is implemented by including conditional instructions in the XML configuration files of the aggregator and builder. To this end, the configuration files may contain variables, logical and arithmetical operators: we have implemented the common comparison operators (more than, less than, equal and different) and the logical operators *AND, OR, XOR* (exclusive or), *NOT*. The following example represents a possible condition: *If the list of concepts in course X is not empty and either the average knowledge of concept A is greater than 3 or there are no students subscribed to the course, then display a particular widget, otherwise display another widget.* In the false case, we present another condition, related to the knowledge level of the current learner and compared with the average level for the course X. In this way, we can implement conditions as complex as needed and we can specify different behaviors at any granularity level. In the conditional expression we can put every variable of the user model, but also variables that represent user preferences and user device configurations.

3 A Possible Application in TEL

We applied the software to data from different LMSes used in a controlled experiment to support a distance learning course. The following examples will show some possibilities of adaptive configuration. The adaptive behavior can be performed by the aggregator and the builder, and is driven by course data (i.e. data not directly related to a single user, such as the number of concepts in a course) and/or user data (i.e. data about learner, like performed activities, acquired knowledge or expressed preferences). All these data are collected by the

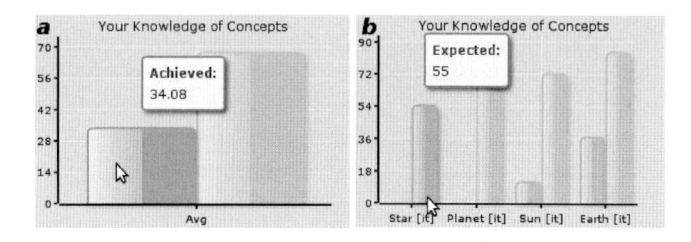

Fig. 1. Example of the produced widgets: different aggregation level of same data

extractor, or can be explicitly declared by the learner through his preferences and personal settings. The first example, based on *user* data (see Fig. 1), adapts at the aggregation level. It presents the knowledge achieved by a student over the concepts of the course. In Fig. 1 on the left there is a compact view, where the average knowledge level of the learner over the concepts of the course is compared to the average knowledge level of the class. The right side of Fig. 1, instead, presents detailed information for each concept of the course. The choice of which of these two widgets should be presented to the user is made by the GVIS engine on the basis of the number of concepts to display: if the number of concepts is too high to be represented in the detailed visualization, GVIS will present the aggregated one. It is important to notice that GVIS will only present data of concepts visited by the learner and this means that the adaptation rule can change the presented object automatically as the learner will visit more concepts of the course. The threshold according to which one of the two alternative visualizations is chosen could be either a fixed number in the XML configuration file or a value that is calculated on the basis of one or more characteristics of the class or activities done on the LMS.

Another visualization we developed, presented in Fig. 2, adapts the type of graph to the preferences of the user and to the number of concepts, in order to optimize the readability of the widget. It shows the information in two different formats: on the left, a bar chart represents the knowledge levels of a learner over the concepts of the course, comparing these values with the expected knowledge level; on the right, a pie chart gives a representation of the knowledge for every concept with their relative weight in the total knowledge achieved in the course. In Fig. 3, another example (based on *course* data) is presented, with an

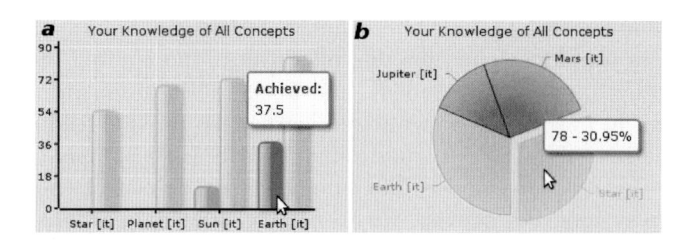

Fig. 2. Example of the produced widgets: different graphical representation of the same base data, aggregated in different way

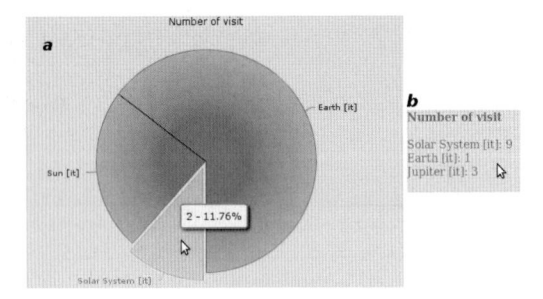

Fig. 3. Example of the produced widgets: graphical versus testual representation

adaptation condition included at the builder layer. In this case the adaptation is driven by the type of hardware used by the learner or by the connection speed. A textual list is well suited for mobile phone devices or handheld based platform, while a graphical widget (on the left) is suitable for larger displays and broadband access.

4 A First Test Case

In order to test the GVIS visualization module in a real environment, we set a testing platform with the Moodle LMS platform that includes a GVIS visualization module. We created a set of six indicators: two for the learners – very compact and seamlessly integrated into the Moodle users interface – and four for the tutor/teacher. This initial pilot phase was conducted applying the GVIS architecture to a Master blended course. Although in this test case we did not aggregate data from different sources, our visualization infrastructure helped to aggregate data coming from different tables in the Moodle database, and to visually represent contextual information about the course and the learners. We developed a specific widget in charge of representing the number of logins and the messages posted in a forum. An interesting outcome was the graphical comparison between the learner's specific information and the average value achieved by the class, that can work as a reference for the self-monitoring process of the user's progress. Some functionalities for the teacher have been implemented in order to support the tutoring, like the combination of accesses to resources of the course done by students and the number of messages posted to the forums. Others widgets were developed for this pilot study: the number of login to the course group by date and by student, and the number of forum post by date. We ran an initial evaluation that allowed learners to provide feedback on their experience with the system. A questionnaire with 16 questions on a 5 point based Likert-scale was developed and submitted at the end of the course with an online survey tool. For brevity, we do not include the questions and the analytical results, but we provide a qualitative description of the surve's results. The majority of the investigated aspects we collected reached at least an almost full satisfaction. Some aspects have different perception by the user and two of them revealed to be problematic: the capability of the tool to leverage mental workload and the possibility that it hinders the collaboration among peers.

5 Conclusions

We designed a tool that allows to aggregate information coming from different sources and to create adaptive graphical presentations of these data in order to support the teaching and learning needs in learning environments. The possibility to include adaptation in the generation of widgets could help avoiding informative overloading, that is a critical aspect in the learning context. The encoding of this information in graphical format is also important in order to make it useful for the learning process. Some open issues still remain, such as providing a set of adaptation templates to be reused, and the availability of an editor for the configurations, in order to support the instructional designers' work. Last, but not least, we consider important to provide an evaluation of the impact of this approach on learning, both from the point of view of self-reflection and awareness, and of instructional effectiveness.

References

1. Laurillard, D., Oliver, M., Wasson, B., Ulrich, H.: Implementing Technology-Enhanced Learning. In: Technology-Enhanced Learning: Principles and Products, pp. 289–306. Springer, Netherlands (2009)
2. Dror, B., Nadine, M., Mike, B.: Visualization and Analysis of Student Interaction in an Adaptive Exploratory Learning Environment. In: Proceedings 1st Int. Workshop in Intelligent Support for Exploratory Environments, EC-TEL 2008 (2008)
3. Van Der Sluijs, K., Hover, K.: Integrating Adaptive Functionality in a LMS. Int. Journal of Emerging Technologies in Learning (IJET) 4(4) (2009)
4. Esposito, F., Licchelli, O., Semeraro, G.: Discovering Student Models in e-learning Systems. Journal of Universal Computer Science 10(1), 47–57 (2004)
5. Van Der Sluijs, K., Houben, G.: A generic component for exchanging user models between web-based systems. International Journal of Continuing Engineering Education and Life-Long Learning 16(1/2), 64–76 (2006)
6. Heckmann, D., Schwartz, T., Brandherm, B., Krner, A.: Decentralized User Modeling with UserML and GUMO. In: Proceedings of the Workshop on Decentralized, Agent Based and Social Approaches to User Modelling (DASUM 2005), pp. 61–65 (2005)
7. Chen, C.: Influence of Perceived Information Overload on Learning in Computer-Mediated Communication. In: Spaniol, M., Li, Q., Klamma, R., Lau, R.W.H. (eds.) ICWL 2009. LNCS, vol. 5686, pp. 112–115. Springer, Heidelberg (2009)
8. Bull, S., Kay, J.: Metacognition and Open Learner Models. In: Metacognition Workshop, Intelligent Tutoring Systems 2008 (2008)
9. Shahrour, G., Bull, S.: Does "Notice" Prompt Noticing? Raising Awareness in Language Learning with an Open Learner Model. In: Nejdl, W., Kay, J., Pu, P., Herder, E. (eds.) AH 2008. LNCS, vol. 5149, pp. 173–182. Springer, Heidelberg (2008)
10. Bull, S., Gardner, P., Ahmad, N., Ting, J., Clarke, B.: Use and Trust of Simple Independent Open Learner Models to Support Learning within and across Courses. In: Houben, G.-J., McCalla, G., Pianesi, F., Zancanaro, M. (eds.) UMAP 2009. LNCS, vol. 5535, pp. 42–53. Springer, Heidelberg (2009)

Introducing a Social Backbone to Support Access to Digital Resources

Martin Memmel[1], Martin Wolpers[2], Massimiliano Condotta[3], Katja Niemann[2], and Rafael Schirru[1]

[1] Knowledge Management Department, DFKI GmbH, Trippstadter Str. 122, D-67663 Kaiserslautern, Germany and
University of Kaiserslautern, Germany
{martin.memmel,rafael.schirru}@dfki.de

[2] Fraunhofer Institute for Applied Information Technology, Schloss Birlinghoven, D-53754 Sankt Augustin, Germany
{martin.wolpers,katja.niemann}@fit.fraunhofer.de

[3] University IUAV of Venice, Faculty of Architecture, Italy
massimiliano.condotta@iuav.it

Abstract. Social media technologies offer potential benefits for a variety of scenarios to support access to digital resources. The involvement of users that do not only consume, but also participate and contribute information, allows for promising approaches such as social browsing and crowdsourcing. Yet, a lot of resources and metadata are contained in distributed and heterogeneous repositories that follow a traditional top-down approach in which only experts can contribute information. A social hub that can aggregate such information, while at the same time offering social media technologies, enables new ways to search and browse these contents, and to maintain underlying structures. We will present how the ALOE system that realises such a social backbone was integrated into the MACE portal. First evaluation results provide evidence about the usefulness of the presented approach.

1 Introduction

Social media technologies offer a variety of potentials to support the access to digital resources. On the one hand, this concerns the creation and provision of resources themselves, on the other hand, this concerns the creation of metadata such as tags, comments, and ratings. As many digital environments do not offer any facilities for end users to contribute resources or metadata, the integration of such functionalities has the potential to significantly improve the user experience as well as the access to the respective digital resources. This paper describes how social media technologies were introduced into the MACE portal by integrating the ALOE system, and provides first evaluation results about the usefulness of the approach.

2 The ALOE System

ALOE[1] is a web-based social resource sharing platform developed at the Knowledge Management group of DFKI. It allows to contribute, share, and access arbitrary types of digital resources such as text documents, music, or video files. Users are able to either upload resources (using the system as a repository) or by referencing a URL (using the system as a referatory; called bookmarking). Users can tag, rate, and comment on resources, they can maintain resource portfolios, join and initiate groups, etc. Furthermore, arbitrary additional metadata can be associated with resources. On the one hand, the system's functionalities are offered via a graphical user interface that can be accessed with any common web browser. On the other hand, a Web Service API is offered that allows to access the ALOE functionalities. ALOE realises a *social backbone* that allows to introduce social media paradigms in existing (heterogeneous) infrastructures. See Figure 1 for an overview of the ALOE system components.

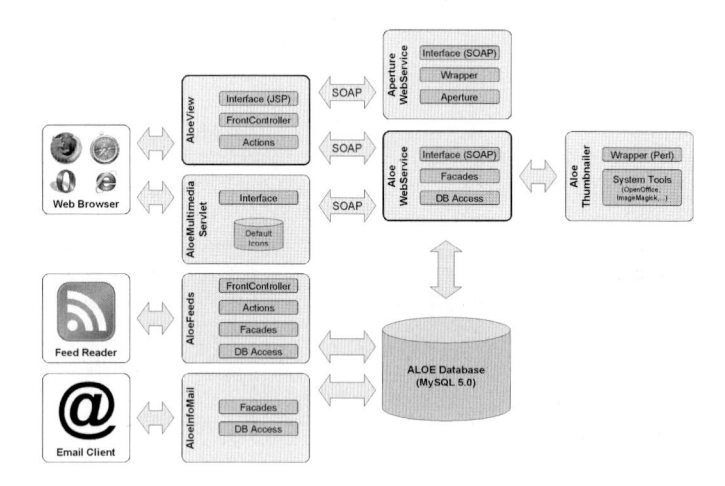

Fig. 1. ALOE – system architecture and components

3 Using ALOE in MACE – A Case Study

MACE (Metadata for Architectural Contents in Europe) is a European Initiative aimed at improving architectural education, by integrating and connecting vast amounts of content from diverse repositories, including past European projects existing architectural design communities [1,2]. Within the MACE portal that is online and publicly accessible[2], searching through and finding appropriate learning resources from a variety of sources is enabled in a discovery oriented way. MACE provides numerous searching and browsing facilities that rely on

---
[1] http://aloe-project.de
[2] http://www.mace-project.eu

the metadata associated with the resources. The system offers a *filtered search* where a user is able to qualify the search with several additional facets, to *browse by classification* based on the MACE taxonomy (see Section 3.3), to *browse by competence* based on a competence catalogue, to *browse by location* allowing to search for contents within a given area, to conduct a *social search* based on tags, and to *browse user portfolios* (social browsing) of resources.

3.1 Integration of ALOE into the MACE Infrastructure

The MACE system builds on a distributed service oriented architecture with a three-tier structure. The front-end with its graphical user interfaces and widgets forms the client tier. The business logic is organised in the application-server tier while the metadata stores form the data-server or back-end tier. Through the integration of ALOE into the MACE infrastructure, a variety of social media technologies are provided. Users can add new contents to MACE, they can maintain personal resource portfolios, they can contribute information about resources (e.g., tags, comments, and ratings), and they can search within this information. Furthermore, it is possible to maintain contact lists and to send messages to other users. Figure 2 provides an overview of the ALOE services and their integration into the MACE infrastructure. The performance, reliability, and scalability of ALOE within MACE was ensured using a variety of strategies and tests. See [3] for a complete overview of the evaluation of the MACE infrastructure and services.

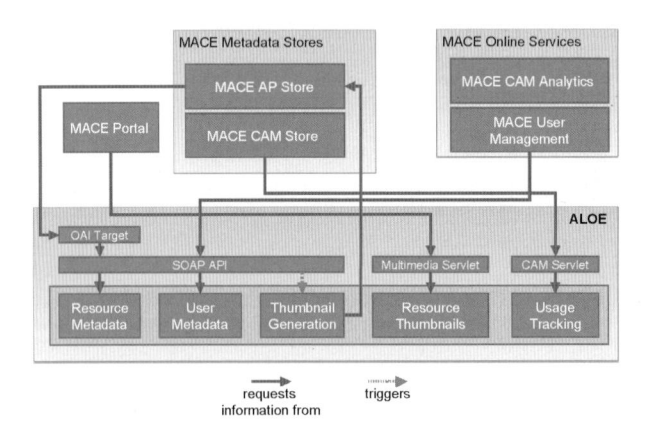

Fig. 2. ALOE services and their integration into the MACE infrastructure

3.2 Contributions by MACE Users

As of April 08, 2010, 914 users were registered in MACE and thus could contribute new resources and metadata. Table 1 provides an overview of the contributions by end users. The numbers presented clearly show that MACE managed to attract a significant number of contributions. We will present information about the usefulness of the contributed metadata in the following sections.

Table 1. End user contributions in MACE (reference date: April, 08, 2010)

Resources		Comments	
Resources contributed	14546	Comments	443
Unique resources contributed	10061	Commented resources	346
Users that contr. at least once	326	Users that comm. at least once	61
Tags		**Ratings**	
Tags added	50797	Ratings	1858
Unique tags added	10212		
Tagged resources	7251	Rated resources	1757
Users that tagged at least once	273	Users that rated at least once	100

3.3 Using Social Tags to Maintain the MACE Application Profile

An architectural project constitutes a great syntheses effort, where different knowledge fields are involved. To find a coherent strategy to approach the knowledge organisation system of such a heterogeneous subject, we relied on several studies about semiotic interpretation of architectural knowledge in order to have the possibility to classify each aspect of the domain with semantic metadata (a detailed description can be found in [4]). The MACE Application Profile (AP) was deleoped respectively to organise all the architectural knowledge of MACE in a meaningful way. It contains a taxonomy whose categories are motivated and supported by the studies and the semiotic model previously mentioned.

Besides the effort to initially create a wide, complete, and shared taxonomy, it is our conviction that it must not be considered fixed and closed. Only with its use by the end users (teachers, students, etc.) it is possible to understand and evaluate its soundness. For this reason, we planned to update the AP every 6 months, i.e., to modify, delete, and especially add new terms, applying an operational procedure to manage the AP maintenance based on the communities' feedback and commonly used tags. This hybrid approach combining a pre-defined top-down hierarchy and a bottom-up folksonomy allows us to utilise the wisdom of the crowds in a controlled manner to profit from existing personal knowledge. The taxonomy can be extended and improved over time, thus having the flexibility to adapt to emerging changes and arising innovations [4]. During the last review (still in a developing phase of the entire MACE system), we extended the MACE AP taxonomy with about 20 new terms. This could be considered a non relevant number of terms, but if we consider the extent of the taxonomy (consisting of 2850 terms) and its purpose (to be as much complete as possible), it is easy to understand that the possibility to find missing terms was rather small.

3.4 Usefulness of Social Metadata from an End User Perspective

Usage Data. For the following calculations, the stored CAM (Contextualized Attention Metadata, see [5]) instances concerning searching and browsing activities were used. Thereby, sessions instead of single actions were considered. That is to say, a search (e.g., clicking on a classification term in the classification based search or entering the name of a country in the location based search) and its refinements (e.g., further clicking in the classification hierarchy) are regarded as one action. A session ends when users access a learning resource or when they leave the page. This approach was chosen to achieve the comparability of the different search and browse types in MACE, as for some actions, like the filtered search, more fine-grained CAM instances were collected as for others. Figure 3 depicts the shares of the different searching and browing facilities as already presented. The data shows that *Filtered Search* (subsuming the simple keyword search) has been the most used tool during the examined period. Browsing in the one's own portfolio and in user portfolios of other users (i.e., social browsing) is also used significantly more often than other facilities that each made out less than 10% of all conducted actions.

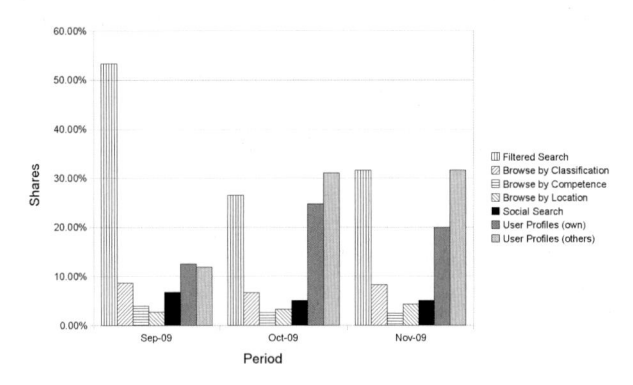

Fig. 3. Shares of search and browse types in MACE

Survey Data. Information about the end users' perception of the usefulness of different services and metadata types was collected by conducting a survey with 14 participants of a MACE competition carried out in August and September 2009 with teams of 20 Urban Design students from the University of Kaiserslautern. Their task was to gather and annotate resources about culturally relevant buildings in the areas Rhineland-Palatinate and Saar-Lor-Lux. For the survey, a questionnaire was used that was made up of a scale based on 2 items. Utilizing a 5-point scale, the users had to rate the importance of *(1) different search and browse facilities within MACE to find contents related to the impromptu*, and *(2) different kinds of resource metadata to judge the relevance of a resource*. Figure 4 summarises the average value of each feature, ranging from 1 to 5 corresponding to a scale ranging from "rather not important" to "very important". Concerning the importance of search and browse facilities, *Keyword Search* and *Browse by Location* were rated as very important, and they were clearly considered as the most important facilities. Still, except for *Browse by Competence*, all other facilities were also rated as important, including *Social Search* and *User Profiles* that are based on social metadata. To judge the relevance of a resource, *Title & Description*, *Tags*, and the *Resource Preview* were considered as the most important kinds of metadata, while all other types were rated similarily as less, but still clearly important. From these preliminary evaluation results, we can conclude that all social metadata is considered as important (especially tags) to judge the relevance of a resource, and that the services based on social metadata are also considered as important means to search and browse.

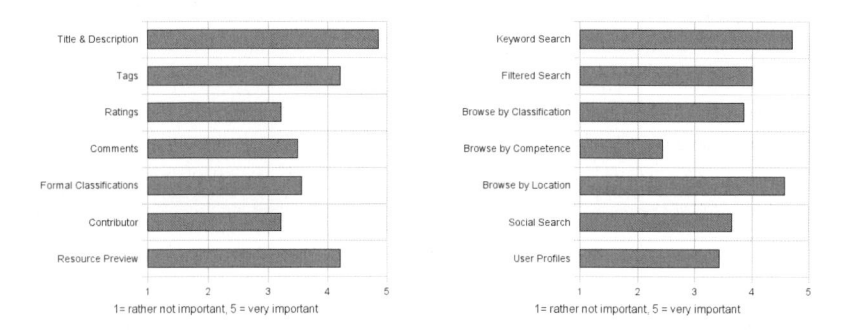

Fig. 4. Usefulness of social metadata from an end user perspective – survey results

4 Summary and Conclusions

Introducing social media technologies has the potential to significanty improve the access to resources in a variety of scenarios. Especially the resources and metadata provided by end users can be used for that purpose. We have presented the ALOE system that realises a social backbone, and we have shown its successful integration into the MACE portal that provides access to distributed learning resources coming from different repositories world-wide. A great many resources and metadata have already been contributed by end users, and first evaluation results indicate that the contributions and the functionalities built upon them improve the user experience in MACE. Furthermore, the contributed tags are used to maintain the MACE AP as an underlying structure of the system.

References

1. Wolpers, M., Memmel, M., Giretti, A.: Metadata in architecture education - first evaluation results of the mace system. In: Cress, U., Dimitrova, V., Specht, M. (eds.) EC-TEL 2009. LNCS, vol. 5794, pp. 112–126. Springer, Heidelberg (2009)
2. Wolpers, M., Memmel, M., Stefaner, M.: Supporting architecture education using the mace system. International Journal of TEL 2(1/2), 132–144 (2010)
3. Stefaner, M., Wolpers, M., Memmel, M., Duval, E., Specht, M., Brner, D., Gruber, M., Jong, T.D., Giretti, A., Klemke, R.: MACE: Joint Deliverable. Evaluation of the MACE system. Deliverable, The MACE consortium (2009)
4. Spigai, V., Condotta, M., Dalla Vecchia, E., Nagel, T.: Semiotic based facetted classification to support browsing architectural contents in mace. In: Naaranoja, M., Otter, A.d., Prins, M., Karvonen, A., Raasakka, V. (eds.) Proceedings of Joint CIB Conference: Performance and Knowledge Management, pp. 273–284 (June 2008)
5. Wolpers, M., Najjar, J., Verbert, K., Duval, E.: Tracking actual usage: the attention metadata approach. Educational Technology & Society 10(3), 106–121 (2007)

Towards an Ergonomics of Knowledge Systems: Improving the Design of Technology Enhanced Learning

David E. Millard and Yvonne Howard

Learning Societies Lab, School of Electronics and Computer Science,
University of Southampton, UK
`{dem,ymh}@ecs.soton.ac.uk`

Abstract. As Technology Enhanced Learning (TEL) systems become more essential to education there is an increasing need for their creators to reduce risk and to design for success. We argue that by taking an ergonomic perspective it is possible to better understand why TEL systems succeed or fail, as it becomes possible to analyze how well they are aligned with their users and environment. We present three TEL case studies that demonstrate these ideas, and show how an ergonomic analysis can help frame the problems faced in a useful way. In particular we propose using a variant of ergonomics that emphasizes the expression, communication and use of knowledge within the system; we call this approach Knowledge System Ergonomics.

Keywords: Design Methodologies, Ergonomics, Knowledge Systems.

1 Introduction

Successful e-learning systems are difficult to design and create. In addition to traditional software engineering problems such as performance, openness, efficiency and interface design there is also a need to take a pedagogical view on the activities and processes enshrined in the software [1], to consider how the system fits into an existing complex ecosystem of physical and digital systems, and to take account of how it is affected by institutional policy and personal preferences [2].

These pressures can create highly specialized software systems that are difficult to transplant to other institutions or contexts, and are extremely brittle in the face of change. If we believe that more specialized pedagogically-informed systems are needed in education then helping technologists build systems that are a good fit to teachers and learners is a critical goal. In our view this can be described as a need for better *Ergonomic Design*, and we believe that taking this wider perspective is helpful in formulating new design principles for Technology Enhanced Learning (TEL) that will reduce risk and help TEL creators design for success.

In particular, through three different case studies, we suggest that since TEL systems can be seen as a particular kind of *Knowledge System* a variant of ergonomics focused on the knowledge models and knowledge processes within them can offer valuable insights into how to align a new TEL system with its users. We call this approach *Knowledge System Ergonomics*.

2 Background

Usability has long been identified as a critical success factor for TEL [3]. Usability pioneers identify a number of key issues for design that apply to e-learning such as matching a system to the real world (using common language and terms), and user control and freedom [4]. Later researchers make the connection between usability and pedagogical considerations, introducing 'learnability' as a TEL design factor [5].

Ergonomics is the study of how to fit a system to a person, and although it is more traditionally thought of in the sense of physical devices and machines, it can equally be applied to digital systems and applications [6]. The environmental considerations of TEL fit well with principles of *macro-ergonomics* where a more holistic approach is taken to designing new systems or processes [7]. When applied in Human-Computer Interaction there tends to be an emphasis on information and cognitive tasks and so this type of approach is referred to as *cognitive ergonomics* [8]. More recently researchers have begun to explore if ergonomics can contribute to education, arguing for an ergonomic perspective on learning, directed at design improvements of physical learning environments [9]; for example, Rudolf et al. demonstrates that improved classroom ergonomics can improve student comfort and productivity [10].

We propose that we gain insight into the design of TEL systems by viewing them as knowledge systems. Definitions of knowledge in the classical world emphasized truth and belief, however with the rise of the Semantic Web and Linked Data broader definitions have become popular that focus on knowledge as information that has a "practical use in action" [11]. This is the perspective that we take: that knowledge is information that it is in an appropriate form for it to be applied to some task.

In this paper we argue that if we see e-learning applications as a form of knowledge system, the problem of designing TEL can be seen as one of *Knowledge System Ergonomics*, a combination of macro and cognitive ergonomics that could help designers create systems that are better aligned with users and usage contexts.

3 Case Study 1: E-Learning Repositories (EdShare)

Description: Over the last decade there has been tremendous growth in the interest in e-learning repositories. The Language Box and EdShare projects at the University of Southampton started in 2007, their objective was to learn from Web 2.0 sites and create a repository for the Language Teaching community, and another as the institutional repository for the University of Southampton [12]. Both projects took a participatory design approach coupled with agile development.

Difficulties and Challenges: Very early it became clear that there was a major disconnect between the needs of potential users, and the sorts of *complex meta-data* represented by Learning Objects; for example, users complained that their were too many fields and that the pedagogical terms didn't match to everyday reality [13]. We also struggled to get users to *reuse materials* in the repository. Initially we allowed users to put two types of item in the repository: *Resources* (that represented a raw set of materials that could be used for teaching) and *Activities* (that described what you might do with those materials). However, we found that teachers struggled to understand the difference between these types. In the end we scrapped Activities and instead introduced the notion of *Remixing* a Resource, this clones a Resource and allows the user to change the copy. This simple remix function was understood much more readily [14]. However, the biggest challenge was in getting users to *engage with the repository*. A major challenge was to understand why people were prepared to use sharing sites but not put their teaching materials into a traditional repository.

Ergonomic Perspective: In the case of Metadata the problem was of terminology and cognitive overload; because of the number of fields, and the unfamiliarity of their names, users were not prepared to spend time uploading content. By designing for minimal manual meta-data, and maximum automatic metadata, and by using everyday practical language we were able to massively reduce the barriers to use.

In the case of Reuse and Remixing, the problem was the sophistication of the information structures, and the way in which they required users to be able to abstract their teaching activities from their teaching content. This type of information abstraction is a key skill for software engineers, but it is alien to most users.

For engagement we found it useful to take a cognitive ergonomics perspective, and to look at the processes that users were involved with, and where exactly the repository should fit. The problem is that research repositories fit at the end of a production process and are therefore providing the service of *Archiving*. But it is not helpful to archive learning materials. Instead we therefore looked at what other services a teaching and learning repository might provide, finally settling on *Hosting* (putting materials online easily and with an inline browser preview), *Organisation* (providing tagging and collection facilities), and *Community* (giving users a profile page as a way of establishing identity, and emphasizing contribution and remixing).

4 Case Study 2: Mobile Tools for Placement Learners

Description: The Mobile Placement Learning and Assessment Toolkit (mPLAT) project aimed to provide a mobile learning toolkit to support practice based learning for nursing students in three different UK Higher Education Institute [15]. Our belief was that practice-based learning would be improved by connecting the student *in situ* with the competency model they were required to learn. We developed two tools: a Profile Placement Tool that provides guidance for mapping the domain and competencies to the opportunities offered in the placement area, and a Learning Contract Builder that drew on student's experience and a placement profile to create an action plan for learning. We deployed the mPLAT toolkit in three separate trials.

Difficulties and Challenges: We undertook significant preparation for the first trial including setting up training sessions, establishing a regular helpdesk, and getting agreement at all necessary management levels, but despite this many students gave up using the tools within a few weeks, and by the end of the trial there were few users.

Through focus group sessions we heard reports of ward staff demanding that the mobile devices were 'put away', some students were accused of 'texting their friends instead of working'. Students also found the device itself technically challenging, and with the generally negative atmosphere did not feel motivated to overcome the difficulties. This happened even though domain partners were sponsors of the innovation and even though the deployment areas were informed about the trial.

In our second trial, the sobering experience of our first trial helped us to recognize that co-design for creating useful, innovative tools is not enough to ensure innovation in practice; it requires a method that we are called *co-deployment* which recognizes the difficulties of deploying tools which may challenge long-held practice, creates initiatives to mitigate them, and brings all stakeholders in the domain community to work together to accept beneficial innovation [16]. In the third trial we also simplified the tools, introducing tagging concepts from web 2.0 to encourage users to link their placement experiences to the competency model. As a result of these changes there was a marked increase in the confidence of the students in the use of the tools, and both students and their mentors found that communication between them improved.

Ergonomic Perspective: An outcome from co-design was that although there was a need for student nurses to become holistic practitioners, there was no pedagogical route in the paper portfolio system for them to achieve it except by reflection on their practice during placements. From a cognitive ergonomics point of view the existing paper system was deficient, giving a clear objective for the technical tool.

Having discovered in the first trial that acceptance of the use of the tools into placements was a significant problem, we found it useful to take a macro-ergonomics perspective, and to look at the cultural norms, practices and environment that students and the nursing professionals were involved with, and where exactly we expected the use of the tools would fit into them. From this perspective, we took forward the principles of co-design to create our co-deployment methodology [16].

Finally, in tackling what we consider as student risk aversion to using novel tools, in the third trial we used a cognitive ergonomics perspective to embed the use of the tool into the processes and activities of the students and practice assessors.

5 Case Study 3: Framework Reference Model for e-Assessment

Description: In 2005 the UK Joint Information Systems Committee (JISC) commissioned the authors to run a project called FREMA (the Framework Reference Model for Assessment) to explore the e-assessment landscape and to help the research community find, understand and articulate key challenges [17].

Due to the maturity of the domain we decided that rather than the project team define a number of narrow challenges we would provide an online information wiki where we could guide the community in reporting its own work, and provide analysis tools to help them discover key issues for themselves. However a standard wiki was not powerful enough for our needs. This is because we not only recorded the type of each entry (e.g. was it a *project*, a piece of *software*, etc) but we also recorded typed relationships between entries (e.g. this software *uses* that standard).

As part of this work we also worked closely with the community to develop a topic map of assessment. In the wiki, typed properties allowed us to attach entries to concepts from our topic map, and we then built a flash-based browser that dynamically queried the wiki in order to provide a graphical index into the site.

Difficulties and Challenges: The concept map became a convenient focus for the FREMA community. But it was a challenge to articulate a *consistent methodology* for building the map. For example, we found that one branch of the map might be decomposed functionally while another might be decomposed around artifacts.

Our use of narrative descriptions to capture entries was a success, and we gathered hundreds of examples, but users *struggled with wiki syntax*, in particular with the complex constructs needed for the Semantic Wiki extensions. We attempted a number of solutions (for example, using templates to make page creation easier, and creating our own SMW extension that acted as a guide that prompted users to complete semantic data and made suggestions, but these were met with limited success [18].

However the biggest difficulty was that we *misunderstood community interest* in the activity of collecting data and building the concept map, as interest in the tool and analysis itself. Towards the end of the project it became clear that it was the activity that acted as a focus for the community, and when that activity disappeared the community dispersed, making the tool ultimately unsustainable.

Ergonomic Perspective: Building a topic map is a process of knowledge construction. Since we did not enforce any one methodology for this process we were relying on an alignment between the way that individuals thought about the assessment domain, and the way that the concept map requires that to be expressed. This can be considered a problem of cognitive ergonomics, but perhaps more than any other of our examples, it is peculiar to knowledge systems in particular, as it is about the expression of knowledge structures that have grown organically in peoples minds through their own experiences, and the difficultly of asking them to express those in a systematic way that may not match their own frameworks of thought.

Ultimately though, the real difficulty was in our misunderstanding of community interest, a problem of macro-ergonomics. We believed that the challenge that needed to be solved was that people needed to better understand the usage of technology in order to better target their work. In fact we learned that it was collaborative activity of defining the domain (through the topic maps) that was perceived as most valuable.

6 Conclusions

We have argued that TEL systems can be considered primarily as knowledge systems, since they are concerned with how knowledge is formed, communicated and applied. Considering knowledge in a system often means focusing on how it is transformed (for example, looking at what users already know, how able they are to express it, how easily it can be interpreted into a machine form, and once there how useful is it).

From our case studies we see evidence of these kinds of transformations (for example, EdShare involved the transformation of tacit knowledge about educational materials into explicit meta-data, and FREMA faced the challenge of transforming the inconsistent and multi-dimensional domain understanding of a community into a single coherent topic map). However we also saw problems concerned with integrating with existing knowledge processes and with how best to use resulting knowledge structures (for example, EdShare had to refocus the services of the repository in order to better fit the requirements and working practices of teachers, and FREMA misunderstood how the community would focus on the activity rather than the tool). We therefore arrive at the following general definition of Knowledge System Ergonomics that draws from both cognitive and macro ergonomics:

Knowledge System Ergonomics - the science of building knowledge structures and systems that fit the ways in which the users of those systems conceptualize, express, communicate, process and apply knowledge.

We believe that a good basis for a design framework of Knowledge System Ergonomics would be **principles of alignment** based on **conceptual**, **cognitive** and **contextual** aspects, to ensure that for each aspect the human, organizational and technical components are aligned. Where misalignment is unavoidable (for example, when knowledge is required at an unusual level of formality that does not naturally occur) processes should be put in place to overcome them (for example, using computational models to bridge the difference, or through appropriate training).

References

1. Mehanna: e-Pedagogy: the pedagogies of e-learning. ALT-J 12(3), 279–293 (2004)
2. Pittard: Evidence for e-learning policy. Technology, Pedagogy and Education 13(2), 181–194 (2004)
3. Chiu, et al.: Usability, quality, value and e-learning continuance decisions. Computers & Education 45(4), 399–416 (2005)
4. Nielsen: Heuristic evaluation. Usability Inspection Methods. John Wiley & Sons, Chichester (1994)
5. Feldstein: What is usable e-learning? eLearn 9 (September 2002)
6. Eason: Ergonomic perspectives on advances in human-computer interaction. Ergonomics 34(6), 721–741 (1991)
7. Hendrick: Future directions in macroergonomics. Ergonomics 38(8), 1617–1624 (1995)
8. Falzon: Cognitive ergonomics: understanding, learning and designing human-computer interaction. Cognitive Ergonomics (1990) ISBN:0-12-248290-5
9. Smith: The ergonomics of learning: educational design and learning performance. Ergonomics 50(10), 1530–1546 (2007)
10. Rudolf, Griffiths: Evaluating the ergonomics of a student learning environment. Work: A Journal of Prevention, Assessment and Rehabilitation 34(4), 475–480 (2009)
11. Schreiber: Knowledge Engineering and Management: the CommonKADS Methodology. MIT Press, Cambridge (2000) ISBN: 0-262-19300-0
12. Davis, et al.: Bootstrapping a Culture of Sharing to Facilitate Open Educational Resources. IEEE Transactions on Learning Technologies 3(1) (2010)
13. Millard, et al.: The Language Box: Re-imagining Teaching and Learning Repositories. In: Proc. of ICALT 2009, Riga, Latvia (2009)
14. Millard, et al.: Phantom tasks and invisible rubric: The challenges of remixing learning objects in the wild. In: Cress, U., Dimitrova, V., Specht, M. (eds.) EC-TEL 2009. LNCS, vol. 5794, pp. 127–139. Springer, Heidelberg (2009)
15. Zhang, et al.: A Mobile Toolkit for Placement Learning. In: Proc of ICALT, Spain (2008)
16. Millard, et al.: Co-design and Co-deployment Methodologies for Innovative m-Learning Systems. In: Multiplatform E-Learning Systems and Technologies: Mobile Devices for Ubiquitous ICT-Based Education. IGI Global (2009)
17. Millard, et al.: The e-Learning Assessment Landscape. In: Proc of ICALT, Netherlands (2006)
18. Kousetti, et al.: A study of ontology convergence in a semantic wiki. In: Proc of ACM WikiSym 2008, Porto, Portugal (2008)

Using Personal Professional Networks for Learning in Social Work: Need for Insight into the Real-World Context

Kamakshi Rajagopal, Desirée Joosten-ten Brinke, and Peter B. Sloep

Centre for Learning Sciences and Technologies (CELSTEC),
Open Universiteit Nederland
{kamakshi.rajagopal,desiree.joosten-tenbrinke,
peter.sloep}@ou.nl
http://www.celstec.org

Abstract. Professionals in social work practice depend on a high level of skills, intellectual ability and a wide knowledge base to find innovative solutions for the complex problems they encounter. They learn by experience and through social interaction using dialogue and discussion with relevant others to create new knowledge. To support their learning, they search for the most suitable and most relevant dialogue partner available in their extensive personal professional network. This is a difficult, high-skilled task, for which little technological support is available. This paper presents a literature review on the learning needs of these professionals and considers the use of technology as a means of supporting this type of learning. It argues for the need for more insight into the strategies used by professionals in building, maintaining and activating connections in their personal professional network for *learning* purposes.

Keywords: Personal Learning Network, social networks, dialogue and discussion as means of learning, expertise identification, user-centred technology design.

1 Introduction

Social work deals with issues of health care, poverty, homelessness, migration and integration in national and international environments supported by government institutions and non-governmental organisations (NGO). Professionals involved in social work practice use, adapt and build a high level of skills, intellectual ability and a wide knowledge base to find innovative solutions for the complex problems they encounter [1]. Their individual expertise is built by the experiences they gain along the way, participating in various projects [2,3,4]. As lifelong learners, the ongoing professional development of social work professionals seems to primarily take the form of learning through experience and learning through social interaction [5]. They build tacit knowledge through experience and reflection and share this knowledge through social interaction with selected others to solve the complex problems encountered [2,6,7,8]. The knowledge built and individual expertise gained is characterized by its applicability in specific contexts, on specific topics and in specific locations.

Dialogue and discussion with colleagues and peers seems to be the tool supporting and enabling this type of learning in social work. This role of discussion has been identified before [9], as have conversations been recognised as a key enabler of knowledge creation in organisational settings [10]. The success of dialogue and discussion in learning depends on two conditions. First, dialogue partners need a basic level of mutual trust to openly share their experience and knowledge and to enable knowledge creation. Second, as the specific experience, expertise and interests of the dialogue partners will greatly influence the relevance of the discussion held and the resulting insights gained by individual professionals, it matters who the dialogue partner is. For an individual learner, the focus shifts to finding suitable dialogue partners for the problems encountered.

In order to have access to the right expertise and experience at the time needed, social work professionals build and maintain extensive personal professional networks, i.e. the network of people set up by an individual specifically in the context of her professional activities. More and more, these real-world networks are mirrored online through various social networking sites. Technology can then take on a role in supporting learning through these online networks.

This paper presents a literature review of the learning needs of professionals in social work and the considerations that need to be made when looking at technology as a means of supporting these professionals in their learning. First, we will try to identify the strategies used in finding suitable dialogue partners and the role of technology in this. Then, we will view the theoretical and practical founding to technology design for this context. Finally, we will give some conclusions and indications of future work.

2 Problem Description

As personal professional networks are only in recent years enjoying increased interest in the academic world [11,12,13,14], there have been few studies on this topic. One of these studies, conducted by Nardi, Whittaker and Schwarz, indicates that individuals need to perform three important primary tasks that form the basis for all other further activities within the network. These are [14]:

- ***Building a network***, i.e. adding new people to the network so that there are resources available when a learning need arises;
- ***Maintaining the network***, where a central task is keeping in touch with relevant persons;
- ***Activating connections*** with selected persons at the time the learning need has to be solved.

Any learning activities in the network will build on the results of these tasks. Although this study gives an indication of the process of networking, there is very little literature available on how professionals go about creating and using their personal professional networks for *learning* purposes. It is unexplored which strategies they use in building and maintaining their network to make it optimal for learning. It is not known why they add certain people (and their related expertise) to the network and why not others. It is unclear which criteria they use for these decisions. It is also not known which strategies they employ in activating connections with relevant others in these networks when they need support in their learning. Social networking technology is certainly used to support these primary tasks: the many online networking and resource-sharing platforms aimed at social work professionals and the many individuals and groups working in this field found on open social networking sites such as Facebook and LinkedIn bear witness to this. These sites often include network visualisation technology and social matching systems to help users get more control over their personal professional networks. However, it is unclear how effective these technologies are in supporting professionals in their strategies for learning from their networks.

When looking at designing technology to support the learning situation of social work professionals, it is important to gain more insight into how these professionals build, maintain and activate their personal professional networks for learning.

3 Need for User-Centred Technology Design

The need for more insight into the networking methods of social work professionals is also supported by theoretical and practical arguments in technology design. The learning environment of professionals involved in social work practice is one of networked learning, with an emphasis on using dialogue and discussion as a tool for learning and finding suitable dialogue partners. To look into the role of technology in this form of networked learning, we will use the concept of a Learning Network (LN), which is defined as a "particular kind of online, social network that is designed to support (non-formal) learning in a particular domain"[15]. The online mirror of the real-world personal professional networks, built and managed by individual social work professionals to support their non-formal learning, can be considered a form of LN which we refer to as Personal Learning Networks (PLN).

The definition of a Learning Network above is a functional definition, describing what such a network does, but silent on exactly how such a LN can be or should be implemented into practice. Implementations of Learning Networks (LNs) in practice (such as the Library School [16] or the VM2 network [17]) show a myriad of underlying design options, concerning:

– *Pedagogy*: LNs can be used to support non-formal learning, informal learning and even formal learning, in diverse learning settings (formal education, adult education, etc.)
– *Organisational structures*: LNs can have various user roles (student, teacher, support staff, learner, peer, group, moderator, etc.) and different levels of user control

– **Supportive technologies**: LNs can include basic functionalities (such as profiling, forum, chat, feed aggregator, etc.) and more advanced services such as navigation services (recommendation of relevant and useful content) [18], positioning services (assessing the position of a learner with regard to content or peers in order to give appropriate advise) [19,20] and communication and collaboration services (connecting learners who may be able to collectively solve problems) [21]

When moving from concepts to practice, design decisions need to be made with respect to pedagogy, organisation and use and functionality of technology in a LN. The technical functionalities in a learning network seem to be very closely determined by the pedagogy and the organisational structure of the network. For example, a navigation service and a positioning service presume a network with people and content, available on one technical platform. To be able to design relevant technology for Personal Learning Networks, it needs to be investigated what the underlying pedagogy and organisation of such a Personal Learning Network are. This presents a theoretical argument for the need for more insight into how professionals build and use their personal professional network for learning. The general approach we take to designing technology in Personal Learning Networks is to start from the individual learner's point-of-view of the network as in the research on Personal Learning Environments (PLE) [22,23,24]. Here, technologies give a high level of user control to the learner at the centre of the network.

In practice, technology seems to be successful in its purpose, when it complements an established way of working and solves acutely faced problems [25,26,27] or when it creates new opportunities to work [28]. To be able to design technology that can complement the natural working methods for social work professionals, it is important to have a clear picture of their current way of working in finding relevant dialogue partners, Technology can then be used to support professionals in effectively and efficiently building and maintaining their personal learning networks and finding suitable dialogue partners in these networks.

4 Conclusions and Further Work

Professionals in social work learn through dialogue and discussion with suitable dialogue partners in their personal professional networks. We think that studying these personal professional networks and their use to support learning in practice is a good starting point to discover these professionals' needs on supportive technology. An empirical study (i.e. an extensive survey and in-depth interviews) is planned, which will give us more insight into the strategies that professionals use to build and maintain their personal professional networks and to activate connections with relevant others within these networks. The specific interest of this study is to discover the strategies that increase the support offered by these networks for learning. On the basis of this study, a theoretical framework can be created on the concept of a Personal Learning Network, in relation to the concepts of Learning Networks and Personal Learning Environments. Such a study will also show the extent to which technology matches the working practice of these professionals now. Starting from this real-world context, existing technological solutions can be improved to offer professionals more effective and efficient support in creating personal learning networks and finding suitable dialogue partners in these networks.

Acknowledgements. This paper provides a theoretical framework that will be part of a PhD study conducted within the LTfLL project. The LTfLL project is partially supported/co-funded by the European Union under the Information and Communication Technologies (ICT) theme of the 7th Framework Programme for R&D. This document does not represent the opinion of the European Union, and the European Union is not responsible for any use that might be made of its content.

References

1. Trevithick, P.: Revisiting the Knowledge Base of Social Work: A Framework for Practice. British Journal of Social Work 38(6), 1212–1237 (2008), doi:10.1093/bjsw/bcm026
2. Hearn, S., White, N.: Communities of Practice: linking knowledge, policy and practice. In: Workshop on estimating and interpreting probability (2009), http://www.odi.org.uk/resources/download/1129.pdf
3. Payne, M.: What Is Professional Social Work?, 2nd edn. Venture Press, Birmingham (2006)
4. Trevithick, P.: Social Work Skills: A Practice Handbook, 2nd edn. Open University Press, Buckingham (2005)
5. Bolhuis, S., Simons, R.-J.: Naar een Breder Begrip van Leren. In: Human Resource Development Organiseren van het leren, Samsom, pp. 37–51
6. White, N.: Networks, Groups and Catalysts: The Sweet Spot for Forming Online Learning Communities. In: Net*Working 2002 (2002), http://www.fullcirc.com/community/networkscatalystscommunity.htm
7. UNESCO-UNEVOC eForum, http://www.unevoc.unesco.org/eforum.php
8. Zunia network, http://www.zunia.org
9. Eraut, M.: Non-Formal Learning and Tacit Knowledge in Professional Work. British Journal of Educational Psychology 70, 113–136 (2000)
10. Von Krogh, G., Ichijo, K., Nonaka, I.: Enabling Knowledge Creation: How to Unlock the Mystery of Tacit Knowledge and Release the Power of Innovation, 292 p. Oxford University Press, Oxford (2000)
11. Grabher, G., Ibert, O.: Bad company? The Ambiguity of Personal Knowledge Networks. Journal of Economic Geography 6(3), 251–271 (2005), doi:10.1093/jeg/lbi014
12. Johnson, M.: Expanding the Concept of Networked Learning. In: Proceedings of the 6th International Conference on Networked Learning, Halkidiki, Greece, pp. 154–161 (2008)
13. Moss Kanter, R.: On Twitter and in the Workplace, It's Power to the Connectors (2009),
http://blogs.harvardbusiness.org/kanter/2009/11/power-to-the-connectors.html

14. Nardi, B., Whittaker, S., Schwarz, H.: NetWORKers and their Activity in Intensional Networks. Computer Supported Cooperative Work (CSCW) 11(1-2), 205–242 (2002), doi:10.1023/A:1015241914483
15. Sloep, P.B.: Fostering Sociability in Learning Networks through Ad-Hoc Transient Communities. In: Purvis, M., Savarimuthu, B.T.R. (eds.) ICCMSN 2008. LNCS (LNAI), vol. 5322, pp. 62–75. Springer, Heidelberg (2008)
16. Bruijnzeels, R., Bitter-Rijpkema, M., Verjans, S.: The Library School: Empowering the Sustainable Innovation Capacity of New Librarians. Paper presented at the The Global Librarian: Satellite Meeting - World Library and Information Congress: 76th IFLA General Conference and Assembly, Bors, Sverige (2010)
17. Goes, M., Delea, P., de Laat, M.: Onderzoek naar de Succes- en Faalfactoren bij het Leernetwerk Consortium VMBO-MBO. Centrum. Heerlen (2010)
18. Drachsler, H.: Navigation Support for Learners in Informal Learning Networks. SIKS Dissertation Series No. 2009-37. Open University of the Netherlands, CELSTEC, Heerlen (October 16, 2009) ISBN 9789079447312
19. Kalz, M.: Placement Support for Learners in Learning Networks. Open University of the Netherlands, CELSTEC, Heerlen (October 16, 2009)
20. Berlanga, A.J., Spoelstra, H., Rajagopal, K., Smithies, A., Braidman, I., Wild, F.: Assisting Learners in Monitoring their Conceptual Development. In: International Conference on Computer Supported Education, CSEDU 2010 (accepted 2010)
21. Van Rosmalen, P.: Supporting the Tutor in the Design and Support of Adaptive e-learning. SIKS Dissertation Series No. 2008-07. The Open University of the Netherlands, Heerlen (2007)
22. Van Harmelen, M.: Personal Learning Environments. In: Sixth IEEE International Conference on Advanced Learning Technologies (ICALT 2006), pp. 815–816. IEEE, Los Alamitos (2006), doi:10.1109/ICALT.2006.1652565
23. Van Harmelen, M.: Personal Learning Environments (2007), http://octette.cs.man.ac.uk/jitt/index.php/Personal_Learning_Environments
24. Attwell, G., Cook, J., Ravenscroft, A.: Appropriating Technologies for Contextual Knowledge: Mobile Personal Learning Environments. In: Best Practices for the Knowledge Society. Knowledge, Learning, Development and Technology for All, pp. 15–25. Springer, Heidelberg (2009)
25. Dourish, P., Bellotti, V.: Awareness and Coordination in Shared Workspaces, pp. 107–114 (November 1992)
26. Dourish, P., Bly, S.: Portholes: Supporting Awareness in a Distributed Work Group. In: Proceedings of the SIGCHI conference on Human factors in computing systems, pp. 541–547. ACM, New York (1992), http://portal.acm.org/citation.cfm?id=142982
27. Gutwin, C., Roseman, M., Greenberg, S.: A Usability Study of Awareness Widgets in a Shared Workspace Groupware System. In: Proceedings of the Conference on Computer-Supported Cooperative Work, pp. 258–267. ACM Press, Boston (1996)
28. Vetere, F., Howard, S., Gibbs, M.R.: Phatic Technologies: Sustaining Sociability through Ubiquitous Computing. In: First International Workshop on Social Implications of Ubiquitous Technology. ACM Conference on Human Factors in Computing Systems, CHI 2005 (2005)

Deep Learning Design for Sustainable Innovation within Shifting Learning Landscapes

Andrew Ravenscroft[1], Tom Boyle[1], John Cook[1], and Andreas Schmidt[2]

[1] Learning Technology Research Institute (LTRI), London Metropolitan University, UK
[2] FZI Forschungszentrum Informatik, Karlsruhe, Germany

Abstract. This paper describes a new approach to designing Technology Enhanced Learning (TEL) in the contemporary, or Web 2.0, landscape and beyond. This embraces the new possibilities that emerging technologies provide for learning, and the pace of change in the development and application of these technologies. In addressing this challenge we outline the framework of Deep Learning Design (DLD) and summarise how it has been developed from, and mapped to, four different TEL initiatives. We argue that this adoption of DLD has led to relatively large-scale and sustainable innovations. It also outlines clear directions for near-future emphases in TEL design and related methodology.

Keywords: learning design, sustainable innovation, contemporary pedagogy, case studies.

1 A Rationale for Deep Learning Design (DLD)

A general perception in the Technology Enhanced Learning (hereafter TEL) community that has been made explicit by some researchers [1], is that changes in the underpinning technologies for learning and teaching is occurring at a pace that we have never before experienced. This is combined with a similar pace in the emergence of new digital tools that offer original opportunities for education. This shifting landscape for TEL necessitates a broader and more profound understanding of *design*, that is more future-proof than relying on the latest or emerging technologies and yet embraces the collaborative, multimodal and ubiquitous nature of learning in 21C. This implies that we need an approach to learning design that is in harmony with the digitally literate learner and teacher in the Web 2.0 age and beyond, and, also recognises attested notions of pedagogy that we can re-configure to make learning more effective [2]. We argue that using technology to make education better is more important than using digital tools to do it differently.

In addressing this difficult but important challenge, this article will outline a new framework of Deep Learning Design (hereafter DLD), that is described in greater detail in [1], that we have developed further through its application to four distinctive TEL projects that are Case Studies of the approach. These focus on: supporting collaborative and critical thinking and learning on the web (Digital Dialogue Games); the production and use of pedagogy rich reusable learning objects on a large scale (Centre for Excellence in Teaching and Learning in Reusable Learning Objects); the use of mobile phones to realize learner-centred and highly contextualised learning experiences (CONTSENS); and the exploitation of social and semantic technologies to promote increased informal learning in the workplace (MATURE).

Our approach has some complementarity with learning design more generally [3]. A main difference however is that DLD is a research driven paradigm for designing contemporary learning that adopts a more humanistic and holistic stance, instead of focusing ostensibly on sharing teaching practice. It incorporates an emphasis on learners' and teachers' active processes and practices within contexts, or is more 'performative' and based on the meditational role of learning technologies [4]. The framework makes use of a combination of Design-based Research [5] and Action Research methodologies. But, unlike Design-based Research, that is quite wideranging in supporting educational research in general and is arguably quite diffuse, DLD has the particular focus of designing learning in the Web 2.0 landscape and beyond.

To summarise, the Deep Learning Design framework is a way of thinking about TEL design and development, and a set of guiding principles for planning, running and assessing TEL projects. In a sense, it could be argued that it 'packages up' some existing and recent notions of good practice, based on successfully executed projects that have led to sustainable innovations, such as the Digital Dialogue Game and Reusable Learning Objects work that is described in Section 3. However a key contribution is that it specifies this proposed practice in a clear and unambiguous way that also supports comparisons across projects. So applying this framework to TEL projects supports the straightforward identification of conformance to, or violation of, principles and practices that have been shown to lead to successful and sustainable TEL innovations.

2 Summarising the Principles of Deep Learning Design

This Section summarises the key principles of DLD that were originally proposed by [1], that have been refined through being applied to the broader and more varied range of projects that are presented in this article.

1. Theoretical and conceptual foundations. There is a commonly held view throughout the TEL community that applications should be informed by learning theory or pedagogical frameworks, and without these, they aren't TEL designs. Instead they are simply interaction designs. This means that theory is the 'anchor' for good design. Also, and perhaps most obviously, good theories have powerful potential to guide design, and therefore instantiating them through technology will increase the likelihood of a TEL interaction leading to the desired learning. Similarly, and related to the points below about opposing pure technological determinism, a theory, like a design, does not have to be technology dependant. So adopting a theoretical stance means that we can appropriately articulate technology to realise a more wideranging and often proven approach to learning, rather than adopting an approach that is simply doable through current or emerging technology.

2. Design as the key development concept. In accepting the condition that new technologies for learning are both constantly emerging and changing, we argue that 'design' is a suitably rich, flexible and yet formal enough concept to help us to engineer, or support, learning in our digital landscape. Additionally, a design based approach is likely to promote a better understanding of the undercurrent processes at play. This stance is partly a reaction to research in the TEL field that has been overly predicated on technologies. It is interesting and important to note that, for most previous technological waves (e.g. Artificial Intelligence and Education, Hypertext, Computer Supported Collaborative Learning), often prestigious researchers and research centres have advocated these as being imbued with great transformative powers that will address the fundamental problems with learning. But as yet, this has not been shown to be the case.

3. Development and interaction in context. DLD recognises that, in an increasingly complex and unpredictable digital world, TEL design and development will benefit from appreciating the social and cultural conditions of particular contexts, and focusing on clear problems or opportunities. So the resulting designs should ideally incorporate an articulation of learning that links cognition, communication and context [6]. This does not suggest that we cannot adapt and reconfigure TEL solutions to work across contexts. It simply foregrounds the necessity to address the complexities of learning-teaching contexts and similarities or variations across them.

4. Evaluation linked to conceptual frameworks and authentic contexts. A final key element of DLD is the adoption of an evaluative framework linked to the theoretical and conceptual foundations and authentic learning activities or contexts. This accepts that in contemporary and often highly contextualized learning situations, this can be challenging. For example, to cover both ecological validity and reproducible empirical rigor, the development of a suitable framework can involve qualitative and/or quantitative methods, and may also include Action Research or more conventional empirical approaches. This stance does not rule-out the value of laboratory studies, in learning science for example. It simply foregrounds the proposal that iterative design linked to evaluation in context is more likely to lead to, or will more directly lead to, sustainable innovation.

3 Four Exemplar Projects of DLD

This Section gives a brief account of how the DLD approach has been developed from, and applied across, four TEL projects. This summarises a more comprehensive account and mapping (to the principles of DLD) that is given in [7]. The first two of these have already led to sustainable innovations, and the latter two outline clear directions for near-future work that that we argue should be taken into account to realize future innovations in their related areas.

The first project represented 'A digital dialogue and social software perspective' (see www.interloc.org.uk). This project built on the social constructivist ideas of Vygotsky and Bahktin, and in particular their notions of dialectic and dialogic [8]. These were articulated through a design paradigm of *Dialogue Games* [9]. The resulting technologies, AcademicTalk and InterLoc, were developed within Action Research teams following an evolutionary prototyping method. This approach has proven efficacy for a range of learning problems and contexts, as documented in a range of research projects over the past ten years that are summarised in [9]. These led to considerable improvements in the design and implementation of the current dialogue game approach that has recently been deployed across five HE Institutions in the UK, with over 350 students and 10 tutors [10]. The evaluation showed that the approach: was valued by tutors and students; was effective in promoting critical thinking; and, generally supported deeper engagement between peers [10].

The second project represented 'A learning objects and reusable learning design perspective' (see www.rlo-cetl.ac.uk) which developed over 200 pedagogy rich multimedia learning objects that were conceived as 'micro contexts for learning'. These were based on the constructivist ideas of Piaget and Bruner, and in particular Bruner's notion of 'ratiocinative amplifiers' [11, 12]. These were resolved into a series of design principles for developing reusable learning objects [13]. A major evolution in these design ideas led to the concept of Generative Learning Objects (GLOs) that are authored with a GLO Maker tool (see www.glomaker.org). These rely on *design patterns* rather than content as the basis for reuse. The individual RLOs and GLO Maker tool were developed through an Agile approach involving tutors, and usually students, working in groups to collaboratively design solutions in their teaching-learning situations. The learning objects have been deployed in a wide range of teaching-learning contexts, where some have demonstrated particularly positive results when used in blended learning situations as diverse as learning computer programming [14] and Study Skills [15].

The third project represented 'A mobile learning and augmented contexts for development perspective' (CONTSENS project). This particularly focused on applying Vygotsky's account of the temporal dimensions of learning to development that revolves around attention and perception [16]. Here notions of time fields and the centre of gravity within related notions of causality are important and so these tools within an Augmented Context for Development could, for example, provide the visualisations that assist the underlying functions that are necessary for learning. In this case the development methodology was a (design-based) evolutionary prototyping approach, which followed the typical cognitive science 'research triangle' incorporating theory, empirical studies and computational studies [17]. Evaluations confirmed that these notions of attention, perception, temporality and causality seemed key processes in the augmented and temporal contexts for development.

These notions of temporality, learning rich contexts, and the development of knowledge and understanding over time are particularly relevant to our final example of DLD, which focuses on digitally mediated informal learning that is related to collaborative knowledge management and development at work. So our final exemplar project represented 'An informal learning and knowledge maturing at work perspective', that is being performed within a large-scale and ongoing European project called "MATURE: Continuous Social Learning in Knowledge Networks" (www.mature-ip.eu). This is an important project to consider because in shifting to informal learning and knowledge maturing in the workplace [18], and emphasising social and semantic technologies, we are applying DLD to another widespread context (of work) and also testing it's applicability to a forward looking and complex initiative with strong 'Web Science' [19] features. In MATURE the design based research approach has also included Use Cases that were linked to personas and particular knowledge maturing activities. This specialised Use Case technique was primarily synthetic, in that it was a *language of design* that all stakeholders could understand and contribute to. Also eight initial Design Studies were performed which investigated how candidate technologies could support the key conceptual, technical and user dimensions of the project. The successful evaluation of this initial design work led to the development of four distinctive 'Demonstrators' that are in the process of being formatively evaluated.

4 Discussion and Future Directions

This article has outlined and illustrated a new framework of Deep Learning Design for TEL. Two of the included projects that are exemplars of this approach (dialogue games and learning objects) have been successful and led to sustainable innovations, especially because they focused on design to solve problems and did not favour a technology and then look for its application. Instead they matched technologies to problems and then refined their approach in light of evaluations. The two later examples (mobile learning and MATURE) have a related motivation, namely exploiting emerging technologies to realise new forms of learning and scope out new directions for TEL that need to be considered in near-future developments.

All these approaches have developed designs within complex and changing contexts, where they have justified and demonstrated the DLD approach. In doing so they have had to embrace the interplay and co-evolution of design and digitally mediated practice, and demonstrated the need for faster and more responsive 'design-development-evaluation' cycles, which is likely to become increasingly common, to ensure that TEL research leads to research-led innovation. A related trend is that advances in Web Science and the notion of the future web as a 'social machine', means that TEL will inevitably require 'social learning machines', and DLD with its emphasis on 'the social' is arguably a very useful framework for developing these.

Acknowledgments

The Authors gratefully acknowledge all colleagues on the DDG, RLO-CETL, CONTSENS and MATURE Project who have contributed to the work. We are also grateful to our funders, the UK JISC and HEFCE, and EC Lifelong Learning and FP7 Programmes.

References

1. Ravenscroft, A., Boyle, T.: Deep Learning Design for Technology Enhanced Learning. In: Proceedings of International Conference on Educational Media (Ed-Media), Toronto, June 29-July 2 (2010)
2. Ravenscroft, A.: Social Software, Web 2.0 and Learning: Status and implications of an evolving paradigm. Editorial for Special Issue of Journal of Computer Assisted Learning (JCAL) 21(1), 1–5 (2009)
3. Lockyear, L., Bennet, A., Agostinho, S., Harper, B. (eds.): Learning Design and Learning Objects, vol. II. Information Science, Hershey
4. Saljo, R.: Digital tools and challenges to institutional traditions of learning: technologies, social memory and the performative nature of learning (2010)

5. Design-based research collective: Design-Based Research: An Emerging Paradigm for Educational Inquiry. Educational Researcher 32(1), 5–8 (2002)
6. Ravenscroft, A.: Towards highly communicative eLearning communities: Developing a socio-cultural framework for cognitive change. In: Land, R., Bayne, S. (eds.) Cyberspace Education, ch. 9, pp. 130–145. Routledge, New York (2004)
7. Ravenscroft, A., Boyle, T., Cook, J., Schmidt, A.: Deep Learning Design for Sustainable Innovation within Shifting Learning Landscapes. LTRI Technical Report, London Metropolitan University (2010)
8. Ravenscroft, A., Wegerif, R.B., Hartley, J.R.: Reclaiming thinking: dialectic, dialogic and learning in the digital age. In: Underwood., J., Dockrell, J. (Guest eds.). Learning through Digital Technologies, British Journal of Educational Psychology Monograph Series, vol. II(5), pp. 39–5 (2007)
9. Ravenscroft, A.: Promoting Thinking and Conceptual Change with Digital Dialogue Games. Journal of Computer Assisted Learning (JCAL) 23(6), 453–465 (2007)
10. Ravenscroft, A., McAlister, S., Sagar, M.: Digital Dialogue Games and InterLoc: Deep Leaning Design for Collaborative Argumentation on the Web. In: Pinkwart, N. (ed.) Educational Technologies for Teaching Argumentation Skills. Bentham Science E-Books (2009) (in Press)
11. Bruner, J.S.: The course of cognitive growth. American Psychologist 19(1), 1–15 (1964)
12. Flavell, J.H.: Piaget's Legacy. Psychological Science 7(4), 200–203 (1996)
13. Boyle, T.: Design principles for authoring dynamic, reusable learning objects. Australian Journal of Educational Technology 19(1), 46–58 (2003)
14. Boyle, T., Bradley, C., Chalk, P., Jones, R., Pickard, P.: Using blended learning to improve student success rates in learning to program. Journal of Educational Media, Special Edition on Blended Learning 28(2-3), 165 178 (2003)
15. Holley, D., Cook, J., Bradley, C., Haynes, R., Smith, C.: Getting Ahead at University: Using Reusable Learning Objects to Enhance Study Skills. Full paper presented at ED-MEDIA 2007 - World Conference on Educational Multimedia and Hypermedia, Vancouver, Canada, June 25-29 (2007)
16. Cook, J.: Mobile Phones as Mediating Tools within Augmented Contexts for Development. International Journal of Mobile and Blended Learning (Due March 2010)
17. Cook, J.: The Role of Dialogue in Computer-Based Learning and Observing Learning. An Evolutionary Approach to Theory. Journal of Interactive Media in Education (JIME) 5 (2002), `http://www-jime.open.ac.uk/2002/5`
18. Maier, R., Schmidt, A.: Characterizing Knowledge Maturing: A Conceptual Process Model for Integrating ELearning and Knowledge Management. In: 4th Conf. Professional Knowledge Management Experiences and Visions, GITO, pp. 325–334 (2007)
19. Hendler, J., Shadbolt, N., Hall, W., Berners-Lee, T., Weitzner, D.: Web Science: An Interdisciplinary Approach to Understanding the Web. Communications of the ACM 51(7), 60–69 (2008)

Evaluation of the Software "e³-Portfolio" in the Context of the Study Program "Problem-Solving Competencies"

Thomas Sporer, Magdalena Steinle, and Johannes Metscher

Institute for Media and Educational Technology
Universitätsstr. 2, 86135 Augsburg, Germany
{surname.lastname}@its.uni-augsburg.de

Abstract. This paper presents the evaluation of an e-portfolio system which has been developed at the University of Augsburg in the context of a study program supporting the acquisition of key competencies. After describing the object of the evaluation and the design-based research approach of the study program's development the results of the evaluation will be presented. It is shown how the software facilitates the students' cooperation and collaboration in self-organized project-groups, in what ways the reflection of the project work can be guided and how the software tool should be enhanced in future.

Keywords: evaluation, e-portfolio, e-collaboration, e-assessment.

1 Introduction

The study program "Problem-solving Competencies" offers students at the University of Augsburg the possibility to gain practical experience and to develop key competencies in extra-curricular projects close to their formal course of study. The program aims to create a learning context within the system of Bachelor and Master which rewards student's commitment beyond the given curriculum and to motivate students to gather learning experiences in non-formal contexts of education. To accredit student's learning activities in the extra-curricular project groups a curricular framework has been established which integrates informal learning into the regular course of studies. It is based on an assessment strategy which promotes the students reflection of their learning experiences via e-portfolios.

2 Introducing the Object of Evaluation: „e³-Portfolio"

The assessment in the study program combines the didactic function of supporting the students' reflection with the accreditation of the project work in the formal curriculum. Throughout the term the students document and reflect the current events in their projects in a project diary about once a week. The process of reflection is facilitated by prompts in form of guiding questions. By the end of term the students compose a project report in which they look back on their activities in the project groups. Contrary to the reflection in the project diary the students contemplate a longer period of time in this project report. The students refer to the reflections collected in the project diary, but reconstruct these reflections to a personal learning history and draw conclusions from their participation in the project [1].

At first the portfolio-based reflection work has been implemented and tested without any ICT-support. However, it turned out to be important for the study program to set up a learning space where all the information is aggregated virtually. Furthermore the multi- and hypermedial possibilities of electronic portfolios were not fully realized in this paper-and-pencil mode. Therefore a custom-made learning environment has been developed which combines e-communities, e-portfolios and e-assessment - hence the name "e³-portfolio" [2]: There the users can (a) organize themselves in groups in the community area. Furthermore it helps the students (b) to collect artifacts of the project work and reflective writings in a portfolio area and it (c) structures the recognition of the students' learning outcomes and working results in the assessment area.

The community area contains information concerning the ideas, the goals and the contents of the projects involved in the study program. This overview helps students to inform themselves about the project groups and to join these groups. To some extend it also makes tools for project and knowledge management available (i.e. community-blog, wiki, etc.). The results of the project work gathered in the community area can then be used as records of the student's achievements in the portfolio area. With the aid of a blog-based project diary the project activities and the learning process throughout the term can be documented. Additionally each participant of the program can set up a personal homepage with information on his or her goals, competencies and interests. The assessment area serves as a tool for the administration and the formal recognition of the participation in the extra-curricular communities of practice in the study program. Here students who want to accredit their project participation for their undergraduate or postgraduate studies can submit their working results and project report at the end of the term. Thereupon they get feedback from a teacher who is responsible for the evaluation of their learning outcomes [1].

3 Instructional Design Approach and Process of Development

The development of the study program followed a design-based research approach. First the design of learning environment described above has been finished, then the corresponding software e³-portfolio was developed. The development process of this software broadly was informed by the "ADDIE-model". However, we did not proceed strictly linear but rather in an agile style which led to an iterative and circular approach within the developmental phases [2]. In addition to the last phase of the summative evaluation the previous phases contained formative elements, too. To give an overview:

• *Analysis*. After the re-design of the study program in the winter term 2006/07 portfolio work has become an essential component of the program's didactic concept. To implement this concept various e-portfolio systems have been tested and in the summer term 2007 the software "ELGG" (www.elgg.org) was used in a trial. During this phase of analysis it turned out that ELGG only met our program requirements with many restrictions. Thus we decided to develop our own e-portfolio system.

- *Design*. Based on the didactic concept we defined the requirements for the software in winter term 2007/08. Therefore we modeled the activities of the study program's stakeholders (participants in the study program, leaders of the project groups, teachers evaluating the learning outcomes, etc.). Using methods of agile software development we mapped out the learning processes and organizational structures, which should be supported by the software. The results of this design phase were documented in the form of user stories.
- *Development*. Since the summer term of 2008 the software was implemented using the agile process-framework "Scrum". The technical realization was carried out on the basis of the open source content management system "Drupal" (www.drupal.org). The first sprints aimed at building a basic installation. Further sprints implemented specific modules (e.g. organic groups, real names) to realize the requirements defined in the user stories. Since not all requirements could be fulfilled by the usage of the existing modules, we additionally developed our own modules [3].
- *Implementation*. After the first sprints were realized the software was released for the students and project groups in a trial phase. The system was introduced at an introductory seminar of the study program and at a workshop with the project leaders. However, using the software was voluntary in winter term 2008/09. After another sprint-release in summer term 2009 the use of e^3-portfolio became obligatory for all participants of the study program to accredit their extra-curricular learning.
- *Evaluation*. During earlier phases of the development process there have been smaller evaluations. However, an extensive formative evaluation was run in winter term 2008/09 at the end of the trial phase. At the end of the summer term 2009 a summative evaluation was carried out which recorded the state of the development. This evaluation aimed at reviewing the software's employment in the study program and to identify issues for its further development.

Since we have presented the first three phases of this developmental process [2] as well as its results [3] elsewhere, we are focusing on the evaluation of e^3-portfolio's implementation in this paper.

4 Formative Evaluation and Summary of Results

At the end of winter term 2009 a group interview with seven users of e^3-portfolio was conducted. The group was selected for the interview because of its heterogeneous use of the software. The group was very active on the platform and most of the group's cooperation and collaboration was organized with its help. Through this group interview we could gather information concerning the group member's patterns of use, the frequency and the motivation of its use. Furthermore, existing problems, bugs and usability difficulties could be revealed and suggestions for future developments could be collected. Additionally to the group interview individual interviews with non-users of e^3-portfolio were carried out. These individual interviews were intended to show which reasons participants of the study program have not to use the software and how the reflective practice built into the study program is judged by the students. Another goal was to find out about usability problems and software functions which would enhance e^3-portfolio.

The interviewed group meets about once a week in a "face to face" setting for an editorial meeting and to discuss current project activities. The community area of e³-portfolio was used for organizational tasks, for the provision of information for all group members and for working collaboratively on documents by them. All members use the group blog and the wiki to work on common tasks, to coordinate appointments and to organize the teamwork (e.g. upload protocols attached to blog-posts). The group-blog is valued by the project members as a shared space and is preferred to other channels of communication and data repository. Another frequently used tool is the wiki. Its handling is considered to be simple and comprehensible.

Since keeping a project diary is rewarded with a certificate and there is the possibility to earn credit points for the project-report the time invested on the reflection of the experience in the projects is generally perceived to be worthwhile. Due to a lack of time the students usually write their diary entries in irregular intervals and tend to reconstruct the events since the last entry. Some voices were saying that there might be too much stress on reflection – especially if there are events in the project without noteworthy results. In this case it is felt to be annoying. It is viewed as an artificial need to create content for the diary and consumes time without any purpose.

Almost all non-users of e³-portfolio kept their diary with the help of a template in Word-format. The preference for that "paper and pencil"-mode was attributed to the easier handling of a word-processing program. The reasons given for that were the existing habits of text production and the better overview of the scope of the diary. Apparently another important reason for not using the platform was the lack of trust in data security. A case was reported in which one user's diary entry was visible for all logged-in users. Hence, some interviewees were so uncertain that they asked other group members to confirm the "invisibility" of their diary entries. In that regard a secure socket layer connection during the login and the transmission of data was expected – regardless of the sensitivity of the data. Closely connected to data security were concerns about the traceability of the writing activities that scared off some interviewees because they got the impression that they are being controlled.

Another technical reason for the disuse was that it is only usable with internet access. The non-users, however, preferred to write offline and did not like to depend on internet access. Furthermore, the supply of a new online service was criticized. Since all services relevant to their studies should be accessible at one central point it was suggested that e³-portfolio should seamlessly integrate into the institutional learning management system. Beyond that the interviews showed that the additional benefit of e³-portfolio is not yet evident for many participants of the study program. There was a somewhat reserved attitude because the use of e³-portfolio was not obligatory when the interviews were conducted.

5 Summative Evaluation and Summary of Results

In the summative evaluation all registered users were asked via mail to participate in an online survey. One fifth of the approximately 150 registered users took part in the survey (n=31). The survey contained questions requiring general information on the participants. Here it was asked if they participate in the project groups and if they participate in the study program. Afterwards questions concerning the working styles in the project groups and usage of e³-portfolio were asked. Further questions were targeted on evaluating the users' satisfaction with the functionality of the software and on gathering ideas for its further development.

The most important channel of communication in the groups turned out to be e-mail. The designation of the second and third most important channels of communication was more heterogeneous. To our surprise we learned that e³-portfolio is considered to be more important than messenger, VoIP and other environments for cooperation and collaboration within the groups. However, half of the respondents indicated to use e³-portfolio only between one or three times per term, about a quarter once a month and about another quarter once a week.

Two thirds of the respondents generally regarded the community area as useful. Like the results of the formative evaluation the most important reasons for using the community area was the use of the group-blog and its function as a document repository function. This was considered helpful to build a common knowledge-base and to document the results of the project work. The second most important option to support the project work was seen in the exchange of knowledge within the group, the coordination of the teamwork and in facilitating decision-making in the group. However, potential for improvement of e³-portfolio was seen in implementing feedback mechanisms, an advanced document repository and an easier way to coordinate appointments like group meetings.

The portfolio area was generally regarded as useful. However, since the use of the platform was not obligatory in summer term 2009, only 16 respondents actually used e³-portfolio to write their project diary. Most of them experienced it to be supportive for their reflective writing but only a minority actually kept their diary weekly. Out of the eleven respondents who composed their project report via e³-portfolio, eight respondents felt supported by the environment. In order to improve its support the following suggestions were made: The usability for writing a diary entry and composing a project report could be improved by extending the formatting options for the text, by introducing an auto-save-function as well as a spell-checker. Furthermore some respondents would like to get feedback on their diary entries by other students.

Concerning the assessment area most respondents stated to get a helpful overview of their achievements and the recent state of the credits points earned in the study program. Out of the persons who had handed in a project diary or project report via e³-portfolio most persons felt to be well informed about the status of their submission. Almost all of them believed to have received high-quality feedback on their project reports through the assessment criteria. However, the respondents made proposals for improvement: The visual presentation of the feedback-form was criticized because it was not structured according to the assessment criteria. Another suggestion beyond the project diary and report was the wish to get feedback on the results of project work as well.

6 Conclusion and Outlook

This paper presented the results of the evaluation of an e-portfolio system which was developed in consideration of the specific requirements of a study program supporting the acquirement of key competencies in higher education. The evaluation contained on the one hand formative elements which helped to adjust the software to the actual needs of its users, to add missing functions and to improve the usability during the trial phase. On the other hand, it involved a summative evaluation of the final product as well as its implementation and introduction in the study program. The evaluation's results show that the portfolio-based assessment is generally considered worthwhile by the students. However, the additional benefit of the "e" in the context of the portfolio work is seen more critical than the recent hype concerning e-portfolios in higher education would suggest.

The students taking part in the formative evaluation tended to be hesitant to switch from the "paper and pencil"-mode of the portfolio work to the electronic version. Hence we learned that on the one hand the benefits and advantages of e-portfolios need to be better conveyed to the students and on the other hand it is important to reduce implementation barriers (e.g. doubts regarding data security or unsubstantiated fears of control). Regarding the faux-pas of the unintended visibility of a student's diary entry during the trial phase and the resulting lack of trust in the software by its users, the agile approach of software development and the employment of the software prototype in an early phase of the implementation need to be reconsidered.

The summative evaluation confirmed some of the formative evaluation's results but led to new insights as well. In summary, e^3-portfolio is so far only used by few participants of the project groups to collaborate and cooperate, even though the respondents attribute an additional benefit to the community area. Here it would be desirable to integrate open interfaces to third party applications (GoogleDocs, Doodle, etc.) which would give the community area the flexibility and adaptability of a personal learning-environment. Until then, e^3-portfolio will presumably be used primarily for handing in the project diary and the project report as well as viewing the feedback from the teachers. For the future, a seamless integration of the assessment area into our university's learning management system should also be realized. With regard to the portfolio area small adaptations need to be realized. However, in general the community area is well developed and is a unique feature of the software.

References

1. Sporer, T., Sippel, S., Meyer, P.: Using E-Portfolios as an Assessment Instrument within the Study-Programme "Problem-Solving Competencies". In: Baumgartner, P., Zauchner, S., Bauer, R. (eds.) The Potential of E-Portfolios in Higher Education, pp. 107–119. Studienverlag, Innsbruck (2009)
2. Sporer, T., Jenert, T., Meyer, P., Metscher, J.: Developing a platform for the integration of informal learning into the formal curriculum of higher education. In: Proceedings of World Conference on Educational Multimedia, Hypermedia and Telecommunications 2008, pp. 3063–3070. AACE, Chesapeake (2008)
3. Meyer, P., Sporer, T., Metscher, J.: e^3-Portfolio – Supporting and Assessing Project-based Learning in Higher Education via E-Portfolios. In: Cress, U., Dimitrova, V., Specht, M. (eds.) EC-TEL 2009. LNCS, vol. 5794, pp. 806–810. Springer, Heidelberg (2009)

Components of a Research 2.0 Infrastructure

Thomas Daniel Ullmann[1], Fridolin Wild[1], Peter Scott[1], Erik Duval[2],
Bram Vandeputte[2], Gonzalo Parra[2], Wolfgang Reinhardt[3], Nina Heinze[4],
Peter Kraker[5], Angela Fessl[5], Stefanie Lindstaedt[5], Till Nagel[6], and Denis Gillet[7]

[1] KMi, The Open University, Walton Hall, Milton Keynes, United Kingdom
{f.wild,t.ullmann,peter.scott}@open.ac.uk
[2] Departement Computerwetenschappen, Katholieke Universiteit Leuven, Leuven, Belgium
{erik.duval,bram.vandeputte,gonzalo.parra}@cs.kuleuven.be
[3] University of Paderborn, Fürstenallee 11, Computer Science Education Group,
33102 Paderborn, Germany
wolle@upb.de
[4] Knowledge Media Research Center, Konrad-Adenauer-Straße 40, Tuebingen, Germany
n.heinze@iwm-kmrc.de
[5] Know-Center and Graz University of Technology, Knowledge Management Institute, Austria
{pkraker,slind,afessl}@know-center.at
[6] Fachhochschule Potsdam, Potsdam, Germany
nagel@fh-potsdam.de
[7] Ecole Polytechnique Federale de Lausanne (EPFL), Lausanne, Switzerland
denis.gillet@epfl.ch

Abstract. In this paper, we investigate the components of a Research 2.0 infrastructure. We propose building blocks and their concrete implementation to leverage Research 2.0 practice and technologies in our field, including a publication feed format for exchanging publication data, a RESTful API to retrieve publication and Web 2.0 data, and a publisher suit for refining and aggregating data. We illustrate the use of this infrastructure with Research 2.0 application examples ranging from a Mash-Up environment, a mobile and multitouch application, thereby demonstrating the strength of this infrastructure.

Keywords: research 2.0, infrastructure, mash-ups, #Res2TEL.

1 Research 2.0

In technology-enhanced learning (TEL), the use of Web 2.0 technologies is now actively researched under banners such as "Learning 2.0" [1], "Personal Learning Environments" [2] or "Open Learning Environments" [3] and the like. In our Research 2.0 work, we aim to leverage the same opportunities for research on TEL. Research 2.0 can be defined as the application of new practices that focus on opening up the research process to broaden participation and collaboration with the help of new technologies that are able to foster continuous engagement and further development.

The basic idea is that, as researchers in technology-enhanced learning, we already know how to make use of for example blogs, wikis and forums to enhance collaborative work, but a full Research 2.0 framework might provide us with a much more powerful structure to make our research more effective.

The proposed components of a research infrastructure build upon the ideas of Research 2.0. By now, the focus is on individual practice and especially on the information management of publication and social media data. Based on this foundation, future extension will strengthen collaborative and community practice for a full "Research 2.0" framework.

The paper is organized as follows. We first outline the tree main components of the research information infrastructure. It follows an outline of a publication format, of services for publication and Web 2.0 data, and a publisher suit. The interplay between these components is shown with three applications, which are build on top of the infrastructure. Finally, we conclude and give a forecast about the next development steps.

2 Components of a TEL Researcher Information Infrastructure

The architecture of the infrastructure foresees three cornerstones [4]. (1) On the server side, services provide the backing data for the tools and widgets. The data are retrievable through a RESTful API. (2) On the client-side, widgets are combined into a coherent user experience with the help of a mash-up environment. Mobile and multi-touch applications use their own environment. (3) Widgets are administered in a directory, thereby subjecting the management of the portfolio to conscious maintenance and development. The fundament of the infrastructure tying these three pillars together is a set of interoperability formats.

Based on these cornerstones of Research 2.0 architectures we implemented data services, tools and widgets, using interoperability formats. We begin with the description of a publication exchange format. This defines a minimum set of guidelines easing the usage across different systems and partner infrastructures. It follows two data services approaches, one for research data including publication data and Web 2.0 data, and a publisher suit. These services are accessible for the use in tools and widgets. We outline three of them, which especially show the strength of the Research 2.0 mash-up architecture for the use in different application fields, including desktop, multitouch and mobile applications. We begin with the interoperability format.

Publication feeds: In order to facilitate the exchange of bibliographic data across the TEL community we use the concept of publication feeds. They are used for a lightweight exchange of publication metadata in a format commonly readable by existing Web 2.0 infrastructure. Hence, they can easily be combined, aggregated, visualized and re-released. This allows for inclusion of external parties who can expose their publication data trough publication feeds as well. An institution only needs to export its publication metadata once to automatically update all the subscribers to this feed (e.g. the STELLAR[1] Open Archive[2]). Publication feeds are RSS 1.0 feeds enhanced with elements from the SWRC and DC ontologies. The feeds are based on the BuRST format [5]. The basis for the publication feed are RSS 1.0, RDF, DC 1.1, SWRC 0.3, and BuRST 0.1. Modifications were applied where the format was outdated or underspecified.

ResearchFM service: The ResearchFM API was proposed as a RESTful API to provide publication and social data of authors in a unified way. Publication data shed light on of communication and collaboration of a research community, e.g. through analysis of co-authorship, co-citations and conference themes. With social media content, there is an unfathomable amount of data being generated almost constantly on the Web from research communities aside from the "official" publications. Heinze et al. [6] point out a number of Web 2.0 tools that are actively used during the daily work of researchers. However, in many community and group work situations the awareness of others is essential for effective and efficient work. This can be especially true in conference settings, since they provide the time and space for exploring new themes, finding like-minded researchers, or finding out what is being discussed online about one's own work. Reinhardt et al. [7] propose the model of Artefact-Actor-Networks (AANs) to store, analyse and visualise the actions, connections and structure of individuals within research communities on both social and artefact level. Therefore, they monitor the community's activities on social media sites based on given tags or given online handles and analyse the content of the gained artefacts. Every artefact is stored together with its metadata, semantic annotations and connections to other artefacts in a semantic database. Furthermore, the relations to actors referring to an artefact (e.g. creating, linking, retweeting, forwarding, discussing about, favouring, tagging) are stored and allow analysing the nexus of a community starting from any artefact or actor in the Artefact-Actor-Network. Furthermore, it allows the identification of semantically similar artefacts or actors from their respective content, extending the possibilities of co-citation measures or co-authorship relations.

As all the collected data is very similar on the one hand, and the tools and widgets use this data in a similar way on the other hand, it became apparent that a lot of benefit could come from a common API in terms of interconnectivity and reusability.

Services for publication data: A suite of publisher services was released to aid institutions and individuals in producing, aggregating and refining publication feeds in producing, aggregating and refining publication feed. The services include a BibTeX converter as well as a feed merger and a feed filtering service: these services can be mashed together, e.g. by using DERI pipes[3]. Additional to the data from the STELLAR Open Archive further TEL specific publication data has been gathered, namely the publication data of two conferences EC-TEL and ED-MEDIA, with others

---

[1] http://stellarnet.eu
[2] http://oa.stellarnet.eu/
[3] http://pipes.deri.org

to follow. This will help to feed more data into the Archive, and form an interesting foundation for tools and widgets to build upon. To have easy access to this data, all tools and widgets will be able to use the unified ResearchFM service.

Build upon the data services and interoperability format three applications are used to demonstrate the wide usage of the Research 2.0 infrastructure.

STELLAR Widget Universe: Builds upon the mash-up idea. It uses Elgg[4], an open source networking and publishing software, as showcasing platform for bringing together widgets and services and the legacy systems of the STELLAR partners. The widgets are delivered through the Wookie widget engine[5]. A plugin for Elgg enables to embed the widgets into Elgg (plugins for Wordpress, Moodle, LAMS exist as well). Researchers can arrange a widget per drag-and-drop on their dashboard. A list shows the gallery of all available widgets from the STELLAR directory. After the selection, the widget is automatically instantiated and can be used by the researcher. All widgets are packaged according to the widget 1.0 specification[6] and can thus not only be run within the reference implementation called Universe, but similarly within STELLAR's stakeholder platform TELeurope[7].

ScienceTable: While the widget universe is browser based, the ScienceTable is a multitouch tabletop application for the collaborative exploration of publication data. This tool allows for an interactive exploration of co-authorship relations. Its layout is completely dynamic, based on a spring graph algorithm. The ScienceTable can be interesting for a researcher exploring his own collaborations or exploring the clusters of co-operating authors in the field. In order to start navigation, search for a specific author is supported. Exploration happens through zoom, pan, drag and tap gestures on a large multi-touch tabletop. Extensions towards citation data are planned for the near future.

The **More!** application [8]: This application is build for mobile devices. Its purpose is to let researchers find information about for example a speaker at a conference and to subscribe to feeds from social tools that keep the attendee informed about ongoing work from the speaker. The application exposes the following information:

- Speaker: full name, photo, e-mail, affiliation and publication list
- Current presentation: slides and paper
- Social tools: Twitter, SlideShare, blog, Delicious, LinkedIn, and Facebook

The following figure gives an overview of the above outlined components of the Research 2.0 information infrastructure. The publication data are collected through the publication feed format. These data and social media data are retrievable through the ResearchFM API, which serves as the backing data for the applications, like the STELLAR universe, the ScienceTable, the More! application and many more.

---

[4] http://elgg.org
[5] http://incubator.apache.org/wookie/
[6] http://www.w3.org/TR/widgets/
[7] http://www.teleurope.eu/

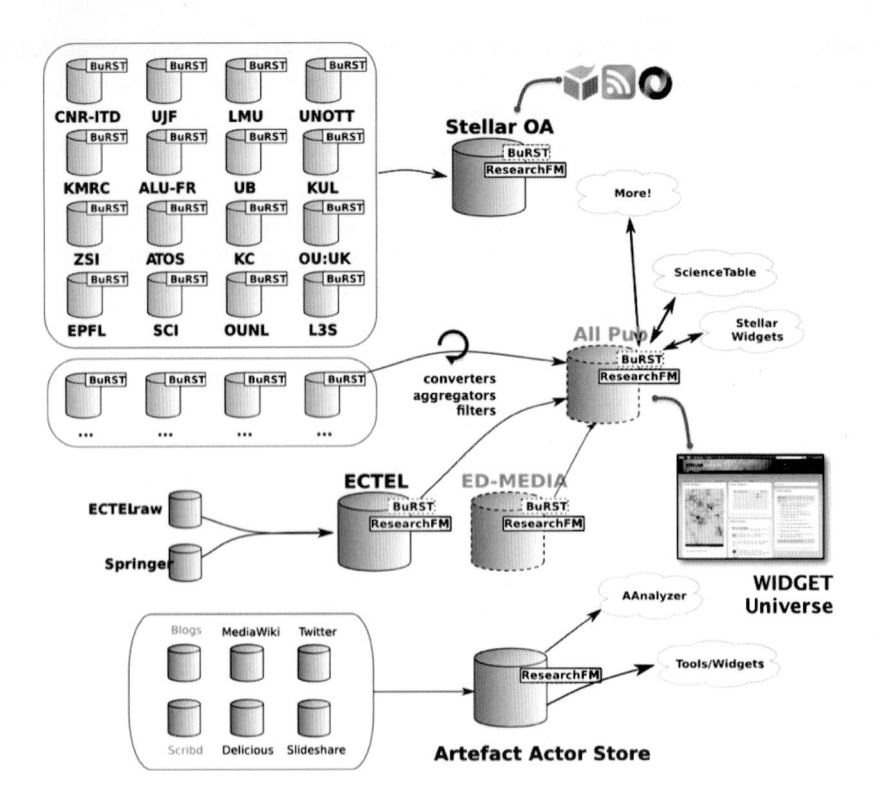

Fig. 1. The Components of the TEL Research 2.0 Information Infrastructure

3 Conclusions and Future Work

We proposed a mash-up infrastructure allowing for continuous innovation, by recombining and repurposing existing technology, and showed concrete implementations. With this, the first steps towards a Research 2.0 framework have been made. The outlined Research 2.0 architecture can help to support the practices of researchers providing them with tools to discover and develop their research field.

The Research 2.0 infrastructure lays the foundation for researchers to experience new practices and provides a rich set of data (publication and social media data) to explore further possibilities. Overall, broadening participation means broadening communication and therefore Research 2.0 must aim at supporting research communities in information processing creating more awareness amongst the members of a research community.

While the components of the infrastructure by now focus on the practice of information provision and distribution, for a full Research 2.0 framework further practices, like collaborative and community practice need to be taken into account. They will serve as a further testbed helping to determine extension and modification needs. However, with the use of Mash-Up environments we see suitable support for the later two, allowing users to engage in collaboratively in a personal research Mash-Up environment.

Although the concepts outlined here focus on the domain of technology-enhanced learning, they might very well apply to several other domains.

Acknowledgment

Special thanks go to Nicolas Balacheff and Jerome Zeiliger from the Laboratory of Informatics Grenoble for their work on the Open Archive. This work was carried out as part of the STELLAR network of excellence, which is funded by the European Commission (grant agreement no. 231913). The Know-Center is funded within the Austrian COMET Program - Competence Centers for Excellent Technologies - under the auspices of the Austrian Federal Ministry of Transport, Innovation and Technology, the Austrian Federal Ministry of Economy, Family and Youth and by the State of Styria. COMET is managed by the Austrian Research Promotion Agency FFG.

References

1. Ala-Mutka, K., Bacigalupo, M., Kluzer, S., Pascu, C., Punie, Y., Redecker, C.: Learning 2.0: The Impact of Web 2.0 Innovation on Education and Training in Europe, http://ipts.jrc.ec.europa.eu/publications/pub.cfm?id=2139
2. Wilson, S., Liber, O., Johnson, M., Beauvoir, P., Sharples, P., Milligan, C.: Personal Learning Environments: Challenging the dominant design of educational systems. Journal of e-Learning and Knowledge Society 2 (2007)
3. Hannafin, M., Land, S., Oliver, K.: Open learning environments: Foundations, methods, and models. Instructional-design theories and models: A new paradigm of instructional theory 2, 115–140 (1999)
4. Wild, F., Ullmann, T.D., Scott, P.: The STELLAR Science 2.0 Mash-Up Infrastructure. Presented at the 10th IEEE International Conference on Advanced Learning Technologies, Sousse, Tunisia (2010)
5. Mika, P.: Bibliography Management using RSS Technology (BuRST), http://www.cs.vu.nl/~pmika/research/burst/BuRST.html
6. Heinze, N., Bauer, P., Hofmann, U., Ehle, J.: Kollaboration und Kooperation in verteilten Forschungsnetzwerken durch Web-basierte Medien – Web 2.0 Tool sin der Wissenschaft. In: GMW 2010 (2010)
7. Reinhardt, W., Moi, M., Varlemann, T.: Artefact-Actor-Networks as tie between social networks and artefact networks. In: Proceedings of CollaborateCom 2009 (November 2009)
8. Parra, G., Duval, E.: More! A Social Discovery Tool for Researchers. In: ED-MEDIA 2010-World Conference on Educational Multimedia, Hypermedia & Telecommunications (2010) (accepted)

Exploring the Benefits of Open Standard Initiatives for Supporting Inquiry-Based Science Learning

Bahtijar Vogel, Arianit Kurti, Daniel Spikol, and Marcelo Milrad

Center for Learning and Knowledge Technologies (CeLeKT),
School of Computer Science, Physics and Mathematics, Linnaeus University,
35195, Växjö, Sweden,
{bahtijar.vogel,arianit.kurti,daniel.spikol,
marcelo.milrad}@lnu.se

Abstract. Mobile devices combined with sensor technologies provide new possibilities for embedding inquiry-based science learning activities in authentic settings. These technologies rely on various standards for data exchange what makes the development of interoperable mobile and sensor-based applications a challenging task. In this paper, we present our technical efforts related to how to leverage data interoperability using open standards. To validate the potential benefits of this approach, we developed a prototype implementation and conducted a trial with high school students in the field of environmental science. The initial results indicate the potential benefits of using open standards for data exchange in order to support the integration of various technological resources and applications.

Keywords: Interoperability, open standards, mobile learning, ODK, sensors, visualization, inquiry-based science learning.

1 Introduction

Mobile devices combined with sensor technologies provide new possibilities for embedding inquiry-based science learning activities in authentic settings [1, 2]. Nevertheless, these technologies rely on various standards for data exchange what makes the development of interoperable mobile and sensor-based applications a challenging task. Therefore, interoperability remains a key feature to resolve while dealing with diverse data exchange issues across different software and hardware components. Interoperability in these settings would enable multiple applications to interact and seamlessly share data. According to Milrad et al., [3], "*interoperability can provide functions such as media integration and flexible, scalable re-use of learning objects*". Interoperability in the field of TEL needs to achieve two basic purposes: 1) the technical interoperability of data exchange and 2) the pedagogical interoperability of learning content and curriculum units. In this paper, we will focus only on the technical interoperability of data exchange in mobile and sensor-based systems with the particular focus on how to support inquiry-based science learning (IBSL). The main research question addressed in this paper is formulated as follows:

How can open standards approaches for data exchange be used to facilitate interoperability across heterogeneous devices used for supporting inquiry-based science learning?

In the following section, we present a brief overview of open standard approaches that could be used to facilitate interoperability.

2 Interoperability and Open Standards

A common approach utilized to facilitate interoperability is the usage of open standard formats for data exchange. Open standards approaches deal with the interoperability of data using transparent descriptions, by which different software systems can easily exchange information [4]. According to Fanning [5], there is a close relation between open standard and open source development. One of the main conclusions of his study is that "*A good open source project is based on open standards*". Dinevski [4] argues that with open source models you can build "*open standards as actual software*" by providing "*higher security, reliability, flexibility and higher quality if compared to closed software system*".

Open standards and open source initiatives have gained momentum in the development of mobile applications with the introduction of Google's Android platform (http://source.android.com). Recently the Symbian platform has also become available as open source code (http://www.symbian.org). These recent trends provided new opportunities for the development of mobile applications based on open standards and open source technologies. One of such emerging applications is the Open Data Kit (ODK) that runs on the Android platform. This application is a set of tools for collecting rich data and, it is especially designed to let users own, visualize and share data easily [6]. The key concept in ODK is to support mobile data collection and exchange tools, making it applicable across different application domains such as health, sports, learning and so on.

Open standards are of key importance for supporting interoperability in distributed TEL environments [7]. In our particular system implementation, we needed to provide support for inquiry-based science learning activities. In these settings, there was a need to insure the data interoperability between diverse applications and devices. Thus, we need to consider how to use and integrate open standards technologies while developing software systems for supporting inquiry-based science learning. In the following section, we will present a number of related research initiatives in the field of IBSL that make use of mobile and sensor-based tools.

3 Technological Resources in Inquiry-Based Learning Systems

Inquiry-based science learning activities have been addressed by members of the TEL community in various projects [1, 8, 9]. The main denominator in these projects has been the integration of a wide range of mobile, sensor and web technologies to support IBSL activities. In the Science Created by YOU project (SCY), learners generate their own learning objects [10]. Additionally, these Emerging Learning Objects are reusable and shareable components created with drawing-based modeling and visualization tools.

The SCY system offers intelligent support for dynamic, ad-hoc collaboration, mobile tools and by providing just in time information and scaffolding to support learning. The Personal Inquiry (PI) project supports inquiry activities with flexible, re-usable tools to support and bridge sequences of activities [11]. The PI system supports location-based inquiry learning across school, field, and home contexts using mobile, sensor and web technologies. The project makes use of digital maps and visualization tools used for bridging representations across field and classroom activities. A common denominator in these projects is the lack of a standard that provides seamless data exchange among the devices and applications used in these activities.

In our previous work, we utilized and visualized sensor data to support different learning processes in the different cycles of IBSL [1]. We have designed and developed a software system that integrates data coming from various technological tools and that include a mobile client for data collection and annotation, mobile sensor probes, a digital pen for notes and audio recording, and geo-temporal visualizations. One central aspect we have identified based on our previous developments is the lack of data interoperability between the different tools and technologies. Under these circumstances, most of the technological resources require to some extent manual synchronization of data for providing data processing and representations. These processes are time consuming and generate significant barriers for the seamless integration of these technologies in educational settings. Each of the technologies in use has a closed system approach that restricts further development. In our case, for example a scientific data logger, typically provides data in binary format that need to be appropriately serialized and decoded in order to get the values correctly. In order to tackle this problem, we argue that data interoperability can be supported by the use of open standards in order to provide more flexible and interoperable software solutions and systems. In the coming sections, we present a specific learning activity, the tools we developed and the technical architecture and its implementation in order to illustrate the potential of using open standards to support IBSL.

4 The Learning Activity

The learning activity presented in this section was conducted as part of the Learning Ecology through Science with Global Outcomes (LETS GO!) project [1, 9]. The aim of the project is to design challenging collaborative IBSL activities supported by mobile and sensor technologies. These combinations of technologies enable the creation of *"mobile science collaboratories"* that can be defined as a set of mobile devices, open software tools, and resources, with an open framework for learner collaboration and inquiry [1, 9]. The activities presented in this section have been developed in collaboration with local teachers in Sweden and USA together with a multi-discipline research team through a co-design process [9].

The learning activity reported in this paper has been conducted over a five weeks period in the winter of 2010 in Sweden. Twelve students (16-17 years old) participated in two hours session once per week. As part of the students' environmental science curriculum, they investigated water quality in surrounding lakes. The activities carried out by the students include classroom lessons, field trips and lab work. Overall, there were four different sessions investigating different aspects of the inquiry-based science learning cycle.

Fig. 1. Technologies used during the learning activity

Figure 1 gives an overview of the water quality learning activity that included workshops for the students to get familiarized with the different technologies (see Fig.1 captions a and b). Additionally, students conducted field experiments at a local lake and collected samples for lab analysis (see Fig. 1 caption c). Students discussed the initial questions given to them about water quality and their findings from the field and lab work. Visualization tools and Google Earth, as a 3D representation tool, were used to support the students' inquiry process (see Fig.1 caption d).

5 Technical Implementation

This implementation followed the specifications detailed in our previous work derived from the functional requirements [1, 9]. The learning design requirements demanded from us was to provide access to sensor networks, live mapping tools, data visualization, and collaboration tools. Software design requirements included usability, low cost, open standards, multiple application support, and support for different types and contexts collaboration [1, 9].

For the mobile client side, we have developed an XForm that was rendered by ODK Collect allowing data collection during the learning activity. XForm is a standard based on a W3C recommendation that is used to build web forms for easy exchange of data across platforms and devices using XML as a data format. The XForm used for this implementation was developed using a simple XML editor. The logic and the structure of our XForm were jointly developed with the subject teachers following the IBSL cycle [1, 10]. The mobile application (ODK Collect) has the capabilities to *render a form, survey into a sequence of input prompts that provide navigation logic, entry constraints* in the mobile application [6]. The XForm supports various types of data and content inputs such as text, audio, pictures, video, visual codes and GPS that makes it possible to annotate the collected sensor data and content with location metadata. Another interesting feature of ODK Collect is that it allows storing the data locally (in the mobile device) and synchronization with a server (ODK Aggregate) could be done once the mobile device has Internet connectivity. ODK Aggregate provides the server companion that runs on the Google App Engine and is used to host XForms, as well as storing the collected data submitted from the ODK Collect. For this particular implementation, we made use of the ODK platform for data collection and developed a visualization tool. The use of XForms facilitated data interoperability across diverse devices and applications that comprise our system. The system overview that describes the integration of the components and resources used in this implementation is illustrated in Figure 2.

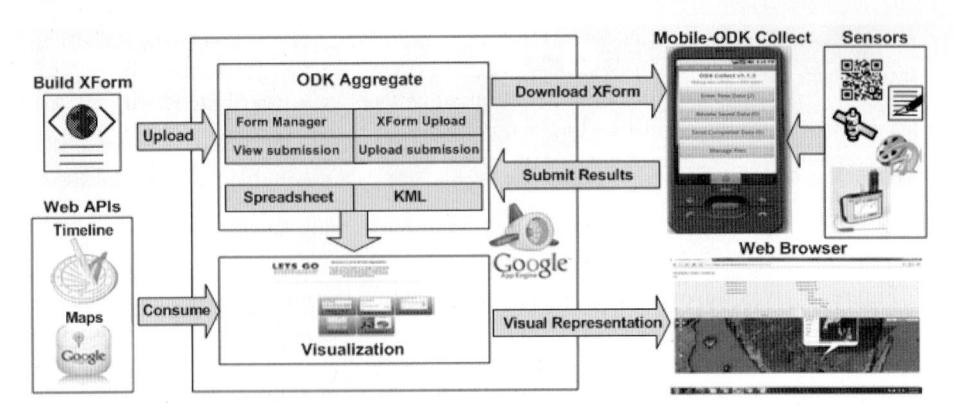

Fig. 2. System overview

The visualization tool was an important component of the system that provided an interactive space to facilitate reflection and collaboration among students that provided a clear overview of the geo-temporal aspects of the collected data [1]. This web-based visualization tool utilizes several web APIs. So far, we have implemented two visualization components that include a timeline and Google maps that uses XML and JavaScript API provided by the Simile project at MIT (http://www.simile-widgets.org/). This tool was integrated with the Google App Engine, as another component of the system. The visualization tool made use of the data collected by the mobile application that were stored as a Google spreadsheet format (.CSV format) in the ODK aggregate. The tool allows users to select geographical data and filter them dynamically using a timeline. Furthermore, the tool visualizes the entire sensor data collected during the learning activities including pH, conductivity, temperature, etc and different annotations and pictures.

6 Discussion and Further Steps

The development and implementation described in this paper demonstrates the growing potential towards the usage of existing open standards to support data collection, data interoperability, analysis and visualization in the context of IBSL. In the activity described in this paper, data interoperability simplifies the integration of data generated by various technological resources and applications. This approach enables rapid development and reuse of technological resources for supporting different learning activities, thus resulting on the seamless integration of data coming from multiple devices. Additionally, this integration has potential benefits for supporting other learning activities. From a practical side, the added value for the classroom is the seamless integration of different sensor data combined with devices that enable powerful visualizations to support the students work. One issue that we will consider in our future work is the full utilization of the visualization component, by incorporating different techniques that provide interactive spaces for discussion, sharing and collaboration. For the next stage of our development, we want to expand our system by incorporating another component from ODK platform, namely the ODK Manage.

This component easily manages the ODK system, by updating the software and forms remotely from the mobile devices, thus further enhancing interoperability issues across different devices. Furthermore, we are in the initial phase of developing a web-based visual authoring tool in which users can design, develop and deploy their own form for mobile data collection tool.

References

1. Vogel, B., Spikol, D., Kurti, A., Milrad, M.: Integrating Mobile, Web and Sensory Technologies to Support Inquiry-Based Science Learning. In: Proceedings of the 6th IEEE WMUTE International Conference on Wireless, Mobile and Ubiquitous Technologies in Education WMUTE 2010, pp. 65–72. IEEE Press, Kaohsiung (2010)
2. Chang, B., Wang, H.Y., Lin, Y.S.: Enhancement of Mobile Learning Using Wireless Sensor Network. In: IEEE Computer Society's Technical Committee on Learning Technology (TCLT), pp. 22–26. IEEE Press, Los Alamitos (2009)
3. Milrad, M., Hoppe, U., Gottdenker, J., Jansen, M.: Exploring the use of mobile devices to facilitate educational interoperability around digitally enhanced experiments. In: 2nd IEEE International Workshop on Wireless and Mobile Technologies in Education, pp. 182–186. IEEE Press, Los Alamitos (2004)
4. Dinevski, D.: Open educational resources and lifelong learning. In: 30th International Conference on Information Technology Interfaces, pp. 117–122. IEEE Press, Los Alamitos (2008)
5. Fanning, B.: What is an "Open Standard"— and how does it relate to "Open Source?". Infonomics, Ebsco 18–19 (2009)
6. Anokwa, Y., Hartung, C., Brunette, W., Borriello, G., Lerer, A.: Open Source Data Collection in the Developing World. IEEE Computer 42, 97–99 (2009)
7. Dalziel, J.: Open Standards Versus Open Source in E-Learning. Educase Quarterly 4, 4–7 (2003)
8. Anastopoulou, S., O'Malley, C.: Issues in Scaffolding Collaborative Inquiry Science Learning. In: Symposium held in CSCL 2009: CSCL Practices, June 8-13 (2009)
9. Spikol, D., Milrad, M., Maldonado, H., Pea, R.: Integrating Co- design Practices into the Development of Mobile Science Collaboratories. In: Proceedings of Ninth IEEE International Conference on Advanced Learning Technologies, pp. 393–397. IEEE Press, Los Alamitos (2009)
10. De Jong, T., Joolingen van, W.R., Weinberger, A.: Learning by design. An example from... the SCY-project. In: Proceedings of CSCL 2009, Rhodes, Greece (2009)
11. Collins, T., Gaved, M., Mulholland, P., Kerawalla, L., Twiner, A., Scanlon, E., Jones, A., Littleton, K., Conole, G., Blake, C.: Supporting location-based inquiry learning across school, field and home contexts. In: Proceedings of the MLearn 2008 Conference, pp. 7–10. Ironbridge Gorge, Shropshire (2008)

Monitoring and Analysing Students' Systematic Behaviour – The SCY Pedagogical Agent Framework

Stefan Weinbrenner, Jan Engler, Astrid Wichmann, and Ulrich Hoppe

COLLIDE Research Group, University of Duisburg-Essen
47047 Duisburg, Germany
{weinbrenner,engler,wichmann,hoppe}@collide.info

Abstract. In this paper we present an agent-based architecture to monitor and analyse students' behaviour while working with a simulation tool. This architecture is based on the blackboard principle and implemented using a Tuple-Spaces approach. The agents are divided into several groups according to their tasks to maximise autonomy and reusability. This separation was done with the idea of perceive-react-cycles in mind. An implemented example scenario that demonstrates how agents interact in generating meaningful context-aware student feedback is described. The visualisation of the agents' analysis results facilitates a deeper understanding of the learners' activities.

Keywords: Agents, Blackboard, TupleSpaces, SCY, Systematic Behaviour, VOTAT, Assessment.

1 Introduction

Current approaches to orientating and supporting science learning emphasise the active role of the learner during the learning experience. One prominent approach that has been investigated intensively is inquiry learning [2]. In inquiry learning, students pose questions, develop hypotheses and test them subsequently by collecting and analysing data. In an inquiry learning cycle this newly gained knowledge is used to pose new questions. If these activities are carried out autonomously, students are challenged to work and think like scientists. There is agreement, that in order to do so, students need to be guided [6]. Students face challenges during all phases of inquiry learning. Besides the challenges of stating a hypothesis [7] students face problems with testing those experiments as well. There is evidence that students tend to work unsystematically by changing several variables at the same time [8]. Consequently students collect data, which are difficult to interpret. Systematic behaviour has been found to be a reliable measure for learning [1].

Previous efforts have shown that providing support to overcome difficulties during inquiry learning is important. Support in form of scripts and prompts have shown effective results on learning [5, 11]. However those forms of support do not take into account the learner's individual behaviour. Therefore, we propose a computational framework to offer just-in-time support that is adapted to the learner's systematic behaviour during inquiry learning.

2 Supporting Systematic Behaviour Just-in-Time

There is a distinction between general and specific heuristics with respect to systematic behaviour introduced by [9]. General heuristics on the one hand can be applied in any context. One example of such a general heuristic is VOTAT (*Vary One Thing at a Time*) a. It suggests to vary only one variable while all others are held constant. A premise of using this heuristic is to be able to determine the dependent and independent variable when running an experiment. The advantage of varying only one variable is that observed changes in an experiment can be attributed to the one variable that has been altered. Specific heuristics on the other hand are context dependent. For instance, selecting equal increments is a valuable heuristics for running specific types of experiments.

2.1 SCY and CO_2 Neutral House Scenario

The context for the work presented in this paper is a new European research project called SCY[1]. The SCY project aims at engaging and supporting students in inquiry learning activities using computer tools such as simulations and modelling software. In SCY-Lab (the SCY learning environment), students work on missions with specific challenges. The configuration of SCY-Lab is adaptive to learners' capabilities and progress helping students to flexibly meet the challenges of the missions. In order to support the cyclic nature on inquiry learning, SCY-Lab provides tools and scaffolds, which provide just-in-time support.

In one of SCY's missions, students are challenged to design a CO_2 neutral house. Part of the mission activities is to test hypotheses by running experiments using SCY's CO_2 House simulation. This simulation software offers a complex set of variables to optimise conditions in terms of insulation to minimise the loss of energy. The following sequence of activities represents a typical usage situation:

The learner starts working with SCYSim CO_2 House for the first time and tries out several variables to reduce heat loss. After gaining some experience with the tool, she decides to select specific variables for making a real experiment. As time goes on, she notices a button but continues with her experiment. As she changes several variables, she notices that the button starts to pulsate. She clicks on the button and a message appears informing her that it is recommended to only change one variable at a time. She takes this information into account and starts collecting a new data set and this time she only changes one variable. She collects several data-points by changing the distance between data points non-canonically (20, 21, 25, 15, 60). The button starts pulsating again. The learner presses the button and receives advice to add data points canonically, keeping the same distance between data points. In her next experiment, she adds data points as follows: 15, 20, 25, 30, 35, 40.

3 Approach and Implementation

SCY-Lab uses agents to analyse and support the learners in their problem-solving and learning activities. The following benefits result from using an agent architecture:

---

[1] SCY – "Science created by You" is an EU project of the 7th Framework Programme. For more information, see http://www.scy-net.eu (last visited in April 2010).

On the one hand, there are several independent sources of information of the learner's behaviour in our scenario, which can be naturally represented by corresponding agents. On the other hand there is no well-defined point in time at which the learner's behaviour is checked, but the agents can supervise the learner's actions continuously. This monitoring allows for contextualised and immediate feedback to the learner. Finally, due to their modular structure and the implicit way of defining data flows, agent frameworks are easily extendable and maintainable.

The conceptual idea behind the communication of this agent framework is based on perceive-and-react cycles. Based on this idea, a set of agent types according to their tasks was developed (Figure 1). The data flow within the framework defines the perceive-and-react cycle. The classification includes different types of agents. In this paper, only the agents that are relevant for the scenario described above are described. In a first step some agents receive action logs, which represent the user's interaction with the system (SCY-Lab). These so-called sensors receive and analyse the logs and provide their results to other stakeholders of the framework. Then, other agents take this information for further evaluations. The results, usually normalised to values between 0 and 100, are again returned to the framework. At the end of this agent chain, a next group of agents, the so-called decision makers, interprets and merges the analysed data to decide, whether a reaction will be sent to the client or not. If a reaction is triggered, the notification service routes it to the corresponding client, which processes and executes it. Possible reactions comprise highlighting, message pop-ups or tool specific actions like adapting the user interface.

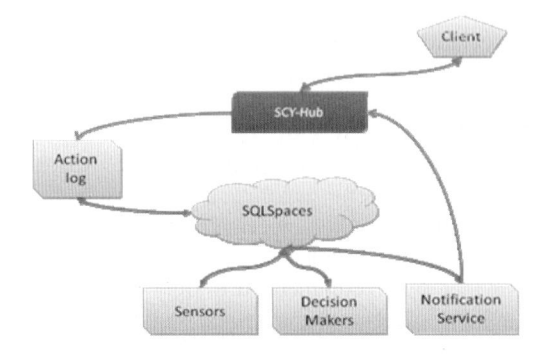

Fig. 1. The SCY Agent Framework

As the architectural design principle we chose the blackboard paradigm [3]. This is characterised by a central server that acts as place, where entries can be written, read and taken. Therefore, there is no direct communication between the clients and the communication is more persistent than a normal, volatile message-passing. In such a system the clients only need minimal knowledge of each other and therefore have the advantages of loosely coupled systems, being robust and flexible. Furthermore, the usage of the blackboard paradigm allows every stakeholder (scenario authors, agents, tools, learners, etc.) to easily share and access information among each other.

3.1 Technical Base

Our implementation of a blackboard architecture is based on the TupleSpaces approach [4], featuring a central TupleSpaces server and loosely coupled clients that use tuples (ordered lists) as entries on the blackboard. We use an implementation called SQLSpaces [10] that has a richer feature set compared to many other implementations. Among others, it offers the possibility to write clients not only in Java, which is the main language of SQLSpaces, but also in other programming languages / environments like Prolog, .Net, PHP and Ruby.

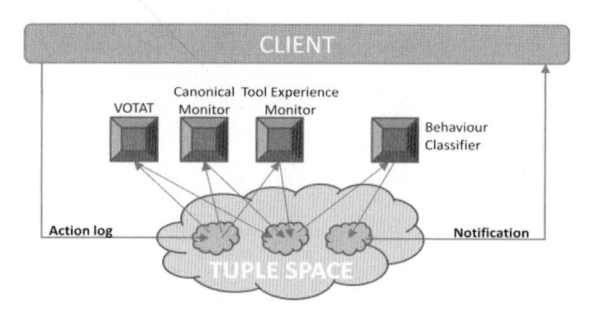

3.2 Implementation for the Scenario

In the scenario described in chapter 2, there are several agents involved There are three sensors that just monitor the actions of the student and collect data. The data is then interpreted by a decision maker at some point in time. The details about these agents and their workflow can be seen in figure 2. The perceive-react cycle starts with the client on the top that logs the actions of the user. These are stored in tuple format as entries of the SQLSpaces server. In this case, we use three several sub-spaces: The action log tuples are written into the actions space, which is represented by the small cloud on the left. After that, the three sensors are notified about new action log tuples and analyse them. The result of this analysis is written in the command space (cloud in the middle), which is the central coordination space for all agents. This space is monitored constantly by the behaviour classifier, that triggers a notification according to its internal rules. The triggering of a notification is done by writing a notification tuple in the last space, the notification space.

Fig. 2. Implementation for the Scenario

The decision of the behaviour classifier whether to react or not is based on the outputs of these three sensor agents:

- *VOTAT*: This agent calculates the degree to which a sequence of action complies with the VOTAT paradigm. For that it takes the amount of different variables within a certain time slide into consideration.
- *Canonical Monitor*: This agent checks whether the value changes of variables are done with equal distances. It also considers only action within a certain time slide.

- *Tool Experience Monitor*: This agent monitors the focus changes within SCY-Lab and counts the time for each user/tool combination. This is done to provide the behaviour classifier with the necessary data to judge whether a learner is still in an exploratory phase or not.

This implementation of the systematic behaviour agent chain shows, that this architecture can be easily used to implement adaptive scaffolds. Especially these implicit agent chains and the loose coupling enables developers to provide intelligent support for learners without the need for heavy-weight and monolithic technologies.

4 Visualizing the Agents' Output

Agents are by nature part of the system's backend, i.e. they are not meant to be shown to the user. Accordingly, the visualisation of agent's output is not trivial. As described in chapter 3, the simplicity of the sensor agents' outputs lead to data that is hard to be interpreted. On the other hand, a visualisation is very helpful to adjust and observe the agents while the system is running. This could be particularly interesting for teachers to monitor students' behaviour. In fact, the teacher is even able to send textual or graphical messages directly to the learner from this visualisation. As we have numerical values produced by the several, we decided to use a dynamic line chart to show the (intermediate) output of the agents.

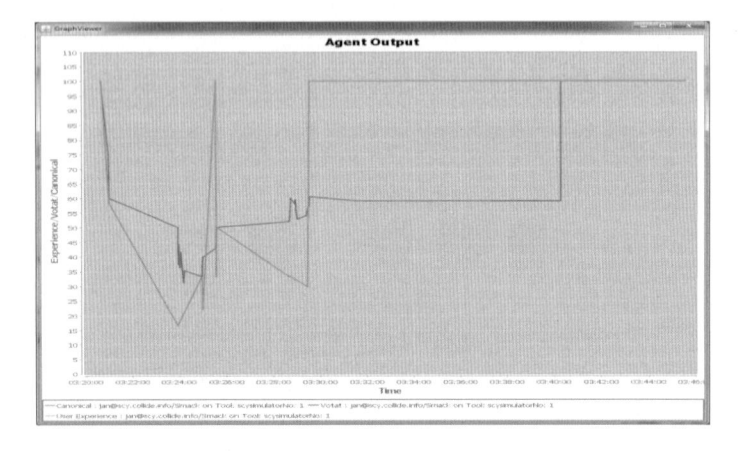

Fig. 3. The visualisation of the agents' output

Figure 3 shows the output of the agents. The x-axis represents a time scale, the y-axis shows the normalised output of the agents on a scale from 0 to 100. The green line shows the experience a user has in the SCY simulator tool. The blue line represents the VOTAT value and the red line shows the canonical value. This graphical representation of the agent's output helps a lot in understanding why and when a notification should be sent to the user.

5 Summary and Outlook

The multi-agent architecture that was described in this paper is based on the blackboard concept and implemented using SQLSpaces. We presented some agents that were used in a pedagogical scenario. Following the idea of perceive-react-cycles, the agents interact in order to give reasonable, contextualised feedback to the students. Finally, a visualisation of the agents' results was described to have a better understanding of the processes inside of what is normally a black box.

There are several ideas how this work can be extended. Although we have already implemented other scenarios in SCY, adding further scenarios is of course planned for the future. Furthermore, a study is planned to evaluate the pedagogical benefits of the support given by our framework.. Finally, the visualisation described in chapter 4 could be extended and used as a base for more sophisticated tools, e.g. authoring tools that allow teachers to configure the agents at runtime.

References

1. Chen, Z., Klahr, D.: All other things being equal: Acquisition and transfer of the control of variables strategy. Child Development 70, 1098–1120 (1999)
2. de Jong, T., van Joolingen, W.R.: Scientific discovery learning with computer simulations of conceptual domains. Review of Educational Research 68, 179–201 (1998)
3. Erman, L.D., Hayes-Roth, F., Lesser, V.R., Reddy, D.R.: The Hearsay-II speech understanding system: integrating knowledge to resolve uncertainty. ACM Comput. Surv. 12(2), 213–253 (1980)
4. Gelernter, D.: Generative Communication in Linda. ACM Transactions on Programming Languages and Systems 7(1), 80–112 (1985)
5. Manlove, S.A., Lazonder, A.W., de Jong, T.: Software scaffolds to promote regulation during scientific inquiry learning. Metacognition and Learning 2, 141–155 (2007)
6. Mayer, R.E.: Should there be a three-strikes rule against pure discovery learning? The case for guided methods of instruction. American Psychologist 59, 14–19 (2004)
7. Njoo, M., de Jong, T.: Exploratory learning with a computer simulation for control theory: Learning processes and instructional support. Journal of Research in Science Teaching 30, 821–844 (1993)
8. Tschirgi, J.E.: Sensible reasoning: A hypothesis about hypotheses. Child Development 51, 1–10 (1980)
9. Veermans, K., van Joolingen, W.R., de Jong, T.: Use of heuristics to facilitate scientific discovery learning in a simulation learning environment in a physics domain. International Journal of Science Education 28, 241–361 (2006)
10. Weinbrenner, S., Giemza, A., Hoppe, H.U.: Engineering heterogeneous distributed learning environments using TupleSpaces as an architectural platform. In: 7th IEEE International Conference on Advanced Learning Technologies (ICALT 2007), IEEE Computer Society, Los Alamitos (2007)
11. Wichmann, A., Leutner, D.: Inquiry Learning: multilevel support with respect to inquiry, explanations and regulation during an inquiry cycle. Zeitschrift für Pädagogische Psychologie 23, 117–127 (2009)

iAPOSDLE – An Approach to Mobile Work-Integrated Learning

Guenter Beham[1], Fleur Jeanquartier[1], and Stefanie Lindstaedt[1,2]

[1] Know Center, Inffeldgasse 21a, 8010 Graz, Austria
[2] Knowledge-Management Institute, TU Graz, Inffeldgasse 21a, 8010 Graz, Austria
{gbeham,fjean,slind}@know-center.at

Abstract. This paper introduces iAPOSDLE, a mobile application enabling the use of work-integrated learning services without being limited by location. iAPOSDLE makes use of the APOSDLE WIL system for self-directed work-integrated learning support, and extends its range of application to mobile learning. Core features of iAPOSDLE are described and possible extensions are discussed.

Keywords: mobile learning, work-integrated learning, smartphones.

1 Introduction

Smartphones are becoming more and more popular in many areas, as computational power, disk space, connectivity, and bandwidth provided by network operators are improving continuously. According to a study released by comScore end of March 2010 [1], the smartphone market increased by approx. 30% between January 2009 and January 2010 in the EU5 countries (France, Germany, Italy, Spain, and U.K.). comScore predicts a considerable growth of the overall market share of smartphones (currently about 23% in EU5 countries), as soon as they get more affordable for the mass market..Looking at the usage of mobile content, text messages are still most frequently used, but surfing websites with mobile web browsers, using downloaded applications, and listening to music are continuously growing. Provided with the functionality of smartphones, new opportunities open up of how technology can be used to support mobile working and learning. Smartphones are thus considered as highly promising for productive use as work integrated learning platforms.

With this paper, we present iAPOSDLE, a smartphone application combining working and learning in a mobile environment. iAPOSDLE makes use of interfaces to APOSDLE[1], a system designed to enhance knowledge worker productivity by supporting informal learning activities during daily work task execution.

2 Mobility in Work-Integrated Learning

Novel approaches to support work-integrated learning aim at assisting knowledge workers in advancing their knowledge and skills directly within their "real" work

---

[1] http://www.aposdle.org

tasks instead of in dedicated (artificial) learning situations [2]. Work-integrated learning (WIL) addresses the challenge of seamlessly integrating working and learning. WIL can be characterised as relatively brief, and unstructured, and it happens spontaneously and often unintentionally. Thus, WIL is a by-product of the time spent at the workplace. Requirements and challenges for WIL support have been presented in [3]. To support WIL, two aspects are especially important: (a) WIL support must be embedded within the "real" computational work environment of the user, and (b) "real" content from the organizational memory should be repurposed as content for learning. Mobile devices have become widely adopted and thus work is not bound to a certain location or office anymore, but can take place everywhere. Such mobile workplaces can range from having a coffee with colleagues to sitting in a train or airplane while travelling to a meeting with a customer. In addition smartphones are increasingly used for work. Hence, mobile applications and smartphones are interesting for supporting learning at mobile workplaces.

2.1 A Scenario for Mobile WIL

Consider the following scenario: Laura is a consultant travelling to one of her clients to run a creativity workshop. During the last week she prepared everything needed for the workshop and would like to seize the time sitting in the train to clarify some last issues about the creativity technique "Morphologischer Kasten" that she will apply in the workshop. She uses her smartphone to connect to WIL services of her company in order to retrieve the missing information. These WIL services are aware of her knowledge about creativity techniques and of the fact that she is travelling. With this information, different services will provide her with information adapted to her knowledge and her work environment (mobile, smartphone). The following section provides an overview over research into the design of mobile learning applications supporting such WIL scenarios.

2.2 Designing Applications for Mobile Learning

In the past years, studies have been carried out to define requirements and guidelines for designing mobile applications, and how to group them based on their functions. In [4] general requirements such as portability, availability, unobtrusiveness, or adaptability are defined. A reference model for mobile social software for learning was proposed by [5]. It defines a classification scheme consisting of the aspects of content, context, purpose, and information flow. The authors applied the reference model on existing mobile educational applications to classify them, investigate possible limitations and provide suggestions on how to improve them. Usability issues of mobile devices have also been investigated by [6]. According to their findings, in the past, the use of mobile hardware and software was limited by usability issues (insufficient battery life, display resolution, cumbersome interaction with software, etc.). Nielsen advises in [7] to focus more on the development of specialized design instead of speculating about the hardware's usability to optimize the mobile user experience. With these findings in mind, reducing complexity of functionality and designing for simplicity have been key design principles when developing our mobile learning application, iAPOSDLE.

3 iAPOSDLE: Mobile Work-Integrated Learning with APOSDLE

With iAPOSDLE, we present a mobile application offering WIL support for use in a mobile work context. iAPOSDLE runs on iPhone smartphones and iPod touches and makes use of services provided by the APOSDLE WIL system. Features of iAPOSDLE are based on the already available APOSDLE desktop client but have been designed to fit the requirements of mobile devices (screen size, bandwidth, memory) and the way how user interfaces are designed for iPhones/iPods. In the following we will present iAPOSDLE's features.

Fig. 1. Browsing an organizations' list of tasks and topics with iAPOSDLE (left); Viewing recommendations based on the current work context (center); contacting a recommended person (right)

3.1 Browsing the Work Domain

iAPOSDLE connects to a specific APOSDLE WIL system through web services. This system provides iAPOSDLE with the work context of the user. In APOSDLE, the work context consists of tasks, topics, and relations between them. When users start iAPOSDLE, it presents them with a list of all these tasks and topics. The leftmost screenshot in Figure 1 shows such a list populated with tasks and topics of an APOSDLE application domain. Users can skim through this list by scrolling up and down and they can switch the view to task or topics only. Additionally an incremental search bar (on top of the list of tasks and topics in the leftmost screenshot in Figure 1) allows fast navigation even in large lists. When having found the task or topic of interest, iAPOSDLE provides a short description (a kind of introduction) by tapping on one of the items. Returning to the scenario from above, our consultant Laura could easily find the topic "Morphologischer Kasten" by entering "mor" in the search box of iAPOSDLE. Laura then taps on the topic to check whether it was the creativity technique she needs more details about. Up until this point, users have specified their work context but did not receive information of how they could accomplish their task at hand.

3.2 Context-Based Recommendations

In WIL, recommending resources for a task at hand essentially means finding knowledgeable persons, textual and multimedia documents (office documents, videos, audio recordings, etc.) within the organisational memory. These resources are repurposed as learning content and presented to the users. In the APOSDLE WIL system, the organisational memory can be accessed through various services. To retrieve persons, documents and multimedia files, iAPOSDLE sends the current work context (task or topic) to the APOSDLE WIL system and receives recommendations.

3.2.1 Snippets – Making Learning Content Suitable for Mobile Devices

Recommendations in the APOSDLE WIL system can be office documents and chat transcripts in PDF format, videos available in different formats, links to web sites, or details about knowledgeable persons known by the system. Transmitting documents and videos between an APOSDLE WIL system and APOSDLE desktop clients does not constitute a real challenge. The situation looks different when it comes to transferring large files over a 3G network to smartphones. iAPOSDLE faces this challenge by reusing a feature of the APOSDLE WIL system called "snippets". Snippets are small parts of textual or multimedia documents with some metadata (e.g., a topic of the work domain) attached to them. They are used to split large documents into smaller parts that are directly accessible. In iAPOSDLE we are using snippets to transfer only small parts of documents from an APOSDLE WIL system to smartphones. That way, we avoid the transfer of large documents when only some paragraphs are related to the current work context of a user. For instance, in the case of Laura, iAPOSDLE would present her with a list of snippets containing e.g., a guideline for applying "Morphologischer Kasten", web links to external resources, and colleagues in her office who already ran workshops using this technique.

3.2.2 Communicating with Knowledgeable Colleagues

All APOSDLE users are regarded as potential sources of knowledge. Knowledgeable persons are identified on the level of topics by the APOSDLE WIL system. For instance, a person can be knowledgeable with respect to the topic "workshop" but might have little knowledge about the topic "creativity technique". For a topic at hand, such knowledgeable persons are recommended together with other materials.

In the aforementioned scenario, Laura might tap on a recommended expert (Bill) and iAPOSDLE would provide her with his contact details. Let us assume, Laura decides to contact him via mobile phone instead of writing an email and having to wait for a response. Therefore she just taps on the presented phone number and her iPhone starts calling Bill. After some seconds Bill answers the phone call and Laura asks him about how she could introduce "Morphologischer Kasten" to her client.

3.2.3 Accessing External Links

Recommended links in iAPOSDLE are external links to online resources. iAPOSDLE uses a feature of the iPhone operation system to open web links in a mobile browser.

To use this feature, Laura taps on a recommended link and iAPOSDLE presents an integrated web browser for displaying the website. Laura decides to visit the online resource about the topic "idea finding" without having to quit the iAPOSDLE application. After scanning through the selected resource, Laura can choose to simply go back to previous recommendations, or continue to learn and work with iAPOSDLE.

3.2.4 Annotating Resources While Being Mobile

The APOSDLE WIL system offers annotations of documents. There are several ways how annotations are created. The authors of [8] already investigated people's motivation to create annotations in mobile media and found that there are many potential uses for annotations. Therefore, we propose a simple annotation feature in iAPOSDLE for adding new resources to the system.

In our scenario, Laura can add annotations by filling out a simple form by pasting or typing in a link, and selecting the topic "creativity technique" and the type "definition". Finally, also Laura's colleagues are able to have a look at the newly created annotation.

4 Conclusion and Outlook

We presented iAPOSDLE, an iPhone application for work-integrated learning. iAPOSDLE provides support while working and learning in a mobile environment. It offers new opportunities to access existing organisational memories and utilises features of the iPhone operation system for communicating with colleagues. We are planning to run an evaluation where participants will be provided with iAPOSDLE in addition to the desktop version of APOSDLE. The evaluation will aim at evaluating the usability, usefulness of implemented features, and conditions under which iAPOSDLE can successfully provide support. In upcoming versions of iAPOSDLE we will be integrating new features dedicated to support users by exploiting context information available on smartphones. For instance, we are planning to add a mobile learning schedule (ad-hoc learning) which tries to find out when users might have some time for short interventions which will then presented to them. The feature for annotating websites will be enhanced with the geo location (e.g., provided by the GPS sensor) to enable users to browse resources by location.

We believe that smartphones are very promising devices for supporting WIL. Nonetheless some technological barriers, such as the complexity of user interfaces, battery life, or content formatted for mobile devices will have to be overcome so that smartphones can unfold their full potential.

Acknowledgements. The Know-Center is funded within the Austrian COMET Program - Competence Centers for Excellent Technologies - under the auspices of the Austrian Ministry of Transport, Innovation and Technology, the Austrian Ministry of Economics and Labor and by the State of Styria. COMET is managed by the Austrian Research Promotion Agency FFG. APOSDLE (www.aposdle.org) has been partially funded under grant 027023 in the IST work programme of the European Community. Most features of iAPOSDLE have been implemented by Sabine Schneider and Max Stricker who are students at Graz University of Technology.

References

1. comScore Press Release, http://tinyurl.com/ylj9bvb
2. Lindstaedt, S.N., Ley, T., Mayer, H.: Integrating Working and Learning in APOSDLE. In: Proceedings of the 11th Business Meeting of the Forum Neue Medien, November 10-11, University of Vienna, Austria (2005)
3. Lindstaedt, S.N., Beham, G., Kump, B., Ley, T.: Getting to Know Your User – Unobtrusive User Model Maintenance within Work-Integrated Learning Environments. In: Cress, U., Dimitrova, V., Specht, M. (eds.) EC-TEL 2009. LNCS, vol. 5794, pp. 73–87. Springer, Heidelberg (2009)
4. Sharples, M.: The Design of Personal Mobile Technologies for Lifelong Learning. Computers and Education 34, 177–193 (2000)
5. Jong, T.D., Specht, M., Koper, R.: A reference model for mobile social software for learning. International Journal of Continuing Engineering Education and Life-Long Learning 18, 118–138 (2007)
6. Kukulska-Hulme, A.: Mobile Usability and User Experience. In: Kukulska-Hulme, A., Traxler, J. (eds.) Mobile Learning: A handbook for educators and trainers, pp. 45–56. Routledge, London (2005)
7. Nielsen, J.: Mobile Usability, http://www.useit.com/alertbox/mobile-usability.html
8. Ames, M., Naaman, M.: Why We Tag: Motivations for Annotation in Mobile and Online Media. In: Rosson, M.B., Gilmore, D.J. (eds.) Conference on Human Factors in Computing Systems (CHI 2007), pp. 971–980. ACM Press, San Jose (April 2007)

A Haptic-Based Framework for Chemistry Education

Sara Comai, Davide Mazza, and Lorenzo Mureddu

Politecnico di Milano
Department of Electronics and Information (DEI)
Piazza L. Da Vinci, 32
I-20133 Milan
{sara.comai,davide.mazza}@polimi.it
lorenzo.mureddu@mail.polimi.it

Abstract. In this demo we present a haptic-based framework for the exploration of the electrical surface of molecules. The geometrical models of molecules are extracted from theoretical data using file formats widely adopted in chemical and biological fields. The addition of information computed with computational chemistry tools allows users to *feel* the interaction forces between an explored molecule and a charge associated to the haptic device. The developed tool can be used to explore electrostatic fields of molecules, either for didactic or research purposes due to its reliance on computational data.

1 Introduction

Molecular analysis has acquired a great importance in recent years. A deep understanding of the *inter-molecular* forces that govern this kind of processes is fundamental, for example, in drug design. Interactions among molecules are usually described by *huge sequences of data*, which describe the attraction/repulsion forces and the positions of interesting sites for binding over molecular surfaces, but difficult to interpret even by experts. Haptic interaction can help by providing the sensing of the involved forces typically not experienceable, due to their existence at nanoscale or atomic levels. At this aim a molecule to be analyzed is shown to the user in a virtual environment, and a *probing* charge is associated with a haptic device (Sensable PHANTOM Omni [3]). Users can feel the interaction forces via the haptic device and explore the electrostatic surface of the molecule to look for binding sites or other properties. Different experiences that address specific molecular features are correctly represented by the tool and tested by users (chemistry students and researchers).

This paper is organized as follows: Section 2 provides an overview of the framework architecture; Section 3 describes some demo experiences that can be done with the tool, while Section 4 reports some users' feedback; finally, Section 5 reports which is the state of the art of the field and Section 6 draws some conclusions.

2 System Overview

Geometrical and electric field data of each molecule are stored in a repository. Figure 1 sketches the architecture of the developed system.

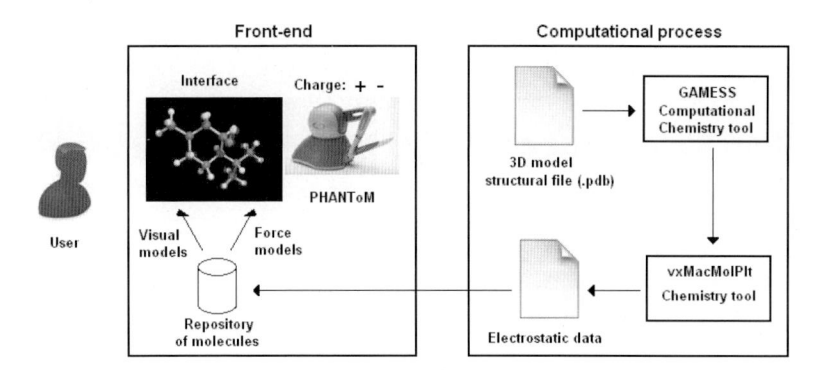

Fig. 1. The architecture of the designed haptic system

Different visualizations of the molecule selected from the repository are possible, to focus the attention on many features of interest. The user is shown a graphical 3D environment where the molecule is shown. The current position of the haptic proxy is also rendered, enriched with visual information that represents the forces, e.g., the force vector exiting the proxy is depicted to highlight force intensity and direction. The surface of the molecule is also colored, using a value-based chromatic scale, to highlight the electrostatic potential value in each specific position. The intensity of returned forces are amplified by an experimentally-determined gain, to scale the force appropriately without losing proportions with reality. Auxiliary key information are also shown in an intuitive way, such as the plot of the electrostatic field along the direction connecting the proxy position to the center of the molecule.

3 Demonstrations

The developed tool has been realized with the twofold purpose of being used for research and didactic activities. In the latter case, the tool can help students to understand the way in which molecules interact, by experiencing it in a more tangible way. Examples of experiences that can be conducted by students are:

Critical points detection. Users can feel where the electric field surrounding the molecule has its typical values (minima, maxima), which act like *holes* of the electronic surface. Holes are specific sites where molecular bindings take place during inter-molecular interactions. With our tool, students can get the information on where such holes are placed in the molecular electric surface,

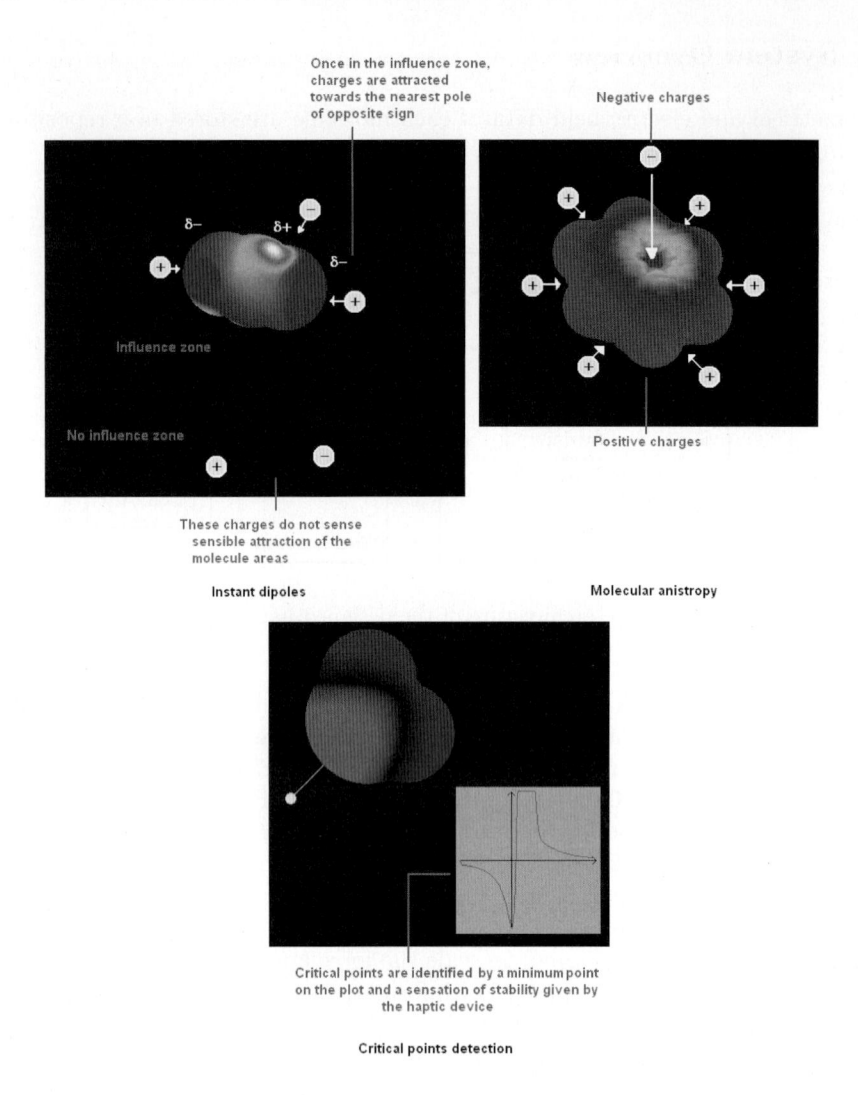

Fig. 2. Graphical explanation of demonstration cases

and so which part of a molecule actually takes part in a binding (e.g., how the binding happens, how the molecule is oriented when it happens and how it must be placed to make the binding happen, etc.). Moreover the system is also able to render the peculiar characteristics of bindings by providing attractions to molecular binding sites till the real binding distance that would occur during the interactions with other molecules. In that position the probe of the haptic device will stop (i.e., a stable point for the haptic probe movement is found), giving the user exactly the sensation that a binding has occurred.

Permanent and instant dipoles. Different molecules exert a different influence on an electric charge, depending also on the distance between the molecule and the charge. For example, when dealing with a *non-polar* molecule, its effect on an electric charge at a high distance can be negligible. Anyway, when the charge starts going below a threshold distance, the electronic density concentrates on the molecule atoms and attracts the electric charge in a particular area around the molecule according to the charge's sign. The tool simulates this behavior by means of different intensities of forces: when the proxy is quite far from the molecule, the intensities of the forces are negligible, because the charge is out of the area of influence of the molecule; near the molecule an attraction or repulsion force is returned to the user, according to the charge's sign. When approaching the atom, the intensity of the force increases. A different situation occurs with a *permanent dipole*, like for example the water molecule, which always exhibits electric poles over its atoms, because of the different electronegativity of the involved chemistry elements. In this case, the interaction with an electric charge is different and force intensities can be felt significantly in the whole surrounding space. Users can feel the differences w.r.t. the previous case where forces can be felt with non-negligible intensity in the whole space around the molecule.

Molecular anisotropy. Molecular anisotropy represents the difference in interaction exhibited by a molecule with respect to the direction of approaching. Indeed, a molecule exerts different influences (in intensity and sign of forces) depending on the direction from where the charge comes.

Figure 2 summarizes the activities from a conceptual point of view.

4 Users' Feedback

The tool has been tested on a user set of 20 students using different molecules stored in the repository. Experiences have been conducted in the form of *guided activities* focused on specific topics of a typical chemistry course and determining how the tool rendered a set of requested features to highlight to better understand a phenomenon.

Users feedbacks have been collected through a questionnaire administered to them at the end of each experience where users were required to say: a) if they were able to experience what they were asked to, thus providing us impressions on tool usability b) if they judged to have understood the phenomena in more detailed way and, if it were the case, we asked them to provide a textual explanation on how they consider their knowledge about the phenomena improved (new features elements of the phenomenon, new details of its dynamics and action, etc ...) and which were the characteristics of the tool that had made them able to improve their knowledge.

The results of the usage of such tool in the didactic activity confirmed the following advantages:

- *increasing of motivation*: students demonstrated more interest for the concepts involved in the faced experiences;
- *internalization of concepts*: students showed more easiness in the assimilation of the concepts introduced with the haptic experience. Also some already partially- or intuitively understood concepts got a further reinforcement or confirmation within students' mind, thus improving their knowledge;
- *spatial and intensity perception*: students can understand the different proportions of the involved objects and how the nature and intensities of interactions can be related to spatial properties (e.g., distances from molecule).

Fig. 3. The tool at work in our laboratory

5 Related Works

[4] provides a survey on haptic rendering techniques: most of the haptic algorithms and applications focus on the rendering of surface tactile feedback, rather than force fields that are distributed in the whole space. In the field of chemical visualization and haptics, our tool is a border-line one and stands along the boundary of old computational chemistry (which privileges awkward numerical outputs, disregarding user-friendliness) and the brand-new bioinformatics (which introduces better and friendly UIs to show results). Most of the developed tools, whenever presenting haptic interaction, exhibit it as a side feature, usually because it has been added later. In our tool, instead, haptic is the main way of interaction. Examples of similar tools include VMD, PyMol, and others (see [2] for a survey), which offer a wide range of representations, but interpretation of data is not so straightforward for non-technician of the field. [1] presents a similar tool, but it is strongly designed on theoretical models and, compared to our systems, it does not allow to use or explore empirical data directly obtained in laboratories.

6 Conclusions and Future Work

We have here presented a framework for experimenting inter-molecular force interactions. The system consists of a computer and a haptic device, which improves the user experience and makes students able to experience what they are used to study on books. The system relies heavily on data obtained by computational chemistry tools widely used in chemical research, which make the simulation of molecular interactions based not on theoretical models, as already done extensively in the past, but on information that can better represent with a high degree of detail the main features of real phenomena, as now considered and known by scientists.

Future extensions of the work go in the direction of implementing other types of interactions, such as the simulation of molecule-molecule ones, seen as an extension of the charge-molecule interaction made in this work.

Acknowledgments

We would like to thank Pierangelo Metrangolo and Antonino Famulari (for the chemistry part), Marzio Ghezzi (for the availability of labs and haptic device) and the students Marco Faverio and Lorenzo Mureddu or their precious contributions in code development.

References

1. Chemical force feedback, http://cff.itn.liu.se/public/
2. Chemistry visualization software survey,
   http://personal.cscs.ch/mvalle/ChemViz/tools.html
3. Sensable phantom omni, http://www.sensable.com/haptic-phantom-omni.htm
4. Day, A.M., Laycock, S.D.: A survey of haptic rendering techniques. Computer Graphics forum 26(1), 50–65 (2007)

Intelligent Tutoring with Natural Language Support in the BEETLE II System

Myroslava O. Dzikovska[1], Diana Bental[1], Johanna D. Moore[1],
Natalie B. Steinhauser[2], Gwendolyn E. Campbell[2],
Elaine Farrow[3], and Charles B. Callaway[4],⋆

[1] School of Informatics, University of Edinburgh, Edinburgh, United Kingdom
{m.dzikovska,d.bental,j.moore}@ed.ac.uk
[2] Naval Air Warfare Center Training Systems Division, Orlando, FL, USA
{gwendolyn.campbell,natalie.steinhauser}@navy.mil
[3] Heriot-Watt University, Edinburgh, United Kingdom
e.farrow@hw.ac.uk
[4] University of Haifa, Mount Carmel, Haifa, Israel
ccallawa@gmail.com

Abstract. We present BEETLE II, a tutorial dialogue system designed to accept unrestricted language input and support experimentation with different tutorial planning and dialogue strategies. Our first system evaluation used two different tutoring policies and demonstrated that BEETLE II can be successfully used as a platform to study the impact of different approaches to tutoring. In the future, the system can also be used to experiment with a variety of parameters that may affect learning in intelligent tutoring systems.

1 Introduction

Intelligent tutoring systems (ITS) have been shown to help learning as part of a technology-enhanced learning curriculum [1], and there has been a lot of interest in developing tutoring systems that understand student explanations (e.g. [2]). However, existing ITS with natural language support typically support only short answer questions; at most, they can analyze student essays but then revert to pre-authored short answer dialogues if remediation is necessary. Accepting longer utterances may be beneficial to learning, because high percentages of self-explanation and contentful talk by students are known to be correlated with better learning in human-human tutorial dialogue [3]. But students also need detailed feedback on their explanations [4], which is very labor-intensive to provide with pre-authored system responses.

We present BEETLE II, a tutorial dialogue system designed to accept unrestricted language input and to support experimentation with different approaches to tutoring. The BEETLE II architecture supports the understanding

---

⋆ This work has been supported in part by US Office of Naval Research grants N000140810043 and N0001410WX20278. We thank Katherine Harrison and Leanne Taylor for their help running the evaluation.

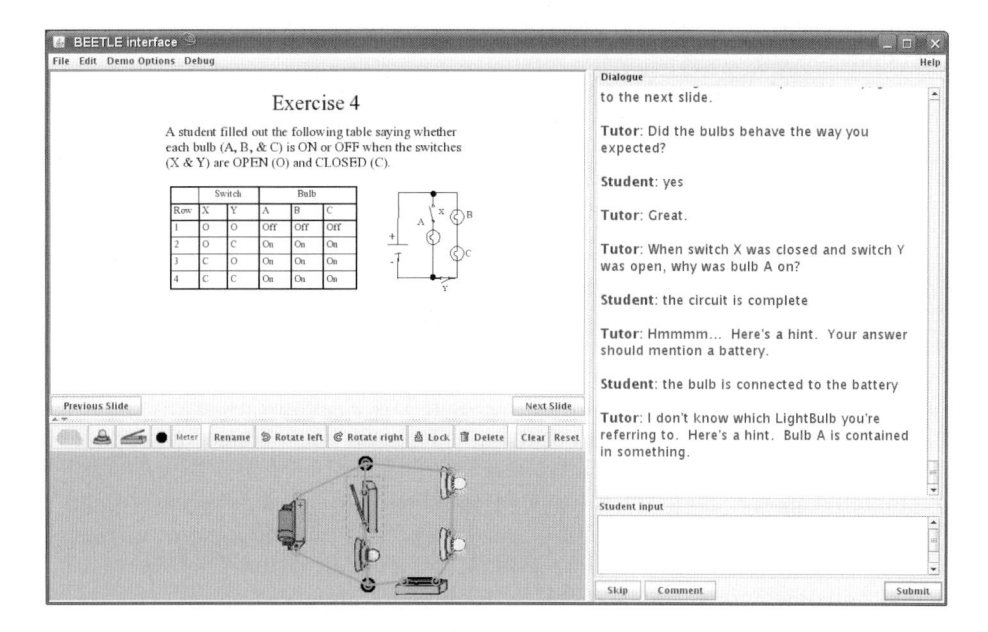

Fig. 1. Screenshot of the BEETLE II system

of student explanations by using techniques from computational linguistics to analyze complex student utterances and generate feedback automatically [5].

Our research goal is to investigate whether contentful talk and self-explanation can be understood and encouraged in a computer system, given state-of-the-art in language technology. The BEETLE II system is designed to ask students to explain their answers, to give detailed feedback and to support students in arriving at the correct explanations without the system resorting to short-answer questions, and without having to hand-author every tutorial response.

We demonstrate a version of the system that has undergone successful user evaluation in 2009. The rest of this paper discusses the BEETLE II design (Section 2) the system architecture (Section 3), the user evaluation (Section 4), and further research questions that can be investigated using BEETLE II (Section 5).

2 Instructional Design

The BEETLE II system delivers basic electricity and electronics tutoring to students with no prior knowledge of the subject. A distinguishing feature of the system is that it is based on a course developed by experienced instructional designers for use in a human-human tutoring study, without taking into account the possible limitations of a computer-based tutor. Two research team members, an experienced electrician and a psychologist, jointly developed a curriculum covering topics including the components of a circuit, how to build a circuit, and how to find faults. The exercises were then transferred into a computer system with

Tutor: Why was bulb A on when switch Y was open and switch Z was closed?
Student: because it had a closed path
Tutor: Right. There is a closed path. Keep going.
Student: it has a closed path with the battery
Tutor: You're on the right track. Here's the answer. Bulb A is still contained in a closed path with the battery.

Fig. 2. Example interaction with the system from our corpus

only minor adjustments (e.g., breaking down compound questions into individual ones).

The instructional design interleaves short presentations of information with interactive exercises, activities and discussion. The activities use a circuit simulator which is realistic enough so that bulbs light up when connected correctly, bulbs may be bright or dim, and measurements may be taken by connecting a simulated meter. Many of the activities follow the "predict-verify-evaluate" (PVE) cycle, in which students are asked to predict the outcome of an activity before conducting an experiment using the simulator, and then discuss the actual outcome and its implications for the underlying principles [6].

A screenshot of the system is shown in Figure 1. The student interface includes an area to display reading material, a circuit simulator, and a dialogue history window. At present, students interact with the system via a typed chat interface to avoid the problems associated with automated speech recognition.

An example dialogue shown in Figure 2 shows how an answer is built jointly by the student and tutor over more than one turn. In response to the first student input, the system rephrases its understanding of the correct part of the answer, and prompts the student to supply the missing information. In the next turn the system combines the information from the tutor's hint and the student's answers and restates the completed answer. We will use this dialogue as a running example to explain system capabilities.

3 System Architecture

The system architecture is modular and combines domain-independent components for parsing and generation with domain-specific reasoners for decision making.

We use a natural language dialogue *parser* [7] to parse the student input. The parser extracts relevant semantic content from each utterance, recognizing paraphrases that can mean the same thing. For our example problem, the parser would recognize that "Bulb A and the battery are in the same closed path", "Bulb A is in a closed path with the battery" and "there is a closed path containing both the bulb and the battery" mean the same thing and constitute the correct answer to the tutor's question. The parser can handle fragmentary input, for example it can determine that in response to the question in Figure 1 "Which bulbs will be on and which bulbs will be off?", the answer "off" can be taken to mean "all bulbs in the diagram will be off".

The output from the parser is passed on to the *domain reasoning* and *diagnosis* components [8,9] to check the validity of the student's explanation. The diagnoser outputs lists of correct, contradictory and non-mentioned objects and relations from the student's explanation. For the first student utterance in our example, the diagnoser will determine that the student correctly mentioned a closed path as part of their explanation, but they forgot to mention that both the bulb and the battery must be in the same closed path.

The *tutorial planner* implements a set of generic tutoring strategies and a policy to choose an appropriate strategy at each point of the interaction. The currently implemented strategies are: acknowledge any correct parts of the answer; suggest a slide to read with background material; prompt for missing parts of the answer; provide a hint (at different levels of specificity); re-state an acceptable answer using better terminology; and give away the answer. The tutorial policy makes a high-level decision as to which strategies to use. In our example the first decision is to restate the correct part of the answer (student correctly mentioned a closed path), and give a contentless prompt for missing explanation parts. The tutorial planner also incorporates an error recovery policy to manage situations when the system cannot interpret the student's input [10].

The tutorial planner's decisions are realized by automatic *text generation* components, using a combination of domain-specific content planning and and a domain-independent text generation system [11] to produce the appropriate text. In our example, the text generation decides that the the chosen tutorial strategy (restate and contentless prompt) should be realized as "Right. There is a closed path. Keep going"

BEETLE II provides extensive logging facilities. All of the students' interactions with the system are logged, including both their text utterances and the experimental circuits they build with the simulator. The students' interactions with the system and the system's responses can be replayed. The system's utterances and its internal decisions are also logged. This provides a detailed corpus for later analysis.

4 Experimental Work Using BEETLE II

The first experimental evaluation involving 81 participants was completed in 2009. Participants were undergraduates recruited from a South-East US University, with little or no prior knowledge of the domain. Each participant took a pre-test, worked through a lesson with the system, took a post-test, and completed a user satisfaction survey. Each session lasted approximately 4 hours.

We implemented two different tutoring policies in the system for this evaluation, which was made possible by our flexible system architecture. In the baseline policy the students were given the correct answer straight away. The system made no attempt at remediation, and never indicated whether the student was understood. In comparison, the full adaptive policy selected a strategy based on student answer analysis and dialogue context, as described above.

Out of 81 students, 76 successfully completed the evaluation (data from 5 participants had to be discarded due to system crashes). All students completed pre- and post- test questionnaires to assess their knowledge. The mean pre-test score was $34.56 (SD = 12.38)$, and the mean post-test score was $73.91 (SD = 15.64)$ for both conditions combined. The difference was statistically significant with $p < 0.0001$, indicating that the students successfully learned the material.

More detailed data analysis, comparison between conditions and comparison to human tutoring are given in [10,12,13].

5 Conclusions and Future Work

Our ultimate goal is to develop a system flexible enough to conduct a systematic investigation into the nature of effective tutoring in technology-enhanced learning environments. The experimental evaluation described in section 4 demonstrates that the BEETLE II system can be successfully deployed in experiments with naive users to test the effect of different tutorial policies. We now have a corpus of interactions between students and the computer tutor that can be analyzed in more detail and used to devise future experiments.

Our initial analyses indicate that additional improvements to remediation strategies, and especially strategies dealing with interpretation problems, are necessary to make the interaction less frustrating to the users [10]. We are planning to do this as part of future work. However, the success of our large-scale evaluation shows that the system can already be used to formulate hypotheses and conduct experimental studies.

Three factors whose effects we intend to investigate in the future are: linguistic alignment between system and user; the choice of modalities for input and output; and the impact of different tutorial strategies.

Techniques from computational linguistics allow us to vary and control the choice of terminology and phrasing that the tutor uses. Current research indicates that better alignment between students and tutors (computer or human) with respect to the terminology they use is correlated with higher learning gain and user satisfaction [14] and that student satisfaction is negatively affected if the system is using different terminology than the student [10]. However, it may be important that students learn specific terminology rather than the system adapt to the students. This can be investigated further through controlled experiments possible with BEETLE II since automatically generated feedback can be adjusted as necessary.

The timing and amount of feedback has been a topic of interest in the e-learning community (e.g.,[15]). The modular nature of BEETLE II will allow us to investigate the relevant issues. For example, it is easy to change the tutorial policy to give feedback immediately, and compare the outcome with exercises which make the student follow a PVE cycle which results in delayed feedback. Other tutoring strategies, such as giving hints at different levels of specificity, can be investigated as well.

References

1. Anderson, J.R., Corbett, A.T., Koedinger, K.R., Pelletier, R.: Cognitive tutors: Lessons learned. The Journal of the Learning Sciences 4(2), 167–207 (1995)
2. Jordan, P., Makatchev, M., Pappuswamy, U., VanLehn, K., Albacete, P.: A natural language tutorial dialogue system for physics. In: Proceedings of the 19th International FLAIRS conference (2006)
3. Chi, M.T.H., de Leeuw, N., Chiu, M.H., LaVancher, C.: Eliciting self-explanations improves understanding. Cognitive Science 18(3), 439–477 (1994)
4. Nielsen, R.D., Ward, W., Martin, J.H.: Learning to assess low-level conceptual understanding. In: Proceedings 21st International FLAIRS Conference (2008)
5. Callaway, C.B., Dzikovska, M., Farrow, E., Marques-Pita, M., Matheson, C., Moore, J.D.: The Beetle and BeeDiff tutoring systems. In: Proceedings of SLaTE 2007 (Speech and Language Technology in Education) (2007)
6. Guzzetti, B.J., Snyder, K.E., Glass, G.V., Gamas, W.S.: Promoting conceptual change in science: A comparative meta-analysis of instructional interventions from reading education and science education. Reading Research Quarterly 28(2), 117–155 (1993)
7. Allen, J., Dzikovska, M., Manshadi, M., Swift, M.: Deep linguistic processing for spoken dialogue systems. In: Proceedings of the ACL 2007 Workshop on Deep Linguistic Processing (2007)
8. Dzikovska, M.O., Callaway, C.B., Farrow, E.: Interpretation and generation in a knowledge-based tutorial system. In: Proceedings of EACL 2006 workshop on knowledge and reasoning for language processing, Trento, Italy (April 2006)
9. Dzikovska, M.O., Campbell, G.E., Callaway, C.B., Steinhauser, N.B., Farrow, E., Moore, J.D., Butler, L.A., Matheson, C.: Diagnosing natural language answers to support adaptive tutoring. In: Proceedings 21st International FLAIRS Conference, Coconut Grove, Florida (May 2008)
10. Dzikovska, M.O., Moore, J.D., Steinhauser, N., Campbell, G.: The impact of interpretation problems on tutorial dialogue. In: Proceedings of the 48th Annual Meeting of the Association for Computational Linguistics(ACL 2010) (2010)
11. Elhadad, M., Robin, J.: Controlling content realization with functional unification grammars. In: Proceedings of the Sixth International Workshop on Natural Language Generation (1992)
12. Steinhauser, N.B., Campbell, G.E., Harrison, K.M., Taylor, L.S., Dzikovska, M.O., Moore, J.D.: Comparing human-human and human-computer tutorial dialogue. In: Proceedings of the the 32nd Annual Conference of the Cognitive Science Society (2010) (poster session)
13. Dzikovska, M.O., Steinhauser, N.B., Moore, J.D., Campbell, G.E., Harrison, K.M., Taylor, L.S.: Content, social and metacognitive statements: an empirical study comparing human-human and human-computer tutorial dialogue. In: Proceedings of EC-TEL- 2010 (2010)
14. Ward, A., Litman, D.: Cohesion and learning in a tutorial spoken dialog system. In: Proceedings of 19th International FLAIRS Conference (2006)
15. Smits, M.H.S.B., Boon, J., Sluijsmans, D.M.A., van Gog, T.: Content and timing of feedback in a web-based learning environment: effects on learning as a function of prior knowledge. Interactive Learning Environments 16(2), 183–193 (2008)

ScenEdit: An Intention-Oriented Authoring Environnment to Design Learning Scenarios

Valérie Emin[1,2], Jean-Philippe Pernin[1], and José Luis Aguirre[1]

[1] Laboratoire Informatique de Grenoble
110 av. de la Chimie - BP 53 - 38041 Grenoble- cedex 9 - France
[2] EducTice - Institut National de Recherche Pédagogique
19 Allée de Fontenay - BP 17424 - 69347 Lyon - cedex 07- France
valerie.emin@imag.fr, jean-philippe.pernin@imag.fr,
jose-lui.aguirre@imag.fr

Abstract. This paper concerns the ScenEdit authoring environment, a graphical tool dedicated to design learning scenarios. The environment allows teacher-designers to structure the design of scenarios by eliciting intentions, strategies and interactions included in the ISIS goal-oriented framework. ScenEdit aims to favor sharing and reusing practices by providing patterns for each type of component (intention, strategy and interactional situation). We present here the main functionalities of the environment through an example of a learning scenario.

Keywords: technology enhanced learning, authoring approach, learning scenarios, goal-oriented approach, learning design patterns.

1 Introduction

For several years some researches have concerned the modeling process of learning situations integrating digital technologies. Educational Modelling Languages (EML) aim to provide interoperable descriptions of learning scenarios. As noticed by IMS-LD authors [1], an EML is not intended to be directly manipulated by teachers or engineers: specific authoring systems [2, 3, 4] must be provided to allow designers to design scenarios at a lower cost. This paper presents ScenEdit [5], a graphical tool dedicated to design learning scenarios based on the ISiS (Intentions, Strategies, and interactional Situations) framework [6] elaborated to structure the design of learning scenarios by teacher-designers. We have co-elaborated ISiS in a participative design approach with experimented and inexperienced teachers. This framework is based on a goal-oriented approach and proposes a specific identification of the intentional, strategic, tactical and operational dimensions of a learning scenario.

2 Context of the Research

The research work presented in this paper was conducted in collaboration between the Laboratoire Informatique de Grenoble and the INRP[1]. This collaboration, part of the

---

[1] Institut National de la Recherche Pédagogique (French National Institute for Research in Education).

ApprenTice PPF Program, closely associates groups of teachers in charge of co-elaborating and experimenting models we want to implement. Our research focuses on authoring environments dedicated to specific designers: teachers who integrate digital technologies in French secondary educational system.

After the evaluation of different authoring solutions in learning design [1,3], we have chosen to develop ScenEdit [5], a graphical authoring environment. ScenEdit is based on the ISiS goal-oriented conceptual model which aims to capture the teachers' intentions and strategies in order to better understand scenarios written by others and to favor sharing and reuse practices. ISiS is not an alternative solution to Educational Modelling Languages [1], but complements them by offering higher level models, methods and tools designed for and with teachers-designers. In parallel with the elaboration of the ISiS model, we have co-designed with teachers a series of software prototypes progressively implementing ISiS concepts.

3 A Graphical Authoring Tool: ScenEdit

ScenEdit is a web-based authoring environment which allows a community of teachers to create, modify and reuse learning scenarios. ScenEdit allows teachers to quickly and easily create structured scenarios by:

- eliciting its intentions in terms of knowledge, competencies and abilities from pre-existing database, common to a certain community of teachers;
- choosing scenario patterns corresponding to common or novel strategies, well adapted to its intentions and to the learning context;
- selecting interactional situations and matching them to the different steps of the strategies;
- managing different components in specific databases, like scenarios, intentions, strategies, interactional situations, etc.

In this version, operationalization features have not been yet implemented.

ScenEdit proposes three workspaces: the **Scenario Edition** workspace, the **ISiS Components** workspace, and the **Context** workspace represented by tabs in the ScenEdit editor as shown in figure 1, to edit a structuring scenario. Figure 1 shows the view provided by the **Scenario Edition** tab, on our scenario example.

Figure 1 shows this scenario implemented with the ScenEdit graphical tool, each type of component (Intentions, Strategies, Situations) is shown with a different symbol: a triangle for a step, a rounded rectangle for an intention, a rectangle for a strategy, a circle for a phase and a picture for a situation. Checkboxes (Intentions, Strategies and Situations) of Figure 1 allows visualizing the desired levels. In this scenario, the teachers' first didactical intention is "to destabilize" a frequently encountered "misconception" of students in electricity which is that "proximity of the battery has an influence on current intensity". Figure 2 shows how this intention is implemented within ScenEdit, by defining mainly 4 elements: the *formulator* of the intention, the *actor concerned* by the intention, and the intention itself: an *operation* on a *knowledge item*.

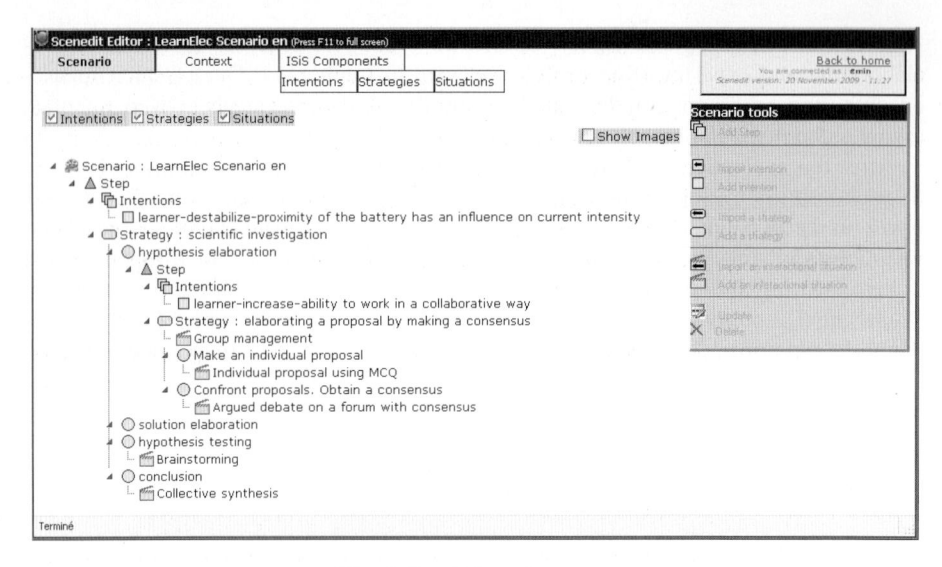

Fig. 1. ScenEdit main screen

Fig. 2. An example of intention in ScenEdit: intention "destabilize- proximity of the battery has an influence on current intensity"

After having defined his intention, the teacher-designer has to choose the appropriate strategy he wants to use to reach the goal.

In this example, the didactical intention is implemented with a specific didactical strategy called "scientific investigation" composed of four phases: hypothesis elaboration, solution elaboration, hypothesis testing and conclusion. Figure 3 shows the visual representation of the intention and the strategy we have implemented with these four phases.

Fig. 3. An example of strategy in ScenEdit : "scientific investigation"

Each phase can be performed through various pedagogical modes and can be refined by another intention according to the type of activity, the availability of computer services, etc. the teacher wants to use. In our example, the first phase: "hypothesis elaboration" is refined by a pedagogical intention called "increase the ability to work in a collaborative way" as shown in figure 1. This intention is implemented with a strategy called "elaborating a proposal by making a consensus" composed of two phases: "Make an individual proposal" and "Confront proposals. Obtain a consensus". For each phase, an interactional situation can be defined: "Individual proposal using MCQ" and "Argued debate on a forum with consensus".

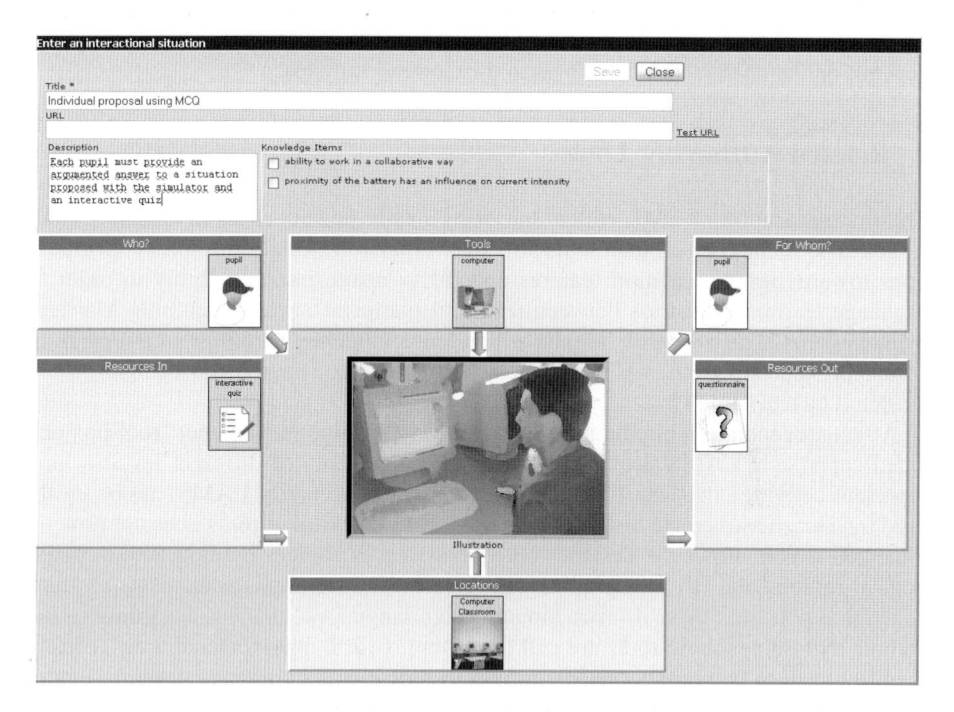

Fig. 4. An example of definition of interactional situation in ScenEdit

Figure 4 shows the form used to define the interactional situation: "Individual proposal using MCQ", in which actors, tools, resources and locations are specified. Finally, during these two phases the teacher is involved in an activity of "Group management" symbolized by an interactional situation called "Group management" as shown in figure 1.

The **ISiS Components** workspace is dedicated to manage the three main components of the ISiS model: (a) Intentions, (b) Strategies and (c) interactional Situations. Each component can be made of re-usable elements that can appear in many scenarios, and for each type the author can either create a new element or import and adapt an existing one from a library. The library contains all the components created inside the scenario and all the patterns provided in the global database.

The **Scenario Edition** workspace allows to create a structuring scenario by assembling and logically linking elements previously defined either in the **ISiS Components** workspace or directly defined in the **Edition** window. In the Scenario Edition tab, the teacher-designer can graphically design the scenario using the hierarchy of levels of ISiS included in the visual representation of the scenario.

The **Context** workspace defines the two different types of context in which a learning unit can be executed: the *knowledge context* and the *situational context*. The *knowledge context* tab allows to define the different contexts of knowledge that can be used in the scenario for defining the *knowledge items* used for intentions and prerequisites. The *situational context* tab allows to define the elements of interactional Situations: actors, tools, resources, locations. The choices available for a component depends on the characteristics defined in the Context workspace.

4 Related Authoring Tools

The first generation of EML editors has been mainly developed from technical challenges. The main goal of such tools was (a) to transform easily designer's specifications towards implementation features and (b) to insure interoperability in order to exchange learning scenarios between technical platforms such as Learning Management Systems. The proposed editors, which reuse modeling techniques coming from computer science (such as UML, for example) were considered too complex to be mastered by teachers [1].

A second generation of editors, such as LAMS [9], proposes another "tool-box oriented" approach. LAMS provides a series of components of different levels which represent activities that can be combined to create a scenario. LAMS can be easily used by a teacher to create different scenarios. But, this kind of tools does not provide a method which allows the designer (a) to motivate its choices by didactical or pedagogical reasons and (b) to capitalize and reuse basic or composed elements. A third generation concerns "visual instructional design languages" [9], but according to the authors themselves these tools are still too complex for a non-technical user: "editing facilities need to be more accessible to non-technical user in order to develop, implement and reach an easier and further use of this type of case studies in reality". Our approach is to combine the previous approaches in the teacher's designing process: (a) to organize the scenario by eliciting formally the intentions and by representing explicitly learning strategies and (b) to favour exploration of reusable components in specific libraries adapted to specific teaching communities.

5 Conclusion

In this paper, we have presented an overview of ScenEdit authoring environment whose purpose is to assist teachers in the design of learning scenarios and to favor sharing and re-use practices. We have worked with teachers to formalize and design patterns of learning scenarios, pedagogical approaches and recurrent interactional situations. ScenEdit, currently, offers some patterns of different levels (intentions, strategies, interactional situations) elaborated from best-practices found in the literature or within communities of practice. With this environment, we expect users will be able to feed databases, in order to share their scenarios with others or reuse them further in related or different contexts. The graphical representation shown in figure 2 is a classical hierarchical tree quite useful to produce a scenario. As the structured scenario can be encoded as an XML file, different outputs can be produced and several possibilities of transformation can be offered: a printable text or form for the teacher is now available, and we plan to provide a printable picture of the edition views, an IMS-LD compliant version for editing with another authoring tool and a SCORM package which can be executed on a LMS. This new online web version will then be experimented more thoroughly, with a wider audience which not necessarily has a great familiarity with ICT and scenario design software and methods.

References

1. Koper, R., Tattersall, C.: Learning Design: A Handbook on Modelling and Delivering Networked Education and Training. Springer, Heidelberg (2005)
2. Koper, R.: Current Research in Learning Design. Educational Technology & Society 9(1), 13–22 (2006)
3. Botturi, L., Cantoni, L., Lepori, B., Tardini, S.: Fast Prototyping as a Communication Catalyst for E-Learning Design. In: Hershey, M.B., Janes, D. (eds.) Making the Transition to E-Learning: Strategies and Issues (2006)
4. Murray, T., Blessing, S.: Authoring Tools for Advanced Technology Learning Environment, Toward Cost-Effective Adaptive. In: Ainsworth, S. (ed.) Interactive and Intelligent Educational Software, p. 571. Kluwer Academic Publishers, Dordrecht (2003)
5. Emin, V.: ScenEdit: an authoring environment for designing learning scenarios. Poster ICALT 2008, IEEE International Conference on Advanced Learning Technologies, Santander, p. 2 (2008)
6. Emin, V., Pernin, J.-P., Guéraud, V.: Model and tool to clarify intentions and strategies in learning scenarios design. In: Cress, U., Dimitrova, V., Specht, M. (eds.) EC-TEL 2009. LNCS, vol. 5794, p. 15. Springer, Heidelberg (2009)
7. Lejeune, A., David, J.P., Martel, C., Michelet, S., Vezian, N.: To set up pedagogical experiments in a virtual lab: methodology and first results. In: International Conference ICL, Villach Austria (2007)
8. Dalziel, J.: Implementing learning design: the Learning Activity Management System (LAMS). In: Proceedings of the ASCILITE 2003 conference, Adelaide (2003)
9. Botturi, L., Stubbs, S.: Handbook of Visual Languages in Instructional Design: Theories and Pratices. Informing Science Reference, Hershey (2008)

Skill-Based Scouting of Open Management Content

Katja Niemann[1], Uta Schwertel[2], Marco Kalz[3], Alexander Mikroyannidis[4],
Marco Fisichella[5], Martin Friedrich[1], Michele Dicerto[6], Kyung-Hun Ha[7],
Philipp Holtkamp[8], Ricardo Kawase[5], Elisabetta Parodi[6], Jan Pawlowski[8],
Henri Pirkkalainen[8], Vassilis Pitsilis[9], AristidesVidalis[9],
Martin Wolpers[1], and Volker Zimmermann[2]

[1] Fraunhofer FIT, Schloß Birlinghoven, 53754 Sankt Augustin, Germany
[2] imc AG, Altenkesseler Strasse 17/D3, 66115 Saarbrücken, Germany
[3] Open Universiteit Nederland / CELSTEC, Valkenburgerweg 177,
6419 AT Heerlen, The Netherlands
[4] Knowledge Media Institute, The Open University, Milton Keynes MK7 6AA, UK
[5] Leibniz Universität Hannover, L3S, Appelstr. 9a, 30167 Hannover, Germany
[6] Giunti Labs S.r.l., via Portobello, Abbazia dell´Annunziata, 16039 Sestri Levante, Italy
[7] ESCP Europe Campus Berlin, BIS, Heubnerweg 6, 14059 Berlin, Germany
[8] University of Jyväskyla, Mattilanniemi 2, Agora Building, Jyväskylä, Finland
[9] Division of Applied Technologies - NCSR DEMOKRITOS, Patriarchou Gregoriou and
Neapoleos str, 153 10 Aghia Paraskevi, Greece
{katja.niemann,martin.friedrich,
martin.wolpers}@fit.fraunhofer.de
{uta.schwertel,volker.zimmermann}@im-c.de
marco.kalz@ou.nl
a.mikroyannidis@open.ac.uk
{fisichella,kawase}@l3s.de
{m.dicerto,e.parodi}@giuntilabs.com
Kyung-Hun.Ha@escpeurope.de
{philipp.holtkamp,jan.pawlowski,henri.j.pirkkalainen}@jyu.fi
{avidal,vpitsilis}@dat.demokritos.gr

Abstract. Already existing open educational resources in management have a high potential for enterprises to address the increasing training needs of their employees. However, access barriers still prevent the full exploitation of this potential. Users have to search a number of repositories with heterogeneous interfaces in order to retrieve the desired content. In addition, the use of search criteria related to skills, such as learning objectives and skill-levels is in most cases not supported. The demonstrator presented in this paper addresses these shortcomings by federating multiple repositories, integrating and enriching their metadata, and employing skill-based search for management related content.

Keywords: open educational resources, content reuse, competences, federated search, management education.

1 Introduction

Management is a large education and training business field in Europe. Training topics range from general management and leadership to very specific issues like managing risks in banking industry. Many enterprises lack the resources and time to cover the resulting specific training needs of their employees by expensive face-to-face courses. Therefore E-Learning using open content has a high potential to support the increasing training needs. Repositories for Open Educational Resources (OER) [1] already provide access to large amounts of open educational material for management topics. However, end-users like learners or teachers are faced with several access barriers when utilizing the content for continuous learning in management. Currently users have to search a number of repositories with heterogeneous interfaces and categories in order to retrieve the desired content. Additionally, the usage of search criteria related to competences and skills, such as learning objectives and competence-levels to be achieved is in most cases not supported.

The demonstrator currently developed within the EU co-funded project OpenScout[1] addresses these two main access barriers. OpenScout aims at providing skill-based federated search and retrieval web services that enable users to easily find, access, use and exchange open content for management education and training.

Thereto, OpenScout builds on technologies developed by the Ariadne foundation[2] and the *eContentPlus* targeted project MACE (Metadata for Architectural Contents in Europe) [2]. The Ariadne foundation develops tools and methodologies for e.g. producing, managing and reusing of computer-based pedagogical elements, whereas the MACE project uses and extends these technologies to connect various repositories of architectural knowledge and enriches their contents with metadata to enable searching and browsing architectural contents. Furthermore, competence services developed in earlier projects like MACE and TENCompetence[3] will be used to implement agreed-upon competence models from the domain that will be discussed and modified by the stakeholder groups within the consortium to ensure their applicability for the target groups of the project.

OpenScout not only adapts existing technologies to specific requirements of the management domain but significantly extends them e.g. by providing an openly accessible tool library for improvement and re-publishing of contents. Furthermore, OpenScout plans to integrate its search services into existing social networks, such as MySpace[4] and LinkedIn[5], as well as into existing LCMSs, like CLIX[6] and learn eXact[7], to enable access from environments familiar to a wide range of users.

The paper is organized as follows. In chapter 2, we describe the demonstrator focusing on the infrastructure and the OpenScout portal. In chapter 3, we give an outlook of further work.

2 Demonstrator

2.1 Infrastructure

This section summarizes the architecture of OpenScout as depicted in Fig. 1. OpenScout already integrates several learning object repositories (LOR), such as

---

[1] http://www.openscout.net
[2] http://www.ariadne-eu.org/
[3] http://www.tencompetence.org
[4] http://www.myspace.com/
[5] http://www.linkedin.com/
[6] http://www.im-c.de/en/products/learning-management-system/product-overview/what-is-clix/
[7] http://www.learnexact.com/

OpenLearn[8], OpenER[9] and SlideStar[10]. Each repository offers an OAI-PMH [3] interface to enable harvesting of the repository's LOM instances which are represented using the OpenScout application profile. The application profile relies on the LOMv1.0 standard [4] and is extended to enable skill- and competence-based search following the European Qualification Framework (EQF). The EQF describes skills as cognitive and practical while competences are described as the ability to use knowledge, skills and personal, social or methodological abilities. Since the domain of management education cannot be described only based on functional skills, OpenScout also uses the broader concept of competences. As a starting point an initial taxonomy for Business and Management Education is used, which will be expanded and tailored to different user groups.

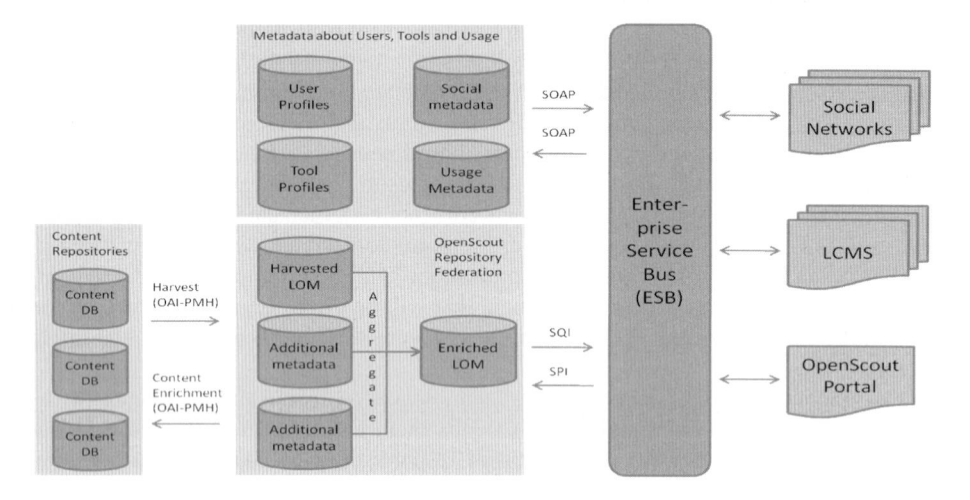

Fig. 1. The OpenScout architecture

The harvested LOM instances are stored in the central OpenScout Repository Federation. Prior harvesting is preferred over direct search for performance and reliability reasons [5]. An OAI-PMH interface is offered to content providers in order to retrieve enriched metadata of their learning objects. The harvested LOM instances are extended with additional metadata like connections between different LOM instances that are generated within OpenScout when objects are used together in a course or when a new object is generated by re-authoring of an existing object.

Additionally, OpenScout maintains user profiles (containing information about the users, e.g. interests and competences), tool profiles (containing data about tools that can be recommended, social metadata (data added by users, e.g. tags and ratings), and usage metadata (data about the user's actions and the usage of objects).

Since the OpenScout web portal accesses different data sources and will mix this data to create new services, it needs a backend layer that allows scalability, and an

---

[8] http://openlearn.open.ac.uk
[9] http://www.opener.ou.nl
[10] http://slidestar.de

easy way to extend services with a plug-in based architecture without affecting the client layer. In order to address these issues, the enterprise service bus (ESB) technology, namely the open source ESB Apache ServiceMix[11] is used. All communication concerning the web services takes place via the ESB. Furthermore, whenever an event occurs (e.g. when a user conducts a search or opens a document), the ESB calls a web service that stores the event as CAM (Contextualized Attention Metadata) [6] instance in the usage metadata database to enable further services, e.g. for recommending learning objects based on trust or users to collaborate with.

2.2 The OpenScout Portal

The OpenScout web portal aims to provide value-added services that build on the OpenScout infrastructure. It is structured as a container of customizable widgets providing the GUI for respective services. The main functionality offered at this stage is the federated search as depicted in Fig 2.

Fig. 2. Federated search

The search functionality is currently extended to support faceted search enabling filtering of the search results, according to the properties of the retrieved learning objects, e.g. content type, competences, language, and repository. The search results are presented together with basic information derived from the LOM description of each learning object. After selecting a learning object, the user is presented with a new container that holds document specific information according to general metadata (date, author, type etc.), social metadata (ratings, reviews, tags), as well as user competences and skills, see Fig. 3. Registered users can add their own ratings, tags and reviews. Competences can only be changed by authorized persons, such as content providers or facilitators. Additionally, the user is presented with recommended tools for working with the selected resource. These recommendations consist of tools for visualization, authoring, and collaboration and are based on the user profile, the profile of the selected learning object and the profiles of the tools.

---

[11] http://servicemix.apache.org/home.html

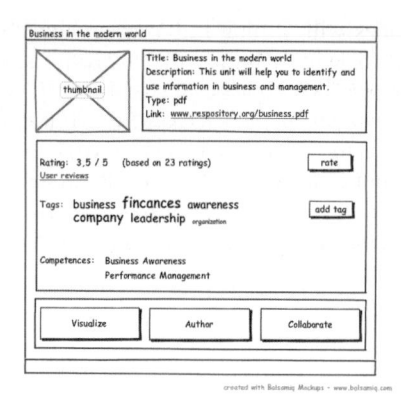

Fig. 3. Presentation of the metadata and tools associated with a learning object

3 Conclusion and Further Work

The paper presents an early prototype of the OpenScout educational services. The purpose of providing a demonstrator at an early stage is to allow various user groups in the management domain, e.g. content providers, educators, content developers or individual learners, to give early feedback so that the final application will support their specific needs. Hence the demonstrator will enable OpenScout stakeholders to evaluate the usability and the added-value of the system. Moreover, the demonstrator will create incentives for content providers to open up their repositories for OpenScout related services and hence to allow more content to be accessed. As a consequence of this evaluating the feasibility of integrating new content repositories into the content federation will be another question to be answered. The usage of the OpenScout services in early stages will furthermore help to collect from the start relevant usage metadata that again helps to develop and improve the intended recommendations. The demonstrator related evaluation objectives will be addressed by running pilots mainly done with non-technical partners. OpenScout will develop target-specific questionnaires for semi-structured interviews in order to collect predominantly qualitative user feedback and to critically assess the degree to which the demonstrator fulfills a consensual set of objectives.

The next step for the demonstrator consists of integrating further management related repositories, e.g. provided by INSEAD[12], one of the world's leading graduate business schools, and by the Avicenna Network[13]. A further next step is to integrate a simple search functionality through gadgets into Social Networks which will bring added-value to the networks and supports viral distribution of the OpenScout service.

Furthermore, we will extend the functionalities of the OpenScout portal. Besides a general user tagging (What is a resource about?) we will implement a so called purpose tagging (What do users do with the resource?) to add additional competence related information [8]. Whilst only authorized persons use the top-down taxonomies

---

[12] http://www.insead.edu
[13] http://pleiad.unesco.org/aquas/index.php

to describe learning resources, the purpose tagging enables end users to describe skills or competences that they see related to the learning objects. Due to the nature of the tags we will implement a post-hoc tagging procedure that asks users about a resource after usage. Additionally, we already collected an initial problem list of SME managers based on a desk analysis of consulting talks in the PLATO network. The relations between problems and competences should help them to identify learning resources that fit to their competence development goals, as stakeholders from SME are more used to find resources related to problems they have in their daily practice than to competences [9].

Acknowledgement

This research has been co-funded by the European Commission within the *eContentplus* targeted project OpenScout, grant ECP 2008 EDU 428016 (cf. http://www. openscout.net).

References

1. Atkins, D.E., Brown, J.S., Hammond, A.L.: A Review of the Open Educational Resources (OER) Movement: Achievements, Challenges, and New Opportunities. The William and Flora Hewlett Foundation (2007)
2. Wolpers, M., Memmel, M., Klerkx, J., Parra, G., Vandeputte, B., Duval, E., Schirru, R., Niemann, K.: Bridging Repositories to form the MACE Experience. Journal New Review of Information Networking 14, 102–116 (2008)
3. OAI: 2002, Open Archives Initiative Protocol for Metadata Harvesting, Protocol Version 2.0 of 2002-06-14 (2002)
4. Institute of Electrical and Electronics Engineers Learning Technology Standards Committee: IEEE standard for learning object metadata. IEEE standard 1484.12.1 (2002)
5. Ternier, S., Verbert, K., Parra, G., Vandeputte, B., Klerkx, J., Duval, E., Ordónez, V., Ochoa, X.: The Ariadne Infrastructure for Managing and Storing Metadata. Emerging E-Learning Technologies. IEEE Internet Computing 13(4), 18–25 (2009)
6. Wolpers, M., Najjar, J., Verbert, K., Duval, E.: Tracking Actual Usage: the Attention Metadata Approach. Educational Technology and Society 10(3), 106–121 (2007)
7. Strohmaier, M.: Purpose Tagging: Capturing User Intent to Assist Goal-Oriented Social Search. In: Proc. of the 2008 ACM workshop on Search in Social Media, pp. 35–42 (2008)
8. Kalz, M., Specht, M., Nadolski, R., Bastiaens, Y., Leirs, N., Pawlowski, J.: OpenScout: Competence Based Management Education with Community-improved Open Educational Resources. In: Halley, et al. (eds.) Proceedings of the 17th EDINEB Conference. Crossing Borders in Education and work-based learning, pp. 137–146 (2010)

The Complexity of Integrating Technology Enhanced Learning in Special Math Education – A Case Study

Ann Nilsson and Lena Pareto

Media production Department, University West, Sweden
{ann.nilsson,lena.pareto}@hv.se

Abstract. We present a study of integrating an educational game in special math education, to explore challenges faced during the process. The game promotes an unconventional approach supporting students having math difficulties, through visual representations, learn-by-exploration and learn-by-teaching models. Our conclusion is that integration in special education is more challenging than in the main stream counterpart, due to social vulnerability of the students, learning/teaching challenges in content, motivation and attitude, a non-typical learning situation, and the challenge of matching learning peers.

Keywords: technology enhanced learning, educational game, mathematics, integration, special education.

1 Introduction

Difficulties with mathematics are often rooted in elementary school [11], but may not become apparent until later. Research suggests that mathematical curriculum for student with learning disabilities should focus on a few important concepts (such as the basic operations of arithmetic) to mastery rather than numerous skills superficially [5]. Special education mathematics instruction still continues to focus on computation rather than mathematical understanding [5]. Problems with math may result in low self-esteem, low confidence and lack of interest. Trying to solve problems without understanding the underlying concepts, creates passive learners and may result in learned helplessness [11]. Repeatedly experiencing negative feelings, such as failure, math anxiety or stress, may result in reduced/low motivation [1, 20] and negative self-confirmation [1]. For students with math difficulties, it is recommended to encourage to "talk math" [4], to use motivational practices such as games [4], and to use board games and other manipulatives as well as instructional software [9].

Educational games as learning tools have documented potential for learning and motivation [7, 22, 4, 9]. We have developed a Technology Enhanced Learning game (TEL game) aiming at conceptual understanding of arithmetic, which is suitable for learners with math difficulties [14] and has shown to benefit low-performing students in an ordinary classroom situation [16]. In this study, *we explore which challenges are faced when integrating the TEL game in a practical special education situation*. Before going into the study, we will describe the TEL game.

2 The Technology Enhanced Learning Game

It is far from evident how to design a game environment which fosters deep mathematical understanding [12]. Our approach is to provide, for the domain arithmetic, 1) a graphical, animated representation, 2) a behavioural model which is explored through game play and 3) an intelligent agent that can be taught to play the game. This yields an engaging game that promotes self-regulation, conceptual understanding and discussions, which is appropriate for learners with difficulties.

The graphical representation is a metaphor for arithmetic: integers are represented as coloured squares and square boxes (Figure 1), where 1's are red squares, 10's are orange square boxes containing 10 red squares, and so forth. Square-boxes are packed and unpacked, to explicitly show carrying and borrowing. Such low-stress algorithms help conceptual understanding [9]. It is a constructive, visually rich representation, which is often essential for learners with difficulties [21]. The metaphor provides a language to talk math, e.g., *"we must unpack the orange square-box, to get more red squares"*. The metaphor explains basic arithmetic in an unconventional way, which means that the relation to math can be hidden until the learner is ready for it: particularly important for learners with math anxiety.

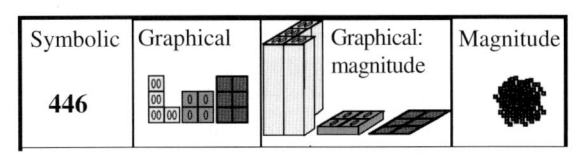

Fig. 1. Representation of positive integers

The graphical representation is used in a simulation model. Mathematical rules are built-in: the model behaves like proper arithmetic. Two-player card and board games are developed on top of the model. Each player act an operation and receives a set of cards with graphical numbers. They take turn choosing a card which is added to a game board, also representing a number. Hence, a game constitutes a sequence of computations, but the task of the players is to choose good cards according to various game goals, such as maximizing number of carryings or number of zeroes. Playing well requires reasoning and anticipating results (i.e., perform mental calculations). Reasoning is fundamental to conceptual understanding and problem solving [6]. Games can be played competitively or collaboratively, but productive strategies are different. Learners can explore how computations behave, how to play strategically, and how to invent solution methods. By inventing methods students learn in a deeper and more lasting way, and should also be allowed for students with difficulties [19].

Guidance and reflection techniques are often required in games to help learners achieve deep understanding [8, 10, 12]. A teachable agent, which is an intelligent agent that can learn [3], can provide both [18]. In our game, students train agents to play the game. The agent learns by observing and asking reflective questions. Teaching the agent is engaging [16], and students are encouraged to reflect on and self-explain their knowledge. The agent's knowledge is determined by the player's playing performance and responses to the questions (for details see [15]). Thus, the agent mirrors the student's knowledge level, but the externalization and disconnection from self makes performance levels easier to accept and talk about (the agent is performing poorly, not the student), which is important for students with low self-esteem and/or confidence.

3 Integration in Special Education – The Case Study

To explore challenges of integrating TEL in practical situations, we conducted a study in special education parallel to a larger study in main stream education. Here, we report results from special education, but use the main stream study as comparison. The study focused on students' attitudes; self-efficacy [2]; and performance in the TEL game compared to conventional math. A special education teacher and six of her students participated: two boys and four girls from 5th to 7th grade. The game play took place under natural circumstances: the teacher instructing students in pairs during regular classes twice a week planned to 40-50 minutes per session. The study involved pre/post-tests, observations, questionnaires and interviews with the teacher.

The pre-test included questions on attitude, self-efficacy, and traditional math problems. The attitude and self-efficacy involved judgments of concentration, subject difficulty, and ability to explain. The math test involved problems on arithmetic operations, the base-10 system, method invention, and negative numbers. The post-test consisted of a combined attitude, self-efficacy and math test, in the two contexts conventional math and the TEL game, in order to make comparisons.

Students played the TEL game for three weeks in class. Each pairs' game playing was observed and video-recorded at three occasions: the first, middle and last session. Recordings were roughly transcribed and analyzed to on students' attitude and ability through verbal statements, facial expressions, gestures and levels of engagement.

The teacher interview concerned her judgment of the students' attitudes and math abilities, and reflections on using the TEL game. Finally, the students' quantitative and qualitative performances in the game were analyzed through game logs.

Results from the pre-test are shown in Table 1: average scores (left part) and generalization to the levels (--,-,0,+,++) for the purpose of overview. Attitudes and self-efficacy were valued on the scale -5 to 5, math results denote percent correct.

Table 1. Results from pre-tests (specific to the left, and levels to the right)

Student/results	D	M	E	L	N	S	(*)	Student/levels	D	M	E	L	N	S
attitude	3,0	-3,3	-3,6	-2,6	-0,7	2,0	*-0,3*	attitude	++	--	-	-	0	+
efficacy	3,3	-1,6	-4,5	1,3	-1,5	-0,9	*1,1*	efficacy	++	-	--	+	-	0
math	29%	65%	37%	50%	48%	24%	72%	math	--	++	-	+	0	--

(*) As comparison, average results from the same test with 53 5th grade students from the parallel study are included. The math results are as expected generally lower for our subjects, but for instance student M is close to average in performance, whereas attitude and self-efficacy is far below. Attitude and self-efficacy are lower in general. For level generalizations, the scale (--,-,0,+,++) is mapped to {[-5,-3), [-3,-1), [-1,1), [1,3), [3,5)} for attitude and self-efficacy, and to {[20,30), [30,40), [40,50), [50,60), [60,70)} for math performance. Note how different the 6 students' profiles are regarding attitude, self-efficacy and performance, e.g., D and M are each other's opposites. Attitude and self-efficacy are generally on similar levels, whereas self-efficacy (perceived performance) and actual performance differ up to 4 levels.

The post-test results are presented as *the difference* of performance in game and math representations, as shown in Table 2. From the attitude test questions of enjoyment of math, efficacy and enjoyment of explaining are reported, and from the math test problems on base-10, calculations, and negative numbers. "0" denotes same results in both representations, "+" better and "–" worse in the game.

Table 2. Results from comparative post-tests (attitude left, math right)

Student/ Diff attitude	D	M	E	L	N	S	avg	Student/ Diff math	D	M	E	L	N	S
enjoyment	4,5	10	6	4,8	5	1,3	5,3	Base-10	+	+	0	0	0	+
efficacy explain	0	5	4,8	4,3	4	-4	2,3	calculation	0	0	+	0	0	+
enjoyment explain	0,5	5,5	6,3	-0,8	5,3	-1,8	2,5	Negative numbers	0	-	0	0	0	0

All students prefer the game to conventional math, 4 of 6 is much more confident explaining in the game and 3 of 6 enjoy it much more. For the math problems, 3 of 6 performed better for the base-10 problem, 2 of 6 in the calculation problem, whereas in the negative numbers problem 1 performed worse.

According to the teacher, all students regard math as a boring and difficult subject. Strong words as *"hates"* and *"detests"* are used. They seem to like the game, except for student L who has a negative attitude in general. It is hard for the students to reason and reflect in the game, and she believes some are mainly guessing. She tries to help by asking questions. She thinks the agent is good, and that the students like teaching it and watch it play, but the agent's reflective questions are too frequent. The vague connection to math and the level of guessing worries her: *"they don't see the numbers being represented"*. She has observed that the students are quiet and don't help each other when playing competitively, more so when playing collaboratively. The reason might be that the students are not used to collaborate in math.

Being withdrawn from ordinary class is delicate, therefore sometimes refused, and it makes the students socially vulnerable. This reinforces exclusion and is questioned by the teacher. Students' parents and other teachers have been informed of the study. Parents reactions of the new form of instruction varied from *"anything as long as it helps"* to worries that the student may fall behind even more. Finally, she admits that she is not convinced herself, which may have effected others.

4 Discussion

Several aspects influenced the students' special instruction sessions: e.g. being withdrawn from ordinary class; taking instruction time to do unconventional math instead of practicing typical problems for tests; being influenced by parents; and the relation to the playing partner as learning companion.

The motivational dilemma and vulnerability when having to leave a movie in class for special math instruction while being called names from classmates, is easy to imagine. Such situations lead to avoidance of help, denial of the teacher among friends, and emotions of shame and distrust in self. Due to such circumstances, one of the students only attended the first observation, and one session only lasted for 6 minutes.

Despite the TEL game's unconventional approach and the students' negative attitude towards math, the teacher frequently pointed out the connection to math. As evident from the video recordings, some students reacted negatively to such instructions, and immediately lost interest or concentration. From this we learn that it is crucial to allow the teachers to become comfortable with the game and learning model prior to instruction, in order to mediate a confident and positive attitude.

While some parents reacted positively to the game, others were stressed by their children playing a game instead of "*doing real math*". They were afraid it would make the student fall behind further, and therefore not supportive of the activity. Parents' attitude is known to have strong influence on their children [17], and similar negative attitudes were shown by their children In fact, one student skipped game playing in favour for doing conventional math tasks difficult even for her peers.

The practice of selecting pairs of students for special instruction based on effective time scheduling, in particular for a pair activity as this game play, is understandable from a practical point of view but not from learning perspective. The relation between play partners can have negative impact on their learning situation: one student's uncertainty was reinforced by the more confident player's occasional lack of certainty. Another student's need for concentration was disturbed by the partner's loud requests for attention and acknowledgement. The mismatch resulted in separating the pair after the first observation. The last pair consisted of one student with a strong behaviour of negative self-confirmation, which may be rooted in a fixed ability belief [13], whereas her partner played intuitively without effort and yet scored a lot. Hence, neither of the pairs was an optimal learning constellation.

A learning situation is affected by the student's social network: the school, teacher, peers and parents. The student's own attitude towards learning, her perception of self, self-efficacy in relation to performance, attitude to the game and special education also influence the learning and motivational effect.

5 Conclusion

Integration of TEL in special education is more challenging than in ordinary classes, due to the social vulnerability of the students; the learning/teaching challenge with respect to content, motivation and attitude; the learning situation, and the challenge of matching learning peers. The latter because of the diversity regarding math level, type of difficulty, attitude and learning needs. Our recommendation is to take time to involve the student's social network, introduce the TEL to the involved teachers until comfortable, and provide support for unconventional approach to mathematics.

References

1. Adler, B.: Dyscalculia & Mathematics. Nationella Utbildningsförlaget, Sweden (2007)
2. Bandura, A.: Self-efficacy: the Exercise of Control. W.H. Freeman, New York (1997)

3. Biswas, G., Katzlberger, T., Bransford, J., Schwartz, D.: TAG-V: Extending Intelligent Learning Environments with Teachable Agents to Enhance Learning. In: Moore, J.D., Redfield, C.L., Johnson, W.L. (eds.) AI in Education, pp. 389–397. IOS Press, Amsterdam (2001)
4. Garnett, K.: Math Learning Disabilities. Division for Learning Disabilities. J. CEC (1998), http://www.ldonline.org/article/5896
5. Gersten, R., Chard, D.: Number Sense: Rethinking Arithmetic Instruction for Students with Mathematical Disabilities. J. Special Education 44, 18–28 (1999)
6. Jonassen, D., Ionas, I.: Designing Effective Supports for Causal Reasoning. Educational Technology Research and Development 56(3), 287–308 (2008)
7. Ke, F.: Alternative Goal Structures for Computer Game-Based Learning. Int. J. Computer-Supported Collaborative Learning 3, 429–445 (2008)
8. Kirschner, P.A., Sweller, J., Clark, R.E.: Why Minimal Guidance During Instruction Does Not Work: an Analysis of the Failure of Constructivist, Discovery, Problem-Based, Experiential, and Inquiry-Based Teaching. Educational Psychologist 41(2), 75–86 (2006)
9. Lock, R.H.: Adapting Mathematics Instruction in the General Education Classroom for Students with Mathematics Disabilities. LD Forum: Council for Learning Disabilities (1996), http://www.ldonline.org/article/5928
10. Mayer, R.E.: Should there Be a Three-Strikes Rule Against Pure Discovery Learning? The Case for Guided Methods of Instruction. Educational Psychologist 59, 14–19 (2004)
11. Miller, S.P., Mercer, C.D.: Educational Aspects of Mathematics Disabilities. J. Learning Disabilities 30(1), 47–56 (1997)
12. Moreno, R., Mayer, R.E.: Role of Guidance, Reflection and Interactivity in an Agent-Based Multimedia Game. J. Educational Psychology 97(1), 117–128 (2005)
13. Nussbaum, D.A., Dweck, C.S.: Defensiveness Versus Remediation: Self-Theories and Modes of Self-Esteem Maintenance. Soc. Psychology Bull. 34(5), 599–612 (2008)
14. Pareto, L.: Graphical Arithmetic for Learners with Dyscalculia. In: 7th International ACM SIGACCESS Conference on Computers and Accessibility. ACM, New York (2005)
15. Pareto, L.: Teachable Agents that Learn by Observing Game Playing Behavior. In: Craig, S.D., Dicheva, D. (eds.) Workshop on Intelligent Educational Games at 14th AIED International Conference on Artificial Intelligence in Education, pp. 31–40 (2009)
16. Pareto, L., Schwartz, D.L., Svensson, L.: Learning by Guiding a Teachable Agent to Play an Educational Game. In: 14th AIED International Conference on Artificial Intelligence in Education, pp. 662–664. IOS Press, Amsterdam (2009)
17. Pourdavood, R., Carignan, N., Martin, B.K., Sanders, M.: Cultural, Social Interaction and Mathematics Learning. Focus on Learning Problems in Mathematics 1 (2005)
18. Schwartz, D.L., Chase, C., Wagster, J., Okita, S., Roscoe, R., Chin, D., Biswas, G.: Interactive Metacognition: Monitoring and Regulating a Teachable Agent. In: Hacker, D.J., Dunlosky, J., Graesser, A.C. (eds.) Handbook of Metacognition in Education (2009)
19. Schwartz, D.L., Martin, T.: Inventing to Prepare for Learning: the Hidden Efficiency of Original Student Production in Statistics Instruction. Cogn. and Instr. 22, 129–184 (2004)
20. Sjöberg, G.: If Not Dyscalculia-What Is It then? A Multimethod Study of Students being in Mathproblems seen from a Longitudinal Perspective. Dissertation, Umeå Univ. (2006), http://umu.diva-portal.org/smash/record.jsf?pid=diva2:144488
21. Vincent, J.: MicroWorlds and the Integrated Brain. In: 7th World Conference on Computers in Education: Australian topics, vol. 8, pp. 131–137 (2002)
22. Vogel, J.F., Vogel, D.S., Cannon-Bowers, J., Bowers, C.A., Muse, K., Wright, M.: Computer Gaming and Interactive Simulations for Learning: A Meta-Analysis. J. Educational Computing Research 34(3), 229–243 (2006)

TAO – A Versatile and Open Platform for Technology-Based Assessment

Eric Ras, Judith Swietlik, Patrick Plichart, and Thibaud Latour

Public Research Centre Henri Tudor
29, avenue John F. Kennedy, 1855 Luxembourg – Kirchberg, Luxembourg
Eric.Ras@tudor.lu
Judith.Swietlik@tudor.lu
Patrick.Plichart@tudor.lu
Thibaud.Latour@tudor.lu

Abstract. The TAO framework is an open-source project that provides a very general and open architecture for developing and delivering tests for the purpose of technology-based assessments. Besides summarizing the main features of TAO, this paper lists TAO's advantages compared to other tools and platforms for technology-based assessment, and reports on its capability for integration into highly flexible learning environments.

Keywords: TAO platform, technology-based assessment, open source software.

1 Introduction

Nowadays, assessments are increasingly considered to be an aid during learning [1]. Hopkins, for example, describes assessments for personalized learning through e-learning products as a "quiet revolution taking place in education [2]".

The TAO platform (*Testing Assistée par Ordinateur*) developed in Luxembourg (joint project of CRP Henri Tudor and University of Luxembourg [3]) has become a core component of large-scale high-stake assessments, such as the recent PISA (Programme for International Students Assessment) and the future PIAAC (Programme for the International Assessment of Adult Competencies) studies with 28 participating countries.

The versatile and generic nature of the TAO platform provides all necessary services to non-IT-professionals to manage *testees*, to create *items* (exercises) and *tests*, to deliver *tests* and manage *test* campaigns, and to manage and analyze *results*. Its modular and distributed character allows the collaboration of different users, in different locations, at different times.

The next sections state the innovations of TAO compared to other technology-based assessment (TBA) tools. We describe its architecture, the underlying workflow, as well as the main features.

2 The Role of IT in Technology-Based Assessment

Assessments cover a wide range of methods that have been changing dramatically with the increasing use of new technologies. In the past, assessment practices were seen as a means for selecting students at university [4] and for monitoring educational systems (e.g., PISA and PIAAC), or they were used for diagnostic purposes.

The emergence of IT in assessment and the usage of web-based assessments have highlighted advantages (e.g., avoidance of time constraints, ease of comparing results, reduction of measurement errors, etc.) and disadvantages (e.g., measurement control, cheating) [5-6]. IT does, for example, allow rich new assessment tasks and provides powerful scoring and reporting techniques [7]. It supports the user in assessment resource development, data collection, and presentation of the results. New constructs such as cognitive and behavioral skills can be assessed; dynamics aspects (e.g., time spent to answer a question, number of clicks, choice of learning materials) can be observed and collected effectively in the near future [5]. A good overview of tools that support the different phases in assessment can be found in [8].

A test consists of several test items. Such an item contains a stimulus, a question, responses, a score schema, and feedback elements [9]. Several authoring tools exist that can be used for simple test items, such as multiple choice, drag and drop, etc. Examples include Flash-Learning Interactions [10], NetQuiz Pro [11], Eclipse Crossword [12], Dyris [13], or tools that are embedded in educational platforms, such as the Gyana service of the portal mySchool [14]. However, those tools do not provide a means for defining the underlying data models for the TBA resources (i.e., testees, test items, tests, etc.). They do not cover the whole bandwidth of TBA services – from test development, deployment, execution, and test result analysis – as TAO does. Furthermore, TAO also allows the development of more sophisticated test items, such as the *Hyper Adaptive Work Area Item* (for the HAWAI item, see next section).

3 TAO Architecture

The global architecture of TAO for the management of TBA resources is close to the common architecture used in many PHP-based applications. On the server side, a database management system is used for data storage. An *application layer,* written in PHP, implements all the specific functions for TBA and relies on the database management system layer (*persistency layer*). This application layer follows a *Model View Controller* architecture and build views that are delivered to the Web browser on the client side. Javascript on the client side queries the application layer that is on the server side and may also update the views if needed (or retrieve a new view from the server).

An innovation for TBA platforms is that TAO uses the semantic Web-related technologies RDF and RDFS to express knowledge about resources at any abstraction level. They allow the system users to define the data model (i.e., define classes of resources and describe their properties) as well as the data itself (e.g., values of properties that describe a particular student). Using RDF repositories instead of a classical database design solves the issue of model variability. The TAO platform makes use of the *generis4* RDF/RDFS repository, developed by the CRP Henri Tudor [15]. It provides a tool infrastructure for modeling and managing all the RDF schemas.

4 Workflow and Features

The workflow has been broken down into these phases: *items, tests, testees, groups, delivery,* and *results* (see Fig. 1). The following sections give a short overview of the six different TAO modules.

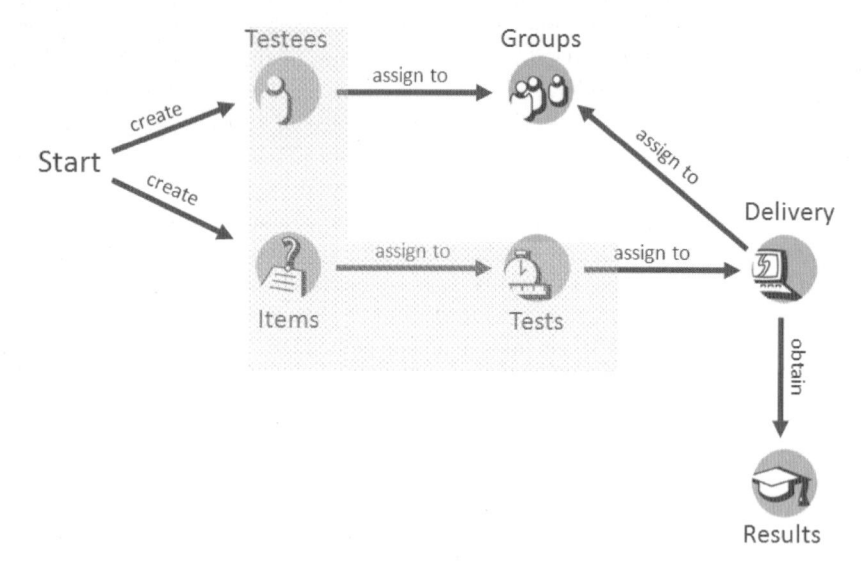

Fig. 1. TAO workflow

2.1 Testee Modeling and Management

The *testees* module allows describing and managing testees (persons who will be assessed). Its flexibility allows the design of datasheets (e.g., name, address, date of birth, gender, etc.). Testees may be organized into groups for specific purposes. In the module, testees are organized into folders: They represent classes offering the possibility to adapt the description of the subclasses through inheritance by defining custom-made properties. This is the basis for modeling personal datasheets within the testees module. Login and password are mandatory for all folders in the testees module. They are needed to authenticate each single testee participating in an assessment and will provide access to a test. TAO offers different types for displaying values of properties, such as short text, long text, formatted text, simple choice lists, drop-down lists, data picker, etc. for defining customized data sheets for all needs.

2.2 Item Management and Authoring

The item module enables the creation and design of *items* (exercises). A series of different templates (item types) are provided to the item authors, such as Multiple Choice Questions (QCM), puzzle design (Kohs), Fill-in-the-gap (C-Test), and HAWAI. The latter is the most innovative item type, and is unique as far as test item authoring tools are concerned. HAWAI is the abbreviation for *Hyper Adaptive Work*

Area Item. The HAWAI item is a very powerful item type enabling the creation of complex item types and providing the whole palette of up-to-date graphical user interface design possibilities. The HAWAI item is based on the BLACK model (i.e., *Business - Layout - Actions - Content -* Knowledge) developed at CRP Henri Tudor, which is a manifest in XML format for describing items. The usage of BLACK and XUL (*XML User Interface Language* developed by the Mozilla project) allows rendering any kind of interface for the delivered test items. The user may influence all these levels of item creation and is free to create any kind of item in various shapes. HAWAI item authoring offers a graphical interface as well as direct access to the code.

2.3 Test Creation

A selection of *items* is combined into a *test* inside the *test* module and the *test* mode (i.e., sequencing, scoring, etc.) and the layout are configured here.

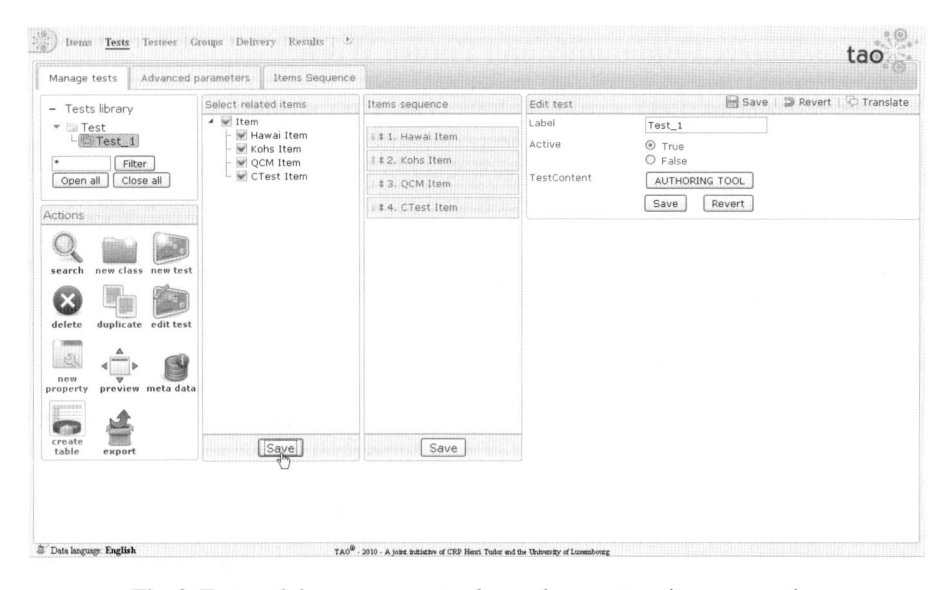

Fig. 2. Test module: management, advanced parameters, item sequencing

In the management area, the *items* are selected in the "select related items" tree. The selected *items* are displayed in the "item sequence", which offers sequencing per drag&drop. The tab "advanced parameters" offers additional parameters for adapting the test to special needs: layout, timing, sequencing mode, scoring, etc. To check whether a test has been created correctly, the preview function displays and runs the test.

2.4 Test Delivery, Execution, and Results Management

The *delivery* module enables the *test* administrator to define *test campaigns* with constraints on test execution (e.g., a test may be available for a given period of time; a maximum number of executions may be assigned to the test, etc.). You may combine several tests into test campaigns and define the sequencing per drag&drop.

Before a test may be accessed by testees, the deliveries have to be assigned to the testees. This is managed in a separate module, the *groups* module. It offers great flexibility to combine testees and delivery resources in various ways. A test is executed via a URL. A login screen appears and the testee needs to authenticate himself. After the login, all deliveries that have been assigned to the testee in the *groups* module are listed for execution. All data recorded during the test execution (scores, endorsements, behavioral data, etc.) are sent to the results module. As the results module is connected to all other TAO modules, it also has access to other data that might be useful for a specific analysis purpose – this is a unique feature of TAO. The results module is based on UTR (Ultimate Table for Result), which enables utmost flexibility for combining various data. The user may design result tables according to his needs, save a table as a template, and filter and export results to make them available for analysis.

4 Open-Source Community and Future Work

The development of TAO started in 2002. The TAO platform always had to be adapted to momentary assessment projects (e.g., PISA studies) and risked losing its highest potential: its versatility and its genericity. A refactoring of the code was done in 2009 to prepare it for open-source software under the GNU public license (GPL v2.0). The TAO website (see http://www.tao.lu) provides all necessary services for an open-source community and invites anyone who is interested to participate in further developments of TAO. Contributions by the open-source community will undergo an evaluation process before being integrated into the TAO platform. This will assure a consistent evolution and guarantee the generic nature of TAO.

Until now, the application domains of TAO have mainly been dedicated to high-stake assessment, i.e., the evaluation of national educational systems with very high requirements regarding data validity and reliability. The advantages of TAO compared to other tools and platforms are the Web service-oriented architecture, its RDF-based data management, and the coverage of all TBA-relevant phases. This makes TAO a candidate for integration into modern technology-enhanced learning environments, such as personal learning environments. Such environments enable self-regulated learning, where the learner self-controls his learning progress. In the future, TAO will support formative assessment, which is a means to support self-regulated learning [16]. In addition, TAO will be extended to support the concept of user-created content, i.e., students create and share test items (elements) for self- and peer assessment.

Acknowledgments

Special thanks go to Romain Martin, Raynald Jadoul, Gilbert Busana, Vincent Koenig, Lionel Lecaque, Bertrand Chevrier, Younes Djaghloul, Somsack Sipasseuth, Cédric Alphonso, and Sophi Battisti for their effort in designing and implementing the platform as well as to Lucie Braye and Hélène Mayer for creating the software demo.

References

1. James, M.: Assessment, Teaching and Theories of Learning. In: Gardner, J. (ed.) Assessment and Learning. Sage, London (2006)
2. Hopkins, D.: Assessment for personalised learning: The quiet revolution. In: Perspectives on pupil assessment. GTC conference, New Relationships: Teaching, Learning and Accountability, London (2004)
3. TAO platform, http://www.tao.lu (Retrieved June 21, 2010)
4. Gipps, C.: Socio-cultural aspects of assessment. Review of Educational Research 24, 355–392 (1999)
5. Csapó, B., Ainley, J., Bennett, R., Latour, T., Law, N.: Technological issues for computer-based assessment of the 21st century skills. Draft White Paper 3. The University of Melbourne, CISCO, INTEL, MICROSOFT, Melbourne (2010)
6. Grundwald Associates LLC Report: An open source platform for internet-based assessment. Grunwald Associates LLC, Bethesda, MD (2010)
7. Scalise, K., Gifford, B.: Computer-based assessment in E-learning: A framework for constructing "intermediate constraint" questions and tasks for technology platforms. Journal of Technology, Learning, and Assessment 4, 3–44 (2006)
8. AL-Smadi, M., Gütl, C.: Past, present and future of e-assessment: Towards a flexible e-assessment system. In: Interactive Computer aided Learning, ICL 2008, Villach, Austria (2008)
9. Sclater, N.: Conceptualising item banks. In: Sclater, N. (ed.) Item Banks Infrastructure Study (IBIS), ch. 2, HEFCE (2004)
10. Verpoorten, D., Glahn, C., Kravcik, M., Ternier, S., Specht, M.: Personalisation of Learning in Virtual Learning Environments. In: Cress, U., Dimitrova, V., Specht, M. (eds.) EC-TEL 2009. LNCS, vol. 5794, pp. 52–66. Springer, Heidelberg (2009)
11. Milligan, C.D., Beauvoir, P., Johnson, M.W., Sharples, P., Wilson, S., Liber, O.: Developing a reference model to describe the personal learning environment. In: Nejdl, W., Tochtermann, K. (eds.) EC-TEL 2006. LNCS, vol. 4227, pp. 506–511. Springer, Heidelberg (2006)
12. Eclipse Crossword, http://www.eclipsecrossword.com/ (Retrieved June 21, 2010)
13. Dyris, http://dyris.free.fr/ (Retrieved June 21, 2010)
14. Gyana - Test authoring tool of the learning platform mySchool, http://www.myschool.lu/home/mS/gyana.asp (Retrieved June 21, 2010)
15. Plichart, P., Jadoul, R., Vandenabeele, L., Latour, T.: TAO, a collective distributed computer-based assessment framework built on semantic web standards. In: Theory and Application AISTA 2004. IEEE Computer Society, Luxembourg (2004)
16. Nicol, D.J., Macfarlane-Dick, D.: Formative assessment and self-regulated learning: a model and seven principles of good feedback practice. Studies in Higher Education 31, 199–218 (2006)

Author Index

Adam, Jean-Michel 408
Aguirre, José Luis 626
Ainsworth, Shaaron 17
Alarcón, Rosa 470
Anastopoulou, Stamatina 17
Anido-Rifón, Luis 482
Anjo, Batel 494
Apostolellis, Panagiotis 451
Arnold, Franziska 390
Aseere, Ali M. 30

Balacheff, Nicolas 109
Banica, Dan 420
Barak, Noaa 396
Barnes, Sally-Anne 151
Beek, Wouter 46
Beham, Guenter 608
Beham, Günter 213
Belgiorno, Furio 457
Bental, Diana 620
Bieliková, Mária 445
Bimrose, Jenny 151
Blat, Josep 276
Bligh, Brett 464
Böhnstedt, Doreen 324
Borau, Kerstin 432
Börner, Dirk 512
Bosson, Jean-Luc 109
Boyle, Tom 578
Bozo, Jorge 470
Bradley, Claire 151
Bredeweg, Bert 46
Brown, Alan 151
Buhmes, Hanno 542
Bull, Susan 476
Burgos, Daniel 396

Caeiro-Rodríguez, Manuel 482
Callaway, Charles B. 620
Camilleri, Anthony Fisher 396
Campbell, Gwendolyn E. 93, 620
Cantador, Iván 488
Castillo, Gladys 494
Chiru, Costin 420
Comai, Sara 614

Conde, José M. 488
Condotta, Massimiliano 560
Cook, John 578
Crespo, Raquel M. 139
Cress, Ulrike 390
Crook, Charles 17
Croset, Marie-Caroline 109
Cuendet, Sébastien 78

Daradoumis, Thanasis 451
Dascalu, Mihai 420
de Hoog, Robert 213
Delgado Kloos, Carlos 139
Derntl, Michael 62
Descalço, Luís 494
Devaurs, Didier 292
de Vries, Fred 396
Dicerto, Michele 632
Dietrich, Michael 357
Dillenbourg, Pierre 78
Diogo, Sandra 494
Do-Lenh, Son 78
Domínguez García, Renato 324
Dotan, Amir 213
Duval, Erik 183, 590
Dzikovska, Myroslava O. 93, 620

Eliasson, Johan 414
Emin, Valérie 626
Engler, Jan 602
Etcheverry, Patrick 536

Farrow, Elaine 620
Fessl, Angela 590
Fisichella, Marco 632
Franco, Andrés 139
Friedrich, Martin 167, 426, 632

Gakhal, Inderdip 476
Gartner, Alexandru 420
Gašević, Dragan 340
Geraniou, Eirini 260, 548
Gerding, Enrico H. 30
Gillet, Denis 590
Giorgini, Fabrizio 500

Glahn, Christian 123
Goguadze, George 357
Gonçalves, Celso 109
Griffiths, Dai 62
Gruber, Marion R. 123
Grundy, Daniel 476
Gutiérrez Rojas, Israel 139
Gutierrez-Santos, Sergio 548

Ha, Kyung-Hun 632
Haferkamp, Nina 506
Harrison, Katherine M. 93
Heinze, Nina 590
Hernández-Leo, Davinia 276
Holocher-Ertl, Teresa 340
Holtkamp, Philipp 632
Hoppe, H. Ulrich 542, 602
Howard, Yvonne 566

Iribarra, Sebastian 470

Jacobson, Michael J. 402
Jeanquartier, Fleur 608
Jeremić, Zoran 340
Jermann, Patrick 78
Johnson, Matthew 476
Joosten-ten Brinke, Desirée 572
Jovanović, Jelena 340

Kalz, Marco 512, 632
Kaschig, Andreas 151
Kawase, Ricardo 632
Kay, Judy 1
Kelle, Sebastian 512
Kennedy-Clark, Shannon 402
Kirschenmann, Uwe 167, 426
Klerkx, Joris 183
König, Florian 197
Koper, Rob 123
Kraker, Peter 590
Krämer, Nicole C. 506
Kummerfeld, Bob 1
Kump, Barbara 213
Kunzmann, Christine 151
Kurti, Arianit 596
Kuuskankare, Mika 518

Latour, Thibaud 644
Laurson, Mikael 518
Lazoi, Mariangela 151

Lee, John 524
Lehmann, Lasse 229
Leony, Derick 139
Ley, Tobias 213
Liem, Jochem 46
Lindstaedt, Stefanie N. 213, 292, 590, 608
Linnebank, Floris 46
Loll, Frank 530
Lopistéguy, Philippe 536
Luengo, Vanda 408
Luong, The Nhan 536

Mabbott, Andrew 476
Maier, Ronald 151
Malzahn, Nils 542
Mandran, Nadine 408
Manno, Ilaria 457
Markus, Thomas 374
Marquesuzaà, Christophe 536
Mavrikis, Manolis 548
Mazarakis, Athanasios 151
Mazza, Davide 614
Mazza, Riccardo 554
Mazzola, Luca 554
McLaren, Bruce M. 357, 530
Melis, Erica 357
Memmel, Martin 560
Metscher, Johannes 584
Meyer, Ann-Kristin 357
Michelet, Sandra 408
Mihaila, Dan 420
Mikroyannidis, Alexander 632
Millán, Eva 494
Millard, David E. 30, 566
Milrad, Marcelo 596
Mittelbach, Arno 229
Monachesi, Paola 374
Moore, Johanna D. 93, 620
Moskaliuk, Johannes 390
Müller, Daniel 245
Mureddu, Lorenzo 614

Nagel, Till 590
Neumann, Susanne 62
Ney, Muriel 109
Niemann, Katja 167, 426, 560, 632
Nieves, Raúl 276
Nilsson, Ann 638

Nodenot, Thierry 536
Nouri, Jalal 414

Oberhuemer, Petra 62
Oliveira, Paula 494
O'Malley, Claire 17
Osburg, Thomas 438

Palmieri, Giuseppina 457
Pammer, Viktoria 213
Paramythis, Alexandros 197
Pardo, Abelardo 139
Pareto, Lena 638
Parodi, Elisabetta 632
Parra, Gonzalo 183, 590
Pawlowski, Jan 632
Paxton, Mark 17
Pearce-Lazard, Darren 260
Perez-Rodriguez, Roberto 482
Pérez-Sanagustín, Mar 276
Pernin, Jean-Philippe 626
Pinkwart, Niels 530
Pirkkalainen, Henri 632
Pitsilis, Vassilis 632
Plichart, Patrick 644
Posea, Vlad 374
Poulovassilis, Alexandra 260
Punie, Yves 308

Rajagopal, Kamakshi 572
Ramberg, Robert 414
Ras, Eric 644
Rath, Andreas S. 292
Ravenscroft, Andrew 578
Rebedea, Traian 420
Redecker, Christine 308
Reimann, Peter 402
Reinhardt, Wolfgang 590
Rensing, Christoph 229, 324
Rutz, Fredrik 414

Salles, Paulo 46
Sandow, Alexander 151
Santos, José Luis 183
Scarano, Vittorio 457
Scheffel, Maren 167, 426
Scheuer, Oliver 530

Schirru, Rafael 560
Schmidt, Andreas 151, 578
Scholl, Philipp 324
Schümmer, Till 390
Schwertel, Uta 632
Scott, Peter 590
Sharples, Mike 17, 464
Siadaty, Melody 340
Sloep, Peter B. 572
Specht, Marcus 123, 396, 512
Spikol, Daniel 596
Sporer, Thomas 584
Steinhauser, Natalie B. 93, 620
Steinle, Magdalena 584
Steinmetz, Ralf 229, 324
Stepanyan, Karen 432
Strohmeier, Stefan 245
Swietlik, Judith 644

Taylor, Leanne S. 93
Todorova, Albena 438
Trausan-Matu, Stefan 420
Tsovaltzi, Dimitra 357
Tvarožek, Jozef 445

Ullmann, Thomas Daniel 590
Ullrich, Carsten 432

Van Assche, Frans 183
Vandeputte, Bram 183, 590
Vidalis, Aristides 632
Vogel, Bahtijar 596

Weinbrenner, Stefan 602
Westerhout, Eline 374
Wichmann, Astrid 602
Wild, Fridolin 590
Windrum, Caroline 396
Wolpers, Martin 167, 426, 560, 632

Xu, Jing 476

Yang, Yang 17

Ziebarth, Sabrina 542
Zimmermann, Volker 632
Zufferey, Guillaume 78

Printing: Mercedes-Druck, Berlin
Binding: Stein+Lehmann, Berlin